THE HEADLAM DIARIES
1935–1951

PARLIAMENT AND POLITICS IN THE AGE OF CHURCHILL AND ATTLEE

THE HEADLAM DIARIES
1935–1951

edited by

STUART BALL

CAMDEN FIFTH SERIES
Volume 14

CAMBRIDGE
UNIVERSITY PRESS

FOR THE ROYAL HISTORICAL SOCIETY
University College London, Gower Street, London WC1E 6BT
1999

Published by the Press Syndicate of the University of Cambridge
The Edinburgh Building, Cambridge CB2 2RU, United Kingdom
40 West 20th Street, New York, NY 10011–4211, USA
10 Stamford Road, Oakleigh, Melbourne 3166, Australia

First published 1999

A catalogue record for this book is available from the British Library

ISBN 0 521 66143 9 hardback

SUBSCRIPTIONS. The serial publications of the Royal Historical Society, *Royal Historical Society Transactions* (ISSN 0080–4401) and Camden Fifth Series (ISSN 0960–1163) volumes may be purchased together on annual subscription. The 1999 subscription price (which includes postage but not VAT) is £60 (US$99 in the USA, Canada and Mexico) and includes Camden Fifth Series, volumes 13 and 14 (published in July and December) and Transactions Sixth Series, volume 9 (published in December). Japanese prices are available from Kinokuniya Company Ltd, P.O. Box 55, Chitose, Tokyo 156, Japan. EU subscribers (outside the UK) who are not registered for VAT should add VAT at their country's rate. VAT registered subscribers should provide their VAT registration number. Prices include delivery by air.

Subscription orders, which must be accompanied by payment, may be sent to a bookseller, subscription agent or direct to the publisher: Cambridge University Press, The Edinburgh Building, Shaftesbury Road, Cambridge CB2 2RU, UK; or in the USA, Canada and Mexico: Cambridge University Press, Journals Fulfillment Department, 110, Midland Avenue, Port Chester, NY 10573–4930, USA.

SINGLE VOLUMES AND BACK VOLUMES. A list of Royal Historical Society volumes available from Cambridge University Press may be obtained from the Humanities Marketing Department at the address above.

Printed and bound in the United Kingdom by Butler & Tanner Ltd, Frome and London

Contents

Acknowledgements

I have incurred many debts whilst working on this volume, and it is pleasure to be able to acknowledge them here. First and foremost, my thanks are due to Captain John Headlam for permission to publish this edition, for his help over the years, and for his patience whilst I have sought to complete it. I am very grateful to the Royal Historical Society for providing a home for this volume in the Camden series, and in particular to their Literary Director, David Eastwood, for his support of the project. I must also mention The Historians' Press, the publisher of the first volume, without whom this project could not have begun; I believe that I speak for many scholars in saying that whilst the Press has made its mark, it will be greatly missed.

The accounts of those who knew the Headlams, or whose parents knew them well, have been invaluable. I am particularly indebted to the late Mrs. Gertrude Ridley, who assisted Lady Headlam's charitable projects from 1927 onwards and was a friend of the family for over seven decades, for answering my enquiries and sharing her recollections in a series of letters during the 1990s. I am also most grateful to Lord Lambton, the late Sir Charles Graham, and Miss B.C. Bell (daughter of H.P. Bell, Sir Cuthbert Headlam's aide for many years).

Mark Thurston of the Local Studies Department, Newcastle City Library, was of great help in locating the personal details of figures in Newcastle local politics. I am most grateful to Jill Davidson, the Conservative Party Archivist at the Bodleian Library, and Richard Temple of the Modern Records Centre, University of Warwick, for information from sources in their care. I would also like to thank Nicholas Crowson for a reference from the Collin Brooks papers, and James Hinton and Chris Wrigley for help with details about persons mentioned in the text. Lin Foxhall and Nicole Davies kindly ensured that I did not trip up when translating phrases from other languages.

It is the nature of prefaces that the largest debts come first and last. My family have put up with this project more than with my other books, for during the final year much of the work was done at home. This intruded on family space to some extent (especially the microfilm reader), but added greatly to the pleasures of the work. One part of this was that my sons, Alastair and Duncan, have been able to take a real interest in what was going on; they also accepted with good grace that our computer was sometimes not available for its proper use of playing games. Last is the very opposite of least: my greatest debt and deepest thanks go to my wife, Gilly, who as always has given me constant encouragement and support.

Abbreviations

Educ.	Education	Nat.	National(ist)
Fed.	Federation	N.E.C.	National Executive
For.	Foreign		Committee
F.S.	Financial Secretary	N.F.U.	National Farmers'
F.S.T.	Financial Secretary		Union
	to the Treasury	N.U.	National Union of
Gen.	General		Conservative &
G.O.C.	General Officer		Unionist
	Commanding		Associations
Gov.	Governor	Parl.	Parliament(ary)
Govt.	Government	Perm.	Permanent
Ind.	Independent	P.L.P.	Parliamentary
I.L.P.	Independent		Labour Party
	Labour Party	P.P.S.	Parliamentary
jt.	joint		Private Secretary
K.G.	Knight of the	Pres.	President
	Garter	Prof.	Professor
kt.	knighted	prop.	proprietor
K.T.	Knight of the	Prov.	Provincial
	Thistle	P.S.	Parliamentary
Lab.	Labour		Sercretary
L.C.C.	London County	rep.	representative
	Council	Res.	Resident
Ld.	Lord	S.A.C.	Supreme Allied
Lib.	Liberal		Commander
L.U.	Liberal Unionist	Sec.	Secretary
Lt.	Lieutenant		(Secretary of State)
Ltd.	Limited	Sen.	Senator
Med.	Mediterranean	suc.	succeeded as
M.F.G.B.	Miners' Federation	U.N.[O.]	United Nations
	of Great Britain		(Organization)
Min.	Minister	Univ.	University(ies)
M.S.	Minister of State	U.S.	Under-Secretary

Newcastle-upon-Tyne: constituencies and wards in 1945

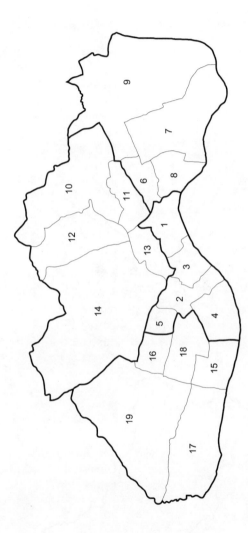

Central Division

1 All Saints
2 St. John's
3 St. Nicholas
4 Stephenson
5 Westgate

East Division

6 Byker
7 St. Anthony's
8 St. Laurence
9 Walker

North Division

10 Dene
11 Heaton
12 Jesmond
13 St. Andrew's
14 St. Thomas

West Division

15 Armstrong
16 Arthur's Hill
17 Benwell
18 Elswick
19 Fenham

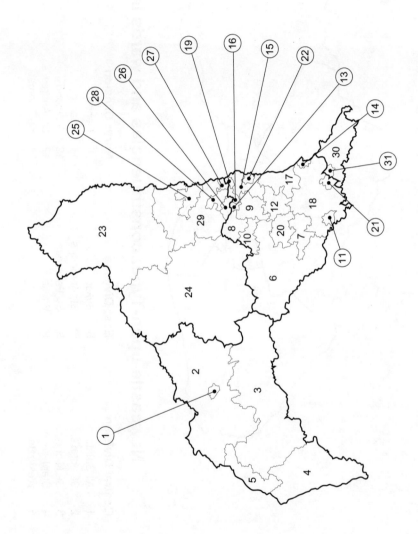

The Northern Counties Area 1930-1949

Cumberland

1 Carlisle (B)
2 Cumberland Northern
3 Penrith & Cockermouth
4 Whitehaven
5 Workington

Durham

6 Barnard Castle
7 Bishop Auckland
8 Blaydon
9 Chester-le-Street
10 Consett
11 Darlington (B)
12 Durham
13 Gateshead (B)
14 Hartlepools (B)
15 Houghton-le-Spring
16 Jarrow
17 Seaham
18 Sedgefield
19 South Shields (B)
20 Spennymoor
21 Stockton-on-Tees (B)
22 Sunderland (2B)

Northumberland

23 Berwick
24 Hexham
25 Morpeth (B)
26 Newcastle
    Central (B)
    East (B)
    North (B)
    West (B)
27 Tynemouth (B)
28 Wallsend (B)
29 Wansbeck

Yorkshire (part of)

30 Cleveland
31 Middlesbrough
    East (B)
    West (B)

(B) = *Borough*
(2B) = *Two-Member Borough*

INTRODUCTION

For the period of his political career, from 1924 to 1951, Sir Cuthbert Headlam's diary consists of more than two and a half million words. The diary is of value for more than just its scale and consistency. Whilst Headlam naturally wrote about his own affairs, he looked outwards as well as inwards. When he was at the House of Commons he would record the gossip of the lobbies, the mood of his party and the standing of its leaders. Headlam knew most of the rising figures in the Conservative Party of the 1930s and 1940s, and recorded his assessment of their characters and fortunes. He also used the diary to analyse the domestic and international situation, and to comment upon topical issues. It is these elements in the diary which are of wider historical significance, and which have been selected for inclusion in the published edition. The remainder, about 85% of the original text, is either more purely personal or is of interest for the picture which it gives of the daily life of a Member of Parliament of this era. The latter material has been synthesised and discussed in this introduction, which is divided into three parts. The first gives an account of Headlam's life and career from 1935 onwards; the years before this are briefly summarised, as they have been described in full in the introduction to the previous volume.[1] The second section moves away from chronological narrative, and takes an overall view of Headlam's character, pattern of life and career, spanning the period of both volumes. The final section concerns the diary itself: Headlam's motives and habits in writing it, the selection and editing of the

[1] S. Ball (ed.), *Parliament and Politics in the Age of Baldwin and MacDonald: The Headlam Diaries 1924–1935* (London, 1992), pp. 1–27; this volume was published by The Historians' Press.

text, and its value as a source. Together, these furnish the context in which the diary can be used and understood.

(i)   *Sir Cuthbert Headlam: the Second Phase*

Cuthbert Morley Headlam came from a minor gentry family which had its roots in north Yorkshire and south County Durham. During the nineteenth and twentieth centuries the Headlams were extensively involved in the respectable professions of the armed services, the Established Church, the law, and public school and university education. Born on 27 April 1876 into a cadet branch, Cuthbert was educated at King's School, Canterbury, and at Magdalen College, Oxford. He had no inherited income to fall back upon, and throughout his life had to make his own living. On leaving Oxford in 1897 he accepted the offer of a Clerkship in the House of Lords. Here he remained until 1924, with the interruption of service on the Western Front between 1915 and 1918 during which he rose to the rank of Lieutenant-Colonel on the General Staff. The Lords' clerkship proved to be a dreary dead end, but after his marriage to Beatrice Crawley in 1904 he was dependent upon its salary. However, in the early 1920s the development of an independent income from journalistic and business activities at last made venturing into politics a possibility, albeit a risky one. Even then, Headlam had not the surplus wealth necessary to fund the large annual subscription usually required from their candidates by Conservative Associations in safe seats. Throughout his career he was to find himself rejected on these grounds in favour of less able men, an experience which contributed to his growing embitterment by the mid-1930s. After several false starts, and armed with a promise of financial support from Conservative Central Office which he could not afford to turn down, Headlam secured adoption through his local family connections for the Barnard Castle constituency of County Durham in June 1924.

In the general election which took place a few months later, after the fall of the first Labour government, Headlam won this highly marginal seat in a straight fight with the sitting Labour M.P. The Barnard Castle division contained a substantial portion of the west Durham coalfield, generally a Labour stronghold, together with pockets of traditional Liberalism in the Pennine dales. It was thus a difficult proposition for the Conservatives, who could only win it when the national tide was strongly in their favour and there was no Liberal intervention. However, representing a northern mining division in the troubled period of the mid-1920s gave Headlam opportunities in debate in the House of Commons on the key issues of the day: the role of trade unions, the political levy, the problems of the coal industry, and the long and bitter strike of 1926–27. His firm but reasonable line was in tune with the sentiments expressed by the Party leader, Stanley Baldwin, and partly as a result Headlam became the first of the large and talented Conservative intake of 1924 to be promoted. In December 1926 he was appointed to junior office as Parliamentary Secretary to the Admiralty, serving there until he lost his seat in the general election of May 1929. Out of Parliament, he attempted to secure adoption for a safer seat, but lack of money thwarted all such efforts. In June 1931 he was the Conservative candidate in the Gateshead by-election; although he did not win this safe Labour seat, the swing to the Conservatives which he achieved was an important indicator of electoral trends even before the August 1931 crisis and the formation of the National Government.

Headlam recovered Barnard Castle in the ensuing general election of October 1931 and was appointed to junior posts, first at the Ministry of Pensions (from November 1931 to September 1932) and then at the Ministry of Transport (from September 1932 to July 1934). The latter was the busier department, but Headlam was kept mainly in the background due to the incompetence of his first Minister, Percy Pybus, who needed much outside help, and then the excess of competence of his second, Oliver Stanley, who needed no help at all. Stanley had also entered the House in 1924, but he was the younger son of the powerful 17th Earl of Derby and was already marked out as a high flier. Although their relations were friendly, Headlam felt humiliated at having to serve under a man who was twenty years younger than himself. Disillusioned with the Party leadership and having been bluntly informed by the Chief Whip that further promotion was unlikely, he resigned and returned to the backbenches in July 1934. Throughout the parliament, he was President of the 'Northern Group' of supporters of the National Government. Headlam felt condemned to fight the hard battles against Labour in the industrial north, where his efforts were neither recognised nor rewarded by the Party hierarchy in London. Not even the award of a baronetcy, gazetted in the Jubilee honours of

June 1935, was a consolation for these disappointments – indeed, Headlam viewed the honour as 'a public recognition of my political failure' [2] As the north-east remained mired in recession during 1934 and 1935 despite the signs of recovery elsewhere, and with the National Government's policies on unemployment relief and the Special Areas in confusion, Headlam was resigned to the loss of Barnard Castle in the coming election. The intervention of a Liberal candidate – the factor which had also been critical in 1929 – was merely the final nail in his coffin. He fought hard and was only 1,320 votes behind the Labour candidate, but defeat by whatever margin still put him out of the House, despite the National Government's victory.

With the loss of his seat in November 1935, Headlam believed that his political career was over. [3] In addition to the habitual pessimism of his temperament, there were several reasons for this view. With a reputation for independence of mind, frankness, and even cantankerousness, he had little expectation that the Party leaders would exert themselves to assist his return to the House of Commons. Although physically fit, his age would also tell against him. Marginal seats preferred younger candidates who would be more able to withstand the pace of a gruelling campaign. Competition was fierce for the safer seats, whose long-serving M.P.s meant that vacancies were much less frequent. By the likely date of the next election in late 1939 or 1940, Headlam would be approaching the age of 65; even if he were to win a seat, he would be unlikely to serve beyond one parliament. Because he would be at best an interim solution, he was only likely to appeal to the nearly hopeless prospects – and they did not appeal to him, after a decade already spent trying precariously to hold on to the Barnard Castle constituency. Headlam was left only with the consolation that he had established himself as the leading Conservative politician in the north-east. Although he did not realise it, this was to be the foundation for the second half of his career, leading to his return to Parliament for a further decade as an M.P. in the 1940s.

However, in the wake of rejection and with his sixtieth birthday only five months away, Headlam's intention was to devote the remainder of his active life to the world of industry and commerce.

---

[2] Headlam diary, 17 May, 31 Dec. 1935; the orginal diaries form the main part of the Headlam MSS deposited at Durham County Record Office.
[3] Headlam diary, 20 Nov., 31 Dec. 1935.

This aim was partly realised, and partly thwarted. Opportunities in London were hard to come by, whilst the sluggish nature of the economic recovery in the north-east limited the openings in the region where Headlam's name carried more weight. In fact, his political prominence was a mixed blessing: he felt that local businessmen did not wish to be linked with him, for fear that this would provoke the hostility of organised labour.[4] They may also have found him too abrasive, but, whatever the cause, his efforts in May–July 1936 to secure the chairmanship of the mineowners' new coal marketing body were unsuccessful. This would have brought a secure annual salary of £4,000, and the disappointment was crushing: 'I have lost all self confidence, and realize that I am a failure.'[5] For the remainder of his life, the problem of scraping together an adequate income was to be his constant concern. Headlam's political career had been made possible in the 1920s by the salary he received as editor of the *Army Quarterly*; although this was becoming an increasingly tedious chore, he could not afford to give it up. The most secure item in Headlam's portfolio was his place on the board of the local electricity generating company, North-Eastern Electric Supply, a well-founded concern which became more prosperous as the demand for power increased during the 1930s. In November 1935 and June 1936 Guy Dawnay, a close friend since the First World War and a successful City of London businessman, made Headlam a director of two of his subsidiary trust and property companies.[6] These brought in £250 per annum each, and until they struck wartime difficulties these were the other dependable element in the Headlams' finances. Oliver Lyttelton, another prominent businessman and acquaintance from wartime days, gave Headlam a directorship in 1935, but this ended in 1937. Help from an unexpected quarter came from the 'diehard' M.P. George Balfour. Although not a particular political or personal friend, he felt that Headlam had been treated poorly by Baldwin and Central Office, and so in May 1938 offered him a place on the board of the Jerusalem Electric and Public Service Corporation, with annual fees of £250. However, in order to

[4] Headlam diary, 22 Nov. 1936, 2 Jan. 1937.
[5] Headlam diary, 27 & 21 July 1936.
[6] These were the Berkeley Property and Investment Co. and the West London Property Corporation, subsiduaries of Dawnay, Day & Co.; Headlam diary, 18 Nov. 1935, 4 June 1936.

maintain their style of living the Headlams needed an income of around £1,500–£2,000, and so financial collapse often seemed to be just around the corner.[7]

The result was a frustrating search for ways to bridge the gap, but of the limited business opportunities which came Headlam's way, all too many became sources of worry or ran into difficulties: 'I certainly don't have much luck in my business undertakings – each in turn seems full of promise, each in succession comes to nothing or disaster.'[8] So it was with the silver and antiques company How of Edinburgh, with Ship Carbon, with the proposal for extracting oil from coal in north Wales (Mold Minerals), with a scheme to link South Shields and Tynemouth by rail tunnel, and with the pump manufacturing business of the Czech refugee Sigmund brothers. The first and last of these consumed a lot of time and energy, and in both cases Headlam's position as chairman of the board of directors bought him much anxiety. The constant near-bankruptcy of How of Edinburgh preoccupied him from late 1936 to August 1938, whilst after a promising start in May 1938 the relationship with the Sigmunds soured during 1939, ending in bitter boardroom wrangles and Headlam's forced resignation in January 1940.[9] The Headlams skirted the shoals of bankruptcy as much by luck as judgement, kept afloat by the help at vital moments of Dawnay in particular. The recurring theme of these years was financial trouble and anxiety: 'It is the lack of £.s.d. which is worrying me into fiddle strings and rendering me so futile and despairing.'[10]

There was frequent talk of having to leave Holywell Hall, the house near Durham which they had rented since 1925, and retire in obscurity to a cottage in the south – and such was the strain that at some points such a fate seemed almost attractive.[11] Yet, despite the cost of maintaining Holywell, which needed a minimum staff of a cook, several maids, a chauffeur and a gardener, the Headlams could not bring themselves to quit. This was due partly

[7] For some of the lowest points, see Headlam diary, 14 July 1936, 2 Aug. 1937, 20 July 1939, 17 Feb. 1940.

[8] Headlam diary, 24 Oct. 1939.

[9] Controlled Engineering (Sigmund Pumps Great Britain Ltd.), a branch of the Czech firm Sigmund Pumps; Headlam diary, 26 & 31 May 1938, 23 Jan., 9 Aug., 31 Oct., 22 Nov. 1939, 23 & 24 Jan., 20 Feb. 1940.

[10] Headlam diary, 14 July 1936.

[11] Headlam diary, 3 Nov. 1939, 5 Mar. 1940.

to the attractiveness of the house, and partly to the lack of suitable alternatives:[12]

> we should be wise to leave it – but the difficulty is where to find another house and what to do – if we leave Holywell we might just as well leave Durham – either returning to London or settling in some cottage in the south – but Beatrice does not want to live in London and we neither of us know of any 'cottage in the south' – so presumably we shall cling on here until we are literally broken.

Instead, efforts were made to cut down the scale of the staff and to economise on entertaining. However, Beatrice was unable to do either for long; the reductions achieved hardly solved the instability in their finances, for 'we have invariably lived beyond our means'.[13] Wartime regulations imposed further cuts, but as long as the Headlams lived at Holywell and had any social life, providing hospitality was unavoidable – 'and that is how the money goes'.[14] Another problem concerned the subsidy which Headlam had received from Party funds; Hamar Greenwood, Party Treasurer from 1933 to 1938, had promised to continue it, but when he stepped down the Chairman of the Party, Douglas Hacking, declared that he knew nothing of this and disavowed it.[15] Matters improved to some extent in 1938 and 1939, but the difficulties persisted even after Headlam returned to the Commons in 1940.

Money was not his only concern during the period out of the House from 1935 to 1940. At the very beginning, he was anxious about the ill-health and depression from which Beatrice suffered during 1935. She had remained to help in his unsuccessful election campaign, but on the day after the result was declared she left to convalesce in South Africa; it was hoped that the sea voyage and change of climate would revive her. Tired and miserable after the loss of the seat, her departure was traumatic for both of them. Headlam missed her intensely, returning to Holywell 'a very desolate and disappointed man in a house from which all the light and happiness have gone'.[16] Despite encouraging letters during the later part of her time at the Cape, Beatrice seemed little better after her

---

[12] Headlam diary, 3 Aug. 1937.
[13] Headlam diary, 5 Feb. 1936.
[14] Headlam diary, 21 Mar. 1940.
[15] Headlam diary, 2, 3 & 9 May 1938.
[16] Headlam diary, 18 Nov. 1935.

return in March 1936, and recurrent troubles led to a good deal of time consulting doctors and trying various remedies over the next few years.[17] Headlam's relationship with his wife was of vital importance, for 'she is the only person in the world who can keep me going: without her I am like a ship without its rudder and seem to have no object in life'.[18] As he wrote at a dark hour in 1940, on their thirty-sixth wedding anniversary, 'so long as we are together, I feel that we can weather whatever storms are ahead of us'.[19] The other family matter was the education of their adopted son, John, who moved from Eton to attend Gordonstoun, then in its early years. His school years were coming to an end as war loomed nearer and the question of his future career was still unresolved when the war began and he prepared for military service.

Headlam's departure from the House of Commons in 1935 had not entailed a complete disappearance from national public life. A legacy from his period at the Ministry of Transport was the chairmanship of a Committee of Imperial Defence sub-committee which was examining the problems which might be faced in unloading and distributing vital imports in wartime. Headlam found this work interesting, but the report was finalised in the spring of 1937. He wrote occasional letters on political and foreign policy issues to *The Times*, of which his friend Geoffrey Dawson was editor, and contributed articles to periodicals such as the *English Review*. This kept him to some extent in the public eye, whilst through the editorship of the *Army Quarterly* he was in touch with military circles, including former wartime comrades who now held senior positions. His military and historical knowledge led to an invitation from the British Council to give a series of lectures about the army in Paris and Lisbon in 1939. However, such activities on the sideline were little consolation: 'I feel so utterly out of things and hopeless', he noted on 15 August 1937. Time hung heavily, leading to apathy, and he frequently complained of an inability to get to grips with his tasks. The feeling of being 'on the shelf' was the main cause of this boredom and depression, and the Headlams felt neglected and forgotten: 'up here where we have worked so hard, we receive no recognition – elsewhere we are considered of no account.'[20] There

[17] Headlam diary, 27 Mar. 1936, 7 Oct. 1938.
[18] Headlam diary, 18 Nov. 1935.
[19] Headlam diary, 22 Mar. 1940.
[20] Headlam diary, 2 Jan. 1937, 4 Dec. 1938.

was little change, and the outlook seemed bleak during these difficult years: 'one just drifts along – never a glimmer of light on the horizon – and every day some minor worry or another, usually due to our penurious state. Life is very difficult and tiring', he wrote in early 1938.[21]

Headlam's anxieties were not only personal; like many others, but from a more informed perspective and perhaps with greater acuity, he saw the international situation deteriorate and the prospect of another terrible world war come ever closer. He had no illusions about the nature of Hitler's regime, even before his attendance as a foreign observer at the Nazi Party rally at Nuremberg in September 1937.[22] He was bitterly critical of the failures of British foreign policy after 1935, and in particular of the continued public reliance upon the League of Nations and the myth of 'collective security'. His condemnation was private rather than public, the result of both party loyalty and the gravity of the situation. Whilst he had doubts that Neville Chamberlain had the qualities of leadership which the crisis demanded, he held him less responsible. The seeds of disaster had been sown before 1937: 'to me Baldwin is the arch-culprit and I fancy that history will so judge', he wrote in April 1939.[23] Headlam regarded the Munich settlement of September 1938 as unavoidable, given the unpreparedness of the country's defences. However, he had no doubt that it was a humiliation rather than a success, and that it gave dangerous encouragement to Hitler's adventurism. By the end of 1938, revolted especially by the outbreaks of Jew-baiting in Germany, he regarded war as inevitable.[24] Even before the occupation of Prague in March 1939, he had come to the conclusion that Hitler would have to be stopped, and that diplomatic efforts were fruitless.

After having invested so much effort and emotion between 1924 and 1935, neither Cuthbert nor Beatrice wanted to abandon their work in the north-east. Whilst they remained living at Holywell it was natural that others would look to them to continue providing the leadership which they had given hitherto. This was not just

---

[21] Headlam diary, 10 Feb. 1938.
[22] E.g., his comments on watching a Hitler Youth parade: Headlam diary, 1 May 1936.
[23] Headlam diary, 8 Apr. 1939.
[24] Headlam diary, 24 Nov. 1938.

political: Beatrice was heavily committed to her charitable projects for unemployed women and girls, while Cuthbert held a prominent position as a regional Vice-President of the wartime servicemen's body, the British Legion. However, his public role was mainly identified with politics, and after 1935 this took on a new dimension. Headlam had emerged as a leading figure in Conservative affairs in the north-east by the beginning of the 1930s. He had an ability to deal with hostile working-class audiences at public meetings, being 'an admirable platform speaker, clear, pithy and fair-minded'.[25] This experience in a hard school led to his frequent use in by-elections around the country while he was a junior minister, and after 1935 he was still much in demand in his own area. Headlam did not like to refuse these requests, and took a particular interest in the lodges of the National Conservative League and the constituency branches aimed at working men and trade unionists. His prominence was a solitary one: apart from the special case of the Prime Minister, Ramsay MacDonald, at Seaham, Headlam was the only minister in 1931–35 with a seat in either Durham or Northumberland. After 1935 the remaining Conservative M.P.s in the north-east were either too young, too old, too ineffectual, or – in Harold Macmillan's case – too idiosyncratic, to provide alternative leadership. This was compounded by the lack of gentry and aristocracy in the region, and the aloofness and unreliability of the most socially prominent family of all, the Londonderrys.[26]

In parallel with developments elsewhere, the Conservative organisation in the region was reshaped in 1930 with the establishment of the Northern Counties Area, one of the twelve into which England and Wales were divided.[27] It comprised the counties of Durham, Northumberland and Cumberland, together with Middlesbrough and the Cleveland district of Yorkshire. The individual county committees continued in existence as a second tier, and Headlam was the natural choice as chairman of the County Durham executive; this office gave him a wider regional role, as it automatically made him a vice-chairman of the Area. In June 1931 his profile and prestige were further raised by his vigorous campaign

---

[25] *The Times*, 3 Mar. 1964.

[26] Ball, *Parliament and Politics in the Age of Baldwin and MacDonald*, p. 9.

[27] S. Ball, 'The national and regional Party structure', in A. Seldon & S. Ball (eds.), *Conservative Century: The Conservative Party since 1900* (Oxford, 1994), pp. 206–12.

in the Gateshead by-election; although he narrowly failed to win this safe Labour seat, the result raised the morale of the Conservative opposition and dealt a blow to Ramsay MacDonald's tottering ministry.[28] Headlam's authority was fully established by the vigour which he brought to the 1931 general election campaign in the county and by his active role in County Council elections.[29] With the bitter taste of the 1935 defeat still in his mouth, and feeling that he had been let down by the party authorities, he at first intended to resign the county chairmanship. However, at the urging of local supporters, he paused and began to reconsider: 'perhaps if I gave it up I should regret it – anyway it is a matter which requires further consideration'.[30] In the end, with some reluctance, he decided to remain and was re-elected as county chairman on 22 February 1936.

This was the first step on the road back to the Commons, and it led not long after to the second. Since its formation the Northern Area had been dominated by the leading figures of Northumbrian Conservatism, Sir Alexander Leith and Sir Alfred Appleby. Their partnership of mutual complacency provoked some hostility, but until age took effect there was little that could be done. However, in July 1936 Leith decided to retire, and his initial suggestion that Appleby should replace him was resisted by the more active members of the Area executive. Quite apart from the feeling that Durham should have its turn, Headlam's talents and commitment had made him the obvious successor. It was thus through a combination of inertia on his part and a local vacuum in the north-east, rather than any plan or ambition, that Headlam resumed political activity in 1936. He expected to hold the chairmanship for four or five years, in line with the emerging consensus in the Party as a whole that these offices should change hands more frequently than had been the case in the past. However, the intervention of the war upset this calculation, and as a result Headlam was to remain in place for almost a decade, finally standing down in May 1946.

The Northern Area was the smallest in the number of constituencies which it contained and the Party was at its weakest here,

[28] Neville Chamberlain to Headlam, 22 June 1931, Headlam MSS, [D/He] 128/11.
[29] Bradford to Headlam, 28 Oct. 1931, Headlam MSS 129/14; Headlam diary, 2 Oct. 1933.
[30] Headlam diary, 15 Dec. 1935.

for there were very few safe Conservative seats; for both these reasons, it had little influence in the counsels of the Party. It resembled only one of the other areas, Wales and Monmouthshire, which was of similar size and economic composition, but even here the Conservatives had a better record. The Conservative Party faced considerable problems in the Northern Area, not just electorally but also in a lack of leadership and resources. Many businessmen preferred to stay on the sidelines and there were relatively few titled families resident in the area to provide social prestige. This meant that the Area was financially weak, and that a heavier burden of work fell upon the Chairman's shoulders than was the case elsewhere. 'I don't suppose that any other Area Chairman does a tenth part of the work I do', commented Headlam on 17 February 1939. After his first few months in the post, he had noted that 'it is certainly no sinecure to be Area Chairman if one really does one's job'.[31] Whilst it could not be said that he relished the challenge, Headlam was not one to shirk his responsibilities. He attended and spoke at a wide range of functions at Area, county and constituency levels, sometimes having two commitments in different places in a day. He was frequently called upon to speak at constituency Annual General Meetings, political education schools and public meetings, to attend social functions, dinners, and clubs, to judge Junior Imperial League speaking competitions, and so on. These engagements were a matter of duty rather than pleasure; after attending a branch inaugural meeting in cold and wet weather, he noted 'I wonder what other Area Chairman attends smoking concerts in tiny villages in his area?'[32]

Two matters particularly concerned him: the encouragement of Conservative trade unionists and workers, and the lack of cohesion in the Area. When he became chairman there was still considerable division between the counties, and he sought to heal the rift by acting in an entirely neutral manner. Cumberland had been both neglected and offended by Leith, and wanted to withdraw from the Area. Headlam made particular efforts to attend events in Cumberland and this, together with his good relations with the leading figures of Sir Fergus and Lady Mary Graham (the former had been his Parliamentary Private Secretary in 1931–32), improved

[31] Headlam diary, 6 Feb. 1937.
[32] Headlam diary, 13 Dec. 1937.

the atmosphere. The Area Chairmanship carried with it a prominent place on the executive committee of the National Union, the representative side of the Conservative Party organisation. This entailed attending committee meetings in London, and to a limited extent kept him in the swim. However, what little novelty and cachet there was in the post soon wore off: 'what a bore it is all becoming!', noted Headlam in early 1938; 'one struggles on with it, however, partly from a sense of duty, partly because one has nothing else to do – and I suppose that possibly one is doing something useful, although one sees little sign of it'.[33]

As he got into his stride as Area Chairman, and lacking other stimulating outlets, Headlam began to consider the possibility of returning to Westminster. Due to his age and the likelihood that the next general election would not occur until late 1939 or the spring of 1940, this meant looking for a by-election opening or at least nursing a better prospect than Barnard Castle. In any case, so strong was his feeling of resentment over his rejection by that constituency that Headlam was adamant that under no circumstances would he stand for it again. He had formally declined the candidacy in February 1936 and, in a deliberate effort to close the door, encouraged the adoption of his younger cousin Agnes Headlam-Morley; she was then a tutor at St. Hugh's College, Oxford, and had made a favourable impression whilst helping in his campaigns.[34] The most attractive route back to the House would have been one of the University seats; these were prestigious and, as the electors were scattered around the country and voting was by postal ballot, they did not entail a conventional campaign. Instead, what mattered were the lists of nominees and influential supporters – especially the heads of colleges – which were published in the press. Headlam took soundings when a vacancy occurred in one of the Oxford University seats in 1936, but his potential support was not enough to counter the prominent Oxford figures, such as Professor Lindemann, who were already in the field.[35]

Headlam also put his name forward for a number of other seats

---

[33] Headlam diary, 1 Feb. 1938.

[34] Headlam to Barnard Castle CA Exec., 3 Feb. 1936, Headlam MSS 135/19ii.

[35] There were rumours in the press in Feb. 1937 that Headlam was interested in the vacancy in the English Universities seat; although he does not appear to have been seeking this, the reports led him to contact the chairman of the Conservative association, but it was clear that they already had a candidate in mind.

during these years, but without success. There were three reasons for this: age, lack of money, and the attitude of the party authorities. The safer seats, such as Guildford and Richmond, were generally looking for a younger as well as a richer man. Money was a particular difficulty: most such constituencies expected that the candidate would pay his election expenses – generally about £1,000 – and that he would make a substantial annual donation to their funds, but Headlam could offer neither. This was the problem that had dogged his political career, and about which he had long felt aggrieved.[36] In addition, the party managers had no particular desire to see Headlam back at Westminster. Constituencies made their own choice, but Central Office was often consulted and could exert a negative influence. In November 1939 the Party Chairman wrote to Lord Derby, the powerful President of the North Western Area, to discourage the selection of Headlam for the candidacy at Stretford. Hacking reported that he had 'discussed the matter with the Chief Whip and he shares my views – in fact he goes so far as to say that Cuthbert Headlam in the House of Commons at this time would be nothing less than a nuisance'.[37] Headlam clearly had a difficult reputation, of which Derby was already aware: he offered to use his influence in favour of the other main contender and, unsurprisingly, Headlam was not chosen. The Central Office correspondence files for the pre-war period no longer exist, but it is unlikely that this was the only such intervention.

Thwarted in his efforts to find a seat elsewhere, Headlam was forced back upon the limited resources of the Northern Area, where his name and position carried weight. In early 1938 the M.P. for Darlington announced that he was not going to stand again; although it would be a hard fight, this was a compact borough seat with a fair chance of success. Headlam wavered, but was reluctant to commit himself as it seemed that the far better prospect of Newcastle North might become available. In the event, he fell between two stools: nothing transpired on the Newcastle front, whilst the Darlington candidacy went instead to a local antagonist,

[36] After rejection by Richmond he wrote a caustic reply on these lines, and sent a copy to Hacking, the Party Chairman; this was perhaps unwise, although the party leadership were publicly opposed to the worst practices of auctioning seats to the highest bidder: Headlam diary, 25 Jan. 1937.

[37] Hacking to Derby, 1 Nov. 1939, Derby to Hacking, 3 Nov. 1939, Derby MSS, 920/DER(17)/31/6, Liverpool Record Office.

Charles Vickery.[38] Having secured nothing else and with the election coming nearer, Headlam acted more decisively when the candidate for Berwick withdrew in January 1939. At once he contacted the local chairman and asked to be considered; perhaps inauspiciously, the letter was despatched on Friday the 13th. Berwick had been in Conservative hands from 1923 to 1935, when its maverick and rebellious 'diehard' M.P. lost it to a Liberal in a straight fight. Although it was a rural division, larger even than Barnard Castle, its attraction was that the election expenses were paid by the Association: Headlam would no longer be dependent upon financial help from either Leith and Appleby or Central Office. He attended the selection committee on 31 January and, after the original seven were reduced to a shortlist of three, Headlam was chosen and formally adopted as candidate at a general meeting on 16 February 1939. This was followed by a campaign of meetings throughout the constituency in March, and he assiduously nursed the seat until the outbreak of war caused the cessation of political campaigning and postponed the election indefinitely.

Berwick was always a second-best, and from the start Headlam felt ambivalent about it. He was conscious of the potential vacancy at Newcastle North, a mainly middle-class and residential district which was the safest Conservative seat in the region. Sir Nicholas Grattan-Doyle, who had held the seat since 1918, was 75 years of age in 1937 and unlikely to fight another general election. He was an obscure figure in the House who had been part of the anti-Baldwin 'diehard' group, and an indifferent local M.P. who lived several hundred miles away in Hertfordshire. He had kept the constituency Association as a small clique, under his own thumb and aloof from the Area. Headlam had long coveted the seat but was aware that Grattan-Doyle regarded it almost as his personal property and wanted to pass it on to his son; a move in this direction was constantly being rumoured in the late 1930s, but it did not occur before the war broke out. However, on 2 April 1940 Grattan-Doyle suddenly announced his retirement and sought to have his son selected for the vacancy, expecting to exploit the wartime party truce to ensure that the latter was returned unopposed. After paying lip service to the possibility of other candidates, the official Newcastle North association swiftly adopted

[38] Headlam diary, 23 Mar. 1938, 27 Apr. 1938.

Howard Grattan-Doyle as its candidate on 13 April. This piece of blatant nepotism, although expected, touched upon Headlam's most sensitive spot: the vagaries and injustices of candidate selection in safe seats. However, he could do nothing on his own, and at first he despaired of the hesitancy of the dissident local Conservatives. With some prodding, opposition began to gather momentum, fuelled by the indignity of the Grattan-Doyles' proprietorial attitude to the seat, dislike of their Roman Catholicism, and resentment of the fact that the son was of military age and would be leaving his unit in France for this safe billet. A group of prominent Newcastle businessmen resident in Jesmond found this combination too much to swallow, and under the guidance of the Area Chairman they formed a rebel Association – which then invited Headlam to become its candidate.[39]

The connection was a natural one: Headlam was the most vigorous Conservative figure in the north-east, and since becoming Area Chairman he had been a much more frequent presence in Newcastle affairs; he was invited to attend or speak at a wide range of functions, not all of them political, and he had been elected to the prestigious Northern Counties Club. The outbreak of war had removed the point of his candidacy for Berwick: instead of taking place in 1940, the general election was now unlikely to come until after the end of the war – a delay probably of several years which would leave Headlam too old to be credible as a candidate. Furthermore, if another wartime coalition should be formed, it was possible that sitting Liberal M.P.s would not be opposed by the Conservatives in any wartime or post-war election. Headlam was frustrated and despondent at having been given nothing useful to do to help the war effort and, although he would have welcomed something with more responsibility, returning to the Commons would give him some role and keep him in touch with events.[40] For these reasons, as well as the scandal of a Grattan–Doyle succession, Headlam was disposed to take up the gauntlet in Newcastle North. At the same time, he was aware of the risks: some – especially outside the region – would disapprove of his actions, whilst failure would mean humiliation and political oblivion.

[39] In addition to the diary, see the account in an untitled memo prepared by Headlam for the National Union inquiry into North Newcastle, 23 June 1951, Headlam MSS 133/18.

[40] Headlam diary, 1, 29 Sep., 4 Oct. 1939.

In accordance with the wartime truce, no Liberal or Labour candidate was nominated, and the by-election therefore unfolded as the bizarre spectacle of the 'official' Conservative candidate selected by the recognised local constituency association being opposed by the Party's Area Chairman standing as the 'independent' nominee of a rebel and unrecognised group. The wartime context was crucial in another respect: whatever the dubiety and resentment felt about the Grattan-Doyle ramp, Headlam could not pursue a course which could be taken as dissent from his party leader, the Prime Minister, at a point of national crisis. It was therefore imperative that Grattan-Doyle did not receive official Central Office support, and above all that he was not granted the endorsement of the usual public letter from the Leader. After some manoeuvring, this vital objective was secured, in part because of the party managers' genuine dislike of what had occurred in the selection process and their scant regard for the retiring M.P.[41] However, given the sensitivities of local Conservative associations over the question of autonomy and central interference, it was a matter that hung in the balance for some days. In this respect, Headlam's superior connections at the higher levels of the party proved to be crucial, and largely neutralised Grattan-Doyle's advantage on paper of being the 'official' nominee. Headlam's interventions in London first secured a delay in the moving of the writ, giving time to ready his supporters in the constituency, and then helped to obtain the public declaration of Central Office's detachment and the withholding of a letter of endorsement from Chamberlain. These last two were, of course, much more than actions of neutrality – they were a slap in the face for the Grattan-Doyle camp, undermining his legitimacy and giving tacit approval to the actions of Headlam and his backers.

The wartime truce helped Headlam in another way, for under normal circumstances the splitting of the Conservative vote might have proved fatal even in this safe seat, and he would have been under local and national pressure to withdraw. Instead, the campaign proceeded almost unregarded by the electorate as the

---

[41] A Central Office memo had described Grattan-Doyle as 'not only an adventurer but a rogue' at the time of his adoption for Newcastle North before the 1918 election, and nothing in his conduct as an M.P. since then was likely to have improved their opinion: undated memorandum, Bonar Law MSS, 41/I/7, House of Lords Record Office.

landscape of the war changed dramatically. The two candidates'
poorly attended meetings were overshadowed by the catastrophe
of the fall of France, and the poll on 7 June took place whilst the
evacuation at Dunkirk monopolised public attention. In this
context, the question of Grattan-Doyle being of serving military
age probably counted for more with the voters than the charges of
nepotism or the social and religious antagonism which had motiv-
ated the local elite. Frustrated at every turn, Grattan-Doyle's
attacks became increasingly intemperate and personal, but this was
counter-productive. In a low poll, with a turnout of only 22%,
Headlam was the victor by the comfortable margin of 7,380 votes
to 2,982.

This was the turning-point, for although the internal wrangles of
Newcastle North Conservatism gave Headlam much vexation
during the next eleven years, he had at last secured a safe seat in
the House of Commons. There was no problem about his status,
and he was immediately recognised as a member of the Conservative
parliamentary party. Headlam was introduced into the House on
11 June by the Chief Whip, David Margesson, and his deputy,
James Stuart, and reported to Beatrice that everyone he met had
been 'very pleasant and quite sure that I had done the right thing',
apart only from a few of 'the National Union bigwigs' who 'were
inclined to look down their noses – but they are very small beer in
the HofC'.[42] Becoming an M.P. gave Headlam more of a definite
role: 'I am a little in touch with things – not so completely out of
everything as I was before I got back to the House.'[43] Nevertheless,
his position was still that of a spectator: in wartime, with an
all-party coalition in office, the opportunities open to a loyal
Conservative backbencher were restricted and passive. Headlam
dutifully attended the House, but found little to hold his interest:
'I am bored stiff in the HofC, and bored still more in the constituency!'[44] Writing at Holywell after almost a year back in the
Commons he noted:[45]

life here is very little different to what it is in time of peace – so far
at any rate as I am concerned – I potter about as usual doing little of

[42] Cuthbert to Beatrice Headlam, 11 June 1940, Headlam MSS 285/3.
[43] Headlam diary, 29 July 1941.
[44] Headlam diary, 5 July 1941.
[45] Headlam diary, 16 Apr. 1941.

any value to myself or anybody else. How one longs for a definite job – something to occupy one's mind and fill up one's time – as things are I have nothing to do but worry myself to death about the war and all its effects.

He was able to follow the progress of the conflict through newspaper reports and radio bulletins, but with no real task to fill the hours 'one is so helpless and has so much time to think!'[46] Cuthbert and Beatrice found the stress more difficult to cope with than it had been during the First World War; they had then been fully occupied with useful work, but now 'we both get depressed and miserable – it is so maddening to be thought useless when we are both full of life and could help so much in many ways up here'.[47]

No opportunity came his way and throughout the war he was to remain 'on the shelf', unable to make a contribution to the national struggle. The resulting frustration was made all the more bitter when Headlam compared himself with the calibre of the people who were given positions of authority, not only locally but also nationally. However, although Headlam sometimes wondered why he bothered to remain in the House, there were compensations. Being an M.P. meant at least some involvement and status, and it was helpful in his business affairs. He could go over the heads of obstructive civil servants and secure interviews with Ministers, whilst the entitlement to free rail travel between Newcastle and London eased his strained finances and was especially useful during the restrictions of wartime. Most of all, Headlam's regular attendance was a matter of his self-respect and sense of duty. Despite the dangers of staying in London during the blitz in 1940–41 and the flying bomb attacks in 1944, and although his presence was rarely necessary given the Coalition's huge majority, he felt that 'I ought to do my job and attend in my place in Parliament – after all, it is my only work in time of war.'[48] Apart from this, his other regular activity was the practice which he began in May 1941 of being available to callers at the constituency office in Jesmond Road, Newcastle, from 2.00 to 4.00 p.m. on Friday afternoons.

Due to the blackout and the problems of transport in the evening, the House of Commons followed a different schedule during the

[46] Headlam diary, 12 Jan. 1942.
[47] Headlam diary, 1 May 1943.
[48] Headlam diary, 22 June 1944.

war, beginning at 11.00 a.m. and usually rising at 6.00 p.m. The
absence of evening sessions suited Headlam; he normally travelled
to London by the overnight sleeper train on Monday night and
attended the House on Tuesday, Wednesday and Thursday, returning north by the sleeper again that evening. The daytime sittings
were awkward in other ways, however, and by 1943 Headlam
was noting that his business commitments were making regular
attendance difficult. He tended to be present for the opening and
closing speeches of debates, making a particular point of hearing
Churchill, but in between he often had to leave the Palace of
Westminster for lunch engagements and other meetings. Even when
not called away he found it tedious to sit through the general run
of speech-making and instead passed his time elsewhere within the
precincts, particularly in the Smoking Room. It was from here that
he observed the mood of the House – or at least of mainstream
Conservative opinion – and recorded the general verdict on debates
and reputations. He felt in some ways out of touch in the House,
not knowing many of the newer M.P.s, whilst his friends of his
own generation were occupied with ministerial office or other
wartime responsibilities. Nearly two and a half years after his return
to the Commons he noted: 'I really must try and get to know more
people and to mix better. It is no use being in the House unless
one does.'[49] Headlam was not a frequent speaker, for, in addition
to the difficulty of getting called, he remained nervous and self-
critical. However, his interventions put the views of most Conservatives in a clear and cogent form. From the responses which
Headlam records, it is evident that they were generally appreciated
by the other M.P.s, and that he had some standing on the Conservative benches.[50]

Headlam's other wartime role evolved from his membership of the
Executive Committee of the National Union. He was encouraged on
at least two occasions to stand for the chairmanship of the committee, but when he did let his name go forward in May 1943
against the incumbent, Sir Eugene Ramsden, he was unsuccessful.
However, his position as an Area Chairman led to his unopposed

[49] Headlam diary, 26 Oct. 1943.

[50] For example, the unsolicited congratulations after his speech in the Beveridge
debate in Feb. 1943, and being cheered and congratulated after speeches in July
1943, Jan. 1945 and Jan. 1949, Headlam diary, 18 Feb. & 14 July 1943, 19 Jan.
1945, 26 Jan. 1949.

election as the Chairman of the National Union as a whole at the Central Council meeting in March 1941. This was a figurehead post which was held for a year, and which by custom rotated amongst the different Areas. The main function of the chairman was to preside over the annual conference, but due to wartime conditions and the political truce this did not meet during Headlam's term. His other task was to attend a number of events around the country, in particular Area annual meetings, but again there was less to do than normal. In December 1941 Headlam was the chairman of the National Union group which met a deputation from the T.U.C. to discuss the latter's request for amendments to the controversial Trade Disputes Act of 1927. He also served on the committee set up by the National Union Executive to consider the financing of the Party after the war, which met on fourteen occasions between November 1942 and March 1944. The report was unpublished and was later over-shadowed by post-war developments, although it pointed the way towards the changes usually associated with the Maxwell–Fyfe Committee of 1948–49.[51] The National Union chairmanship and his continuing Area role put Headlam at the centre of events, in many ways to a greater extent than would have been the case if he had been given office in the government. The preoccupations of a ministerial workload, especially with the extra demands and cares of wartime, would have prevented him from taking the broad view of issues and events which is reflected in the diary.

The Headlam diary gives an uniquely detailed view of the daily life and concerns of a Member of Parliament, and this is of especial interest during the wartime period when so much was different from usual. Social life in London was very limited, especially for M.P.s of Headlam's generation; many people had moved out of the city or were engaged in war work elsewhere, and those who remained did little entertaining due to the shortages and rationing. The blackout made getting around difficult and even dangerous, whilst public transport was limited and often crowded and taxis were almost impossible to find. The daily routine soon became monotonous: 'one's life is limited to the HofC until 6 p.m. – and then to one's Club or one's flat'.[52] During the bombing of London

---

[51] Special Finance Committee, Report, 16 Mar. 1944, Conservative Party Archive [CPA], CCO/500/3/1, Bodleian Library.
[52] Headlam diary, 19 Dec. 1944.

in November and December 1940 the Commons met in Church House nearby; referred to simply as 'the annexe' for security reasons, this was a modern building thought to be more able to withstand a direct hit. However, it lacked facilities and was generally unpopular with M.P.s, and the usual chamber was returned to until the heavy attacks at the end of April 1941, when 'the annexe' was again used. Shortly after this, on 10 May 1941, the Commons chamber was completely destroyed by an incendiary bomb. After a few weeks' temporary residence at Church House, the Commons moved into the chamber of the House of Lords on 24 June 1941. Apart from a further sojourn in 'the annexe' during the worst of the flying bomb threat from 20 June to 3 August 1944, M.P.s were to use the Lords until the reconstructed House of Commons was opened in October 1950. The furniture in the Lords was moved into the facing rows of the Commons, and a Speaker's chair and clerks' table was installed at the north end.[53] This strange mixture of the odd and the familiar added to the unreal atmosphere of wartime, especially for Headlam for whom the Lords' chamber brought back memories of his years as a clerk before 1924.

Headlam had returned to the Commons shortly after the formation of Churchill's wartime ministry, in which all the main parties were included. Despite occasional murmurings during the darkest days of 1941 and 1942, the Prime Minister had the support of the country and of almost all M.P.s. In these circumstances there was unlikely to be any repeat of the events of May 1940, and parliamentary activity had little purpose. As all National Government and Labour M.P.s were officially supporters of the coalition, the role of leadership of the 'opposition' fell upon the most senior Labour figure who was not in office. As a former minister, Headlam found himself in the odd position of being entitled to sit on the opposition front bench, but he was reluctant to do so. He found the House 'an odd place', sparsely attended and with no life in it.[54] For most of the war the role of Parliament was a passive one, a forum in which events were reported whilst the important decisions were taken elsewhere. Until questions of post-war policy began to emerge late in the war, debates were held as much to keep M.P.s occupied as for any other purpose and many felt, like

---

[53] J. Tanfield, *In Parliament 1939–1950: The Effect of the War on the Palace of Westminster* (House of Commons Library, document 20; London, 1991).

[54] Headlam diary, 12 June 1940.

Headlam, that there was little point in making speeches. However, this left the stage clear for a motley group of disgruntled and second-rate Conservatives, procedural obscuritanists, maverick independents and left-wing Labour M.P.s (of whom the most effective was Aneurin Bevan). Headlam regarded the antics of the handful of persistent critics of the government with antipathy and contempt, and was not attracted to joining the likes of Eddie Winterton. This left him very few outlets, and the feelings of futility and frustration led inevitably to tiredness and depression. Headlam was aware that he could make himself a more active and prominent figure in the House, but he lacked the motivation to do so. The government had his loyal support and his doubts and criticisms were made in private and not in public. He was often unimpressed by the quality of individual ministers, but felt that they were doing their best and that in any case there were not more capable men available to replace them. He was aware that he was unlikely to be offered a post, and was certainly unwilling to make trouble in order to promote his claims.[55] A further problem was the vagaries of Speaker Fitzroy; not only did Headlam find it difficult to catch his eye, but he seemed constantly to call the same few Members and to give far too much scope to the awkward squad. Fitzroy died in 1943, and his successor, Douglas Clifton-Brown, was the M.P. for the Northumberland division of Hexham and a friend of Headlam's. However, Headlam was unable to benefit fully from this change, as he fell seriously ill and was absent from the House from the end of November 1943 until late April 1944, apart from one visit in mid-February which brought about a relapse.

The main themes of politics during the Second World War run through the entries which Headlam made in his diary. First and foremost was the concentration on the progress of the conflict, both in the clashes of arms and the provision of materials. These were linked, for the problems of production and supply led directly to reverses in the field from 1940 to 1942 – British forces always seemed to be outnumbered, lacking in suitable equipment and without sufficient air support. Headlam's military experience gave him a clearer insight than many, and he was especially worried about the shipping situation; until the Battle of the Atlantic was won, there could be no certainty of ultimate victory. The resolve

[55] Headlam diary, 2 & 26 May 1943.

of the general public impressed and moved him, but it was a mixed blessing and he became concerned about the dangers of complacency after Russia and the U.S.A. entered the war in 1941. This particularly affected war production, with absenteeism and an increase in industrial disputes which confirmed Conservative reservations about giving too much power to trade unionism. The worst problem was literally on Headlam's doorstep: the shortages of coal and the intransigence of the miners, with strikes in the autumn of 1943 and spring of 1944. Headlam's other reservation concerned the progressive intelligentsia; he felt that their discussion from early in the war of past iniquities and future reconstruction was divisive and distracting, and thought that their faith in planning and controls was misguided and unrealistic. These issues came to the surface in the coal-rationing scheme of 1942 and in the debate on the Beveridge Report on post-war welfare policy in 1943, when Headlam's short but effective speech was in tune with mainstream Conservative opinion.

Above all of this was the commanding position of Churchill as Prime Minister. Headlam's pre-war view of Churchill had been typical of most Conservative M.P.s: distrustful of his motives and judgement. From his acceptance of Churchill as Premier in May 1940 to the conclusion that he was the one indispensable figure in the government, the changes in Headlam's opinion chart the sea-change in Conservative sentiments. The growth in confidence began with Churchill's indomitable leadership during the Battle of Britain in 1940, became more marked from the middle of 1941 onwards, and was strong enough to withstand the low points of early 1942. It derived from the quality and resonance of his broadcasts and Commons speeches, rather than confidence in his strategic judgement. As Headlam neither forgot his previous doubts nor overlooked the defects of Churchill's personality, his tributes to the Prime Minister's leadership carry all the more weight. A particular problem was Churchill's reliance upon a personal court of cronies, of whom Lord Beaverbrook was especially distrusted.

The downfall of Chamberlain and the effects of the war displaced many of the former Conservative leaders. The most prominent figures of the pre-war years were dropped or shunted aside, bearing the blame for the failures of appeasement and rearmament. Hoare, Simon, Inskip and Halifax left active politics, whilst the careers of others, such as Walter Elliot and even Oliver Stanley, never fully recovered. In their place, the star of the 'anti-appeasement' rebels was rising. This brought Anthony Eden to the position of Churchill's unquestioned heir, although Headlam was not alone in harbouring doubts about his strength of purpose and ability to lead. Duff Cooper came back to cabinet office and, at a lower level, Harold Macmillan's feet at last were placed upon the ministerial ladder. By 1944 three figures had emerged below Churchill as the leading Conservatives of the next generation; they had arrived by different routes, and all three were on friendly terms with Headlam, who was able to observe and judge them from close quarters. First was Eden, whose primacy was accepted rather than respected. Second was Oliver Lyttelton, who was found a safe seat in the Commons when he was brought directly in from business to be President of the Board of Trade in 1940; although he stumbled at first, by the later stages of the war he had found his parliamentary feet and was thought a possible leader. Third was Oliver Stanley, who recovered ground and was appointed Colonial Secretary in 1942 after threatening to vocalise backbench unrest – although, typically, he could never bring himself to take effective action. Below these three, but rising fast, was 'Rab' Butler, author of the 1944 Education Act. He was the most concerned with the issues of reconstruction, and was chairman of the Conservative Party's 'Post-War Problems Central Committee' from July 1941. This worked through a series of sub-committees focusing upon different themes, and Headlam was invited to become chairman of the Constitutional Affairs group. This proved to be a minefield, partly due to the personalities involved and partly to the thorny nature of such topics as House of Lords reform, and the eventual report was quietly sidelined.

Churchill's concentration upon the prosecution of war, together with what Conservatives resentfully considered to be the exploitation of the political truce by their opponents, meant that there was little to counter the advance of the Labour Party between 1940 and 1945. Suffering from widespread apathy and with their party organisation in decay, Conservatives had little to cling to other than the belief that Churchill's prestige would bring electoral triumph when victory came. As the end of the war visibly approached after the liberation of France in late 1944, the Coalition began to show cracks along party lines. The Tory Reform Committee, a group of younger Conservative M.P.s, attempted to

refurbish the party's credibility in domestic policy, but its pro-
gressivism alarmed many Conservative stalwarts. Headlam observed
these trends, and unlike many of his parliamentary colleagues
placed little faith in Churchill's electoral appeal. From mid-1944
he anticipated a Labour victory, although he did not expect the
scale of the landslide which came in July 1945. Newcastle North
proved safe enough to keep his own head above water, and he had
a comfortable majority of 7,153 even though he faced both Liberal
and Labour opponents. However, he was left as almost the only
Conservative M.P. in the north-east: every seat in Co. Durham was
won by Labour, and the only other successful Conservatives were
the Speaker at Hexham and, ironically, a victory at Berwick over Sir
William Beveridge, who had sat as a Liberal since a by-election in
1944. Several of the Conservative leaders had lost their seats elsewhere, and Central Office was seeking vacancies through which they
might return and strengthen the new opposition front bench.
Headlam declined the offer of a peerage to vacate Newcastle North,
partly because he could not afford the loss of income which this would
entail, and partly because of the struggle which he had fought to
remain as candidate and a feeling of obligation to those who had
supported him. However, he requested and was granted a Privy Councillorship. This is the honour which is most prized amongst M.P.s as
it confers status in the House, where 'Right Honourable' Members
take precedence in debate. It would not be conferred unless the standing of the recipient merited it, and it is therefore a sign of Headlam's
reputation and effectiveness; he was not one of the 'shadow cabinet'
leadership, but he was a respected and senior backbench figure.

The financial reservation about the peerage reflected the continuing ups and downs of Headlam's business career during the
1940s. The decade opened with the most severe crisis, with the
severing of the link with the Sigmunds and a falling away of the
directors' fees from other companies due to the effects of the war.
In February 1940 Beatrice's bank, Coutts, were demanding that
she sell her remaining inherited securities in order to reduce her
overdraft, though this was the worst possible time to get a good
price for them. Increased taxation added to the problems: 'How
we shall weather the storm I cannot see', wrote Headlam, 'I have
never been so consumed by anxiety as to the future as I am today.'[56]

[56] Headlam diary, 17 Feb. 1940.

His return to the Commons and the resulting salary helped matters, and from the summer of 1940 they took in paying guests at Holywell; these were mainly the families of officers stationed in the area, in particular at the army base at Brancepeth Castle. The paying guests enabled them to carry on, 'though now and then one does get fearfully bored with them'.[57] By this and other expedients, including turning the garden over to growing vegetables, the Headlams climbed out of the depths of the trough. However, 1941 brought further problems, of which the worst was the abrupt end of his position as editor of the *Army Quarterly*; after the death of the publisher in August 1941, his son installed a new editor and gave Headlam six months' notice. During this time the director-ship in Dawnay's unit trusts company appeared threatened when the business changed hands, but the new owner asked Headlam to remain on the board. His spirits were lifted in November 1941 when, on Dawnay's recommendation, he became a director of the large and successful Liverpool, London & Globe Insurance Company, which balanced the loss of the *Army Quarterly* income.

The silver lining to the fiasco of the involvement with Sigmunds was the forging of a strong link with the city entrepreneur John Grey, who had been ousted together with Headlam in 1940. Apparently wealthy and reputable, Grey had been impressed with Headlam's ability and judgement, and felt something of an obli-gation towards him. After working together on various schemes, Headlam accepted an invitation in April 1942 to join the board of his private company, J.N. Grey & Partners. The £600 per annum which this brought in helped to carry the Headlams through to the post-war world, when some of the other companies began to revive. However, in 1947 the Labour government's nationalization programme meant the extinction of the dependable North-Eastern Electric Supply Company, whilst the British withdrawal from Pal-estine threatened the Jerusalem concern. The next two years were again stressful times, with recurrent worries over a new venture – a pig farm at Holywell. With meat rationed and imports from overseas restricted by the balance of payments crisis, the potential profits were tempting. It was the scheme of Beatrice and Headlam's former secretary and agent, Harry Bell, but the latter was spending

[57] Headlam diary, 14 June 1941.

part of the year in the Channel Islands, having married the daughter of the Dame of Sark, and Beatrice had to oversee a good deal on her own. Matters did not go smoothly at the start and there were continual difficulties in getting suitable workers; as Beatrice's capital was at risk, this led to anxious times in 1948. The corner began to be turned in 1949, just as the next crisis arrived as a bolt from the blue. Headlam had always considered John Grey to be honest, although 'a rough diamond and inclined to be too optimistic'.[58] However, financial difficulties led Grey to cut corners and in March 1949 the auditors refused to pass the company accounts; with its reputation tarnished, this meant the end of the business. At one stage proceedings for fraud looked likely, and Headlam found himself shuttling between meetings with the bankers on one hand and Grey on the other. The latter's mood swung erratically, but in the end he decided to ignore all the warnings and try to ride out the storm, leaving Headlam no alternative but to break with him. As this trouble reached its peak in May 1949, Headlam was fortunately offered the chairmanship of the unit trust group with an increased salary. Even so, matters remained difficult during the next year, and the Headlams once again feared that they were almost on the rocks when in March 1950 their share of the estate of his brother Geoffrey turned out to be worth much more than expected, paying off the mortgage on Holywell and most of the bank overdraft.[59] However, although the Headlams had kept afloat during the 1940s, their future was still far from secured. Age and the end of his status as an M.P. were bound to erode his remaining directorships, and financial need was a major factor in Headlam's reluctance to retire from Parliament.

The Parliament of 1945–50 was Headlam's first experience of opposition. The scale of the defeat had shaken the Conservative Party and left it uncertain of its policies, and with the huge Labour majority there was little that could be accomplished in the House of Commons. Headlam endured the boredom of the backbenches: 'just hanging about with nothing to do except to vote in divisions does not amuse me – and yet I suppose even this form of work is

---

[58] Headlam diary, 3 Apr. 1942.
[59] Fearing that their occupancy would be threatened by the nationalization of the coal mines, Headlam had arranged to purchase Holywell in 1946 for £880; see also below, p. 56.

better than no work at all'.[60] For the first half of the parliament, whilst Labour were enacting their manifesto pledges and the Conservatives began the process of reviving their organisation and restoring their credibility, the opposition kept a low profile. This was tactical rather a lack of party spirit or critical views; whatever their number, Headlam was unimpressed by the ranks of new Labour M.P.s. His view of 'the comrades' was a mixture of amused condescension and contempt, due more to their rawness and niavety than their social origins – although, like most upper-class Conservatives, Headlam tended to respect working-class Labour M.P.s and dislike the middle-class and intellectual element. For this reason as well as his personality and manner, the most detested of the Labour leaders was the 'dirty doctor', Hugh Dalton, Chancellor of the Exchequer from 1945 to 1947 and well known to Headlam as the M.P. for Bishop Auckland. Headlam acknowledged the competence of Stafford Cripps and the ability and debating skills of Aneurin Bevan, but thought few other ministers to be capable: he had never had a high opinion of Attlee, found Morrison to be glib and predictable, and did not subscribe to the view that Ernest Bevin was a steady helmsman at the Foreign Office.

Concern about the intentions of Soviet Russia and the development of the Cold War was a dominant theme of these years, giving Headlam more anxiety than any matters of domestic policy. The government appeared to be abdicating their responsibilities in the withdrawals from India and Palestine, and wasting the asset of British prestige. At home, Labour's troubles grew after the chaos of the severe winter of 1946–47, whilst the nationalised coal mines failed to produce enough fuel for domestic and industrial needs. However, although the economic difficulties grew worse and led to devaluation in September 1949, there was little sign that public opinion was moving away from Labour. This in turn added to the stresses within the Conservative opposition, in particular over Churchill's leadership. It was clear that he was the only possible leader, but his lengthy absences together with a tendency to go too far when he did attack, produced much restiveness. Eden, Lyttelton, Stanley (until his sudden death in 1950), Butler and Macmillan jostled for position, whilst the ambitions of the progressive Tory Reformers grated on the less articulate traditional right. Frustration

---

[60] Headlam diary, 14 Apr. 1947.

at the lack of progress surfaced in the 1922 Committee, especially after the failure to win the Hammersmith South by-election in February 1949. By this time the parliament was visibly running out of steam; ministers were exhausted, and both sides were jaded and bored. It was only a matter of marking time until the election, which was announced during the Christmas recess and took place in February 1950.

The final phase of Headlam's parliamentary career, from 1945 to 1951, was played out against a backdrop of continual strife in the constituency. The defeat of Grattan-Doyle in 1940 did not end the troubles, for many of his former supporters remained aggrieved. Central Office, concerned to prevent the division among local Conservatives from becoming permanent, intervened to urge the amalgamation of the old and new Associations. After difficult negotiations, during which Headlam fell out with his own chairman, Vick, this took place in January 1941. As Headlam feared, it was premature: it proved to be a fusion without reconciliation, and only the blanket of inactivity resulting from the wartime political truce concealed the tensions which still persisted. Matters marked time during the middle period of the war, during which the Conservative Party nationally sank into apathy and decay at the grass-roots. In January 1944 the Newcastle North chairman, Geoffrey Sykes, retired due to illness, and into his shoes stepped the figure whose ambition to become the M.P. for the division was to cause many of the problems of the next seven years. William Temple, an Alderman on the City Council, 'was a ludicrous figure and always walked about Newcastle with a huge bundle of briefs, or so-called briefs, slung over his shoulder.'[61] As his intrigues became more apparent he alienated an increasing number of Association members, but he also retained a solid core of support – in part due to Headlam's brusque manner and tendency to offend people. Headlam began to consider standing again in February 1943, and during 1944 and 1945 he became increasingly concerned about the inactivity of the association and the evasiveness of its chairman. By August 1944 he was suspicious of Temple: 'He is, I think, an unpleasant piece of work and not a person in whom one can put much trust.' However, a frank talk seemed to clear the air: Temple admitted that he wanted to become the M.P. but that, as he was

---

[61] Lord Lambton to the editor, 14 May 1998.

not yet ready, it would suit him for Headlam to stand at the next election, as this would leave the door open for him after that.[62] With further prodding, steps were taken in 1945 to revive the organisation and to appoint an agent.

Thus, although Headlam was aware that some of the association executive were hostile towards him, he was taken by surprise when there was a sudden attempt to remove him as candidate at the end of May 1945, just as the election campaign was about to begin. The initiative seems to have been taken by Lawson, the former chairman of the Grattan–Doyle association, and the women's branch chairman, Mrs. Fenwick. Temple's role is unclear, but on 2 June he headed a deputation from the executive committee which informed Headlam that they were unwilling to recommend him as candidate and hoped that he would stand down. However, despite a whispering campaign over the previous months, Headlam's enemies had struck too late. The adoption meeting was already scheduled and, whatever the reservations about his age or popularity, bringing in a new candidate at this stage was even more likely to lead to the loss of the seat. Headlam was confident of finding support amongst the wider membership at the adoption meeting, and resolved to outface the coup. Whilst his supporters whipped up the rank and file, he mobilised his superior social connections. Lord Ridley took the chair at the meeting on 8 June, putting the local worthies in the shade, and the challenge fizzled out. Temple proposed Headlam as candidate and he was adopted almost without objection. During the campaign there was some friction with the newly appointed agent, Colonel Scanlan, the son of a former Newcastle city councillor, who returned from wartime service at the last moment. He proved to be both stubborn and inefficient, but at first Headlam was unconcerned about this as he did not expect to contest the seat again.[63] However, during 1946 he became increasingly dubious about the activities of both the agent and the chairman, and more convinced of the latter's unsuitability to be the next M.P. Relations remained amicable on the surface, but after a dinner with Temple in January 1947 Headlam noted: 'He is now all over me and no doubt expects me to back him as my successor – but how can I?'[64]

---

[62] Headlam diary, 30 Aug. 1944, 1 Sep. 1944.
[63] Headlam diary, 18 July 1945.
[64] Headlam diary, 20 Jan. 1947.

The 1945 Parliament was now approaching mid-term; as the Labour government struggled with the crises of 1947, and the prospect of the next general election began to loom on the horizon, the question of the candidacy became more pressing. Headlam was ambivalent about remaining in Parliament: 'except for reasons of finance, I don't feel much inclined to go on in the HofC – and yet without my parliamentary work there is really nothing for me to do'.[65] He also resented the idea of being 'elbowed out' by Temple or by Dudley Appleby, Sir Alfred's son, and was determined that such a plum seat should not go to a second-rate candidate. From this feeling was born Headlam's quest to secure a prominent front-bencher as his successor. However, finding a suitable person who was in need of a new berth was not a simple matter, and in the meantime Headlam kept his own hat in the ring. This prevented any early decision – which would have been likely to favour Temple – and had the twin merits of buying more time and postponing the moment of decision about Headlam's own curtain call. Another factor in the equation was that the parliamentary salary and expenses were vital to the Headlams' finances and their loss would make it difficult to continue living at Holywell.[66] For this reason as much as any, Headlam was moving towards a decision to stand again when in June 1947 he faced a fresh blow: the 'nerve-racking' news that the Commission which was revising constituency boundaries intended to abolish one of the Newcastle divisions – and that it was the North which was to go.[67] This threat receded in the autumn when the Commission decided to keep all four Newcastle seats, but the changes to the area which the North division covered meant that it would be less of a safe seat. Money was a factor in the decision to go on, but pride was even more important. As Central Office were informed by the Area Agent in May 1947, 'Headlam will fight again to prevent Chairman getting seat.'[68] Temple was showing his hand more openly and, with the close support of Scanlan, preparing the way for his own nomination at next election. With a mixture of evasiveness and inefficiency, the chairman and agent combined to keep Cuthbert and Beatrice as much in the background as possible. The Headlams were not

[65] Headlam diary, 16 Mar. 1947.
[66] Cuthbert to Beatrice Headlam, 19 June 1947, Headlam MSS 288/22.
[67] Headlam diary, 14 & 15 June 1947.
[68] 'Notes following Mr Galloway's talk', 31 May 1947, CPA CCO/4/2/7.

informed of meetings, which were often deliberately fixed on days when it was known that they could not attend.[69] In some cases Headlam only found out about an Association event when he read about it in the press, and only his vigilance and tenacity enabled him to attend key gatherings such as the annual dance.[70] At the same time Temple assiduously courted local support, building up a majority on the Executive Council.

This was the state of affairs in April 1948, when J.P.L. Thomas, the Party Vice-Chairman responsible for candidates, raised privately with Headlam the possibility of his being succeeded by Walter Elliot, a leading front-bencher whose University seat was to be abolished at the end of the Parliament. Although the financial factor was still a worry, Headlam foresaw that his age would be used against him by Temple or one of the other local competitors; if the election did not come until 1950, Headlam would then be nearly 75. He disliked the idea of another squalid public struggle as much as his disliked the idea of the seat going to 'a rotten Town Councillor type of candidate'. The introduction of a major figure from outside would avoid this, and so Headlam decided to stand aside and secure the seat for Elliot if he wanted it.[71] However, hesitancy on both their parts, together with the continuing intrigue in the constituency, led to Elliot's possible candidacy fading away towards the end of 1948; in 1950 he instead contested and regained Glasgow Kelvingrove, the seat which he had lost in 1945. Thomas noted in November 1948 that 'Headlam is now going to continue at North Newcastle at all costs owing to his loathing of Alderman Temple!'[72] In fact, Headlam continued to blow hot and cold for some time; the decision to stand again evolved gradually, but it seems to have taken definite shape by the middle of 1949.[73] Another consequence of the events of 1948 and 1949 was that the party officials in Newcastle and in London lost confidence in Temple. The Area Agent called him 'an inveterate liar', and considered that the constituency Executive was unrepresentative and 'really a

[69] Headlam diary, 21 June 1949; Headlam's memo for the National Union inquiry, 23 June 1951, Headlam MSS 133/18.
[70] Headlam's memo for the National Union inquiry, 23 June 1951, Headlam MSS 133/18.
[71] Headlam diary, 15–17, 28 Apr. 1948.
[72] Postscript on note by Thomas of an interview with Temple, 9 Nov. 1948, CPA CCO/1/7/71.
[73] Headlam diary, 31 Mar., 21 June 1949.

political caucus of not too good a reputation'.[74] The repeated failure of both Temple and Scanlan to reply to letters or settle their bills during 1949 and 1950 was 'just another example of the disgraceful way in which this Association is administered'.[75] Central Office were fully informed by both Headlam and their Newcastle staff of Temple's efforts to secure the seat for himself; they were also aware that there were doubts about Temple's business activities, and considered that 'he would be a most undesirable M.P'.[76] This had the effect that, despite some friction, the Area Office in Newcastle was supportive of Headlam, whilst the Party Chairman and Central Office turned a frosty face towards Temple's ambitions.[77]

In a comment which sums up the whole Newcastle North saga during the 1940s, the Area Agent reported in May 1949 that 'The atmosphere in this Association is unbelievably bad. Suspicion, antagonism, and distrust seem to be the order of the day.'[78] The approach of the next general election, likely to be in late 1949 or early 1950, brought the simmering pot to the boil. The next attempt to remove Headlam began on 24 October 1949, when in a sudden move the Executive Council voted by twenty-eight to nine to drop him as candidate. A few days later Temple announced the summoning of an emergency General Meeting for 19 November, intended to ratify the Executive's decision. In the interval Headlam's supporters rallied, knowing that whilst the Temple clique was strongly entrenched on the executive, the wider membership would dislike anything which smacked of disloyalty and personal ambition.[79] Furthermore, the branches in the districts which had been added to the constituency in the 1949 boundary revision wanted nothing of these old sores; they had also been courted by Headlam's

[74] Galloway [Area Agent]'s remark on Temple in Thomas [Party Vice-Chairman] to Chapman-Walker [Party Chairman's Office], 3 Nov. 1948; on the Executive in note by Maxse [Deputy Party Chairman] of interview with Galloway [Area Agent], 'North Newcastle', 26 Oct. 1949, CPA CCO/1/7/71.

[75] Galloway [Area Agent] to the Accountant [Central Office], 3 Dec. 1949, CPA CCO/1/8/71/2.

[76] Hay to Party Chairman, 27 Oct. 1949; note by Maxse [Deputy Party Chairman] of interview with Galloway [Area Agent], 'North Newcastle', 26 Oct. 1949, CPA CCO/1/7/71.

[77] Woolton [Party Chairman] to Scanlan, 10 Nov. 1949, CPA CCO/1/7/71.

[78] 'North Newcastle', Area Agent's annual Basic Report to Central Office, 31 May 1949, CPA CCO/1/7/71.

[79] Galloway [Area Agent] to Grenville [personal assistant to the Party Chairman], 5 Nov. 1949, CPA CCO/1/7/71.

supporters, and knew him better than Temple. It was clear that the larger the attendance at the meeting, the less likely it was that the deselection would be approved – for this reason, Headlam's supporters were resentful and suspicious of the shortness of the notice given and the fact that it was to be held on a Saturday. Despite these hindrances, their efforts were successful and the general meeting on 19 November overturned the decision not to readopt Headlam by 481 votes to 301.

Temple sought to keep matters open until a further Special General Meeting in January, ostensibly intended to adopt Headlam as candidate. In the intervening weeks, against a background of rumour and intrigue, the balance of opinion swung further towards Headlam.[80] This was marshalled by some of the most active workers, and was largely based upon indignation at the manoeuvres of the Temple clique and antagonism to Temple himself.[81] The latter did not accept defeat until the adoption meeting on 10 January 1950, by chance the day on which the general election was announced. Bowing before the storm, Temple proposed Headlam as candidate and called for unity, although he also allowed a vote. This was a comfortable triumph for the Headlam camp, with 704 votes in favour to only 201 against.[82] Thus Headlam entered what was to be his last election campaign, already tired and strained from struggle over the nomination. This and the prospect of campaigning in dark and wintry weather left him 'depressed at the prospect of another election', even though 'it ought not to be any more strenuous for me than the last one, and it was not very tiring'.[83] He was then laid up with a cold in the first week of the campaign, but Beatrice continued with a full programme of small meetings held in supporters' homes.

Headlam was returned comfortably at the head of the poll, with a majority of 8,465. His success did not bring down the curtain upon the infighting in Newcastle North, but instead heralded the final act of the drama. Hopes of ousting Temple at the Annual General Meeting in June 1950 were dashed, but although he held

---

[80] Galloway [Area Agent] to Watson [Central Office], 29 Dec. 1949, CPA CCO/1/7/71.

[81] Postscript recording comments of Ridley, on note by Woolton [Party Chairman] of an interview with Headlam, 2 Nov. 1949, CPA CCO/1/7/71.

[82] Galloway [Area Agent] to Watson [Central Office], 11 Jan. 1950, CPA CCO/1/7/71.

[83] Headlam diary, 28 Jan. 1950.

on to the chairmanship by a small margin, Headlam's leading supporters Lord Ridley and Robin Houston were elected President and Treasurer respectively. From this point on, however, the focus moved away from Headlam and the unjust treatment which he had received, and concentrated more upon the problem of Temple and the self-respect of Newcastle North Conservatism. During 1950 Headlam lost ground steadily, partly because his age and health were now severely limiting his value as a rallying-point against the Temple clique, and partly on personal grounds. He 'had become very much more unpopular', and by November had 'now practically no supporters'.[84] Central Office were aware that whilst Headlam was acting as encourager and advisor to the anti-Temple forces, the latter would not wish to have him as their candidate.[85] After dragging on through the second half of 1950, matters moved to a spectacular and public climax. Unable to work with Temple, Ridley and Houston resigned their posts in February 1951 and a few weeks later spearheaded the formation of a breakaway Conservative Association; Headlam was consulted upon each twist and turn, but as the sitting M.P. he limited himself to prompting from off-stage.[86] The new Association applied for recognition by the National Union, and on 14 June the National Union Executive delegated three of its members to act as a committee of enquiry.[87] This group was effectively judge and jury, for their recommendation would almost certainly be adopted, and so their visit to Newcastle in the first week of July prompted an extensive and bitter rehearsal of all the troubles since 1940.[88]

Once again the infinitely superior social and political connections of Headlam and, in particular, Ridley easily trumped the parochial milieu of the Temple faction. The saga of recent years, which also included the blacklisting of the 'old' Association for its repeated

[84] Maxse to Woolton, 17 Nov. 1950, CPA CCO/1/8/71/1.

[85] 'North Newcastle', memo by Thomas to the General Director, 25 Apr. 1951, CPA CCO/1/8/71/1.

[86] See for example Bazin to Headlam, 20 Apr. 1950; Headlam to Bazin, 14 May 1950; Cuthbert to Beatrice Headlam, 5 Feb. 1951, Headlam MSS 133/5, 133/11, 290/6.

[87] N.U. Exec., 14 June & 19 July 1951; the members of the committee were Geoffrey Summers (the chairman; a former President of the N.U.), Stanley Bell (Chairman of the North Western Area) and Mrs. Warde (a Vice-Chairman of the N.U.).

[88] The minutes of the enquiry meetings are in CPA NUA/6/2/8; the report is attached to the minutes of the Special Meeting of the N.U. Exec., 19 July 1951.

failure to pay for literature ordered from Central Office, also meant that the party organisation in London and at the Area Office were entirely behind the 'rebel' camp, a fact of which the inquiry team were fully aware.[89] Headlam's political skills and experience played their part in securing the desired outcome; as well as submitting a carefully measured written account,[90] he was also, in the later congratulatory words of the chairman of the inquiry, 'most restrained and forbearing in your criticism of Alderman Temple and his colleagues'.[91] The result was scarcely a surprise: when the Executive Committee of the National Union met on 19 July to consider the enquiry's damning indictment of the old Association, the latter was cast out into the darkness and the new Association was enshrined in its place. During this period the vexed question of the candidacy was also finally resolved, for at the inaugural meeting of the new Association on 2 July Headlam publicly announced that he would not stand again at the next election.[92] The first meeting of the new Association's Executive on 10 August invited Gwilym Lloyd George to become the candidate, and he immediately accepted.[93] The younger son of the former Prime Minister and a Liberal Minister in the wartime Coalition, he had remained allied with the Conservatives after 1945 but lost his Welsh seat in the 1950 general election. When the general election came in October 1951 he successfully contested Newcastle North as a 'National Liberal and Conservative', holding the seat whilst serving as Minister of Food from 1951 to 1954 and as Home Secretary from 1954 to 1957.

The diary covers only part of Headlam's final term as an M.P., which lasted until October 1951. The situation in the House was now very different, as Labour had only seventeen more M.P.s than the Conservatives and their allies. Labour remained in office but, with an overall majority of only five and a tired and fractious cabinet, their position was precarious. Clearly another and more decisive election could not be long postponed, but equally neither

[89] Note by Thomas [Party Vice-Chairman] of an interview with Ridley, 10 May 1951, CPA CCO/1/8/71/1; Pierssene [General Director, Central Office] to Headlam, 28 Apr. 1950, CPA CCO/1/8/71/2.

[90] Headlam's memo for the National Union inquiry, 23 June 1951, Headlam MSS 133/18.

[91] Summers to Headlam, 24 July 1951, Headlam MSS 133/20.

[92] *Newcastle Journal*, 3 July 1951.

[93] Galloway [Area Agent] to Thomas [Party Vice-Chairman], 11 Aug. 1951, CPA CCO/1/8/71/1.

side wanted to embark upon it at once. During the first few months
of the new Parliament the Conservative opposition followed an
unsteady path in which there was some bark, but no real bite. The
outbreak of the Korean War in June 1950 also complicated the
role of the opposition, but pressure was applied in the second half
of 1950 and steadily increased from the start of 1951. There was
no pairing with Labour M.P.s throughout the Parliament, and snap
divisions and other tactics were used to embarrass the government
and wear down its supporters. For this strategy to work, a high
level of attendance was needed on the Conservative side. This
would have posed problems even if Headlam's health had been
good, but both Cuthbert and Beatrice were seriously unwell in the
late spring and early summer of 1950.[94] He had another bad attack
of bronchial pneumonia and was confined to bed for several weeks
from May to early July, whilst Beatrice had an accident and burned
herself in early April. Although by August Headlam 'had made a
wonderful recovery', he felt low for some time afterwards and there
were also incidents of forgetfulness over engagements, tiredness
and financial anxiety.[95] It was during this period that the Conservative leaders considered the problem of the M.P.s who were
older and least dependable in attendance, and the shadow cabinet
decided to press Headlam and two others to retire in October and
create by-election vacancies.[96] As he did not keep the diary in the
second half of 1950, it is unknown whether this request was ever
made, or whether Headlam declined to go, but the writing was
clearly on the wall. At the start of the Parliament, Headlam had
noted of his own position in the House: 'I am not disliked or not
respected, but I am just a somewhat interesting survival – someone
who is lingering on the stage somewhat unexpectedly – and nothing
more.'[97] In the early summer of 1951, suffering from eczema and
finding the overnight train journeys more tiring than before, he
finally took the decision to stand down. He remained an M.P. until

---

[94] The Deputy Area Agent, Miss de Jonghe, reported after a visit to Holywell on
28 June that 'Sir Cuthbert and Lady Headlam have both been very ill indeed, and
both appear to be in a very low state of health, particularly Sir Cuthbert.' Memo,
'Newcastle North', Galloway [Area Agent] to Watson [Central Office], 28 June 1950,
CPA CCO/1/8/71/1.

[95] Headlam to Maxse, 5 Aug. 1950, CPA CCO/1/8/71/1.

[96] Note in the Shadow Cabinet files quoted in J. Ramsden, *The Age of Churchill
and Eden 1940–1957* (London, 1995), p. 220.

[97] Headlam diary, 6 Mar. 1950.

the dissolution came in October 1951, when his parliamentary career came to an end at the age of seventy-five.

Money remained the great problem of Headlam's final years. There was not only the fall in income due to the loss of his parliamentary salary, but the fact that in retirement and old age his directorships would also inevitably dwindle away. 'It is a truly depressing thing in one's old age to have to face penury – for there is no way now in which one can possibly hope to increase one's income.'[98] This financial anxiety, rather than a desire to keep a public role, led Headlam to return to the question of a peerage after his retirement from the Commons in 1951. He told his older brother 'I should like to return to the HofL', but knew that 'my chance of going there is not a good one, particularly as I refused the offer in 1945'.[99] Nothing came of it, either in 1951 or when he enquired again when his contemporaries Eden and later Macmillan became Prime Minister. In part he was too obscure, and was not entitled to the almost automatic preferment which those of cabinet rank could request, but it was also the case that Central Office was hostile: he had turned them down when his seat was wanted in the Party's interests, and granting a peerage later would encourage M.P.s to feel that they could ignore such requests with impunity.[100]

The Headlams continued to live at Holywell during the 1950s, although 'the house and garden are far too big for us nowadays'.[101] Whilst there was 'nowhere else to go', there were also positive reasons for staying in the north – they had a niche in county society, and there were Beatrice's continuing social and charitable interests, and Cuthbert's involvement in political affairs and his remaining connections with the British Legion and other civic bodies. For all these reasons, they did not wish to leave Holywell; as Headlam had noted nearly twenty years before, 'both Beatrice and I feel that we shall stick on here as long as we can – we don't admit it to each other but we both know that to leave this place would mark the beginning of the end'.[102] Although his directorships fell by the wayside, the Headlams kept afloat due to the profits

---

[98] Headlam diary, 1 Jan. 1949.
[99] Cuthbert to Maurice Headlam, 5 Dec. 1951, Maurice Headlam MSS, Eng. Hist. c.1099, f. 15, Bodleian Library.
[100] Lord Lambton to the editor, 14 May 1998.
[101] Headlam to Maxse, 5 Aug. 1950, CPA CCO/1/8/71/1.
[102] Headlam diary, 20 Mar. 1942.

from the pig farm which continued to operate through the 1950s. The produce was sold to various government departments, and in particular to the army camp at Brancepeth Castle. Holywell had also become a registered market garden during the war years, and these commercial activities allowed the Headlams to offset much of the running costs of the house and cars against the businesses. This enabled them to continue to live in a fairly grand style, and to employ staff. In March 1954 they celebrated their Golden Wedding. During these final years in retirement Cuthbert spent much time writing in his study; as he no longer kept the diary, it is unclear upon what he was engaged, but it was most probably articles for journals. His remaining directorships, including that of the APAL Travel Agency, still took him to London, though less frequently than before. Here he was also an intermittent presence at the Literary Society, seeming to have attended rather more in the last years after the Headlams moved south and London was easier to reach by train. His mood, at least in public, tended to be a bleak one, leading to further isolation. 'Nobody was keen to sit next to him', wrote Rupert Hart-Davis after a Literary Society dinner in 1956; 'Before dinner Cuthbert managed to deliver several of those unfair and depressing remarks which should never be made anywhere, particularly not at convivial evenings. "When you're eighty", he said to me, "there's nothing to do but wait for death".'[103]

In 1960 the Headlams finally left Holywell, which was purchased by Tony Lambton mainly as a way of helping them financially. With greater infirmity and diminishing income, the house had become too much of a burden; they had also felt for some time that they would see their friends more easily if they lived in the south, and Cuthbert had always liked the idea of retiring to Bath.[104] As always, it was Beatrice who instigated and organized their move; from an long-standing friend of hers, Lady Hobhouse, the Headlams bought in 1960 an old house in Shepton Mallet. The property needed to be large to accommodate the Headlams substantial old-fashioned furniture, and it took a convoy of five lorries to bring their goods down from Durham. However, whilst the new house had a fine view – a more important feature for Beatrice than the

---

[103] Hart-Davis to Lyttelton, 13 Oct. 1956, in R. Hart-Davis (ed.), *The Lyttelton–Hart-Davis Letters, Volume 1* (London, 1978), p. 195; see also *Volume 2* (London, 1979), p. 59.

[104] Gertrude Ridley to the editor, 9 Jan. & 19 Feb. 1997.

degree of modern comforts inside – it seemed as if it rained continually, and there was little to occupy them socially in the area. After three years they moved from Shepton Mallet to Bath, where they had more friends, and purchased 19 Camden Crescent for around £1,200. This was a large, five-storey house in classic Georgian crescent style. It was situated on the side of a hill with splendid views across the city; this, and the old wisteria on the front with which Beatrice fell in love, decided their choice, although in other respects the house was far from suitable. As well as being large, it had been requisitioned as offices during the war and had not been used as a home since; it needed re-wiring and plumbing, and lacked central heating. The Headlams could not afford such work, as by this time they were very short of money. Cuthbert would have preferred a small house or flat in London, but they could not afford a property there which would be large enough to suit Beatrice.

The passage of the years was also taking its toll of their health and energy. Beatrice, who had remained the more active, especially due to the responsibilities of the pig farm, was coping with shingles and arthritis by 1959.[105] Cuthbert suffered periodically from chest infections but was still able to get about and to visit London occasionally. However, by the end of the decade he was becoming frailer and had lost more weight: 'he looked incredibly thin and weightless' in 1960; 'there is *nothing* of him inside those clothes'.[106] Nor was the outlook better: in early 1962, in the last surviving letter, Cuthbert wrote of feeling 'just overpowered by everything' and 'not being able to see the wood for the trees either in world affairs or our own'.[107] A few weeks later he presided for the last time at a Literary Society dinner in London – 'very thin and shrunken, with one foot in a carpet slipper'.[108] The latter was a result of the continuing problems with his leg, which developed a sore which the doctors were unable to heal; this hampered his mobility, as he detested the idea of being taken out in a wheelchair. Relations and old friends continued to visit them in Bath, but they were mainly of the Headlams' generation, and were diminishing in

---

[105] Morrison to Headlam, 25 Sep. 1959, Headlam MSS 136/10.

[106] Lyttelton to Hart-Davis, 14 & 19 July 1960, in R. Hart-Davis (ed.), *The Lyttelton – Hart-Davis Letters, Volume 5* (London, 1983), pp. 107, 109.

[107] Cuthbert to Beatrice Headlam, 27–28 Jan. 1962, Headlam MSS 292/5.

[108] Hart-Davis to Lyttelton, 15 Apr. 1962, in R. Hart-Davis (ed.), *The Lyttelton – Hart-Davis Letters, Volume 6* (London, 1984), p. 183.

number. Cuthbert's decline was linked to the problems with his
chest and lungs, which his smoking made more troublesome. He
had perhaps never entirely recovered his strength after the serious
bronchial illness which he suffered in the winter of 1943–44, after
which he was prone to chest infections.

In the severe winter weather of early 1964 a cold developed into
bronchial pneumonia and Headlam was confined to bed, taking
oxygen from a respirator. He knew that the end was near when he
ceased to feel the pain in his leg, and after three or four days in
bed he died suddenly but peacefully in his own home on 27
February. Preparations had been in hand for a party to celebrate
the Headlams' Diamond Wedding anniversary on 22 March 1964;
as always Cuthbert disliked the idea, but had acceded to Beatrice's
wishes. Gertrude Ridley, a friend of the family who had come to
Bath to help with the arrangements, recalled that 'he was not well
and now and then had lapses of memory – but he was quite lucid
when I left, though he cried when I said I would be back for the
party and said he would not be there! There was no party, when I
got home after my long train journey they phoned to tell me he
had died.'[109] The funeral was held on 2 March at Walcot parish
church in Bath, followed by interment at Lansdown cemetry; a
memorial service, partly conducted by the Archbishop of Canterbury, and attended by Harold and Dorothy Macmillan and
many current and former M.P.s, was held at St. Margaret's,
Westminster, on 6 May 1964. The hand-to-mouth existence of the
final years was underlined by the small amount which Headlam
left, his estate proving to have a net value of only £1,152.[110] After
she was widowed Beatrice lived on in the house for a further two
years, but she was becoming increasingly frail and the stairs were
becoming too much to cope with. She was persuaded by her family
and doctors to move into a nursing home in Bath, in the Circus;
she stayed there for about two years, and died, with her son at her
side, on 6 April 1968.

[109] Gertrude Ridley to the editor, 11 Sep. 1990.
[110] *The Times*, 17 June 1964.

(ii)   Character and Career

A Character Portrait

Cuthbert Headlam was 'a natural leader of men' who found himself condemned to marginal and subordinate positions, in which over time his frustration hardened into bitterness.[111] Although intelligent, possessing a clarity of thought and literary skills, he never found a stimulating or constructive outlet. He was particularly effective as a public speaker, and his ability to command the respect of a hostile audience without enraging it was of especial value in the Labour-dominated north-east. Headlam's platform style was described by a neutral observer in 1940 as 'alert and commanding in a reasonable and cultured manner'.[112] His approach was 'both intelligent and honest'; he did not patronise his listeners, and was particularly good at handling questions – both in turning aside the clumsy thrust of the heckler, and in responding to the point of the genuine inquirer.[113] Agnes Headlam-Morley, who had been present at many of his election meetings from 1924 to 1940, recalled in an obituary tribute that:[114]

> He never attempted rhetoric: his speeches were simple, well-argued statements on politics and economics. He had sincerity, great charm and a beautiful voice. He took every question seriously at its face value, and, in spite of a quick, sometimes sardonic, wit, he never allowed himself a trace of sarcasm.

Headlam's powers of analysis are shown in many of the diary entries. His judgements were shrewd, if tinged with pessimism, on both domestic politics and questions of foreign policy or military strategy.[115] These talents were never fully stretched in any of his jobs; his role was always a restricted one, and he had to endure instead the boredom of routine and relatively unimportant tasks.

---

[111] *The Times*, 5 & 3 Mar. 1964; Lord Lambton to the editor, 14 May 1998.

[112] 'Newcastle by-election candidates', June 1940, Mass-Observation MSS, Box 8, File B, Sussex University Library.

[113] 'Newcastle By-Election', File Report 195, p. 17–18, Mass-Observation MSS.

[114] *The Times*, 5 Mar. 1964.

[115] Examples are the potential danger from Germany during the Abyssinnian crisis and before Hitler's first move (14 Jan. 1936), the prediction of the location of the Allied invasion of Europe (4 June 1944), the future of the wartime coalition (20 July 1944), Churchill as an electoral asset (12 Apr. 1945), and electoral pospects (4 Dec. 1947).

After 1935 he was depressed by the lack of any challenging or useful work: 'The fact of having nothing to do is what makes one so wretched and discontented – and unpleasant, I fear.'[116] His interests were engaged by the larger picture and, despite his knowledge of military matters, he did not seek recognition as an expert on any special topic. Foreign policy, defence, and the empire were of most concern, but he became easily bored with the details of social legislation and was uninterested in finance and economics.

Much of the blame for his failure to rise to the top in politics was put by Headlam on factors outside his control. A regular refrain was that lack of money had meant that he was too old when he had begun his political career, and that he could not find a safe seat. He felt that age and circumstances had condemned him always to be the junior, and that bad fortune had placed him in posts where there was little scope. However, he was aware that other and more personal factors also played their part, and acknowledged his own shortcomings. Some of these were ascribed to the family characteristics of the Headlams:[117]

> We are at the same time critical and modest, opinionated and diffident, entirely lacking in veneration for those whom the world considers great, unless they really are great ... Successful people, as a rule, are 'yes' men ... None of us belongs to this type. We are clever and capable, honest and respectable, witty and amusing (when we so choose), generous and sympathetic – but we say what we believe and say it without hesitation often at the wrong time and often to the wrong people. Nor is any of us particularly thorough, systematic or hardworking. If given a job, one can do it – and do it well – but one cannot make a job or go on for ever seeking for one.

He was not tidy or methodical in his working habits, although he may have exaggerated the extent of this: 'I never know where anything is and spend half my time looking for letters and papers which I remember require attention, but have mislaid.'[118]

A crucial factor was his lack of confidence, the roots of which may be found in his unhappy schooldays at Canterbury.[119] This

---

[116] Headlam diary, 4 Aug. 1937.
[117] Headlam diary, 21 Mar. 1938.
[118] Headlam diary, 6 Jan. 1942.
[119] Headlam diary, 30 Sep. 1936, 26 Apr. 1949.

lack of assuredness worried him from his first days as an M.P. in 1924:[120]

> When will this feeling of depression and of one's own insufficiency wear off? And the comic thing is that the world, I believe, usually regards me as a man who has a good opinion of himself. There was never anyone who had less confidence in his own powers than I. I am far too much of a critic not to underrate my own ability.

Although it was hidden behind an appearance of arrogance, he remained throughout his life 'very shy and diffident about my abilities'.[121] Despite his success on the public platform, he found speaking in the House of Commons an intimidating experience. He was perhaps too severe in his self-criticism, but his nervousness persisted and inhibited his performances. On some occasions he gave up the struggle to be called, feeling that others had already made the points which he had in mind. When he did speak, his efforts were sound but often shorter than he had intended. All this limited his impact, for success in debate was the foundation of all reputations; 'it is timidity in the House which has done me in', wrote Headlam on leaving office in July 1934.[122] He was no less severe about his literary efforts, whether factual or fictional. In this respect his education and enjoyment of reading were a hindrance, for he had very high standards which were almost impossible to live up to. Time and again he felt that he had nothing original to say, and he certainly did not consider himself important or interesting enough to write anything autobiographical.[123] This made completing any task of drafting a slow and painful process, even when it was only an attempt to earn money: 'How often have I destroyed my masterpieces simply because on reading them over I have felt that they were not worth publishing – though perhaps in some cases publishers might have thought otherwise.'[124]

Handicapped by 'an inferiority complex which prevents one from hobnobbing with the mighty and makes one feel out of it', Headlam was always reluctant to push himself forwards.[125] This was also a

---

[120] Headlam diary, 15 Dec. 1924, 27 Jan. 1939.
[121] Cuthbert to Beatrice Headlam, 20 Apr. 1948, Headlam MSS 289/4.
[122] Headlam diary, 6 July 1934, 22 July 1935.
[123] Headlam diary, 1 Jan. 1947.
[124] Headlam diary, 3 Jan. 1945.
[125] Headlam diary, 6 May 1934.

matter of integrity: 'how could I as a self respecting man suck up to men in whom I have no confidence or liking? too much against the grain '[126] There was some comfort in the notion that honesty did not pay, and that promotions went to sycophants and to the shallow and the predictable. Headlam was not only unwilling or unable to ingratiate himself, but was also impatient with mediocrity – perhaps too openly so in the case of some of those in positions of influence and authority. A laudatory profile in the press at the time of his first ministerial appointment in 1926 contained this telling passage, clearly based upon personal knowledge:

> He has one trouble. He loathes mediocrity, suffers fools a deal worse than anyone I ever met, and has a tendency, not to think only, but to show that he thinks, that he could do the boss's work better than the boss can.[127]

This did not change, for his obituary declared that 'Cuthbert Headlam was almost god-like in his lack of respect for persons. He feared nobody ...'.[128] Whilst he was loyal to his subordinates, Headlam came to feel that his own loyalty and services were unappreciated by those above him. This contributed to his alienation from the Party leadership during 1931–35, and to his increasing bitterness thereafter.

These feelings gave an added edge to his personal manner. On many occasions he could seem impatient and abrupt, and this aspect of arrogance was remarked upon even by those who were fond of him and knew him well. Sir Fergus and Lady Mary Graham, respectively his former P.P.S. and a leading figure in the Northern Area, described him as 'abrasive'; Lord Lambton, who saw much of him from 1945 onwards, comments upon 'a sense of superiority which made him disliked'.[129] Boredom and frustration combined with his shyness to render Headlam awkward and offhand on social occasions; the result could be an 'extraordinary

[126] Headlam diary, 26 July 1936; the comment referred in particular to three Conservative leaders: Hoare, Cunliffe-Lister and Hailsham.

[127] *The Sphere*, 25 Dec. 1926.

[128] *The Times*, 3 Mar. 1964.

[129] Comments of Sir Fergus and Lady Mary Graham recounted by their son, Sir Charles Graham, in a letter to the editor, 6 Sep. 1990; Lord Lambton to the editor, 14 May 1998.

rudeness'.[130] His intelligence was sometimes a liability, for he had 'a tongue as sharp as his wit' and was prone to a sardonic style which ranged from the amusing to the caustic.[131] Like most people, he was generally unaware of how he seemed to those whom he encountered. He was taken aback when told by the Whip, James Stuart, in 1936 that he had made 'enemies', and was disconcerted when Beatrice warned in 1948 about his 'unpopularity – by reason of my rough tongue'.[132] This was married to a quick temper: Gertrude Ridley, Beatrice's assistant in the 1930s and a family friend for many years, recalled that 'easily irritated, he could fly into a rage when annoyed'.[133] Temper was a trait for which the Headlam family were well known: Sir Alec Douglas-Home wrote in his memoirs that Cuthbert's brother Geoffrey, the Eton school-master, 'was one of three Headlam brothers who were known as "Sometimes angry", "Always angry", and "Furious"'.[134] 'Tuppie', as Geoffrey was known, was 'Sometimes'; it is not clear who were the other two, but as another source refers to the eldest brother Maurice as 'the least crabbed', it is likely that Cuthbert was one of them.[135] Headlam did not hold on to his anger, which went as swiftly as it came. Beneath the sharp exterior, 'he was a kind man but not one to know easily'.[136] He was never spiteful or cruel, and was not intolerant: 'The longer I live the more I realize the impossibility of passing a final judgement about the character of any man or woman.'[137] Without pride and aware of human frailty, he was reluctant to condemn others. He responded to those whose downfall was public with sympathy for their shame and humiliation, even feeling sorry for the loathed 'dirty doctor' Dalton when he had to resign as Chancellor in 1947.[138]

Physical courage was not lacking, as was shown by his wartime service and his willingness to stand up in front of hostile audiences, but a cautious and pessimistic streak ran through his character. If

[130] Lord Lambton to the editor, 14 May 1998.
[131] *The Times*, 3 Mar. 1964.
[132] Headlam diary, 18 Feb. 1936; Cuthbert to Beatrice Headlam, 20 Apr. 1948, Headlam MSS 289/4.
[133] Gertrude Ridley to the editor, 4 Sep. 1990, 11 Nov. 1993.
[134] Lord Home, *The Way the Wind Blows* (London,1976), p. 29.
[135] Lyttelton to Hart-Davis, 22 Dec. 1955, in R. Hart-Davis (ed.), *The Lyttelton – Hart-Davis Letters, Volume 1* (London, 1978), p. 48.
[136] Gertrude Ridley to the editor, 4 Sep. 1990.
[137] Headlam diary, 26 Mar. 1949.
[138] Headlam diary, 22 Apr. 1936, 3 Apr. 1943, 13 Nov. 1947.

this negative outlook on the world was not already shaped in childhood or adolescence, it was certainly ingrained by the wearisome years which he spent as a Clerk in the House of Lords, and especially when he was passed over for promotions shortly before and after the First World War. Pessimism, at least about his own prospects, was the public face which he presented even at the promising start of his political career, as the congratulatory letters of his fellow M.P.s when he was given office in 1926 attest.[139] Together with his analytical temperament, this led to a sober viewpoint and an emphasis upon realism rather than idealism. Looking back in old age, he observed: 'I never felt myself a young man – by which I mean that I have never been carried away by youthful urges and inspirations and enthusiasms – have always been old for my years.'[140] Three decades earlier, while serving on the Western Front, he told his wife, 'I am always surprised when I find myself liked by anyone ... they look upon me as a curious old buffer with a "cynical" manner.'[141] This was largely a defensive veneer, for in fact he felt emotions keenly. Headlam sometimes had difficulty in suppressing his feelings and conforming to the expected convention of masculine behaviour, being often moved to tears. What affected him most were the moments which evoked the essence of the nation and the truths of life and death – certain occasions of public ceremony, 'God Save the King' sung heartily, attending funerals, or hearing of brave deeds.[142] His emotional warmth was focused mainly upon the private sphere of his family; he had a caustic wit, but those who knew him better saw a kinder sense of humour. He could be 'most affable' on occasion, even in his final years, although it always tended to be 'the sun of January rather than of June'.[143] As an obituary notice remarked, 'When in mellow mood he could be the most charming and amusing of companions, but, in general, a feeling of frustration too often overshadowed his life.'

[139] McDonnell to Headlam, 21 Dec. 1926, W.E.D. Allen to Headlam, 10 Jan. 1927, Glyn to Headlam, 29 Dec. 1926, Hudson to Headlam, 27 Dec. 1926, Headlam MSS 126/245, 3, 81,119.

[140] Headlam diary, 27 Apr. 1947.

[141] Cuthbert to Beatrice Headlam, 17 July 1916, Headlam MSS 151.

[142] Headlam diary, 14 Apr. 1945.

[143] Lyttelton to Hart-Davis, 13 June 1957 and 13 May 1959, in R. Hart-Davis (ed.), *The Lyttelton – Hart-Davis Letters, Volume 2* (London, 1979), p. 115, *Volume 4* (London, 1982), p. 65.

After the loss of his seat in 1935, this sense of disappointment was reinforced by anxiety and physical ageing. These combined to dull his energies, with financial problems causing continual stress and tension: 'it is the perpetual worry of how to pay one's butcher's bills that wears one out'.[144] He found having to remind those who had offered to help find directorships a humiliating process; he had to swallow his pride, and inevitably it introduced a certain awkwardness into the friendship. Although he tried to avoid dwelling on the financial problems, they were a recurring source of stress. Together with the sense of futility and boredom, this led to lassitude and depression. A few weeks before returning to Parliament in 1940 he wrote:

> One is certainly growing older – one no longer seems to have the energy or power of rising to the occasion that one had in the past. Little worries upset one more than ever, and the big worries, which used to stir one to greater efforts when one was younger, now seem overpowering – too big to cope with.[145]

As he grew older, Headlam did not get any easier. The advancing years only entrenched his existing characteristics more deeply, as infirmity combined with anxiety to remove the last veneers of patience with which he faced life's disappointments and irritations. Headlam was aware of this, and described himself in early 1936 as 'too old, too disagreeable, too difficult'.[146]

However, this self-critical view must not be taken as the whole truth. The journalist and editor Collin Brooks found himself in Headlam's company during a sea passage from Portugal in May 1939, and noted in his own diary that 'Cuthbert Headlam is a nice little old-maid of a man'.[147] Brooks was travelling with his employer, Lord Rothermere; as neither were persons whom Headlam would have felt any particular need or wish to charm, this rare vignette from a third party is at least an equally valid indication of the impression which he made upon acquaintance. Nor, despite the anxieties of ageing, was it all pessimism. On his sixty-fifth birthday he wrote: 'Sometimes I feel as if I did not mind if the years to

---

[144] Headlam diary, 7 Feb. 1936.
[145] Headlam diary, 31 Mar. 1940.
[146] Headlam diary, 7 Feb. 1936.
[147] Collin Brooks diary, 21 May 1939; I am indebted to Dr Nicholas Crowson for this reference.

come were limited: at other times I feel desperately anxious to survive in order to see what is going to happen! ... when the wind is not N.E. I really don't feel very ancient and that is a comfort.'[148] At least until the end of his parliamentary career he remained interested in the issues and events of the day: 'I am not at all anxious to leave this world so long as I retain my faculties. There is so much of interest in it, even to a mere onlooker like myself.'[149] However, there is no doubt that the predominant tone of the later years was sour, especially after 1951. A fellow diner at the Literary Society at the end of the 1950s referred to Headlam as 'the old acid drop', whilst Lord Lambton recalls that 'he simply could not keep his bitterness out of his conversation'.[150]

Headlam did not love the House of Commons in the way in which many of its Members come to do: his feelings were more ambivalent. During his time as an M.P. he was often bored and frustrated, and in his second period after 1940 it was hard to find congenial companions of a similar age or outlook. However, when out of the House he felt even more irrelevant and on the shelf. It is this combination which explains his interest in returning in the late 1930s and his reluctance to depart in the late 1940s, despite the grumbling and chafing at the tedium and demands of being a backbencher. Apart from periods of illness and despite the constant long journeys, Headlam was a regular attender during the parliamentary session. His presence was dutiful rather than enthusiastic, but although moments of excitement and interest were in the minority there remained an element of fascination. 'A strange place the HofC', he noted in 1942; 'one can never tell what is going to happen there – possibly in this lies one of its main attractions.'[151] As he grew older there was no alternative activity or source of income to attract him away; however dull the House might be, Headlam knew that 'I should miss it terribly if I had to give it up'.[152]

Religious faith was a matter about which Headlam was unostentatious. As several members of his and Beatrice's families were

[148] Headlam diary, 27 Apr. 1941.
[149] Headlam diary, 28 Sep. 1942.
[150] Lyttelton to Hart-Davis, 12 Nov. 1959, in R. Hart-Davis (ed.), *The Lyttelton – Hart-Davis Letters, Volume 4* (London, 1982), p. 159; Lord Lambton to the editor, 14 May 1998.
[151] Headlam diary, 6 Sep. 1942.
[152] Headlam diary, 14 Feb. 1945.

Church of England clergymen, his moderate Anglican outlook was hardly surprising. However, although his observance was conventional in form, it was something more than simply observing the conventions: 'our life on earth is certainly a sore trial – and each day one lives, one realizes more and more that without some kind of confidence in the hereafter existence here would be intolerable.'[153] The presence of God was accepted, giving both meaning and comfort, but he had no inclination for soul-searching or debate. Headlam rarely discussed his religious feelings, but on Good Friday in 1936 he wrote: 'I feel my utter incompetence and lowliness, and can only trust that God understands it and forgives my shortcomings, my lack of simple faith and complete unworthiness.'[154] In fact, a basic Christian belief was what he did possess, added to which was the appreciation of a cultured man of his class and era for a well-conducted service, with good music and a coherent sermon. Headlam was aware of the religious issues of the day, and became involved when they came directly into politics, as in the Prayer Book controversy in 1927–28 and the Education Act in 1944. Apart from this, his outlook was tolerant and non-sectarian.

> My view is simply based on what seems to be common sense. If you believe that what Christ taught should be the basis on which you should endeavour to plan your conduct in life, what else really matters? If you endeavour to act up to His principles as set out in the Gospels and believe in his divinity, you are, so I hold, a Christian whether you call yourself a Catholic, or a Protestant, or a nonconformist. Then why should Christians quarrel among themselves about the interpretation of dogmas?[155]

However, although his prejudice was mild in comparison with many of his background and generation, Headlam always commented when he came into contact with Jews. He was not antagonistically anti-Semitic or hostile to the race as a whole, and indeed sympathised with Zionist aspirations, but he was always aware of a difference and subscribed to the common stereotype of Jewish character and integrity. For this reason he was always uneasy about the connections which he formed with various Jewish businessmen

---

[153] Headlam diary, 3 Aug. 1936.
[154] Headlam diary, 10 Apr. 1936.
[155] Headlam diary, 25 Apr. 1943.

shortly before and during the Second World War: 'I cannot bring myself to like being associated with Jews.'[156]

A Pattern of Life

In appearance Headlam was tall and slender; a handsome and imposing figure, especially on the platform. He was described as 'a sparely built, keen-featured man' by a Mass Observation reporter at the time of the 1940 by-election.[157] Although gaunt, he aged fairly well and looked younger than his years; the same observer thought him to be 'probably between 56 and 60', when he was in fact 64. Headlam had always been thin, but became more so with age. Illnesses accelerated the trend: he lost a stone due to German measles in February and March 1940, and after a severe bout of influenza in August and September 1942 his weight fell again to around nine and a half stone: 'I am 0 but skin and bones, and all my muscles have disappeared.'[158] He did not regain this weight and remained very thin, especially after the serious bronchial illnesses of 1943 and 1950. Apart from these incidents, and especially up to 1943, his health was generally robust. As he got older, he suffered from problems with his teeth and feet. The latter 'have always been a curse to me through life', and Headlam thought that 'half my gloom and grumpiness I veritably believe is due to fatigue caused by my rotten feet'.[159] He described the problem as 'bad joints' and a thinness of the feet which led to corns and the need for regular treatment by a chiropodist.[160] His dental difficulties were due more to natural ageing; there were intermittent problems in the later 1930s which led to a series of extractions, some of which left a painful legacy. This did not end when his last nine teeth were removed on his dentist's advice in May 1943, for after this he had to rely upon dentures which were often badly fitting, sore and wearisome.

The other recurring source of trouble was his susceptibility to chest infections, which had its origins in the gas used on the Western Front in the First World War. The resulting tendency to respiratory

---

[156] Headlam diary, 13 Apr. 1944.
[157] 'Newcastle by-election candidates', June 1940, Mass Observation MSS, Box 8, File B.
[158] Headlam diary, 16 & 22 Sep. 1942, 23 Mar. 1940.
[159] Headlam diary, 16 May, 26 Aug. 1940.
[160] Headlam diary, 30 Sep. 1936, 20 July 1939.

illness was made worse by his smoking, which was heavy but not unusual for the period. His average consumption would seem to have been about sixty cigarettes a day, and he also sometimes used a pipe. The addiction was strong: on New Year's Day 1943 he made a resolution to give up cigarettes, but had smoked at least a dozen by lunchtime. The very serious bronchial illness at the end of 1943 forced changes in his diet and habits; his doctor forbade cigarettes, but as pipe-smoking was permitted 'provided that the tobacco is very strong, or cigars if they are the best', the gain was probably limited.[161] Although by February 1944 his blood pressure returned to a more normal level and his weight had recovered to nine stone and five pounds,[162] he suffered a sharp relapse at the end of that month and had to return to the nursing home again in May 1944. For the next fifteen years his health was fairly good for his age and the medical resources of the era, but he was always prone to chest infections which could turn to pneumonia, as in the two most serious attacks in the early summers of 1948 and 1950. By the end of the 1940s he had some lapses of short-term memory, mainly minor but embarrassing matters of forgetting appointments or engagements.[163] However, these could well have been due to stress and tiredness, for there is no sign of any dimming of his analytical ability or his facility with language.[164]

A constituency and home in the north of England meant constant travelling to and from London, to attend the House and for business affairs. During the 1930s in particular the Headlams were often weekend guests at the houses of friends, generally in southern England, and this involved further journeys. Headlam also travelled to speaking engagements in various parts of the country, especially when he was a junior minister and during his year as Chairman of the National Union. A good part of his life was therefore spent in motion, sometimes by car but more usually by train. Whilst he was used to this and could relax with a novel or doze, still 'as one gets

[161] Headlam diary, 5 Jan. 1944.
[162] Headlam diary, 12 Feb. 1944.
[163] Headlam diary, 8 Jan. 1948.
[164] This judgement is based upon the diary, various recollections, and the press reports and internal Conservative Party papers relating to the North Newcastle troubles of 1947–51; whilst Headlam's age is a barrier to being the candidate again in 1951, it is clear that he remained effective in private meetings and at public occasions.

older these long journeys tire one'.[165] During his term as Chairman
of the Northern Area, awkward combinations of commitments
sometimes required two return trips between Newcastle and the
capital in the same week. Otherwise, his usual pattern was to take
the sleeper service to the south on Monday night, arriving in
London on Tuesday morning and leaving by the same means late
on Thursday evening. Headlam generally slept well on the train,
unless his compartment was directly above the wheels. Even so,
this amount of travelling was wearing, and it became more so
during the war: 'secretly, I am beginning to wonder whether I shall
be able to continue it much longer', he wrote in May 1941.[166] For
a period there were no sleeper carriages, and after this only limited
spaces, with M.P.s having to obtain vouchers from an official at
Westminster. Wartime train journeys were an endurance test: in
the blackout and with much extra traffic on the lines, passenger
services were unpredictably delayed and often crowded. Headlam
found the latter especially trying, for he had always much preferred
solitude to conversation, and found the journey most relaxing when
he had the carriage or compartment to himself.[167] The Headlams
gave up their rented flat at 3 Sloane Court in December 1935 and
for the next nine years when staying in London they usually lodged
at their respective clubs; in Cuthbert's case, the Travellers'. From
December 1944 until 1947 they shared the cost of a flat in
Westbourne Terrace, near Paddington, with a couple by the name
of Price whom they had met when Mrs Price had been a paying
guest at Holywell. After this, Headlam rented a small flat or a
room at various locations, generally for a few months at a time;
the best of these was a spell as the paying guest of an old family
friend, Dodo Hanbury-Jones, at 41a Smith Square.

   Whether at home or away, Headlam was most contented when
he was able to read quietly alone, free from interruptions and social
discourse. At Holywell he spent most of his time in his study, at
his happiest when he could 'rejoice in my books'.[168] He read widely,
enjoying history, biography, and novels; the latter were mainly the
standards of the nineteenth century, and contemporary works were
more rarely satisfying. Modern fashions did not appeal to tastes

[165] Headlam diary, 7 Sep. 1936.
[166] Headlam diary, 30 May 1941.
[167] Headlam diary, 18 Oct. 1937.
[168] Headlam diary, 5 Feb. 1936.

which were formed in the late-Victorian world, but he did not turn his face away from the innovations of the age. In the 1930s and 1940s he visited the cinema quite often in the company of others and, although critical, he appreciated the entertainment value of some of the films which he saw – however, it was the news theatre, with its shorter programme and 'pictures of real life', which he really enjoyed.[169] Headlam was quite content with the amenities of metropolitan life and would have been happy with a quieter life in a small London flat, although he would have missed having a garden. This was one of Holywell's most attractive features: 'sometimes I feel that I should like to stay in my garden all the time', he wrote in June 1933.[170] He was an active rather than an expert gardener, attending mainly to the pruning of the roses and to weeding, upon which he could peacefully spend several hours.

Another feature of Holywell was the pleasant walks which could be taken with the many dogs – mostly dachshunds – which the Headlams kept. Beatrice in particular was devoted to these pets, with the inevitable sadness at their deaths – 'how one loses one's heart to a dog', wrote Headlam after one such event.[171] His favourite physical recreation was fly-fishing, especially for salmon. Headlam fished in the rivers of the border counties and eastern Scotland, often by the invitation of friends such as James Stuart, and on a stretch of the Test in Hampshire courtesy of Guy Dawnay. His efforts rarely resulted in a catch, but this mattered little – what was relaxing was the combination of activity with tranquillity and companionship with little conversation. 'I love being alone by a river – it is the most restful and calming thing in the world, and one sees and hears animal life to perfection – with no one to bother one – nature all to oneself – I would rather have a good stretch of fishing than anything else in the world.'[172] Disappointment here rarely vexed him: 'some day perhaps the luck will change and this is always the consoling thought of the true fisherman'.[173] Apart from this, he played some lawn tennis, though without much enthusiasm. Headlam was never attracted to golf, nor was he more

---

[169] Headlam diary, 15 Sep. 1937.
[170] Headlam diary, 25 June 1933, 10 Sep. 1936.
[171] Headlam diary, 15 Dec. 1947, 12 June 1938.
[172] Headlam diary, 17 June 1943.
[173] Headlam diary, 26 June 1936.

than a tepid follower of cricket, although from time to time he
watched part of a match at Lords.

Most of all, however, 'it is always pleasant to be "quietly" at
Holywell'.[174] The house had engaged the Headlams' affections from
the time when they had first seen it in 1925. It was an old building,
with part of the structure dating from the fourteenth century; its
name was even older, as centuries before it had been the last resting-
place of the body of St. Cuthbert on its journey to burial in Durham
Cathedral. Holywell was not the easiest or most comfortable of
houses; it was draughty and damp, factors made worse by the
northern climate and more recent human activity. Owned by a
colliery, the property was an island of about six acres entirely surrounded by coal mines. Working tunnels which passed under the
house and grounds caused regular problems of subsidence: ponds
appeared in the gardens, walls were crooked and doors jammed.
Whatever the discomfort, Holywell was both accessible, being only a
few miles from Durham, and remote; it was unusual and had charm.
Headlam found that there was 'a strange fascination about Holywell –
it is a house with an atmosphere of its own – a sort of personality',
although it could be lonely and dreary when Beatrice was away.[175]
The financial crises of the 1930s and the heavy taxation of wartime
led to constant fears that they would not be able to afford to continue
at Holywell, although they hated the idea of leaving. Labour's victory
in 1945 paved the way to the nationalisation of the mines, and
Headlam became concerned that this would affect the house and
leave them homeless. Up to this point they had rented, but before
nationalisation took effect Headlam arranged to purchase the estate
for £880. Life at Holywell was 'rather disorganised':[176]

> timekeeping was erratic, especially with meals; staff came and went
> and Lady H. had an ability to pick up the waifs and strays from miles
> around, and they seemed to often become pregnant. Few of the staff
> were reliable, for whatever reason. The house was usually over-run
> with dogs, as ill disciplined as the staff, most sleeping in Lady H.'s
> bed.

[174] Headlam diary, 10 Sep. 1936.
[175] Headlam diary, 20 Mar. 1942, 23 Mar. 1943, 13 Apr. 1941.
[176] Caroline Bell to the editor, 23 Oct. 1990, 'from memory of parental tales': her
father, Henry Parkin ('Harry') Bell, Headlam's private secretary and aide for many
years, lived at Holywell from 1925 until his marriage in 1948; her parents continued
to winter at Holywell until 1954, and kept in touch thereafter.

The house was expensive to run, needing several servants and the maintenance of two or three cars. Finding and keeping staff was a constant problem, due partly to the remoteness of the area and partly to the low wages which were all that the Headlams could afford.

These problems fell mainly on Beatrice's shoulders, but the strain worried her husband. The support which he gained from his marriage was of vital importance to Headlam; on Beatrice's birthday in 1939 he wrote simply: 'She is so wonderful that one feels everything in life depends upon her.'[177] The love and affection which he felt for Beatrice recur throughout the diary, in particular on her birthday and their wedding anniversary. After forty years together, he was sure that 'no man ever had a more perfect wife ... I have always adored her and been proud of her.'[178] A strength of the marriage was their mutual affection: Beatrice was devoted to Cuthbert, whose ability and cleverness she admired. The post-humous daughter of a wealthy businessman, Beatrice Crawley had been rather spoiled as a child; her assistant for many years, Gertrude Ridley, noted that she was 'used to getting her own way but was kind-hearted and loving'.[179] Their characters were complementary, but very different. Beatrice was lively, with an 'energetic rest-lessness'.[180] She had great charm and enjoyed company, and was both popular and successful as a hostess: 'Beatrice has the power of making things go and getting the most incongruous gathering of people to play up'.[181]

Although she was not always concerned with practicality, Beatrice had verve and ideas. The charitable and employment schemes which she started in outbuildings of Holywell in the later 1920s were examples of this, and were the reason for the award of a C.B.E. in 1929.[182] These ventures grew in scale during the depression years of the 1930s, and remained active after 1945. Before and after the war, questions of funding and state regulations involved endless frustrating negotiations with local officials and Ministry of Labour

---

[177] Headlam diary, 27 May 1939.
[178] Headlam diary, 22 Mar. 1944.
[179] Gertrude Ridley to the editor, 11 Sep. 1990.
[180] Headlam diary, 20 Apr. 1949.
[181] Headlam diary, 8 Jan. 1939, 22 Mar. 1948.
[182] For a fuller account of these, see Ball, *Parliament and Politics in the Age of Baldwin and MacDonald*, pp. 10–11.

civil servants. Despite a flow of well-connected young women as voluntary helpers, the burden of responsibility rested on Beatrice's shoulders. Cuthbert worried that she took on too much – 'she never gives herself a moment's respite and seems incapable of resting' – but he could never persuade her to slow down.[183] The whirl of activity took its toll of Beatrice's nervous strength, and periodically she was confined to bed with minor illnesses which were probably stress-related.[184] Different medical advisors and remedies were tried, but with little effect as her lifestyle remained the same. Her husband found his role as spectator a frustrating one:[185]

It has always been the same since we married – one doctor or healer after the other – and never any really satisfactory result – and all the time she is living on her nerves and overdoing things the moment she feels a little better ... one can do nothing to help her because she won't be helped. I feel such a useless creature – it makes me miserable to see her suffering.

After the problems of 1935 which led to the trip to South Africa, the next most worrying time was Beatrice's long period of poor health and low spirits in the first half of 1941. This began with a car accident on 22 March in which her nose was broken and she was severely shaken, and the shock led to unusual low spirits from which she did not recover until late June. Because financial stringency was the cause of much of the stress, Headlam felt constantly guilty that he could not provide his beloved with more comfort and security, especially for her old age. However, despite their advancing years and recurrent illnesses, he drew much strength from their marriage: 'her courage, her high spirit, her unfailing optimism have been marvellous'.[186]

Their partnership was closer than most of those around them: 'we have been very happy – very lucky – in a hundred ways we have much for which to be thankful', he wrote on their anniversary in 1945. They had no children of their own, but had adopted a son, John, in the early 1920s. Headlam was a fond parent, for

[183] Headlam diary, 5 Sep. 1945.
[184] Hugh to Maurice Headlam, 11 Nov. 1950, Maurice Headlam MSS, Eng. Hist. c.1118, f. 147.
[185] Headlam diary, 7 Oct. 1938.
[186] Headlam diary, 22 Mar. 1945.

whom the usual concerns about schooling and finding a career were followed by the greater worry of John's active service in the army during the Second World War. The one problem between Cuthbert and Beatrice was her extravagance: 'though they were a devoted couple, he was often annoyed with her for spending so light-heartedly – and there were quarrels'.[187] She had been brought up to think little about money, and accumulated debts which her elder brother Ernest from time to time helped to clear; after his death, she had to be more careful. Beatrice was Cuthbert's essential foundation, for 'life without my beloved would be unendurable'.[188] As the years advanced, however, this was a prospect which had to be faced, and on Beatrice's 69th birthday he noted: 'what a sad business it is this nearing the end and knowing that in the natural course of things one of us must be left alone'.[189]

A Failed Career?

It would be easy to dismiss Headlam's career as a study in failure, but it would be fairer to view it as a success within limitations. The latter were interlinked, and ran through his whole life. The first, most remarked upon by Headlam himself, was lack of money. This had the effects of delaying the start of his political career, so that he was older than most of his rivals for office, and of preventing him from finding a safe perch in the House of Commons – until 1940, when it was too late. By then he had to settle for a regional eminence and for the intermediate status of an elder statesman amongst the backbenchers. The lack of a secure seat was the second factor to put a ceiling upon Headlam's rise, as it caused the broken nature of his two decades as an M.P. Headlam himself felt that his absence from the House between the general elections of 1929 and 1931 had been a crucial interruption. It is true that before the 1929 defeat Headlam had been the best placed of the intake of 1924, with reasonable prospects of steady if not spectacular advance, whilst his belated inclusion in the National Government in November 1931 was only too obviously an afterthought. However, it may be that the period of exile mattered less than Headlam believed, for it was not until 1933 and 1934 that Duff Cooper, Oliver Stanley,

---

[187] Gertrude Ridley to the editor, 11 Nov. 1993, 11 Sep. 1990.
[188] Headlam diary, 22 Mar. 1948.
[189] Headlam diary, 27 May 1949.

Harry Crookshank and other younger men clearly overtook him. In order to explain this, the focus must be widened to include other and more personal factors.

The first of these was the lack of opportunities to shine in the junior offices to which Headlam was assigned. The Admiralty posting from 1926 to 1929 put him in a department which at that time was playing a crucial role in international relations in terms of Anglo-American friction, efforts to secure multilateral disarmament, and the role of the League of Nations. However, Headlam's role was only that of a privileged spectator: such matters of great substance were decided at cabinet level where the Admiralty case was put by the First Lord alone. Furthermore, beyond the details of its annual spending estimates, the Admiralty had hardly any parliamentary business. Apart from the string of constituents' personal cases which M.P.s raised at question time, naval affairs took up little of the time of the House and involved nothing to catch the eye of a public more interested in domestic issues and social policies. The two dismal posts held by Headlam in the National Government from 1931 to 1934 were the bottom of the heap in British politics, and gave him scarcely any more scope. At Pensions his berth was an embarrassing revival of a lapsed office in a time of supposed economy, whilst at Transport he was thwarted by the very different aptitudes of his two superiors. Lack of opportunity was not however the only problem, for when Headlam did have the chance to speak he was not always able to make good use of it. It seems clear that his best parliamentary performances were as a new Member in 1925–26 and after his return to the backbenches in 1934–35. In office, his speeches on key occasions were of more variable quality. Although allowance must be made for Headlam's tendency to severe self-criticism and perfectionism when analysing his own efforts, it is clear that he was a more effective speaker on the public platform than he was at Westminster. This was mainly due to his intense desire to succeed and the nervousness which resulted from this, but it was also partly related to another weakness which Headlam was generally less ready to acknowledge.[190]

Headlam rarely found his work to be congenial or satisfying. He once observed: 'I am ambitious and yet have no push or capacity

---

[190] Cuthbert to Beatrice Headlam, 20 Apr. 1948, Headlam MSS 289/4.

for really hard work – this is the real trouble.'[191] Although the judgement was harsh, it contained more than a grain of truth. The problem was not one of laziness – by most standards, Headlam was diligent, reliable and effective – but of motivation. One of the causes of the problem was having high standards and a clear view of what ought to be possible in any given role or task, establishing aspirations which were difficult to live up to. This also applied to writing, as his appreciation of good literary style made it 'a long and laborious task' to complete even short items. 'I never remember writing anything which I have not re-written several times – and never do I recollect anything that I have written which has really pleased me!', he noted on 6 January 1939, adding a fortnight later: 'I am always the most severe critic of my own work.'[192] Headlam also lacked confidence in the quality and originality of his thought. He was not sufficiently blinkered or egotistical: when preparing material, especially for articles or books, his awareness of the previous work of others inhibited and discouraged him. In later years, his concentration was affected by anxiety over money in particular: 'when I am worried I cannot get on with any work or spend my time usefully'.[193]

Throughout his junior ministerial career, Headlam considered most of his activities to be both tedious and pointless – a frame of mind which made it all the harder to apply himself to the detailed grind of departmental administration. The affairs of the Admiralty were partly familiar to Headlam from his wartime experience in the Army general staff, and in the late 1920s he had the added incentive of the fact that his star seemed to be rising. However in the early 1930s, feeling himself imprisoned in backwaters of bureaucratic tedium, he found it all the more difficult to get sufficiently interested in the minutiae of his work. Yet this has always been essential for the mastery of any ministerial post in British parliamentary politics: nothing impresses the House of Commons more at the junior level than visible competence and an unshakeable command of facts and figures. This characteristic was also apparent in other spheres of Headlam's life: in missing a First at Oxford, in the boredom he found in his duties in the House of Lords and in his tendency to put off the tasks of authorship,

---

[191] Headlam diary, 25 June 1933.
[192] Headlam diary, 20 Jan. 1939.
[193] Headlam diary, 15 July 1938.

journalism or the editorial duties of the *Army Quarterly*. It was the problem of having a more incisive mind and a greater felicity with language than most of his tasks ordinarily required, so that he had never had to develop the self-discipline necessary to get through mundane work with at least an appearance of cheerfulness. Hard work alone cannot make a man successful at the highest level of politics, as Headlam's Oxford contemporary Arthur Steel-Maitland so clearly demonstrated as Minister of Labour in 1924–29. However, it does enable the painstaking and solid to prosper, such as Philip Cunliffe-Lister, George Cave, Walter Guinness or Harry Betterton, and also explains the greater success of men of less evident ability who possessed common sense and good nature, such as William Bridgeman or John Gilmour.

Two final factors circumscribed Headlam's political success. The first of these was an inclination to too much independence of thought. Headlam never voted against the Party line, not from any fear of the sanctions of the whips but because he was suspicious of such gestures as disloyal and pointless self-indulgence. However, this apparent orthodoxy did not prevent him from exercising his own judgement. Though very much in the mainstream of Conservative politics, Headlam was often critical of his leaders' abilities and dubious about the proclaimed merits of their proposals. He did not hide his opinions in private conversation around the Palace of Westminster, and at one acutely sensitive point ruffled his seniors' feathers by making public his reservations about the cabinet 'agreement to differ' on tariffs of 1932. He believed that 'had I been cannier, more careful in my conversation, more of a toady, I should not have been dropped as I was'.[194] This habit of critical observation elided into the final problem of temperament, which others perceived as an abrasiveness in his manner and personality. In reality, the diary reveals a generous spirit and Headlam was far from being intolerant or narrowly judgmental of either colleagues or political opponents. Nor had he the arrogance imparted by the assumption of knowing the right answers, and in the privacy of the diary he was often willing to acknowledge the perspectives of others and the possibility that they might be right. However, he had no great fund of patience and was easily bored or irritated by uninteresting company or foolish conversation. Like

[194] Headlam diary, 5 Oct. 1941.

other shy men, he could sometimes seem abrupt, whilst to some his self-deprecation and general pessimism appeared as dourness: '*joie de vivre* is not a conspicuous element in his make-up'.[195]

Headlam was not unpopular and did not lack friends, although they were mainly amongst his own cohort of the parliamentary intake of 1922–24 and he found it difficult to get to know the new and younger M.P.s of the 1930s and 1940s. Throughout, he had more dining acquaintances than close intimates amongst his fellow M.P.s, but that was no more than the norm for men of his social class and generation: the curiously semi-distant relationships with Harold Macmillan and Oliver Stanley were good examples of this. Nevertheless, Headlam's natural sharpness became more acute and more embittered as his career stagnated between 1930 and 1934; it also became more apparent to others, and he became less comfortable to be with. This clearly had some effect on how he was regarded by the Party hierarchy, and not least by his contemporary and one-time friend David Margesson, the powerful and influential Chief Whip from 1931 to 1941. Headlam had also found it difficult to get on close terms with either of his Party leaders up to 1940, finding both Baldwin and Neville Chamberlain to be insular and introverted. In his last years this sense of disappointment was allied with ill-health and depression, and rendered him all the more isolated: 'he's a misery to himself and a ghastly nuisance to everyone else'.[196]

The factors above indicate why Headlam never rose beyond the junior ministerial ranks nor, despite his tenure of an Area Chairmanship for ten years, ever became a powerful force behind the scenes. However, they do not mean that he had no success in his career, nor that he might not under other circumstances have reached at least the junior rungs of the cabinet. A key factor in the stagnation of his career was the formation of the National Government in August 1931. With the other parties in the coalition taking a share of both cabinet and junior posts, the number of places to be filled by Conservatives was sharply reduced. If this had not happened, it is possible that Headlam might have been given a much better junior post, from which he could have moved

[195] Lyttelton to Hart-Davis, 21 Feb. 1957, in R. Hart-Davis (ed.), *The Lyttelton – Hart-Davis Letters, Volume 2* (London, 1979), p. 61.
[196] Hart-Davis to Lyttelton, 14 Nov. 1959, in R. Hart-Davis (ed.), *The Lyttelton – Hart-Davis Letters, Volume 4* (London, 1982), p. 162.

further upwards. The coming into office of a purely Conservative government had seemed likely before the August crisis erupted; in such a case, as a considerable number of the 1924–29 Conservative cabinet were no longer able or likely to serve, it is possible that Headlam might have had a minor cabinet post or a ministry of his own. Given his age, his inability to really dominate in the House of Commons, and the rapid advance which younger men such as Eden, Stanley and Cooper were making, it is unlikely that he would have come to the topmost perches. However, he might well have been Minister of Transport, rather than the junior, and have tasted the fruits of cabinet rank.[197]

(iii)   The later Diaries 1935–1951

The Diary and its Author

Headlam never thought that his diaries would interest anyone else, and at one point considered leaving definite instructions for them to be destroyed after his death.[198] Fortunately Beatrice did not share his low opinion of their value, and instead the diary volumes and some other papers were deposited at Durham County Record Office in June 1967.[199] It is a curious feature that although many people passed through the House of Commons in the first half of the twentieth century, remarkably few useful collections of papers have been left by backbench M.P.s and junior ministers, of any party. The archives of those who reached cabinet rank are not only greater in number but also in many cases much more extensive in scale. However, the records of junior rank Conservatives for the period from the end of the First World War to the 1950s are very often disappointing, consisting of little more than brief congratu-

---

[197] This point is also argued in Ball, *Parliament and Politics in the Age of Baldwin and MacDonald*, p. 21.

[198] Headlam diary, 21 Nov. 1944,

[199] The diaries form the heart of the collection, with the main series consisting of 37 volumes for 1910–1915, 1919–45 and 1947–51, listed as D/He 9–46; the wartime gap is covered by the other substantial deposit of Cuthbert's regular letters to Beatrice, D/He 137–182. The remainder of the collection, including two further small deposits added in 1987 and 1989, consists of appointment diaries, press cuttings, photographs, ephemera, congratulatory letters and some general correspondence.

latory letters, press cuttings, invitations and other ephemera.[200] Diaries are even rarer, with only two of any real range or depth: those of Sir Henry 'Chips' Channon and the Liberal National M.P. Robert Bernays, both of which have been published.[201] The Headlam diary matches these, and in some respects is of greater value. Bernays was a member of a small party and his diary covers only a few years in the 1930s; Channon's has tremendous atmosphere and he moved in a higher social set, but he was never as representative of the party mainstream or had as wide a range of contacts as Headlam. The latter's diary has three great strengths; it was kept in regular form over a long period, it was written with style, and the content is often analytical in nature.

There are several parallels between Headlam's diaries and the late-twentieth-century journal of Alan Clark.[202] This is more than just the fact that both were junior ministers (with Clark holding the more important posts, and better known to the public of his day), as it concerns the form and purpose of the diaries themselves. Both began their diary in early adult life and had been in the habit of writing for ten to fifteen years before entering the House of Commons, which affected the content rather than the basic approach; both were authors of published works (indeed, in the same field of military history) and thus had a sense of prose style which was automatically carried into their unpublished diaries. Neither wrote in the expectation that their diary would be of interest to anyone else, let alone that they would be published. In both cases the diary was used to express comments and reactions which did not have any other outlet, and acted as a repository of confidences and reflections and even as a purgative for frustration, anger or despair. There is even a certain similarity in tone: an avoidance of self-deception and humbug, an interest in the role of personalities in politics, and a sharpness from which not even friends are exempt.[203]

[200] The other significant collections are the Nancy Astor MSS (Reading University Library), Duchess of Atholl MSS (Blair Atholl), Page Croft MSS (Churchill College, Cambridge), Emrys-Evans MSS (British Library), and Hannon MSS (House of Lords Record Office).
[201] R.R. James (ed.), *Chips: The Diaries of Sir Henry Channon* (London, 1967); N. Smart (ed.), *The Diaries and Letters of Robert Bernays, 1932–1939* (Lampeter, 1996).
[202] A. Clark, *Diaries* (London, 1993).
[203] These comparisons derive in part from comments made by Alan Clark at the 20th Century British History Seminar, Institute of Historical Research, 7 Dec. 1994.

Headlam kept a regular diary from 1910 onwards, although during his wartime service it was replaced by an extensive series of letters to his wife which are also preserved in his papers.[204] He was therefore already in the habit of diary-keeping when he became an M.P. for the first time in 1924, and he simply continued in the same form. Headlam used a bound 'desk diary' volume which had a full page for each day, of size seven and three-quarter inches by five inches. For most of the period these pages were printed with narrow feint lines, although due to economy measures the later wartime volumes are printed on thin paper and have no lines (and in the 1945 volume, Saturday and Sunday share a page). Almost without exception, Headlam completely filled the allotted page, writing between 260 and 290 words for each day.[205] In many instances a significant proportion or even the whole of the entry is taken up by a topic which had aroused his interest or concern on the day in question. The matters which most often stimulated such discussions were the strategic picture during the Second World War, the state of international relations both before and after the war, the domestic political situation, and the character and standing of the leading personalities. The other form of entry, more common at weekends and during parliamentary recesses, simply narrates the passage of Headlam's day, concluding after dinner or with any events in the evening. The location where he was writing is given at the top of each page, and this also indicates that the diary was normally written at the very end of the day, shortly before going to bed.[206] It was generally written on a regular daily basis, although there are a few cases where the entry was made a day later (this sometimes led to the wrong page being used by mistake, but Headlam would then correct the printed header in his own hand[207]). This was usually the fullest extent to which he would retrace his steps, and normally if a day's entry was not made at the time then

---

[204] For the origins and early years of the diary, see Ball, *Parliament and Politics in the Age of Baldwin and MacDonald*, pp. 29–30.

[205] During a few periods of illness there are shorter entries, such as 19–24 Sep. 1937.

[206] See e.g. entry for 9 Mar. 1947, which ends with the words: 'To bed – for I am nearly asleep.'

[207] Such cases are indicated by footnotes in the main text; for a rare example of a confusion where the printed date was not amended, but the error noted in the next entry, see 24–25 Sep. 1943.

the page was left blank.[208] Thus, whilst there are scattered gaps, the diary remains an immediate and contemporary account.

Both form and content suggest that the text for each day was written in one burst, probably in less than ten minutes, but the tone is ordered and often reflective. This was partly due to Headlam's analytical mind and partly to his habitual sensitivity to style and language: 'I like to find the word I need ... and I like, too, to make the story run – to get the prose to move smoothly.'[209] Even so, revisions to the text are nearly always on a small scale – the most common being the insertion of a word above the line in order to clarify a meaning or to correct a grammatical slip. There are a few instances where a sentence or two has been crossed out and it is impossible to tell at what time the deletion was made. In general, revisions are conspicuous by their rarity and there is no particular pattern to them. Although Headlam occasionally refers to looking over past volumes of his journal, he did not seek to amend the entries with the benefit of hindsight.[210] The journal was not kept for self-justification, and still less with any thought of publication.[211] Instead, Headlam thought from time to time of consigning it to the flames, and he expected it to suffer this fate after his death. In November 1944 he commented:[212]

> I have been reading some of my old diaries recently and have found them interesting – but I fancy that they would interest no one else ...
> I am more convinced than ever that I am not another Pepys and that the only sensible thing to do with my diaries is to burn them. I have not yet made up my mind to do this job myself – it would be almost like infanticide – but I feel that it is a job for my executor which I shall direct him to carry out as expeditiously as possible after my

[208] In a few very busy periods entries may have been made a few days afterwards. An indication of this occurs during the 1950 election campaign, when at the foot of the page for 22 Feb. Headlam added a note recording that an item of family news mentioned at the end of the entry was wrongly included, as the message was actually received on 24 Feb. However the fact that he corrects himself, and that such errors are very infrequent, suggests that it was an infrequent practice. The entries for the 1950 campaign are otherwise written as if penned on the day in question, and do not appear to be influenced by hindsight.

[209] Headlam diary, 6 Jan. 1939.

[210] The alteration made to the last few lines of 15 July 1939 is almost unique in this respect. Mention of looking at past volumes is infrequent but does occur, e.g. reading the 1938 volume again: Headlam diary, 19 Apr. 1949.

[211] Nor did Headlam consider writing his memoirs: see Headlam diary, 1 Jan. 1947.

[212] Headlam diary, 21 Nov. 1944; see also 2 Sep. 1936.

demise – a pity perhaps that I should have expended so much time in writing these diaries...

Given this attitude, why did Headlam regularly keep a diary through so many years? Habit forms part of the answer, but most of all the diary offered an outlet for personal expression which was otherwise lacking: 'why go on dilating on my worries – probably because it relieves my feelings', he noted on one occasion.[213] He had many acquaintances, but no very close friends – and certainly none in proximity to his residence in County Durham (hence his perseverance with the awkward and boorish Harold Macmillan). His most constant and satisfactory relationship was with his wife, but Beatrice was a busy and active woman, more sociable and outgoing than her husband. Whilst she listened to and sympathised with him, the division of social roles between the genders which was customary in their class and generation inevitably affected the quality and quantity of their communication, even if to a much lesser extent than in many other marriages. Headlam's was a rather isolated and lonely life; he was not on bad terms with his family, but was not especially close to his relatives either. The one whom he saw most frequently, especially in the 1930s, was his brother Geoffrey Wycliffe Headlam, who was always known by the nick-name 'Tuppie'. Although less aloof and distant than Maurice, 'Tuppie' appears to have been a self-contained character whose occupation as an Eton housemaster augmented his parochialism and self-absorption. If Headlam's own family did not encourage him to warmth and intimacy, personal and political friendships did not fill the gap.

Headlam combined the reserve of shyness with the asperity of relative disappointment; whilst the former may have diminished as he grew older, the latter markedly increased. So too did his isolation – a fact which of he was aware, but unable to alter. Whilst these personal circumstances were not unique, Headlam also possessed an analytical intelligence and a natural literacy which encouraged the expression of private thoughts on paper. Keeping a diary affords a chance to recover mastery over the hazard of the day's events; to reflect, assess, criticise, and give vent to emotion. Headlam was often away from home as a result of his itinerary of

[213] Headlam diary, 3 Aug. 1937.

weekend visits and political speech-making. The possession of a seat in the north entailed frequent lengthy and tedious train journeys, and many diary entries are marked at the top of the page as has having been written whilst travelling between Durham and London. He had begun a regular diary several years before entering Parliament, and the pattern of his political life provided many solitary opportunities which facilitated its continuance. For all these reasons, the diary was a habit which was peculiarly hard to break. Despite chafing sometimes at the labour, and periodically resolving to abandon it, it was a part of his routine. On 1 January 1939 Headlam noted, 'I registered a vow last year that I would give up keeping a diary this year – but long habit has been too strong for me and here I am beginning again.'

Headlam normally wrote a full-page entry for more than 90% of the days in the year, but there are some major gaps in the later years. The first and longest of these runs from mid-October 1945 until the start of 1947, and there are further gaps from August to December 1948 and from June to December 1950. The final section consists of only a few weeks from January to March 1951, but even with these blanks the diary covers thirty-eight of the seventy-five months of the 1945–51 Labour governments. Missing days become slightly more frequent after 1935 and there are scattered short gaps in the diary of one or two days with occasional longer ones, although an interval of more than a week is very unusual.[214] The short interruptions are unheralded and the diary resumes without explanation, as if they had never occurred. Most of the longer cessations are due to periods of illness, although they cannot all be explained in this way.[215] The lack of entries from 23 November to 3 December 1935, after the election defeat and whilst Beatrice was away, are probably a reflection of physical and emotional tiredness. From 27 November to 23 December 1943 Headlam was seriously unwell but he resumed the diary during his convalescence, apart from a shorter gap due to a relapse from 17 to 22 February 1944. He was ill again in early May 1945 and during his recovery the

---

[214] Unexplained gaps of five or more days occur on 25–29 May, 12–17 Oct. 1936; 6–10 Apr., 16–21 May, 21–28 June, 24 Aug-2 Sep. 1937; 26 Aug-6 Sep. 1938; 21–26 May, 26–29 June, 9–14 July 1939; 18–22 Sep., 17–21 Dec. 1941; 21–29 Mar. 1942; 17–23 June, 19–23 Dec. 1947.

[215] The two long gaps for which there is no apparent explanation are 10–31 Aug. 1936 and 22 Oct.-7 Nov. 1937.

entries are mostly only a few words in note form; however, the blank pages for 12–19 and 25–29 June are due not to ill-health but to the pressure of the general election campaign.

The long break in the diary which extends from 15 October 1945 to the end of 1946 probably began unintentionally; there is no comment which foreshadows the cessation, although there had been some short gaps since the general election and a longer one from 18 to 30 September. However, Headlam resumed the diary on 1 January 1947, and his opening comment that 'I gave up keeping a diary in the autumn of '45 and I don't quite know why I am starting one again this year' indicates that no volume for 1946 ever existed. During 1947 he kept the diary slightly less regularly than before, but there were still full entries for more than 80% of the year. Although seventy days were left blank, the gaps consisted mainly of single days and were very rarely of more than three days together.[216] However, he noted on New Year's Day 1948 that he was continuing the diary 'very half-heartedly – I had difficulty in keeping one going last year from day to day'. Age was beginning to take its toll: 'as one grows older one seems to get more and more feeble and less able to express oneself on paper – one seems, too, to take less interest in what happens and to forget things so quickly that one cannot record them'.[217] All began well in 1948, with only eight blank days in the first four months, but after this the diary faltered and there was a second long interruption. It was not kept from 2 May to 19 June 1948, during a period of illness and recuperation in the Channel Islands. The diary then resumed for two months (in which there were thirteen missing days), before ceasing for the rest of the year on 19 August. This second abandonment was probably the result of stress and depression, as it followed a difficult period in early August during which Headlam was suffering from excema on his legs and was worried by several family matters. The 'last straw' came on 19 August when a letter suggesting that he might have to retire from some of his remaining directorships 'destroyed my peace of mind'.[218]

---

[216] The 70 blank days in 1947 were distributed as follows: Jan. (4), Feb. (3); Mar. (3); Apr. (7); May (7); June (9); July (8); Aug. (7); Sep. (8); Oct. (2); Nov. (0); Dec. (12).; apart from 17–23 June and 19–23 Dec., the gaps are mainly of single days or of two days.

[217] Headlam diary, 1 Jan. 1948.

[218] Headlam diary, 19 Aug. 1948.

The diary was resumed once again on 1 January 1949 and, despite Headlam's lack of enthusiasm, it was kept as regularly as at any time in the past. Between 1 January 1949 and 22 April 1950 there are only twenty-six blank days, an average of less than two a month, and Headlam even continued writing when he was unwell in June 1949. However, the pattern changes at the end of April 1950; during May the entries become steadily less frequent and then, apart from a single entry of seven lines on 21 June, the 1950 volume is completely empty from 24 May to the end of the year. Once again, illness was the cause, as both Cuthbert and Beatrice were seriously unwell in May and June.[219] On this occasion, however, when he recovered later in the summer he did not return to the diary. This was perhaps the real end of the diary, as the final short period at the start of 1951 was almost inadvertent. Headlam was prompted into restarting as a result of his stationer having automatically sent him the volume for 1951, but this did not last for long. The diary was kept regularly for the first six weeks of the year, but then dwindled away whilst Headlam was resting at Holywell after contracting a cold. Although he was recovering and expecting to return to London in the following week, the diary ceases after a full-page entry on 2 March 1951. There is no particular explanation of the stoppage, other than lack of motivation, and he did not keep a diary again.

Selection and Editing

The same principle has been followed in selecting the extracts for both volumes of the published edition.[220] All material which seems to be of historical significance and interest has been included, and nothing has been left out due to considerations of space. This has led to a longer second volume as Headlam wrote more extensively about wider issues and affairs during this period, partly because he had no specific duties and partly due to the gravity of the events which were unfolding. The passages selected contain all the comments on political and parliamentary developments, gossip, personalities and reputations. Alongside this is Headlam's discussion

---

[219] Memo, 'Newcastle North', Galloway [Area Agent] to Watson [Central Office], 28 June 1950, CPA CCO/1/8/71/1.

[220] The comments in this section on selection and editing also apply to the first volume; see note 1 above.

of the international situation; although his knowledge of these matters was at second hand, the perspective of a senior and representative Conservative M.P. is significant in itself. Finally, material which illuminates the working of the Conservative Party machine, sheds light on the regional affairs of the north-east, or reveals the reality of politics at the grassroots, has also been included, although on a more representative basis. Where a topic is mentioned at one stage, later references to its development or resolution have been included in order to maintain narrative continuity. However, given the length of the diary, Headlam often said much the same thing in much the same words, and duplications of this sort have been omitted. The main exclusion is the extensive material about Headlam's ordinary routine and personal affairs, most of which has no significance other than for his own personal story. The diary does provide a remarkably complete picture of the daily life of a Member of Parliament, but illustrating this through extracts would require a great deal of space for comparatively little return. Rather than dilute the essential text in this way, these aspects are reviewed in the introduction.

The extracts selected have been reproduced as far as possible exactly as they appear in the original text. Headlam wrote well-constructed and flowing prose in a legible hand, and instances where editorial intervention has been necessary to ensure comprehensibility are few and far between. Most such cases are due to the omission of a single word – usually a preposition – and where the sense of the passage has been affected the most likely missing word is shown in square brackets. There are also a few occasions where an odd construction has been retained in its original form, and to show that this is not an error the term *sic* appears in square brackets. However, whilst the text is generally clear, Headlam's punctuation marks are often ambiguous. He frequently used dashes to separate clauses (and would often link several in succession in this way), but he used a very similar marking to denote a dash, a comma and a full stop. Although his capitalisation could be erratic, the locations of full stops are usually apparent from the syntax and sense of the passage. However, deciding whether a comma or a dash was intended is more of a matter of judgement, and indeed Headlam may not have definitely had one or the other in mind. Where there is doubt, the selection of a dash or a comma in the published text has been influenced both by the shape and position of the original mark and by whichever choice results in greater clarity and sense. This is not unreasonable, as Headlam had a strong sense of good prose style, and would not have intended to write ungrammatically or awkwardly.

Headlam's spelling has been left as it stands provided that it is not likely to cause confusion; this includes following his practise in the use of 'z' or 's' in words such as 'deputize', 'realize', 'organize', and so on. However, some standardisation in the spelling of names and places has been required. For example, Headlam normally wrote the name of the American President as 'Roosevelt', but sometimes rendered it as 'Roosefelt'. Other cases where he varied between two forms include 'Cranbourne' for Cranborne, 'Jugoslavia' for Yugoslavia, 'Trueman' for Truman and 'Hogge' for Hogg, whilst Hinchingbrooke varied in several ways. In these cases, all the references have been put in the form which Headlam used most frequently. Hyphenation in surnames can also be variable, and this has been standardised into the normally expected form. However, simple errors of spelling have been corrected even if the mistake was one which Headlam made constantly: thus 'Denis' Herbert has been amended to Dennis, Harold 'Nicholson' to Nicolson, Donald 'Somerville' to Somervell, and 'Willinck' to Willink. Headlam wrote morale without an 'e' in the early years of the war, but with an 'e' later on – to avoid confusion, all have been rendered as 'morale'. Numbers were sometimes written with commas inserted between the thousands and millions, and sometimes not; for clarity, they have all been put in the former style and commas have been placed as required. Otherwise, the text has been left as it stands, including inconsistencies in the use of quotation marks around titles such as '1922 Committee', of capitalisation and ampersands in the frequent use of the phrase 'and Co.' (or '& Co.'), and capital letters in terms such as Government, Party, Independent, and so on. Generally understood contractions (such as 'govt.') and common abbreviations (such as 'B.B.C.') need no explanation. However, less well-known initials are expanded in the text, with the rest of the word appearing in square brackets after the first letter; in such cases the full stop which Headlam placed after the initial has been removed. Other points of elucidation, including the translation of phrases in other languages, are dealt with in the footnotes.

Content and Themes

As a historical source, the main value of the Headlam diary lies in the account which it gives of political opinions behind the scenes in the House of Commons. The official record of debates may have the text of a speech, but it cannot capture the atmosphere in which it was delivered or reveal what M.P.s thought about it afterwards. Further than this, Headlam records the gossip of the lobbies and Smoking Room, with their fluctuating views of reputations, potential leaders, and election prospects. He naturally had most insight into the moods of the parliamentary Conservative Party and saw their opponents mainly through this prism, but this is a useful perspective. The analytical dimension of the diary, when the recording of the day's events is left aside in order to discuss an issue or dissect a personality, adds to its value. Taken as a whole, it provides a remarkable insight into the life of a Member of Parliament whose background and outlook was fairly typical of most of the dominant party of the era. Headlam stood in the mainstream of his party. Although never on the right-wing, he was regarded by the 'diehards' as having 'sound and sane Conservative views';[221] he was also on good terms with, and was listened to, by the leading lights of progressive Toryism such as Harold Macmillan, Oliver Stanley, and Duff Cooper.[222] Located firmly near the centre of gravity of the parliamentary party, it is reasonable to assume that Headlam's outlook was broadly representative and was shared by others. Whilst his observations may have been above average in their articulateness and clarity, they were typical in their assumptions and sentiments. Headlam eschewed public dissent and gestures of revolt in the voting lobby; as James Stuart remarked when standing down as Chief Whip in 1948, 'you were a very good boy always in my days'.[223] Whilst his perspective was that of the loyal centre, it was not one of unthinking dutifulness. In private conversation he was often sharply critical of his leaders and their strategies, and this gives the text a cutting edge.

Although never a household name, Headlam's views have some significance. He was one of the twelve regional Conservative Party chairmen during the period of 'appeasement' in the late 1930s, and

---

[221] Kindersley to Headlam, 22 Dec. 1926, Headlam MSS 126/127.

[222] For balance, see Skelton to Headlam, 18 Dec. 1926, Headlam MSS 126/198.

[223] Stuart to Headlam, 9 July 1948, Headlam MSS 135/194.

then served as a respected and senior backbench M.P. during the wartime Coalition and post-war Labour governments. He was one of the most senior Conservatives outside the ranks of the wartime government; as an ex-minister he was entitled to sit on the front opposition bench after 1940, and his standing was recognised by the conferring of a Privy Councillorship in 1945. Although for several reasons outside the innermost circle, Headlam was more in the picture than the average Conservative backbencher. He was involved in the wartime policy review conducted by 'Rab' Butler, and in the negotiations with the T.U.C. over the Trade Disputes Act. On the depleted Opposition benches in the 1945–51 Parliament, his experience of the House and his position as one of the tiny handful of Conservative M.P.s from the north-east meant that he was more than just a face in the background behind Churchill, Eden and the other leaders.

Three themes dominate this volume, during which Headlam focused much more upon international affairs than was the case in the period covered by its predecessor. First is the policy of appeasement and the increasing likelihood of war as the situation worsened from 1936 to 1939. Second is the inevitable concern from 1940 to 1945 with the conduct of the war, especially during the unrewarding and difficult period up to 1943. Third is the adjustment to the reduced circumstances of the post-war world; at home, in the measures of the Labour government, and abroad, in the decline from world power status and the emergence of the Cold War. The hallmark of the diary is the shrewd assessment of persons and reputations; as someone who met Headlam in a social context wrote, 'I found his talk of good astringent quality, and though his valuation of his fellow men was a long way from being gushing, it was not indiscriminate.'[224] Headlam not only had his own opinions of his leaders, but listened to those of others. As always, the two most constant topics discussed among M.P.s were the fortunes of those aspiring to the top rank and the prospects of victory or defeat in the next election. Headlam was on familiar terms with many of the leading Conservative figures of the 1940s. Oliver Stanley, Anthony Eden, Harold Macmillan, Duff Cooper, Harry Crookshank and the Chief Whip, James Stuart, had all come into the

---

[224] Lyttelton to Hart-Davis, 13 May 1959, in R. Hart-Davis (ed.), *The Lyttelton–Hart-Davis Letters, Volume 4* (London, 1982), p. 65.

House at the same time as him in 1924, and were to a greater or lesser extent friends as well as colleagues. Oliver Lyttelton, a rising star of the war and post-war years, had been known to Headlam for many years before office in the wartime Coalition brought him into the Commons in 1940. In these cases and several others, including Butler, Headlam was a shrewd observer of their characters and careers. There is one further dimension to the diary: the insight which it provides into the working of the party machinery, at both national and regional level. If the diary is one amongst a very few sources for junior ministers and backbench M.P.s, it is unique in giving a picture of the private thoughts and attitudes of an Area Chairman, the key figure in the increasingly significant middle tier of the Conservative Party structure.

Headlam's commentary is not just extensive and continuous; it is also shrewd and intelligent, and in several cases the judgements are notably perceptive. He had fewer illusions than many about both the probable results of British foreign policy in the later 1930s and the prospects for the Conservatives in the 1945 election. Yet whilst his instinct was to look forward with caution, he had the imagination to see the larger picture. One such example is his assessment on 18 February 1939 of how the war might unfold, which is aware of Britain's present weakness but concludes with the prophetic observation that 'even with the Germans on the shores of the Black Sea it will only be the beginning of the war'. Another instance, written in the depths of wartime crisis on 18 March 1942, looks still further ahead to Britain's post-war future as 'a mere island in the North Sea', dwindling to become either an unimportant appendage of a dominant United States or a small cog in a European federation. The prose style in the diary is crisp and succinct, and a sense of place and occasion is conveyed with immediacy. The final word, on both Headlam and the diary, may be left to someone who knew him in later years: 'he is a dry wine, but very far from flavourless'.[225]

---

[225] Lyttelton to Hart-Davis, 13 June 1957, in R. Hart-Davis (ed.), *The Lyttelton – Hart-Davis Letters, Volume 2* (London, 1979), p. 115.

1

NORTHERN AREA CHAIRMAN
November 1935 to August 1937

Headlam lost his parliamentary seat, Barnard Castle in County Durham, in the general election of November 1935. On the day after the result was declared his wife, Beatrice, departed for South Africa; she had been unwell for some time, and it was hoped that the sea voyage and the warmer climate would restore her health.

Saturday 16 November 1935   This has been one of the worst days of my life, saying goodbye to my beloved Beatrice was almost more than I could bear. She, poor darling, was wonderfully brave and good – but we both broke down at the last. It was a horrible business and I only hope and pray it will be made up to us by her coming back to me refreshed and invigorated by her visit to S.A. If only I could have gone with her, how happy we should have been to get right away from all our worries ... but this parting was like the war all over again and one felt that it was asking too much of us. ... I feel utterly miserable and alone...

Wednesday 20 November   It has been a dreary, dreary day and mercifully it is now over and I am about to go to bed where I trust I shall go to sleep very quickly and forget the pervading melancholy of the present time. ... I wrote a letter to Baldwin,[1] more to show I am alive than for any other reason. I don't suppose for a moment that he will lift a finger to help me in any way, but there is no

---

[1] Stanley Baldwin (1867–1947), Con. M.P. Bewdley 1908–37; F.S.T. 1917–21; Pres. Bd. of Trade 1921–22; Chanc. of the Exchequer 1922–23; P.M. 1923, 1924–29, 1935–37; Lord Pres. 1931–35; Con. Leader 1923–37; K.G. 1937, cr. Earl Baldwin of Bewdley 1937.

harm in letting him have the opportunity of remembering that I am completely stranded. ... Had I won in 1929 I should have had a fair chance of making a political career – now of course the chance has gone for ever and I doubt very much whether I shall ever sit in the HofC again. Well, the only thing to do is to turn my whole attention to business and try and pick up as many directorships as I can – if only one can make a little money, one's declining years ought not to be too bad – if only we keep our health.

Tuesday 10 December   Rab[2] says that Anthony Eden[3] made an excellent speech in the House today defending the Hoare-Laval proposals to Italy – as one reads what they are supposed to be in the press it looks as if they were giving Italy far too much...

Wednesday 11 December   I lunched with Oliver Stanley[4] ... Oliver deplored his inability to help me in any way – but no doubt meant to be friendly. He is a curious, aloof creature. He told me that Sam Hoare[5] had been given no instructions by the Cabinet to arrange peace terms with Laval,[6] and that they were all knocked of a heap

---

[2] Richard Austen Butler (1902–1982), Con. M.P. Saffron Walden 1929–65; U.S. India 1932–37; P.S. Labour 1937–38; U.S. For. Office 1938–41; Pres. Bd. of Educ. 1941–45; Min. of Labour 1945; Chanc. of the Exchequer 1951–55; Lord Privy Seal 1955–59; Home Sec. 1957–62; Dep. P.M. 1962–63; For. Sec. 1963–64; Con. Party Chairman 1959–61; Chairman, Con. Research Dept. 1945–64; Chairman, N.U. 1945–46, Pres. 1956; Master of Trinity College, Cambridge 1965–78; cr. Baron Butler of Saffron Walden 1965, K.G. 1971.

[3] (Robert) Anthony Eden (1897–1977), Con. M.P. Warwick & Leamington 1923–57; P.P.S. to G. Locker-Lampson 1924–26, to Austen Chamberlain 1926–29; U.S. For. Office 1931–34; Lord Privy Seal 1934–35 & Min. for League of Nations 1935; For. Sec. 1935–38, 1940–45, 1951–55; Dominions Sec. 1939–40; Sec. for War 1940; P.M. & Con. Leader 1955–57; K.G. 1954, cr. Earl of Avon 1961.

[4] Oliver Frederick George Stanley (1896–1950), Con. M.P. Westmorland 1924–45, Bristol W. 1945–50; P.P.S. to Lord Eustace Percy 1924–29; U.S. Home Office 1931–33; Min. of Transport 1933–34; Min. of Labour 1934–35; Pres. Bd. of Educ. 1935–37; Pres. Bd. of Trade 1937–40; Sec. for War 1940; Colonial Sec. 1942–45; younger son of 17th Earl of Derby.

[5] Samuel John Gurney Hoare (1880–1959), Con. M.P. Chelsea 1910–44; Sec. for Air 1922–24, 1924–29, 1940; India Sec. 1931–35; For. Sec. 1935; 1st Lord of Admiralty 1936–37; Home Sec. 1937–39; Lord Privy Seal 1939–40; Amb. in Madrid 1940–44; Con. Party Treasurer 1930–31; suc. 2nd Bart. 1915, cr. Viscount Templewood 1944.

[6] Pierre Laval (1883–1945), French statesman, Dep. 1914–19, 1924–27; Sen. for the Seine 1927–36, for Puy-de-Dôme; Min. of Public Works 1925; Min. of Justice 1926; Min. of Labour 1930; P.M. 1931–32, 1935–36; Foreign Min. 1934–36; chief Min. of the Vichy Govt. 1942–44; executed 1945.

when they heard about them. I asked him why then they let them
go forward – to which he replied darkly that things were in a pretty
rocky condition – which means of course that they at last realize
that the enforcement of an oil embargo (if, indeed, it could be
effected) would mean war with Italy in all probability – and that
we are not in a position either in Egypt or in the Mediterranean to
fight – but surely they might have foreseen all of this before they
began playing with sanctions? It really frightens me that we should
have such a crew running the show.

Tuesday 17 December   How on earth the Government can have
so misunderstood public opinion it is difficult to imagine, but then
of course not one of them really is up against it in his constituency –
with the exception of course of Walter Elliot.[7]

Wednesday 18 December   [Christmas party] at Londonderry
House last night ... Mrs. Baldwin was there and Hailsham[8] and
other ministers -and people were all sitting in corners and whispering – the 'crisis' is a pretty real one and I shall not be surprised
if Sam Hoare had to go...

Thursday 19 December   Sam Hoare has resigned, and speaks in
today's debate as a private member. Rumour has it that all the
young gents in the Cabinet – Walter [Elliot], Oliver [Stanley], Duff
[Cooper][9] and Anthony [Eden] presumably – were against him and
that the whips have had the wind up for some days – so Mr. B.
has thrown Sam to the wolves. Of course one is sorry for the
victim, but Sam has never had a set back and it may do him good.
Personally I smile – for I have never cared about Sam and I know

[7] Walter Elliot Elliot (1888–1958), Con. M.P. Lanark 1918–23, Glasgow Kelvingrove 1924–45, 1950–58, Scottish Univ. 1946–50; P.S. Health for Scotland 1923–
24, 1924–26; U.S. Scotland 1926–29; F.S.T. 1931–32; Min. of Agric. 1932–36;
Scottish Sec. 1936–38; Min of Health 1938–40.
[8] Douglas McGarel Hogg (1872–1950), Con. M.P. St. Marylebone 1922–28;
Attorney-Gen. 1922–24, 1924–28; Lord Chanc. 1928–29, 1935–38; Sec. for War
1931–35; Lord Pres. 1938; Con. Leader in the Lords 1931–35; kt. 1922, cr. Baron
Hailsham 1928, Viscount 1929.
[9] (Alfred) Duff Cooper (1890–1954), Con. M.P. Oldham 1924–29, St. George's
1931–45; F.S. War Office 1928–29, 1931–34; F.S.T. 1934–35; Sec. for War 1935–37;
1st Lord of Admiralty 1937–38; Min. of Information 1940–41; Chanc. Duchy of
Lancaster 1941–43; British rep. with Free French 1943–44, Amb. in Paris 1944–47;
cr. Viscount Norwich 1952.

what a persistent wire puller and self-seeker he has always been: he meant to be Foreign Secretary; he has been Foreign Secretary – and now he has made a mess of the job. I suppose he will be succeeded by Anthony, though rumour again has it that Sir Austen[10] is to be called back into the cabinet and of course some people suggest the perfect Edward Wood.[11] Not one of these men is really what is wanted – indeed, I can't think of any man in politics at the moment who is fit for the job.

Friday 20 December   Sam Hoare seems to have scored a success in the HofC last night, but Mr. B. appears to have not been at his best. *Mea culpa*[12] was his cry. The Socialists do not seem to have made the best use of a wonderful opportunity. Attlee[13] and Dalton[14] are a sorry pair.

Sunday 22 December   I went to lunch at Wynyard ... Charley[15] told me all about his exit from the cabinet in which business Mr. B. does not play a nice part. Of course he is a mean little man –

[10] (Joseph) Austen Chamberlain (1863–1937), M.P. Worcs. E. 1892–1914 (L.U. to 1912, then Con.), Con. M.P. Birmingham W. 1914–37; Postmaster-Gen. 1902–03; Chanc. of the Exchequer 1903–05, 1919–21; India Sec. 1915–17; Member of War Cabinet 1918–19; Lord Privy Seal 1921–22; For. Sec. 1924–29; 1st Lord of Admiralty 1931; Con. Leader 1921–22; K.G. 1925.

[11] Edward Frederick Lindley Wood (1881–1959), Con. M.P. Ripon 1910–25; Pres. Bd. of Educ. 1922–24, 1932–35; Min. of Agric. 1924–25; Viceroy of India 1925–31; Sec. for War 1935; Lord Privy Seal 1935–37; Lord Pres. 1937–38; For. Sec. 1938–40; Amb. in Washington 1941–46; cr. Baron Irwin 1925, suc. 3rd Viscount Halifax 1934, cr. Earl of Halifax 1944, K.G. 1931.

[12] translation: I am to blame.

[13] Clement Richard Attlee (1883–1967), Lab. M.P. Limehouse 1922–50, Walthamstow W. 1950–55; U.S. War Office 1924; member of Simon Comm. 1928–30; Chanc. Duchy of Lancaster 1930–31; Postmaster-Gen. 1931; Lord Privy Seal 1940–42; Dominions Sec. 1942–43; Lord Pres. 1943–45; Dep. P.M. 1942–45; P.M. 1945–51; Dep. Labour Leader 1931–35, Leader 1935–55; cr. Earl Attlee 1955, K.G. 1956.

[14] (Edward) Hugh John Neale Dalton (1887–1962), Lab. M.P. Peckham 1924–29, Bishop Auckland 1929–31, 1935–59; U.S. For. Office 1929–31; Min. for Economic Warfare 1940–42; Pres. Bd. of Trade 1942–45; Chanc. of the Exchequer 1945–47; Chanc. Duchy of Lancaster 1948–50; Min. of Planning 1950–51; Chairman, N.E.C. 1936–37; cr. Baron Dalton 1960.

[15] Charles Stewart Henry Vane-Tempest-Stewart (1878–1949), Con. M.P. Maidstone 1906–15; U.S. Air 1920–21; Leader of the Senate & Min. of Educ., N. Ireland 1921–26; 1st Comm. Works 1928–29, 1931; Air Sec. 1931–35; Lord Privy Seal & Con. Leader in the Lords 1935; Pres., Northern Counties Area 1930–49; Ld. Lt. Co. Durham 1928–49; Mayor of Durham 1936–37; styled Viscount Castlereagh 1884–1915, suc. 7th Marquess of Londonderry 1915, K.G. 1919.

nevertheless, getting rid of colleagues must always be a horrid job. Tonight I was rung up by the *Daily Express* to be told that Anthony Eden has been made Foreign Secretary: did I know anything about his childhood days in Durham. I said I did not and rang off. I suppose it is the right appointment, but somehow or other Anthony does not strike me as the strong man who is wanted at the Foreign Office at the moment. He is too amiable; too much identified with the League [of Nations] and not the man to deal squarely with Germany or, indeed, with Italy. He has had a meteoric career, but I should not be surprised to see him fall just as quickly as he has risen – I hope I may be wrong for he is a very good fellow.

Tuesday 31 December   And so ends 1935 – not a successful year even though I have been created a Baronet[16] – indeed, to have been so honoured is a mark of political failure – failure mainly due to the fact that I am a very poor man and so could not afford to obtain a safe seat. Had I not been thrown out in 1929 I honestly think success would have crowned my political gamble. They could hardly have treated me as they treated me in 1931 had I done well in the 1929–31 Parliament – and there is no reason why I should not have done well. Now that I have again lost my seat, politics are over for me – and there seems little chance of my being given a job of any kind – while my prospects of making a living out of directorships do not seem rosy. But worst of all in 1935 has been Beatrice's loss of health and depression – pray God that South Africa will restore her health and spirits, and then we can try again for worldly success even so late in life.

Sunday 19 January 1936   The news of the King[17] is no better. There can be no doubt that he is dying – and I suppose it can only be a matter of hours or days before the end comes. He will be a tremendous loss, for he has attained exactly the position of lofty eminence which is so valuable politically – his prestige is such that one feels that he can exercise the control which is so requisite in political life today. His experience and popularity are such that no politician or body of politicians could afford to neglect his opinion –

---

[16] Headlam had been created a Baronet in June 1935.
[17] George Frederick Ernest (1865–1936), Prince of Wales 1901–10, King George V 1910–36; he died on 20 January.

and his opinion would always be given in the interests of the people as a whole and not of a section.

Tuesday 21 January   The P[rince] of W[ales][18] has also a splendid press – no King can ever have started under better auspices and it is to be hoped that he will be equally as successful as his father. How well I can remember walking with him at Bethune in the autumn of 1915 when he explained to me how absurd it was to have to be a King – how royalty was out of date – how England should be a republic – my answer to him was that far from being out of date there was no time in English history when the Crown was more essential than it was today – it was the *real* link which united the Empire, and in the Sovereign still rested a tremendous influence – for if he were wise, impartial and experienced he could by reason of his detached and permanent position advise and often guide the policy of statesmen in the interests of the nation, and check the follies of political parties. The history of his father's reign fully justifies all I said.

Saturday 25 January   I came down here [Birch Grove House] in the evening where everything is as much as usual – Harold[19] has broken his ankle and limps about – but otherwise he is just the same.

Monday 3 February   Beatrice writes ever so much more cheerfully and says that at last she is feeling much more like her old self – this good news has cheered me more than I can say – this long separation will be well worth it if only my darling is the better for it. ... I wrote my official reply to the B[arnard] C[astle Conservative] Association's invitation to stand again: declining the honour – in

---

[18] Edward Albert (1894–1972), Prince of Wales 1910–36, King Edward VIII 1936, cr. Duke of Windsor 1936.
[19] (Maurice) Harold Macmillan (1894–1986), Con. M.P. Stockton 1924–29, 1931–45, Bromley 1945–64; P.S. Supply 1940–42; U.S. Colonies 1942–43; Min. Res. N.W. Africa 1942–45; Air Sec. 1945; Min. of Housing 1951–54; Min. of Defence 1954–55; For. Sec. 1955; Chanc. of Exchequer 1955–57; P.M. & Con. Leader 1957–63; cr. Earl of Stockton 1984.

a private letter to Claude Pease[20] I suggested Agnes[21] as my successor – but I doubt whether they will adopt her – if Charles Vickery[22] produces a fat subscription the bait will be too much for them to resist. It really is sickening that money should count more than anything else in the adoption of a candidate for the HofC.

Sunday 9 February   My own opinion is that everything depends upon our foreign policy – if we can succeed in staving off a European war, we shall survive in some form or other, until the Socialists have the sense to drop their extremists and then they will turn us out.

Wednesday 19 February   In the afternoon I had a meeting of the chairmen of the divisional Conservative Associations: only about half a dozen attended (West Hartlepool, B[arnard] C[astle], Sedge-field, Durham Group, Houghton-le-Spring). I told them that I should not carry on as County Chairman unless I got some kind of an understanding that I should not be let down as I was before the last election. We drafted a somewhat insipid resolution on the subject with which I suppose I must be contented, though God knows I have had enough of political management for the rest of my life. We considered how best to raise money, but I cannot say that anyone had any practical suggestion to offer. Clearly if none of the business people will give adequate subscriptions and none of the small people subscribe at all, there will never be money available.

Friday 21 February   But what a thousand pities that we thought it necessary to embark upon the Sanctions policy. It really does little to help the Abyssinians, makes bad blood between us and Italy, does not help our trade, and will assuredly lead to trouble if

[20] Claud E. Pease (1874–1952), Chairman, Barnard Castle C.A. from 1930; Chairman, Horden Collieries; Dir., Barclays Bank 1924–52.
[21] Agnes Headlam-Morley (1902–1986), Fellow of St. Hugh's College, Oxford Univ. 1932–86; Montague Burton Professor of International Relations, Oxford Univ. 1948–71; prospective Con. Cand. Barnard Castle 1936–44; daughter of Sir James Wycliffe Headlam-Morley, and Headlam's second cousin.
[22] Charles Edwin Vickery (1881–1951), army career 1900–35, incl. service with Egyptian army 1907–12, special mission to King of the Hedjaz 1916–17, British Agent at Jeddah 1919–20, Col. Royal Artillery Northern Command 1933–35; war service with B.E.F. 1939–40; Con. cand. Blaydon 1935; member of Durham County Council 1937–51, High Sheriff 1945–46.

Germany decides to make use of the occasion. Supposing Hitler[23] marches into the demilitarized zone – and he well may – what is to be our policy?[24] The French will naturally appeal to the Locarno Powers[25] – Italy is one of them. Is Italy, who has infringed the Covenant [of the League of Nations] herself, to be called upon to stand against Germany who will also have become an offender? and if sanctions are applied against Italy, are sanctions not to be applied against Germany? and yet now Italy is doing all her trade through Germany. The whole situation is too absurd, and yet how few people in England appear to appreciate its absurdity or to anticipate what may be in store for us.

Tuesday 3 March   I attended the Northern Area Executive Committee meeting this afternoon at the Conservative Club in Newcastle. Sir Alec[26] and Sir Alfred[27] as usual ran the show and decided everything according to their pleasure. I am quite sick of both these gents, and of the Conservatism [*sic*] wire-pullers' organization which they so ably represent. I know that it is useless to hope for anything better in politics. These people are necessary cogs in the machinery. They are useless as workers or speakers; but they are useful, I suppose, in getting money out of people's pockets. What one does resent about them is the way in which they lay down the law and pose as leaders – Alec is one of the most futile politicians I ever met, helpless and hopeless – and old Alfred is just a snob and wire-puller who manoeuvres in the dark – and yet these 2 men seem to be perpetual chairmen of the Party and have to be taken seriously.

Thursday 5 March   Cecil [Hanbury][28] tells me that no one yet

[23] Adolf Hitler (1889–1945), leader of the National Socialist German Workers Party 1921–45; Chancellor of Germany 1933–45; Head of State 1934–45.

[24] German armed forces moved into the demilitarised zone of the Rhineland on 7 March 1936.

[25] The Locarno Pact of 1925, signed by Britain, France, Germany and Italy, guaranteed the existing frontiers between Belgium, France and Germany.

[26] Alexander Leith (1869–1956), steel merchant; Food Comm., Northumberland & Durham 1917–19; Chairman, Northumberland Prov. Div. to 1930; Chairman, Northern Counties Area 1930–36; Chairman, N.U. 1922–23; High Sheriff, Northumberland 1923–24; cr. Bart. 1919.

[27] Alfred Appleby (1866–1952), solicitor, head of Appleby & Lisle Ltd. to 1951; appointed Con. Agent, Newcastle C.A. 1889; Chairman, Newcastle C.A. during the 1920s; Chairman, Northumberland C.A. 1930–46; Vice-Chairman, Northern Counties Area 1930–46; Coroner, City & County of Newcastle 1906–51; kt. 1923.

[28] Cecil Hanbury (1871–1937), Con. M.P. Dorset N. 1924–37; kt. 1935.

knows who is to be the Defence Minister – the latest selection is
W. Morrison,[29] the Financial Secretary to the Treasury – my own
view is that, unless they give the job to one of the more important
Ministers, they might just as well not have a Defence Minister at
all – a minor man could not possibly stand up to the Service
Ministers. I fancy that the new Minister is intended to be a kind
of Min. of Munitions – and that all his 'co-ordinating' work will
be devoted to the matter of *materiel* – not to that of strategic co-
operation.

Thursday 26 March   I had a talk with Douglas Hacking[30] at the
Central Office this morning. He was really very kind and pleasant –
and I think that he should prove a tactful, and possibly intelligent,
Chairman of the Party – a great improvement on that silly little
ass Stonehaven.[31]

Friday 27 March   Anthony Eden seems to have scored a great
success in the HofC last night: the speech was a *tour de force* and
disarmed all opposition. It was designed to show how much we
had done to keep the peace: but I don't think that anyone has
denied this – what one doubts is whether our policy has been, and
is, calculated to establish an era of peace in Europe.

Saturday 28 March   Eden's speech has produced a reaction in
favour of our foreign policy (whatever that may be!) ... It has
placated all the League of Nations Union[32] 'fans' and taken the

[29] William Shepherd Morrison (1893–1961), Con. M.P. Cirencester & Tewkesbury
1929–59; Chairman, 1922 Ctte. 1932–35; F.S.T. 1935–36; Min. of Agric. 1936–39;
Chanc. Duchy of Lancaster 1939–40; Min. of Food 1939–40; Postmaster-Gen. 1940–
42; Min. of Town & Country Planning 1942–45; Speaker 1951–59; Governor-Gen.
of Australia 1960–61; cr. Viscount Dunrossil 1959.
[30] Douglas Hewitt Hacking (1884–1950), Con. M.P. Chorley 1918–45; P.P.S. to
Sir J. Craig 1920–21, to Sir L. Worthington-Evans 1921–22; Whip 1922–25; U.S.
Home Office 1925–27, 1933–34; Sec. Overseas Trade 1927–29; F.S. War Office 1934–
35; U.S. Dominions 1935–36; Con. Party Chairman 1936–42; Vice-Chairman, N.U.
1930–33; Chairman, North West Area 1932–34; cr. Bart. 1938, Baron Hacking 1945.
[31] John Lawrence Baird (1874–1941), Con. M.P. Rugby 1910–22, Ayr Burghs
1922–25; P.P.S. to Bonar Law 1911–16; U.S. Air 1916–19; P.S. Transport 1919;
U.S. Home Office 1919–22; Min. of Transport & 1st Comm. Works 1922–24; Gov.-
Gen. of Australia 1925–30; Con. Party Chairman 1931–36; suc. 2nd Bart. 1920, cr.
Baron Stonehaven 1925, Viscount 1938.
[32] Established to promote the ideals of the League in Britain, this was a large and
powerful pressure group with branches in every constituency.

thunder out of L.G.[33] and the other critics and no doubt given Mr. B. a new lease of life – his stock was getting pretty low.

Wednesday 1 April   I had an interview with Tom Inskip[34] this evening at the C[ommittee of] I[mperial] D[efence] office. The new Minister for co-ordinating defence was, as usual, friendly and sympathetic. ... I don't think that he has an idea what he is intended to do – and will, I suppose, be entirely in the hands of Hankey.[35] Harry Crookshank[36] (with whom I am staying) thinks that S.B. has put Tom Inskip into this office with the idea at the back of his mind that he (Inskip), if successful, might be the man to succeed him if and when he retires. Inskip might be a good Leader of the Party until someone better turns up – but I don't see Neville Chamberlain[37] allowing him to pass over his head – nor do I see S.B. retiring yet awhile, unless some new crisis arises and he makes another mess.

Thursday 2 April   The Government had a beating last night in the HofC – an unimportant affair[38] – but still not a good thing – a good many Conservatives voted against the Government and in a

[33] David Lloyd George (1863–1945), Lib. M.P. Caernarvon Boroughs 1890–1945; Pres. Bd. of Trade 1906–08; Chanc. of the Exchequer 1908–15; Min. of Munitions 1915–16; Sec. for War 1916; Coalition P.M. 1916–22; cr. Earl Lloyd-George of Dwyfor 1945.

[34] Thomas Walker Hobart Inskip (1876–1947), Con. M.P. Bristol Central 1918–29, Fareham 1931–39; Solicitor-Gen. 1922–24, 1924–28, 1931–32; Attorney-Gen. 1928–29, 1932–36; Min. for Co-Ordination of Defence 1936–39; Dominions Sec. 1939, 1940; Lord Chanc. 1939–40; Lord Chief Justice 1940–46; kt. 1922, cr. Viscount Caldecote 1939.

[35] Maurice Pascal Alers Hankey (1877–1963), service in Royal Marines 1895–1912; Sec., Ctte. of Imperial Defence 1912–38; Sec., War Cabinet 1916–18; Cabinet Sec. 1919–38; Clerk of Privy Council 1923–38; Min. without Portfolio 1939–40; Chanc. Duchy of Lancaster 1940–41; Paymaster-Gen. 1941–42; kt. 1916, cr. Baron Hankey 1939.

[36] Harry Frederick Comfort Crookshank (1893–1961), Con. M.P. Gainsborough 1924–56; U.S. Home Office 1934–35; Sec. for Mines 1935–39; F.S.T. 1939–43; Postmaster-Gen. 1943–45; Min. of Health 1951–52; Lord Privy Seal 1952–55; Leader of the House 1951–55; cr. Viscount Crookshank 1956.

[37] (Arthur) Neville Chamberlain (1869–1940), Con. M.P. Birmingham Ladywood 1918–29, Edgbaston 1929–40; Postmaster-Gen. 1922–23; Min. of Health 1923, 1924–29, 1931; Chanc. of the Exchequer 1923, 1931–37; P.M. 1937–40; Lord Pres. 1940; Con. Leader 1937–40.

[38] An amendment calling for equality of pay for women employed in the Civil Service was carried against the government by 156 to 148 votes.

thin House this did not do – how very furious David Margesson[39] must have been! a good experience for him!

Thursday 23 April From what James Stuart[40] told me the other night the Government's stock is not very high and they expect to lose the Peckham bye-election. There are rumours that Mr. B. intends to resign shortly but James thinks that he has no such intention and will certainly not do so before the Coronation. I should imagine that James is right. I don't suppose that Mrs. B. would dream of her Stanley not being P.M. at the Coronation, and then of course Neville – the only possible successor at the moment – is not so popular that he cannot be kept waiting.

Wednesday 20 May Runciman[41] introduced the Coal Bill yesterday in the HofC – a most whole-hogging piece of work which naturally stirred up a lot of opposition – ultimately the Government had to give way and promised to reintroduce the Bill later in the Session. . . . it is an odd affair, not calculated to increase the Govt's prestige. I can't help fancying that Mr. B.'s days are numbered – and yet he has a wonderful facility for weathering storms!

Thursday 21 May Cherry[42] came to see me this morning about a Labour Party appeal for subscriptions which has been sent to all C[ounty] C[ouncil] employees and which is causing uneasiness to our people who consider it a form of blackmail. We are going to publish it in the press . . .

Saturday 23 May Alec Leith appeared at Holywell[43] this after-

---

[39] (Henry) David Reginald Margesson (1890–1965), Con. M.P. Upton 1922–23, Rugby 1924–42; Ass. Whip 1924–26; Whip 1926–29, 1931; Chief Whip 1931–40; Sec. for War 1940–42; cr. Viscount Margesson 1942.

[40] James Gray Stuart (1897–1971), Con. M.P. Moray & Nairn 1923–59; Scottish Whip 1935–41, Chief Whip 1941–48; Scottish Sec. 1951–57; Scottish Con. Party Chairman 1950–62; cr. Viscount Stuart of Findhorn 1959.

[41] Walter Runciman (1870–1949), Lib. M.P. Oldham 1899–1900, Dewsbury 1902–18, Swansea W. 1924–29, St. Ives 1929–37 (Lib. Nat. from 1931); P.S. Local Govt. Bd. 1905–07; F.S.T. 1907–08; Pres. Bd. of Educ. 1908–11; Pres. Bd. of Agric. 1911–14; Pres. Bd. of Trade 1914–16, 1931–37; Lord. Pres. 1938–39; cr. Viscount Runciman of Doxford in June 1937, suc. 2nd Baron Runciman in August 1937.

[42] R.C. Cherry (d.1956), Sec., Durham Municipal & County Federation 1928–56.

[43] Holywell Hall, a few miles west of the city of Durham, was the Headlams' residence from 1925 to 1950.

noon ... to sound me about the succession to the chairmanship. I took the line agreed upon between me and Ledingham.[44] Alec was all butter and might have been my dearest friend. We shall see what happens. He had a lot of gossip about J.H.T.[45] who is supposed to be in a very bad way financially and to owe his bookmaker £10,000 – which I should think was an absolute lie. However, it is notorious that he is a bit of a gambler.

Sunday 31 May   Harold [Macmillan] is much as usual – never tired of political gossip and as much occupied as ever with his economic and financial theories. He certainly has mastered the idiom and the jargon of the economists, but his theories seem to me more and more vague and unpractical.

Tuesday 2 June   The Thomas report[46] came out this evening: it finds that there was a leakage and attributes it to Thomas. It does not surprise me because I know the man: he may not have betrayed the secret in so many words but that he gave enough away to make it possible for people to expect what was going to be done, seems to me perfectly certain. Thomas is not my type – a common, second rate man too much inclined to drink – a snob and a vulgarian. He has only got what he has long deserved – but, nevertheless, one is terribly sorry for him as one always is for anyone who has come a cropper. The only satisfactory thing about a sordid business is that it has been so swiftly and effectively cleared up. If only old Asquith[47] had dealt with the Marconi case[48] in a similar manner, we might have been spared L.G!

Monday 8 June   I went to a cocktail party this afternoon given

---

[44] R.J.W. Ledingham, Con. Agent, Stafford 1926–34; C.O. Agent, Northern Counties Area 1934–39; military service 1939–45; C.O. Agent, West Midlands Area 1945–56.

[45] James Henry Thomas (1874–1949), M.P. Derby 1910–36 (Lab. to 1931, then Nat. Lab.); Gen. Sec., National Union of Railwaymen 1918–31; Colonial Sec. 1924, 1935–36; Lord Privy Seal 1929–30; Dominions Sec. 1930–35.

[46] Into the leakage of information before the Budget speech of 1936.

[47] Herbert Henry Asquith (1852–1928), Lib. M.P. Fife E. 1886–1918, Paisley 1920–24; Home. Sec. 1892–95; Chanc. of the Exchequer 1905–08; P.M. 1908–16; Lib. Leader 1908–26; cr. Earl of Oxford & Asquith 1925.

[48] A scandal in 1913 concerning profits made after government purchase of shares in the Marconi company, involving several ministers including Lloyd George.

by Sir H. and Lady Cayzer[49] at a house in Cadogan Gate ... There
were a few second rate M.P.s there including Henry Page Croft,[50]
George Penny,[51] *Sir* Pat Hannon,[52] and Irene Ward[53] – the last
named was kindly and patronizing to me. She is much above
herself.

Thursday 2 July   In 'certain sections' of the press the report is
being spread that Mr. B. means to retire in a few weeks' time, etc.,
etc. I don't believe a word of this – that little man means to carry
on just as long as he likes – and probably at the moment his going,
or being forced to go for that is what it would mean, would cause
a political catastrophe because there is really no one else who can
hold the HofC as he can, or who could maintain the somewhat
shaken facade of the National Government. It is odd, too, what a
hold the little man still has upon the 'man in the street'. People
still regard him with affection and trust him: they consider him 'so
honest', etc., and yet how he has allowed things to drift and what
a devilish dangerous position we are in today as a result of his
complacent disregard for what has been going on in Europe during
the last 10 years or so!

Friday 10 July   We have lost Derby as was generally expected.
The Times is a little depressed, but assures its readers that the lack
of enthusiasm for the Government candidate does not mean that
the voters wish to return to 'party politics' – really this stupid

[49] Herbert Robin Cayzer (1881–1958), Con. M.P. Portsmouth S. 1918–22, 1923–
39; Pres., Chamber of Shipping 1941–42; cr. Bart. 1924, Baron Rotherwick 1939.
[50] Henry Page Croft (1881–1947), Con. M.P. Christchurch 1910–18, Bournemouth
1918–40; U.S. War Office 1940–45; a leading protectionist, Chairman, Organisation
Ctte., Tariff Reform League 1913–17, Chairman, E.I.A. Exec. Ctte. 1928–45; a
leading 'Die-Hard' and Principal Organiser of the National Party, a breakaway
right-wing faction, 1917–22; cr. Bart. 1924, Baron Croft 1940.
[51] Frederick George Penny (1876–1955), Con. M.P. Kingston-upon-Thames 1922–
37; Ass. Whip 1926–28, Whip 1928–37; Con. Party Treasurer 1938–46; kt. 1929, cr.
Bart. 1933, Baron Marchwood 1937, Viscount 1945.
[52] Patrick Joseph Henry Hannon (1874–1963), Con. M.P. Birmingham Moseley
1921–50; Vice-Pres., Tariff Reform League 1910–14; Gen. Sec., Navy League
1911–18; Dir., British Commonwealth Union 1918–28; Sec., E.I.A. 1925–50; Pres.,
Industrial Transport Association 1927–37; kt. 1936.
[53] Irene Mary Bewick Ward (1895–1980), Con. cand. Morpeth 1924, 1929, Con.
M.P. Wallsend 1931–45, Tynemouth 1950–74; Treasurer, Womens' Advisory Ctte.,
Northern Counties Area 1926–32, Vice-Chairman 1932–34; cr. Dame 1955, Baroness
1974.

pretence that we have done with party politics because a few so
called Liberals and the 2 MacDonalds (*père*[54] *et fils*[55]) are members
of the Cabinet is becoming a serious menace to the Conservative
Party – what is the position going to be if we lose the next general
election?

Monday 13 July   We had a meeting of the Area Executive
Committee this afternoon. Leith announced his resignation and old
Appleby made a fulsome speech about him – or rather read one
for it was all carefully typewritten ... then the fun began – what
about a successor? Leith (who of course had intended to propose
Appleby as his successor and get him nominated there and then)
now announced that the successor could not be nominated by this
meeting and Appleby then proposed that a special meeting of
chairman of constituencies should be called to nominate a successor.
I suggested that according to the rules this job should be done by
the Executive Committee, and eventually it was decided to call
another meeting of the committee for the purpose – but there was
a lot of talk before this was done – proposals were made to limit
the period of office of the Chairman, to make it a rule that the
Chairmanship should alternate between the counties, etc. It was all
rather odd and unpleasant, but directed mainly, I gathered, against
Appleby. I took little part in the performance – the whole business
annoyed me – it seemed too beastly of Leith and Appleby considering all I have done for the Party – however, there was no
doubt that the meeting today was entirely on my side.

Wednesday 15 July   I lunched with Harry Crookshank who has
the gout. He appears to be a little embittered about the treatment
of his Coal Bill and a wee bit disgruntled – presumably, he has not

[54] James Ramsay MacDonald (1866–1937), Lab. M.P. Leicester 1906–18, Abera-
von 1922–29, Seaham 1929–31, Nat. Lab. M.P. Seaham 1931–35, Scottish Univ.
1936–37; Lab. Party Sec. 1900–12, Chairman 1912–14; Lab. Leader 1922–31; P.M. &
For. Sec. 1924, P.M. 1929–35; Lord Pres. 1935–37.
[55] Malcolm John MacDonald (1901–1981), Lab. M.P. Bassetlaw 1929–35 (Nat.
Lab. from 1931), Nat. Lab. M.P. Ross & Cromarty 1936–45; U.S. Dominions 1931–
35; Colonial Sec. 1935, 1938–40; Dominions Sec. 1935–38; Min. of Health 1940–41;
High Comm. in Canada 1941–46; Governor-Gen. of Malaya & Singapore 1946–48;
Comm.-Gen. in S.E. Asia 1948–55; High Comm. in India 1955–60; Governor,
Governor-Gen., & High Comm. in Kenya 1963–65; Special Representative in Africa
1965–69; son of Ramsay MacDonald.

achieved merit and resents his treatment – all the bright young men's stars are a bit dimmer than they were. He says that Baldwin may go much sooner than is generally anticipated – that he is really losing his grip.

Monday 20 July   I had a long talk with Ledingham ... He showed me a private letter he had received from Charley this morning – a real beauty – calmly suggesting that as he (Charley) had heard that there was opposition to both his 'friends' (Sir A.A. and myself) would it not be a good thing to make Lady Grey[56] chairman! C. is assuredly a very odd kind of friend and supporter. I was selected *nem. con.*[57] for Area Chairman at the meeting this afternoon – proposed by Sir A.A.; seconded by Mabel Grey – the meeting went off all right, but Leith might have omitted a final speech of gush over Sir A.A. and he might have shaken me by the hand and wished me good luck – as everybody else did.

Thursday 3 September   ... we entertained a lot of women from the B[arnard] C[astle] division to tea – they came for some kind of committee meeting – and were much as usual. The trouble is that I never can distinguish one from the other – there is an astonishing similarity among Conservative women. I made them rather a good little speech – and they all appeared pleased to see me again – and expressed regret that I was no longer their candidate.[58] They are the salt of the earth – but somehow or other the salt has lost its savour for me, and I felt a sense of relief when tea was over and the ladies began to depart – a sense, wholly pleasurable when the last of them had gone! Is this a sign of age and disillusion? Did I ever care about them? I can answer neither question with any confidence – all I know is that I cannot bear anything or anybody connected with Barnard Castle – and yet this is silly and unreasonable – for these old bodies did their best for me and were loyal always. If there had been more of them, I might still be M.P. I

[56] Mabel Laura Georgina Palmer (1884–1958), daughter of 2nd Earl of Selborne, married 1906 Charles Robert Grey, suc. 5th Earl Grey 1917; Vice-Chairman, Womens Advisory Ctte, Northern Counties Area 1926–32, Chairman 1932–38; Vice-Chairman, Northern Counties Area 1932–38.
[57] translation: without opposition.
[58] Headlam had been Con. M.P. for Barnard Castle 1924–29 and 1931–35.

must get over this absurd anti-B.C. mania: it does one no good to bear a grudge against people or things.

Wednesday 9 September ... to Whitburn Hall (Hedworth Williamson's[59] place near Sunderland). Here I addressed quite a good gathering of Houghton-le-Spring Conservatives. 'Circe'[60] (Londonderry) also spoke – she was to have opened the show but of course arrived far too late to do so. I found her rather trying – she spoke after me and made some rather silly remarks about the Government – of course her nose is out of joint, but why display it?

Friday 11 September Hitler's claim to Colonies is very tiresome and the sooner our Government says definitely that we have no intention of surrendering any colonies, the better it will be. There is no earthly use in our giving them up to the Germans – even if we were in a position to do so. It would only make Hitler and co. more certain than ever that they could go on asking for more – a policy of Danegeld never has paid and never will. I don't for a moment suppose that Hitler is doing more than trying it on – he has got to adopt an aggressive attitude to prove to his own people that he is a devil of a fellow and he has got away with [it] so often now that he thinks that he can go on on the same lines indefinitely.

Saturday 12 September I went to the allotments exhibition at Dryburn this afternoon – a really splendid show of flowers and vegetables. ... Jack Lawson,[61] M.P., seized the opportunity to make a violent attack upon the Government. (I wonder what the Labour people would have said had I made use of a similar occasion to make a political speech: this afternoon one man had the courage to shout out 'no politics' when Lawson began his tub-thumping –

[59] Hedworth Williamson (1867–1942), suc. 9th Bart. 1900; Chairman of family firm of that name, excavators of quarries in Sunderland and Westmorland; a landowner, a courtier and friend of Edward VII and George V.

[60] Edith Helen Vane-Tempest-Stewart (1879–1959), married 1899 Viscount Castlereagh, suc. 7th Marquess of Londonderry 1915; founder & Pres., Womens' Legion 1914–18; Pres., Womens Advisory Ctte., Northern Counties Area 1930–46; known as Circe by family and friends.

[61] John James Lawson (1881–1965), Lab. M.P. Chester-le-Street 1919–49; F.S. War Office 1924; P.S. Labour 1929–31; Sec. for War 1945–46; Ld. Lt. Co. Durham 1949–58; cr. Baron Lawson of Beamish 1950.

but there were immediately cries of 'Give order', 'Turn him out', and he wisely desisted). It was interesting to watch the psychological effect of Lawson's speech – before he began his dose of sob stuff and clap trap everyone was in a good temper – interested entirely in the prize-giving – friendly and keen. After Lawson's effort I (who was standing among the crowd) heard nothing but unpleasant remarks about the Government and the mine owners. Everyone became sulky and disagreeable; it did them no good to be reminded how miserable and down-trodden they all were! What a tragedy it is that the Labour Party exists!

Monday 14 September   It is odd how little independence of thought or judgement the average Minister possesses. The permanent officials, and at the Admiralty and the W[ar] O[ffice] the professionals, win hands down always – at least so it seems to me – but then, as a rule, in my time at any rate, the political chiefs in these offices have always been amateurs, and not really *au fait* with their jobs.

Tuesday 15 September   I fancy Mr. B. must be rather seedy: at any rate Neville is to deputize for him at Margate[62] and he is not to begin work again until Parliament meets. I have no love for him or belief in him – but, all the same, I realize his political value in the country and his going (if he does go) at an early date may lead to big changes – it may even lead to the departure of Ramsay Mac[donald]!

Friday 18 September   Anthony E[den] and Edward Wood are off to Geneva – and the farce begins again – talk, talk, talk – and all the time the nations are arming – and the Teuton faces the Slav as he did in 1914, and Fascism stands opposed to Communism. To us in this country it all seems so silly and unreal – and yet, whether we like it or not, it all affects us terribly. We go on talking – some of us really believing that it is possible to find agreement between the contending influences that are perplexing and upsetting Europe today: others realizing the hopelessness of pacts for peace and collective security so long as no nation will abide by such guarantees: none of us bold enough to say that the time has come for us to

[62] The location of the Conservative Party Conference on 1–2 Oct. 1936.

admit that the League has failed and must be scrapped or recreated on new lines – and that really G.B. must trust to herself alone, and keep out of other people's messes.

Saturday 19 September   We attended the Area Council meeting this afternoon and I was duly elected Chairman in succession to Sir Alec. I think that everyone entirely approved my election and they certainly gave me a very hearty reception. ... Geoffrey Dawson[63] has no news – but he seems to think that S.B[aldwin] intends to hold on until after the Coronation – apparently he has made up his mind on the matter and G.D. says that when once he does make up his mind he generally adheres to his decision. I expect that Mrs. B. is anxious to be in the front row during the Coronation festivities. G.D. thinks that Ramsay Mac. will disappear when S.B. goes – and there seems to be no doubt as to Neville's succession – at the moment there is clearly no one else with the slightest claim to dispute his leadership.

Thursday 24 September   Later in the afternoon I presided at a meeting of chairmen of divisions to discuss details regarding the 'Leith dinner'. No one except Sir Alfred seemed to be very interested in it – it is to cost about £125 + a present of £50. I doubt whether we shall be able to raise the money – but Sir Alfred is quite prepared to finance it out of his secret fund if we cannot get all we want – and yet he was grudging £100 to a very hard working, keen chairman of a division who wanted the money to pay an organizer.

Thursday 1 October   The [Conservative] Conference was terribly dull – Sam Hoare and Walter Elliot were the only Cabinet Ministers present. The former told us all about rearmament in his own precise way and everybody cheered – but both he and Walter failed to get the conference to accept their point of view about other matters – e.g., handing back colonies to Germany and agricultural tariffs.

Sunday 18 October   We discussed the Area problem – whether Cumberland should, or should not, remain in the Northern Area.

---

[63] (George) Geoffrey Dawson (1874–1944), known as Robinson until 1917, when he assumed the surname Dawson; editor of *The Times* 1912–19, 1923–41; a contemporary of Headlam at Magdalen College; a confidant and friend of Baldwin.

Mary Graham[64] was all for remaining: Fergus[65] assured us that no one in Cumberland wanted to belong to the Northern Area – they saw no use in the association: could not be bothered to come to Newcastle; etc., etc. Personally I don't care what Cumberland does, but I would rather the Northern Area did not break up the moment I become chairman – so I shall try and keep the thing together if I can – of course Alec Leith did a lot of harm – first, by never going near Cumberland, and secondly by announcing without rhyme or reason, entirely off his own bat, that Cumberland ought to cease to belong to the Northern Area.

Wednesday 21 October   John Simon,[66] after saying he would like to spend the night here tomorrow, has wired to say that he has to back in London on Friday morning and so must return to town immediately after the meeting. I expected this – no eminent Minister will ever stay five minutes longer in the north than he can help. I had strongly urged upon Simon the sound policy of staying in Durham on Friday and having a look round – but neither he nor Baldwin nor any of them has the sense to see the wisdom of evincing interest in our Special Area.[67] Lennox-Boyd,[68] M.P., spent the night here. He is touring Durham this week – speaking every night somewhere or other and doing well I am told. He is a pleasant creature – full of vim – a member of the Right Wing to which I ought to belong – and should, I think, if it were not lead by Winston,[69] Page Croft, etc.

[64] Mary Spencer Revell Reade (1897–1985), married 1918 (Frederick) Fergus Graham (q.v.), suc. 5th Bart. 1932; Chairman, Northern Counties Area 1948–51.

[65] (Frederick) Fergus Graham (1893–1978), Con. M.P. Cumberland N. 1926–35, Darlington 1951–59; member of Cumberland C.C. 1925–74, Alderman 1934–74; Ld. Lt. Cumberland 1958–68; suc. 5th Bart. 1932.

[66] John Allsebrook Simon (1873–1954), Lib. M.P. Walthamstow 1906–18, Spen Valley 1922–40 (Lib. Nat. from 1931); Solicitor-Gen. 1910–13; Attorney-Gen. 1913–15; Home Sec. 1915–16, 1935–37; For. Sec. 1931–35; Chanc. of the Exchequer 1937–40; Lord Chanc. 1940–45; kt. 1910, cr. Viscount Simon 1940.

[67] The Special Areas Act (1934) was intended to promote employment projects in the 'depressed areas' of Durham, S. Wales, W. Cumberland and S.W. Scotland.

[68] Alan Tindal Lennox-Boyd (1904–1983), Con. M.P. Mid-Beds. 1931–60; P.S. Labour 1938–39; P.S. Home Security 1939; P.S. Food 1939–40; P.S. Aircraft Production 1943–45; M.S. Colonies 1951–52; Min. of Transport 1952–54; Colonial Sec. 1954–59; cr. Viscount Boyd 1960.

[69] Winston Leonard Spencer Churchill (1874–1965), M.P. Oldham 1900–06 (Con. to 1904, then Lib.), Lib. M.P. Manchester N.W. 1906–08, Dundee 1908–22, Con. M.P. Epping (later Woodford) 1924–64; Pres. Bd. of Trade 1908–10; Home Sec. 1910–11; 1st Lord of Admiralty 1911–15, 1939–40; Chanc. Duchy of Lancaster

Thursday 22 October   I took the chair for Sir John Simon in the City Hall at Newcastle tonight. A very fine meeting: the hall packed: and not an opponent present I should say, J.S. spoke for an hour and to me it seemed a dull, common place effort – however, the audience seemed greatly impressed by it ... but of course J.S. puts his case clearly and his language is superb. He was very pleasant to Beatrice and me: full of apologies for not staying the night, etc. The Liberals were all over him – little Magnay[70] alluded to him as 'my beloved leader' – too absurd. We got away soon after 9 o'clock. Harry Crookshank rang me up this evening and asked me if I wanted to stand for Oxford University. I said 'yes' – and he seemed to think that I should have a good chance against Lindemann[71] and Salter.[72] I have left myself in his and Agnes's hands – and we shall see what happens. I should like to become Burgess for the University – but it is no use being too optimistic about my chances.

Saturday 24 October   The luncheon at Carlisle went off very satisfactorily. I spoke for 35 minutes and I do really believe that my effort was appreciated. There were about 100 people present – not a bad gathering for a single constituency in the north.

Wednesday 28 October   I lunched at the Beefsteak – sat next to Harold Macmillan who was more self-centred and disgruntled than ever – Ned Grigg[73] there too: he was full of talk as ever – his book *The Faith of an Englishman* is just out and he was very important about it ... later I visited Harry Crookshank at the Mines Depart-

1915, Min. of Munitions 1917–19; Sec. for War & Air 1919–21; Colonial Sec. 1921–22; Chanc. of the Exchequer 1924–29; P.M. 1940–45, 1951–55; Con. Leader 1940–55; K.G. 1953.

[70] Thomas Magnay (1876–1949), Lib. cand. Blaydon 1929, Lib. Nat. M.P. Gateshead 1931–45.

[71] Frederick Alexander Lindemann (1886–1957), Prof. of Experimental Philosophy, Oxford 1919–56; Personal Assistant to W. Churchill 1940–41; Paymaster-Gen. 1942–45, 1951–53; cr. Baron Cherwell 1941, Viscount 1956.

[72] (James) Arthur Salter (1881–1975), Ind. M.P. Oxford Univ. 1937–50, Con. M.P. Ormskirk 1951–53; Sec.-Gen., Reparations Commission 1920–22; Gladstone Prof. of Political Theory, Oxford 1934–44; P.S. Shipping 1939–41; P.S. War Transport 1941–43; Chanc. Duchy of Lancaster 1945; Min. for Economic Affairs 1951–52; Min. of Materials 1952–53; kt. 1922, cr. Baron Salter 1953.

[73] Edward William Macleay Grigg (1879–1955), Lib. M.P. Oldham 1922–25, Con. M.P. Altrincham 1933–45; private Sec. to Lloyd George 1921–22; Gov. of Kenya 1925–30; P.S. Min. of Information 1939–40; F.S. War Office 1940, U.S. 1940–42; Min. Res. in Middle East 1944–45; kt. 1920, cr. Baron Altrincham 1945.

ment and discussed the Oxford seat. He was friendly but not hopeful.

Thursday 29 October   Walter Elliot has been made Secretary of State for Scotland (rather a confession of failure?) W.S. Morrison succeeds him at the Ministry of Agriculture, Colville[74] becomes Financial Secretary to the Treasury and Hore-Belisha[75] has been given a seat in the Cabinet.

Wednesday 4 November   I dined at the Beefsteak ... Cromer[76] looks like death, but he says that he is better. As he was present we did not discuss H[is] M[ajesty] and Mrs. S[impson][77] – this unhappy business is the one subject of discussion at the moment – everyone has some new detail to tell of, and everyone is extremely fussed about it. The paying off of Mrs. S. is what is making people nervous.

Wednesday 11 November   I attended the meeting of the [Durham] County Council this morning – there were no excitements, every-thing very amicable. The government is now so orthodox and economical that there is little to be said against it – and therefore a 'truce' at the next election is clearly indicated. ... My own opinion is that Smith[78] and the saner men will welcome it – but that the wild men will have none of it. There will be no 'truce' – but we

---

[74] David John Colville (1894–1954), Con. M.P. Midlothian N. 1929–43; Sec. Overseas Trade 1931–35; U.S. Scotland 1935–36; F.S.T. 1936–38; Scottish Sec. 1938–40; Gov. of Bombay 1943–48; Ld. Lt. Lanarkshire 1952–54; cr. Baron Clydesmuir 1947.

[75] (Isaac) Leslie Hore-Belisha (1893–1957), M.P. Plymouth Devonport 1923–45 (Lib. to 1931, Lib. Nat. 1931–42, Nat. Ind. 1942–45); P.S. Trade 1931–32; F.S.T. 1932–34; Min. of Transport 1934–37; Sec. for War 1937–40; Min. of Nat. Insurance 1945; cr. Baron Hore-Belisha 1954.

[76] Rowland Thomas Baring (1877–1953), diplomatic service 1900–11; Managing Dir., Baring Bros. 1913–14; Ass. Private Sec. to the King 1916–20; Lord Chamberlain 1922–38; Lord in Waiting 1938–52; British govt. Dir. of Suez Canal Co. 1926–50; suc. 2nd Earl of Cromer 1917.

[77] Bessiewallis ('Wallis') Warfield (1896–1986), married 1916 Winfield Spencer (divorced 1927), married 1928 Ernest Simpson (divorced 1936), married 3 June 1937 the Duke of Windsor (formerly King Edward VIII, abdicated 10 Dec. 1936); she then became Duchess of Windsor, but was never granted the title of 'Royal Highness'.

[78] W.N. Smith (1868–1942), Lab. member of Durham C.C. 1917–42, Vice-Chair-man 1921, Chairman 1926–29, 1932–42.

shall have something of a war cry and the discord between the 2 sections of the Labour Party will be increased.

Saturday 14 November   The Cumberland County meeting this afternoon went off quite satisfactorily and was better attended than Fergus [Graham] had led me to expect. A resolution to secede from the Area was moved – but withdrawn after I had had my say. As a matter of fact it was rather a half-hearted business and meant as a kind of demonstration against Alec Leith who never took the trouble to go to Cumberland. How we are to improve the organization in Cumberland, however, without money I really don't know – and how we are to raise money for Area purposes is a still more awkward problem. ... [At Crofthead, at dinner] the conversation was mainly concerned with H.M. and Mrs. Simpson. It really is a miserable business and to me inexplicable. The only reasonable explanation is that the man has temporarily lost his reason – really believing that he is so popular with the proletariat that he can get away with it and marry the lady. He will have a rude awakening if once the Press gets going.

Tuesday 17 November   This evening we had the great banquet to Sir Alec. It really went off very well. We sat down 240 to dinner and practically all the Conservative big noises were present. Alec was tremendously pleased with himself: he sat between the Londonderrys ... Charley L. made a very dull speech and, needless to say, dragged in foreign politics. He always feels whenever and wherever he makes a speech that it must be a 'pronouncement'. Alec was terribly bad, and went on for 25 minutes. Then I proposed the 'Conservative Party' and Douglas Hacking, who had come up specially for the dinner, replied – I am told that he and I were the only 2 speakers who could be heard.

Wednesday 18 November   Frank Mitchell[79] fairly let himself go about H.M. which was odd for a courtier – clearly King G.'s men are not for King E. – and no wonder. Frank darkly hinted that a climax to the Simpson business was inevitable within a short space of time, and he seemed certain that H.M. would rather abdicate

[79] Frank Herbert Mitchell (1878–1951), Ass. Private Sec. to the King 1931–37; Groom in Waiting 1937–51; Sec. of the Order of the Garter 1933–51; kt. 1937.

than give her up – I simply cannot believe it – I think when he finds that the Govt. won't allow him to marry her, he will give in.

Sunday 22 November   Ledingham and his wife came to luncheon. Afterwards he, the Greys and I discussed the problem of finance for the Area and were all agreed that we must have money and more or less agreed upon the best method to proceed upon to get it. Clearly the thing is to amalgamate all the existing funds – but a proposal to do this is bound to be strenuously opposed by Appleby and Leith who will raise Northumberland against us – so I propose to suggest a new fund for the Area and shall, at the next Executive, propose the appointment of a small committee to consider the subject. It will be interesting to see how A. and L. behave – I feel pretty sure that they will be obstructionists. What a worrying and annoying business political management is!

Wednesday 25 November   I wrote to David Margesson the other day recommending old Leech,[80] M.P., for a knighthood – I did so of course in my capacity as Area Chairman. He has replied in the most official manner saying that Leech has not been long enough in the HofC to put him high enough on his list for a knighthood. It really is preposterous that length of service in the House should be the criterion. This means that people who are in a position to go into Parliament young, and to secure safe seats, are those who are honoured – whereas men like Leech, who have done fine work socially, professionally, in municipal politics, and, may be, in the end won difficult seats, stand a less good chance. It is all of a piece – at any rate so far as things are managed on the Conservative side – money and social influence alone prevail. I suppose that it does not really matter in the long run: so long as 'Conservatives' are elected, the Government does not really care who they are: and so long as Conservative Associations throughout the country are willing to sell their seats to the highest bidders, it is ridiculous for people like me or Leech to bother about politics. A time must come, however, when poor men will realize it is uscless to attempt to take an interest in politics, or to hope to do their bit in the government of the country – and then they will either join the

[80] Joseph William Leech (1865–1940), Con. M.P. Newcastle W. 1931–40; Dep. Lord Mayor of Newcastle 1929–30, Lord Mayor 1932–33, Sheriff 1930–31; kt. 1938.

'progressive' parties or retire altogether from the unequal contest. But, even so, no doubt the rich young men will carry on! (and continue to collar the fat directorships into the bargain!)

Wednesday 2 December   The fat is in the fire today. The Bishop of Bradford has made a speech at his diocesan conference in which he suggests that H.M. needs the Grace of God – and the *Yorkshire Post* and other papers have taken this to mean that they can begin discussing Mrs. Simpson. It remains to be seen what happens – but clearly the Press is now going to take up the matter and the whole silly business will now be discussed *ad nauseam*. It really is disgusting the way the monarchy has been brought into the gutter just because this obstinate little devil has fallen a victim to a lady at the age of 42. Clearly he believes that he is so popular with the proletariat that he can get away with it – and no doubt he will have a bigger backing among the younger generation than some people appear to think. Nevertheless, I simply cannot believe that the country as a whole – the nonconformist conscience in particular – will tolerate such a marriage. If it comes, too, to a question of the Government resigning, I don't see how we as a democratic nation can put up with such a King. It is a beastly affair and I cannot help feeling that someone has blundered, and blundered badly, in ever having allowed it to become public. Surely Mr. B. could have done more and yet after what Frank Mitchell told us the other night perhaps he could not. He has been dealing with a mad man.

Thursday 3 December   The King's affair is now the one subject discussed in the press – the newspapers are very good to him – but all of them seem to be agreed that the marriage would be impossible – if he really insists on marrying the woman, he will have to abdicate – my own view, probably inspired by hope, is that he will see reason – but in any case he has given a shake to monarchy – however, if he pulls himself together and does the right thing, I should not be surprised to see his popularity increased tenfold – for we live in a strange world today.

Friday 4 December   *The Times* said in its leader about the King's marriage ... that the objection to Mrs. S. was not that she was a commoner ... I think that this assertion is not wholly true – so long as you have a Queen, she must be head of Society and no one really wants anyone in that position unless she is a lady. Supposing then the King had pitched upon some young woman of virgin purity, but with a cockney accent or something of that kind – it is ridiculous to suggest that she would have made a suitable Queen but that is exactly what *The Times* suggests. Let us be honest and speak the whole truth – pretence is no good and if you want a King and a Court, you must recognize the fact that it implies class distinctions and forms and etiquette – not social equality.

Saturday 5 December   The 'crisis' is so terrific that Circe feels that she and Charley must be in London – so the weekend party at Wynyard has to be deprived of its host and hostess. Charley rang me up this morning to convey this news: he says that Winston and Beaverbrook[81] have been called in by the King and are going to use this opportunity to have another go for S.B. This is possible for neither Winston nor B. are men who would stop at anything to secure their own ends – but it only shows (if they intervene in this business) how little they know of public opinion – the country is not behind H.M. and the sooner he realises it the better it will be. He can give up Mrs. S. and stay – or he can abdicate. The real tribute to him – or to the monarchy – is that such an effort is being made to keep him.

Sunday 6 December   ... of course there yet may be some way out of the impasse which will save abdication. I confess, however, that I can see no such way – and I feel myself that it would be a pity to find one. The King has shown himself so obstinate and unbalanced in this affair that it would be a mistake in my opinion to let him get away with it – it would only mean some other 'crisis' in the future. He is clearly not the right kind of man to be a constitutional monarch and, unpleasant though all this business is, it may be a blessing in disguise. The Yorks[82] should do the job

[81] (William) Maxwell Aitken (1879–1964), Con. M.P. Ashton 1910–16; prop. of *Daily Express* 1916–64, of *Sunday Express* 1918–64, of *Evening Standard* 1923–64; Min. of Information 1918–19; Min. of Aircraft Production 1940–41; Min. of Supply 1941–42; Lord Privy Seal 1942–45; cr. Bart. 1916, Baron Beaverbrook 1917.

[82] Albert Frederick Arthur George (1895–1952), Prince 1895–1920, cr. Duke of York 1920, suc. King George VI 1936; married 1923 Elizabeth Angela Marguerite Bowes-Lyon (1900-), daughter of 14th Earl of Strathmore, styled Lady Elizabeth Bowes-Lyon 1900–23, Duchess of York 1923–36, Queen 1936–52, Queen Mother 1952-.

admirably – and once the King is out of the country I don't myself believe his disappearance will cause any trouble – except perhaps politically to Mr. B. But it is a sad, bad business, and when I look back upon H.M. in the days of the Guards Division I cannot help but feel very, very sorry for him.

Monday 7 December There was no definite news this morning about the King and apparently his decision, whatever it may be, is not to be announced for a few days. In view of the difficulties of the situation, probably this is the right thing. It would not do for it to appear that the Government were forcing H.M. to come to a decision – such a line of action might well strengthen the sympathy which some people are said to have for him. The Beaverbrook and Rothermere[83] Press are trying their best to arouse such sympathy – but they might, I am sure, spare themselves the trouble. Public opinion – in all classes of society – is against him. The feeling is that he has let us all down – and no one really approves of a morganatic marriage with a woman of the type of Mrs. Simpson – the American press campaign has had far more effect in this country than people like Beaverbrook and Rothermere and Duff [Cooper] and Diana[84] have any idea of. ... our party for tomorrow's dance is beginning to assemble – neither Charley nor Circe nor any member of their family is to be at it. Quite absurd – for none of them is required in London to help solve the King's problem for him. However, no doubt it is more amusing to be listening to all the gossip in London and helping to pull strings than to attend a charity ball at Wynyard.

Tuesday 8 December The Ball was a great success – over 400 present – everyone annoyed or amused at the absence of the Londonderrys and their family. Beatrice looked charming and acted as a sort of hostess though she did not receive the guests.

Wednesday 9 December I caught the early train this morning

[83] Harold Sidney Harmsworth (1868–1940), prop. of *Daily Mirror* 1914–31, of *Daily Mail*, *Evening News* & Associated Newspapers Ltd. 1922–40; Sec. for Air 1917–18; cr. Baron Rothermere 1914, Viscount 1919.

[84] Diana Manners (1892–1986), daughter of 8th Duke of Rutland, styled Lady Diana; married 1919 (Alfred) Duff Cooper, cr. Viscount Norwich 1952; recognised as one of the aristocratic beauties of her age, she moved in the most fashionable social circles.

... and slept most of the way to London. I went straight (via the Club) to Palace Chambers[85] for an Executive Council meeting at 2.30. It was as deadly and futile a performance as usual – the usual people – the usual placid self satisfaction and ignorance of realities among the members of the Committee. I did not open my mouth on this occasion – there was really nothing worth talking about. The deputation of Area leaders with 'Resolutions' to 'the Leader' was put off in view of the Crisis – so I did not see Mr. B. There seems no doubt now that H.M. will abdicate tomorrow – and clearly the general opinion is that in the circumstances it is better he should go.

Thursday 10 December   The streets crowded – Baldwin told the HofC that the King was determined to abdicate – and so a Bill is to be presented to that effect – a miserable business – however, Baldwin has managed the whole thing admirably and I think that we are through it with dignity, calm and common sense. I don't think either that the monarchy need suffer – the King has bowed to his ministers backed by public opinion. It is his affair: he is abdicating because he prefers to marry Mrs. Simpson to remaining King of England – a queer decision – and the only charitable view of this sorry affair is that the poor little man is not responsible for his actions.

Saturday 12 December   Beatrice and I listened to the proclamation of George VI on the wireless this afternoon. We heard Sir G. Wollaston,[86] Garter King of Arms, splendidly – a fine voice for so small and insignificant a man. We also heard the declaration made in Canada – in French and English – of course not quite so clearly. At 10 o'clock we listened to the late King's broadcast. He spoke from Windsor Castle – and his voice was firm and loud. I expect that what he said will appeal to many people – but I confess that it left me rather cold – in a way it was a *tour de force* – but I cannot get over what the man has done. There can be no excuse for such a performance. However, it is all over now – and it is no use giving it another thought. What its ultimate effects may be no

---

[85] The location of Conservative Central Office, in Westminster Bridge Road.
[86] Gerald Woods Wollaston (1874–1957), Norroy King of Arms 1928–30; Garter Principal King of Arms 1930–44; Norroy & Ulster King of Arms 1944–57; Earl Marshal's Sec. 1944–54; kt. 1930.

man can say – it may be that this episode may strengthen the monarchy. Much will depend upon the new King and Queen. From what I know and have heard of them they give me confidence – and it is clear that the people are out to help them.

Sunday 13 December   On the whole the Sunday papers have dealt with the crisis decently – and I think that the general opinion seems to be to try and forget this amazing episode in our history as quickly as possible. I am sure that this is the best way to deal with it: the less said about it the better. Beatrice and I listened tonight to Cosmo *Cantuar*[87] who broadcasted [*sic*] a sermon from the B.B.C. headquarters. We did not think it a very happy effort; it was pontifical and unctuous and snobbish. However, I suppose he felt that he must draw a moral and adorn a tale – and disliking Edward VIII (as one knows he did) he did not refrain from rubbing it in. I fancy that a good many people will disapprove of this: once a man is down, it never does any good to kick him and people may well ask (unfairly perhaps) why if the Archbishop felt so strongly about the King and his entourage he did not speak out long ago.

Tuesday 15 December   To Carlisle for the annual constituency dinner – not very largely attended for a big town, but those responsible seemed satisfied. I proposed the toast of the Association – Spears,[88] as Member, spoke on the subject of the abdication in a most statesmanlike speech – but he is not a pleasing speaker to listen to.

Friday 18 December   I presided this afternoon over the Area Executive Committee in Newcastle. There was a fairly large attendance, but both Sir Alec and Sir Alfred were conspicuous by their absence! I opened up the subject of Area finance and we appointed a committee to look into the subject. One or two people suggested

[87] (William) Cosmo Gordon Lang (1864–1945), Bishop of Stepney 1901–09, Archbishop of York 1909–28, Canterbury 1928–1942; cr. Baron Lang of Lambeth 1942; referred by the Latin for Canterbury, *Cantuar*.
[88] Edward Louis Spears (1886–1974), Nat. Lib. M.P. Loughborough 1922–24, Con. cand. Bosworth 1927, Carlisle 1929, Con. M.P. Carlisle 1931–45; Head of British Military Mission in Paris 1917–20; P.M.s Representative in France, 1940; Head of Mission & Min. to Syria & Lebanon 1941–44; kt. 1942, cr. Bart. 1953.

that there was money available if only we could get at it – alluding to Appleby's fund -but I expressly ruled this out and said that what we wanted for our purposes was a special fund of our own. We shall see what happens – my own feeling is that Appleby and Leith will fight like devils to keep us off their funds and will not raise a finger to help us raise a fund for ourselves. They like being the financial big noises: it is the source of their control, and, so long as they continue to be interested in politics, they will cling to the purse strings. I am very tired of it all and more tempted each day that passes to give up the unequal contest of trying to lead the Conservatives of the north of England. One could do it all right if it were not for the wire-pullers and businessmen – the former collect the money and delight in hanging on to it and do no other work – the latter are too stupid to realize that unless they bestir themselves, the Socialists will ride rough-shod over them – they have surrendered without a fight.

Tuesday 22 December   I dined at the Beefsteak – only 3 or 4 people there – including the futile Harold Macmillan – no use as a man or a friend. He professed to be pleased to see me, etc. – but, as usual, was entirely self-centred.

Monday 28 December   L.G. has sent an outrageous telegram to the Duke of Windsor – designed, I suppose, to make trouble for Mr. B. – but of course he is out of the picture, and I should imagine gaga. It is rather a deplorable picture all the same – for this man at one time was akin to God in the estimation of many people, certainly the most powerful Minister of modern times – and now he is utterly futile – spiteful and childish. Since the fall of the Coalition it seems to me that he has played his cards extraordinarily badly. Always supposed to be a political wizard, he has proved himself quite incapable of playing his cards correctly. An old man in a hurry to regain power, he found himself up against a much more astute politician in the man whom he so foolishly underrated and despised – Mr. B. has beaten him to a frazzle – and, on the whole, to the inestimable advantage of the country – for, like Winston, L.G. had no thought but for himself.

Thursday 21 January 1937   I went at 6.45 to the Central Office to be 'interviewed' by the Richmond (Surrey) Selection Committee –

the usual body of men and women – and the usual financial inquiries. Would I pay my election expenses? How much would I subscribe to the Association? It sickened me – however, I said I would give £100 to £150 a year and pay my expenses – the offer was visibly not good enough – the same old story.

Wednesday 10 February   At noon I went to the Central Office to a meeting of Area Chairmen presided over by Douglas Hacking. Much discussion about 'co-ordinating committees' – to keep together the 3 parties.[89] I said that as we had no Nat. Labour Party in the Northern Area and only Samuelite Libs.,[90] I saw no good in attempting the formation of such a committee. Hacking admitted that our position was peculiar. I lunched in the HofC – the luncheon given by Ebbisham[91] to meet Bingley,[92] his successor as President of the Nat[ional] Union.[93] What inspiring leaders we do have in our Party!

Saturday 13 February   Later on in the afternoon I attended the annual meeting of the Labour Advisory Committee[94] – a very wide awake body. I was told that Leith in all his seven years of office had never been present at one of their meetings. He really was a perfectly useless political leader and yet no doubt he did the job to the satisfaction of all the other perfectly useless people who 'lead' the Conservative Party up here. It is odd how we contrive to keep going as a party – the reason why we do is presumably that our people prefer 'King Log' to 'King Stork' – and just jog along,

[89] In the National Government: Conservatives, Liberal Nationals (followers of Sir John Simon), and National Labour (followers of Ramsay MacDonald).

[90] The wing of the Liberal Party, led by Sir Herbert Samuel, which joined the National Government in August 1931 but resigned over free trade in September 1932; they opposed the Government in the 1935 election, and became the post-war Liberal Party.

[91] George Rowland Blades (1868–1953), Con. M.P. Epsom 1918–28; Con. Party Treasurer 1931–33; Pres., N.U. 1936; Senior Sheriff of London 1917–18, Lord Mayor 1926–27; kt. 1918, cr. Bart. 1922, Baron Ebbisham 1928.

[92] George Richard Lane-Fox (1870–1947), Con. M.P. Barkston Ash 1906–31; Sec. for Mines 1922–24, 1924–28; Member of Indian Statutory (Simon) Commission 1928–30; cr. Baron Bingley 1933.

[93] National Union of Conservative and Unionist Associations; the representative wing of the Conservative Party to which local constituency Associations are affiliated, and which holds the annual Party conference.

[94] The Conservative Party's organisation for trade unionists.

trusting to luck when an election comes along – work and organization are entirely uncongenial to them.

Tuesday 16 February   I have no opponent, so I am doomed again
to be a County Councillor – I felt that having arranged 2 meetings
for to-night I had better hold them – as H.P.[95] has told me that
my cancelling all my meetings last year was unpopular.

Tuesday 2 March   I have spent my usual day – nothing has
happened. Life is as dull as ever and never a glimpse of anything
coming my way – constituency after constituency comes along and
passes to some other fellow – and no further directorships loom in
sight, or jobs of any kind. I suppose that I am definitely on the
shelf.

Friday 5 March   I went this morning to see Mr. Armstrong[96] and
Miss Turner[97] at their office. They were both as charming as ever,
though much depressed at the result of the L[ondon] C[ounty]
C[ouncil] election. They had fully expected a victory for the Municipal Reform[98] people – however, Herbert Morrison[99] has got away
with it: not entirely surprising: he has done very well during his 3
years of office: has not shown himself an extremist: his propaganda
was excellent – that of the Municipal Reformers futile. It consisted
of anti-Red propaganda where Reds were practically non-existent.

---

[95] Henry Parkin Bell (1901–1976), known as Harry, Headlam's private Sec. 1925–
40, & Con. Agent, Barnard Castle 1929–37; Ass. Gen. Manager, N.E. Trading
Estates 1937–40; war service 1940–44; Sec., Northern Industrial Group 1944–48;
married 1948 Jehanne Beaumont, youngest daughter of the Dame de Serk, and lived
on Sark 1948–76; member of Chief Pleas 1948–76, of the Douzaine 1974–76;
Constable of Sark 1953–54; Dep. Seneschal 1956–69.

[96] Horace Victor Armstrong (1887–1979), Con. Agent Horsham & Worthing
1919–24, Scarborough & Whitby 1924–26; Ass. Organiser, Junior Imperial League,
Yorks. & Northern Counties Areas 1926–28; C.O. Agent, Northern Counties Area
1928–34, Metropolitan Area 1934–38; Sec., N.U. 1938–52.

[97] Barbara L. Turner (1902–1975), Woman Organiser, Northern Counties Area
1930–33, Wessex Area 1933–36, Metropolitan Area 1936–39; service in A.T.S. 1939–
45; Sec., Fed. of Univ. Con. Associations 1949–67.

[98] The Conservative organisation for contesting London local elections.

[99] Herbert Stanley Morrison (1888–1965), Lab. M.P. Hackney S. 1923–24, 1929–
31, 1935–45, Lewisham E. 1945–50, Lewisham S. 1950–59; Min. of Transport 1929–
31; Min. of Supply 1940; Home Sec. 1940–45; Lord Pres. 1945–51; For. Sec. 1951;
Dep. Labour Leader 1945–55; member of L.C.C. 1922–45, Leader 1934–40; cr.
Baron Morrison of Lambeth 1959.

Armstrong agrees with me that if we had a G.E. now the Nat. Govt. would be beaten.

Saturday 6 March   Ledingham came here to luncheon and prattled away in his usual way. I am sorry to say that I find him more and more tiring which is unfortunate as I am doomed to have a lot to do with him during the next few years. I consider him to be honest and well meaning, but even these two admirable qualifications fail to make him a congenial personality.

Sunday 7 March   A eulogy of Anthony Eden in *The Sunday Times* – it seems that he is rapidly assuming a great control over the HofC. It is astonishing what a good press he has – whatever his foreign policy may be – and of course it is quite different now to what it was a year ago – never has a Foreign Secretary so completely eaten his words – he seems to give satisfaction to the journalists. I suppose I am a bit jealous of his success if the truth were known – and so I may view him with a jaundiced eye – but, for the life of me, I cannot regard him as a strong man or one who really knows where he is going. He still prattles away about collective security and the League of Nations – at the same time he is wise enough to see at last that neither of these things mean anything at all – that the beginning and end of the business is that we should be strong enough to defend ourselves quite independently of others. The long and the short of it is that collective security is only another name for an alliance on the continent sufficiently strong to preserve the balance of power, and that the League of Nations is a sham and a delusion so long as some of the Great Powers are outside it.

Sunday 14 March   Why do we always live in an atmosphere of make-believe and imagine that because we don't want war, there will be no war? It is, I suppose, the tragic legacy of Liberalism which makes us so foolish, and the penalty we pay for being a democracy. Sooner or later it must inevitably be our undoing: we cannot count on always being able to muddle through: some day we shall be caught napping – and then the deluge. One cannot visualize an England of no account – reduced to the condition of Holland or Portugal – and yet their empires collapsed very much for the same reasons which may (God forbid) lead to the collapse of ours.

Thursday 25 March   This morning Beatrice and I went to the Castle [in Durham] to see Anthony Eden made a D.C.L.[100] It was not a very inspiring ceremony – such a performance should undoubtedly be conducted in Latin. Charley Londonderry did not do his part very well – possibly because it was against the grain. He could see no particular reason why Anthony should be so honoured! I remember his saying this to me some little time ago – and possibly there is something in this – he is young and yet to prove his worth – however, he looked very nice and pleasant – and may yet turn out to be a great Foreign Secretary.

Wednesday 14 April   I went to London this morning by the early train and attended the Executive Committee this afternoon at Palace Chambers. S.B. made a valedictory speech to us – nothing to expatiate about – at least so I thought – but dear, old Mrs. Fyfe[101] was almost reduced to tears and most of my fellow members on the committee appeared to be impressed. I do so wish that I had been endowed with the bump of veneration – so that I might accept the commonplace when dished out to me by a man in an important position, as if it were something really worth hearing. When S.B. left us we elected old George Stanley[102] as Chairman *vice* George Herbert[103] who has been made a Groom in Waiting. The latter is a real loss to the committee – a pleasant, level-headed sensible man – G.S. is too stupid, too deaf, and too old for a Chairman's job – however, he is presumably the type of man we all like! He is not likely to cause any kind of trouble and the committee will not be disturbed in its equanimity. ... At the

[100] Eden, who came from a long-established family of Durham gentry, was being awarded the honorary degree of Doctor of Civil Laws by Durham University; as Chancellor of the University, Londonderry presided at the ceremony.

[101] Mrs C. Fyfe, member of N.U. Exec. Ctte. from 1934.

[102] George Frederick Stanley (1872–1938), Con. M.P. Preston 1910–22, Willesden E. 1924–29; Comptroller of the Household 1919–21; F.S. War Office 1921–22; U.S. Home Office 1922–23; P.S. Pensions 1924–29; Gov. of Madras 1929–34; Chairman, N.U. Exec. Ctte. 1937–38; brother of the 17th Earl of Derby.

[103] George Sidney Herbert (1886–1942), second son of 14th Earl of Pembroke, styled Hon. George Herbert; member of N.U. Central Council from 1924, Chairman 1931–32; Chairman, N.U. Exec. Ctte. 1932–37; Aide-de-Camp to the King 1936–42, Groom in Waiting 1937–42; cr. Bart. 1937.

Beefsteak were some of my richer friends including Bertie Horne[104]
and Harold Macmillan. The latter was trying hard to be affable to
me (after my recent remarks to Dorothy)[105] but he could not get
away from himself.

Thursday 22 April   Neville's proposed tax on industrial profits
seems to be upsetting the Party. I wonder whether it is wise to put
on such a tax even for a special purpose? He may intend it to be
temporary and moderate, but his successors, especially Socialist
ones, may make use of the precedent in a hundred unpleasant ways.
Personally I have not come to a decision as to his wisdom – and
of course it is foolish of people to go off the deep end until they
see his actual proposals in the Finance Bill.

Friday 23 April   I attended a meeting of the Area Education
Committee this afternoon presided over by Mr. Donald Scott[106]
who takes it all very seriously. It was a long business – presumably,
however, it was time well spent – one hopes so – but I personally
am rather doubtful as to the value of the Conservative education
'stunt'. It seems to me somewhat ineffective and, so long as the
Conservative Party is what it is, I fail to see what use there is in
'educating' our young working class people. We offer them nothing
for it except to utilize them as hack speakers for some miserable
pittance: it does not occur to us to give them a real chance in
politics – either national or local. No Conservative Association (if
it could get anyone else) would dream of running a working man
candidate for the HofC and few employers are prepared to make
it possible for their intelligent young employees to take up local
politics. Personally if I were a keen young working man, I should
not be a Conservative.

---

[104] Robert Stevenson Horne (1871–1940), Con. M.P. Glasgow Hillhead 1918–37;
Min. of Labour 1919–20; Pres. Bd. of Trade 1920–21; Chanc. of the Exchequer
1921–22; kt. 1918, cr. Viscount Horne of Slamannan 1937.
[105] Dorothy Evelyn Cavendish (1899–1966), daughter of 9th Duke of Devonshire,
married 1920 (Maurice) Harold Macmillan.
[106] (Robert) Donald Scott (1901–1974), Con. M.P. Wansbeck 1940–45, Penrith &
the Border 1950–55; jt. P.S. Agric. May-July 1945; Chairman, Northumberland
County Con. Assoc. 1945–50; Vice-Chairman, Northern Counties Area 1945–50;
Chairman, Con. Party Political Educ. Ctte. 1949–50; kt. 1955.

Saturday 15 May   Old Snowden's[107] death is announced in tonight's evening paper. He died very suddenly – heart failure – but of course he has been ill for several years. A great man in his way – but not nearly so big a C[hancellor] of [the] E[xchequer] as he is likely to be represented in his obituary notices – an old fashioned Liberal posturing as a Socialist – a controversialist – unyielding, dogmatic and bitter – a very able, lucid speaker and a first class debater. It always seemed to me that he made mincemeat of Winston in the 1924–29 Parliament. Personally I liked him though I did not know him well. In private conversation he was friendly – quite unlike his vitriolic HofC manner. His has been a great career and shows how careers are open to talent in this old out-of-date country.

Tuesday 25 May   [in Berlin] I lunched with Henderson,[108] the British Ambassador, *tête-à-tête*. He strikes me as a very intelligent and sensible man who *may* do some good with the Germans – at any rate, he appreciates their point of view which most of our diplomats don't. He also sees that, unless we get busy, there is bound to be a mess.

Friday 28 May   S.B. has gone and N[eville] C[hamberlain] reigns in his stead. I don't suppose this change will make any difference to me – and apparently 'the National character' of the government is to be continued. The one matter of importance, however, is foreign affairs and I only hope that N.C. will take a more personal interest in them than S.B. did.

Monday 12 July   I went off to Carlisle for the Area Executive Committee ... the meeting was not well attended, even by the Cumberland people – however, Wilkin[109] was there and he brought old Appleby with him. The latter very indignant because Burns-

---

[107] Philip Snowden (1864–1937), Lab. M.P. Blackburn 1906–18, Colne Valley 1922–31; Chanc. of the Exchequer 1924, 1929–31; Lord Privy Seal 1931 32; cr. Viscount Snowden 1931.

[108] Neville Meyrick Henderson (1882–1942), diplomatic service; Min. to Egypt 1924–28, to France 1928–29, to Yugoslavia 1929–35; Amb. in Argentine & Paraguay 1935–37, in Berlin 1937–39; kt. 1932.

[109] Albert Scholick Wilkin (1883–1943), businessman; Managing Dir., A.S. Wilkin Ltd; Chairman, Newcastle Central C.A. 1931–43; kt. 1939.

Lindow[110] and Nunn[111] had put up a resolution advocating an enquiry into methods financial and organization[al] of the Party – as it was worded the Resolution was a difficult one for us to adopt, so I let it go altho' I approved what it advocated – unfortunately Burns-Lindow put his case very badly and gave Appleby plenty of opportunity for criticism – in which Luke Thompson,[112] somewhat surprisingly, joined.

Saturday 17 July   The P.M.'s meeting at Ormesby Hall has been a huge success. Beatrice and I went over there for luncheon.[113] The party consisted of our host and hostess (Pennymans), Sir Eugene Ramsden[114] M.P. (Chairman of the Yorkshire Area) and his wife (rather a nice American or Canadian woman, I think), ourselves, young Wrightson,[115] the candidate for Sedgefield, and Commander Bower[116] M.P. (Cleveland) and his wife. Neville and his wife arrived about 3.30 – and they did the right thing walking about and being introduced to all the Conservative local leaders – S.B., I gather, would never do this. Zetland[117] was in the Chair for the meeting. I had never met him before and was not much impressed with him today – an uninspiring little man – and he spoke too long for a chairman. Neville's speech was a good one, but not quite long enough. Eugene and I did our moving and seconding in under ten minutes between us – Bower also was commendably brief. The audience was said to be about 6,000 which was not as large as I had anticipated on a really fine day. The Chamberlains, both of them, were very friendly to us.

[110] Isaac William Burns-Lindow (1868–1946), High Sheriff of Cumberland 1935.

[111] William Nunn (1879–1971), Con. M.P. Whitehaven 1931–35, Newcastle W. 1940–45, Con. cand. S. Shields 1929, Whitehaven 1950.

[112] Luke Thompson (1867–1941), Con. M.P. Sunderland 1922–29, 1931–35; kt. 1934.

[113] Ormesby Hall near Middlesbrough, home of the Pennyman family, was the venue for a major rally jointly organised by six local constituencies.

[114] Eugene Joseph Squire Hargreaves Ramsden (1883–1955), Con. M.P. Bradford N. 1924–29, 1931–45; Chairman, Yorkshire Area 1933–46; Chairman, N.U. 1938–39, Chairman, Exec. Ctte. 1938–43, Pres., N.U. 1951–52; kt. 1933, cr. Bart. 1938, Baron Ramsden 1945.

[115] John Wrightson (1911–1983), Con. cand. Sedgefield 1937–40; suc. 3rd Bart. 1950.

[116] Robert Tatton Bower (1894–1975), Con. M.P. Cleveland 1931–45; Chairman, Society for Individual Freedom 1950–53.

[117] Lawrence John Lumley Dundas (1876–1961), Con. M.P. Hornsey 1907–16; Gov. of Bengal 1917–22; India Sec. 1935–40; styled Lord Dundas 1876–92, Earl of Ronaldshay 1892–1929, suc. 2nd Marquess of Zetland 1929, K.G. 1942.

Friday 30 July   Mr. Beattie,[118] the Durham Agent, came to see me this morning and we discussed the organization of his six constituencies – the usual bricks without straw business. How tired I am getting of it all – it really is futile trying to keep the Conservative cause alive up here without local support of any kind. One agent cannot possibly look after six constituencies – more especially when there are really no Associations worth two pence in most of them. No money, no workers, no organization is the rule in Durham County and I can see no means of ever having anything better.

Saturday 7 August   I went to Gosforth Park – the race course – where the Princess Royal[119] presented new Colours to the Red Cross people of Northumberland and Durham. It was a lovely day for the show – but the crowd was surprisingly small – and the quality was not in much evidence. Mabel Grey ran the business as President of Northumberland, but of course the Londonderry woman ought to have been there to represent Durham. She sent her usual telegram of regret this morning so Charlie Grey[120] told us – could not fly over from Ireland because of weather conditions.

Saturday 14 August   To Alnwick for a mass meeting addressed by Morrison, the Minister for Agriculture. He spoke well – and I gather that he has given great satisfaction by going round and seeing farms and receiving deputations. This is the proper way for Ministers to behave when they visit provincial areas – not rushing up to address a packed meeting and then rushing off again because they 'must get back to London'.

---

[118] George Beattie, war service 1914–18; assisted voluntarily at Houghton-le-Spring & Chester-le-Street C.A.s 1918–25; trainee Con. Agent Royton 1925; Con. Agent S. Shields 1925–29, Berwick 1929–37; Durham Group (6 constituencies) 1937–38; appointed Chief Con. Agent, Manchester City Fed. 1938.

[119] Victoria (1897–1965), eldest daughter of King George V, Princess Royal; married 1922 6th Earl of Harewood.

[120] Charles Robert Grey (1879–1963), Con. cand. Bradford Central 1910; styled Viscount Howick 1894–1917, suc. 5th Earl Grey 1917.

2

APPEASEMENT AND MUNICH

September 1937 to October 1938

In September 1937 Headlam was amongst a group of foreign observers at the Nazi Party's annual rally at Nuremberg.

Tuesday 7 September 1937   This morning we all attended the first meeting of the Party Conference in an enormous building – a temporary structure – designed to hold, so they told us, about 15,000 people – it was literally packed today. We had excellent seats near the front just below the platform ... The proceedings began with music (perhaps the best part of the show: a superb band) – then at last the Nazi swells began to arrive – then came a procession headed by an apparently endless supply of flags – then came Hitler followed by all the other leaders – Goering,[1] Goebbels,[2] Hess,[3] Rosenberg,[4] etc. – great enthusiasm prevailed. They seated themselves on the platform and one had a fine view of them – one

[1] Hermann Goering (1893–1946), German fighter 'ace' in First World War; Pres. of *Reichstag* 1932–33; appointed P.M. and Min. of Interior for Prussia 1933, Reich Air Min. and commander of the *Luftwaffe* 1935, Reich Council Chairman for Nat. Defence 1939; tried at Nuremberg 1945–46, sentenced to death but committed suicide 15 Oct. 1946.

[2] Joseph Paul Goebbels (1897–1945), Nazi Party chief in Berlin 1926–30; in charge of Nazi propaganda from 1929; Min. of Propaganda 1933–45; Reich Comm. for Total Mobilization, 1944–45; committed suicide 1 May 1945.

[3] Rudolf Hess (1894–1987), Hitler's political secretary from 1920; Dep. Leader of Nazi Party 1933–41; Min. without Portfolio 1933–41; flew to Britain in the hope of negotiating peace 10 May 1941, arrested and interned; tried at Nuremberg 1945–46, sentenced to life imprisonment and held in Spandau Prison, Berlin, until his death.

[4] Alfred Rosenberg (1893–1946), leading ideologist of National Socialism; head of Nazi Party Foreign Affiars Dept. 1933–45, of Nazi Party ideological education 1934–45; Min. for Occupied Eastern Territories 1941–45; tried at Nuremberg 1945–46, sentenced to death.

was rather terrified at their appearance – they looked *capabales de tout*[5] and no doubt are. Hitler himself is a bigger man than I thought – by which I mean he is of average size: otherwise, he is exactly like his pictures. A boring beginning was the reading out of the names of all the martyrs of the movement – not so many after all – then came a speech from Hess – another from Sleicher[6] (don't know the man's name: he is the anti-Jew propagandist): then the reading of the Führer proclamation ... a reference to the colonial question much applauded.

Wednesday 8 September   There was nothing arranged for us to do this morning so I pottered about the town with some of our party. It was terribly crowded – every kind of Nazi uniform of course, police of different varieties, regular soldiers, airmen, etc., etc. – and peasants in their local costumes from every province in Germany – lots of colour and a cheerful population. There can be no denying the popular excitement and enthusiasm – though some of the people who were here last year say that all this part of the business is not so great as last year. But there is evidently a mass of public opinion behind the regime and the Führer is supreme. He has only to lift his finger and the people will follow him – it is an ominous business and one cannot but feel very uneasy about it. ... Tonight there was a dinner to the foreign guests, presided over by Rosenberg. I was accorded a long conversation with him after dinner ... I asked a good many questions which he failed to answer – he asked some which I answered – but it was a futile business. They are just out to see what they can get by pressure – and if they can't get it, they are quite ready to fight when they are ready.

Friday 10 September   ... the more one sees and hears here, the more clear it is that trouble is brewing. ... We went to tea this afternoon with Hitler at his hotel – the whole or nearly the whole of the foreign visitors. We shook hands with the great man, also with Hess, his second-in-command. The impression of those of us who were here last year is that the Führer treated us somewhat

---

[5] translation: capable of anything.
[6] Julius Streicher (1885–1946), Nazi Party *Gauleiter* of Franconia 1925–40; editor of the anti-semitic newspaper *Der Stürmer* 1923–45; tried at Nuremberg 1945–46, sentenced to death.

coldly – I confess that I did not notice it – all I know is that when he shook me by the hand he fixed me with a penetrating eye and that I gazed back at him with equal steadiness wondering why *he* had become a national hero and *I* was just on the shelf?

Saturday 11 September   This morning we went to the Hitler Youth demonstration – a remarkable show. The enthusiasm was splendid: there is no doubt that young Germany is being brought up to believe in the new creed – a profound belief in national socialism and an implicit obedience for the Führer. ... it is impossible to conceive a better organized and run business than we have here, or a more overwhelming exhibition of popular enthusiasm.

Sunday 12 September   The endless discussion continues among us [the British observers] – what actually does Germany want? If and when one finds out what she is really after, how are her demands to be met? Some of us are confident that a 'gesture' would solve all the difficulties – give her back the colonies. Even if this apparently easy – but really most difficult – policy could be adopted, it would not, in my opinion, do much good. It would merely make Hitler & Co. think that they could continue getting things which they wanted merely by adopting a truculent attitude. It seems to me that the only policy now is for us to try and get on friendly terms with the Nazi Government: express our willingness to discuss the whole economic position with them directly – and then if it is found possible to let them have some territory, to make certain that we get a good return for what we give – but to prepare for war all the time and for all we are worth.

Monday 13 September   The military display this morning – 15,000 all arms on parade – enabled us to see that the Germans are provided with up-to-date implements of war and know how to use them. It was of course a long drawn out business, but a very interesting one. The enthusiasm was tremendous and after the parade was over Hitler, standing up in his car with Blomberg[7] standing behind him, went slowly all round the arena. His reception

[7] Werner von Blomberg (1878–1946), German army career; Min. of Defence 1933–35, of War 1935–38; C. in C. of the *Wehrmacht* 1935–38; dismissed due to the scandal following his second marriage in Jan. 1938, when his new wife was revealed to have a police record as a prostitute.

was magnificent – I try to think that the man deserves it and really means peace not war.

Wednesday 20 October   I went into Newcastle again to meet Magnay, M.P., and Dr. Grant of Seaham, Ramsay Mac.'s friend, for our 'Co-ordinating Committee' – Magnay turned up: Grant was ill in bed with a cold – however, his absence did not really matter. We fixed up the seats without much difficulty – Magnay is a silly little ass – but quite amenable – he knows as well as we do that the Simonite Libs. are wholly dependent on the Conservatives and that it is as much as they can do to find candidates.

Monday 8 November   I lunched at the Travellers with Philip Kerr[8] (Lothian). He and I (who seldom share the same opinions) are at one about Germany. He despairs of Eden and the F.O. clique and can see little hope of a settlement between the 2 countries unless the P.M. takes up the business himself – if there is no settlement, another war is inevitable. Kerr (after some terribly long letters in *The Times*) thinks that he has done all he can, and is off to see what he can do in India.

Wednesday 10 November   I spent a good deal of time today at the Central Office – I attended a meeting of Area Chairmen in Douglas Hacking's room at which we discussed a report on the Junior Imperial League.[9] It struck me as a lot of hot air – without money the League can never be of much more value than it is at present and it appears that money is not forthcoming. The idea of the Central Office is of course to centralize it as much as possible – to have a certain number of organizers to be sent about the country and to do away with the Area Organizers – at least no longer to go on helping to pay for them. I cannot agree with this proposal.

Monday 15 November   Edward Wood is off to Germany on

[8] Philip Henry Kerr (1882–1940), co-founder and first editor, *Round Table* 1910–16; private Sec. to Lloyd George, 1916–21; Sec., Rhodes trust 1925–39; Chanc. Duchy of Lancaster 1931; U.S. India 1931–32; Chairman, Indian Franchise Ctte. 1932; Amb. in Washington 1939–40; suc. 11th Marquess of Lothian 1930, K.T. 1940.

[9] Founded in 1906, this was the Conservative Party's organisation for young persons (normally ages 14–25) until it was replaced by the Young Conservatives in 1946.

Wednesday – and one hopes for the best – but I am not very sanguine of great results. If we are not prepared to give Germany some kind of freedom to move in Europe (which we are not either keen or in a position to prevent), I don't see what we have got to offer Hitler – for I cannot believe that any British Government will dare to give away colonies – I don't believe either that it would get the support of its own followers in the HofC, let alone that of the country as a whole. It looks to me like an impasse – Edward Wood's expedition will probably turn out as futile as Haldane's visit to Berlin before the war.[10] However, I may be quite wrong: they may be nearer to a settlement than one knows. In any case I think that Edward is the best an they could have selected for the job. I think that his personality and manner will make an appeal to Hitler – and that is always something to the good. Simon was too smug for him, I fancy, and Anthony Eden too much the F.O. young man.

Saturday 20 November   Topping[11] and I left Holywell soon after 10 a.m. – we had a meeting at Tilley's [tea rooms] of Conservative school teachers over which I presided. We arranged to form a 'Teachers' Circle' which presumably will be of some value to the party – anyhow it is what Topping wished us to form. ... Then I presided over a meeting of Conservative club men at the Old Assembly Rooms and we formed a Clubs Advisory Committee which again was to please the Central Office.

Friday 26 November   Today has been taken up by the Raby bazaar, to raise funds for the [Barnard Castle] Conservative Association ... There were not many people at Raby and I was afraid that no money would be made – however, Beatrice tells us tonight that they have cleared over £200 which is not so bad. ... What a nuisance it is to have to raise money by bazaars – why cannot people subscribe their 6d or 1/- every year and so produce the

---

[10] The 'Haldane mission' of 1912; an unsuccessful attempt to reach an understanding on the naval race during a visit to Germany by the Lord Chancellor, Lord Haldane.

[11] (Hugh) Robert Topping (1877–1952), Con. Agent Dublin 1904–11, Glamorgan S. 1911–18, Cardiff, Llandaff & Barry 1918–23, Northwich 1923–24; C.O. Agent, North West Area 1924–28; Con. Principal Agent 1928–30, Gen. Dir. 1930–45; kt. 1934.

required funds? Then the wretched Agents could get down to the propaganda and organization work for which they are intended.

Monday 29 November   This afternoon I gave a lecture entitled 'Problems at Home and Abroad' at a political school organized by the Central Division, Newcastle. It was at the County Hotel and Wilkin was in the chair. There were only about fifty or sixty people present – mainly middle-aged and ageing women – I keep on wondering what practical value there is to the Party in these ever-lasting political schools. Central Office, as Ledingham says, has gone mad about them and all the leading wire-pullers in London (who know little or nothing about rough and tumble politics) are 'educational' enthusiasts. I feel that if we were to concentrate our forces on more active propaganda we should be doing a deal more practical good. None of the people to whom these lectures are given is likely to take any really active part in politics either canvassing or on the platform – at least as I gaze upon them I cannot believe that any of them will – bar, of course, the few who already do so. However, there it is, education is apparently the *dernier cri*[12] among those in authority and we must not be behind hand in it in this part of the world, or we shall be considered retrograde!

Wednesday 1 December   The meeting in Dumfries this afternoon was what I expected – about seventy women ... it is boring to have to address a small meeting of women who never utter a sound of approbation or disapprobation from the first moment to the last – and are all waiting for their tea!

Sunday 5 December   The Japanese appear to be treating us with the contempt we deserve in Shanghai – behaving as if the international settlement belonged to them. It is difficult to see how our prestige, and with it our trade and commerce, is going to survive all this business – what the end of it all is going to be *Dieu seul sait*[13] – but, in our present circumstances in Europe, we clearly cannot send our Fleet to the Pacific, and, unless the U.S.A. are prepared to play, I don't see how we are going to put the Japanese

[12] translation: the last word.
[13] translation: God only knows.

in their place. It is a bad world at the moment and our position is extremely uncomfortable – but no one here seems to care what happens. We are an odd Imperial race! ... Charley Londonderry, wearing his Air Force uniform, came here from Usworth late in the afternoon and he and I and Ledingham discussed the best method of raising money for the Conference next year. Charley was very affable, but how I wish that he could even for a few moments forget that he is Lord Londonderry. He really is at heart such a good fellow that it is a pity he can never relax – a greater pity still that he should imagine that just because he happens to be a very rich nobleman he is more important and intelligent than he really is!

Wednesday 8 December ... attended the Executive Committee at Palace Chambers. It was as dull a business as usual – the only item in the agenda which caused any kind of flutter was caused by the resignation of Geo[rge] Godwin,[14] Secretary of the National Union, and the method of appointment of his successor. Now Geo. Godwin some little time ago told me in confidence that he was retiring and that the intention was to replace him by a minion of the Central Office – this he considered would be a mistake (he has no love of Topping and considers that this man's determination to get everything into his clutches should be checked so far as the National Union is concerned – and I agree with him) – apparently he told young Williams[15] and one or two others 'in strict confidence' the same story – so when today some of the 'hack' men who are always put up to do the Central Office work, got up to propose that the appointment of Godwin's successor should be left to our officers + Hacking – there was a certain amount of opposition in which I joined – eventually a compromise, proposed by me and supported by Lord Salisbury[16] was accepted – nevertheless, I could see that Hacking, Topping & Co. were not best pleased.

[14] George Godwin, Sec., Reigate Constitutional Club 1903–06; Con. Agent Reigate 1906, Guildford 1906–21; Sec., National Union 1921–1938.

[15] Alfred Martyn Williams (1897–1985), Con. M.P. Cornwall N. 1924–29, cand. 1931, 1932; High Sheriff, Cornwall 1938.

[16] James Edward Hubert Gascoyne-Cecil (1861–1947), Con. M.P. Darwen 1885–92, Rochester 1893–1903; U.S. For. Office 1900–03; Lord Privy Seal 1903–05, 1924–29; Pres. Bd. of Trade 1905; Chanc. Duchy of Lancaster 1922–23; Lord Pres. 1922–24; Con. Leader in the Lords 1925–31; styled Viscount Cranborne 1868–1903, suc. 4th Marquess of Salisbury 1903.

Tuesday 4 January 1938   I went to Sunderland this evening ...
and addressed the Methodist 'Men's Forum' on the international
situation. ... The audience was entirely working men and their
politics were left wing – however, they gave me a very good hearing
and their questions were not unduly violent. It is odd how they all
differentiate between Hitler and Stalin:[17] one is a gangster, the other
a good democrat.

Saturday 22 January   Oliver and Maureen[18] [Stanley] seem pleased
to see us – the former as usual very heavy in hand – one always
has to do all the talking with him and he never appears to take the
slightest interest in one. He is an odd creature and I cannot see
him ever leading the Party even though no doubt every string will
be pulled for him when the time comes.

Sunday 23 January   Despite the weather I went a walk with Oliver
this morning ... I doubt whether he has the slightest interest in me
or in anyone else but himself. He tells me that none of the young
men in the HofC is displaying much promise: he thinks that should
Neville go, Tom Inskip would succeed him and that, if by chance
Sam Hoare were selected as leader, he (Oliver) would give up
politics – would he, I wonder? He seems to approve of young
Morrison whom he considers very clever. He says that some sort
of a trading agreement is likely to made with the U.S.A. and that
at the moment the U.S.A. govt. is friendly – but wisely he feels
that we cannot trust it to play the game by us in the Far East or
anywhere else. He is all for a German agreement, but says that it
will take a long time to arrive at one.

Saturday 29 January   ... to discuss with Tommy Bradford,[19]
Ledingham and Cherry how best the Conservative agents can help
the municipal people in local elections. My idea is that, if we can

[17] Josef Vissarionovich Djugashvili (1879–1953), adopted the alias of Stalin ('man
of steel'); Commissar for Nationalities 1917–22; Gen. Sec. of Communist Party from
1923, effectively dictator from 1928, but only formally head of state 1941–53.

[18] Maureen Helen Stanley (1900–42), eldest daughter of 7th Marquess of Londonderry, married Oliver Stanley 1920; styled Lady Maureen.

[19] Thomas Andrews Bradford (1886–1966), Con. cand. Seaham 1922, Durham
1923, 1931 (withdrew before nomination); Treasurer, Co. Durham C.A. 1930–37,
Chairman 1937–45; Vice-Chairman, Northern Counties Area 1937–46; Chairman,
D.M.C.F. 1948–56; High Sheriff, Co. Durham 1942; kt. 1939.

utilize the machine *sub rosa*,[20] we can gradually collar the Federation for all practical purposes and only have Conservative candidates. then possibly we shall get our voters to turn out better at elections than they do now: they hate voting for Liberal candidates even at local elections. ... I presided over a meeting over the Grand Lodge (N.C.L.).[21] It was suggested that I be made Grand Master (*vice* Charley Londonderry) seeing that I did all the work – but I declined the honour – fancy Charley's feelings if he had been deposed for me. ... The Teesside lodges still seem to be flourishing, but everywhere else, except perhaps at Sunderland, the League is to all intents and purposes moribund.

Monday 31 January   I spoke tonight at the annual meeting of the Darlington Conservative Association ... There was a miserable attendance – at any rate for a place like Darlington (and with a speaker like me!) – of course Peat,[22] the M.P., and his family were conspicuous by there absence. I spoke for about half an hour on foreign affairs ... Foreign affairs nowadays is the only thing which seems to exercise the minds of people. They are mostly in work, I suppose, and for the time being are not worrying as much as usual about their grievances and their dole.

Wednesday 9 February   I ought to be in London today for the meeting of the Executive at the Central Office, but I have given it a miss – it won't really matter my not being there – indeed, for all the good I do there, I need not really attend at all – I am always in a minority and am no doubt looked upon as nothing but a bore. I probably am: for I disturb the smug equanimity of the proceedings – a serious offence in a body which is always agreed to do exactly as the caucus wants. Henry Page Croft spoke in Durham tonight on behalf of the [Joseph] Chamberlain Centenary celebration ... It was not a great gathering, but the audience listened spellbound to Henry for about an hour – one wondered

---

[20] translation: in secret.

[21] The National Conservative League was a semi-official organisation for Conservative working-men, with membership of the 'lodges' by invitation; it was active in Co. Durham between the wars, and Headlam had actively supported it.

[22] Charles Urie Peat (1892–1979), Con. M.P. Darlington 1931–45; P.P.S. to O. Lyttleton 1941, to H. Macmillan 1941–42; P.S. Supply 1942–45; partner in Peat, Marwick Mitchell & Co., accountants.

why – but was glad that they were so easily pleased. I have never discovered why H.P.C. should be such a successful platform speaker. He is not a tub thumper – he is not even eloquent – I think that it is because he is obviously sincere and says what he has to say simply and in words which the audience can understand.

Saturday 12 February   ... I had to go on to our Area Labour Advisory Committee annual meeting. There was trouble there. They have a silly custom by which each county in turn is entitled to produce the annual chairman. In order to do this the county representatives meet and elect their nominee before the Labour Committee meets. The nominee is then accepted by the Committee. Today there was a contest and the Darlington man who was supposed to be going to be unopposed was beaten by one vote by a gent from Sunderland. Then in the full Committee the Darlington man was put up and elected by the full Committee – much heart burning on the Sunderland side. Clearly everything was in order – but it was an unfortunate episode which I fancy Ledingham might have prevented by the exercise of a little tact – but he was caught napping. I took no part in the business which was clearly no affair of mine. It all comes from our maintaining these absurd county distinctions and I did go so far as to say that when I got on my feet to make my speech.

Saturday 19 February   There are strong rumours that there is trouble in the Cabinet and that Anthony Eden and Neville are at loggerheads. I should not wonder whether these rumours may not prove true.

Sunday 20 February   The excitement tonight is that Anthony Eden has resigned his job – what a fuss there will be about it! and yet really how little he deserves the reputation he has got as Foreign Secretary. He crashed badly over sanctions and the European situation has gone from worse to worse since he has been in power. Three years ago we could have got almost any bargain we liked with Germany: now it is not going to be easy to get a decent agreement – and the same applies with Italy.

Tuesday 22 February   The debate in the HofC last night appears to have been a success for the Govt. – Anthony's speech does not impress me. There was really no cause for him to resign on the matter of this decision to begin negotiations with Italy – I suppose really he is not in agreement with a policy such as Neville clearly is out for, and still is a League of Nations man – probably, too, his head is a bit swollen and he dislikes the P.M. taking so active a part in foreign affairs! Personally I am glad that he has gone – during his reign at the F.O. things have steadily deteriorated and I don't believe that so long as he remained there, there was any chance of their improving – and the odd thing about it is that he is not a strong man – he is more of a prig than a swashbuckler – and that is why the dictators dislike being lectured to by him.

Friday 25 February   I attended this evening a meeting of the Durham Group Executive to interview a prospective Liberal Candidate for Durham. His name is Spencer and he does not seem a bad sort of man – common and commonplace – rather a nice looking, pleasant-mannered wife (looks Jewish). He gave us an address – twenty minutes of platitudes, repeated over and over again and not well expressed – but Tommie Bradford and all the others present were quite pleased with it. Spencer is of course a Conservative: all his views on protection, foreign policy, etc., are similar to my own but he calls himself a Liberal – and this is all that matters nowadays – how ridiculous it is to go on 'pretending' – we all might be a pack of children – we are even asked to go on pretending that there are such animals as 'National Socialists', and the 'Co-ordinating Committee' in London have asked us to find some seats for them in this part of the world where we cannot even find a Nat. Socialist to second a vote of thanks at a big public meeting.

Wednesday 2 March   I went to South Shields again this evening and Mr. Pilkington, the Liberal National, was promised the support of the Conservatives. It was much the same kind of performance as the one the other day in Durham. The man Pilkington made a Conservative speech, assured us that he was an out and out supporter of the Nat. Govt., supported Neville's foreign policy, etc., etc. He lead us to understand that he was a man of unimpeachable honour, honest God-fearing, etc. – of course I did not like him or his manner of speech – he smelt of 'Liberalism' and the lower middle class and chapel – but the South Shields people appeared to be quite satisfied with him and no doubt he is good enough for them.

Thursday 10 March   I met Edward Halifax in the Park this morning – I said 'Edward, may I congratulate you?'[23]
   'No,' he replied, 'you certainly may not!'
   'May I condole with you?'
   'Yes, you may.'
   'How easy the job would have been 3 or 4 years ago!'
   'Yes, indeed.'
   'Can it be done now, I wonder?'
   'I wonder too!' – and so we passed on.

Friday 11 March   The event today is that Hitler is marching into Austria – it is what I have always expected would happen – the taking over of Austria by the Germans – but had we not been such fools it need never have happened in this unfortunate way. How well I remember discussing this question with Austen Chamberlain, Anthony Eden & Co. when I came back from Berlin early in 1935 – none of them would tolerate any intercourse with Hitler & Co. because of the episode in the previous summer when the Nazis had their bloody purge[24] – and at that date we could have settled all outstanding questions with Hitler for the asking!

Saturday 12 March   The German invasion of Austria is proceeding according to plan – the people appear to be welcoming the invaders which no doubt is the wisest thing they could do. The Austrian government has been deposed and the Nazis reign in their stead. The Sunday newspapers express our indignation at the method of aggression which Hitler has adopted, but there is no apparent anxiety of the English people to rush to arms in defence of the 'aggressed' nation – and I am pretty confident that there would be a similar disinclination on their part to fight even if the Germans played the same game in Czechoslovakia even though the Czechs put up a fight. The truth of the matter is that we are not going to war unless we can see with our own eyes that this country is directly threatened – and yet the Labour men and the Liberals

[23] Halifax was appointed Foreign Secretary after Eden's resignation.
[24] The 'Night of the Long Knives', 29 June 1934.

will go on prating about collective security and pretending that
they mean something by the expression!

Saturday 19 March   I called on Charley Londonderry at the
Station Hotel [Newcastle]. He was friendly, but gloomy – he came
up last night to attend the luncheon to Douglas Hacking and the
Area meeting. He presided at the luncheon: I at the meeting. The
luncheon was well attended – quite a number of the chairmen of
Associations turning up – and they asked quite intelligent questions.
Hacking is rather a dull dog, but he is doing well as Chairman of
the Party because he is taking trouble – and going about in the
Areas. The meeting in the Old Assembly Rooms was a very good
one – about the largest I remember. There must have been about
four hundred people present I should say.

Wednesday 6 April   The principal event today is a conversation
I had with the P.M. in his room at the HofC. I asked him if he
would put my name on his list for the vacant Suez Canal directorship
and he said he would, but that, as I could imagine, the list was a
long one – I gathered from this that it was unlikely that I should
be the new director. I told him a little of our difficulties and he was
sympathetic – at least he lets you do a little of the talking which
S.B. never did! ... Having disposed of these personal matters, we
discussed the affairs of the world. I asked him whether Anthony
had really resigned because of the Musso[25] business – because
Musso was not told to show himself a good boy before he was
forgiven. He replied that this was about what it amounted to. He
also assured me that in his opinion, unless we had come to an
agreement with Italy, there would have been war this year. He
struck me as a bit too confident about having public opinion in
this country on his side – in my opinion the floating Liberal vote,
on which the Nat. Govt. depends, is heartily against the Italian
agreement and that if we had a general election tomorrow we might
be in the soup.

Thursday 7 April   I came down here [Government House, Farn-

[25] Benito Mussolini (1883–1945), founder & *Duce* of Italian Fascist Party; Pres.,
Council of Ministers 1922–26; P.M. 1926–43; For. Min. 1924–29, 1932–36; Head of
German puppet regime in N. Italy 1943–45; often referred to in Britain as 'Musso'.

borough] this afternoon to stay the night with Jack Dill[26] ...
Bartholomew[27] – now G.O.C. Northern Area – is also here. We
had quite an interesting evening. Dill has aged a good deal, but he
still appears to be keen and intelligent. ... Neither of them is very
happy about the situation – that is to say, neither of them feels
that the Army is in a condition to face a war – mainly because
there is so little of it and what there is is so ill-provided with the
arms and equipment which are required today. Neither of them
has any use for Hore-Belisha whom they regard as a mountebank
and a politician.

Saturday 9 April   It was the final of the Area speakers' competition today in Newcastle and the judging went on from 2.15
p.m. to 6 p.m. ... had a meeting with Ledingham and some of the
Agents about their 'scheme' for raising a central fund for the
financing of impecunious constituencies. This scheme is to be
considered by the Topping sub-committee at the Central Office and
I suppose that I shall have to father it. The speaking this afternoon
was much the same as usual – and we all said the usual thing about
it – how much it had improved! The odd thing about these
competitions is the interest which the competitors and their friends
appear to take in them. The speeches are listened to with intense
interest and real anxiety is evinced as to the winning of the prizes.
I suppose, therefore, that there is some value in the competitions,
even if they are not calculated to provide the Party with a useful
band of orators.

Sunday 10 April   There is such a spate of books nowadays about
current topics that one simply must read some of them – either
from the 'Left Book Club' or the 'Right Book Club'. Most of them
are pretty poor stuff – written off by journalists who either like or

---

[26] John Greer Dill (1881–1944), army career, Commandant, Staff College 1931–
34; Dir. of Military Operations & Intelligence 1934–36; Commander British Forces
in Palestine 1936–37; C. in C. Aldershot 1937–39; G.O.C. 1st Army Corps 1939–40;
C.I.G.S. 1940–41; Head of British Joint Staff Mission to U.S.A. 1941–44; kt. 1937.
[27] William Henry Bartholomew (1877–1962), army career; Dir. of Recruiting &
Organisation 1927–28; Commandant, Imperial Defence College 1929–31; Dir. of
Military Operations & Intelligence 1931–34; Commandant, Royal Artillery 1934–
37; Chief of General Staff, India 1934–37; G.O.C. Northern Command 1937–40;
Aide-de-Camp Gen. to the King 1938–40; Comm. for Civil Defence, N.E. England
1940–45.

dislike dictators – it is odd how, on the whole, people in this country are inclined to dislike any form of government which is not what they consider 'democratic' – so long as there is something with calls itself a parliament, the tendency here is to regard it as a sign of salvation – however gross the tyranny may be, however little influence the so-called parliament may have. At the moment Stalin's form of government is preferred to that of Mussolini or of Hitler because on paper he has revived a form of 'parliamentary government'. Franco[28] is considered a ruthless military adventurer because he is attacking what is considered by many people in this country [to be] a popularly elected parliamentary government. The truth of the matter of course is that very few people in England really trouble to understand foreign politics and are guided in their judgement of them by their own political ideas and the political clichés of this country. They imagine that the so-called 'Liberal govt.' in Spain,[29] for example, means that it professes a political faith such as is held by Sir H. Samuel[30] & co.

Wednesday 27 April   I then went to see Ledingham who was as garrulous as ever – apparently the money is coming in well for the Conference fund which is as I hoped and expected. We discussed Darlington and North Newcastle, etc. It is difficult to decide whether to go for Darlington – I cannot make up my mind. It would be a hard fight and the seat can never be a really safe one. It would be maddening to be booked for it and then for North Newcastle to come into the market.[31] But there is no certainty about N. Newcastle – Grattan-Doyle[32] won't give it up until the last minute and he is all out to run in his son. I could of course fight the son – but it would be an unpleasant business. I don't really know what to do.

---

[28] Francisco Franco y Bahamonde (1892–1975), Spanish soldier, Chief of Staff 1935–36; Gov. of Canaries 1936; led military attack on Republican Govt. July 1936, became leader of Nationalist forces in Spanish Civil War Oct. 1936; ruled Spain with dictatorial powers as Caudillo 1939–75.

[29] The Republican Government, based in Madrid.

[30] Herbert Louis Samuel (1870–1963), Lib. M.P. Cleveland 1902–18, Darwen 1929–35; Chanc. Duchy of Lancaster 1909–10, 1915–16; Postmaster-Gen. 1914–15, 1915–16; Pres. Local Govt. Bd. 1914–15; Home Sec. 1916, 1931–32; High Comm. Palestine 1920–25; kt. 1920, cr. Viscout Samuel 1937.

[31] Newcastle North was one of the few safe Conservative seats in the north-east.

[32] Nicholas Grattan Grattan-Doyle (1862–1941), Con. M.P. Newcastle N. 1918–40; kt. 1924.

Saturday 7 May   Charley Londonderry turned up here this afternoon and stayed for a long time, discussing men and things. ... He
also said that Neville [Chamberlain] was somewhat caustic about
some of his colleagues and that all Hore-Belisha's military 'reforms'
are the result of Neville's pushing – well, even if they are, they
don't amount to much! Charley sees no hope of peace unless we
settle things quickly with Germany and he wants this to be done
by Neville Henderson in Berlin in the same way as the Italian
agreement was done by Perth[33] and Ciano[34] in Rome. ... I doubt
whether at the moment this country would stand any conversations
with the Nazis. The Austrian affair has upset people and until the
Czech position is clarified I doubt whether it would be advisable
to begin any definite talks with Germany.

Sunday 8 May   The man Lawson[35] (chairman of North
Newcastle) and his wife came here today ... I discussed the North
Newcastle situation quite frankly with Lawson and told him plainly
that should N. G[rattan]-D[oyle] try to run in his son he would
most likely be opposed by an independent Conservative – possibly
myself. He seemed to take it all in, and no doubt was wondering
all the time whether it would be better for him to stick to G-D. or
to follow us. He evinced surprise to learn that I should like to
return to the HofC. It will be interesting to see what is the outcome
of this conversation: no doubt G-D. will be fully informed although
both Lawson and I insisted upon our talk being absolutely confidential!

Friday 13 May   The air debates in Parliament yesterday leave
one with the feeling that there is a lot to be said against the Air
Ministry and that our air position is unsatisfactory in the extreme –

---

[33] (James) Eric Drummond (1876–1951), entered diplomatic service 1900; Private
Sec. to P.M. 1912–15, to For. Sec. 1915–19; Sec.-Gen., League of Nations, 1919–
33; Amb. in Rome 1933–39; Chief Advisor on For. Publicity, Min. of Information
1939–40; Scottish rep. peer in House of Lords 1941–51; Dep. Lib. Leader in Lords
1946–51; kt. 1916, suc. 16th Earl of Perth (Scottish peerage) 1937.
[34] Count Galeazzo Ciano (1903–1944), Italian For. Minister 1936–43; Amb. to
the Vatican 1943; married Mussolini's daughter 1930; voted for Mussolini's over-
throw July 1943; arrested by Gestapo, executed 11 Jan. 1944.
[35] James Coldwell Lawson, member of Newcastle City Council, St. Thomas' Ward
1927–43, Alderman 1943–45.

neither Cunliffe-Lister[36] in the Lords nor Eddie Winterton[37] in the
Commons came out of the debate with added laurels and clearly
the Party is not very happy – obviously the programme of construction is behind hand and, even if it is completed by the time
stated, we shall be immeasurably inferior in strength to the
Germans. It is all very disquieting and I expect that the Government
will be obliged to set up a Ministry of Supply. I wonder whether
Swinton will go – probably not – he belongs to the inner clique
and is a friend of Neville's.

Saturday 14 May　　　There are rumours of a reconstruction in the
Cabinet and it is rather ill-omened, I think, to find that S.B. spent
an hour and a half at No. 10 Downing Street yesterday and that
Sam Hoare was in and out there all day. The latter of course is the
busiest wire-puller of the lot – always on the look out for what
may be to his own advantage. But surely Neville is not going to be
such a fool as to reintroduce S.B. into the Cabinet! His reappearance
would not please a large section of the Party nor would it appeal
to public opinion – probably S.B. is too canny a bird to run the
risks of a come-back!

Sunday 22 May　　　... at Hackwood this afternoon where we 'took
tea' with the Camroses who now own the place, I found Lord
Camrose[38] in a state of great alarm – it seems that it has really
been 'touch and go' all the weekend, and the Cabinet appears to
have been in session all today. Neville Henderson in Berlin has
been good I fancy. Ribbentrop[39] was rude and foolish to him when

[36] Philip Cunliffe-Lister (1884–1972), Con. M.P. Hendon 1918–35; P.S. Trade
1920–21; Sec. Overseas Trade 1921–22; Pres. Bd. of Trade 1922–24, 1924–29, 1931;
Colonial Sec. 1931–35; Sec. for Air 1935–38; Min. Res. W. Africa 1942–44; Min.
Civil Aviation 1944–45; Chanc. Duchy of Lancaster 1951–52; Commonwealth Sec.
1952–55; changed surname from Lloyd-Greame 1924, cr. Viscount Swinton 1935,
Earl 1955.

[37] Edward Turnour (1883–1962), Con. M.P. Horsham 1904–51; U.S. India 1922–
24, 1924–29; Chanc. Duchy of Lancaster 1937–39; Paymaster-Gen. 1939; Father of
the House 1945–51; styled Viscount Winterton 1883–1907, suc. 6th Earl Winterton
(Irish peerage) 1907, cr. Baron Turnour 1952.

[38] William Ewart Berry (1879–1954), newspaper prop.; Chairman, Financial Times
Ltd. 1919–45, Allied Newspapers Ltd. 1924–36; prop. & editor-in-chief of *Sunday
Times* 1915–36, of *Daily Telegraph* 1928–54; Principal Adviser, Min. of Information
1939; cr. Bart. 1921, Baron Camrose 1929, Viscount 1941.

[39] Joachim von Ribbentrop (1893–1946), Nazi politician; Amb. in London 1936–
38; For. Minister 1938–45; tried at Nuremberg 1945–46; executed 16 October 1946.

he saw him yesterday when he asked if the Nazis really meant to invade Czechoslovakia – whereupon Henderson said he should advise his nationals to leave Germany:[40] he did so and I should imagine that no course of action could have been better – anyway, according to the wireless, the situation seems to be easier tonight.

Tuesday 14 June   The Education Committee was as dull as usual – only my friend Donald Scott really takes any interest in it, I fear, but we must pretend to believe in the value of 'political education' (whatever it may mean) so long as the powers-that-be in Palace Chambers ordain its necessity – in other words we shall have to waste money on it so long as Lady Falmouth[41] and Dame Regina Evans[42] so wish!

Wednesday 15 June   I spent most of the day in the Central Office. In the morning I brought forward in Topping's sub-committee the Northern Agents' proposals for a central fund to help poor constituencies – and somewhat to my surprise there was really no opposition to the policy, though there were of course differences of opinion as to the method of procedure to be adopted. I don't suppose that anything will come of it all, because unless the thing is vigorously pushed by the Leader of the Party, it is certain to be killed by the dead weight of the opposition of the richer con-stituencies. In the afternoon there was the usual Executive Com-mittee meeting, presided over by Eugene Ramsden (now a Baronet). There were no excitements – a little breeze about the report of Kingsley Wood's[43] committee on the organization of the London Area published in the press. I felt it my duty to warn the Londoners that to give them an organization of their own independent of the

---

[40] A public signal that war could soon be declared.

[41] Mary Margaret Desirée ('Daisy') Wood [her father assumed the surname Meynell in lieu of Wood in 1905] (1894–1985), married 1915 Evelyn Hugh Boscawen, suc. 8th Viscount Falmouth 1918; Con. Party acting-Dep. Chairman 1930–31, Vice-Chairman 1931–39; Chairman, Red Cross Civilian Relief Overseas Dept. 1943–46; Dep. Chairman, British Red Cross Soc. 1952–54.

[42] Regina Margaret Evans (d.1969), Chairman, N.U. Womens' Advisory Ctte. 1934–35, N.U. Central Council 1934; Chief Commandant, Auxiliary Territorial Service 1939–43; Chairman, London Hostels Assoc. 1949–69; cr. Dame 1936.

[43] (Howard) Kingsley Wood (1881–1943), Con. M.P. Woolwich W. 1918–43; P.S. Health 1924–29; P.S. Educ. 1931; Postmaster-Gen. 1931–35; Min. of Health 1935–38; Sec. for Air 1938–40; Lord Privy Seal 1940; Chanc. of the Exchequer 1940–43; kt. 1918.

Central Office would not be agreeable to the other Areas. This roused some of the London representatives on the Committee – but I fancy that the warning was rather necessary, and for once I seemed to have pleased the powers that be by giving it.

Friday 1 July   I attended the [Northern Area] annual Agents' and Women Organizers' luncheon at Tilley's. Charley Londonderry was in the chair and Patrick Gower[44] from the Central Office was the chief speaker. ... Charley made a very poor speech which, nevertheless, seemed to please the Agents and Organizers who all slobbered over him. He now seems not to attempt to prepare his orations and he is not a clever enough or a well-informed enough man to do this – the result is a dull rambling speech with constant repetitions and nothing to catch hold of.

Saturday 16 July   The N[ational] C[onservative] L[eague] Grand Lodge, between 30 and 40 strong despite the weather, came here this afternoon and, after our brotherly meeting and my usual address, they all had tea and appeared to enjoy themselves. They made the usual complaints about being victimized because they belong to the N.C.L. – no doubt there is something in what they say, but equally I sometimes think that they must be rather trying employees. However I sympathized with them and said that I would do what I could to help them if any particular cases were brought to my notice – but I know very well that mine managers are not going to put themselves out for the sake of any Conservative working men. They don't mind the Socialists being as active politicians as they choose – but woe betide the Conservative worker if he airs his politics and causes any kind of disturbance. It is all rather absurd, but there it is – 'His Majesty's Govt. must be carried on' – the pit must be kept working.

Monday 8 August   On the wireless tonight Bob Bourne's[45] death is announced – I wonder what he died of – a good fellow, hard

[44] (Robert) Patrick Malcolm Gower (1887–1964), civil service career; Private. Sec. to Chanc. of the Exchequer 1919–21, to Lord Privy Seal 1921–22, to P.M. 1922–28; Chief Publicity Officer, Con. Central Office 1929–39; Chairman, Charles F. Higham Ltd. 1939–56, Pres. 1956–64; kt. 1924.
[45] Robert Croft Bourne (1888–1938), Con. M.P. Oxford 1924–38; Dep. Chairman of Ways & Means 1931–38.

working and painstaking, not a personality in any way. He was a master of HofC procedure, but I doubt whether he would ever have been elected Speaker – his voice and manner were so uncongenial to everyone and he lacked charm.

Wednesday 7 September   The news today is not particularly reassuring: the Nazis are now congregated at Nuremberg and it remains to be seen whether or not Hitler is going to be truculent about Czecho[slovakia] – so far he has not disclosed his intentions – his first speech has been the usual anti-Jewish tirade. I am afraid that he may be going to take another plunge on the supposition that neither we nor the French will move. If he does, and again gets away with it, then it seems to me that a big European war is inevitable in the near future – I firmly believe that now is the moment for us to call the man's bluff.

Saturday 10 September   The news on the wireless this evening sounds rather ominous – Hitler and Goering have been giving tongue in Nuremberg ... It really is astounding that men should be quite ready to plunge the world into another war – more especially men who passed through the last one. ... Surely the time has come when we should make up our minds – better fight the Germans now than later, if fight them we must – but, honestly, I don't believe they would fight if they knew for certain we should be against them.

Wednesday 14 September   Late tonight has come the sensational news that the P.M. is to fly to Germany tomorrow to see Hitler. It is, I think, a very wise move whether the result of the conversations are successful or unsuccessful – because it does show to the world what tremendous efforts we are making for peace. I wonder who had the imagination to think of this move: Neville himself I should say – he is a brave man, there is no doubt about that. But how desperately near war it must be for this step to have been taken.

Saturday 17 September   Neville, rather to everyone's surprise, returned to London today. He has expressed himself as thoroughly satisfied with his talk with Hitler, and assures us all the he and H. now entirely understand each other's point of view. Neville of course has come home to consult his colleagues and probably the

French – also Runciman who arrived in England today from Prague.[46] I suppose the trouble now is to reconcile the Czechs to some form of plebiscite ... At present Neville has the whole country behind him, but if he surrenders Czechoslovakia to Hitler, he will lose Liberal and Labour support.

Monday 19 September   ... to the Central Office ... Hacking had no news – but seemed rather dubious about what appears to be Neville's policy – *viz.* to surrender – or make the Czechs surrender – their frontier and to allow the Reich to absorb the Sudetens. If this is really the outcome of Neville's visit to Hitler, it seems to me that he might just as well have stayed at home – the surrender would have looked less like a surrender. I am the last man to say that this may not be the only solution of the problem but coming now (clearly as a result of a threat of force) it seems to me a poor business, calculated to enhance enormously Hitler's prestige, to lower ours and to make war absolutely certain before long. They say that Daladier[47] has agreed to back this scheme (worse still for France's prestige than ours) and that our Cabinet favours it. One can only suppose that our military preparedness must be a deal worse than one imagined it – we could not adopt such a policy otherwise, even to save a war, surely?

Thursday 22 September   I don't believe that anything Neville can say or do now will prevent the Germans smashing up Czecho in one way or another – I am pretty confident in my own mind that they are acting in collusion with the Poles and the Hungarians and that they mean to cut up Czechoslovakia once [and] for all. I don't see how the French can tolerate this – it would be the end of their leading role in Europe and a confession of weakness which would not be lost on Hitler & co. If they go in, I equally cannot see how we can stand out of the fight. There is a bad time in store for us, there can be no doubt about it and God only knows what the

---

[46] Walter Runciman, who had retired from the Cabinet in May 1937, was sent to Czechoslovakia in August to act as mediator between the Czech government and the representatives of the German population in the Sudetenland region of Bohemia.

[47] Edouard Daladier (1884–1970), Radical Dep. for Vaucluse 1919–40, 1946–58; Min. for Colonies 1924–25; Min. of Works 1930–31; Min. of War & Defence 1932, 1933, 1936–37, 1938–40; For. Min. 1934; P.M. 1933, 1934, 1938–40; imprisoned by Vichy regime 1942–45; Pres. of Republican Left Party 1947–54; Pres. of Radical-Socialist groups in the Assembly 1956–58; Pres., Radical Party 1957–58.

outcome of it all may be. The American press appears to be covering us with abuse as having betrayed democracy – I think that we can afford to treat this with the contempt it deserves, but it shows pretty plainly that we cannot reckon upon American intervention for some time to come.

Sunday 25 September   Neville still appears not to have lost hope and the Germans are giving Prague 6 days in which to evacuate the 'Sudeten areas'. Whilst there is life, there is presumably hope – but one must face the situation and be ready for the worst. If only between us -the French and ourselves – we had a really superior Air Force, I suppose that we might hit the Germans pretty hard – but I suppose we have not – *hinc illae lacrimae*[48] – and the real villain of the peace is that wretched little Baldwin. We have been caught with our trousers down – not for the first time in our 'rough island story'. This time we shall be lucky if we get out of the mess without war – war for the first 6 months would be most unpleasant and the trial would be a severe one for our industrial population[49] – one knows that we should win in the end if we had the guts – but clearly we must preserve the peace if we can – and this obviously is what Neville is out for – even if it means his being called a 'traitor', etc. If only he had become P.M. a year earlier, we might well have been spared all this humiliating business – for, even if we are nor actually pledged to go to the assistance of the Czechs, we were a party to the calling into existence of their unhappy country and are supposed to stand up for the smaller nations.[50]

Monday 26 September   One can't help comparing one's feelings in these days with what one felt in 1914 – then one felt that war was inevitable – had felt it for years – today one does not feel this inevitability – on the contrary one knows instinctively that it can be avoided *now* if not indefinitely – whether it will be or not remains to be seen – but clearly *no* nation wants a new Great War – and even dictators cannot afford to neglect public opinion however

[48] translation: hence these tears. This is a classical quotation, originally in Terence, *Andria*, 1.1.99, but probably encountered by Headlam in texts read at school, either Cicero, *Pro Caelio*, 25, or Horace, *Epistles*, 1.19.41.

[49] The general expectation was that any war would open with immediate and heavy aerial bombing of town and cities, causing great loss of life.

[50] Czechoslovakia was created in the peace settlement after the First World War.

much they may pretend to despise democracy – in the long run it is public opinion which makes or unmakes them. Neither Hitler nor Mussolini is a fool: neither of them can afford to risk a big war: the former has got all he wants, the latter does not really like Germany to be too strong. Diplomacy should be able to find a way of allowing them to draw back before it is too late – we cannot prevent the Czechs being annihilated even if we go to war on their behalf: the French clearly can and will do very little to help them and the Russians by all accounts are worthless from a military point of view and dangerous politically.[51] I believe that Neville by going direct to Hitler took the right course. His visits may fail of course – but their having taken place has weakened Hitler – and, if he chooses to fight, his people will know *he* made the war however much the Nazis may try to disguise it – will he dare take this risk now that he knows what will be against him at home and abroad?

Wednesday 28 September   Neville's speech in the HofC appears to have been a triumph and his announcement at the close that Hitler had invited him, Daladier and Musso to Munich tomorrow for a talk looks as if peace might still be preserved.

Thursday 29 September   ... clearly there will be no war now – it would, I think, be quite impossible for Hitler to stage a war now – Neville's persistence and his two visits to Germany must have impressed the German people of our desire for peace just as it has impressed the rest of the world – and his calling upon Mussolini at the last moment has been a clever move – for Musso is no more anxious for war than we are – because the Italians don't want war with us on the side of Germany – of that I am sure ... the only trouble is that Hitler gets away with yet another coup at the expense of a smaller nation without a blow. But if Neville has made him understand that he really won't be allowed to do it again and has got some kind of a larger agreement for a European settlement out of him – why then he has deserved well of his country and all the world.

Friday 30 September   They came to an agreement at Munich early this morning – and so peace has been preserved – for how

---

[51] The Red Army was weakened by Stalin's purges of the officer corps.

long remains to be seen. If Neville is right, it may be indeed be for our time – and yet, if I were P.M., I should not stop preparing for war at home and abroad. The Czechs have been put down the drain because there was no means of helping them … throughout the world Neville has obtained a prestige which should help his country materially. If he has really brought the signed message from Hitler saying that all differences of opinion henceforth between Germany and England can be settled amicably – it may mean much or it may mean little – but at any rate, it is a confession made and that is something.

Saturday 1 October   The chorus of praise of Neville continues and all the world agrees that he has saved us from war, and he has I think for the time being at any rate – and so long as there is peace there is hope. His policy is of course the right one – but its success depends upon Hitler first and foremost – and can one trust the man? Duff Cooper evidently cannot as he has resigned – which rather amuses me as it was he who told me that the 3 golden rules in politics were 'never ask for anything, never refuse anything, never resign' – and as he has resigned I regard him as a very honest man for he is not well off and can ill afford to give up £5,000 a year. He belongs to the school which does not trust the German – and the whole history of modern Germany proves it to be right – but if one is not prepared to fight the Germans, one has to negotiate with them. Our only policy is to treat them as civilized beings but to see to it that we are strong enough to stand up to them if they don't play the game – they recognize force and nothing else.

Monday 3 October   The opposition to Neville is beginning to make itself heard. The usual idiots – Bob Cecil[52] etc. – have sent a memorial to *The Times* screaming that we have given way to violence and let down a gallant little democracy – but the Labour Party won't risk a vote of censure – and they dare not try and

---

[52] (Edward Algernon) Robert Gascoyne-Cecil (1864–1958), Con. M.P. Marylebone E. 1906–10, Hitchin 1911–23; U.S. For. Office 1915–18 & Min. of Blockade 1916–18; Lord Privy Seal 1923–24; Chanc. Duchy of Lancaster (with responsibility for League of Nations affairs) 1924–27; Pres., League of Nations Union 1923–45; styled Lord Robert Cecil 1868–1923, cr. Viscount Cecil of Chelwood 1923; awarded Nobel Peace Prize 1937.

force an election. Neville may be too optimistic (and I believe he is) but he is not the ass the Labour Party is!

Tuesday 4 October   Duff Cooper made his valedictory speech in the House yesterday as a Minister – and one could not help agreeing with much that he said. His contention was that we had given way to force and that no one in his senses could believe anything that Hitler said – one feels in one's bones that the latter contention is right. Perhaps in the past had we been nice to Hitler we might have been able to deal with him and he might have played the game by us – I always thought so and at any rate the game was worth trying – but we never were nice to him – and then allowed him to rearm and do as he liked, with the result that he has brought off three very successful coups without a drop of blood being shed. No wonder the man thinks that he can do what he likes and feels that bluff and lying pay. Is it likely that he will now step in time with us? and is it likely that he will postpone his next coup until we are ready?

Thursday 6 October   The Commons debate is over and the Government has secured a big majority, and so this incident in our foreign policy is concluded. What its consequences may be remain to be seen. It has not been a particularly happy experience. We have saved the peace – for the time being at any rate – and, in view of the fact that we were in no position to fight, this is an achievement. But we have not cut much of a figure, even if we have not actually let down the Czechs. Shall we learn the lesson? Shall we really organize the people to be ready next time to face a war should it come? I doubt it – once this scare is over we shall subside again into our usual complacent serenity. In any case I doubt whether the Nazis will allow us much time to prepare ourselves – they have scored all along the line and know it.

Friday 7 October   The German occupation of the Sudeten area continues, and the international committee is said to be controlling things! I confess that I am pretty unhappy about everything – but I suppose that one should be thankful that we are not at war and try and believe that things will go all right.

Saturday 8 October   The correspondence in *The Times* continues –

carefully selected letters no doubt all explaining in one way or another how right we have been in allowing the Germans to obtain control of Czechoslovakia. How absurd this is when one comes to think of it – perhaps it was better for us not to fight a war now, but surely no sensible Englishman can view with equanimity the continuing expansion eastward of a great power like Germany, especially under its present rulers – and to argue that we could not have gone to war in defence of the Czechs because they have been oppressing minorities is absurd – we should have been defending a small nation against the aggression of a bigger nation – but we should have been fighting in our own defence against a power which threatened us. However, of course had we fought the Czechs would have been the chief sufferers, no one can deny that – now when war does come they can sit still and watch what happens.

Sunday 9 October   Our futile foreign policy not only brought Nazism into being, but also allowed it to become so powerful that it has now become a menace to world peace. Baldwin, MacDonald, Simon, Hoare, Eden & co. are the men who have lead us into our present somewhat futile and humiliating position – and now we are content to point out how much better it is for Czechoslovakia that we did not go to war on her behalf...

Monday 10 October   This afternoon I went to Newcastle to preside over a meeting of our Conference sub-committee. We agreed that we should like to have the Conference in Newcastle next year – whether we get it or not remains to be seen. Ledingham tells me that feeling among Conservatives about the Czech business is mixed – a great many people are very uncomfortable about the whole thing and dislike giving way to Hitler exceedingly. He is sure that if the question arises of handing back colonies to Germany, there will be a split in the Party. Personally I have always been against any such policy and am more against it now than ever – Germany is quite powerful enough in Europe without being given anything more.

Thursday 13 October   I dined tonight at the Beefsteak ... George

Clerk[53] was there – most talkative and interesting. He told us the details about the Hoare-Laval business. He, Sam and Vansittart[54] met Laval – they agreed on the division of Abyssinia – the Italian Ambassador in Paris present: he agreed: rang up Ciano. he agreed: Mussolini agreed – then Sam instead of returning to London chose to go to Switzerland: the *Quai d'Orsay*[55] officials dying to get rid of Laval let the cat out of the bag – and the whole admirable scheme flopped – but for this the Ethiopian gent might still be an Emperor,[56] Mussolini might not have been Germany's friend and all our troubles might have [been] spared us.

Monday 17 October   I went up by the early train to see Tom Inskip ... he struck me as a helpless and hopeless man for his job: no wonder we are in our present state of unpreparedness with a man of this type to 'co-ordinate' defence – (I don't mind betting that he will go to the Woolsack[57] pretty soon!). Poor Edward Stanley's[58] death is reported today. he was a kindly, gentle soul – without an enemy in the world – and a man of good abilities and common sense, with everything in the world to make life worth living.

Tuesday 25 October   We drove to Grasse [on the French riviera] and had luncheon with Sir John and Lady Power.[59] She is rather a nice, sensible woman: he of course is a common little creature with an over-weaning conceit – to listen to him one might imagine that

---

[53] George Russell Clerk (1874–1951), diplomatic service; Min. to Czechoslovakia 1919–26; Amb. in Constantinople 1926–33, in Brussels 1933–34, in Paris 1934–37; kt. 1917.

[54] Robert Gilbert Vansittart (1881–1957), entered diplomatic service 1902; Ass. U.S. For. Office 1928–30, Perm. U.S. 1930–38; Chief Diplomatic Adviser to For. Sec. 1938–41; kt. 1929, cr. Baron Vansittart 1941.

[55] The location of the French Foreign Ministry, by which it is commonly known.

[56] Haile Selassie (1892–1975), Emporer of Ethiopia 1930–74; exiled in Britain during Italian occupation 1936–41; deposed by army coup 1974.

[57] Be elevated to Lord Chancellor; Inskip was a prominent lawyer.

[58] Edward Montagu Cavendish Stanley (1894–1938), Con. M.P. Liverpool Abercromby 1917–18, Fylde 1922–38; Whip 1924–27; P.S. Admiralty 1931–35, 1935–37; U.S. Dominions 1935; U.S. India 1937–38; Dominions Sec. 1938; Con. Party Dep. Chairman 1927–29; Chairman, Junior Imperial League 1928–33, & Pres. 1933–38; styled Lord Stanley 1908–38, eldest son of 17th Earl of Derby, elder brother of Oliver Stanley.

[59] John Cecil Power (1870–1950), Con. M.P. Wimbledon 1924–45; Treasurer, Royal Institute of International Affairs 1921–43; cr. Bart. 1924.

he was one of the men who really counted in the formation of British foreign policy. If one believed him all the great ones come to him for advice and it has only been when they neglected it that troubles have arisen! ... However, he meant to be very pleasant and civil and entertained us for all he was worth. He told us that the experts had assured the Government that had we gone to war the other day, we might have expected a quarter of a million casualties in London alone during the first fortnight so grotesquely inadequate were the air defences. If this is true, it shows how necessary it was to maintain the peace – but how truly disgraceful it is that we should be in such a helpless position – after all, we have been rearming for three years now and by this time surely, had there been any proper direction of defence, the defence against air raids should have been as adequate as was possible?

Thursday 27 October   Harold [Macmillan]'s book is so terribly dull (*The Middle Way*) that I find it almost impossible to read – let alone digest.

Friday 28 October   It seems that Jim Stanhope[60] is to be First Lord of the Admiralty and De La Warr[61] is to succeed him at the Board of Education. It is rather galling to see Stanhope get the Admiralty – galling for me – he has succeeded where I failed -and all because S.B. was so fond of him and disliked me.[62] I like Jim Stanhope, but I have no opinion of his ability – he is a very conscientious, hard-working hack – and it seems to me absurd that he should go on steadily rising in the hierarchy as he does. De La Warr of course is nothing at all except a representative of 'National Labour' – why at a moment like this when men of real ability and drive are called for Neville should make appointments of this kind

---

[60] James Richard Stanhope (1880–1967), P.S. War Office 1918–19; Civil Ld., Admiralty 1924–29; P.S. Admiralty 1931; U.S. War Office 1931–34; U.S. For. Office 1934–36; 1st Comm. Works 1936–37; Pres. Bd. Educ. 1937–38; 1st Lord of Admiralty 1938–39; Lord Pres. 1939–40; styled Viscount Mahon 1880–1905, suc. 7th Earl Stanhope 1905, suc. 13th Earl of Chesterfield 1952, K.G. 1934.

[61] Herbrand Edward Dundonald Brassey Sackville (1900–1976), Lab. Peer (Nat. Lab. from 1931); U.S. War Office 1929–30; P.S. Agric. 1930–35; P.S. Educ. 1935–36; P.S. Colonies 1936–37; Lord Privy Seal 1937–38; Pres. Bd. of Educ. 1938–40; 1st Comm. Works 1940; Postmaster-Gen. 1951–55; Chairman, Nat. Lab. Party 1931–43; styled Lord Buckhurst 1900–1915, suc. 9th Earl De La Warr 1915.

[62] Stanhope and Headlam had both been junior ministers at the Admiralty in 1926–29.

defeats me – I suppose he feels that the more dullards he has in high places, the easier it will be for him to run the show as he likes.

3

THE APPROACH OF WAR

November 1938 to August 1939

Friday 11 November 1938   Armistice Day – and what a world today after those strenuous years of war. How little one thought that all that expenditure of blood and treasure would have so little result – that 20 years after we shall be, to all appearances, on the brink of another war. How helpless and hopeless we have all been since 1918 – in my heart of hearts during the war I always felt that we should learn nothing from our experiences – that as soon as peace came the cranks and fools would again obtain control – and they did – they shrieked for disarmament and pinned their faith in the League of Nations. They shut their eyes to the inevitable – and now here we are again *vis à vis*[1] with Germany as we were in 1914 – only today our position is infinitely more dangerous as a result of air warfare – God knows what may be in store for us – pray that yet again he will see that England is preserved despite her follies and her thoughtlessness.

Sunday 13 November   The papers are full of the Nazi Jew-baiting – the Jews are to be fined £80 millions, not to be allowed to go to places of entertainment or to do business in Germany, and the hundreds who are being sent to concentration camps are to be made to pay for their keep while in detention. It really is too appalling that such brutalities should go on in the 20th century – I don't see how we can go on trying to come to terms with a government capable of such atrocious injustice and cruelty. Public opinion in England simply won't stand it.

[1] translation: face to face.

Wednesday 16 November   The German press has been let loose on us in revenge for the outcry against the persecution of the Jews in Germany – we are accused of having committed every imaginable brutality in South Africa, Ireland, India, Palestine, etc. It is all too ridiculous, but typical of Nazi mentality and I suppose calculated to stir up public opinion in Germany against us – of course all this makes a policy of appeasement out of the question for the time being – or possibly at all – and then what will happen?

Monday 21 November   I went to Newcastle after luncheon for the Area Executive committee meeting. It was rather 'dramatic' – Alfred Appleby turned up and thought fit to explain why he and Leith refused to open their purse strings (the purse strings of their respective funds) to assist the Area in propaganda work. It was not a very successful effort and I fancy that he did himself considerable harm – however, this does not help me get money and money we must have if the Area is to do anything useful.

Thursday 24 November   I feel so utterly despondent at the moment that I have no vim left in me. It is not so much about my own personal concerns that I am in the glooms – it is because I cannot see a glimmer of light on the political horizon. I simply cannot see how another war is to be avoided, unless we keep giving way to the Berlin–Rome axis. The state of France is quite lamentable and we ourselves are so terribly unready: I don't see how any government here could risk a war now – or for some time to come – and unless one is prepared to fight, one cannot hope to be able to cope with dictators. They may be bluffing, but one is not in a position to call their bluff unless one has confidence in one's own ability to stand up to them if it should be necessary. One always had a lingering hope that we were more ready for a war than was generally supposed – but the recent crisis showed one only too clearly that we are not ready, or even approaching readiness, for a war.

Wednesday 30 November   Harry [Crookshank] tells me that the split in the Party over foreign affairs is pretty grim – he himself is anti-Neville I gather – indeed, resigned but was prevailed upon to stay after Neville had withdrawn all the palaver about 'peace with honour' and 'peace for our time'. He tells us that Anthony Eden when at the F.O. was always urging the Cabinet to go ahead, full speed, at rearmament – but they wouldn't – Anthony, therefore, is in the right and Anthony is the coming man. I wonder?

Thursday 1 December   Charley Londonderry and the youngest daughter were on my train – needless to say, a compartment was reserved for them and the Station Master escorted them to it – the same ceremony at York where we changed! ... I told Charley about the Leith–Appleby money business: needless to say he did not in the least appreciate what it was all about: he is no more use to me than a sick headache in the north: he grows, I think, if possible more stupid and vain every day and more entirely self-centred – and yet one can't help liking the man – he really does try to be a good citizen!

Thursday 15 December   I had no engagement today except to dine with the Central Newcastle Association people at the County Hotel, Newcastle – an annual function. Last year Basil Dufferin[2] was the guest of honour – this year it was to have been Rob Hudson[3] – but he had to scratch at the last minute as there is some Exports Credits Bill in the House tonight – his substitute in Newcastle was Sir George Broadbridge[4] (I think the name is right – ex-Lord Mayor of London and now M.P. for the City of London). He is a common little man with a cockney accent and he made a terribly dreary (*Hints-for-Speakers*)[5] speech which bored everyone stiff. It does seem to me a pity to send such second rate people (just because they happen to be M.P.s) to functions of this kind.

Saturday 17 December   I attended the annual meeting of the Durham County British Legion this afternoon in the Town Hall

[2] Basil Sheridan Hamilton-Temple-Blackwood (1909–45), P.P.S. to Lord Irwin (Viscount Halifax) 1932–36; Whip in the Lords 1936–37; U.S. Colonies 1937–40; suc. 4th Marquess of Dufferin & Ava 1930, killed in action in Burma 25 March 1945.
[3] Robert Spear Hudson (1886–1957), Con. M.P. Whitehaven 1924–29, Southport 1931–52; P.S. Labour 1931–35; Min. of Pensions 1935–36; P.S. Health 1936–37; Sec. Overseas Trade 1937–40; Min. of Shipping 1940; Min. of Agric 1940–45; cr. Viscount Hudson 1952.
[4] George Thomas Broadbridge (1869–1952), Con. M.P. City of London 1938–45; Sheriff of City of London 1933–34, Lord Mayor 1936–37; kt. 1929, cr. Bart. 1937, Baron Broadbridge 1945.
[5] A Central Office publication containing basic material for speeches.

... Whatever any of the politicians may say or do, the man in the street has made up his mind about Hitler & co. He will have nothing more to do with them, regarding them as gangsters and brutes unworthy of intercourse with decent people – and they [*sic*] fail to appreciate the hold such people have obtained over the German people. They believe that the German working men are being ground down under a ruthless tyranny and are longing to be rid of their oppressors.

Tuesday 20 December   Dined with Ross Taylor[6] (M.P.): a very decent fellow. He is giving up the HofC after this Parliament: tired to death of the place, its intrigues, etc. He knows little of this uprising of the junior Ministers – according to Edward Stanley of Alderley,[7] Rob Hudson went to Neville privately and said that he and other junior Ministers including Basil Dufferin and Don Strathcona[8] were dissatisfied with Tom Inskip, Hore-Belisha, etc. Neville shocked and surprised: consulted Sam Hoare who gave the whole business away to Beaverbrook – hence the publicity.

Saturday 24 December   The Duchess of Atholl[9] has been beaten and all the Government's supporters are in high fettle, which is natural as she was definitely seeking confirmation of her disapproval of Neville's foreign policy. It is suggested that the snow on the hills was the main cause of her defeat. This may be so – but it scarcely explains a majority of over a 1,000 against her.

Saturday 7 January 1939   Agnes [Headlam-Morley] is full of Germany as usual – all the people she has just seen in Berlin, she says, are disgusted with the Nazi regime and ashamed of the treatment of the Jews, etc., etc. I have no doubt that this is the case; no decent people can care about such a form of government

[6] Walter Ross Taylor (1877–1958), Con. M.P. Woodbridge 1931–45.
[7] Edward John Stanley (1907–1971), suc. 6th Baron Stanley of Alderley 1931, assumed style of 6th Baron Sheffield 1957.
[8] Donald Sterling Palmer Howard (1891–1959), Con. M.P. Cumberland N. 1922–26; P.P.S. to H. Betterton, 1923–24, to W. Bridgeman 1925; U.S. War Office 1934–39; suc. 3rd Baron Strathcona and Mount Royal 1926.
[9] Katharine Marjorie Stewart Murray (1874–1960), married 1899 Marquess of Tullibardine, suc. 8th Duke of Atholl 1917; Con. M.P. Kinross & W. Perth 1923–38 (resigned Con. whip May-October 1935 & from April 1938 and sat as Ind. Con.); P.S. Educ. 1924–29; the first woman to hold office in a Con. ministry.

as Hitler's – unfortunately 'decent people' don't cut much ice anywhere nowadays, least of all in Germany.

Friday 13 January Little Mr. Glossop[10] has retired from his candidature at Berwick after paying visits on 30,000 constituents: apparently he has been offered a safe seat nearer home and has decided quite wisely to take it. The spirit moved me to write a line to Leonard Milburn[11] saying that I should like to have my name considered – why I wrote I cannot make out as I have always said that I would never stand again for a big agricultural constituency – Berwick is a good deal bigger than B[arnard] C[astle] and will take a lot of working – nor is it anything like a safe seat. Its advantage is that money does not enter into the picture, as the Association pays the election expenses – so if they take me and I take the plunge, I shall not have to go hat in hand to Alec Leith and the Central Office.

Saturday 14 January I drove to Carlisle and back today for the [Cumberland] annual county committee meeting ... I lunched with Fergus Graham at the County Club which was, as usual, full of pot-bellied, blue-nosed old gents at the top of their form. ... [Spears] is annoying all the Carlisle people because he is becoming more and more anti-Government – it is rather tiresome especially for Fergus in North Cumberland, as Spears's speeches are used by the Liberals against him.

Sunday 15 January The Bishop,[12] Mrs. Henson ... and the Chaplain lunched here today – their farewell visit – rather a sad business. The poor little man is so dreadfully sorry to be going away – presumably he is right to resign if he feels that he is no longer fit for his job, but to the outsider he seems as vigorous and full of life as ever. He is one of the most remarkable men I have ever met, and intellectually immeasurably superior to most of his

---

[10] Clifford William Hudson Glossop (1901–1975), Con. M.P. Penistone 1931–35, Howdenshire 1945–47, prospective cand. Berwick 1936–38; N.E. Area Meat & Livestock Officer 1940–44.

[11] Leonard John Milburn (1884–1957), High Sheriff of Northumberland 1928–29; suc. 3rd Bart. 1917.

[12] Herbert Hensley Henson (1863–1947), Canon of Westminster 1900–12, 1940–41; Dean of Durham 1912–18; Bishop of Hereford 1918–20; Bishop of Durham 1920–39: one of the most prominent clergymen of the inter-war era.

contemporaries in high places. Had he only been more judicious – more judicially minded – he would have reigned at Lambeth.[13] He is too vigorous a controversialist, too much of a partisan not to have made a host of enemies and critics. The world does not care for people who speak out too openly, even if they speak the truth – Henson has always enjoyed a conflict of words, and has always spoken his mind. I dislike his leaving here intensely because – even if I disagree with him and I often do so – I enjoy talking with him. He has a great sense of humour and is very human when you get to know him well. He will be greatly missed, I think, even if his successor is the wonder he is painted – because he is such a live wire, so full of pluck and original in his outlook.

Wednesday 18 January   I don't fancy that world peace has come any closer as the result of the Rome talks.[14] Everything now depends on what happens in Spain – if Musso plays the game and carries out what appears to have been his pledge to Neville to remove his troops from Spain as soon as Franco has won, all should be well ... Our policy should be to get on the right side of Franco and leave it to him to rid himself of his Italian and German allies – this will be a difficult business (a) because people in England are so foolishly hostile to Franco, and (b) because Franco may find it embarrassing to rid himself of his allies in view of the strength of the Fascist element among his own supporters. Our best hope is our ability to give financial assistance to Spain when it is required.

Friday 20 January   L.G. let himself go in a speech yesterday – a really scandalous performance – abusing Neville in the most disgusting way. No one pays any attention here to this horrid little man who is rightly regarded as being in his dotage – but he has been Prime Minister and a great power in the land, and abroad his remarks are noted and made use of. It is a pity, therefore, that he cannot be restrained – or, better still, removed to another world, where he could go on telling all and sundry how much abler, and wiser, and braver he had been on earth than other men. I think when history is properly written his place will not be very high – when historians weigh him in the balance his claim to fame will

---

[13] Lambeth Palace, official residence of the Archbishop of Canterbury.
[14] The visit of Neville Chamberlain and Lord Halifax to Rome, 10 Jan. 1939.

not be very high – for he played his own game throughout his career – he had I suppose political acumen – but no balance and no judgement – power to influence the crowd, but not to convince the wise.

Saturday 21 January   I went to Newcastle and attended the Northumberland county annual meeting, presided over by Alfred Appleby who was looking seedy ... There was a poor attendance. Ledingham expressed himself strongly in favour of my standing for Berwick. I can't make up my mind about it – but am inclined to stand – though if I do so decide, I feel pretty confident that North Newcastle will soon become vacant, and then how angry I shall be!

Tuesday 31 January   I went to Alnwick ... and was 'interviewed' by Leonard Milburn and his Committee. It was rather a futile business, but inevitable. They interviewed seven people altogether ... This took all the afternoon ... I returned and gave a short address to the 'Council' – about 70 people present. It was not a very excellent performance but apparently it was better than that of either of the others – at any rate, I was selected for recommendation to the Association on the 16th of February. So there it is: I have burnt my boats and, as sure as eggs are eggs, old Grattan-Doyle will now die or resign his seat or something, and I shall miss any chance of North Newcastle. This Berwick seat will mean a lot of work and is by no means an easy proposition.

Thursday 2 February   Beatrice and I attended the luncheon and annual meeting of the Area Women's Advisory Committee at the County Hotel today – a dreary business. Circe was in the chair – somewhat of a surprise visit – they say the reason of it being that some of the women had been suggesting that Mabel Grey should take her place as President! We had a speech from Circe – quite a long story – as usual read out (indifferently) from notes. ... Circe at luncheon ... as usual full of herself and critical of M.[15] who, she told me, was overdoing it like R.[16] – odd for a mother to speak so openly about a matter of this kind. She professes herself to be

---

[15] Maureen Stanley, Lady Londonderry's daughter.
[16] Edward Charles Stewart Robert Vane-Tempest-Stewart (1902–1955), Con. cand. Darlington 1929, M.P. Co. Down 1931–45; styled Viscount Castlereagh 1915–49, suc. 8th Marquess of Londonderry 1949; known as Robin, he had a drink problem.

extremely nervous as to what may happen to M. during her approaching lecturing trip to the Balkans. I of course think it ridiculous to send her on such a trip – to promote English culture forsooth! – she is the wife of a Cabinet minister – not too discrete and young and attractive – one feels that she is quite capable of making a bloomer and then the fat might well be in the fire.

Friday 10 February   ... attended a meeting of the N.E. Board Development Executive Committee ... Eustace Percy[17] present, looking as fat and dirty as ever – pompous and unforthcoming. He certainly evinces no friendliness towards us: I cannot imagine why this should be.

Saturday 11 February   I went into Newcastle this afternoon and attended the annual meeting of the Area Labour Advisory Committee at which I gave a short address. It was a very good meeting, well attended. They passed a sound resolution abolishing the county Labour committees – I hope that this may be the beginning of the end of the county organizations.

Thursday 16 February   Beatrice and I went to my adoption meeting at Berwick today ... There was a gathering of about seventy ladies and gents which I addressed – and I was duly adopted – everyone was very friendly – but I doubt whether I shall succeed in winning the seat – opinions on the matter very tremendously – some say that I shall walk in, others that I have not got a ghost of a chance. Well – only time can show which is the correct opinion – my own view is that, *if there is a contest*, it will be a very close one.

Saturday 18 February   I don't believe for a moment that Hitler does not intend to carry on with his *Mein Kampf*[18] programme, despite his assurances to Neville. His obvious game is to act

[17] Eustace Sutherland Campbell Percy (1887–1958), Con. M.P. Hastings 1921–37; P.S. Educ. 1923; P.S. Health 1923–24; Pres. Bd. of Educ. 1924–29; Min. without Portfolio 1935–36; Rector of King's College, Newcastle 1937–52; styled Lord Eustace after suc. of father as 7th Duke of Northumberland in 1899, cr. Baron Percy of Newcastle 1953.
[18] The book containing Hitler's ideas and programme, written whilst in prison in 1923–24, which became the key text of the Nazi Party.

quickly – to keep moving – not to wait until we are stronger. To me it seems that this Year of Grace 1939 is the crucial year – if we can get through it without a war, we shall be lucky – if we have a war, we shall have to go through a very bad time. We are miserably unprepared, and my own belief is that the Germans, and probably the Italians, are ready. They will simply march through the Balkans – I doubt, indeed, whether any of the Balkan peoples will even venture to stand up to them. And then? God only knows – I don't – by all the rules we ought to be down and out – and yet somehow or other I feel that even with the Germans on the shores of the Black Sea it will only be the beginning of the war.

Monday 27 February   I was asked to take the chair at a meeting of Northumberland constituencies to consider the holding of a big demonstration at Gosforth Park in the summer to be addressed by a Cabinet Minister. We began by going through the names of the Cabinet – and eventually it was decided that only 2 of them were worth having – *viz*. Halifax and Chatfield[19] (I wish the others could have heard the discussion).

Wednesday 15 March   From what one reads in the papers today the newest Hitler coup is upon us. These wretched Slovaks are clearly going to secede from the Czechs – and of course this will give Hitler his chance to walk in. ... I fear that this will be the death knell of poor Neville's policy of appeasement, and equally of course all his opponents will say 'I told you so!' It is also the end, I should imagine, of any further dealing with Hitler – the man henceforward should be treated as outside the pale – and when we are strong enough should be fought.

Saturday 18 March   A fine speech by Neville at Birmingham last night – he stood by his Munich policy – and then let Hitler have it straight from the shoulder – clearly the 'appeasement policy' is now at an end – it remains to be seen how long it will be before war comes, for I cannot see any stopping the German bid for world hegemony short of stopping it by force of arms. ... But we are to

[19] (Alfred) Ernle Montacute Chatfield (1873–1967), entered Navy 1886, Rear-Admiral 1920, Vice-Admiral 1930, Admiral 1935; 4th Sea Lord 1919–20; 3rd Sea Lord 1925–28; C. in C. Atlantic 1929–31, Med. 1931–32; 1st Sea Lord 1933–38; Min. for Co-ordination of Defence 1938–40; kt. 1918, cr. Baron Chatfield 1937.

blame for Hitlerism – there's no doubt about that – and by *we* I mean the English nation, and its cranks, faddists, fools and futilities who have misled it and deceived it since the Armistice.

Thursday 23 March   Hitler has now possessed himself of Memel.[20] This of course was inevitable and one has been expecting it for some time past – the Lithuanians had no kind of right to be there and it has really been in the hands of the German population for the last year or so – still his seizing it immediately after his Czech coup is maddening and has increased the tension. It is a very nerve-wracking time – especially so, I imagine, for people of my age. One feels so futile nowadays with nothing to do – no work of national importance whatsoever and seemingly no chance of getting it. Even in Durham County no one appears to feel disposed to ask me to take on any job. There is an enormous committee in being to promote and organize nat. service.[21] Charley is its president, but has handed it over to Alderman Smith and his friends. The Ministry of Labour appears to be running the show – why I cannot imagine – was there ever such confusion and stupidity as reign here today – and with such leaders as Sir J. Anderson[22] and Ernest Brown[23] is it to be wondered at? I suppose we must grin and bear it all – and wait and see.

Friday 24 March   I attended the opening of the Area Political School by Ben Cruddas[24] at Whitley Bay this afternoon, and proposed a vote of thanks to him. Then I went on to Lesbury where I addressed quite a good meeting of Conservative workers and others ... I talked with all and sundry after the meeting, and

[20] A Baltic port which had been part of Prussia and then Germany until 1919.

[21] In preparation for military conscription if needed, but at this point compulsory service was not applied and registration was voluntary.

[22] John Anderson (1882–1958), civil service career; Chairman Bd. of Inland Revenue 1919–22; Perm. U.S. Home Office 1922–32; Gov. of Bengal 1932–37; Nat. M.P. Scottish Univ. 1938–50; Lord Privy Seal 1938–39; Home Sec. 1939–40; Lord Pres. 1940–43; Chanc. of the Exchequer 1943–45; kt. 1919, cr. Viscount Waverley 1952.

[23] (Alfred) Ernest Brown (1881–1962), Lib. M.P. Rugby 1923–24, Leith 1927–45 (Lib. Nat. from 1931); P.S. Health 1931–32; Sec. for Mines 1932–35; Min. of Labour 1935–40; Scottish Sec. 1940–41; Min. of Health 1941–43; Chanc. Duchy of Lancaster 1943–45; Min. of Aircraft Production 1945.

[24] Bernard Cruddas (1882–1959), Con. M.P. Wansbeck 1931–40; High Sheriff of Northumberland 1942.

then went on with Milburn ... to the 'Supper Club' at Alnwick – about forty men representing the town's social and business activities. Here I was given a meal and spoke again ... afterwards I answered a few questions and talked with the gents ... one feels that the country is now really roused and that no government can afford to shut its eyes to the force of public opinion – if Hitler continues his present policy, war is inevitable.

Monday 27 March   ... it looks to me more than likely that I shall never stand for the Berwick division – I feel more or less certain in my own mind that some sort of combination will be formed in the national emergency that will make it necessary for me to stand down and allow Seely[25] a walk-over. I have no luck as a politician.

Wednesday 29 March   The Government has plumped for doubling the T[erritorial] A[rmy] and we are to have no compulsion for our splendid patriotic democracy – as usual the call is made on the willing citizen and the shirk and slacker get away with it. It is a pitiable business – but all the silly press seem delighted. Ye Gods – are all the good men to be sacrificed again as they were in the last war just because the T.U.C. and the Labour Party and the old-fashioned Liberals dislike conscription and consider it beneath the dignity of an Englishman to serve his country unless it pleases him? ... The country is ready for conscription whatever the politicians may think to the contrary.

Thursday 30 March   ... attended the Conservative National Union meeting in the Central Hall, Westminster, where I proposed Charley Londonderry as President for the year – he was present and made a courteous reply![26] Neville was to have come and made

[25] Hugh Michael Seely (1898–1970), Lib. M.P. Norfolk E. 1923–24, Berwick 1935–41; P.P.S. to A. Sinclair 1940–41; U.S. Air 1941–45; suc. 3rd Bart. 1926, cr. Baron Sherwood 1941.

[26] This position was held by the various Areas in rotation, and due to this unwritten convention normally no other nomination would be made.

a speech, but sent word by Alec Dunglass[27] that he could not get away from the Cabinet meeting – there have been two meetings of the Cabinet today, so presumably they are making up their great minds what to do if the Germans go for Danzig[28] which seems to be the next move anticipated. The doubling of the T.A. has got a good press – it is a ridiculous step unless it is a prelude to conscription – I doubt whether they get the men – they certainly will not be able to maintain such a force very long in normal times – and then all the drill halls, etc., which they will now build will be pulled down or sold, until another scare comes. The soldiers at the W[ar] O[ffice] are just as silly about conscription as are the trade union leaders – and neither the soldiers or the trade unionists should be considered. If they (the Govt.) had only asked for an enabling bill or made the National register compulsory, I could have understood their doubling the T.A.

Friday 31 March   Neville made a declaration in the House this afternoon of great importance – stating that we and the French would 'in the event of any action which clearly threatened Polish independence which the Polish Government accordingly considered it vital to resist with their national forces . . .'[29] feel ourselves bound 'at once to lend the Polish Govt. all support' in our power. So now possibly the next European war may arise in defence of the Polish corridor![30] How odd that would be – apparently all sides in the HofC were delighted with this announcement.

Saturday 1 April   . . . a leader in *The Times*, written it would

---

[27] Alexander Frederick Douglas-Home (1903–1995), Con. M.P. Lanark 1931–45, 1950–51, Kinross & W. Perth 1963–74; P.P.S. to N. Chamberlain 1935–40; U.S. For. Office 1945; M.S. Scotland 1951–55; Commonwealth Sec. 1955–60; Lord Pres. 1957, 1959–60; For. Sec. 1960–63, 1970–74; P.M. 1963–64; Con. Leader in the Lords 1957–60; Con. Leader 1963–65; styled Lord Dunglass 1918–51, suc. 14th Earl of Home 1951, disclaimed peerage 1963, cr. Baron Home of the Hirsel 1974, K.T. 1962.

[28] Situated at the mouth of the River Vistula on the Baltic, Danzig was a Prussian city from the partition of Poland in 1793 to the Treaty of Versailles in 1919. It was then internationalised as a 'Free City', administered by a League of Nations Commissioner, as part of giving Poland a 'corridor' of access to the sea.

[29] The ellipsis in is Headlam's original text.

[30] The Versailles Treaty created the 'corridor' in order to ensure that Poland had independent access to the Baltic, but the territory was mainly German in population and also divided East Prussia from the rest of the Reich.

appear to water down the P.M.'s assurance to Poland – a pity – but *The Times* is a terrible wobbler, and its article may not be inspired – it is to be hoped not at any rate.

Sunday 2 April   The foreign situation absorbs me: I cannot see how war is to be avoided much longer, unless we retire into our shell and allow Hitler and Musso to divide Europe between them – not since the days of Napoleon have two such filibusters appeared on the scene. My own view is that we shall have to take them on sooner or later, and that perhaps the sooner the better – for each new act of aggression (if we do nothing) will make it more difficult to induce the smaller nations of Europe to come in against them. The trouble of course is that we are still unready for war and really have no important ally except France whom we cannot help properly and who would have to bear the brunt of things at the beginning of a war. If only Russia were trustworthy, and the U.S.A. would play the game, I would not hesitate to challenge the next act of aggression – as things are, however, I can quite understand the difficulty in which the Government is faced. It must feel a deal stronger before it can act with decision – and, meanwhile, we must try and preserve our equanimity and go on preparing for war. Rather a sorry position – but there it is. Time presumably is on our side – for neither Germany, nor Italy, nor Japan is really sufficiently strong financially or politically for [*sic*] keeping up a state of war indefinitely – at least I hope not.

Friday 7 April   Italy has had a go at Albania – she has apparently sent 30,000 troops there – seized the ports – and is pushing forward into the interior. This information came on the wireless – and this in spite of our recent agreement with her regarding the *status quo* in the Mediterranean. It is all pretty intolerable, but there it is – we have just got to make up our minds to the fact that Hitler and Musso are two desperate and untrustworthy knaves who will stick at nothing to gain their ends and that it is useless trusting to any agreement made by them.

Saturday 8 April   ... Musso's men are in complete control of the country – a very successful coup for the B[erlin]-R[ome] Axis – and no reply to it from us so far as I can see, short of going to war – and presumably we shall not go as far as that. It will be interesting to see what happens next and how long it will be before the next coup comes. It is all very humiliating – but we have only our own foolish selves to thank – Bob Cecil, Gilbert Murray[31] & Co., Baldwin-Simon-Eden-MacDonald, the Labour Party and the Paci fists are all equally responsible for the present situation – but to me Baldwin in the arch-culprit and I fancy that history will so judge.

Monday 10 April   The Government has summoned Parliament to meet – evidently this Albanian coup has upset Neville & co. – the policy of appeasement is finally at an end – but unless we have conscription I don't see how we are to cry halt to the aggressors – and, even if we do, it will be some time before we can put an army in the field. President Roosevelt[32] has made a pronouncement asking Hitler to be a good boy – it will be interesting to see what the reply will be – what is wanted is a definite assurance that the U.S.A. will intervene.

Monday 17 April   We have agreed to support Poland if she is attacked and considers her national independence threatened. This is a big step forward ... They mean, I suppose, that we shall declare war on Germany if she goes for Poland – does this mean that we are to fight for the retention of the Polish corridor? Surely not – and yet the Poles might well say that its being taken by Germany meant the end of their national independence. I give it up – one can only hope and believe that Neville and Edward Wood[33] are not fools and know what they are about. It is always a consolation to know that those in charge of affairs have information which is not possessed by the man in the street, and are therefore in a position to make decisions which otherwise would appear to be ludicrous and futile. The negotiations with Russia are reported to be going on satisfactorily and also those with Turkey – the latter to my mind are of real importance, for a good understanding with

---

[31] (George) Gilbert Aime Murray (1866–1957), Prof. of Greek, Glasgow Univ 1889–99; Regius Prof. of Greek, Oxford Univ. 1908–36; Lib. cand. Oxford Univ. 1918–29; Chairman, Exec. Council, League of Nations Union 1923–38; Pres., United Nations Association 1945–49.

[32] Franklin Delano Roosevelt (1882–1945), Ass. Sec., U.S. Navy 1913–20; Gov. of New York State 1929–33; Pres. of U.S.A. 1933–45.

[33] Lord Halifax, the Foreign Secretary.

Turkey is essential for us in the eastern Mediterranean.

Thursday 27 April   This morning I went to the British Council and saw Charles Bridge[34] and George Lloyd[35] – the former is General Secretary, the latter Chairman. They both take themselves and the B.C. very seriously – and the latter was as usual the 'dynamic' personality! I suppose there is something to the man, but I confess that he does not ever impress me very greatly. I got my ticket money, etc., and the blessing of the B.C.[36] The Government has decided upon a mild measure of conscription – oddly enough it is to be vigorously opposed by the Labour Party, acting by order of the T.U.C. Personally I am sure that the country will be behind the Govt. and would gladly fight an election on it – however, one is not likely to be called upon to do so.

Saturday 29 April 1939   ... undoubtedly the Jews have far too much influence – politically and in the press – both in England and in the U.S.A.

Friday 12 May   Tonight we have all dined at the 'Aviz', the swell hotel of Lisbon, as the guests of Lord Rothermere. He gave us a very good dinner and was very friendly – I forgot, I think, to note that I met him at lunch at the Embassy last week and was agreeably surprised by the man. He is grotesque to look upon and obviously a coarse type – but less aggressive than one imagined – perhaps age has mellowed him. He is a veritable Cassandra, prophesying war in the very near future and the end of the British Empire – but, if I recollect rightly, this has always been his attitude.

Thursday 18 May   This morning I had an interview with Edward Halifax at the F.O. and gave him my impressions of Portugal. He seemed more familiar with things there than I expected – but, as

---

[34] Charles Edward Dunscomb Bridge (1886–1961), army career 1904–28, Gen. Staff 1915, Lt.-Col. 1918; Military Attache, Warsaw & Prague 1927–28, Rome 1940; Sec.-Gen., British Council 1934–40.

[35] George Ambrose Lloyd (1879–1941), Con. M.P. Staffs. W. 1910–18, Eastbourne 1924–25; Gov. of Bombay 1918–23; High Comm. for Egypt & the Sudan 1925–29; Colonial Sec. 1940–41; Con. Leader in the Lords 1941; Chairman, British Council 1937–40; kt. 1918, cr. Baron Lloyd 1925.

[36] From 29 April to 16 May 1939 Headlam visited Portugal to deliver a series of lectures on the British Army.

usual with all of us, took it for granted that we could count with complete assurance on our old Allies.[37] I emphasized the importance of playing up to them a bit – e.g., an invitation to the President to stay here from the King, a D.C.L. Oxon.[38] for Salazar.[39] ... He seemed fit and well – and he gives one confidence – a man of character not to be bustled – at the moment the only possible Conservative P.M. should Neville pass out. He seems to think that the situation is a bit less gloomy for the time being. He clearly dislikes the Russian alliance as much as I do – but considers that it should be effected, if reasonably possible, in order to satisfy public opinion here and to maintain unity as far as possible.

Saturday 3 June   The more I think over things, the more I am convinced that the only solution of all the German worry is in a conference – though I doubt myself whether it is not too late in the day for one. The Nazis have now got blood to the head and have put themselves in a position regarding Danzig which will make it difficult to back down unless some face-saving can be done and this may not be easy to bring about now that we have pledged ourselves to the Poles – still in his heart of hearts every sane Englishman must realize that it would be grotesque and wicked to start a European war over the matter of Danzig and the Polish Corridor. But I don't see the country standing for another Hitler coup. People now regard him as a reincarnation of Napoleon. The agreement with Russia still hangs fire and I personally should not feel particularly unhappy if it were not brought off.

Saturday 10 June   [at Birch Grove] Dorothy Macmillan as friendly as ever – also Harold – as usual he is disparaging the Government. He assures me that a break-up of the Conservative Party is inevitable – that the feeling against Neville is gaining strength, etc. He is more than ever disgruntled – even trade, his trade,[40] is bad – there is no hope anywhere. Tonight Beatrice and I ... went to Glyndebourne ... there were other people we knew there including

---

[37] The Anglo-Portugese Alliance had been in existence since 1642.

[38] The honorary degree of Doctor of Civil Laws, from Oxford University.

[39] António de Oliveira Salazar (1889–1970), Portugese Min. of Finance 1928–32; P.M. 1932–68, with dictatorial powers; For. Minister 1936–47.

[40] The publishing firm of Macmillan.

David Margesson's wife[41] whom we have not seen for ages – she does not live with David any longer for which I don't blame her.

Sunday 11 June   This morning I spent (as usual when I am here) in the gloomy library reading the Sunday newspapers ... After dinner we had to watch a film (no endless films) depicting Dorothy's travels in Kenya – this is a new form of horror which unhappy guests are expected to enjoy in country house parties.

Wednesday 14 June   As I was in London I felt that I better stay for a meeting of the Executive Committee at Palace Chambers. It was a more than usually dull affair – opened by a speech from Sir John Anderson on A[ir] R[aid] P[recautions]. He told us nothing that we did not know and displayed a quite uncalled-for optimism. He was sleek and common – but no doubt he is a superman – incidentally, he is becoming extremely pot-bellied. I gather that it is the intention (all being well) to have a general election at the end of October – but I should imagine that the chance of all being well is very slight. This Tientsin[42] episode is worrying everyone – it is such a humiliating position for us to be in – we are now the plaything of the Germans, Japanese and Italians and they just toss us about as it suits them – playing their game very cleverly it must be admitted. How long is it to last?

Thursday 15 June   The Government announced its intention last night to set up a Ministry of Information which is all to the good – but why Eric Drummond (Perth) of all men should be put at the head of it, I cannot imagine. He is apparently supposed to know all about propaganda because he was so long at Geneva as Secretary of the League of Nations! It really is too absurd – if they had appointed the Secretary of the League of Nations *Union*[43] there

---

[41] Frances Leggett (d.1977), daughter of Francis Leggett of New York; married D. Margesson 1916, divorced 1940.

[42] The crisis began when the manager of the Japanese-sponsored Federal Reserve Bank was assassinated at the Grand Theatre in the British territorial concession at Tientsin in northern China. In order to force the British authorities to hand over the Chinese nationals arrested for the crime, the Japanese military began a blockade of the settlement on 14 June 1939 during which they inflicted humiliations upon British citizens attempting to enter or leave.

[43] An unofficial organization which fostered public support for the League of Nations, known for its large membership and effective propaganda .

might have been something to it – but why an ex-official, an ex-Ambassador, should be supposed to be a good man for propaganda purposes I cannot imagine – George Lloyd would have been an infinitely better selection. But it is always thus – one of the clique is invariably chosen and anyone who has a mind of his own is left on the shelf.

Friday 16 June　　The situation at Tientsin is becoming very annoying. Presumably the Government will take some action, but at present all we are told is that it is in touch with the French and American Governments neither of which I should imagine is likely to take any steps to influence the Japanese to behave themselves. It is a bad look-out, because obviously we cannot take anything like a firm attitude ourselves – action, I mean, which might lead to war -unless we can count on American naval assistance. I must admit that, if I were at the F.O., I should be in considerable doubt what to do – and yet I have it in my bones that the right course to pursue is to take a big risk – tell the Japanese that we were not going to be brow beaten and that, if they do not raise the blockade, we shall take whatever steps may be necessary to raise it ourselves. In other words, I believe that we should risk a war. I don't fancy that the Japanese want one – and I do believe that if we did have to face war, we should be more likely to get American assistance than if we go on taking things lying down. Probably I am all wrong!

Sunday 18 June　　The Japanese tension continues – what exactly their game is it is difficult to say – but presumably they are seeing just how far they can go, presuming that we are in no position to go to war with them – and therefore that the more they can succeed in making us 'lose face' the more they are likely to impress the Chinese. No doubt, too, they are acting in collusion with Rome and Berlin. It is a sorry position for us to be in – but time is on our side – and we can afford to lie low temporarily, provided that, when the time comes, we are determined to see things through. It is because one rather doubts our determination to stand up for ourselves that one feels gloomy at times – one belongs to a different age and one does not understand the present day attitude of mind in this country. War may be futile and immoral – whatever you like – but the British Empire was won by wars, and, unless we are prepared to defend it in arms, we shall lose it sure enough to more virile nations.

Friday 23 June   The Japanese are becoming ruder and ruder, and it is quite intolerable that they should be allowed to do as they are doing – stripping Englishmen in the presence of Chinese coolies and women, etc., etc. Tientsin is still blockaded and the situation is critical – it looks as if we should be obliged to take some vigorous action – and then presumably the fat will be in the fire. Presumably the Berlin-Rome axis is responsible for the whole of this nasty business and one feels that it is useless going on hoping that anything but war will end their troubling us.

Sunday 25 June   There is no news in the press except a speech by Neville at Cardiff in which he tells us that he is not going to stand the Japanese insults much longer. It seems to me he has stood them far too long – but what exactly he intends doing I cannot imagine.[44] We are in a very unpleasant position.

Saturday 15 July   I had breakfast at the Station Hotel and spent from 11 o'clock to a quarter to one listening to Sir R. Topping explaining how to run an election. We had quite a good attendance for this performance and it was not quite so deadly as might have been expected. Appleby gave us luncheon at the Station Hotel. He asked me to take the other end of a long table and sat with Topping and Alec Leith at the other end. The two old sinners were all over Topping – no doubt the hunt for the baronetcy is well on, and presumably it will be successful. .... The Area meeting (Council) went off all right this afternoon – a motion by Donald Scott in support of the Government's foreign policy was accepted unanimously, but an addition moved by Rebe Bradford[45] deploring the Churchill–Eden agitation aroused a good deal of discussion and was withdrawn. Many people think that the inclusion in the cabinet

---

[44] Despite this speech, the crisis was eventually ended by British concessions and a compromise accord was reached on 24 July.

[45] (Honor) Rebe Bradford (d.1943), Vice-Chairman, Womens Advisory Ctte., Northern Counties Area 1926–38, Chairman 1938–43; Vice-Chairman, Northern Counties Area 1938–43; became Lady Bradford after kt. of husband, Thomas Andrews Bradford, 1939.

of these 2 gents is urgently necessary for the national welfare.[46]

Wednesday 19 July   How I wish that I was still in the HofC no tongue can tell. It is maddening being out of everything at a time like this. In the HofC one always heard the news and could get at those who were able to give it – nowadays I see no one and no one ever writes to me. Out of sight, out of mind – not a single one of my political friends has proved worthy of the name of friend.

Monday 24 July   ... talked with Orme Sargent[47] of the F.O. after dinner. He was giving nothing away – but clearly was not hopeful. To me it looks as if we were heading straight for war. I doubt whether anything we can do or say will make much difference. Hitler and Co. are persuaded that the game is in their hands – and the Russians, I believe, are just playing with us. Japan is in the game, too, and the U.S.A. won't play on our side.

Friday 28 July   Ledingham discussed North Newcastle and seems entirely at a loss how to prevent G[rattan] D[oyle] running in his son – and I, too, can see no way of preventing him unless we can get some help from people in the division.

Sunday 30 July   The more one hears about the Nazis, the more one loathes them. They are utterly foul and their creed is the Devil's own – surely they cannot last for long even in Germany?

Tuesday 1 August   The Nazis are more and more active in Danzig and their mobilization in Germany continues. How it can end in anything but war I fail to see. I suppose the issue now depends on the Poles – if they really mean business, we shall have no alternative

---

[46] The final sentence was written in a more critical form and then amended to this wording; the deleted words are partly obscured, but the original text appears to have read: 'It is odd why some people should think that the inclusion in the cabinet of these two gents should be so urgently necessary for the national welfare.' The alterations are in Headlam's hand, and could have been made at a later date with benefit of hindsight. It is more probable, however, that they were made at the time of the entry or very shortly afterwards: Headlam did not return to his diary entries and revise or sanitise them, and much sharper comments on both Churchill and Eden exist elsewhere without any changes having been made to them.

[47] Orme Garton Sargent (1884–1962), entered For. Office 1906, Head of Central Dept. 1928–33, Ass. Under-Sec. 1933–39, Dep. Under-Sec. 1939–46, Perm. Under-Sec. 1946–49; kt. 1937.

but to go in with them. I fancy that Hitler and co. fancy that they are strong enough to smash up the Poles in a few weeks, before we can do anything effective to help them. Then when the Germans have collared the corridor and Danzig and are probably in Warsaw, they think that we shall accept the *fait accompli*. This, it seems to me, is just what we cannot do – a German success in Poland will only be the opening phase in the war – but it must be very difficult to make the Nazis realize this.

Sunday 6 August   One cannot help feeling gloomy these days – nothing seems to go right and there is always this war cloud hanging over us all. I suppose that really we are at war and this is the new technique – which they call 'a war of nerves'. I don't think that it really affects the mass of the people in this country – they hardly realize what it all means and are not disturbed by things which don't actually touch them – as long as prices don't go up and nothing happens, they just carry on as usual. The people it does affect are those who do appreciate what is in the air – more especially those who have something to lose if war comes – and these are the people unfortunately who count – whether they will stand the strain indefinitely remains to be seen, but there are a good many more of them in England than in Germany and Hitler & co. know this well enough.

Tuesday 15 August   Poor little Anthony Crossley[48] was killed today in a flying accident – his aeroplane on its way to Copenhagen caught fire and dropped into the sea – the pilot was saved, but the passengers perished. A ghastly tragedy ... I liked Anthony and no doubt he was very able – but he was a difficult man to get to know – shy, I think – yet assertive. .... I don't think that he would have gone far in politics for he was not well balanced – in letters he might have achieved greater success.

Saturday 19 August   The crisis is rapidly developing, and my own fear is that war will break out almost immediately. It looks to me as if the Nazis were determined on their Polish coup and still

[48] Anthony Crommelin Crossley (1903–1939), Con. M.P. Oldham 1931–35, Stretford 1935–39; P.P.S. to C. Headlam 1932–34; a member of the 'Eden group' of anti-appeasers.

believe that they can bring it off without a general European war. If they can – why, then, they will be masters of Europe – we simply cannot let them get away with it again.

Tuesday 22 August   Well – what I feared has happened. The Soviet has done the dirty on us and a Russian-German Non-Aggression Pact is announced today. It will be interesting to see how the Socialists and Liberals take their medicine! I am thankful to say that the Cabinet has announced its intention to stand by Poland and according to the papers the Poles have not been unsteadied by the new from Moscow. It looks, however, now as if war were certain.

Thursday 24 August   I attended the meeting of the Berwick Association this afternoon. We were to have discussed election plans – but, in view of the situation, we adjourned without doing so – *sine die*.[49] I doubt whether I shall ever fight this division.

Monday 28 August   ... it looks as if war between Germany and Poland may begin at any moment, and then presumably we and the French will declare war on Germany. It is not a nice look-out – but, on the whole, it would appear to be the best solution of the problems because so long as Hitler and his regime last there can be no peace in Europe. Unless the Soviet joins forces with the Nazis (and I don't regard this as out of the question) the war should not be a long one. No doubt the Germans will overrun Poland (though possibly not so easily as they seem to imagine) – but that cannot be helped. I base my view on the fact that Hitler really has not a united country behind him, and has world opinion (which counts in the long run) against him. Nor do I believe that economically the Germans are as strong as they were in 1914. They will fight hard for a bit, but unless they carry all before them in the first rush, I don't fancy that they will be able to last as they did in the last war.

Thursday 31 August   No fresh news today – no reply from Hitler to our last note. I fear that this means war – I suppose that the man has allowed things to go too far and feels that he would lose

---

[49] translation: without a day, i.e. without arranging a further meeting.

face by agreeing to any form of negotiations at the last moment. But I doubt very much whether he ever intended anything but war from the moment he came to terms with the Bolshies at any rate. He no doubt still imagines that, once he has crushed the Poles, we shall all come to heel and that then he will be able to rest on his laurels for a bit until he is ready to strike again. Such a possibility may well be influencing him – but for us to come to heel would be an act of suicide – and the same applies to the French. If he makes war on Poland we must go to war with Germany at once, and continue the war to the bitter end. It is a gloomy prospect – but there is no alternative and I am thankful to say this seems to be the opinion of all the people in this country of every political persuasion.

4

THE PHONEY WAR

September 1939 to May 1940

Friday 1 September 1939   Hitler began his war against Poland last night or early this morning – so presumably it is only a matter of days or hours before we are at war. It is a ghastly prospect – more especially I think to people who passed through the last war, because they can appreciate more vividly what is in store for all of us than can the present generation – and to many of them, who like myself are too old to hope for any war employment, the outlook is gloomy in the extreme – nothing for them to do but sit and wait and hope that those whom they love may be spared. Last time God knows it was all horrible enough when war came – but then at any rate one knew what one had to do – and there it was – this time one is out of everything. Well – it is no use repining: one has only got to grit one's teeth and pray that a successful end may come sooner in this war. That we shall finish Hitler in a few months seems to me ridiculous to believe. He has a magnificent fighting machine and he is absolutely ready for war. He will, I fear, eat up the Poles very quickly and then – if he can't get us to make peace – will go all out to pulverize us into surrender. His people will stick to him for a time – so long as he is successful – this in my opinion is certain.

Saturday 2 September   Apparently Neville is making a last bid for peace – if Hitler will withdraw his troops from Poland, we are ready to talk – this policy no doubt is good moral propaganda – but of course it is futile – Hitler, if he would, cannot now afford to draw back. ... If only the Poles had had the sense to stand firmly behind the Czechs last year instead of trying to grab what they could from them they would have done much better for themselves and might have saved Europe another war. They have only themselves to blame for what is coming to them now.

Sunday 3 September   As no answer has been received to our message to Hitler we are at war with him today, and never before in our history has the country been so firmly united behind the Government. The Empire, too, appears to be equally united against Hitler. The moral opinion of the world is on our side. We start this war, therefore, under good auspices and with God's help we shall win it before so very long – but what a time is ahead of us.

Thursday 7 September   Went on to Newcastle where I saw Miss Hodgson:[1] we are closing down the Conservative office completely and she is packing off to do land work – all strength to her arm.

Friday 8 September   Mr. Potts[2] and Miss Hodgson lunched here. He came to explain to me how it was proposed to utilize political organizations in co-operation with the Ministry of Information's Regional Committees – apparently the R.C. up here is to be run by the man Berry[3] who runs the Berry Press in Newcastle.

Saturday 9 September   I saw Ledingham for a few minutes at his office – in uniform and very patronizing! He is an ass and a bore – but means well no doubt. Miss Hodgson is still in charge in Picton Street, but has a land job and is itching to be off. The sooner she goes the better – but it is rather absurd the Central Office expecting the constituency organizations to function in any way without leaving some sort of organization of their own in being in Newcastle.

Tuesday 12 September   The Germans are now well into Warsaw and I suppose will have full possession of the place very shortly – whether or not the Polish army is still in being and capable of further defence remains to be seen. Our B[ritish] E[xpeditionary] F[orce] is now officially in France, but does not appear to have

[1] K. C. Hodgson, Woman Organiser, Northern Counties Area, 1936–1946.
[2] Joseph Spearman Potts (b.1881), Organizing Sec., Northern Tariff Reform Assoc. 1905–14; Con. Agent Macclesfield from 1914; C.O. Agent, Northern Counties Area to 1928, North West Area 1928–46.
[3] V. Ewert Berry, Managing Dir. *Newcastle Journal*, 1936–48.

been engaged as yet. Clearly, however, it is going to share in the French advance if it continues! Presumably henceforward the German defence will become stronger and I quite expect to hear very soon that the French are withdrawing – what is going to happen then remains to be seen. I simply cannot see what Hitler's plan of campaign is going to be – an attack on the Maginot Line[4] would be a very costly undertaking and its success extremely problematical – a push through Belgium and Holland or Switzerland does not look to the ordinary man any more alluring. To draw the Allies on into Germany and then smash them presupposes that the Allies are duds – are they, I wonder? If not, what then? The Russians perhaps? The steam roller of the last war on the other side.

Thursday 14 September   Commander Marsden,[5] M.P., ... has some naval job up here. He lunched with us: very severe on the reappearance of Anthony Eden in the Cabinet: he says that in the HofC he is regarded now merely as a 'Glamour boy'.[6] After luncheon ... to Alnwick where there was a meeting of the Council of the [Berwick] Association. If I had not been there, I fancy that they would have sacked Knowles [the Agent] there and then and closed down for the duration: I got them to keep him on for 3 months and then reconsider the situation.

Sunday 17 September   The Russians have marched into Poland to ensure the safety and happiness of their fellow Russians and assure the world that they intend to go no further – it is all very overwhelming and one can hazard no guess as to what will happen next – the only thing that one can be fairly certain about is that neither the U.S.A. nor any other neutral state will take any notice of this fresh outrage to international usage and the sanctity of pacts! The Japanese are said to have made a pact of non-aggression with the Bolshies in Asia and are reported to be embarking upon a fresh drive in China – they are no doubt hoping to make hay while the sun shines. Well – well one can only carry on and hope

---

[4] The French fortifications on the Franco-German frontier.

[5] Arthur Marsden (1883–1960), naval career 1898–1921; Con. M.P. Battersea N. 1931–35, Chertsey 1937–50.

[6] The derogatory term applied to the 'anti-appeasers' by the Whips and the M.P.s who supported Chamberlain's policy in the late 1930s.

that right will triumph – but it is beginning to look like a long and grim struggle.

Tuesday 19 September   London is amply protected by a balloon barrage – hundreds of balloons in the air – a good many buildings are sandbagged and trenches and A.R.P. stations abound – otherwise things seem to be more or less normal.

Wednesday 20 September   ... so long as Stalin remains in the east and prevents the Nazis from over running the Balkans, perhaps there is something to be said for his knavery. But my fear is that his main object is to lengthen the war – to exhaust us and the French and the Germans, and then Bolshevize Europe.

Friday 22 September   I went into Newcastle today and lunched with old Appleby who wrote to tell me that there was to be a meeting of the North Newcastle Association next week to consider a successor to Grattan-Doyle. The old rascal is evidently seizing this opportunity to run in his son – Appleby was all for my coming forwards as a rival candidate and I expressed myself as quite ready to do so. I don't suppose that in the circumstances G.D. will resign, but it will be interesting to see what happens. Topping is to be consulted!

Saturday 23 September   Roosevelt has sent a message to Congress asking for the repeal of the Neutrality Law – and from what one reads in the press, it seems certain that he will get what he wants. It is said that this will help us more than the Boche – because we can bring what we want from the U.S.A. and he cannot. This may or [may] not be true – but one thing is certain – the American industrialists will be the gainers and this is all that really matters to Roosevelt and his friends. It is the old story over again – put R. for Wilson[7] in somewhat similar circumstances, and you have it. The U.S.A. must remain neutral as long as possible, certainly until the next Presidential election, and make all the money that is to be got out of us or anyone else – it is not a very idealistic policy, but it is reasonable enough. In this war of course there really should

---

[7] (Thomas) Woodrow Wilson (1856–1924), Gov. of New Jersey 1910–12; Pres. of U.S.A. 1913–21; awarded Nobel Peace Prize 1919.

be no neutrals if the principles behind the Covenant of the League of Nations or the Kellogg Pact[8] stood for anything at all except windy sentiment. But no one ever really thought they would when they were tested – except of course the fatuous creatures in this country who supported the League of Nations Union and refused to recognize facts or to appreciate national needs and human passions.

Monday 25 September ... I had a word with old Appleby: he does not think that there will be any definite decision about North Newcastle on Wednesday – to me it seems pretty certain that there will be unless a good number of people present at the meeting take a strong line against Grattan[-Doyle] – and there are not likely to be many people at the meeting anti-Grattan unless they are whipped up.

Wednesday 27 September Needless to say the P.M. has refused to help me in the G.D. affair: I had a letter to this effect from Alec Dunglass this morning. So G.D. has got away with it and his son has been declared a right and proper person to represent Newcastle (North) whenever G.D. chooses to resign. It is a disgusting episode – but it looks as if one was helpless to stop it – no one in Newcastle (North) seems to care a jot – Ledingham is away busy being a soldier: I cannot take any direct action and no one else will. Appleby talks a lot – but is quite futile and silly.

Thursday 28 September ... this truly appalling increase in taxation which Sir John Simon announced yesterday. It will mean the final collapse of the upper-middle class in this country and the final end of the old social regime – well, I suppose that this has been inevitable for some time past – and all that one can hope is that the new world will be better than the old – but I am glad that I shall not be called upon to live in it.

Sunday 1 October Winston broadcasted tonight – the sort of speech which will be liked.[9] I notice that the 'cheap press' (Sunday

---

[8] The Kellogg-Briand Pact of 1928 affirmed the rejection of war as a method of settling disputes, but placed no obligations upon the nations who signed it.
[9] Churchill had been appointed First Lord of the Admiralty on 3 Sep. 1939.

illustrated muck) is beginning another campaign to make him P.M.
It is not the time for this sort of thing – but I suppose it cannot be
helped.

Monday 2 October   But how the Nazis propose to fight this war
is still a mystery to me – one cannot see how they can hope to win
the war unless they really mean to let the Russians co-operate with
them against us – I mean by this in Europe. Even then it would
entail a long and laborious war which neither Nazis nor Bolshies
could, I should imagine, stand.

Wednesday 4 October   I don't know how I shall get through the
winter here with nothing to do and nothing to hope for, and
suffering all the time from the nervous tension inevitable in
wartime – it will be a trying ordeal.

Thursday 5 October   The outcry against waste and extravagance
all round continues in the press, and there are signs that the 'supermen' who are in charge of things are becoming slightly disconcerted.
The Ministry of Information is to be overhauled and paid jobs in
A.R.P. work are to be reduced – but of course there are too many
new Offices and far too many officials everywhere. The bill is going
to be colossal – and of course thousands of ordinary people are
already being cast out of their jobs – private employment and
businesses of all kinds – simply because their employers are already
hard hit by new taxation and are still more fearful of a state of
penury after the war. Ninnies like Sam Hoare on the wireless the
other night beg people to be patriotic and not to dismiss their
servants, clerks, etc., but how can people be expected to do
otherwise when they can no longer afford to keep up their estab-
lishments? Troubles of all kinds lie ahead of us – and one thing is
certain only – that is, that the Bolshies will have it all their own
way after this war.

Friday 6 October   I had talks with Appleby and the new Central
Office man[10] *re* North Newcastle. They both agree that nothing can
be done unless people in the division become aroused – and of

[10] Ledingham's wartime replacement as Area Agent, A.J. Tydeman (for biographical details, see 30 October 1939).

course unless there is someone to arouse them, they won't become aroused. No – G.D. has dished me and again I am made to realize how little I count in politics even in the Area where I have worked so hard and long.

Wednesday 11 October   The Russian move in the Baltic is continuing and the apprehension in Finland is growing apace. I don't know what our attitude is going to be if the Bolshies invade Finland, if she does not give way to their peaceful pressure. Personally I feel that it is rather pitiful [we] are shutting our eyes to Russia's aggression while we make such a to do about that of Germany. My own view, too, is that the Bolshies are a greater menace to us than are the Nazis. I should sever diplomatic relationship [*sic*] with Russia if I were in power – but of course if I were 'in the know' I might take a different view. The man in the street, however, I feel certain must share my present view. This Russian method of grab is almost more intolerable than Hitler's.

Thursday 12 October   Chamberlain spoke today in the HofC – a short and very effective reply to Hitler – reciting the former's[11] broken pledges, saying that his peace offer meant nothing and that before we could consider any kind of peace we must have something more effective to go upon. He differentiated between the Nazi Government and the German people – against whom we had no quarrel and whom we were prepared to treat on terms of equality. Of course this line of talk is the obvious one – but equally of course the German people won't listen to it – not until Hitler is beaten in the field or until the economic situation gets really insupportable. ... We had a meeting of the Area Executive this afternoon and discussed how we were to keep the party organization in being during the war: we decided to have a meeting of divisional chairmen as soon as possible.

Monday 16 October   Really the German attitude in the Baltic is bewildering. It is astounding that Hitler should acquiesce in allowing the Russians to make it a Russian lake. ... The only supposition is that he considers that for the time being he must give way to Stalin in order to have his hands free for the war against us – when

---

[11] A mistake, as Headlam clearly means the latter, i.e. Hitler.

he has crushed us and the French he imagines, presumably, that he can turn on the Russians and win back all he is now giving away to them ... I cannot myself see how he can win a lightening war in the west, particularly when he is beginning it so late in the year – and surely he cannot win a long war? But it is going to be a very desperate business and I rather regret the way in which people are taking things in this country – a little too optimistically, I feel, in view of the desperate characters who are running Germany.

Tuesday 17 October   It looks as if the German offensive were beginning on the Western Front – the report tonight from our side is that the French have been forced back a bit, but have succeeded in checking the German attack so far. Today apparently there were two air raid warnings in Newcastle ... The air invasion has clearly begun ... *Royal Oak*, so the Admiralty announce, was in harbour at Scapa Flow when she was sunk – which is rather alarming.[12]

Monday 23 October   I find the Crookshanks *mère fils et fille* exactly the same as ever – the women garrulous, Harry as self-centred. He has not got a good word for the P.M. I suppose he feels that he ought to have been in the Cabinet by now and is not. He gives one little gossip for he is very much a Minister and on guard – and perhaps, being still a junior minister he really knows very little of what is going on. He finds Simon almost as difficult a chief to work for as Oliver Stanley: he says that he never knows until the last minute what he is expected to do and when he has to make a speech. This must be very trying in an office like the Treasury and means that he must always mug up everything – Simon, he says, is rarely in the House.

Tuesday 24 October   I lunched ... at the Senior today – all the nobs were there including Chatfield and Hankey. The latter looked dirtier and sicker than ever and I wondered more than ever why he had been made a member of the War Cabinet – presumably he is of some use – knows a lot of precedents, etc. They say, too, that he can deal with Winston – if he really can do that, he is, indeed, valuable! Harry Crookshank tells me that Winston will be Neville's successor for a certainty.

---

[12] A battleship sunk by a German U-boat which entered the main fleet base.

Thursday 26 October   ... I went to the Central Office (which is slowly returning to Palace Chambers from Ealing where it retired on the outbreak of war). Hacking had asked me to visit him ... but had little to suggest as to how to keep young G.D. from stepping in when old G.D. wishes to retire. We agreed that the only possible course was a revolt against the plot in Newcastle (N), and the formation of a new association – and the trouble is, as I told H., that no one in the division will do anything to help. Hacking is greatly worried about the Party's position. He was told by those in authority that all propaganda was to be conducted by the Ministry of Information and on that understanding he advised Conservative associations to close down in the interests of economy: now the Ministry of Information is a washout and the Labour and the Liberal organizations are working hard. He does not know what to be at, poor man – but begged me to keep things going as far as I can in the Northern Area. He was very civil, but is a feeble creature.

Friday 27 October   I am rather glad to get out of London for it is a truly dismal place nowadays: houses shut, shops closed down and few people about. My own view of course is that all this air raid precaution business is being terribly overdone – I admit that we may have heavy attacks from the air before the war is over, but I don't believe that they can be very often repeated in strength enough to justify our present dislocation of industry and life in general. I am afraid that if we continue doing things as they are being done now London and other big towns will go under: no trade, no rents, no civil life – people are being scared to such a degree that they are fleeing the towns and the results will be very bad for all our municipal undertakings. If the war lasts for some years, they will have to alter some of these onerous regulations and get the machine going again.

Sunday 29 October   Surely when this war is over some measures will be taken to prevent the recurrence of yet another German war? All the pundits are now busily trying to make out that the Nazis are the whole cause of the war – that the German people are quite different to them – but the truth of the matter is that it is because the German people are what they are that they just follow their leaders whoever they may be and are ready to go to war without

question whenever they are ordered to do so. This is the whole
lesson of history since the Prussians gained a footing in Germany -
until a real attempt is made to break up the German states into
separate units and successfully accomplished, I don't believe that
we shall ever have a real and lasting peace in Europe.

Monday 30 October   I went into Newcastle this morning – saw
the man Tydeman[13] (the Central Office man) who seems perfectly
helpless and hopeless as regards Newcastle [North] -he has not an
idea in his head as to how the G.D. ramp is to be countered, and
assures me that nothing can be done. ... I lunched with Wilkin
whom I saw in the train the other night and asked him to get busy
re Newcastle (N) – needless to say he now has cold feet and tells
me that the women run the show and that they are dead set on
young G.D. – really it is a hopeless business! with no one to help
one. I presided this afternoon over a meeting of the chairmen and
women of the Area – quite a good gathering – most constituencies
represented. They all seemed keen to carry on, and so I hope that
we shall get going again.

Thursday 2 November   The war continues and there is nothing to
show that it is going on except this endless propaganda. Presumably
it has its effect on the public both here and in Germany, and also
in neutral countries – but it is difficult to understand why it should,
for it seems too futile to impress the meanest intelligence. The issue
in this war is even simpler – by which I mean more obvious than
it was in the last war – it is whether Germany should rule the
world – nothing more or less. England and France fought from
1914–1918 to save themselves and Europe from German hegemony:
today they are doing the same thing – but today the situation is
complicated by the fact that Russia is on the side of Germany – or
rather the political and social ideas for which Germany and Russia
stand are of a similar character. Thus a German victory would
mean a social and political world revolution which would destroy

---

[13] Albert James Tydeman (1884–1966), Con. Agent, Woolwich 1911–19, Green-
wich 1919–21, St. George's, 1921–27; Assistant C.O. Agent, Metropolitan Area
1927–29; C.O. Agent, Western Area, South East Area 1929–39; transferred as Acting
C.O. Agent, Northern Counties Area 1939–46, returned to South East Area (Home
Counties South), 1946–51.

our present form of civilization and religion. All this is so evident that one gasps to find neutrals in such a contest.

Wednesday 15 November Geoffrey Dawson, whom I saw in London, told me that he personally never believed in this Dutch invasion,[14] but that last week the G[eneral] S[taff] at the W[ar] O[ffice] were convinced it was imminent. He also told me that Winston was determined that the Germans intended to drop people from parachutes in this country to work mischief and had ordered all his home defence people should wear side arms. The idea of invasion is also fairly widely held.

Thursday 16 November ... to Berwick where was held a meeting of the Divisional Executive – a small attendance. After some palaver it was decided to carry on the Association for another 6 months at any rate – but neither Milburn nor Craster[15] was very enthusiastic in the matter – indeed, I doubt whether things would have gone as they did, had I not been present. Why I should bother about the beastly constituency I hardly know – for it does not look very likely that I shall ever be candidate for Berwick, unless the war ends a deal earlier than I anticipate.

Saturday 18 November There is the usual chatter in the papers today about troubles in Germany – a supposed split among the Nazis, a monarchist rising, etc., etc. I don't suppose much of this gossip is supported by fact and it seems to me to be a pity to publish such stuff. It can only have the effect of making the public believe that revolution is imminent in Germany which is most unlikely at this early stage in the war. Personally, I don't believe that Hitler's regime will be in any real danger until the German Army is beaten in the field – and goodness only knows when that happy event will occur – not yet awhile anyway.

Wednesday 22 November ... I went to call on the Stanleys,

[14] During this period it was thought that the Germans were preparing to attack Holland and Belguim.
[15] John Montagu Craster (1901–1975), Chairman, Berwick C.A. 1946–49, 1953–56, Pres. 1965–67; Chairman, Northumberland Sea Fisheries Ctte. 1929–70, Assoc. of Sea Fisheries Cttes. 1939–70; Pres., Fisheries Organisation Soc. 1959–75; High Sheriff of Northumberland 1944; member of Northumberland County Council 1947–57, Alderman 1957–67; kt. 1955.

hoping to have a word in private with Oliver – but the room was full of Brendan Bracken,[16] foreign gents and painted women playing bridge and drinking cocktails, and I had not a chance of a word in private with either Maureen or Oliver – somehow all these people sickened me – what does war mean to them?

Thursday 30 November   The Russians have invaded Finland today on land, at sea, and in the air. It is a monstrous business – so monstrous, indeed, that the U.S.A., it is reported, are thinking of withdrawing their ambassador from Moscow! I fear that the Finns will have to surrender unconditionally against such an overwhelming onrush – and then what will be the next Stalin-Hitler move?

Saturday 2 December   ... it is difficult to believe that any Germans can view with satisfaction the advance of Russia and her increased strength in the Balkans. Sooner or later I should imagine that a Russian-German clash is certain. Meanwhile this strange war goes on – and one thing is clear – that is that it is costing us far too much in £.s.d. for us to be able to carry it on indefinitely in this kind of way.

Sunday 3 December   It seems to me that Hitler's policy in this war is crystal clear – he has only one objective, the defeat of Britain – until he has accomplished this, nothing else matters – and in this absolute concentration upon a single aim lies our danger. I am confident that we can beat Hitler, but it is going to be a hard and long job – and it would be foolish for us to running after the Russians and dispersing our forces which is exactly what Hitler would like us to do. The old controversy between Westerners and Easterners is likely to be repeated in this war before it is over.[17]

Tuesday 5 December   This morning I went by appointment to see

[16] Brendan Rendall Bracken (1901–1958), Con. M.P. Paddington N. 1929–45, Bournemouth 1945–50, Bournemouth E. 1950–51; P.P.S. to W. Churchill 1940–41; Min. of Information 1941–45; 1st Lord of Admiralty 1945; Chairman of *Financial News* 1926–45, of *Financial Times* 1945–58; cr. Viscount Bracken 1952.
[17] The strategic debate during the First World War: the 'Westerners' considered that the Western Front was the decisive theatre and wished to concentrate all resources there; the 'Easterners', seeking an alternative to the stalemate and casualties in the West, hoped to undermine Germany by defeating her allies in eastern and southern Europe.

Geoffrey Lloyd,[18] now Minister of Mines – one of the rising hopes of the grand old Tory Party. He was quite civil and friendly – not too patronizing – but clearly, and quite properly no doubt, the Minister. I went to see him regarding the refusal of his control to allow the export of coal, coke and anthracite to Yugoslavia for which sterling was to have been paid. It transpired that his control had no objection to the deal, but that the Ministry of Economic Warfare had turned down the transaction because the policy for the moment was to send all available coal, etc., to Italy in order to keep her sweet. One would have thought that there was enough coal for all and sundry and that the more we exported, the better it would be for our foreign trade.

Tuesday 19 December I had a talk with Harry Clive[19] yesterday at the Travellers. He is just back from Brussels – rather disgruntled at having to give up his job at such an interesting moment. It does seem rather silly to change an ambassador in the middle of a war - always supposing that the ambassador is any good and gets on with the Govt. to whom he is accredited. Harry says that the Germans were fully intending to attack Holland on Nov. 11th – then the announcement that Belgium would stick to Holland took them by surprise – and von Reichenau[20] (the only political general they have) told Hitler that he could not guarantee a quick victory – and the invasion was called off.

Wednesday 27 December ... it is fairly obvious that no offensive can be contemplated by the Germans at present – the weather conditions being such as they are. War correspondents are hard put to it to find anything to write about and the tripe they do send home makes one almost weep – but presumably the public like it.

---

[18] Geoffrey William Lloyd (1902–1984), Con. M.P. Birmingham Ladywood 1931–45, King's Norton 1950–55, Sutton Coldfield 1955–74; private Sec. to S. Baldwin 1929–31 & P.P.S. 1931–35; U.S. Home Office 1935–39; Sec. for Mines 1939–40, for Petroleum 1940–42; P.S. Fuel & Power 1942–45; Min. of Information 1945; Min. of Fuel & Power 1951–55; Min. of Educ. 1957–59; Pres., Birmingham C.A. 1946–76; cr. Baron Geoffrey-Lloyd 1974.

[19] Robert Henry Clive (1877–1948), diplomatic service; Min. to Persia 1926–31, to the Vatican 1933–34; Amb. in Tokyo 1934–37, in Brussels 1937–39; kt. 1927.

[20] Walter von Reichenau (1884–1942), German army career; Chief of Staff, Min. of War 1933–35; G.O.C. 7th Army Corps 1935–38, Army Group IV 1938–39, 10th Army 1939–41, 6th Army 1941, Army Group South 1941–42.

The Finns claim they have fought the Russians to a standstill and the silence of Moscow seems to confirm this. It is a fine performance and one that deserves final success – but how we are to give any effective help to the Finns beats me.

Saturday 6 January 1940   The news today is that Hore-Belisha has resigned and that Oliver Stanley reigns in his stead at the W[ar] O[ffice] – no reason has been given for the former's going, but I imagine that the cause of it must be that the soldiers could not bear with the little beast a moment longer. Neville appears to have offered him the B[oard] of T[rade] which he has declined for some reason or another – no doubt he expects or intends a bigger come-back. The appointment of Oliver to the W.O. means, I presume, that he is now entirely rehabilitated and once again in the running for the leadership. What a lucky man he has been! and when I remember his abject collapse after his Min. of Labour trouble (Feb. 1935)[21] I wonder very much whether he will be able to stand the strain of the W.O. in wartime – still more, whether he possesses the guts to become leader.

Sunday 21 January   ... tonight we listened to Winston on the wireless. He was as usual full of vim and bounce – but he is undoubtedly a tonic, despite all his *faux pas*. ... I suppose that, if Neville falls by the way, Winston is certain to be P.M. It would be a marvellous achievement for him to get the prize for which he has longed so ardently after so many ups and downs. I have no liking for him or real belief in his judgement, but I should not grudge him his triumph. He would, I believe, be an admirable war P.M. – better, at any rate, than any of the others available at the moment, except *of course* Edward Halifax!

Friday 26 January   The Finns claim to be holding up the Russians on all their fronts – but in course of time it is inevitable that the Russians will get through by sheer weight of numbers unless the Finns can be reinforced. How this is going to be done God only knows. The Americans are helping the Finns splendidly – they are lending them a good many million dollars to be expended on goods

---

[21] The crisis resulting from the lower benefit rates introduced by the Unemplyment Assistance Board; see volume 1, pp. 319–21.

made in the U.S.A. 'not of military nature' – really the Yanks are more despicable in this war than in the last.

Saturday 27 January   ... a fighting speech by Winston at Manchester. I wish that he and not O.S[tanley] were coming to Newcastle.

Thursday 1 February   An excellent speech by the P.M. reported in the press today. He spoke at some City show and took a strong line, emphasizing our determination to see the war through and giving evidence to show the growing strength of our war effort. It was a cheering speech – calculated to impress the world outside this island. I wonder how long Neville will last? The longer the better in my opinion both because he seems to me to be the right sort of war P.M. and also because I don't want Winston – and if anything happens to Neville, I can see no other choice at the moment but Winston – the country wants him. How odd this seems when one looks back a few years – the very οι πολλοι[22] who now cheer him to the echo were clamouring then for his head on a charger.

Saturday 3 February   ... to the City Hall, where we listened to a very good speech by Oliver Stanley. It was a fine 'non-party' meeting presided over by the Lord Mayor, and attended by the 2 Judges of Assize and many naval and military and air force officers in uniform. Tydeman assured me that there was an audience of 2,500 – certainly the hall was packed – about half a dozen I.L.P.,[23] Pacifists and Mosleyites[24] were ejected. ... I had a little talk with Oliver – he was very kind and pleasant and promised to try and find something for me – but I don't expect anything to result from this! He has made the same promise before! He tells me that Hore-Belisha was sacked for his insolence to Gort[25] and co. and that the

---

[22] translation: the masses; a common designation from the radical democracy of classical Athens.

[23] The Independent Labour Party had been a key element in the founding of the Labour Party and provided much of its left wing in the 1920s; after 1930 it moved further to the left, and was disaffiliated at the 1932 Labour Party conference.

[24] Members of the British Union of Fascists, led by Sir Oswald Mosley.

[25] John Standish Surtees Prendergast Vereker (1886–1946), army career, awarded Victoria Cross 1918; Commandant, Staff College 1936–37; C.I.G.S. 1937–39; C. in C. British Expeditionary Force 1939–40; Inspector-Gen. for Training 1940–41; Gov. & C. in C. Gibraltar 1941–42, Malta 1942–44; High Comm. & C. in C. Palestine & Transjordan 1944–45; suc. 6th Viscount Gort (Irish peerage) 1902, cr. Viscount Gort (U.K. peerage) 1945.

mess he has made will take a lot of clearing up which confirms what Jack Dill has told me.

Tuesday 6 February   This morning I paid a visit to the G[eneral] P[ost] O[ffice] H.Q. to see George Tryon[26] ... George has aged a great deal and to me seemed to be just as charming and just as ineffective – presumably he is entirely in the hands of his officials as he was at the Ministry of Pensions.

Wednesday 7 February   This morning I visited Ned Grigg at the Ministry of Information which is located in the new buildings of London University in Russell Square. They are rather impressive. I went to see Ned on the advice of Horace Wilson[27] (whom I spoke to at the Travellers the other day saying that I had nothing to do and was in despair) but I might have saved myself the trouble. Ned was quite friendly, but said that he was being moved from the ministry and so not in a position to help me. He, I could see, was thoroughly disgruntled – no doubt by the arrival of Sir J. Reith[28] to take on a job which no doubt he had expected to get himself.

Monday 12 February   John Buchan's[29] death is announced in today's paper. ... He might, I have always thought, have filled a big place in English literature had he not written so much and been a little more discriminating in what he wrote. His power of work was simply amazing and I cannot imagine how he kept up his output as he did at such a comparatively high standard. He never

---

[26] George Clement Tryon (1871–1940), Con. M.P. Brighton 1910–40; U.S. Air 1919–20: P.S. Pensions 1920–22, 1940; Min. of Pensions 1922–24, 1924–29, 1931–35; Postmaster-Gen. 1935–40; Chanc. Duchy of Lancaster 1940; 1st Comm. Works 1940; cr. Baron Tryon 1940.

[27] Horace John Wilson (1882–1972), Ass. Sec., Min. of Labour 1919–21, Perm. Sec. 1921–30; Chief Industrial Adviser 1930–39; Perm. Sec., Treasury & Head of Civil Service 1939–42; kt. 1924.

[28] John Charles Walsham Reith (1889–1971), Gen. Manager B.B.C. 1922–27, Director-Gen. 1927–38; Nat. M.P. Southampton Feb.-Oct. 1940; Min. of Information Jan.-May 1940; Min. of Transport May-Oct. 1940; Min. of Works 1940–42; Dir. Combined Operations, Material Dept., Admiralty 1943–45; Chairman, Commonwealth Telecommunications Bd. 1946–50; Chairman, Colonial Development Corporation 1950–59; kt. 1927, cr. Baron Reith 1940, K.T. 1969.

[29] John Buchan (1875–1940), Con. M.P. Scottish Univ. 1927–35; Gov. Gen. of Canada 1935–40; author of popular fiction; cr. Baron Tweedsmuir 1935; 'I met him about my first day at Oxford and have known him, more or less, ever since': Headlam diary, 10 Feb. 1940.

struck me as a 'big man', but he had the knack of impressing all and sundry with the idea that he was a big man – and this really amounted to the same thing for his capacity as an administrator and politician was never put to the test. He also had the faculty of getting to know the right people – and sticking to them. He was justified for he made a great career for himself and to judge by what one reads in the press has succeeded in making everyone recognize him as one of our great ones. He was a kind-hearted, little man – ready to help and advise all and sundry – and he will be missed by many friends.

Monday 19 February I dined tonight at the Turf Club with Charley Londonderry who was very friendly – like me he is a disappointed man so far as politics are concerned, though of course he was longer at the game and was probably lucky ever to get into the Cabinet. However, he was badly treated and he has every right to feel disgruntled. He has nothing to do now and, like me, feels that the world is crumbling before his eyes. We talked about the usual things – Robin, the future of the Londonderry family and their possessions, etc. – but he was very human and hospitable. He is closing down Londonderry House and removing the furniture to save paying rates which he told me are £4,000 a year!

Monday 26 February I am afraid that the Finnish resistance is really collapsing ... it is a sad, bad business – and one regrets more than ever our impotence to help – if only those damned Swedes would come into the picture, it would be a different affair. I suppose they feel pretty certain that the Russians will leave them alone for fear of the Germans – their role is to supply a buffer state between Berlin and Moscow – but Norway is in a far more dangerous position – so it seems to me. One wonders what our reaction would be if the Germans were to overrun Norway? Such a manoeuvre might give us a chance – if only we were prepared for it – one feels, however, that under the present control at the W.O. we are never likely to be prepared for anything. I simply cannot believe in the efficiency of Ironside.[30]

[30] William Edmund Ironside (1880–1959), army career; C. in C. British Forces in Russia 1918–19, in North Persia 1920–21; Commandant, Staff College 1922–26; G.O.C. 2nd. Div. 1926–28, Meerut District, India 1928–31; Q.M.G. India 1933–36; G.O.C. Eastern Command 1936–38; Gov. & C. in C. Gibraltar 1938–39; C.I.G.S. 1939–40; C. in C. Home Forces 1940; kt. 1919, cr. Baron Ironside 1940.

Thursday 29 February   I have read a good deal today[31] – one or two left wing books abusing Chamberlain over Munich. All the writers seems to forget our state of military unpreparedness at that date – especially our weakness in the air – they apparently were quite ready to allow the Czechs to be massacred, and assure us that Russia would have saved the situation. It is all very childish and yet no doubt thousands upon thousands of people in this country are quite ready to accept all the nonsense. Chamberlain of course will have to take his share of blame for our unpreparedness, but history will show that the Munich Agreement not only was inevitable – the only policy for us – but possibly lost Germany the war.

Sunday 3 March   A certain amount of air activity is reported today on the Western Front – but there are no signs apparently of an enemy offensive on a large scale. When it does come, however, and come it will, it will come as a surprise and one only hopes that our people won't be caught napping. I wish to goodness that there were more of our troops in France – for in a crisis I cannot help feeling nervous about the French: their conduct of the war so far does not inspire me with a feeling of confidence.

Wednesday 13 March   This afternoon I attended the meeting of the Conservative Exec. Committee at Central Office and earned disapproval because I said that active propaganda was essential for the Nat. Govt. so long as Labour propaganda was so active.

Wednesday 20 March   I presided over the Area Executive in the afternoon at the Conservative Club: a very small gathering: so far as I can see the Conservative Party is as dead as makes no difference for the time being.

Friday 29 March   The more I think over the situation in France, the less I like it. I have always distrusted the French: in the last war they – or their Government – were on 2 or 3 occasions nearly giving in – and I can see no Clemenceau[32] today ready to keep the

---

[31] Headlam was in bed, recovering from German measles.
[32] Georges Clemenceau (1841–1929), Dep. 1876–93, Sen. for Var 1902–20; Min. Home Affairs 1906; P.M. 1906–09, 1917–20.

other miserable politicians going should a real crisis arise. .... I was to have attended a dance at Alnwick tonight – but gave up the unequal contest. I really think I better let the Berwick association know that I don't feel disposed to go on being their candidate. I have not actually made up my mind about it – but the more I think about it the less disposed I am to go on 'nursing' the seat indefinitely – Goodness only knows how long the war is going to last, and by the time it is over I don't suppose I shall feel inclined to go racing about making speeches all over the Berwick division: it is certainly not an old man's job.

Saturday 30 March   It seems to me that the Germans have been given long enough time to mature all their plans for an offensive and that the testing time will not be long delayed. I wish that I felt more confident about ourselves and the French. I suppose that our Regular divisions in France are good enough – but from what one hears one has not equal confidence in our other divisions and, in any case, our people are too few to make much difference in a big clash. Everything really depends on the French unfortunately.

Tuesday 2 April   Grattan-Doyle has announced his intention of applying for the Chiltern Hundreds[33] – Beatrice rang me up tonight to let me know that Wilkin and Appleby were getting busy: apparently Sir A. Sutherland[34] and other business men are up in arms and say that they simply will not have young G.D. as their M.P. I wish to goodness they had said all this a few months ago: I am to be asked to come forward as Conservative Candidate – it will be interesting to see how the business develops, but it is not going to be easy for me!

Wednesday 3 April   I then attended Jack Gilmour's[35] memorial at the Scottish church in Pont Street – a largely attended ceremony –

[33] A formal means of vacating a seat in the House of Commons.
[34] Arthur Munro Sutherland (1867–1953), shipowner and coal exporter; Pres., Chamber of Shipping 1930; Pres., Shipping Federation Ltd. 1938–50; Sheriff of Newcastle 1917, Lord Mayor 1919; High Sheriff of Northumberland 1943; kt. 1920, cr. Bart. 1921.
[35] John Gilmour (1876–1940), Con. M.P. Renfrewshire E. 1910–18, Glasgow Pollok 1918–40; Ass. Whip 1913–15, 1919–21, Scottish Whip 1921–22, 1923–24; Scottish Sec. 1924–29; Min. of Agric. 1931–32; Home Sec. 1932–35; Min. of Shipping 1939–40; suc. 2nd Bart. 1920.

the whole Cabinet, L.G. and a host of M.P.s and civil servants. Gilmour was liked by everyone – a real good sort and a first class administrator, at least so I am told – at any rate he knew his own mind and was not simply run by his officials as so many ministers are. He was a poor speaker and ineffective in the HofC. L.G. was at the service, and appeared to be still full of vitality – the P.M. also looked very fit – not a day older than he did when I first knew him. I saw Magnay on the way out of the church – of course he has done nothing about putting a letter in the press respecting the North Newcastle position. He pretended that he was going to do something but as I now hear that McKeag[36] talks of standing as an Independent Liberal, I don't suppose he will. ... A telephone message from Beatrice this evening: apparently Wilkin is busy about North Newcastle and things are moving.

Thursday 4 April   I looked in this morning at the Central Hall, Westminster (walking there from the Travellers with Emrys-Evans[37] M.P. and Bonar Law[38] M.P. who are both rebels against the Government) where the National Union Council was holding its meeting. Bonar Law always struck me in the HofC as a very sensible and capable fellow – and it is surprising to me that he has never been given a job – too honest and outspoken, I imagine, to please the whips. I only stayed at the conference for about three quarters of an hour as I had to catch the one o'clock train, so I missed the P.M.'s speech. It appears to have been a good one – full of confidence and vim. It certainly reads well and should binge up people. All I heard at the conference were little speeches puffing the various officers. I was made a Vice Chairman – proposed by Mrs Higgins of Newcastle who was all over me and made me blush. She described me as 'our leader in the north' with Charley Londonderry sitting just behind her. I felt quite embarrassed – however, after I had listened to what was said about all the others

[36] William McKeag (1897–1972), Lib. cand. Durham 1924, 1929, Lib. Nat. M.P. Durham 1931–35, Lib. cand. Newcastle N. 1945, Newcastle E. 1950; Dep. Ass. Adjutant-Gen. 1939–45; Lord Mayor of Newcastle 1951–52, 1953–54.

[37] Paul Vychan Emrys-Evans (1894–1967), Con. M.P. Derbyshire S. 1931–45; U.S. Dominions 1942–45.

[38] Richard Kidston Law (1901–1980), Con. M.P. Hull S.W. 1931–45, Kensington S. 1945–50, Haltemprice 1950–54; F.S. War Office 1940–41; U.S. For. Office 1941–43, M.S. 1943–45; Min. Educ. 1945; Chairman, Nat. Youth Employment Council 1955–62; cr. Baron Coleraine 1954; son of Andrew Bonar Law, P.M. 1922–23.

including old Almeric Paget[39] I felt that I deserved as much as they got – and perhaps more! ... Saw Leonard Milburn in the train and discussed North Newcastle: he was very nice about it and said of course I ought to take the chance if it came my way. it won't!

Friday 5 April   I went into Newcastle this morning. Wilkin met me at the Station Hotel – very full of all that he had done. He certainly is trying to do all he can to pull the strings: it is a thousand pities that he did not get to work earlier – now I very much fear we are too late to defeat this horrid business. We lunched *chez* Sir Arthur Sutherland who lives in a huge villa in Jesmond – it is typical of every house I have ever seen belonging to a very rich man who has risen in life – heavy very much polished mahogany furniture: very thick carpets: ugly vases of enormous size: great Victorian pictures in very golden frames: much glass and cutlery on the table, etc., etc. The luncheon party consisted of Sutherland, self, Wilkin, Appleby and Allsop (chairman of the Conservative Club, a decent fellow). They all seemed keen to defeat Doyle, and ultimately I drafted a letter which they are to get influentially signed and sent to the chairman (Lawson), the woman chairman and old Oliver[40] of the North Newcastle Association – whether it will have any effect it remains to be seen – I doubt it. Sutherland is on his last legs I should imagine – but was full of energy in the business. I liked him better today than I have ever done before and can understand his success in life better after seeing him at work. Appleby was, as usual, tiresome and half-hearted – I never trust the man.

Saturday 6 April   I went into Newcastle again this morning and lunched at the N[orthern] C[ounties] Club – Charley Londonderry was my guest. He was very pleasant and wanted to know how he could help me win North Newcastle! He came to the Area Meeting with me (quite well attended, 200 present so Tydeman said) and

---

[39] Almeric Hugh Paget (1861–1949), Con. M.P. Cambridge 1910–17; Whip 1911–17; Pres., Eastern Area 1909–46; Pres., National Union 1928–29, 1940–41; cr. Baron Queenborough 1918.

[40] Thomas Oliver (1853–1942), physician; Prof. of Physiology, Univ. of Durham College of Medicine, Newcastle 1889–1911, Prof. of Medicine 1911–27, Pres. 1926–34; Vice-Chancellor, Durham Univ. 1928–30; Pres., Royal Institute of Public Health & Hygiene 1937–42; kt. 1908.

made quite a good speech. We got through our resolutions all right and then when the show was over I talked with various people regarding the N.N. situation. The Chairman of the N.N. Women's Branch was there and she said that they had chosen 'Howard'[41] and meant to stick by him, that unless I opposed him, nobody else would, etc., etc. I did not say much, saying only that the great object was to avoid an election if possible. The letter is to be sent to the Association on Monday, so Wilkin says, and then they may, or may not, ask me to see them. Personally I don't see the Doyles giving way and I don't know whether I dare fight an election, knowing so little about the feeling of the constituency as a whole. It is a very trying situation.

Sunday 7 April   I have written to Leonard Milburn today about Newcastle North. As a matter of fact no question really arises *re* Berwick unless I become M.P. for N.N. – and that at the moment is a very doubtful business. I don't see Grattan-Doyle standing down and I shall find it a difficult decision to make if it comes to standing against him. Agnes of course, like Beatrice, is desperately keen for me to seize the opportunity of getting back into the HofC. But I wonder whether, if it came to a fight, I should win? There is nothing really to go on – and obviously such organization as there is will be against me. It would be a great flop to stand for the seat as an independent and then be defeated by young G.D. It would be the end of my political leadership in the north – well – would this matter much? I am now just on 64 and in many ways am getting tired and done – politics are exacting and unremunerative – the only point in them nowadays (so far as I am concerned) is that they keep me going – if only some lucrative business came along how much better it would be to give up public life altogether and to earn a little money even at this late hour – but no business (lucrative) ever does come my way – there is the rub!

Tuesday 9 April   The Germans took possession of Denmark this morning and also invaded Norway. The Danes made no kind of resistance. The Norwegians are said to be resisting – but Oslo surrendered this afternoon – the Norwegian government has

---

[41] Howard Grattan-Doyle (1908–1947), Con. cand. Newcastle N. 1940, later Lt.-Col., Judge Advocate's Branch; died after a horse-riding accident, 1 Jan. 1947.

removed to a place called Hamar and the Army is between that place and Oslo. The Allies are going to the assistance of Norway – of course we are too late. ... Everyone is very excited and hopeful – but honestly I cannot see why.

Thursday 11 April   I went into Newcastle by train this morning and was there until 5.30 p.m. when I returned by train. Lunched at the Conservative Club with Allsop and Richley. They both are, I think, whole hearted supporters of mine and are busy collecting names for the letter to the Executive. They assure me that in a straight fight I should beat young G.D. easily – Tydeman, on the other hand, whom I also saw today, assured me that I should be beaten. I don't know why he should say this and I can't understand his attitude in the whole business which is decidedly pro G.D. He let out today that he had known about Hacking's letter to old G.D. for a long time past – it seems scandalous that the Central Office should let their agent know about this letter and not let the Chairman of the Area know about it.

Friday 12 April   I lunched at the Conservative Club with Wilkin, Allsop and the other man who is busying himself in this business, one Richley. Wilkin was a bit gloomy, and feels, I think, that the press agitation he started has had the effect of embittering the G.D. clique. I always fancied it would and would never have begun it myself – however, there it is. This afternoon I visited Sir Thomas Oliver (in bed): he was reported to be very strongly determined to uphold young G.D.'s cause – however, after I had explained my position in the business, he said that he thought my proposition a fair one and I only hope that he will let his committee know his views – but of course he is laid up and he cannot be at the Executive meeting called for tomorrow. I fear that it will be run by the women. Saw Appleby (now apparently all out for me and a fight if necessary), and talked to a few people on the telephone.

Saturday 13 April   This morning Wilkin rang me up and begged Beatrice and me to go into Newcastle – so we went and wasted a lot of time at the Conservative Club discussing things with Wilkin, Allsop, Richley and Tydeman – the last named determined that I shall be beaten if I stand. ... Later in the day we heard from Newcastle that the N.N. Executive had had its meeting and upheld their allegiance to young Grattan-Doyle by 20 votes to 2 – rather disappointing, but what one had to expect – now I shall have to make up my mind one way or the other. I hate the idea of an election especially when there is no way of judging one's chances: at the same time I hate even more, I think, giving way to this beastly little clique in North Newcastle. I have stood out strongly all my political life against this corrupt method of choosing candidates and I feel that it would be rather cowardly not to stand up to it now that there is a chance – but before I decide I must be sure of the financial position – it's no good saying that I will fight unless I am provided with sinews of war! Wilkin seemed a bit gloomy at the end of the telephone tonight – but why he expected any change of view on the part of the N.N. Executive I cannot imagine.

Monday 15 April I went into Newcastle in the car with H.P. this afternoon: we met Wilkin, Appleby, Allsop and Richley at the Conservative Club. Wilkin very nervous of what might happen if young G.D. got a letter from the P.M. and I did not. At first I thought that they would all back down – but they warmed up later on – I am to see Hacking in London (and so is Appleby) on this matter of the P.M.'s letter. Tydeman, whom I also saw today, assured me that even if Grattan-Doyle stood down (which he did not think likely) the Association would never accept me as a candidate which may be quite true – altogether tonight it does not look likely that I shall ever become M.P. for N.N. – certainly I am not a lucky politician!

Tuesday 16 April I went to London this morning by the early train – travelled up with Douglas Clifton-Brown[42] ... He had little political gossip – said that Ronnie Cross[43] was doing very well and that people were beginning to spot him in place of the dethroned W. Elliot, Morrison, etc. – early days yet I should imagine to begin

[42] Douglas Clifton Brown (1879–1958), Con. M.P. Hexham 1918–23, 1924–51; P.P.S. to J. Macpherson 1920–22; Dep. Chairman of Ways & Means 1943; Speaker 1943–51; cr. Viscount Ruffside 1951.
[43] Ronald Hibbert Cross (1896–1968), Con. M.P. Rossendale 1931–45, Ormskirk 1950–51; P.P.S. to R.S. Hudson 1932–35, to W. Elliot 1935; Ass. Whip 1935–37, Whip 1937–38; P.S. Trade 1938–39; Min. of Economic Warfare 1939–40; Min. of Shipping 1940–41; Gov. of Tasmania 1951–58; cr. Bart. 1941.

spotting another winner. He also said that Sam Hoare was still planning to succeed Neville when the time came, but that he was sure that the Party would never accept him as leader.

Wednesday 17 April   I saw Douglas Hacking at the Central Office. He has sent a Central Office list of candidates to the N.N. Association! He won't see young G.D. and ask him to stand down because he is sure that the young man would not do so and he does not wish 'to make him a martyr'! He was very doubtful whether it would be possible to leave the election an open one! This of course means that a letter from the P.M. may be sent to young G.D. despite everything: in that case I cannot of course stand against him – a man like Hacking simply makes one despair.

Thursday 18 April   A letter today from Lady Hunter-Weston in answer to my note of condolence on Hunter-Bunter's[44] death – he fell off the roof of his house not so very long ago where it seems he was accustomed to do his physical jerks. He was an odd personality: a fine soldier, I suppose, in his day: brave, optimistic, kind-hearted – but vain and futile in many ways – very human nevertheless – always nice to me.

Friday 19 April   I went into Newcastle this morning by train and wasted most of the day. Wilkin was anxious to see me so I felt I must go – but he really had nothing new to tell me. He is, I fear, beginning to get cold feet – but I told him definitely that, provided the P.M. did not back young G.D., I was ready to fight the election (the sinews of war of course being forthcoming).

Saturday 20 April   I heard from Tydeman this evening that the N.N. Executive turned down the Central Office list of candidates this afternoon and reaffirmed their choice of young G.D.. Wilkin, who rang me up later in the evening, was rather gloomy – I fancy that he had still been hopeful that the Executive would change their minds – but why should they? The only interesting question which awaits an answer is whether the Central Office will recognize young

---

[44] Aylmer Gould Hunter-Weston (1864–1940), military career; G.O.C. 8th Army Corps 1915–18; Con. M.P. Ayrshire N. 1916–18, Bute & N. Ayrshire 1918–35; kt. 1915.

G.D. as the 'official candidate' – technically, I suppose, the N.N. Executive have carried out the rules after being pressed. I cannot stand against young G.D. if he receives the P.M.'s blessing – but if he does get it, I really think that the time will have come for me to give up working for the Conservative Party.

Sunday 21 April   I am worried about this North Newcastle episode because I hate being in the public eye and subjected to criticism – never had any man so thin a hide as I have – never, therefore, was anyone less fitted for public life. However in this particular instance it is inevitable that I should come in for criticism, because, if one makes a stand on a matter of principle – however right and honourable that principle may be – one is certain to be misjudged and attacked. Naturally the N.N. Association people are furious with me for trying to upset their little game – and of course they abuse me. What one cannot tell (until after an election) is how far their abuse will effect the average elector. The pity is that one cannot tell the whole story against G.D. on the platform.

Monday 22 April   I have spent most of today in Newcastle discussing the situation with my supporters. They all seem ready to carry on, but Wilkin is, I think, disappointed that the other side is not going to give way – and he is quite decided in his original advice to me not to stand if the Central Office decide to back young G.D.. In this I think that he is right because, if the P.M. sends a letter to young G.D., I doubt whether I should get much support, and as a friend and follower of the P.M. I could not very well go against him. It is all very trying and I suppose I should have been wiser not to have intervened. If there is an election and I win it I shall of course be justified in my action: if there is no election because Neville supports G.D. I shall look rather a fool, and if I am beaten I shall look even more a fool. I dined with Wilkin tonight, and then attended the annual meeting of the Central division, and here I made a short speech stating my intention to accept the invitation addressed to me to come as a candidate for N.N. – thus burning by boats. Young G.D. was being adopted by his Association about the same time I imagine. My speech was well received by the Central Newcastle people (mainly women) who offered to work for me.

Tuesday 23 April   This morning I saw Wilkin and others, and emphasised the necessity of getting to work as quickly as possible to form a new Association. If we really can get together a new association of any size and importance within the next ten days, it surely should be plain to Hacking & co. that there is so serious a split in the party that it would be unwise to allow the P.M. to back either candidate. I fear that my unpopularity at Central Office will be greater than ever as a result of all this business, but I need not worry much about this as the people there have never lifted a finger on my behalf politically or otherwise. I owe them nothing – nor, as a matter of fact, do I owe Neville anything as he has never helped me in anyway and I might starve for anything he cared. I feel that, in view of all the work which I have put in for the party during the last 15 years, they might stand behind me now instead of acquiescing in this beastly piece of nepotism run by a packed association out of which every decent person has been driven.

Wednesday 24 April   ... Nairne Sandeman[45] ... died very suddenly in the HofC a few days ago ... He was a very kindly man and I liked him greatly. In the House he was generally liked: he was not brilliant but he was absolutely honest and like most stupid people was usually dead right: he always had a supreme contempt for Stanley Baldwin both as a man and minister – and events have shown how correct he was in both respects.

Thursday 25 April   I saw Hacking this morning at the Central Office. He was as helpless as a sick headache – he has not even approached young G.D. to stand down: he is obsessed with the fear of being charged with interfering with a decision of a local association and kept on telling me that the leader must support a candidate adopted by a local association, never mind what the outside opposition of the Party was or how improperly the candidate and his association had behaved. Of course if he intends to give an official backing to G.D. I shall have to give way and a pretty fool I shall look – however, it cannot be helped.

Friday 26 April   I went to see James Stuart this morning and

---

[45] Alexander Nairne Stewart-Sandeman (1876–1940), Con. M.P. Middleton & Prestwich 1923–40; cr. Bart. 1929.

explained to him the N.N. situation – my object being to get the whips to delay the issue of the writ, if possible, in order to give us time to try and arrange matters. He quite agreed with me that the 'political truce' was not intended to facilitate the perpetration of 'crimes' such as this.

Saturday 27 April   I am 64 years old today – and in the privacy of these pages will admit I am beginning to appreciate my age. I get tired easier and feel less inclined to work – but I feel that this latter sign of years is due more to my having nothing definite to do than to my inability to concentrate. If only I had a job of work, I should be just as capable of doing it as ever I was – at least such is my conviction.

Monday 29 April   H.P. says that my Newcastle supporters are busy trying to form a new association and that the petition asking me to become candidate has been signed by about 400 people. It certainly is not easy to get things going quickly – and I doubt very much whether my particular supporters are the right people for this particular job. They are mostly busy men and have neither the time nor inclination to get down to a job of work of this kind – which, admittedly, is a tiring and disagreeable one – any form of canvassing is beastly.

Tuesday 30 April   This morning I went into Newcastle with H.P. and we saw Wilkin, Allsop & co. They still seem keen on going on with the business, but not one of them is really taking a lead and I am not very happy about the situation. Richley took me this afternoon to see 2 female supporters (members of the old association). They seemed confident that I ought to win if it comes to an election even if there is a three cornered fight, but I doubt whether they really can gauge public opinion – the view of the man in the street. They think that people are tired of Grattan-Doyle and want a change, and that it is a mistake to think that there will be any sentimental feeling for the son of his father among the women voters. I rather doubt this – but nothing can prove whether my ladies are wrong or right except an election. The other side are full of fight and will not hear of any compromise.

Wednesday 1 May   I went into Newcastle this morning – saw

Tydeman who was very civil and rather on his guard – begging me not to believe all I heard said about him! ... Later saw Dudley Appleby[46] and found him apparently keen to carry on. He and others are to see Hacking tomorrow morning – also, later in the day, the other side are to be interviewed – so tomorrow, I presume, Hacking will come to a decision as to his attitude in this affair. I personally have not much hope of his adopting an attitude favourable to me. Came home by the 5.30 – feeling tired and sick of the whole business. My political life is certainly not an easy one!

Thursday 2 May I have spent most of today in Newcastle. ... In the morning Hacking met a very strong deputation of my supporters and they fancy that they impressed him considerably! After luncheon he suggested to me that both young G.D. and I should stand down in favour of some other candidate to be chosen by our respective supporters – a futile proposal which, however, I told him I would consider. He saw the G.D. people later in the day and they apparently were absolutely adamant. What his views were when he returned to London, no one knows, but, if he is well advised, he will council the P.M. to keep out of the business.

Friday 3 May The papers full of futile criticism about the Norwegian situation[47] – as usual the majority of them entirely fail to appreciate the difficulties that had to be faced ... It is the old, old story – the initiative cannot rest in our hands so long as the neutrals persist in their neutrality.

Saturday 4 May I went into Newcastle again this morning and saw Tydeman and Dudley Appleby. The former assured me that the Doyle faction was confident of beating me and he clearly agrees with them. Dudley Appleby lunched with me and we concocted a letter for the press – a sort of final appeal to G.D. to stand down. I don't for a moment suppose that it will have any effect. Personally I feel very gloomy about the whole business and have the notion that I have been a fool to embark upon it – the people who are

---

[46] Dudley Fitz-Mowbray Appleby (1904–1966), member of Newcastle City Council, Jesmond Ward 1929–39, four times Under-Sheriff; Con. cand. Wallsend 1950, Sedgefield 1955; Chairman, Political Ctte., Northern Counties Club 1945–50.

[47] The evacuation of British forces from the Trondheim area was announced by Chamberlain in the House of Commons on the previous day.

supporting me do not inspire me with confidence – they don't really know the feeling of the electors and they won't do any real work. The other side have been busy for a long time and are fanatics.

Sunday 5 May   I am now beginning to wonder whether we are going to be able to remain in Norway at all – the capture of Narvik is taking such a long time, the German northern advance seems [to] be continuing and their command of the air is so complete. I fancy that the government will come in for a pretty severe attack on Tuesday next. The sooner some of these damned Labour people are made to join the cabinet the better it will be. If we are to have an inquest (political in character) after each setback we get (and no doubt there will be many setbacks), it will be almost intolerable for the Government. I have had a feeling of revulsion for N.N. all day, wishing that I had never embarked on the business – however, no doubt I shall revive again, more especially if I am attacked in the Executive committee next Wednesday which I should imagine is almost certain.

Monday 6 May   … the more I think of it, the gladder I am that we have drawn out of the Norwegian affair – and I cannot help thinking that in doing so the Government knew what they were about. Of course the public cannot be really well informed about matters of strategy and that is why it is so ridiculous for people to air their views so loudly and to raise trouble in Parliament. For all any one of us knows the Germans may be on the brink of some big coup either against the Low Countries or in the Balkans, or possibly on both of these possible fronts – how much more difficult, then, would it be for us to cope with them if we had large forces tied up in a theatre like Norway. I suppose the real truth of the matter is that in a democratic country like ours war is made almost too difficult for soldiers and statesmen.

Tuesday 7 May   I travelled from Durham by the early train with Clifton-Brown. He was pleasant and more communicative than usual. Amongst other things he told me that Harry Crookshank had been offered his job (Deputy Chairman of Committees) and refused it. This news surprised me – but clearly H.C. cannot be in favour with the powers that be: I wonder why?

Wednesday 8 May   I lunched at the Beefsteak where people were wondering what the result of last night's performance may be – Duff Cooper, who is very bitter against Neville, is going to vote against the Government tonight so he told me – and so is Ralph Glyn[48] of all people in the world. 'C.M.G.[49] if we are to win the war' is now a battle cry – how odd it all is – and the cause of all this sudden outbreak – the immediate cause at any rate – a very wise refusal on our part to be in a large scale expedition in Norway just when the storm is going to burst in the Low Countries! It really is ridiculous. I attended the central Executive this afternoon – the meeting held in the Central Hall, Westminster, as apparently the Party is saving money by sub-letting the upper floor in Palace Chambers. At the end of the proceedings Hacking informed the committee that as at present advised he proposed in view of the cleavage of opinion in the Party in N. Newcastle to advise the leader not to intervene in the contest in favour of either candidate. I felt that I was expected to say something and so fulfilled expectation – perhaps unwisely – everyone looked down his nose – but no one attacked me openly.

Thursday 9 May   ... lunched with Charles Peat, M.P. He says that last night's debate or rather division was a disgraceful business – but he like everyone else I have met is convinced that Chamberlain will have to go.[50] The Socialists won't serve under him and they scored heavily as a result of last night's division. Personally I don't see that Neville's departure will make much difference so far as the prosecution of the war is concerned.

---

[48] Ralph George Campbell Glyn (1884–1960), Con. M.P. Stirling E. 1918–22, Abingdon 1924–53; Sec. Unionist Reorganisation Ctte. 1911; P.P.S. to Ramsay MacDonald 1931–37; cr. Baron Glyn 1953.

[49] 'Chamberlain Must Go', an echo of the famous initials 'B.M.G.' used by Leo Maxse in the campaign against Balfour's leadership of the Party in 1911.

[50] At the end of the 'Norway debate' of 7–8 May 1940 the Labour vote of censure was defeated by 281 to 200, but the fall in the Government's normal majority (due to 33 of its supporters voting against it and about 65 more abstaining) made Chamberlain's position unrenable.

5

RETURN TO PARLIAMENT

May to October 1940

Friday 10 May 1940   Neville Chamberlain announced his resignation on the wireless tonight: a dignified effort – Winston is to rule in his stead – so at last that man has gained his ambition: I never thought he would – well – let us hope that he makes good. I have never believed in him: I only hope that my judgement of the man will be proved wrong. He certainly possesses courage, imagination and drive[,] and age and experience and responsibility may give him judgement – then all should be well. One is sorry for Neville but I should imagine that he has only himself (and David Margesson[1]) to blame for his fall: he should long ago have cut the dead wood out of his administration. The Germans invaded Holland and Belgium early this morning – troops dropped from the air appeared to be very busy in both countries. ... No doubt we were ready for this coup. The war has now really begun and we are in for a period of strain and tension.

Saturday 11 May   The situation in the Low Countries is somewhat obscure – but clearly the German attack is being pushed for all it is worth, especially from the air. ... the Germans are immensely strong and their numerical superiority in the air is staggering – it is really inexplicable that we should be so behindhand in aeroplane construction – well, we are going to have to pay the penalty for our futility unless I am much mistaken. The first appointments in Winston's government are out tonight – he is P.M. and Min. of

[1] The Chief Whip since 1931; a disciplinary martinet who was unswervingly loyal to the Party leader, he dismissed or contained signs of concern amongst M.P.s rather than acting as a channel of communication upwards.

Defence, Neville, Attlee, Halifax and Greenwood[2] in the War
Cabinet. Alexander,[3] Admiralty; Eden, War Office; Archie Sinclair,[4]
Air Ministry. To me it is not an impressive combination and I fancy
that it will not propitiate the more angry of the Conservatives – it
will be interesting to see what is the fate of Sam Hoare, Simon,
Oliver S., etc. ... I have been trying to write an election address,
not an easy job.

Sunday 12 May   Winston has announced some more appointments – Simon is to be L[ord] C[hancellor], and so he has definitely
given up the hope of becoming P.M. – this means the retirement
of Tom Inskip into private life. George Lloyd is to have the
Colonies, Herbert Morrison Supply and Duff Cooper Information
which means the departure from that office of Reith, the superman!
I should have made Lloyd Information and given nothing to Duff.
I suppose he had to be rewarded for leading the revolt against
Neville – perhaps this is a trifle unkind but though I like Duff
personally I have no opinion of him as an administrator.

Monday 13 May   It has been a lovely day – no official bank
holiday[5] but I gather that most people are taking one, mainly
because they had made all their arrangements for a holiday before
they were informed that there was not to be one – the usual official
stupidity. The French assert that the Allies are taking up positions
for the defence of Brussels – but it all looks fairly hopeless and the
news that the Queen of the Netherlands has arrived in England
shows clearly enough that Holland is down and out. I suppose it
was a hopeless military effort to go to the assistance of the Dutch

---

[2] Arthur Greenwood (1880–1954), Lab. M.P. Nelson & Colne 1922–31, Wakefield
1932–54; P.S. Health 1924; Min. of Health 1929–31; Min. without Portfolio &
member of War Cabinet 1940–42; Lord Privy Seal 1945–47; Paymaster-Gen. 1946–
47; Min. without Portfolio Apr.-Sep. 1947; Lab. Dep. Leader 1935–45, Treasurer
1943–54; Acting-Leader, P.L.P. 1942–45; Chairman, Lab. N.E.C. 1952–53.
[3] Albert Victor Alexander (1885–1965), Lab. M.P. Sheffield Hillsborough 1922–
31, 1935–50; P.S. Trade 1924; 1st Lord of Admiralty 1929–31, 1940–45, 1945–46;
Min. without Portfolio 1946; Min. of Defence 1946–50; Chanc. Duchy of Lancaster
1950–51; Lab. Leader in the Lords 1955–64; cr. Viscount Alexander of Hillsborough
1950, Earl 1963, K.G. 1964.
[4] Archibald Henry MacDonald Sinclair (1890–1970), Lib. M.P. Caithness &
Sutherland 1922–45; Scottish Sec. 1931–32; Sec. for Air 1940–45; Liberal Party
leader 1935–45; suc. 4th Bart. 1912, cr. Viscount Thurso 1952, K.T. 1941.
[5] The normal Whit Monday bank holiday had been cancelled.

once the German invasion had begun – no wonder the Germans did little or nothing to prevent us rushing out of our positions on the French frontier – it must have been exactly what they wanted us to do! and now presumably we are going to reap the consequences. ... I have spent most of the day in the garden trying to forget about the war and North Newcastle – but it is not easy to divorce oneself from realities even by weeding: one feels so utterly useless in these days, and one has so little confidence in the men who are running the show – was there ever such a mess in every department of the national life, so little real leadership or common sense?

Tuesday 14 May   I was in Newcastle most of the day – the usual talk – most people with cold feet – but the colder they get – the more I feel decided not to withdraw which shows, I suppose, that there is a little guts in me even in my declining years! ... The German advance continues. They have captured Rotterdam ... In Belgium there is fighting on a wide front from north of the Albert Canal to the French frontier – and, worse still, the enemy's pressure round Sedan is said to be very heavy – the Maginot Line proper has not yet been attacked – but what use will it be to the French if it is turned – an event which now looks very likely – was there ever such a catastrophe! One wonders how the French people will respond to it – will they fight on even if Paris falls – or will they give up the unequal contest? ... Anthony Eden, our new Minister of War, has made an appeal on the wireless tonight for the immediate raising of Local Defence Volunteers[6] – their job being to guard us against German parachutists, etc. – a good move, I think – at long last the middle-aged and elderly will be given their chance of serving their country – but how can they be armed?

Thursday 16 May   ... reading between the lines of the French official reports, one realizes that the Germans are making rapid progress and that no real attempt is being made to check them. Their tanks are rushing ahead – driving into the blue – causing disorganization and panic deep behind the French line of defence ... if the breakthrough in France is as serious as I imagine it to be, we shall have to come out of Belgium just as quickly as we can, if

---

[6] The name was changed to Home Guard in July.

we are to escape disaster – our force is too small – far too small – to stand on its own. We shall be amazingly lucky if it manages to escape in the circumstances.

Friday 17 May   ... at the rate at which the Germans are going our lines of communication must be in great peril – if they are cut, we shall be in a sorry mess – Dunkirk would appear to be our one possible port of evacuation, if the worst comes to the worst – but let us hope that I am unduly nervous – possibly things are not so bad as I imagine.

Sunday 19 May   The news today is very serious and it looks to me as if the German break-through must be on a very large scale – far larger than is stated officially. Winston spoke tonight on the wireless: a fine, courageous effort – but there was no mistaking the supreme gravity of the situation. ... This Newcastle election business also adds to one's worries: I feel that there ought not to be an election – equally that I ought not to stand down – but there is nobody to take on the job of settling the business with the other side.

Tuesday 21 May   Heavy German pressure continues – clearly this mechanized drive is pushing its way ahead at terrific speed – and it looks to me as if it must reach the Channel ports – and then? Well – in 1918 -we imagined that if we lost the ports it was all up, and that at all costs we must not be divided from the French – now we have got to face both these possibilities – and to keep up our faith in victory nevertheless. ... I came in here today and have been seeing people, etc., etc., at our central office where H.P. has taken over full command – what I should have been able to do without him God only knows – the man Richley is a washout and no one else of those who begged me to come forward is lifting a finger in the doing of work – Vick,[7] the Chairman of our new Association is trying his best – but the situation is not exhilarating!

Wednesday 22 May   Tonight my adoption meeting was held – it

[7] Henry Hampton Vick, member of Newcastle City Council, St. Nicholas' Ward 1935–40; Chairman, North Newcastle (1940) Con. Assoc., May–Dec. 1940; and then briefly Chairman of the amalgamated North Newcastle CA, Jan. 1941 (see chapter 6).

was well attended and clearly those present were whole-heartedly out for me. I spoke for about half an hour and Beatrice approved the speech. She has been canvassing today and tells me that she was everywhere welcomed and so she is in good heart – but of course no one can tell in this huge constituency what opinion really is – we cannot hope to make anything in the nature of a real canvass – and I am afraid that many people who might otherwise support me may not vote as a protest against an election in war time.

Thursday 23 May   I have done a bit of canvassing today – a tiring and to me irksome job. Beatrice is working herself to fiddle strings: a marvel of energy and optimism. I am so hopelessly strung up by the war news that I feel quite incapable of taking any interest in this damned election. I feel I have been let in for it, too, by people who are not even troubling to give me adequate support - none of the eminent people who asked me to stand is lifting a finger to help me – and now it seems somewhat doubtful whether we shall get anything like the money (£400 to £450) which H.P. says is the minimum needed. He is splendid as always.

Saturday 25 May   I spent rather a futile morning – Wilkin did his best to assure me that the necessary money would be forthcoming (Appleby having written to tell me that all I could count on was £275!) – it really is a monstrous business: I was a fool, however, to trust such people, I suppose, and [ought] to have got them to put up £500 at least before I embarked upon this enterprise.

Monday 27 May   Today the news is very serious – the German advance is proceeding with terrific pace and the evacuation of Boulogne is announced. It all seems incredible and one can scarcely visualize the situation – on paper one does not see how the B.E.F. can escape – it makes one almost sick with anxiety. ... It is difficult to fight an election in the present situation and the critics of this election are becoming more and more vocal – even Tommie Bradford is going about saying that I ought not to have taken it on. I resent his attitude very strongly: what ever he may think, he should keep it to himself – needless to say, he has not approached me personally in the matter. There would be no election I feel sure if it were not for the little man Lawson, chairman of the North

Newcastle association, who has definitely told Vick that he is out for my blood! My offer to young Grattan-Doyle was a good one, and if I were allowed to see the young man and talk things out with him I feel sure I could make him see sense. An election is unfortunate at a time like the present, but my reason for fighting it remains good even if there is a war on.

Tuesday 28 May   I lunched with Vick today. He still holds firm though I fancy from what I am told that he is less firm when I am not present, and I gather, too, from what Wilkin tells me Appleby is beginning to hedge. It is odd how cowardly most people are and how little they are prepared to face criticism from what ever quarter it may come. I went to see Berry the manager of the *Newcastle Journal* and I think I got him to see that this election cannot now be avoided and that it is up to him to back me. He is a poor sort of a creature – half baked and I should say entirely ignorant of politics and most other things. His little editor is far more of a man.

Wednesday 29 May   Berry produced a short leader in today's *N.J.* in which after regretting the election he backs me – so my visit was a success. Today is nomination day and accompanied by Harry Bell I went to the Town Hall and was duly nominated, depositing with the Sheriff £150 which H.P. had provided me with. Grattan-Doyle was also nominated – I had hoped faintly that he would scratch at the last moment.

Thursday 30 May   Another lovely day: really the weather is superb – how grand a summer we should be having if it were not for this beastly war. We seem to be holding our own in France – by which I mean that our people appear to be holding the Germans off from Dunkirk and are carrying on the evacuation – a whole fleet of every kind of craft appears to have been assembled for the purpose. It really looks as if the greater part of the B.E.F. might yet be saved – I am beginning to feel more cheerful – but one must not be too optimistic. I have been busy all day and seen a good many people who are supposed to count in the division. Some of them adopted the line that there ought not to be an election and therefore that they would not vote – as a rule, however, they changed their point of view after I had explained things to them. I fancy that most decent people in the division are anxious to get rid of the Doyle connection and may seize this opportunity – such is the feeling one gets from all one hears. ... On the other hand we are told that the Doyle people are quite confident of winning and this is why they are fighting the election.

Friday 31 May   Another lovely day – far too hot for electioneering ... The canvassers are full of confidence and their reports are so optimistic that one begins to feels there must be [a] snag somewhere. There does seem a favourable feel in the air, but the question none of us can answer is whether people will actually take the trouble to vote. Without workers and cars it is impossible to drag them to the poll, and with this war on one is nervous that the electors will be even more apathetic than usual. ... The news from Dunkirk is satisfactory – our odd assortment of seacraft are working splendidly and bringing off the troops from under the enemy's noses – it is a grand performance which stirs one's blood and makes one prouder than ever of being an Englishman.

Sunday 2 June   It may well be when history is written that this escape of the B.E.F. was the turning point of the war – the first really serious German setback.

Monday 3 June   News has come today that George [Duke of] Northumberland[8] has been killed – a very sad affair – and a great loss to the north. I liked him and believed that in [the] course of time he would have developed into a very useful public man – he was intelligent and had a great sense of humour. ... The casualty lists are now beginning to come in and look like being very heavy – but the B.E.F. are being evacuated in a marvellous way and I feel a deal happier about things than I did last week. ... I had a quiet little meeting tonight – small attendance, but friendly. My opponent appears to be starting a campaign of abuse which is not likely to carry him very far. How I wish that it was all over: there is no great kudos about this election to be gained by me – but I do want to have my action justified – then I can afford to snap my fingers at my critics.

---

[8] Henry George Alan Percy (1912–1940), P.P.S. to Lord Londonderry 1935, to Lord Swinton 1936; suc. 9th Duke of Northumberland 1930.

Tuesday 4 June   The evacuation from Dunkirk continues: it really has been a marvellous achievement ... Canvassing continues – Agnes was helping Beatrice today – both of them are elated at their friendly reception: indeed, things look almost too good to be true. ... The desire to be rid of the Grattan-Doyle incubus seems widespread: at any ordinary election I should romp in.

Wednesday 5 June   Winston made a very fine speech in the HofC last night – he called the evacuation from Dunkirk 'a miracle of deliverance', and he was right. It has been an amazing epic of invincible courage and naval efficiency – but of course we have suffered the biggest military disaster in our history and it would be absurd to deny it. ... Beatrice who has been canvassing all day is still full of hope: everywhere she has met with supporters – whether they will actually vote remains to be seen. I have done a bit of canvassing too – mainly with Jews. We had 2 meetings tonight – both small but quite successful – no interruptions of any kind and some quite good questions. This closes my speaking campaign – which has not been an exacting one or much disturbed the efforts of the war workers!

Thursday 6 June   The Germans have begun their new offensive for Paris ... It is a trying time and one's nerves are like fiddle strings – mercifully this is the last day of the electioneering. Beatrice has been wonderful again all day: really she has the grit and determination of a hero – and her optimism is supreme. All our little band of workers seem hopeful – but one really cannot tell what people are thinking and of course there is no time to get fully round this vast division. Lunched with Wilkin at the Station Hotel. He is as nervous as I am – but he has proved a tower of strength throughout this business.

Friday 7 June   Another of these grilling days: not a cloud in the sky. I have been driving round most of the day with H.P. – committee rooms and polling stations. Voting has been very slack and clearly it is going to be a light poll – this we expected – no one can tell whether it will help us or not – my own view is that the heavier the poll the better for us. Apparently G.D.'s meeting last night was rather a bear fight: he and his friends were very rude to me and our supporters seem to have heckled them severely – the meeting finally breaking up in disorder. Well, the fight is over and now it only remains to hear the result. Beatrice has been wonderful and so has H.P. If we win, theirs is the victory – not mine.

Saturday 8 June   Well – it is over – the fight for N.N. fought and won: Poll 10,362 – myself 7,380 – G.D. 2,982 – majority 4,398. It is a grand result: I had not dreamt of such a big a majority on a small poll. But even the poll is not so bad considering all things: probably Labour and Liberals did not vote, old register, thousands of removals and absentees, no political excitement, 'a war on', brilliant summer day, no motor cars, etc., etc. Our win is an immense relief to both of us – and a vindication of my action. Beatrice and I got to the count about 10.15 [a.m.]. The moment I saw H.P. I knew everything in the garden was rosy – but how rosy neither he nor I suspected until the figures were announced. Young G.D. came and spoke to me: he was quite civil and had I been allowed to have a talk with him before nomination day I feel sure that I could have got him to see reason and stand down – I suppose that this is why his father and friends would not let us meet. After the result we met our workers: speeches: mild excitement and drinks – everyone highly elated.

Sunday 9 June   The contest has been a tremendous nervous strain and now that it is over one realises it more than ever. We took a big risk for if I had been defeated, it would have meant my retirement from politics and of course would have been a real slap in the eye. Everyone would have turned on me and all the smug Central Office people would have rejoiced exceedingly – why they dislike me so keenly I never can understand, for surely no one has ever worked harder for the Party than I have? I suppose it is because I always say what I mean and don't accept blindly all the things those in authority lay down. Now it will be a little awkward for Hacking, Topping & co. to say that I was wrong to stand up to the Grattan-Doyle ramp – it will be interesting all the same to see whether they will raise any objection to my being received into the fold. So far as I can see there can be no objection to my being given the whip as the Central Office stood out of the election and I stood as a supporter of the Government.

Monday 10 June   I lunched at the Beefsteak to meet James

Stuart.[9] He can see no reason why he should not introduce me: he is going to consult David Margesson and let me know. ... Musso has declared war against the Allies: just what might have been expected.

Tuesday 11 June   I was introduced today by David and James and so am completely accepted by the Party which is both gratifying and amusing! It is odd to find oneself back in the HofC so unexpectedly – I don't somehow or other feel elated to be an M.P. once again. I suppose it is because I am a nobody and have no hope of being anything else – and yet it is a satisfaction to be back here – at any rate it gives one a position and a chance of seeing and hearing what is going on at a critical period in our history – God only knows how critical! Every decent M.P. I have met seems really pleased that I won the election and professes to be glad to see me again – not one of them (except George Balfour[10]) has lifted a finger to help during my absence.

Wednesday 12 June   I attended the HofC again today. It is an odd place – no life in it at all – and a sparse attendance. The 'opposition' is lead by that poor, little creature Lees-Smith[11] who takes himself very seriously. Apparently ex-ministers of all parties are permitted to sit on the front opposition bench and Eddie Winterton and Herbert Williams[12] do so. I doubt whether I shall – at the same time it is silly not to maintain an active Conservative group as otherwise the Socialists have it all their own way. But Winterton is a futile fellow to lead a group and there seems to be no one else. ... I dined at the Beefsteak again and sat next to

[9] Deputy Chief Whip, and a friend of Headlam's since they entered the Commons together as new M.P.s in 1924.

[10] George Balfour (1872–1941), Con. M.P. Hampstead 1918–41; founder & Chairman of Balfour, Beatty & Co. Though not a particular political or personal friend, Balfour felt that Headlam had been treated poorly by Baldwin and Central Office, and in May 1938 secured for him a directorship in the Jerusalem Electric & Public Service Corporation which paid £250 p.a.: Headlam diary, 25 May 1938.

[11] Hastings Bertrand Lees-Smith (1878–1941), Lib. M.P. Northampton 1910–18, Lab. M.P. Keighley 1922–23, 1924–31, 1935–41; Postmaster-Gen. 1929–31; Pres. Bd. of Educ. Mar.-Aug. 1931; Acting Chairman, P.L.P. 1940–41.

[12] Herbert Geraint Williams (1884–1954), Con. M.P. Reading 1924–29, Croydon S. 1932–45, Croydon E. 1950–54; P.S. Trade 1928–29; Chairman, London Area 1939–48; Dir., E.I.A. 1926–28, 1931–41; kt. 1939, cr. Bart. 1953.

Harold Nicolson[13] who is now Under-Secretary to Duff [Cooper] at the Ministry of Information. He strikes me as the last man in the world to make a success as a Minister – conceited, futile and self-satisfied. He talked a lot of nonsense tonight about France and was laying down the law about everything. The trouble is that all this clique (Winston, Duff, F.O.,[14] etc.) have never realised the weakness of France, and still scarcely appreciate the truth.

Thursday 13 June   I have got and am still getting a lot of letters of congratulation from all sorts and conditions of men – it amuses me to hear from complete strangers telling me how glad they are that I have defeated the official candidate – certainly the Central Office is one of the most unpopular bodies in existence. Why it should be is not difficult to understand and as long as the Conservative Party organization remains such a narrow clique it will never be popular or really efficient. How it is all to be remodelled I don't know – but, unless it is, it is doomed.

Saturday 15 June   Fergus [Graham] appears to be one of the three selected candidates for West Newcastle now vacant due to old Joe Leech's death. I should like him to get it, but I don't suppose he will – William Nunn is the man they appear to fancy – of course he carries more guns than Fergus.

Tuesday 18 June   I travelled to London this morning for the meeting of the HofC. Winston made a very fine and courageous speech – I am not one of his admirers – by which I mean that I have never believed in his judgement or his fitness for the office which he now holds – but this does not imply that I do not admire his courage, his abilities, his quickness of uptake and his fervid patriotism. In many ways he is the right man for the present situation – his personality is what counts at the moment – and provided only that he does not run amuck as an amateur strategist, all may be well. At the moment he certainly commands the respect

[13] Harold George Nicolson (1886–1968), diplomatic service 1909–30; New Party cand. English Univ. 1931; Nat. Lab. M.P. Leicester W. 1935–45; P.S. Information 1940–41; joined Labour Party 1947, Lab. cand. Croydon N. 1948.
[14] The meaning of 'F.O.' is unclear: it does not fit any particular person, and is not likely to mean the Foreign Office as a whole; it might however be a reference to Anthony Eden, a former Foreign Secretary and prominent 'anti-appeaser'.

of the HofC and is very popular in the country. He looks very fat and unhealthy – but they tell me that he is in excellent form. I wish that he was not so intimate with Beaverbrook and that he had a better P.P.S. than Brendan Bracken. It is little short of a scandal that the latter should have been made a Privy Councillor – there appears to be pretty general agreement on this matter. The cabinet as a whole is not a very inspiring body and Attlee, who acts as Winston's second in command, is poor stuff – feeble, inaudible, ineffective. He welcomed me in a most friendly manner today in the smoking room which was nice of him, as I really scarcely know him – so did Maxton[15] and some of the Labour people whom I used to know.

Wednesday 19 June   The Franco-German armistice discussions are going on, and so is the German advance in France. It is rather appalling to know that the whole coastline of France is now in German hands – we must brace ourselves for a trying time for it is undoubtedly ahead of us. London is going to have a hell of a time before long.

Thursday 20 June   There was a secret session today, but, so far as I could see, anything said might with perfect safety might have been said *coram publico*.[16] All the old bores whom I used to listen to are still boring.

Friday 21 June   Presumably it is the scare of invasion which is fussing everyone today – personally I simply cannot believe that even Hitler will attempt a full scale invasion of this country without command of the sea – unless at any rate he has full command of the air. Whether or not he will be able to get that still remains to be seen – in France, at any rate, our flying people, although in a great minority, appear to have held their own with the Germans, and I have a supreme confidence in their ability to hold up an attack on this country.

Saturday 22 June   The German-French terms for the Armistice

---

[15] James Maxton (1885–1946), M.P. Glasgow Bridgeton 1922–46 (Lab. to 1931, then I.L.P.); Chairman, I.L.P. 1926–31, 1933–39.
[16] translation: before the public.

are made public today – they are much as expected, but their implications are serious for us. ... it means that we shall have to endure a real bombing from the air for however superior in quality our air force may be in quantity it cannot compete with the enemy. It remains now to see how our people will stand up to what is in store for them – if they can bear it, and I hope and believe that they can, all will still be well. Gradually we should be able to build up a larger air force than the Germans and give them hell – until then we shall just have to grin and bear it. What cheers me now is that to no one I meet nowadays – to whatever class he may belong – does it seem to occur that we shall not win the war. One strange result of the collapse of the French is that it has given our people a new confidence in themselves – they seem happier to be no longer impeded by allies!

Monday 24 June   I travelled to London by the early train this morning with Douglas Clifton-Brown. He is now Deputy Chairman of Committees and is said to stand a good chance of being elected Speaker when Algy Fitzroy[17] goes. The latter ought to retire: he is clearly bored stiff with his job and has aged a good deal since I was in the House. Douglas tells me that there is really a surprising lack of bright young men in the House nowadays and that it is quite impossible to pick a winner among them. The best of them are now serving in the forces – so no wonder I find the others pretty poor stuff. I dined tonight at the Beefsteak and sat beside Harold Macmillan. He is very much the Minister nowadays, but says that he has arrived too late to rise very high. I can see no reason (except his own personality) for his not getting on – even to the top of the tree – but he is his own worst enemy: he is too self-centred, too obviously cleverer than the rest of us. He never will let the other man have his say and he invariably knows everything better than the other man. He was by way of being loyal to his present chief (Herbert Morrison), but made me realize that he agrees with what I have already heard – *viz.* – that H.M. is not as much a success as Minister of Supply – and cuts very little ice – except of course for having told other people to 'go to it!'

[17] Edward Algernon Fitzroy (1869–1943), Con. M.P. Northants. S. 1900–06, 1910– 18, Daventry 1918–43; Dep. Chairman of Ways & Means 1922–23, 1924–28; Speaker 1928–43; after his death his widow was cr. Viscountess Daventry 1943.

Thursday 27 June   There was another 'secret session' today: the Ministry of Supply was discussed – nothing in the least interesting was disclosed and Mr Herbert Morrison got away with it very easily. Of course there is no serious opposition and the futile points raised by the various speakers could be easily disposed of.

Monday 1 July 1940   The losses in material of every description in France have been appalling and apparently there were no supplies in existence at home to replace them – or, at any rate, not nearly enough. This is pretty disgraceful and one feels that there has been no real drive behind our war effort for the last nine months. Chamberlain will have to bear the blame for this – for he should have realized, when the Labour people refused to come in with him, that it was useless to carry on. Unless they would cooperate, he could not count upon the full support of the trade unions and a whole-hearted effort by the workers. He should, therefore, have resigned long ago. Poor man – one feels sorry for him – he did his level best but he lacked the divine spark and was lacking in the human touch – too much convinced that he could stand alone and lacking those qualities which arouse the enthusiasm of one's supporters. He was also, I think, a bad judge of men – how otherwise can one account for his appointing Hore-Belisha to the War Office and Burgin[18] to the Ministry of Supply? Two more unsuitable men for their respective jobs it would be impossible to find.

Tuesday 2 July   Duff Cooper told me this afternoon that they were all convinced that 'the invasion' would begin tomorrow night! He was quite serious!

Wednesday 3 July   I heard tonight at the Beefsteak where I dined that Duff and Gort were sent to northern Africa by air to try and induce the French General commanding in Morocco not to obey the Pétain[19] Government's orders – apparently he refused to see

---

[18] (Edward) Leslie Burgin (1887–1945), Lib. M.P. Luton 1929–45 (Lib. Nat. from 1931); P.S. Trade 1932–37; Min. of Transport 1937–39; Min. of Supply 1939–40.

[19] Henri Philippe Pétain (1856–1951), entered French army 1876, comm. French forces at Verdun 1916; C. in C. French armies Western Front 1917; Marshal of France 1918; Vice-Pres., Higher Counc. of War 1920–30; Min. of War 1934; P.M. 1940–42, absorbed Presidential powers as Chief of State, July 1940; head of state, Vichy regime 1942–44; sentence of death for treason, commuted to life imprisonment 1945.

them. To me his attitude was entirely understandable, and I cannot imagine a more futile proceeding than to try and influence him by English pressure – more especially in view of the complete failure of a similar effort made by Duff and G. Lloyd at Bordeaux. Other people at the Club held different views and possibly they were right in suggesting that at any rate 'it was worth trying'.

Thursday 4 July   Winston made a very effective speech in the HofC this afternoon – telling us of our dramatic seizure of the French fleet – and the unhappy affair at Oran where our ships had to destroy a number of French vessels. ... I think that every man in the HofC felt that in the circumstances the government had no alternative but to act as it did. There was a wild scene of enthusiasm when Winston sat down this afternoon: everyone standing up and cheering. As I watch the scene I could not help visualizing a similar scene (at which I was not present) when a similar ovation was given to Neville Chamberlain, 'the man of Munich'.

Tuesday 9 July   We had a secret session – Dr. Dalton told us all about the splendid work his department (Economic Warfare) is doing now that he has taken charge of it – never was such a humbug – but he got away with it today, and everyone was impressed – those of us, at any rate, who did not know what lies he was uttering. I intervened and spoke not too badly for about a quarter of an hour – but I did not say nearly enough – of course our failure to do trade in the Balkans is notorious and its evil effects are all too noticeable politically. I dined with James Stuart at the house. He has lost all his vim, and tells me that he would like to give up his job and have done with politics – when people have been successful politically and have jobs, one always doubts assertions of this kind.

Wednesday 10 July   In the HofC Alexander told us a little about the work of the Navy. I suppose that this man is able and fit for his job, but he does not impress me: I believe him to be a flat catcher – but in this Government I presume that he will play second string to Winston who is the only man who counts. I am told that the people at the Admiralty like Alexander. ... I dined at the Beefsteak – the usual people, the usual gossip – it is odd how intelligent people have so little to say worth recording!

Thursday 11 July   Every day that passes makes one prouder and prouder of the R.A.F. Beaverbrook spoke in the HofL today and assured their lordships that there is no shortage of aeroplanes – but that of course we can never have enough. He asserted that everything was being done to speed up production and that American supplies were coming in. This all sounds splendid – but I wish that I could put more confidence than I do in the word of a Beaverbrook – I utterly distrust the man and I have little faith in his so-called 'dynamic' abilities!

Friday 12 July   Beatrice and I went into Newcastle and attended a meeting of our N.N. Association. It was quite a good gathering and I made a speech which went down well. Sooner or later we ought to be able to make a good show – but I could wish that we could find a better chairman than Vick. One is grateful to him of course for having stepped into the breach when he did – but he is such a feeble creature and so utterly lacking in guts that one feels that he is quite incompetent to run the show or to deal as he should with Lawson and the other association. He is a man who is afraid of his own shadow and who's only wish is to be a friend of everybody however big a scoundrel anybody may be.

Sunday 14 July   Winston spoke on the wireless tonight – a fine effort – less bombastic than usual and full of vim. The recent successes of the RAF have clearly cheered him up a lot. He assured us that we now have a million and a half men under arms in this country, and, in addition, another million in the Local Defence force which he preferred to call the Home Guard. (To do him justice he did not try and make us believe that this latter force was yet armed!). It is clear, I think, now that we are in a position to resist an invasion should the Germans risk one ...

Tuesday 16 July   London is rapidly become like a besieged town – or, rather, is being converted into a defended zone. Whether all the barbed wire defences and machine-gun posts in the Whitehall area are erected to cover the last stand of Winston and the rest of us against the invading Germans, or whether to prevent the government offices being raided by 'Fifth Columnists' and parachutists, one does not know. They are certainly formidable obstructions to most of us especially in the hours of darkness when one is confronted by barriers in the most unexpected places. I am told that Winston is mainly responsible for them and takes the deepest interest in them. He appears to spend a lot of time inspecting our defences all over the country. It is certainly his hour – and the confidence in him is growing on all sides.

Monday 22 July   After luncheon I went to the HofC quite forgetting that the House did not sit on Monday nowadays.

Tuesday 23 July   Kingsley Wood's budget speech this afternoon was a dull, uninspired affair – a 1/- more on the income tax, a rise in surtax, and on beer, and tobacco – it is going to mean a quite considerable addition to my financial worries. Dined at the Beefsteak: I found Harold Nicolson more trying than ever – never have I come across a more conceited, self-satisfied and common-place man.

Thursday 25 July   Lord Joicey[20] appears to have committed suicide – shot himself with a shotgun on his own lawn. I saw him only a few days ago at the Club in Newcastle – he seemed to be quite normal – but I am told that latterly he has been the complete pessimist – a terrible thing to do all the same and very cruel to his poor wife. I suppose that this will mean the closing down of Ford Castle – the Joicey estate can hardly have got over the last death duties.

Sunday 28 July   It is odd how seldom one finds any really trustworthy people connected with politics – so seldom do people interest themselves in local political associations from motives of principle or patriotism: it is usually for what they can get out of them either in the way of office which gives them a little local importance or in order to get some honour or reward however trumpery. Women on the whole, I think, are more tiresome and easily upset than men – and greater intriguers.

Tuesday 30 July   There was a secret session today, before which there was a debate in which Eddie Winterton 'as an old member'

---

[20] James Arthur Joicey (1880–1940), suc. 2nd Baron Joicey 1936.

aired his views about secret sessions, etc., and Josh Wedgwood,[21] who is now of the stock bore of the HofC, speaking on every possible occasion and always making the same speech, took a prominent part. I spoke in the subsequent debate economic warfare, not too badly, but it was an unprepared effort and I could have done much better had I known it was coming – I mean the particular subject which was to be discussed. It was not an enlivening discussion and did not do anything to convince one that those in charge of things know their business. It is fairly obvious that the Treasury still has a stranglehold on everything, and still adopts a policy which may do well enough in time of peace but which is quite hopeless in a time of war. We shall win this war, I suppose, in due course, but we are doing everything in our power to handicap ourselves in the struggle, and God knows the odds against us are heavy enough already without our adding to our own difficulties.

Wednesday 31 July   There was a debate in the HofC today on the defence regulations to which I cannot say I listened very much. It was mainly conducted (as all debates now are) by the Labour Party – it is odd how the Conservatives, even the stock bores who usually keep talking, have passed out of the picture. I am told that many of the best of them are now away with the forces and of course some of them are not – and never were – talkers. No doubt, too, those who might intervene in debate more often feel, as I do, that there is no object in making speeches nowadays – all the same, I feel that we are mistaken and ought not to allow the Socialists such a free run. There is of course 'a party truce', but it is only observed by one side – every speech made by the Labour people in the HofC is a party speech and is propaganda. Of course our side ought to organize itself and arrangements should be made for certain M.P.s to speak in all important debates to put forward the Conservative point of view. The trouble is that Winston appears to be the only man to lead us and he is quite incapable of the job. There are some other ex-cabinet ministers – Walter Elliot, Colville,

---

[21] Josiah Clement Wedgwood (1872–1943), M.P. Newcastle-under-Lyme 1906–42 (Lib. to 1919, Lab. 1919–31, Ind. Lab. 1931–42); Chanc. Duchy of Lancaster 1924; Vice-Chairman, P.L.P. 1922–24; cr. Baron Wedgwood 1942; Chairman of Ctte. on House of Commons Records 1929, and principal promoter of resulting History of Parliament project.

Dorman-Smith[22] – but not only are they masquerading as soldiers but they are also, none of them, suitable men to lead a party.[23] It is altogether a bad look out for the future and it looks as if everything we ought to stand for will go by default.

Thursday 1 August   ... the one thing which emerges is that our R.A.F. is holding its own in the air *blitzkrieg*[24] – it is doing magnificently and is clearly superior to the enemy both in personnel and material – if it were only larger, we might well give the enemy such a knock as would remove any danger of invasion. What worries me is that our production still seems to be very slow – everyone tells you the same story about it, and no one is able to account for the slowness. Opinions differ about Beaverbrook – some say that he really is getting a move on, but has to get rid of any number of duds before he can hope to get things going – others assert that he is merely making confusion worse confounded. Everyone agrees that personally he is a crook and laments the influence he is supposed to have over Winston.

Sunday 4 August   It has been a superb day and how happy we all might be if it were not for this beastly war and the knowledge that there are hundreds of thousands of unpleasing Germans waiting about on the other side of the Channel for the chance of invading us! The invasion scare is a very real one there can be no doubt about it – and I think that everybody realizes it – though whether our military preparations are up to much seems open to doubt – certainly the local defence units have little or no equipment and the reason for this is said to be that there is nothing like enough equipment for the regular army. If Hitler had the guts to come across by any means he could *now*, he might give us a very ugly

---

[22] Reginald Hugh Dorman-Smith (1899–1977), Con. M.P. Petersfield 1935–41; Min. Agric. 1939–40; Pres., N.F.U. 1936–37; rejoined army 1940–41; Gov. of Burma 1941–46; kt. 1937.

[23] After being dropped from office in May 1940, several former Ministers sought useful war work by joining the armed forces; most had previous experience from serving in the First World War, but were now too old for front-line duties.

[24] translation: lightning war. Originally used to describe the tactics of rapid advance by armoured units with close air support used by Germany in the invasions of Poland and France, the shorter form *blitz* was used by the British public to refer to the German bombing of cities (especially London) in 1940–41.

time of it – the longer he waits, the less chance of success he has – for surely production should improve every day.

Wednesday 7 August   I lunched with Jack Dill today – it was nice to see him again and to feel that he is in charge, for he still gives one the same feeling of confidence that he gave one at G.H.Q. in April, 1918. He does not attempt to minimize the extreme gravity of the situation and he expects a full-blooded invasion any day. He is a bit happier about the Army – he says that the training is improving and that supplies are coming in more adequately, but that we shall not be ready to carry out any offensive operation for a long time to come on a large scale. ... Apparently Archie Wavell's[25] force is not nearly large enough to give us much cause for confidence: it can, I gather, barely be expected to hold its own. I asked him how it was that our people in France did not spot the feebleness of the French: he admitted that he supposed they ought to have done so: he said that he personally had never had much opinion of Gamelin,[26] but that the majority of the other generals with whom he came in contact seemed keen enough – the troops in the Maginot Line, he said, seemed smart and alert – other troops did not strike him as so good. Of course Dill is being worked to death and I rather gathered that Winston was a nuisance.

Thursday 8 August   This afternoon I went to a cocktail party at the Ritz given by some American gent. I was invited to it by Maureen Stanley – she was at the top of her form – busy 'vamping' Sir John Reith. The latter was as pleased as Punch and I heard him asking her to call him John! Maureen had little or no gossip: she is out of the picture now that Oliver is no longer in the Cabinet – she told me that he is well and happy in some job at Chester. She assured me that her one and only object was to enter the HofC – I dissuaded her, visualizing all the horror of being a

[25] Archibald Percival Wavell (1883–1950), army career; G.O.C. Palestine & Trans-jordan 1937–38; C. in C., Southern Command 1938–39, Middle East 1939–41, India 1941–43; Supreme Comm., S.W. Pacific 1942; Viceroy of India 1943–47; kt. 1939, cr. Viscount Wavell 1943, Earl 1947.

[26] Maurice Gustave Gamelin (1872–1958), French army career; served on staff of C. in C. 1911–17; Military Ass. to High Comm., Syria 1925–28; Chief of Staff 1931; Inspector-Gen. 1935–37; Chief of Gen. Staff 1938–39; C. in C. 1939–40; tried by Vichy govt. 1941, imprisoned at Buchenwald Concentration Camp 1943–45.

woman M.P. and having to associate with Nancy,[27] Irene [Ward], Thelma,[28] 'Red Ellen',[29] Miss Rathbone,[30] etc.

Sunday 11 August   There has been another air battle reported in the south and we are reported to have destroyed 60 German machines: 19 of our own lost. The Germans are making fantastic claims which show they dare not publish the truth – a good sign if it really is the case. I honestly believe our people dare not minimize our losses or magnify our successes.

Tuesday 13 August   ... spent the afternoon at the HofC – I find it a very dull and depressing place *socially*: such friends as I have there are Ministers and they are usually conspicuous by their absence – there are few other people who were in the House with me about whom I care about in the least and of course I don't know the new people. Our Conservative lot strike me as a very feeble collection, but I am told that the very best of our people are on war service of one kind or another and don't come near the House. There is a sprinkling of men in uniform, nevertheless, who are very regular attendants – noticeably Victor Cazalet[31] who is the same as ever, but a lot fatter. I had dinner tonight at the HofC with Maxton and Campbell Stephen[32] – I have always liked the former: the latter has not got an attractive personality. It is difficult to take either of them seriously politically – but, nevertheless, the I.L.P. group has become an institution in the HofC for which

[27] Nancy Witcher Astor (1879–1964), Con. M.P. Plymouth Sutton 1919–45; married 1906 Waldorf Astor, suc. 2nd Viscount Astor 1919; the first woman to sit in the House of Commons.
[28] Thelma Cazalet (1899–1989), Con. M.P. Islington E. 1931–45; P.P.S. to K. Lindsay 1937–40; P.S. Educ. 1945; adopted surname Cazalet-Keir after marriage 1939.
[29] Ellen Cicely Wilkinson (1891–1947), Lab. M.P. Middlesborough E. 1924–31, Jarrow 1935–47; P.P.S. to Susan Lawrence 1929–31; P.S. Pensions 1940; P.S. Home Security 1940–45; Min. of Educ. 1945–47; Chairman, Lab. Party N.E.C. 1944–45.
[30] Eleanor Florence Rathbone (1872–1946), Ind. M.P. English Univ. 1929–46; member of Liverpool City Council 1909–35; Pres., Nat. Union of Societies for Equal Ctizenship 1919–29.
[31] Victor Alexander Cazalet (1896–1943), Con. M.P. Chippenham 1924–43; P.P.S. to P. Cunliffe-Lister 1924–27, to J.H. Thomas 1931; Liason Officer with Polish Forces 1940–43.
[32] Campbell Stephen (1884–1947), Minister in United Free Church, 1911–18; I.L.P. M.P. Glasgow Camlachie 1922–31, 1935–47; rejoined P.L.P. 21 Oct. 1947, died 25 Oct. 1947

everyone (outside the Labour Party) has a kindly feeling. ... I put down a motion today advocating drastic overhaul of [the] Min. of Information and reduction of F.O. staff – I don't suppose that I shall be given a day to debate this motion!

Friday 16 August   Our R.A.F. is wonderful and, personally, my opinion is that we owe it to Trenchard.[33] He must have laid the foundations very surely for such results to be possible. He always insisted upon a very high standard in the personnel, and this established a high morale. In material, too, I believe that he insisted on being supplied only with the best of everything.

Saturday 17 August   In this war we seem to know even less than we did in the last war how things are going in Germany. I suppose the Gestapo has succeeded in blocking every channel of information pretty effectively, in addition to which of course there are really no foreign observers in Germany today – no neutral journalists. ... Our people who are being bombed seem to be behaving with marvellous courage and *sang froid*.[34]

Monday 19 August   Yesterday, after a comparatively quiet day on Saturday, the enemy made a big attack in the air – 600 aeroplanes are said to have tried to get through the London defences – they were held up, however, in the suburbs. The Air Ministry states tonight that 140 of the German machines were brought down – a truly splendid effort on the part of our people – I cannot believe that the German air force can stand up against such losses much longer – are we nearing the end of the *blitzkrieg*, I wonder? If the Germans stop it or reduce its strength, it will mean I am sure that the invasion need not be expected – even Hitler would scarcely embark upon such a venture, except as a last hope, without having obtained a command of the air ... The only other news of any interest today is that Canada and the U.S.A. are going to set up a united joint Board of Defence for the two countries: certainly the war is bringing the English-speaking races together in a way which one would have thought impossible a few years ago – if the outcome

[33] Hugh Montague Trenchard (1873–1956), army career; Chief of Air Staff 1918, 1919–29; Commissioner of Metropolitan Police 1931–35; kt. 1918, cr. Baron Trenchard 1930, Viscount 1936; the founding father of the Royal Air Force.
[34] translation: coolness, unconcern; literally: cold blood.

of it all is going to be a real union between the Brit. Empire and the U.S.A., this war will not have been fought in vain – Hitler may yet prove to be a blessing in disguise.

Tuesday 27 August   Lunched at the Beefsteak – Malcolm Robertson,[35] the latest M.P., there and delighted to be in the HofC. He will be a great and popular frequenter of the smoking room whatever else he may be – that is sure! He is a cheery, confident man who knows his own mind – which is something. I am all for a man who is capable and courageous enough to air his views, even if I disagree with them.

Wednesday 4 September   There is no doubt that if the Germans go on bombing us and unless we can devise some method of fighting them at night, they will do an immense amount of damage and slaughter thousands of people – whether or not they will break down civilian morale remains to be seen: so far, at any rate, there is no sign of any such happening – but, personally, I doubt whether they have as yet even begun to do their 'damn'dest'.

Monday 9 September   I went into Newcastle this morning and lunched Wilkin at the Station Hotel. I wanted to have his views as to our best policy for getting the Association going. The women, lead by Beatrice, are screaming for an H.Q. Vick is against incurring any expenditure until we have some money. He says that no one will subscribe now and therefore that we just better hang on. He says that the rival Association is dying: our women say that, on the contrary, it is very much alive, and that some of our people are deserting to it.

Wednesday 18 September   ... the other Association is carrying on and rumour has it that they are approaching 'a prominent Newcastle businessman' to be their candidate against me at the next election. I don't regard this as a serious menace, but, nevertheless, it is a nuisance that the beastly people should continue their vendetta

---

[35] Malcolm Arnold Robertson (1877–1951), diplomatic career; British High Comm. to Inter-Allied Rhineland Commission 1920–21; Consul-Gen., Tangier 1921–25; Min., Buenos Aires 1925–27, Amb. 1927–29; Chairman, Spillers Ltd. 1930–47; Chairman, British Council 1941–45; Con. M.P. Mitcham 1940–45; kt. 1924.

against me. I suppose that the horrid little drunkard Lawson is at the bottom of it all.

Friday 20 September   Things seem to have been quieter over London today – it is beginning to look as if the *Luftwaffe* had had about enough of the business – they have certainly got it in the neck. ... Our airmen have had a gruelling time, but each day that passes the more magnificently they seem to carry on the fight. It is odd to see how so much we owe to so small a number of young men – here are millions of us doing nothing while the battle is being decided above our heads by a chosen band of warriors drawn from here, there and everywhere – upon them depends our safety and perhaps the independence of our country. They must be a superb body of men ... one would like to know the difference in material strength of our R.A.F. and the *Luftwaffe*: some day presumably we shall know – and then, more than ever, I expect, we shall salute the gallant men who are now doing such untold services for their country.

Thursday 3 October   Neville Chamberlain's resignation is announced tonight. The news has not come as a surprise as report has warned us that he was not well and could not last long. Poor man – one is sorry for him -for he failed to carry out his policy and preserve peace – but of course the job was an impossible one when he took it in hand. Things had been allowed to go too far by Baldwin, MacDonald, Simon & Co. – Neville cannot be blamed for his failure when at the helm, however much he may share in the blame due to the other people – after all, he was the most influential man in Baldwin's cabinet. As regards the Munich Agreement I have always held that he was right – humiliating though it was, we could not have risked war in 1938 as the state of things in London today shows only too plainly. What Neville's place in history will be it is hard to say – not so high or so low as some people imagine today. One thing is fairly evident even now and that is that neither his knowledge of foreign politics nor his upbringing and experience fitted him to deal with foreigners or to take charge directly of foreign affairs, more especially as he seems to have taken advice mainly from Horace Wilson who was equally ignorant and inexperienced.

Friday 4 October   The changes in the Cabinet are not particularly exciting – to me the interesting one is the introduction of Oliver Lyttelton[36] as Pre[sident] of the B[oard] of T[rade]. It is amusing after all the contempt he has poured upon the HofC to see him entering it – but of course he enters it easily and as a Cabinet minister, and can say quite fairly that he is being forced in owing to be[ing] one of the 'supermen'. I think that he is likely to be very successful in the House – he has a sense of humour, great ability and plenty of self-assurance – indeed, he may be the man to lead the party – who knows? The move of Sir John Reith (+ a peerage because presumably he has been a complete failure in the HofC) to yet another post is typical of our method of never getting rid of a man once the press has insisted upon him being a superman! Moore-Brabazon[37] should do well at the Min. of Transport, if he will take the trouble. He is very able, but lazy and ill-mannered. Duncan[38] for Morrison at the Ministry of Supply should be an improvement, and Morrison for John Anderson at the Home Office cannot make matters worse in that job. Bobbety Cranborne,[39] Sec. of State for the Colonies,[40] is probably a reward for having stuck to Eden: but he is a capable and charming fellow and should do well. Tom Inskip becomes L[ord] C[hief] J[ustice] after being L[ord] C[hancellor] which I should think is making legal history. He now gets £8,000 for a year for the remainder of his days – which is not so bad for a man of his legal calibre – he has been a lucky man.

[36] Oliver Lyttelton (1893–1972), business career; Controller of Non-Ferrous Metals 1939–40; Con. M.P. Aldershot 1940–54; Pres. Bd. of Trade 1940–41, 1945; Min. Res. Cairo 1941–42; Min. of Production 1942–45; member of War Cabinet 1941–45; Colonial Sec. 1951–54; Pres., Institute of Directors 1948–51, 1954–63; cr. Viscount Chandos 1954; a friend of Headlam's since the First World War.

[37] John Theodore Cuthbert Moore-Brabazon (1884–1964), Con. M.P. Chatham 1918–29, Wallasey 1931–42; P.S. Transport 1923–24, 1924–27; Min. of Transport 1940–41; Min. of Aircraft Production 1941–42; cr. Baron Brabazon of Tara 1942.

[38] Andrew Rae Duncan (1884–1952), business career; Coal Controller 1919–20; Vice-Pres., Shipbuilding Employers' Fed. 1920–27; Dir., Bank of England 1929–40; Chairman, Central Electricity Bd. 1927–35, British Iron & Steel Fed. 1935–40; Nat. M.P. City of London 1940–50; Pres. Bd. of Trade Jan–Oct. 1940, 1941–42; Min. of Supply 1940–41, 1942–45; kt. 1921.

[39] Robert Arthur James Gascoyne-Cecil (1893–1972), Con. M.P. Dorset S. 1929–41; U.S. For. Office 1935–38; Paymaster-Gen. 1940; Dominions Sec. 1940–42, 1943–45; Lord Privy Seal 1942–43, 1951–52; Commonwealth Sec. 1952; Lord Pres. 1952–57; Con. Leader in the Lords 1942–57; styled Viscount Cranborne 1903–47; summoned to the Lords as Baron Cecil of Essendon 1941, suc. 5th Marquess of Salisbury 1947, K.G. 1946.

[40] Cranborne was appointed Dominions Secretary, not Colonial Secretary.

Saturday 5 October   We had the Area half-yearly meeting this afternoon: not at all a bad attendance in view of war conditions. I moved 2 resolutions – 1 expressing our confidence in Winston (would that I possessed it more strongly myself) and 1 bidding farewell to Neville. ... Topping had had a talk with Vick and Lawson this morning and apparently the latter's tone has completely changed and he is ready to make it up and be friends. It is a tiresome business and one hates the interference of Topping & co. – nevertheless, it is easy to overrate the importance of a matter of this kind – certainly not worthwhile to get angry with busybodies.

Tuesday 8 October   Went to the HofC ... it met at 11 a.m. Winston made an admirable speech – full of vim, but not too much buck. He is under no illusions as to what we have ahead of us, and clearly means the people to face facts. He told us that the mistake of letting the French ships through to Dakar was the fault of a local commander – he got away with this, but surely this is no excuse for our not having taken Dakar weeks ago – when we decided to go for the French fleet? ... There have been air raid warnings all day, and the guns are going vigorously as I write.

Wednesday 9 October   The House discussed A.R.P. work in London today and I confess that I did not listen to the debate. I had an early luncheon with Jock McEwen[41] – a nice fellow. (He was dropped from some under-secretaryship when this Govt. was formed – but does not seem to bear any malice against those in authority). ... I decided not to attend the party meeting this afternoon summoned to elect a leader in succession to Neville Chamberlain – it was certain that Winston would be elected ...

Friday 11 October   I went into Newcastle this morning and lunched with Vick at the Conservative Club. I talked very frankly to him: said that he could not be a friend at one and the same time with me and Lawson: warned him not to commit himself in any way when he met Lawson: and told him not to worry his head

---

[41] John Helias Finnie McEwen (1894–1962), Con. M.P. Berwick & Haddington 1931–45; P.P.S. to R.A. Butler 1933–36, to W. Elliot 1936–38; Ass. Whip 1939; U.S. Scotland 1939–40: Whip, 1942–44; Chairman, Con. Foreign Affairs Ctte. 1938–39; Chairman, 1922 Ctte. 1944–45; Pres., Scottish Unionist Ass. 1949–50; cr. Bart. 1953.

about Ramsden, Topping & Co. He took it all very amiably but then he is that type of man – just a jelly!

Tuesday 15 October   There was nothing doing at the House and very few members present. The general opinion of those who were there was that it is ridiculous to meet 3 times a week when there is so little to do: that 2 days a fortnight would be ample for the next few months. There is little necessary legislation for the time being and the whips have to arrange little debates to keep us going on such subjects as physical education for children, malnutrition, etc. – any subject of importance is *verboten* apparently. ... The bombing here last night was pretty bad in the West End. The swine got the poor old Travellers[42] (so it is just as well I decided not to come to London yesterday) – incendiary bombs have burnt the roof and bedrooms – so my London home is gone – the Carlton Club got a direct hit and is badly shattered. There were over 100 members in the Club at the time and not one of them was scratched which seems to indicate that God approves of Conservative legislators.

Wednesday 16 October   Lunched at the House with James Stuart and Harold Macmillan – the latter and a good many other junior ministers was at the Carlton when the bomb dropped – both admitted that they found the air raids very nerve-shaking and infinitely preferred the shelling in the trenches of the last war. They are both brave men, and one realises from what they say how marvellous the man in the street is to stand the strain as well as he is standing it – but one cannot help wondering how he will stand it all through the winter. The underground and the shelters are pretty beastly places to sleep in night after night. ... The difficulties of communications are making all forms of business almost impossible in London.

Sunday 20 October   The German drive in the Balkans continues – they now are in full possession of Rumania and presumably will soon be equally strong in the other Balkan states. One feels that all this is largely our own fault – but it seems useless to me to keep abusing (as people do) Edward Halifax and our diplomatists entirely for this. They have failed to make full use of propaganda and the

---

[42] Headlam's club; at this time, he normally slept there when staying in London.

economic means at our disposal, but they have always been in the difficult position of not being able to help these wretched little countries by force of arms – whereas the Germans can always threaten force. In the past, too, our diplomacy has always been able to play off the Russians against the Germans in the Balkans, but today the Russians, if not actually in collusion with the Germans (which I personally suspect) show no signs of resisting their access to the Black Sea. It is a difficult situation with which to deal – too far gone now, I fear, for us to be able to hope to effect anything by diplomatic means. If we can prevent Greece [from] being overrun peacefully by Germany, it will be an agreeable surprise. Meanwhile we are told that we are spending money at the rate of £9,000,000 a day: it is a grotesque state of things and means higher and yet higher taxation.

Thursday 24 October   ... went to the HofC at 11 a.m., the present hour of meeting. The air debate was not interesting and Archie Sinclair's speech told us nothing we did not know before – he is a feeble fellow to be in charge of a fighting service in a great war. ... I caught the 5.25 from King's X and had Tom Magnay M.P. as my travelling companion: tiring but not so tiring as Irene Ward.

Friday 25 October   ... attended a meeting of our Executive Committee at Vick's office. We decided to accept the proposal to negotiate with the other Association, but subject to no stipulations of any kind. Lawson is certain to refuse this and then I can see no reason why we should bother with him and his Association any more – but no doubt old Vick will still hanker after 'coming to terms', hoping to please Topping & co.

6

WINSTON'S WAR

October 1940 to June 1941

Monday 28 October 1940   The news today is that the Italians issued an ultimatum to the Greeks last night or in the early hours of this morning demanding the surrender of certain unspecified parts and that the Greeks refused to discuss the proposal. There is now war between Italy and Greece. I am agreeably surprised that the Greeks have had the guts to stand up to Musso: I shall be still more agreeably surprised if they can stop his armies from over-running Greece.

Thursday 31 October   People in England are now crying out for more bombing of Italian towns and expecting the impossible. It is always so: we stint the services in peacetime and then call upon them in wartime to do anything and everything which comes into our heads. We are a strange race which, if God did not love, must inevitably go under. We come through our troubles not because we deserve to do so, but because God likes us I suppose because we do possess qualities of courage and endurance when we are up against it, and possess the qualities, too, which make the world a better place – a sense of justice and fair play, a willingness to see the other fellow's point of view, and a horror of cruelty and unfairness between man and man. I believe that in their heart of hearts even these dictators realize that the British Empire is a real necessity in the world which they cannot replace.

Tuesday 5 November   Winston in his speech today gave us the civilian casualty list as a result of air raids: very grave figures, I thought, but he made light of them. He told us, too, that the submarine and mine war was extremely serious, though he was confident that the Navy would be able to cope with it. M.P.s are getting rather rattled by it and no wonder: they are very perturbed, I am glad to say, about 'Eire'[1] – but it would seem that the Govt. is not inclined to take any drastic action. Beamish[2] told me today that some little time ago he put a question down on the subject and Cranborne begged him to withdraw it because they did not want to upset the Irish! Ye Gods – are we to be compelled to lose our men and ships and food and munitions indefinitely for fear of annoying De Valera[3] & Co! It is preposterous.

Wednesday 6 November   In the HofC Ned Grigg read out a long W[ar] O[ffice] report relating to the Home Guard which might just as well have been published as a white paper – Ned is terribly important nowadays – office has had the same kind of effect upon him as it has had on Harold Macmillan, making him bigger than ever for his boots!

Wednesday 13 November   The House sat today at what is termed 'The Annexe' – in other words the new Church House at Westminster.[4] We are to dodge about between this place and the HofC in order to mystify the German bombers. To me it seems rather absurd – but it is said to be Winston's idea and so everyone is satisfied – for the time being anything and everything that Winston says is right. He had a great moment today when after questions he announced that the Fleet Air Arm had bombed the Italian Fleet in Taranto harbour and crippled badly 3 battleships, 2 cruisers and

[1] Formerly the 'Irish Free State', the name 'Eire' was adopted in the constitution introduced by De Valera in 1937. Eire remained a member of the Commonwealth until 1949, but was the only Dominion to adopt a position of neutrality during the war; this made protecting the Atlantic convoys much more difficult.

[2] Tufton Percy Hamilton Beamish (1874–1951), naval career 1888–1922; Con. M.P. Lewes 1924–31, 1936–45.

[3] Eamonn de Valera (1882–1975), Sinn Fein M.P. Clare E. 1917–21; member of Dail for Co. Clare 1921–59, Pres. of Dail 1919–22; Pres., Sinn Fein 1917–26; Pres., Fianna Fail 1926–59; Min. for External Affairs 1932–48; Taoiseach 1937–48, 1951–54, 1957–59; Pres. of the Republic 1959–73.

[4] The Commons sat at Church House on 7, 19 & 21 Nov., 10–12 & 17–19 Dec. 1940; one reason for the move was that Church House was a modern building with a stronger structure than the Palace of Westminster. It was unpopular with M.P.s but was used again during heavy bombing in late April 1941 and, after the destruction of the Comons chamber, from 13 May to 19 June 1941; it was also used from 20 June to 3 Aug. 1944 during the flying bomb attacks.

2 auxiliary vessels. Needless to say, the House went wild with delight. ... In the afternoon I attended the National Union Executive at Caxton House at which Winston spoke, as leader of the Party. I had a word with Hacking about N.N. and begged him to keep out of our local affairs.

Saturday 16 November   The Greeks still seem to be doing well, but it is too much to hope that they can hold up the Italians for any length of time unless we can help them on land as well as in the air – and help them effectively. This, I should imagine, will be no easy task for us, unless Wavell's army is a great deal bigger than I imagine it to be. In addition to this, we must be prepared for a German move to back up the Italians – probably through Yugoslavia, because I fancy that Hitler and Molotov[5] are not going to make the mistake of drawing in the Bulgars to attack the Greeks – if they did, the Turks would surely come into the picture?

Sunday 17 November   ... to Hexham to see an exhibition of platoon drill by some Essex b[attalio]n. ... It was a disappointing show ... One feels rather nervous and unhappy when one sees the modern soldiers: they seem so very raw and untrained, even after all these months of war. The weak lot are of course the second line T[erritorial] A[rmy], Hore-Belisha's boys: their officers are said to be quite impossible.

Monday 18 November   The similarity between things today and the situation in 1807 is remarkable – but I could wish that we had a Canning at the F.O. instead of Edward Halifax. The latter appears to have no policy, no initiative, no drive, no anything.

Tuesday 19 November   I saw Bobbety Cranborne at the HofC (Annexe) this morning and spoke to him *re* the Irish ports. He told me that the P.M. was now attending personally to the matter and that it was still hoped that De Valera might be got to see sense – but I could see that the hope was a very meagre one. I said that there was a general feeling, especially among sea-faring men, that

[5] Vyacheslav Mikhailovich Skriabin (1890–1986), Bolshevik revolutionary, adopted the alias of Molotov ('the hammer'); Member of Politburo 1921–57; P.M. 1930–41; For. Minister 1939–49, 1953–56; Dep. P.M. 1941–57; Min. of State Control 1956–57; Amb. to Mongolia 1957–60; negotiated Nazi-Soviet Pact of August 1939.

things could not be allowed to go on as they were much longer. He agreed. I also saw Dudley Pound[6] (1st Sea Lord) at the House. He is being much attacked at the moment and he told me that there was a terrible lot of intriguing going on — certainly it is a beastly world, but whether Pound is good enough for his job I of course do not know. He was on the Board of Admiralty with me as A[ssistant] C[hief of the] N[aval] S[taff] and struck me as a keen, hard-working man whose only fault seemed to me to be that he was inclined to do far more work than he need – i.e., that he did himself what it was the job of other people to do for him – a common fault among the high-ups in the Services ...

Wednesday 27 November   Greenwood and Bevin[7] and Morrison all did badly in the HofC today. I am convinced that none of these men is fit for his job. The first named is really entirely hopeless, and the 2 others are far too conceited and self-satisfied to be successful as ministers. Bevin is clearly out to be a kind of labour dictator and for the time being has a wonderful press – our journalists really make one sick! – but, as I fancy I have noted before, I doubt whether the man will make a success of it in Parliament, and I gather that he has already put most of his own side against him. He has a swollen head and appears to be a bully.

Thursday 28 November   The sitting was disturbed by an air raid, the Speaker leaving the chair. This prevented my hearing the whole of Anthony Eden's speech which was tiresome as it was delivered in secret session and I shall never know, therefore, all the great War Secretary told the House – what I did hear, however, did not amount to much – but clearly we are still very short of *materiel* in the Middle East – A.A. guns, for example, have to be taken out of our front-line positions in the desert to be sent to the Greeks! It is really amazing how we are still so behind in our production. He assured us that the troops under Wavell were in high fettle – that

---

[6] (Alfred) Dudley Pickman Rogers Pound (1877–1943), naval career; Assistant Chief of Naval Staff 1927–29; 2nd Sea Lord 1932–35; Chief of Staff, Med. 1935–36, C. in C. 1936–39; 1st Sea Lord 1939–43; kt. 1933.

[7] Ernest Bevin (1881–1951), Gen. Sec., Transport & General Workers' Union 1922–40; Chairman, T.U.C. Gen. Council 1937; Lab. M.P. Wandsworth Central 1940–50, Woolwich E. 1950–51; Min. of Labour & Nat. Service 1940–45; Member of War Cabinet 1940–45; For. Sec. 1945–51; Lord Privy Seal 1951.

he believed that the dangerous period on the Sudan front was over and led us to suppose that the Abyssinians were shortly going to give the Italians trouble – it was a characteristic speech from a second-rate man. A.M. Lyons,[8] M.P. for Leicester, came to me in the Lobby – he rather suggested that we should get together and form a group – I hardly know the man, but he is a K.C. (Jew of course) and said to be honest and clever – I am to talk things over with him as soon as may be. ... Travelled home by the 3.50. Nunn, M.P., conversed with me the whole journey – very intelligently – he is intensely gloomy about the conduct of the war and our prospects.

Saturday 30 November   ... there is nothing I can do to keep Conservatism alive without workers and without money. ... chaos is looming ahead: all the cranks and faddists are getting ready to put things right, and all the so-called Conservatives are playing up to them – we are to have a 'better Britain' after the war; 'there must be no going back to the *status quo*', etc., etc. – and no one appears to know what is to be done except that there must be no more profit-making and that everything must be nationalized. It is all a repetition of what happened in the last war and no doubt will lead to a similar confusion or confusion worse confounded.

Monday 2 December   I had a talk with Tydeman *re.* the row which is raging about M.P.s being allowed to disapprove of speakers (M[inistry] of I[nformation] speakers) in their constituencies – of course the whole rumpus has been engineered by the Labour Party, ably supported by asses like Eustace Percy – but it is a serious business, calculated to bring down Duff Cooper, I imagine. Tydeman, I need scarcely say, was of little help. He is still entirely incapable of understanding the Labour people's methods of political warfare and quite hoodwinked by them. ... I spoke at a meeting ... urging the citizens of W. Hartlepool to buy Government securities. They asked me to come because Howard Gritten[9] M.P. had let them down. I was begged by the Conservative leaders to get rid of H.G. for them – they say that he is always letting them

---

[8] Abraham Montagu Lyons (1894–1961), Con. M.P. Leicester E. 1931–45; Recorder of Great Grimsby 1936–61.
[9] William George Howard Gritten (1870–1943), Con. M.P. The Hartlepools 1918–23, 1929–43.

down and that if he goes on much longer there will be no hope of retaining the seat.

Tuesday 3 December   ... the Min. of Information Regional Committee which began at 2.30. The Labour clique was present in full force and moved Charlton Curry[10] into the chair – the first slap at me, clearly arranged beforehand probably with the connivance of Morgan.[11] Then when I objected very properly to a misleading entry in the minutes of the last meeting, they voted solidly against me – then Charlton Curry moved his resolution condemning the veto by M.P.s – a lot of nonsense was talked, the usual threats of breaking the party truce being made by the Labour people – I stood out of the business and then the resolution was carried – Wilkin, Tydeman and a few others refraining from voting. It was a sorry business and I must now consider my position. I should like to resign from the committee but my doing so would be certain to be misrepresented and might do harm. I think that my best course will be to remain a member and then not to attend the meetings – resigning later on 'owing to my inability to attend'.

Wednesday 4 December   David Margesson has thought fit to send out a 3 line whip for tomorrow's debate on the I.L.P.'s peace motion: so I feel that I must go to London tonight ... That ass Hugh Dalton made a speech today asserting that the Germans would find themselves in difficulty for their oil supply in a few months time if they went on fighting – even if this were true, which I don't for a moment believe to be the case, no Minister should publish it abroad. I look upon Dalton as a public menace in his present job – indeed, I look upon Bevin and Greenwood and Morrison as equally menacing – not one of them is fit for his high position.

[10] Aaron Charlton Curry (1887–1957), Lib. M.P. Bishop Auckland 1931–35 (Lib. Nat. to 1933); member of Newcastle City Council 1941–57, Alderman 1951–57, Lord Mayor 1949–50, 1956–57.
[11] Arthur Eustace Morgan (1886–1972), Principal, Univ. College Hull 1926–35; Vice-Chancellor, McGill Univ., Montreal 1935–37; Chief Special Officer for Nat. Service, Min. of Labour 1939; District Commissioner for Special Areas, Durham & Tyneside 1939; Regional Information Officer, Min. of Information, Newcastle 1939–41; Ass. Sec., Min. of Labour & Nat. Service 1941–45; Educational Controller, British Council 1945–50; Warden, Toynbee Hall 1954–63.

Thursday 5 December   I tried hard to speak in the debate today – but that damned Speaker did not call me. It really is intolerable the way in which he keeps on calling the same people: everybody is sick to death of him and it is high time he retired. Today he would insist on calling member after member from the Labour side. McGovern,[12] who moved the amendment, Campbell Stephen and Maxton all spoke at great length. Their speeches were good of course (they have so much practise) but they all talked rubbish and the amendment demanding a peace conference was defeating by 300 and something (340 I think) to 4. The whole business was [a] great waste of time and energy. I find that a lot of people are dissatisfied with the Government – but as there are no leaders of a possible ginger group except Hore-Belisha and Eddie Winterton I don't see how an effective group can be formed. I gather that production is not nearly good enough: that the work people in airplane and other government factories are beginning to go ca'canny: that the dockers at the ports are giving trouble, not clearing ships half fast enough: Communists active – I only hope that much of this gossip is exaggerated, but it is alarming none the less.

Tuesday 10 December   The HofL got a hammering last night – members' staircase, cloak room, cloisters and Public Bill Office suffered severely.[13] We sat in 'the Annexe' – tried to get in on an unexpected debate on the adjournment – on the internment of British subjects: failed as usual.

Thursday 12 December   Philip Lothian has died suddenly in the U.S.A. – very sad and, I should imagine, a real catastrophe for us – for he has clearly been a great success at Washington not only with the President, but with the press and public. He will be a difficult man to replace there. I have known him slightly for many years – had I known him better, I should no doubt like him more – as it was I found him too superior: there was literally nothing he did not lay down the law about. But there is no doubt that he was a very able and well-informed man – and when talking with him

---

[12] John McGovern (1887–1968), Lab. M.P. Glasgow Shettleston 1930–59 (I.L.P. 1931–47, whip withdrawn 1954–55).
[13] From bomb damage.

one realised the cogency of his arguments even if one disagreed with him. He was essentially 'a Round Table man', and some of us have never been able to stomach this particular type. We (L. & I) agreed completely on one thing: the wrongness of our policy towards Germany for the ten years preceding this war.

Saturday 14 December　　Beatrice and I attended a meeting of our N.N. Association's committee this morning at the Station Hotel in Newcastle. Vick reported on the 'amalgamation' business – would resign if it were not brought about at once, etc.: Lawson & Co. now 'loyal' to me – it was all rather pitiful and mean – but it looks as if we shall have to take in the other side and trust to luck – our women much disgruntled as is only natural. I wish to God that we could get rid of Vick – but there is literally no one else to take his place – Beatrice very angry about the whole business: so am I – but I don't honestly think that it matters much – all we have to do is to watch our new members closely and insist upon running the show with our people as much as we can.

Tuesday 17 December　　Back to the House after luncheon – Kingsley Wood introduced, or rather moved 2d [reading] of Government Insurance Bill – a very complicated and expensive scheme it seems to me, but everyone appeared to be pleased with it.

Wednesday 18 December　　To the House in the morning – I went specially to see Duff about the Regional Officer in Newcastle – but had to content myself with Harold Nicolson as Duff was in bed with flu. I tried to explain things to this creature and he said he would look into the matter as he was coming up North on a visit of inspection. I am sure, however, that he will do nothing and that Morgan will be left – if so, I shall resign as I cannot go on *auspice*[14] such a man and with the Labour party in full control of the machine.

Thursday 19 December　　Winston spoke in the Annexe this morning – not the usual prepared speech – he was optimistic – but it did not strike me that he was as optimistic as usual. He is right

[14] translation: under the leadership (or inspiration) of; as used in Horace, *Epistles*, 1.3.13.

not to be carried away by our recent successes against Italy[15] and to warn us that we are still in danger of invasion. The truth is, I fancy, that οἱ ἔντελλοι[16] are worried to death by the shipping position which is very serious – the public at large does not realize how serious – we simply have got to get more ships of war to cope with the submarine menace. I spoke to L[loyd] G[eorge] for the first time today thus breaking my pledge – I could not well keep it for he came and sat beside me on the front opposition bench before I realised who he was. He was quite friendly – but I doubt whether he knew who I was. Both he and Winston spoke very sympathetically about Lothian whose death is universally considered a tremendous loss – he went down so well with the Yanks and seem to have understood them so well. Edward Halifax is generally expected to be going to succeed him – and presumably he is the best man available – this I suppose would mean the return of Anthony to the F.O. How fortune aids some people.

Saturday 21 December   Wilkin ... told me that after I left the Regional Committee the other day they appointed Charlton Curry chairman for a year – certainly Morgan and the Labour Party have played their cards very cleverly – it amazes me that Tydeman has never let me have this piece of news.

Tuesday 24 December   ... a letter from Vick resigning the chairmanship – ill health being the reason for his leaving us. Apparently he saw his Doctor this morning who warned him that he must avoid all worry, etc., etc. Personally I think that we are well rid of him – but it will be interesting to see whether the rest of the world agrees with this view. ... Tonight Winston delivered a Philippic on the wireless on Musso. He was addressing the 'Italian people' – whether or not his indictment of the *Duce* will have any affect in Italy will remain to be see – but it was certainly well done – a terrific attack which will have given satisfaction to all who heard it in this country.

[15] As well as the Greek counter-offensive into Albania, there had been air attacks on the Italian fleet and on Naples, and Wavell's continuing advance in Tripolitania.

[16] translation: those in command. This phrase is based upon classical works which Headlam read in his schooldays, and derives from Cassius Dio, *Historiae Romanae 1*, 1.1.2.1 and 80.5.3.4.

Monday 30 December   I had a straight talk with Tydeman this morning, telling him that he was always going behind my back and keeping things from me – of course he denied all I said, but when I gave him chapter and verse for all I meant he was obliged to admit that I might have misunderstood him, etc., etc. I don't suppose that this conversation will make him love me any more, but, at any rate, we now know how we stand with each other.

Tuesday 31 December   Everyone it seems is pleased with Roosevelt's speech – clearly the President means to help us all he can – short of joining in the war – and the idea of being our armoury and supply furnishers seems to appeal to the Yanks as their share in the war for democracy. They are a quaint lot – they are told that if we lose the war they will be the next on Hitler's list – that they will then have to fight for their existence, etc., etc., and yet they seem quite content to leave the actual fighting to us: they will do anything to help except fight. For the time being we don't want American soldiers – but it seems to me we are terribly in need of American sailors and ships. President R., I am glad to say, spoke very clearly to De Valera and co. – but I am much afraid that De V. dare not agree to our taking over his ports – that wretched southern Ireland is a veritable thorn in our flesh – and I personally can see no hope of our getting hold of the ports except by taking them: we can't do this until the Americans are actually in the war with us, when they will be the first to insist upon our doing so I should imagine. ...

It has been a difficult year in every way, but we have much to be thankful for. In May, June and July we passed through a crisis which, now that one looks back upon it, was one of the most serious in our history. We survived it – and then our airmen saved us from being overwhelmed by the *Luftwaffe*. Since then we have kept our end up and the campaign in the Western Desert and the Greek successes in Albania have done much to restore our prestige – combined of course with the courage and endurance of our people under the air attacks – but the situation remains very grim, and a very critical time lies ahead of us. If we can hold our own at sea, keep our communications going, withstand the German air attack for another six months or so, we should then be on the road to victory. We can only grit our teeth and make up our minds to stick to it, however hardly we may be tried.

Saturday 4 January 1941   Beatrice ... attended the meeting of the amalgamation delegates at the Conservative Club in Newcastle: I was not present. It was a regular ramp and Councillor Temple[17] entirely failed to control the proceedings: he allowed Vick to attend and the fat man went all out on the side of the old Association – some of our people also ratted. The result was (as Temple was fool enough to allow a division) that Lawson was recommended as President, Vick as Chairman ... A most unfortunate affair – the beginning of a lot more trouble, I fear. It does madden one that we should have to go through all this business again – one feels that one cannot give way to the very people whom one fought in the election and who behaved so abominably.

Sunday 12 January   Charley Londonderry turned up here this morning and spent about 2 hours with me. He was at his best and no one can be pleasanter than he when he is in one of his friendly moods – I think that in his queer way he really is fond of me and bears no ill will against me for the many little tiffs we have had. Today, as usual, he discussed himself, his family, his affairs, his political failures, etc. He is proposing to write a book to show how we might have avoided war, had we been wiser – and asked me to come in with him. I said I would help him all I could, but warned him that I was a devastating critic! His principal criminal appears to be Neville Chamberlain who, he thinks, might have saved the situation in *1935* had he faced facts and not got frightened.

Tuesday 14 January   The Greeks seem to be pressing on ... How long they will be able to continue their advance, however, is a matter which worries me – in this weather and in such a terrain the strain on the troops must be terrific and the Greek army is a very small one. A German attack must be anticipated sooner or later and it would be a sad business if it were to fall upon a worn out and exhausted Greek army. In a few weeks' time the Germans will be able to move large armies in the Balkans, and one does not see how the Greeks can be expected to stand up to them. Presumably

---

[17] William Temple, member of Newcastle City Council, Arthur's Hill Ward 1932–45, Alderman 1945–60; Con. cand. Newcastle E. 1924, but stood in breach of a local pact with the Liberals; formerly Chairman, Newcastle W. C.A.; Chairman, North Newcastle C.A., 1944–51, when the Association of which he was Chairman was disaffiliated from the National Union.

these obvious dangers must be appreciated by our great ones – and possibly they have made arrangements to deal with the situation when it arises – but a German attack will come very suddenly and in overpowering strength – and I cannot help feeling nervous. In Libya we are closing in round Tobruk – and there are still no reports of Italian opposition. The situation gets odder and odder, but clearly German air support for Musso is increasing in the Mediterranean and there seems to be no longer any doubt that German troops are pouring into Italy – very soon Italy will be just as fully under German control as is Rumania. Personally I should much prefer the Italians to run their own war effort.

Friday 17 January   My old friend Luke Thompson (formerly M.P. for Sunderland: he wanted me to succeed him but Sam Storey[18] decided otherwise because he fancied that he would be safer if he surrendered one of the seats to a Liberal in which he was probably right) has been killed. He was trying to work a winch and got caught up in the machinery. He was one of the few men in politics up here who was perfectly honest, capable and did his job.

Sunday 19 January   There was a regular blizzard last night and we are snowed in here today – quite impossible to get to the main road either way ... Beatrice and I therefore had to deny ourselves the pleasure of hearing Maggie Bondfield[19] give her 'lecture' in Newcastle this afternoon – I am rather sorry as I was anxious to hear how 'political' her remarks were. I am feeling a bit gloomy: this bother about the two Associations is so tiresome and is certain to be misrepresented to my disadvantage. I am glad to be rid of

[18] Samuel Storey (1896–1978), Con. M.P. Sunderland 1931–45, Stretford 1950–66; P.P.S. to F. Horsbrugh 1939–42; Chairman, Con. Social Services Ctte. 1942–45; Chairman of Standing Cttes. 1957–64; Dep. Chairman of Ways & Means 1964–65; Dep. Speaker 1965–66; cr. Bart. 1960, Baron Buckton 1966.
[19] Margaret Grace Bondfield (1873–1953), Lab. M.P. Northampton 1923–24, Wallsend 1926–31; P.S. Labour 1924; Min. of Labour 1929–31; Chief Woman Officer of General & Municipal Workers' Union 1916–21; Pres. T.U.C. 1923; Chairman, Women's Group on Public Welfare 1939–49; the first woman junior minister & cabinet minister.

the man Vick[20] – but I quite realize that he may be a nuisance. He has a certain following and very few people will credit that he is both foolish and dishonest.

Monday 20 January   I find the HofC a depressing place nowadays – I have no inclination to speak – the effort to get in is too boring and fatiguing, and there really is nothing to say. But I fancy my real trouble is that I am out of touch with things and have no one to hob-nob with – most of the people I know are in the Government or away from the House and those M.P.s who do come to the House are unknown to me or people whom I have no use for. I suppose, too, that having no prospects, I have no urge to make an effort.

Tuesday 21 January   The Boothby[21] Committee's report is published today – a condemnation of the unhappy Bob which Eddie Cadogan,[22] a member of the Committee, tells me was absolutely unanimous.[23] Personally I am very sorry that such a catastrophe should have happened to this particular man because he is very able and should have done well – but of course he has a very foolish side to his character and cannot be described as a white man. I gather ... that his reputation in the City is none too good

[20] Vick's resignation of the chairmanship of the new North Newcastle constituency association was accepted at the executive meeting held the previous day; after it was decided by 6 votes to 5 that he was therefore no longer a member of the executive, he resigned from the association, taking several members of the committee with him.

[21] Robert John Graham Boothby (1900–1986), Con. M.P. Aberdeenshire E. 1924–58; P.P.S. to W. Churchill 1926–29; P.S. Food 1940–41; kt. 1953, cr. Baron Boothby 1958.

[22] Edward Cecil George Cadogan (1880–1962), Con. M.P. Reading 1922–23, Finchley 1924–35, Bolton 1940–45; Sec. to the Speaker 1911–21; Member of Indian Statutory (Simon) Commission 1928–30; kt. 1939.

[23] Boothby was chairman of a committee representing British citizens and residents who had claims against the Czechoslovak assets in Britain frozen after the German occupation in March 1939. Due to a previous arrangement with a personal friend (Richard Weininger, a Czech citizen), Boothby had a financial interest in promoting certain claims which he failed to disclose when speaking on the matter in the House. When Weininger was interned in 1940, the arrangement was discovered from his papers and, as it affected a serving Minister, the Treasury Solicitor informed the Prime Minister. On 17 Oct. 1940 Churchill moved that a Select Ctte. be appointed to investigate Boothby's conduct, and he was suspended from ministerial duties in the interim. After the critical report he had no alternative but to resign from office, but he remained an M.P.; from 1941 to 1942 he served in the R.A.F.

and in other ways he has misbehaved himself sadly.

Wednesday 22 January   I lunched at the HofC – sat next to Charles Waterhouse[24] who is as gloomy about Conservative pro spects as I am, indeed, gloomier – for the only leader he can see after Winston is Sir John Anderson! Donald Scott made an excellent maiden speech today, pleading for agricultural workers for the land. He really made an admirable debut: I am so glad. Winston who wound up the debate (on man-power) for the Government was at the top of his form: I have never heard him make a more effective speech. He certainly is a very different man now that he is P.M. – wiser, pleasanter, and cleverer. In the past one never felt sure of him – felt that he was playing his own game – doubted his judgement – distrusted him. In this crisis he seems to be a different man: one feels that he can't be beat!

Thursday 23 January   ... to the House, where the Committee stage (first day) of the War Damages Bill was being taken – a dull business. Denville[25] had asked me to back an amendment which he had put down saying that it was sent him by the Town Clerk of Newcastle – I agreed – now I learn from the T.C. that he knows nothing about the amendment except that Denville asked his opinion of it. Denville himself has not an idea what it is about, but thought that I might! I have told him that the wisest course he can adopt is to drop the amendment.

Tuesday 28 January   In the HofC Bob Boothby made his apo-logia. Winston whom I spoke to in the Lobby (and who was quite civil) told me that he considered Bob's speech a magnificent parliamentary achievement. Personally I considered it far too long and too much a special pleading and I think that this was the general opinion. When a man has made a mess of it – however unwittingly – and has had judgement passed against him, the only thing to do in my opinion is to bow to adverse fate and have done

---

[24] Charles Waterhouse (1893–1975), Con. M.P. Leicester S. 1924–45, S.E. 1950–57; P.P.S. to P. Cunliffe-Lister 1928–29, to H. Betterton 1931–34; Ass. Whip 1935–37, Whip 1937–40; Ass. Postmaster-Gen. 1939–41; P.S. Trade 1941–45; leader of the Suez Group of Con. M.P.s in the 1950s.
[25] Alfred Arthur Hinchcliffe Denville (1876–1955), Con. M.P. Newcastle Central 1931–45; a theatrical manager & producer.

with it. Bob, they say, intends to get a vote of confidence from his constituents and remain in the HofC – a foolish thing to do – he ought to make 'a gesture' and join up – why shouldn't he? He is young – or youngish – has no ties and it is the obvious thing to do as Winston hinted in the House.

Tuesday 4 February   ... I went to the HofC where they were engaged on the War Damages Bill, a measure which I doubt whether anyone understands (judging from Kingsley Wood's, Donald Somervell's[26] and Harry Crookshank's contributions to the debate which I happened to hear), and which I am equally certain will cost us all a lot for any trifle gained.

Wednesday 5 February   George Lloyd has died at the age of 61 – rather a sudden end – apparently from some strange affection [*sic*] of the blood so Tommie Lascelles[27] told me tonight. He had just been made leader of the House of Lords and was Colonial Secretary – sad that he should have to go just when he had come back into office and was doing well. I have known him slightly for many years. He was a man who had the courage of his convictions right or wrong; drive and energy; a patriot who believed in the divine mission of England – but somewhat difficult to work with by all accounts, a bit of a poseur and I should say lacking in judgement – though I really have no right to say so as I was never associated with him. I liked what I knew of him and wish I had known him better.

Sunday 9 February   Winston gave a wonderful broadcast tonight which filled us all with delight – 40 minutes of the best – strong, witty, wise and on the whole encouraging. He reviewed the last five months of the war: told us we had much to be thankful for, and warned us not to be careless or to fancy we were out of the wood. He clearly anticipates an intensified sea attack, invasion and a

[26] Donald Bradley Somervell (1889–1960), Con. M.P. Crewe 1931–45; Solicitor-Gen. 1933–36; Attorney-Gen. 1936–45; Home Sec. 1945; Lord Justice of Appeal 1946–54; Lord of Appeal in Ordinary 1954–60; kt. 1933, cr. Baron Somervell 1954; Headlam mis-spelt his surname as Somerville.

[27] Alan Frederick Lascelles (1887–1981), known as 'Tommie'; Ass. Priv. Sec. to Prince of Wales 1920–29; Sec. to Gov.-Gen. of Canada 1931–35; Ass. Priv. Sec. to the King 1935–43, Priv. Sec. 1943–52; Priv. Sec. to the Queen 1952–53; Chairman, Pilgrim Trust 1954–60; kt. 1939; in 1919–20 he had been aide-de-camp to Lord Lloyd, then Gov. of Bombay.

German move in the Balkans. There is no doubt that Winston is a born leader of men and I only wish that I were one of his gang!

Monday 10 February   Euan Wallace[28] has died at the age of 48. I knew that he was laid up in a nursing home and had had some kind of operation – but I had no idea that he was so bad. I always got on well with him and liked him – as a politician and M.P. he was not in the first rank – but he wore the 'old school tie', had lots of money and rose to be a Cabinet Minister – *persona grata* with David Margesson. Colin Forbes Adam[29] wrote his 'Special Area' report which brought him into notice: it was a good one.

Tuesday 11 February   The Navy bombarded Ostend early this morning – it is said that the bombardment was highly successful and that we had no casualties. One might imagine that, as a result of all the damage done to the 'invasion ports', the Germans could no longer invade us – and yet we are always being told that Hitler has everything ready for an invasion whenever he gives the word. I rather fear that the second idea is the correct one – I don't suppose that the damage done by our people is as big as they make out – nor do I imagine that all the German barges, etc., are lying at our mercy in the ports: they are tucked away in safe seclusion, I expect, for the day. Well – come it may – and horrible may be what it brings – but I cannot believe that we shall not succeed in driving back the invaders – and then? Will the war last much longer? One wonders whether the Germans will still go on believing in Hitler, if he fails in his invasion – it will certainly take some explaining away. There are some people here and in the U.S.A. who seem to be convinced that once the invasion has failed the war will be over – let us hope that they are, or may prove to be, right. For myself I am still one of those who doubt whether there will ever be an invasion proper – raiding and bombing, yes – and an intensified submarine, etc., blockade – but not a full-blooded

---

[28] (David) Euan Wallace (1892–1941), Con. M.P. Rugby 1922–23, Hornsey 1924–41; P.P.S. to L. Amery 1922–23, 1924–28; Ass. Whip 1928–29, Whip 1929–31; Civil Ld., Admiralty 1931–35; U.S. Home Office 1935; Sec. Overseas Trade 1935–37; F.S.T. 1938–39; Min. of Transport 1939–40; Comm. for Civil Defence, London 1940–41.

[29] Colin Forbes Adam (1889–1982), Indian civil service career 1912–27; District Comm. for Special Area of Durham & Tyneside 1934–39; Chairman, Yorkshire Con. Newspaper Co. 1960–65.

attempt at landing. I fancy that Hitler believes he can beat us in the East and means to go all out in that theatre.

Tuesday 18 February   I fired off my A.T.S.[30] questions in the House this morning where they aroused some attention – apparently there is a lot of trouble among the ladies at the War Office and I may have walked into a hornets' nest: but it does not much matter if I have.[31] I lunched at the HofC, with Tommie Dugdale[32] whose health is said to have broken down in Palestine: he looks 'in the pink'. He has been summoned back here as second-in-command to James Stuart[33] and no doubt will do the job well – he is intelligent, nice mannered and is generally popular.

Wednesday 26 February   Had tea with Oliver Lyttelton – as usual he was ponderously jovial – and, as usual, he was self-assured and as confident as Pre[sident] of the B[oard] of T[rade] as he was as a metal magnate. He is of course a very able man and I think that if he can manage the HofC he might well become a leader for the Conservative Party, should he put his mind to politics. He has a great chance, for he is the right age and really has no competitors – visible at any rate. Rob Hudson, I am told, gave the '22 Committee[34] a very gloomy account of our shipping position this afternoon –

[30] Auxiliary Territorial Service: the uniformed organisation in which women served in the army, taking non-combat roles (mainly as drivers and clerical staff) in order to release more men for front line duties.

[31] The friction within the A.T.S. related particularly to its Chief Commandant, Dame Regina Evans (q.v.); Headlam's questions raised the general dissatisfaction within the A.T.S., the issue of an age limit for senior posts, and the preference within the ranks for a male commanding officer with previous military experience.

[32] Thomas Lionel Dugdale (1897–1977), Con. M.P. Richmond 1929–59; P.P.S. to P. Cunliffe-Lister 1931–35, to S. Baldwin 1935–37; Whip 1937–40; Dep. Chief Whip 1941–42; Con. Party Vice-Chairman 1941–42, Chairman 1942–44; Min. of Agric. 1951–54; Chairman, Yorkshire Area 1948–52; cr. Bart. 1945, Baron Crathorne 1959.

[33] Appointed Conservative Chief Whip and Parl. Sec. to Treasury 14 Jan. 1941.

[34] The Conservative Private Members' (1922) Ctte., usually referred to as the '1922 Ctte.' or 'the '22'. The name originates from its foundation by a group of M.P.s elected for the first time in 1922, but from 1926 onwards the membership consisted of all Con. backbench M.P.s and it acquired a semi-official status. The weekly session was attended by a whip who briefed M.P.s on the forthcoming business of the House and reported back the feeling of the meeting to the Party leaders; the circumstances of the wartime Coalition led to the 1922 Ctte. playing a more significant role in expressing Con. opinion during periods of political tension.

presumably designed to spur us up 'to dig for victory'.[35]

Thursday 27 February   I spent most of today at the HofC – second reading of the HofC Disqualification (Temporary Provisions) Bill – Winston apparently is very angry with some of us for venturing to criticize this measure which is being introduced in order to enable Winston to get rid of young MacDonald[36] (or anyone else in the Government) by giving him a job overseas and allowing him to retain his seat in the HofC. He assured us today that this arrangement is likely to assist him in winning the war. I have 2 objections to the Bill – 1st that on a certificate signed by the 1st Lord of the Treasury a gent should be able to retain his seat on accepting an office of profit under the Crown, and 2nd that I can see no earthly reason why a constituency should be disfranchised for the duration of the war in this way. Winston took all the interest out of the proceedings by making the passing of the 2nd reading a matter of confidence in the Government – a very childish exhibition of temper. The Speaker called me quite early in the debate rather to my surprise – I spoke from the front opposition bench and did pretty well – but as usual I was too short a time on my feet – still the House listened to me and several people congratulated me. The Attorney-General[37] who moved the second reading of the Bill was ineffective – Pickthorn[38] who moved an amendment made a clever speech, but was too long – Winston who wound up the debate in a speech of 55 minutes had his usual success.

Wednesday 5 March   We had the Army Estimates in the HofC today and David Margesson delivered a very long speech – read it very well – and everyone appeared to approve. Reading speeches seems to be the fashion in the HofC nowadays – and for Ministers, if they read them cleverly, it is obviously a good plan, because they can say exactly what they want (or their department wants them) to say – David has a good voice and delivery, and is evidently

[35] A wartime propaganda slogan which passed into common usage, originally used to promote greater use of land for agricultural production.
[36] Malcolm MacDonald had been appointed High Commissioner in Canada.
[37] Sir Donald Somervell (q.v.).
[38] Kenneth William Murray Pickthorn (1892–1975), Con. M.P. Cambridge Univ. 1935–50, Carlton 1950–66; P.S. Educ. 1951–54; Fellow of Corpus Christi, Cambridge 1914–75; cr. Bart. 1959.

going to do his best to make a success of his job so far as the HofC is concerned. I went to tea with Lady Londonderry late in the afternoon. She was much the same as usual – it is amazing the way she keeps her vitality. She poured forth a lot of stuff about the A.T.S. – she has no use for the Dame[39] – but clearly she is much influenced by being out of the picture.

Saturday 8 March ... I cannot say that on looking back upon the day's effort, I can honestly say that I have done anything calculated to win the war or to promote the 'New World' which is to come after it. The amount of rubbish which is being spoken and written about this world to be is calculated to cause a deal of trouble later on and, of course, the people who are mainly responsible for all this prattle are the usual crew – the political intelligentsia and the good social workers. What always annoys me is that none of this crowd ever alludes to all that has been done within the last fifty years in the way of what is called 'social reform', or dreams of mentioning the vast sums of money which have been poured out to improve the condition of the people. From the way men like J.B. Priestley[40] speak one might imagine that nothing was being done for the great mass of the population and that this country was preserved solely for an idle crowd of parasites who never lifted a finger for the public good – all this is sheer nonsense – and the foolish talk about equality can only lead to an increase in discontent and unrest when peace comes again.

Tuesday 11 March Roosevelt signed the Lease and Lend Bill today which is a sign, I take it, that the Yanks are, to all intents and purposes, now in the war on our side – what a long time they have been in making up their minds! If only they had come to this decision last year, what a difference it would have made – still, it is always useless to reflect upon the 'might have beens' and it is a mercy that they have taken the plunge. One is now less anxious

---

[39] Dame Regina Evans (q.v.) was Chief Commandant, Auxiliary Territorial Service 1939–43.
[40] John Boynton Priestley (1894–1984), author and playwright. His radio broadcasts were enormously popular during the early wartime years; however the left-wing tone and criticism of the conditions of the 1930s in his first series of June-Oct. 1940 aroused Conservative disquiet, and Priestley was more outspokenly critical of the ruling classes in the second series which began in Jan. 1941.

about our shipping difficulties – the Yanks must produce more tonnage and more escort vessels if we are to survive the submarine blockade.

Thursday 13 March   Shinwell[41] made an excellent speech in the Secret Session *re* shipping – Cross, Minister of Shipping, who replied for the Government, was not very inspiring – clearly the situation is very alarming and one does not see how we can carry on against an intensified submarine war unless we get more ships (merchant) and more destroyers from the U.S.A.

Friday 14 March   ... went into Newcastle ... I had a meeting at King's College, where were all the intelligentsia who are proposing to devote their attentions to after-war problems as they affect this area. A man named Goodfellow[42] is responsible for this gathering – he is the author of a recently-published pamphlet on *Tyneside: the Social Facts*; a left-winger because, as he frankly told me, he thought he had better prospects on the Labour side: he is not my 'cup of tea'. The gathering included Dr. Morgan, Colonel Methven,[43] Alderman Adams[44] M.P., various professors, trade union leaders, etc. The usual types and opinions – I liked Professor Jack[45] who took the chair. Whether I shall go on with these people remains to be seen – I cannot say that I am greatly tempted to do so, as their views in the main are not likely to be mine and as they propose to issue a report, it might mean my having to write a

[41] Emanuel Shinwell (1884–1986), Lab. M.P. Linlithgow 1922–24, 1928–31, Seaham 1935–50, Easington 1950–70; Sec. for Mines 1924, 1930–31; F.S. War Office 1929–30; Min. of Fuel & Power 1945–47; Sec. for War 1947–50; Min. of Defence 1950–51; Chairman, P.L.P. 1964–67; cr. Baron Shinwell 1970.
[42] David Martin Goodfellow, extra-mural lecturer, Durham University; member of Newcastle City Council, All Saints' Ward 1941–45; author of *Tyneside: The Social Facts* (Co-Operative Printing Soc., Newcastle, 1940), *A Modern Economic History of South Africa* (Routledge, London, 1931), and *Principles of Economic Sociology* (Routledge, London, 1939). Goodfellow had a London University Ph.D., where he had been a pupil of R.H. Tawney.
[43] Lt.-Colonel M. D. Methven, General Manager of the Gateshead Trading Estate.
[44] David Adams (1871–1943), Lab. M.P. Newcastle W. 1922–23, Consett 1935–43; member of Newcastle City Council from 1902, Sheriff 1922–23, Lord Mayor 1930–31.
[45] Daniel Thomson Jack (1901–1984), Prof. of Economics, King's College, Newcastle (Univ. of Durham) 1935–61, Sub-Rector 1950–55; Chairman, Air Transport Licensing Bd. 1961–70; a long-serving member of the Industrial Disputes Tribunal; kt. 1966.

minority report – and the fat would be in the fire.

Sunday 16 March ... they are getting on with the digging – the old herbaceous border and the long strip along the new one are already dug up, but the big lawn remains to be done – how sad it all is – but we must 'dig for victory' and be prepared to live on vegetables for the next few years. So far, I must admit that I have not been in the least inconvenienced by rationing, but a bad time is in store for us I am certain. Hitler and co. are a long way from being finished and will give us a lot of nasty bangs before they are done – indeed, sometimes I wonder how we are going to beat them – though I would not say so aloud for all the world. They are a much more serious proposition than the Kaiser and his lot, and so few people here seem to realize it – and how nearly the Kaiser beat us when we had all the world's ships fighting on our side – well, I presume that sooner or later the Yanks will be all in with us and that should do the trick.

Thursday 20 March I lunched at the HofC and listened to the 'Women's debate' for a little. It convinced me more than ever that the HofC is no place for women: I told Megan Lloyd George[46] that my hope was that this debate should be the first and last of such performances which made her smile. She is rather a nice little thing.

Saturday 22 March The Grahams told me that Topping and Tydeman held a meeting at Carlisle on their own the other day and that Topping failed miserably both as a speaker and an answerer of questions. I am very angry that I was not told about this meeting and am writing severely to Tydeman.

Thursday 27 March I was duly elected Chairman of the Central Council of the National Union of Conservative and Unionist Associations at the Caxton Hall, Westminster, this morning – proposed by Lady Hillingdon[47] and seconded by Donald Scott

---

[46] Megan Arfon Lloyd George (1902–1966), Lib. M.P. Anglesey 1929–51, Lab. M.P. Carmarthen 1957–66; Dep. Leader Lib. Party 1949–51; styled Lady Megan after cr. of father as Earl Lloyd George of Dwyfor 1945.

[47] Edith Mary Winifred Cadogan (1895–1969), daughter of Viscount Chelsea; married 1916 Arthur Robert Mills, suc. 3rd Baron Hillingdon 1919; Chairman, N.U. Central Women's Advisory Ctte. 1935–38; cr. Dame 1939.

M.P. Winston (our leader) arrived about 12.30 – he made his usual speech which we are all agreed is superb – he kept us at his *bonne bouche*[48] to the end, when he informed us that Yugoslavia 'had found her soul' – a *coup d'état*, the young King installed, the Regent sent packing, the Ministers who had signed the treaty with Germany locked up. It all sounds very satisfactory and everybody was most enthusiastic at Caxton Hall. ... The afternoon 'session' was rather boring – there was the usual resolution about party candidates – the usual arguments in favour of youth and ability being given a chance; the usual Central Office reply from Douglas Hacking who always strikes me as more stupid and commonplace every time I meet him.

Tuesday 1 April   ... to me our shipping losses appear to be our only *real* danger – just as they did in the last war. How nervous one was in those days – and how much greater the need for nervousness seems to be in this war. The odds against us are so much greater than between 1914 and 1918 – it is the complete French debacle which has let us down so badly this time – if only we had more warships and more merchant vessels, things would not be so bad – well, it is useless to repine! Only one thing is sure – we have got to win the war, and, thank God, we have a people which does not even visualize the possibility of defeat and knows how 'to take it'. Whatever faults we may have as a nation, no one can dispute the bravery of our people and their power of endurance. The astounding courage of all sorts and conditions of men and women and children is past belief and makes one prouder than ever of being an Englishman.

Wednesday 2 April   The defeat of the Home Secretary's order for the opening of theatres and music halls on Sundays yesterday by 8 votes seems to have surprised people – but of course the good people worked up their people, and the other side left things to chance – the prayer book business over again.[49] I should have voted for the Home Secretary's regulation, had I been in the House.

Thursday 3 April   I spent from noon to 2 p.m. sitting on the

---

[48] translation: hanging on his lips.
[49] For the rejection of the revised Prayer Book in 1927, see vol. 1, pp. 134–7, 146–9.

Select Committee *re* qualification for offices, etc. Dennis Herbert[50] in the chair: the Attorney-General giving evidence. It was not a very interesting performance – the A.G. does not strike me ever as being a very capable person and he did not alter this impression by anything he said today. It does not look as if this committee were going to be a particularly entertaining business.

Sunday 6 April   The curtain is now about to go up in the Balkan theatre – the Germans are reported to be crowding through Hungary and massing on the Thrace-Bulgar frontier. One wonders whether we have really forced Hitler into a false move: it all depends on the strength of our forces in Greece, what the Turks do, and how well the Greeks and Yugoslavs can hold up the enemy's initial attacks.

Wednesday 9 April   Today Winston announced in the HofC that the Germans had reached Salonica – a most unpleasant business – one had hoped that they would not make such speedy progress and wonders why they have not been held up a bit longer … Their success of course comes largely from the other chaps not being ready, not, indeed, having made proper, concerted plans. It is the story of Holland and Belgium over again, and we again have been called in too late – so far our troops in Greece have not been engaged – but a fight cannot be long delayed – and then, I suppose, we shall find ourselves completely outnumbered and have to withdraw if we began [*sic*] – pray God we are not in for another 'miracle' of Dunkirk. The most serious part of Winston's speech, however, was the gravity of our shipping position – the prospects for next year, unless the Americans can really produce the requisite new shipping, are not particularly bright.

Thursday 10 April   … I went to the HofC – there I found the intelligent people gloomy and the stupid people cheery – the former of course appreciated the danger of the Balkans situation, the latter did not. They all said that Winston made a fine speech yesterday and commiserated with him on having to change what he hoped

---

[50] Dennis Henry Herbert (1869–1947), Con. M.P. Watford 1918–43; Dep. Chairman of Ways & Means 1928–29, Chairman of Ways & Means and Dep. Speaker 1931–42; Pres., Law Society 1941–42; kt. 1929, cr. Baron Hemingford 1943.

would be a song of victory into the old, old story of catastrophe. People are becoming a bit fed up with the Turks who are still lying low. Eden and Dill are reported back in London – presumably their long jaunt in the East has been a failure, and one wonders how far the Russian influence has been against them?

Friday 11 April   I have been reading a good deal .. and at the same time have felt a slight urge to write something myself – I should like ... to show up the incredible ineptitude of the men who have been responsible for our government since the last war – and, above all, to impress upon the public at large the weaknesses of this democracy about which we are all so busily explaining the merits. I should like, too, to have a dig at the 'intelligent' people who shut their eyes to what was so obvious to the rest of us, and deceived the people so grossly, making them believe in all the League of Nations nonsense and assuring them that all we needed to preserve the peace was 'collective security'. What a load of responsibility men like Gilbert Murray and Bob Cecil have to bear - and the amusing thing is that they still believe that all their hot air meant something. Idealists and humanitarians are responsible for more misery and suffering today than are the Nazis – for but for them, the latter could never have been in a position to do the damage – disarming and a refusal to face facts are the main causes for our sufferings.

Tuesday 15 April   [In Greece] we are still reforming our line – which means of course that we are being pushed back – to the sea. It sickens one to think of all the gallant lives which are being and will be wasted in this futile expedition to Greece ...

Sunday 27 April   ... the end appears to be rapidly approaching in Greece. The Germans claim to be at the gates of Athens, and our troops are still retreating – where they are making for is not told us. Winston has made an admirable speech on the wireless tonight – just the right sort of thing – fully appreciating the gravity of the situation, yet striking the right note of confidence and encouraging us all to stick it. He certainly is an amazingly good war leader so far as the preserving of the national morale is concerned.

Tuesday 29 April   The House is meeting in the 'Annexe' this week, as some damage was done to the 'usual place' in the blitz – the Speaker's house a good deal damaged and most of the windows facing the river smashed. But I gather that we ought soon to be back in our proper home – I hope so, at any rate, for the Church House is a horrible place, nowhere to sit and a positive rabbit warren in which it is almost impossible to find one's way; how anyone can have designed such a place I cannot imagine. I found most people rather gloomy today – oddly enough it does not seem to have occurred to many M.P.s that we could not hope to stop the Germans in the circumstances, and that if we could not stop them we must be driven into the sea. People were also greatly upset by our having been driven out of Libya – I suppose in view of our exiguous forces the thing to note is that we were able to get Libya at all, not that we were forced out of it.

Thursday 1 May   ... I had to attend a luncheon given in honour [of] Sir Emsley Carr[51] who has completed 50 years service with the *News of the World* of which he is editor. It is a foul paper and I cannot understand why a reputable man is its editor. I remember a remark of the late Marquess of Cholmondeley[52] when one day he asked in the Prince's Chamber, HofL, who the new peer was – it was Lord Riddell,[53] they told him, owner of the *News of the World* – 'oh, I know the paper', replied the Marquess, 'good stuff: all c–t and crime.' Today's gathering was at the Dorchester and all the swells were there – political and press. Winston had a big reception – John Astor[54] in the chair. I was well placed close to the

---

[51] Emsley Carr (1867–1941); editor, *News of the World* 1890–1941, Chairman 1934–41; Chairman, Press Gallery of House of Commons 1929–30; Pres., Institute of Journalists 1932–33; Sheriff of Glamorgan 1938; kt. 1918.

[52] George Henry Hugh Cholmondeley (1858–1923), Lord Great Chamberlain of England 1884–1923; suc. 4th Marquess of Cholmondeley 1884.

[53] George Allardice Riddell (1865–1934), Chairman, *News of the World* 1903–34; liaison officer between the British delegation and the press at the Paris peace conferences, 1919–20; kt. 1909, cr. Bart. 1918, Baron Riddell 1920.

[54] John Jacob Astor (1886–1971), Con. M.P. Dover 1922–45; prop. of *The Times* 1922–66; Chairman, Phoenix Assurance Co. 1952–58; Chairman, 4th-7th Imperial Press Conferences; cr. Baron Astor of Hever 1956.

top table and sat between Geoffrey Shakespeare[55] M.P. (a dull dog) and W.W. Hadley,[56] editor of the *Sunday Times*, rather a nice old gentleman. We had a first class luncheon – perfect food (nothing rationed) and excellent drink, etc. The speeches took rather long – old Sir Carr spread himself a bit ...

Saturday 3 May   Presided over the annual meeting of the Area Council in the Old Assembly Rooms this afternoon. There was quite a good attendance considering all things – 150 or thereabouts. Charley Londonderry gave us one of his 'statesmanlike' orations – I moved a resolution of confidence in the Government, and there was one other resolution deploring the increase of juvenile crime, etc., which was cast out after discussion.

Tuesday 6 May   ... then went to the HofC – the debate (confidence in Govt. and its war policy) was not very interesting. I missed Eden's speech, but the general opinion was that it was a bad flop.

Wednesday 7 May   I intended speaking in the debate today, but made a mess of things. Clifton Brown would have called me, so he said, had I been in the House at a particular moment – why they can't say 'yes' or 'no', I never can understand – it would save one such a lot of worry and fatigue – and why the same people are always called is another matter which always puzzles one. L.G. spoke for just over an hour – he said a good deal of what I had intended saying, but he could not help being tactless and I should imagine will have offended the Americans and Turks. I am not one of his admirers, but he is certainly a wonderful man for his age. The *on dit*[57] is that he has been invited to join the Government –

---

[55] Geoffrey Hithersay Shakespeare (1893–1980), Lib. M.P. Wellingborough 1922–23, Norwich 1929–45 (Lib. Nat. from 1931); private Sec. to Lloyd George 1921–23; Lib. Nat. Chief Whip 1931–32; P.S. Health 1932–36; P.S. Educ. 1936–37; F.S. Admiralty 1937–40; Sec. Overseas Trade 1940; U.S. Dominions 1940–42; director of Abbey National building society 1943–77, Dep. Chairman 1965–69; cr. Bart. 1942.

[56] William Waite Hadley (1866–1960), journalist; editor of *Merthyr Tydfil Times* 1892–1893, *Rochdale Observer* 1893–1908, *Northampton Daily Echo & Mercury* 1908–23; parl. correspondent & leader writer, *Daily Chronicle* 1924–30; editor, *Sunday Times* 1932–50.

[57] translation: rumour.

but I should doubt it. Winston, in winding up for the Government, made an effective speech from a debating point of view but said little to convince me that he knew much more about how to win the war than I did myself. However, he had a personal triumph and we voted 447 to 3 in his favour.

Thursday 8 May   This morning I wasted time sitting on my Select Committee (offices or places of profit under the Crown) and listened to Dennis Herbert 'examining' Campion,[58] Clerk of the House – D.H. certainly enjoys all the business tremendously – I mean all the historical side of it, precedents, etc., – and he dislikes it very much when any other member of the committee ventures to ask a question. To me all the old traditions and precedents are meaningless nowadays in view of the entirely changed position of an M.P. and the substitution of Govt. for [the] Crown. In the past the point of view of an M.P.s constituents did not enter into the picture – now of course they must be considered. So long as M.P.s don't take on jobs which mean their leaving the country or being unable to represent their constituencies there is, in my opinion, little against their being employed by the Govt. I cannot see much danger from 'placemen' to our constitutional liberties with the press and public opinion to show up scandals.

Tuesday 13 May   The one topic of conversation today has been the sudden arrival in Scotland of Rudolph Hess, the Nazi leader, piloting his own machine. No one seems to know the meaning of his coming – it has clearly upset the Nazis who declare that he is *non compos mentis*[59] – indeed, until they heard he was here, they asserted that he had committed suicide. I should say that the most likely supposition is that he had fallen out with Hitler and was fearful of being purged, but it may be, as some people think, that he felt that he might be able to bring about some peace agreement if he could meet our leaders – presumably we shall know soon what is the truth as he [is] said to be making a statement.

Wednesday 14 May   The HofC (the Chamber and the Lobby)

[58] Gilbert Francis Montriou Campion (1882–1958), clerk in House of Commons from 1906; Clerk Assistant 1930–37; Clerk of the House of Commons 1937–48; kt. 1938, cr. Baron Campion 1950.

[59] translation: not in possession of his wits, i.e. insane.

have been entirely destroyed: I have not been to see the mess but I am told it is terrific.[60] There is a hole in the roof of Westminster Hall, but luckily the roof has not been destroyed – 'Big Ben' is pitted all over his face and had a narrow escape, but still carries on. We are once again at the Church House – pretty beastly – there is talk of our having the HofL and their Lordships moving to the Royal Gallery, but I doubt whether we shall be left in peace wherever we go. ... I spent most of the early part of the afternoon at a meeting of the Executive Committee of the Party – guided by Douglas Hacking it showed its usual feebleness on the subject of any amendment of the Trade Disputes Act[61] – amendment is now being pressed on the Govt. (so we are told) by the T.U.C. – it is sheer blackmail which I have no doubt Winston and Beaverbrook would pay quite cheerfully.

Thursday 15 May   Hess is still the universal topic of conversation, but no official statement regarding him has yet been made.

Wednesday 28 May   I went to the Central Office again this morning and afterwards lunched with Topping at the Constitutional Club – seemingly he and I are now on very good terms. The man is undoubtedly very capable, but I don't trust him very far. He has far too much authority in the Party and runs Hacking entirely – also Tommie Dugdale, now Vice-Chairman, and Eugene Ramsden.

Thursday 29 May   The news from Crete is worse than ever today and it looks as if the end cannot be delayed much longer – the enemy's air superiority is evidently becoming more and more overwhelming. It is said that we have succeeded in putting reinforcements into the island – but, personally, it seems to me a foolish thing to do – unless there is still a chance of beating the Germans. The question now is how many of our people we shall be able to get off the island, not how many more we can put on. Things in

[60] The chamber of the House of Commons was destroyed by an incendiary bomb on the night of 10–11 May 1941. After sitting at the 'Annexe', Church House, from 13 May to 19 June, the Commons moved to the chamber of the House of Lords. Apart from a short period at Church House during the peak of the flying bomb attacks (20 June to 3 Aug. 1944), the Commons continued to sit in the House of Lords until their own rebuilt chamber was opened in Oct. 1950.
[61] The Baldwin government's Trade Disputes Act of 1927, passed after the 1926 General Strike, was greatly disliked by the Labour Party and the trade unions.

Iraq are going better and our relieving force is said to be nearing Baghdad. Presumably keeping the Germans so busy in Crete prevents them from supporting their adherents in Iraq and so all this waste of life in Crete may not be entirely in vain. There is a good deal of criticism again in the HofC Smoking Room and it is not altogether surprising – nevertheless, I resent that so much of it should come from Liberals and Socialists who have in the past invariably opposed any form of preparation for war and never lifted a finger to help the armed forces – now these miserable people attack the generals and admirals and suggest that they are incompetent – because poor fellows they have been unable to make bricks without straw. I hate all these amateur strategists who presume to sit in judgement on their betters and blame them for disasters which really they themselves and their like are responsible.

Friday 30 May　I lunched at the Station Hotel with Wilkin. He approves my idea of having a monthly meeting for Conservatives to be addressed by one or other of the City [of Newcastle] M.P.s. I have discussed the subject with Denville who is agreeable and must speak to Nunn when I next see him. Probably I shall have most of the talking to do – but perhaps this is just as well.

Sunday 1 June　The Cretan episode now appears to be at an end: we have been driven out of the island and the only consolation I can find is that there are any of our troops left to escape. I fancy that there will be a good deal of criticism over this business – after our experience in Greece without air support why was it considered possible to hold Crete without any air support?

Wednesday 4 June　I have felt rather 'blue' all day – for the life of me I cannot see how we are going to beat the Boche, except after the lapse of many years. Of course the German nation may crack, but I don't think this in the least likely unless the German Army gets a bad knock or unless something entirely unexpected happens – I don't believe in a food shortage or the effects of our blockade – of course intensive bombing of the civil population might have a big effect on German morale – but it will be a long time, I fancy, before we are really strong enough in the air to do such a job thoroughly – and, in the meanwhile, what a lot we are going to be called upon to endure! I don't think a tenth of the

people in this country have an inkling of all that may be in store
for them. The Labour Party conference shows you how little
even the Trade Union leaders and their political associates really
appreciate the position!

Thursday 5 June   I also went into Newcastle this afternoon to
attend a meeting summoned by Lambert,[62] the Regional Commissioner, to enlighten M.P.s on the fire-fighting arrangements in
the area. There were 11 M.P.s present – 7 Labour and 4 Conservative – I was the only Newcastle representative. I cannot say
that I was much impressed by Lambert's knowledge of what is
going on: but his officials (most of them) were able to answer such
questions as they were asked. It amused me to find our old friend
Vick in charge of the fire-fighting arrangements for the area – was
there ever such a choice! He retires, I am told, to his dugout the
moment he hears an alert and nothing will budge him – and we
know that he cannot make up his mind about anything. In this
war there appears to be a fixed policy of appointing the weakest
men to the key positions.

Saturday 7 June   I don't think that we can ever expect any
friendliness with Pétain & Co. Their whole line of country is that
it was we who let France down and it seems to me unlikely in the
extreme that they should change their attitude of mind. Whether
or not they will go so far as to ally themselves actively with the
Germans against us remains to be seen – clearly the Germans want
the French fleet and it is Pétain's best bargaining counter – but it
seems incredible that the French people would tolerate his handing
over the fleet to the Germans to be used against us? However,
incredible though it may sound, our people would be very foolish,
I think, not to visualize such a possibility. The French do not love
us, and now have a grievance against us – or a fancied grievance –
and people who have done the dirty on an ally are always more
bitter against the former ally, being conscious in their heart of
hearts that their own conduct won't bear much looking into!

[62] Arthur William Lambert (1876–1948), businessman; member of Newcastle City
Council 1910–30, Alderman 1930–44, Sheriff 1924–25, Lord Mayor 1926–27, 1928–
29; Chairman, N.E. Coast Exhibition 1929; Comm. for Civil Defence, N.E. England
1939–45; kt. 1930.

Monday 9 June Our advance in Syria seems to be going on all right ... some of the Vichy troops are stated to be coming over to the Free French. I wonder what the future of Syria is to be? To me it would be sheer folly to leave it to the French – there ought to be some kind of federation in that part of the world – Palestine, I am really beginning to believe, this side of Jordan should be a Jewish state, and the whole federation should become a Dominion within the British Empire. ... Apparently we lost another cruiser (*Calcutta*) and two more destroyers in the sorry Cretan show over and above the ships already reported casualties. The Navy must be getting terribly short of cruisers and destroyers.

Tuesday 10 June The debate on Crete in the House today was interesting if not particularly illuminating – Winston was, I thought, very good – making the best of rather a bad job. He was as usual successful in his effort. He is so immeasurably more able in debate than any of his critics. His line was that although we had failed to hold Crete, it may well be that the stiff defence will have upset German plans elsewhere – and that, at any rate, the time taken by the enemy in defeating us has enabled us to strengthen our defences elsewhere in the Middle East. He assured us that the lessons learnt (at what a cost!) would be taken to task and studied. I tried to fire off a little speech which I had prepared carefully – but, needless to say, the Speaker did not call me – as usual the Labour people and Liberals caught his eye, and the usual Conservative bores. ... Winston's report of the battle of the Atlantic in his speech today was cheering – we seem to be holding our own well.

Wednesday 11 June There was nothing of much interest at the HofC – Winston's speech yesterday has done a good deal to allay criticism both in Parliament and in the press – but, nevertheless, people are somewhat aghast at yet another failure, wondering how it is that we are always deficient in fighter aeroplanes and seem unable to appreciate the danger from the air to ships in narrow waters.

Thursday 12 June There has been a meeting at St. James's Palace (needless to say an address by Winston) of all the Allies – they decided to continue the struggle until Germany has been defeated. What else could they decide? I only hope that we are really striving to come to some kind of agreed settlement of Europe after the war now that we have got all these foreign governments actually with us in London – surely it should not be beyond the wit of man to fix up some kind of workable plan for the new Europe – and yet I instinctively distrust all these people, especially Benes[63] and the Poles. ... However, I don't suppose that we need to be in too much of a hurry about the post-war settlement: we have a long and arduous time ahead of us before we have beaten the Germans – indeed, for the time being, the more we concentrate on winning the war and the less we occupy our time rebuilding a better world, the better. People in this country – especially the intelligentsia – will not take our position sufficiently seriously – and I don't suppose they ever will until they have had some closer acquaintance of the Germans and their methods.

Friday 13 June ... nothing new at Holywell – it is all very peaceful, and it is hard to realize that a bloody war is in progress upon the result of which the future of this country and the world depends. That we may be beaten – or, at any rate, may be compelled to make an unsatisfactory peace – never seems to occur to our ignorant and unimaginative public. Perhaps it is just as well, or a lot of them who now go on as usual might get the wind up – and yet possibly it might help to get a real move on, if the bulk of the population were more alive to our real danger. There is not half enough drive in our war industries and all most workers think of is their wage increases and of their grievance in having to pay taxes, etc. There are no very visible signs of the will to win spirit or of any eagerness to make sacrifices.

Friday 20 June ... in Newcastle ... attended an A.R.P. demonstration got up for the benefit of Herbert Morrison and Ellen Wilkinson who both clearly enjoyed being in the limelight. The show took place on the football ground and was attended by all the civil people and Sir Arthur Lambert, whose futility strikes me more and more each time I meet him. Pray God that he may never be called upon to act.

[63] Eduard Benes (1884–1948), Czech For. Minister 1918–35; P.M. 1921–22; Pres. 1935–38, 1946–48, & of govt. in exile 1941–45.

Saturday 21 June   The rumours about a German invasion of Russia continue – but apparently there is no confirmation of an American report that the invasion had actually begun. It is an odd situation but, whatever may happen, we should, in my opinion, be very foolish to expect anything from the Bolshies. If they are forced to fight with Hitler, they won't be fighting to help us and will be guided by nothing but what they believe to be their own interests. I don't fancy that their military machine will prove a very strong one or last very long – but there is always the possibility that Hitler may overreach himself – Russia was too vast for Napoleon.

7

THE INVASION OF RUSSIA

June to December 1941

Sunday 22 June 1941 The Germans began an invasion of Russia early this morning – I confess that this move has surprised me: I always imagined that Stalin would give way to Hitler and give him all he wanted – but perhaps the military people in Russia have prevented his doing this or perhaps Hitler asked even more than Stalin could stomach. I don't suppose that the 'conquest' of Russia will take very long – and what then – presumably either Hitler will make some kind of peace offer to us based upon our acceptance of the 'New Order', or he will try his hand at an invasion here or push on in the [Middle] Eastern theatre. Winston spoke on the wireless tonight and was very fierce and determined – never should we make peace with Hitler, etc., we were in this struggle to the bitter end however long it might last. This is the right attitude to adopt for the time being at any rate – meanwhile it remains to be seen what the Yanks are going to do – without them it is difficult to see how we are going to beat Hitler in this war. However, one feels that God is on our side – that's the great thing.

Monday 23 June I had to go into Newcastle again this morning to attend a luncheon given by the Lord Mayor to R.C. Morrison,[1] a Labour M.P. who appears to be in charge of the Govt.'s Waste Food department. It was not a very gay affair – but it is just as well I went as the inevitable Irene Ward was much in evidence,

[1] Robert Craigmyle Morrison (1881–1953), Lab. M.P. Tottenham N. 1922–31, 1935–45; P.P.S. to H. Gosling 1924, jt. P.P.S. to Ramsay MacDonald 1929–31; Chairman, Waste Food Board, Min. of Supply, 1941–45; Whip in Lords 1947–48; P.S. Works 1948–51; cr. Baron Morrison 1945.

also Alderman Adams M.P. ... The news of the fighting in Russia is conflicting ... The main thing, so far as we are concerned, is that these two nations should kill as many of each other as possible, destroy each other's mechanized armament and take as long about the business as they possibly can.

Tuesday 24 June　　We sat in the HofL today for the first time – an odd sensation for me to find myself seated in that chamber in which I used to stand about so much.[2] Anthony Eden read out a long and not very striking speech stating that we should do all that we could to assist the Russians – that so long as they were fighting the Germans we should consider them as our allies whether they liked it or not – or words to that effect. Roosevelt is taking a similar line – and no doubt the Russians are grinning at us both.

Wednesday 25 June　　There was a shipping debate in Secret Session today – I listened to Winston's speech. Things still seem none too good and the Govt. must have been through a nerve-racking time the last few months. The losses have been far too heavy – but the trouble also has been that repair work and turning ships [around] have been too slow. The bombing of Clydeside and Merseyside did not improve matters as may be imagined. According to Winston things are better now and repair work has been greatly expedited – but, clearly, the battle of the Atlantic is being a grimmer affair than any of us has imagined.

Thursday 26 June　　I sat from 12.15 to 2.15 in Dennis Herbert's Select Committee – a dreary business. The only witness [was] Sir Percy Harris,[3] who was utterly futile – but Dennis Herbert took over an hour to go through his brief.

Tuesday 1 July　　I spent most of the day at the HofC – nothing of much interest as going on there – and there were not many people about. No one seemed to have any gossip. The vigorous

---

[2] Headlam was a Clerk in the House of Lords from 1897 to 1924 (apart from his military service during the First World War).

[3] Percy Alfred Harris (1876–1952), Lib. M.P. Harborough 1916–18, Bethnal Green S.W. 1922–45; Lib. Chief Whip 1935–45 & Dep. Leader 1940–45; member of L.C.C. 1907–34, 1946–52, Chief Progressive Whip 1909–14, Dep. Chairman 1916; cr. Bart. 1932.

Russian resistance to the German invasion is pleasing everyone, but no one believes that it will last very long – however, only time will show whether they are right or wrong.

Wednesday 2 July   Archie Wavell has been removed from the Middle East command being replaced by Auchinleck[4] who has been C-in-C in India where Wavell now takes his place – Oliver Lyttelton is to go to Cairo as 'Minister of State' to supervise things as a member of the War Cabinet. Everyone today has been gossiping about these changes – no one seems to know why Wavell has been removed – whether he is being sacked as a failure or being sent to India because we expect a Nazi invasion there. My own view is that probably he is a tired man and really needs a rest. Oliver's appointment is an odd one – the first time in our history, I fancy, that a political adviser has been appointed to accompany an army in the field. Many people are loud in their disapproval of this new departure – but I can see some sense in it and I should say that Oliver was the right man for the job if the job is to be made – because he knows a good deal about soldiering, has great capacity and is unlikely to rub up the soldiers in command.

Thursday 3 July   I spent all day at the HofC – I wanted to speak in the debate on propaganda, but was not called. Considering that I had put down a motion on the subject some time ago, and in view of the infrequency of my desiring to speak, my standing, etc., I feel that I ought to have been called – more especially as I had spoken to Dennis Herbert about speaking the day before yesterday and written to him yesterday – so angry was I that I wrote to him expostulating. He did apologize, but assured me that he had never got my letter which is odd – I don't think that he is a liar, but am sure that he is too old for his job. The debate was a very poor one. John Anderson who opened it with a declaration of Government policy was helpless and hopeless. He may be a 'super man', an administrator, etc., but he is an extremely poor orator -pompous, ineffective. Duff who wound up did well – he clearly did not approve of the Cabinet's plan, but said that he would try and work

---

[4] Claude John Eyre Auchinleck (1884–1981), army career; G.O.C. Northern Norway 1940, Southern Command 1940; C. in C., India 1941, 1943–47, Middle East 1941–42; Supreme Comm., India & Pakistan 1947; kt. 1940.

it. No one approved of the compromise which has been arrived at – but no one took the line which I was going to take – viz., that the M[inistry] of I[nformation] is too big and expensive and should be cut down – that we should drop its home propaganda and concentrate on our foreign propaganda for all we are worth in every possible way.

Monday 7 July　　The HofC is really too depressing for words – I know so few people there – or perhaps what I mean is that I care for so few – and all the Conservatives seem to me quite futile and useless. They never do anything or act together in any way with the result that the Party is ceasing to exist. The trouble of course is that there is no one to lead them – Eddie Winterton ought to do so but he is quite hopeless and useless and plays away at the idea of forming an alternative National Govt. He is too childish for words. I suppose if I were younger and more self-assertive, this would be the moment for me to come forward – but, frankly, I no longer possess the energy and drive and power of work which would be required to galvanize into life the inert mass, and, literally, there seems to be no one who would either be willing or capable of helping one. The only individuals who are being busy in the HofC now are men who are out for themselves and hope by making themselves a nuisance to be taken on by Winston. It is a depressing state of things.

Tuesday 8 July　　I lunched at the House and attended a meeting regarding Conservative candidates in James Stuart's room in the afternoon. It was not very exciting: the only person who appeared to take any interest in the proceedings was Topping.

Wednesday 9 July　　Winston made rather a flippant little speech about the American taking over of Ireland in the House this morning – it made people laugh, but shocked others a good deal. The House discussed production today but I heard little of the debate except Harold Macmillan's reply. I gather that most speakers were very critical, not unnaturally. Harold was in his best form: did very well in his way but really made little reply to criticism. He told us how much better production was now than it was, but he did not explain why it had taken such an infernal time to get going and why it was still so unsatisfactory. This afternoon I went to a meeting of the Nat[ional Union] Executive at the Caxton Hall. I tried to get the committee to approve of a resolution advocating the calling of a party conference at an early date – but got little or no support. It was held that a party conference would make things difficult for Winston – was there ever such nonsense!

Thursday 10 July   Lunched at the HofC – no gossip worth recording – but clearly no one is satisfied with the Government's reply to critics in the production debate. Moore-Brabazon made a clever and amusing speech today and assured us that before long we would be able to bomb Berlin a deal harder than London has ever been bombarded – but no one was much impressed by his fulsome praise of the Beaver[5] – his description of the little man holding 4 conversations at one and the same time quite coherently did not impress us much. The general view is that he may be all right at the Min. of Supply for a few weeks in order to bother people out of their inertia, but that it would be fatal to leave him there for any length of time as he has not an idea of organization, etc. ... Dined with Jennings[6] M.P. – he assured me that Grattan-Doyle had tried to sell him N. Newcastle for £10,000! it seems incredible.

Monday 14 July   A letter from Stafford[7] this morning to let us know that Aidan[8] is missing – apparently he went back to active R.A.F. work and was last seen flying a Hurricane somewhere in the Libyan desert. I am afraid that it doesn't sound likely that the poor boy will ever be seen again. It was very gallant of him to

[5] Lord Beaverbrook, who became Minister of Supply on 29 June 1941; Moore-Brabazon had suceeded him as Minister of Aircraft Production on 1 May 1941, and between then and 29 June Beaverbrook had been a Minister of State (i.e. without portfolio).

[6] Roland Jennings (1894–1968), Con. M.P. Sedgefield 1931–35, Sheffield Hallam 1939–59; kt. 1954.

[7] (Arthur) Stafford Crawley (1876–1948), clergyman; Vicar of Benenden, Kent 1905–10, of East Meon, Hants. 1922–24; Chaplain to Archbishop of York 1910–22, 1924–28; Sec., York Diocesan Bd. of Finance 1924–28; Diocesan Sec., St. Albans 1929–34; Canon of St. George's Chapel, Windsor 1934–48, Chaplain to the King 1944–48; Beatrice's brother, father of Aidan.

[8] Aidan Merivale Crawley (1908–1993), educational film producer 1936–39; war service in R.A.F., prisoner of war 1941–45; Lab. M.P. Buckingham 1945–51, Con. M.P. Derbyshire W. 1962–67; P.P.S. to G. Hall & A. Creech Jones 1945–50; U.S. Air 1950–51; resigned from Lab. Party 1957; Chairman, London Weekend Television 1967–71, Pres., 1971–73; Headlam's nephew.

return to active flying for by all accounts he was no expert and had already had many narrow escapes. ... He was a wonderful athlete and possessed a good brain. Before the war he was going through a curious political phase and how it would have ended one could not say – but it seemed to me when I last saw him that he had come on a lot and he might well have developed into a useful man. Well – perhaps he may yet turn up and do well. Pray God he may.

Tuesday 15 July   The news of importance today is that the Yanks have taken over Ireland – are to garrison the island. This seems to me to be a big step forward – for surely if they garrison Ireland they must take over the guarding of the sea approaches? Winston implied as much in his statement in the House today.

Wednesday 16 July   I attended the meeting of the [National Union] Executive this afternoon at the Caxton Hall, Eugene Ramsden presiding. He did so with his usual self-sufficient manner which I find so exasperating. They were all against my proposal for a conference. The opposition was lead by Colonel and Mrs. Mayhew[9] (Grattan-Doyle's pals) – and, oddly enough, all the others were deeply impressed by what this absurd couple said. Seemingly a party conference would put Winston in a very difficult position: how could he talk party politics, etc., etc. It was all very silly but I saw that all the old women (male and female) were against me, and of course neither Douglas Hacking nor Eugene Ramsden gave a sign of life – no doubt they had stirred up the opposition. I withdrew my resolution and told them that we were riding for a fall – which I honestly believe is the case.

Thursday 17 July   I spent the morning at the HofC. We were considering Ernest Brown's Pharmacy Bill – it is one of those agreed bills about which nobody appears to be agreed – the herbalists and patent medicine people are greatly alarmed. Ernest Brown and his much more able Parly. Secretary (Florence Horsbrugh[10]) assure me that their alarm is groundless. I intervened

---

[9] John Mayhew (1884–1954), Con. M.P. East Ham N. 1931–45; kt. 1945; married 1907 Guendolen Gurney (d.1946).
[10] Florence Gertrude Horsbrugh (1889–1969), Con. M.P. Dundee 1931–45, Manchester Moss Side 1950–59; P.S. Health 1939–45, Food 1945; Min. of Educ. 1951–54; member of Cabinet 1953–54, the first woman Con. cabinet Minister; cr. Dame 1954, Baroness Horsbrugh 1959.

twice in the debate quite shortly – just to show I was alive. But how boring it all is! I find no one in the House to hobnob with. Yesterday I attended a luncheon given to George Windlesham[11] who has been turned out (none too soon) of the Vice-Chairmanship of the Party – he is succeeded by Tommie Dugdale who ought to do the job much better. George made a speech of some length – and spoke under, what is usually described [as], the influence of deep emotion – Kingsley Wood, who was there, told me that the poor man is deeply hurt.

Friday 18 July   I went into Newcastle ... I addressed a meeting of Conservatives at the office of the Central Division. This is the first of our monthly meetings – and it was not too bad a gathering. Sykes[12] took the chair as Wilkin did not arrive in time and I spoke on the war for about 40 minutes. Beatrice told me that I did well and the people – mainly women – seemed interested.

Monday 21 July   There are changes in the Government calculated no doubt to strengthen our war effort – Duff [Cooper], for example, is leaving the Min. of Information and is being sent as Chancellor of the Duchy of Lancaster to the Far East to coordinate things in general! No doubt he will be heavily paid and will be allowed to take Diana with him to cast a glamour East of Suez. He has failed in every job he has been given: is clearly incompetent as an administrator, but belongs to the Winston clique. Brendan Bracken succeeds him and it will be interesting to see how he performs. Harold Nicolson is sacked, but made a Governor of the B.B.C. R.A. Butler goes to the Board of Education *vice* H. Ramsbotham[13] who is made a peer and given Betterton's job at £5,000 a year – ample reward for faithful minor services and general inadequacy. Young Law succeeds R.A.B. as Under-Secretary at the F[oreign]

[11] George Richard James Hennessy (1877–1953), Con. M.P. Winchester 1918–31; P.P.S. to T. Macnamara 1921–22; Whip 1922–28, Dep. Chief Whip 1928–31; Con. Party Vice-Chairman 1931–41; cr. Bart. 1927, Baron Windlesham 1937.

[12] Geoffrey Sykes, Chairman of Newcastle North C.A. 1941–44.

[13] Herwald Ramsbotham (1887–1971), Con. M.P. Lancaster 1929–41; P.S. Educ. 1931–35; P.S. Agric. 1935–36; Min. of Pensions 1936–39; 1st Comm. Works 1939–40; Pres. Bd. of Educ. 1940–41; Chairman, (unemployment) Assistance Bd. 1941–48; Governor-Gen. of Ceylon 1949–54; cr. Baron Soulbury 1941, Viscount 1954.

O[ffice] and Duncan Sandys[14] (Winston's son-in-law) goes to the W[ar] O[ffice] as Financial Secretary *vice* Law. So the family and friends are well looked after by Winston in the old, unabashed Whig manner of the 18th century – and we are all supposed to say 'how right and proper!'

Thursday 24 July   Vichy[15] is reported to have given way to Japan and surrendered bases in Indo-China – it seems that the French are ready enough to fight against us to preserve their possessions, but are not prepared to do so against the Japanese. It really is a monstrous business and one wonders how things can ever be put right between this country and France when this war is over. I suppose the truth of the matter is that the French and English peoples cannot really become friends – the old hatred and rivalry between them has too deeply national prejudices [*sic*] on both sides of the Channel.

Friday 25 July   ... into Newcastle ... I visited the Labour Ministry H.Q. and was then taken down to Wallsend where I inspected the ministry's Training Centre. It seems a well-run show ... they have all sorts and conditions of men and women to train as fitters, welders, etc., and the manager told me that it is amazing how very quickly most of them pick up the work. It is much to be hoped that our overlords – the T.U.C. people – will allow these training centres to be kept running after the war. I shall be surprised if they do.

Saturday 26 July   I have had a long and tiring day. I left Durham at 8.26 a.m. and got to Manchester at 1.30 p.m. – lunched at the Grand Hotel with the Chairman of the Lancashire, Cheshire and Westmorland Area and a party of local Conservative bigwigs: addressed the Area conference[16] (about 170 present): caught the 5.10 p.m. from Manchester to York where I missed my connexion –

[14] Duncan Edwin Sandys (1908–1987), Con. M.P. Norwood 1935–45, Streatham 1950–74; F.S. War Office 1941–43; P.S. Supply 1943–44; Min. of Works 1944–45; Min. of Supply 1951–54; Min. of Housing 1954–57; Min. of Defence 1957–59; Min. of Aviation 1959–60; Commonwealth Sec. 1960–64, & Colonial Sec. 1962–64; cr. Baron Duncan-Sandys 1974; founder of European Movement 1947.

[15] The French government located at Vichy, led by Marshal Petain.

[16] i.e., the Annual General Meeting.

I ultimately got back here about 11.45 p.m. In addition, the trip cost me about £2.10[shillings] – and all this for the Party! Surely I am a madman, seeing how little the Party has done for me and what a rotten lot we all are! My speech was a success, I think. The stations and trains were over-crowded with holiday-makers – quite on the pre-war bank holiday scale. Clearly the public are paying no attention to the Government's request to them to stay at home . . .

Monday 28 July		One only hopes that we are using this respite to advantage and that the supplies are mounting up. The trouble is that a good many people seem to be under the impression that everything in the garden is beautiful now that the Russians are fighting the Germans – indeed, there is a dangerous feeling about that the war will soon be over and that there is no need for us to keep going full steam ahead. To me this seems to be a very dangerous attitude of mind and the Govt. should do all it can to disillusion people. I don't believe that the Russians will be able to stand up to the Germans very long – though I admit that they seem to be doing a deal better than I for one expected. My belief is that the Germans will be in possession of the Ukraine before many weeks are past and then our troubles will begin again. I hope to God that we are stronger than we were in the Middle East – it has yet to be seen, too, whether Stalin & co. are really prepared to carry on the war once their armies have had a good beating and they have lost Leningrad and Moscow and Odessa – I should imagine that they are quite capable of swallowing another Brest-Litovsk.[17]

Tuesday 29 July		In the House there was a 'Production' debate, opened by Winston. I did not hear his speech as I was in the City, but no one thought much of it: of course Winston's oratory and make-up are not suited to such a subject as 'production' – you can't get away with it by phrases when you are called upon to explain why the supply of the most necessary and obvious things is terribly behindhand. Bevin who wound up for the Government

[17] The separate peace treaty which the Bolshevik regime signed with Germany in March 1918 at the town of Brest-Litovsk, under which large territories were ceded by Russia.

was, I thought, better than usual. He scored over that ass Austin Hopkinson[18] and pleased his own friends by cracking up the unskilled working man – and he made a kind of case for high wages and no compulsion. There is no doubt, I fear, that we are now governed by the T.U.C. industrially and God only knows what the mess will be after the war.

Wednesday 30 July   I lunched with Douglas Jerrold[19] at the Atheneum Club. He is interested in our policy committees and would like to join in with us I gather – it seems that he was engaged in similar work with George Lloyd. He is a very strong Tory and strikes me as a sensible and practical man – but I doubt whether he will be acceptable to our lot – he is too strongly right wing I am afraid.

Friday 1 August   There was a debate on India today in the House and I thought that Amery[20] spoke well: it really is absurd that people here or in India should worry their heads about Home Rule for India at such a time as this – but the ignorance and folly of the Socialists and some Liberals is beyond belief.

Tuesday 5 August   In the House today they discussed the coal situation. I did not hear Grenfell,[21] but by all accounts he made a hopelessly bad speech and Andrew Duncan who wound up for the Government and whom I heard was not particularly happy. They tell me that he hates the HofC and is nervous when speaking there.

Wednesday 6 August   Attlee spoke instead of Winston (who is said to have gone to America!) in the debate on the progress of the war. He read out a statement which told us nothing more than we

[18] Austin Hopkinson (1879–1962), Ind. M.P. Prestwich 1918, Mossley 1918–29, 1931–45 (accepted Coalition Lib. whip 1918–22, supported Nat. Govt. 1931–38).
[19] Douglas Jerrold (1893–1964), author and historian; Chairman, Eyre & Spottiswoode Ltd, publishers; editor, *English Review* 1930–36, *New English Review* 1945–50.
[20] Leopold Charles Maurice Stennett Amery (1873–1955), Con. M.P. Birmingham (S., later Sparkbrook) 1911–45; U.S. Colonies 1919–21; F.S. Admiralty 1921–22; 1st Lord of Admiralty 1922–24; Colonial Sec. 1924–29 (& Dominions 1925–29); India Sec. 1940–45.
[21] David Rhys Grenfell (1881–1968), Lab. M.P. Gower 1922–59; P.P.S. to C. Attlee 1924, to M. Jones 1929–31; Sec. for Mines 1940–42; member of P.L.P. Exec. 1931–40; Father of the House 1952–59.

already knew and he read it very badly. After he sat down Nunn spoke well on the Japanese situation and King-Hall[22] spoke well (but far too long) on political warfare. Then the spirit moved me to stand up in order to back up the two others and Douglas Clifton Brown called me – of course I was entirely unprepared but I spoke quite decently for a quarter of an hour: it would have been much better no doubt had I fired off one or other of the speeches I had prepared – but I had not got them with me. I had a talk with R.A. Butler this morning *re* our Conservative committees on policy[23] and he agreed that we ought to put out some kind of basic instructions for them – he is going to try and write something and then let me see it. He tells me that Kingsley Wood and others are saying that he ought not to be chairman of this show as he is a Minister. This has always been my opinion – but then I wanted to be chairman myself!

Friday 8 August   Womersley's[24] decision to give pensions to people who have lost their health as a result of service in this war after having been passed into the Services as fit is a kindly one, but it is going to give M.P.s a lot of bother, and I don't suppose that many of the applicants will get their pensions – however, writing letters to Ministers to satisfy their constituents is one of the recognised jobs of M.P.s and one has to do as others do.

Sunday 10 August   One does not know what to think of the Russian situation. Clearly the Germans are making ground and will have Odessa I should imagine in a short space of time – but, unless they succeed in turning the Russian retreat into a rout and smashing up the Russian armies, I don't see that the capture of Odessa and Leningrad and Kiev and even Moscow need mean the

[22] (William) Stephen Richard King-Hall (1893–1966), M.P. Orsmkirk 1939–45 (Nat. Lab to Feb. 1942, then Ind. Nat.); Dir. of Publicity, Min. of Fuel & Power 1942–43; founder of *National News Letter* 1936, and Hansard Soc. 1944; kt. 1954, cr. Baron King-Hall 1966.

[23] In May 1941 the National Union Exec. Ctte. approved the establishment of the Post-War Problems Central Ctte., of which Butler was appointed chairman by Churchill. This body established a series of sub-committees under their own chairmen, to consider and report on different areas of policy; Headlam was invited to chair the Constitutional Affairs Sub-Ctte.

[24] Walter James Womersley (1878–1961), Con. M.P. Grimsby 1924–45; P.P.S. to K. Wood 1931; Whip 1931–35; Ass. Postmaster-Gen. 1935–39; Min. of Pensions 1939–45; kt. 1934, cr. Bart. 1945.

collapse of Russia, unless of course Stalin and co. give up the struggle and come to terms with Hitler. In my opinion such a *dénouement*[25] would not be in the least surprising – but then I have no faith in the Bolshies, and am quite certain that their treaty with us means nothing to them. The one and only thing which we have got to keep clearly in our heads is that, if we are to win this war, we have got to win it for ourselves – in other words, that the British Empire is standing on its own and cannot depend on any other country.

Monday 11 August   I went into Newcastle after luncheon and attended the Research Group – I was in the chair and we discussed town planning for $2\frac{1}{2}$ hours – a paper by Goodfellow – but did not get much forwarder. Personally I am not a 'planner' – by which I mean that I distrust what is generally meant by planning and the people who are so keen about it. Let us by all means have a certain amount of method in our general madness, but do not let us attempt to regiment everything or to believe that the results of such regimentation will be much better than they are at present. However 'planning' is the fashionable pastime at the moment and all the bureaucrats and intelligentsia are all out on the war path – so perhaps it is just as well that a few of us of the old school who believe in individualism and freedom should stand by and prevent too much nonsense being talked and too much damage being done.

Wednesday 13 August   ... Anthony Eden told me the other day that we were still very short of bombers – it is strange that this should be the case and one cannot help feeling depressed that our production is so slow – production of the most essential war implements. It is no use fussing and one must try and believe that those in authority are really doing their best to get a move on. I feel that it is wrong to keep airing this matter of production in the House because it serves no useful purpose and presumably it must cheer the enemy to hear how behindhand everything is – but I do rather resent the attitude of Ministers when one approaches them privately and puts up the questions regarding bad management, waste and idleness that come one's way. They are always perfectly satisfied that everything possible is being done to speed up things,

[25] translation: outcome.

etc. – they invariably deny the perfectly well authenticated stories that one gives them, and stand up for their wretched officials – the vast majority of whom nowadays have not even the excuse of being regular civil servants, and are just odds and ends raked in from industry to try and run the show. We are suffering, especially in the Ministry of Supply, if half one hears is to be believed, from a plethora of inadequate persons, many of whom are neither honest nor capable – and there appears to be little or no higher supervision.

Thursday 14 August   Attlee broadcasted today and after all the excitement about what he was going to say what he actually said was rather flat – Winston and Roosevelt have had a heart to heart somewhere in the Atlantic (Winston travelled in the new battleship *Prince of Wales*), and they have concocted an 8 point pronouncement somewhat vague and woolly in character as some kind of a rejoinder to Hitler's 'New Order'.[26] I expect that they will be a good deal criticized here, but may please the Americans for whom presumably these pious aspirations are primarily intended.

Friday 15 August   The press today is of course full of the Winston-F.D.R. '8 points' – they get a chorus of praise – now, indeed, we know what we are fighting for – all the old tags which we have always advocated – but, presumably, they have tickled the Yanks to death – and it was for the Yanks, I suppose, that this business was intended. They don't seem any more inclined to come into the war than they did – it remains to be seen what their reaction will be should the Japanese take the offensive against us. They really are a strange and unpleasing people: it is a nuisance that we are so dependent on them.

Sunday 17 August   Stalin has welcomed the coming of a British-American delegation to Moscow to discuss what can be done to help him – and the delightful Lord Beaverbrook is said to be going there to represent us. It is odd that such a man should be chosen for such an important job – I suppose he amuses Winston and gives him lots of cigars and brandy – money is a great asset to

[26] The 'Atlantic Charter', a statement of basic principles for the post-war world, was drafted at the Churchill-Roosevelt meeting of 9–12 Aug. 1941 at Placentia Bay, Newfoundland.

success in this world – money, cheek, cunning and bounce.

Sunday 24 August   Winston broadcasted tonight and, as usual, made an eloquent, forcible and well-constructed attack upon the 'Nazis' – but I cannot say that he told us anything new, or led us to hope that the Yankees were any nearer to coming into the war than they were before he saw Roosevelt – however, his speech was more for the Yanks than for us – and will, I imagine, have a good effect in the U.S.A.

Wednesday 3 September   The third year of the war begins today – and all one can say with any truth is that the third year is beginning in rather better conditions than did the second year. We have still a lot of trouble ahead of us and it seems to me useless to imagine that the Germans are anywhere near beaten – but we are a deal stronger than we were in September last year and the fact of Russia's being in the war against Germany is a great asset, provided she can last the course. ... I am certain that a lot more work and energy is called for if we are to win the war. I should feel happier, too, if I had complete confidence in Winston and his associates. W. is a great leader in his way – courageous, determined, an oratorical genius – but I don't believe that he has a power of organization and I don't trust him as a strategist – and he insists, so one is told, on being the war boss and won't take advice from anyone. I only hope that Jack Dill, and Pound and Portal[27] can deal with him – but certainly no one in his cabinet can.

Saturday 6 September   Moore-Brabazon seems to have got into hot water. He is reported to have said in a recent speech that it was all right the Russians and Germans killing each other: all the better for us, or words to that effect. It is what a good many of us think, but it is not wise to say so *coram populo*[28] – keep such opinions for a diary!

Sunday 7 September   It always seems odd to me in the peaceful surroundings of Holywell to know that our virulent enemy is only

[27] Charles Frederick Algernon Portal (1893–1971), air force career; C. in C. Bomber Command 1940; Chief of Air Staff 1940–45; Controller, Atomic Energy, Min. of Supply 1946–51; kt. 1940, cr. Viscount Portal of Hungerford 1945.

[28] translation: before the people.

a comparatively few miles away from us, and that men are battling fiercely all over the world. How ridiculous it all seems at first sight – but this war is not only the testing time of the present generation, it is also being fought for two quite different conceptions of life. Is the world to go back to a period of the rule of force in which Germany will be holding down all opposition – or are we going to preserve the ideals for which the British Commonwealth of Nations stands? There never was a clearer issue or a more inevitable struggle – and how will it end? One simply refuses to believe, if there is a God in heaven, that Hitler will be successful – but, on the face of things, the fight is going to be one to the death and one wonders now and then whether, when the strain becomes greater and greater, men will be able to last out – whether, sooner or later, the question will be raised – 'Is it worth going on?' There is only one answer to such a question: Germany must be crushed once [and] for all or Satan will have triumphed on Earth.

Tuesday 9 September Winston made a very good and clear statement of the situation in the House today: some people complained that it was dull – but I considered it to be about the best he has made. It was soberly optimistic and he evidently believes that we have seen the worst of the battle for the Atlantic, although there are bound to be ups and downs in losses at sea. I think, too, that he must be certain in his own mind that the Americans will soon be in the war – for all practical purposes, except manpower, they are now. To keep the Russians going is now the main object of our war policy: and I don't fancy that it is going to be too easy for us to do this. We have already sent a good many aircraft, so Winston says.

Wednesday 10 September Today George Balfour's Bill to supply electricity in the Highlands got a bad time in the House – all sorts and conditions of men united in their opposition to the attempt to spoil mountain beauty for private gain. The motion to read the Bill again in 3 months' time was accepted by the promoters without a division – they would have been beaten had they challenged a division. I should have voted for the Bill not because I like what it proposed – I hate doing more than has already been done to spoil the Highlands – but because I feel that the promotion of tourist traffic has already ruined the amenities and because in these days electric power is essential for the development which all these wretched Scots are always clamouring for.

Thursday 11 September   The House had a dull sitting, so I am told, but I did not enter the chamber – still busy with my committee. Dennis Herbert is a very tiresome and irritable chairman and his deafness is a nuisance: it is certainly high time that he ceased to be Chairman of Committees – this is the general opinion – and it holds good, too, of the Speaker who is also too old for his job – inasmuch as it bores him.

Sunday 14 September   ... into Newcastle this after[noon] where I felt that I must go to listen to Attlee – I should say that there were about 1,700 in the Hall. The speech was a good one – but Attlee is a poor speaker – bad voice, bad delivery. Eustace Percy proposed a vote of thanks, and Bowman,[29] the trade unionist man, seconded it. It is really becoming somewhat marked the way in which the Conservatives are being given no part or lot in these M[inistry] of I[nformation] big meetings – I shall have to take the matter up, if it persists – Eustace and the L[ord] M[ayor] are of course responsible for the business.

Sunday 28 September   I went ... to speak at the meeting organized by the Newcastle left-wingists in favour of Anglo-Soviet cooperation. The meeting was in the City Hall – Lord Mayor in the chair – audience (largely Communist) about 1,000 I should say – speakers Sir Bernard Pares[30] (supplied by the Minister of Information!), Horner[31] leader of the South Wales miners (said to be a Communist), myself and David Adams M.P. Pares spoke for three-quarters of an hour: a very pro-Bolshie bit of work which

[29] This is probably John ('Jack') Bowman (1889–1981), Statutory District Sec., Tyne Area, Amalgamated Engineering Union, 1924–53; Dir., N.E. Trading Estates Ltd. from 1956 (also see entry for 3 Mar. 1945), but could be James Bowman (1898–1978), Gen. Sec., Northumberland Miners' Assoc. 1935–49; Vice-Pres., Nat. Union of Mineworkers 1938–49; Chairman, Northern Div., Nat. Coal Bd. 1950–55; Dep. Chairman, Nat. Coal Bd. 1955–56, Chairman 1956–61; kt. 1957, cr. Bart. 1961.

[30] Bernard Pares (1867–1949), Prof. of Russian, Liverpool 1908–17, London 1919–36; Dir., School of Slavonic & E. European Studies 1922–39; temp. civil servant 1939–40; lectured in U.S.A. for Min. of Information 1942–44; kt. 1919.

[31] Arthur Lewis Horner (1894–1968), Pres., S. Wales Miners' Fed. 1936–46; Gen. Sec., Nat. Union of Mineworkers 1946–59.

surprised and annoyed me – Horner and Adams both utilized the opportunity for political propaganda. I was very careful not to say anything anti-Bolshie, but I made it quite clear that I disliked and disbelieved in Communism and that in my opinion the Russian resistance to the German invasion was in defence of Holy Russia and not of Marxian principles. I am afraid that this Anglo-Soviet organization in Newcastle is Communistic and likely to cause us a lot of bother in the future. I saw Wilkin on the platform ... but few other people whom I knew – as usual our Conservatives gave the meeting a miss.

Tuesday 30 September　　Winston spoke on the war situation in the House today – a really admirable speech which cleverly and effectively knocked out his critics. He was cautious in what he said, but clearly was in a confident mood – a long war ahead of us, but things improving. Clearly he expects the Russians to hold on – let us hope he is right. I did not hear the subsequent speeches as I had to be at our 'offices' [Select] Committee – Dennis Herbert as trying as ever, but we got on with the report – indeed, practically finished with it.

Wednesday 1 October　　I went to see Armstrong at the Central Office this morning and went through with him the agenda for tomorrow's [National Union Central] Council meeting. Derek Gunston's[32] resolution *re*. buying of seats is the only thing that may lead to discussion – but it will of course be passed. It really means very little in practice – for money will always count where candidates are concerned, and there are really only 2 ways of stopping any preference for the man with money – (1) that election expenses should be paid by the State and it be forbidden by law for a candidate or M.P. to subscribe to his local association; or (2) a system such as that in the Cirencester and Berwick divisions where the Association pays the election expenses and the Member is not called upon to subscribe to the Association. ... Spoke at the 1922 Committee meeting this afternoon in favour of Conservative M.P.s

[32] Derrick Wellesley Gunston (1891–1985), Con. M.P. Thornbury 1924–45; P.P.S. to Sir Kingsley Wood 1926–29, to Neville Chamberlain 1931–36, to Sir E. Grigg 1940–42; cr. Bart. 1938.

joining Horder's[33] A[nglo-]S[oviet] [Public Relations] Com[mittee].

Thursday 2 October   I spent most of today presiding over the Conservative Central Council at the Caxton Hall. The proceedings passed off all right and I was congratulated by several people on my able chairmanship and by Topping and others on my speech moving a resolution of confidence in Winston and his Government. Some criticisms of the terms of this resolution were expected, but they did not mature – Pickthorn, Herbert Williams and H. Strauss[34] who were the critics did not turn up – wisely perhaps. I lunched with Tommie Dugdale at a restaurant in Leicester Square, an excellent meal which I enjoyed. Oliver Lyttelton and Bobbety Cranborne were also lunching there – the former is over here from Cairo for a few days, reporting to the Cabinet. He was as usual delighted with himself and he certainly has a grand billet if ever anyone had. He told me that on the whole things were shaping well in his Middle East – armies at last assuming proper proportions and well-equipped.

Sunday 5 October   As I get older – and I am ageing rather fast at the moment – I find I am inclined to ruminate a good deal – to let my mind wander back to the past and bother about all the might-have-beens. I suppose that if I had been different temperamentally I might have made a bigger name for myself than I have done. Even going late into the HofC as I did, and even lacking £.s.d., I have no doubt that had I been cannier, more careful in my conversation, more of a toady, I should not have been dropped as I was. Worldly wisdom is essential for success in almost every walk of life – in this country, I mean – and by worldly wisdom I mean the cultivation of the people who matter which often necessitates flattery and the veneration of the second rate. In worldly wisdom, or at any rate the exercise of it, I – like most of my family – am entirely lacking – and yet what does success really matter – should I have been

---

[33] Thomas Jeeves Horder (1871–1955), Senior Physician, St. Bartholomew's Hospital 1921–36; Physician to King George V, King Edward VIII, King George VI & Queen Elizabeth II; Chairman, Min. of Health Advisory Ctte. 1935–59; Medical Advisor, Min. of Food 1941; kt. 1918, cr. Bart. 1923, Baron Horder 1933.

[34] Henry George Strauss (1892–1974), Con. M.P. Norwich 1935–45, English Univ. 1946–50, Norwich S. 1950–55; jt. P.S. Works & Planning 1942–43; P.S. Town & Country Planning 1943–45 (resigned, Mar. 1945); P.S. Trade 1951–55; cr. Baron Conesford 1955.

happier, I wonder, had I become a Cabinet Minister?

Tuesday 7 October   Lunched at the House where there was nothing much doing – the principal item in the programme being the Bill to continue the life of this Parl[iament]. I made a little intervention asking whether it was quite clear, if we passed the Bill, that the Govt. would have to come again to Parl. next year if its life had to be prolonged still further – it did not seem to me and others that the wording of the Bill made this clear. Morrison (Home Secretary) assured me that they, the Govt., would have to come for fresh authority next year.

Wednesday 8 October   Lunched at the House – a very dull day. Everyone is gloomy about Russia's prospects – and the ginger people are all for having a go at the Germans somewhere at once. They never consider where we are to attack them – with what forces – and how we are to find the shipping – but, admittedly, now is the moment to strike if it were possible – but one does not want to court another catastrophe.

Thursday 9 October   There was a 'secret session' this morning, while we discussed our future sittings. Winterton, Aneurin Bevan,[35] Mander,[36] etc., objected to the Government's very sensible proposal to shorten the hours of sitting in the winter months. I intervened on the side of the Government quite effectively – at any rate I drew Eddie Winterton all right much to the House's pleasure. I pointed out that he and the 2 other members who were anxious for longer hours were the members who took up far too large a share of the available time. My suggestion that, during the war at any rate, there might be a time limit for speakers was not so popular – and yet all that the average Member has to say might well be said in ten minutes or a quarter of an hour. Lunched at the House next to Sir John Power who kept on assuring me what a clever, hard-

---

[35] Aneurin Bevan (1897–1960), Lab. M.P. Ebbw Vale 1929–60, expelled for supporting a Popular Front, Mar.-Dec. 1939; editor of *Tribune* 1942–45; Min. of Health 1945–51; Min. of Labour Jan.-Apr. 1951; member of P.L.P. Parl. Ctte. 1952–54, 1955–60; member of N.E.C. 1944–54, 1956–60; Labour Dep. Leader 1959–60, Treasurer 1959–60.
[36] Geoffrey Le Mesurier Mander (1882–1962), Lib. M.P. Wolverhampton E. 1929–45; P.P.S. to Sir A. Sinclair 1942–45; High Sheriff of Staffordshire 1921; kt. 1945; joined Lab. Party 1948; Headlam wrote his name as 'Maunders'.

working, important man he was – apparently (according to his own assertion) he is *the* authority on foreign affairs. He has often told me all this before. ... Had a talk with Rab Butler this morning *re* policy committees.

Tuesday 14 October   We had the final meeting of our Select Committee today, and pretty things were said in public to old Dennis Herbert: in private no words were bad enough for him. He certainly was the most autocratic, rude and tiresome chairman I have ever come across. His deafness was very tiresome – however, all's well that ends well and the report is not a bad one – I suppose that it will be debated in the House. There was a division today – an event which requires recording in these days: what it was about I really don't know, but as it was challenged on an amendment to a Govt. agricultural Bill by Mrs. Tate,[37] I voted for the Govt. without any hesitation – as good a reason for a vote as could be found, so it seemed to me.

Wednesday 15 October   ... by appointment I went to 11 Downing Street where I had a heart to heart with Kingsley Wood. He admitted that my case – being called upon to pay income tax and sur tax on director's fees which have never been paid to me – was a bad one. He was most conciliatory, but said that if he found that letting me off would mean a great loss of revenue, he would have to stick to the letter of the law. We discussed the approaching meeting of the 7 Conservatives (of whom I am one) and the 7 T.U.C. people *re* amendment of the Trade Disputes Act, and he gave me the inner history of the business. ... to Twyford to see Maureen Stanley – I was delighted to find her on the road to recovery, but she looks older and thinner and has been pretty bad I gather. She had nothing much in the way of news – but is actually contemplating going to the U.S.A. by air with her maid to spend the winter there. To me this seems madness: she clearly intends going and assured me that Oliver wants her to go.

Thursday 16 October   I went to the House – nothing much doing, the usual people talking – Sam Hoare addressed the 'All Party'

[37] Mavis Constance Tate (1893–1947), Con. M.P. Willesden W. 1931–35, Frome 1935–45.

Committee this afternoon. He seemed well and pleased with himself ... He told us that when he first went to Madrid[38] it was fully expected that Spain was about to enter the war against us, and he was told to keep the aeroplane that took him to Madrid to bring him home again. He said that Spain is in a very bad way economically – desperately short of food – and that typhus, Malta fever and diptheria are raging – that the Spaniards are frightened to death of the Germans and quite incapable of resisting them, should Hitler decide to march through Spain.

Friday 17 October   I have taken a regular feeling of repulsion for the B.B.C. announcers and can scarcely listen to their voices – I think that it is their glib and utterly un-understanding announcements of the war news from Russia which drives me wild – poor creatures I suppose they are not responsible for what they read to us – but somehow or other one feels that if they read their stuff differently it would not seem so bad!

Tuesday 21 October   Two American cargo ships have been sunk by the Germans, but the Americans show no undue resentment ... Sooner or later, presumably, the U.S.A. will be forced into the war, but I see no immediate prospect of this happening unless the Japanese do something desperate. For some reason or other the Yankees seem more ready to fight the Japanese than the Germans – probably because they affect them more nearly and also because they fancy them as easier meat.

Monday 27 October   It amuses me to see how the big boss Bevin is at last beginning to wake up to the fact that compulsion is the only way of getting people to do war work. His vain efforts to keep up trade union ideas during this national crisis would be amusing if the lag in production were not so great. It is now evident to most of us that things cannot be allowed to go on as they are, and Winston will be well-advised to hand Bevin to the wolves rather than allowing him to go on messing about much longer – I don't fancy that his removal would upset anybody.

Wednesday 29 October   I lunched at the Beefsteak ... Harold

[38] Hoare was British Ambassador to Spain from May 1940 to Dec. 1944.

Macmillan sat next to me: more self-satisfied and important than ever. He told me that all the production trouble was due to Supply and Labour being under two separate ministries (I should say that it was due to there being two such ministers as the Beaver and Bevin) – and to everything being run on peace time Civil Service lines with endless committees *auspice* Sir John Anderson – the quintessence of officialdom.

Monday 3 November   The Lord Mayor[39] ... is terribly cast down at not getting a third term – all the more I should imagine as it is entirely his own fault – I fancy that no one would have opposed him, had he been less addicted to the bottle.

Thursday 13 November   ... to the House – the debate on the Address – I listened to a speech by Shinwell – a clever debating performance, but he did not say anything very different to what he always says – all his little crowd (Eddie Winterton, Lindsay,[40] etc.) applauded him but nobody else. Clearly Winston is still cock of the walk and can go on employing whom he likes – for there is no one to take his place in the present Parliament – take his place *from* him, I mean.

Monday 17 November   Morrison, our Herbert of the Home Office, has produced a new regulation under the Defence of the Realm Act enabling him and our Bevin to start wet canteens in factories.[41] All the Temperance people are up in arms and there appear to be far too many of them in the North Newcastle division – a lot of them are writing to me as their M.P., commanding me to do all I can to knock out this regulation which it is asserted will mean death and damnation to hundreds of young people. How silly it all is: granted that people are not to be prevented from getting beer anywhere, I cannot imagine a better way of controlling its consumption than by supplying it in factory canteens – besides

[39] Adamson Dawson Russel, member of Newcastle City Council, St. John's Ward 1935–45, Lord Mayor 1939, 1941.

[40] Kenneth Martin Lindsay (1897–1991), Nat. Lab. M.P. Kilmarnock 1933–45 (Nat. Ind. from 1942), Ind. M.P. English Univ. 1945–50; Civil Ld., Admiralty 1935–37; P.S. Educ. 1937–40; Gen. Sec., Political & Economic Planning 1931–35; Dir., Anglo-Israel Association 1962–73.

[41] i.e., empowered to serve alcholic drinks.

there are now lots of factories which are far from public houses.

Sunday 23 November   There is little fresh about Libya in the papers – but I don't fancy that things are going for us quite according to plan – though it is only by reading between the lines that one gets this idea. ... In Russia the battle for Moscow is as violent as ever and the Russians admit that they are very hard pressed – Hitler will lose a lot of prestige if he does not get possession of the city and his troops will have a bad winter. It is a very interesting situation – one feels that if Moscow does not fall after all this bitter fighting, it may be the beginning of the end of German national morale. Such a happening would be in the nature of a major defeat: even the German Army would find it difficult to explain away. The effect of such a failure would be great throughout Europe which now is convinced that the Germans are invincible – once this myth has been exploded, things may begin to happen – however, it is no use indulging in an undue optimism. We are in very grave danger and will continue to be, so long as we are not far stronger militarily than we are today.

Wednesday 26 November   I had a talk with Rab Butler at the HofC this morning – he agrees with my proposed terms of reference to the sub-committee on constitutional reform of which I am to be chairman. We then discussed the personnel of the s[ub]-c[ommittee] and here there are a good many difficulties as it is hard to think of suitable people. I can only think of Agnes H[eadlam]-M[orley], of Kenneth Pickthorn and Douglas Jerrold – an odd trio! Rab suggested Onslow[42] which would make an even odder quartet!

Thursday 27 November   As a result of my known views on the subject and after a conversation I had yesterday with Erskine Hill,[43] chairman of the 1922 Committee, I was asked to join a Conservative group which is being formed to act together in the House. This is a good move and I agreed to join it. Vansittart gave an address

---

[42] Richard William Alan Onslow (1876–1945), diplomatic service 1901–14; Whip in Lords 1919–20; Civil Ld., Admiralty 1920–21; P.S. Health 1921–23, Educ. 1923–24; U.S. War Office 1924–28; Paymaster-Gen. 1928–29; styled Viscount Cranley 1876–1911, suc. 5th Earl of Onslow 1911.

[43] Alexander Galloway Erskine Erskine-Hill (1894–1947), Con. M.P. Edinburgh N. 1935–45; Chairman, 1922 Ctte. 1940–44; cr. Bart. 1944.

this afternoon to the Foreign Affairs Committee on France. He was interesting – he told us that in 1935 the French G[eneral] S[taff] was ready to move but the French politicians would not – that it was the F. politicians who were determined to take no action when the Germans went into the Rhineland and that they were not under pressure from us; that in 1938 again it was the French politicians who were determined not to go to the help of Czechoslovakia.

Saturday 29 November   ... Harold Balfour[44] ... has only just come back from Russia and told me at the HofC last Thursday that in his opinion the Germans were not going to take Moscow. He spoke highly of the Russian air force, both of the personnel and the machines.

Sunday 30 November   It looks as if these wretched Japanese were really going to make their plunge. There are reports which seem to mean an early move on their part on Siam and that the Japanese fleet has put out to sea – I am afraid that we shall have a lot of trouble from that fleet before long. How good it is no one seems to know – but on paper it is very powerful and probably it is a deal bigger than we know of. The really interesting thing now will be to see what the American line of action will be – they can hardly sit still and let Japan invade Siam and attack the Burma road – presumably their fleet will have to take action – and then we shall join in with them.

Tuesday 2 December   Winston introduced the Government's man-power proposals today. They are well devised, I think – probably because they represent to all intents and purposes my own views – I am sure it would have been unwise, for the time being at any rate, to conscript married women. The atmosphere in the House today was not very bright – the failure of the first Libyan attack upset people, who expected far too easy a run for their money, and now one hears nothing but gloomy remarks about the poor quality of our tanks, etc., etc.

Wednesday 3 December   Nothing of much interest at the HofC –

[44] Harold Harington Balfour (1897–1988), Con. M.P. Thanet 1929–45; U.S. Air 1938–44; Min. Res. W. Africa 1944–45; Pres., E.I.A. 1956–60; cr. Baron Balfour of Inchrye 1945.

man-power debate – the usual people talking. It looks as if nothing could prevent a war between the U.S.A. and Japan. I can't make up my mind whether the entry of the U.S.A. into the war is going to help us or not – they are so utterly raw and unprepared – and it would mean our having to hold the baby for quite a long time and probably a reduction in American materiel assistance as they would want all they could make for themselves.

Thursday 4 December In the House we went on with the man-power debate. Bevin wound up for the Government and made the best speech I have heard him deliver. Some 30 or 40 people – mainly extreme Labour – divided against the Government because they held that if you conscript labour you must nationalize property, coal mines, railways, etc. Clearly under their existing powers the Govt. can 'nationalize' anything and everything in the country – that they don't do so means that they don't think such a policy would strengthen the war effort. Labour of course only advocates nationalization because it is their declared policy – they are trying, in other words, to utilize the war as a means of introducing Socialism.

Saturday 6 December ... I went into Newcastle ... listened to Archie Sinclair deliver an oration in the City Hall. He spoke, or rather read a speech, for 55 minutes – rather wearisome – but he has a pleasant voice (I always like his little stammer) and he said what he ought to say – but how ridiculous it is that a man of his calibre should hold an important office in a time of national emergency such as this – however I gather that he is only a rubber stamp and no doubt does well enough.

8

DARK DAYS

December 1941 to May 1942

Sunday 7 December 1941 We heard on the wireless tonight that the Japanese have made a violent attack on the American naval base at Pearl Harbour in Hawaii and other places in the Hawaiian group of islands – American ships sunk, aircraft destroyed, heavy casualties – they are also invading Thailand and the Malay Peninsula – and all the time their Ambassador and special agent are in Washington carrying out negotiations with Roosevelt – I suppose the little swine have been preparing this coup for some considerable time – and, after all, they are only doing what they did when they fought Russia[1] – rushing into Port Arthur and torpedoing the Russian ships before they declared war – and now they have more excuse for their methods for Hitler has used them all along in this war. I always expected that the Americans would have some nasty surprises in a war with Japan, and one only hopes that they have not been hit too hard – because if they are not going to be of much help to us for some time, we are going to have a difficult time in the Pacific – I suppose we shall lose Hong Kong – and may have to defend Burma. But of course everything depends upon our being able to hold Singapore – and surely we can do this? What difficulty Willie B[ridgeman][2] and I had in prevailing even upon our own side that we must go on with the fortifying of Singapore in those years 1927–29 when people used to ask us why we needed a fleet![3]

[1] The Russo-Japanese War of 1904–05.
[2] William Clive Bridgeman (1864–1935), Con. M.P. Oswestry 1906–29; Sec. for Mines 1920–22; Home Sec. 1922–24, 1st Lord of Admiralty 1924–29; cr. Viscount Bridgeman 1929.
[3] Headlam served as junior minister at the Admiralty from December 1926 to June 1929, under Bridgeman as First Lord.

Monday 8 December   Apparently there was a summons to Parliament on the 12 (midnight) wireless . . . but mercifully not conveyed to me – so I missed hearing Winston's speech today telling us that we were at war with Japan. This afternoon (or morning, I forget which) we all listened to Roosevelt announcing the villainies of Japan in the American Congress – he did the job remarkably well and only took eight minutes to do it; we heard him admirably. Clearly the Japanese must have caught the American navy napping – Roosevelt admits that a lot of damage has been done at Pearl Harbour in Hawaii – 'an old battleship' and a destroyer sunk, large numbers of aircraft destroyed, 3,000 casualties on Oahu Island, etc., etc.,. The Japanese are busy trying to land troops here, there and everywhere – Siam has already submitted to them – and presumably Burma will now be attacked. It is the old, old story – the enemy prepared, the Allies unprepared – and no doubt we are in for a beastly time of it for a bit. Singapore has been bombed, also the Philippines and the American base on Guam Island has apparently been taken by Japan. In Russia things seem to be going well – the Germans have now decided not to take Moscow until the spring – the winter it seems is not a suitable time for military movement.

Wednesday 10 December   The news today from the Pacific has startled everyone – *Prince of Wales* and *Repulse* are reported sunk. Winston made the announcement in the HofC this morning, but I . . . only got to the House just before luncheon. No details are as yet available – but the impression is that Japanese dive bombers – suicide squads – did the job.[4] It is a very serious situation – this successful crescendo of attack on our and American shipping will enable the Japanese to do much as they like in the Pacific for some time to come and greatly facilitate their land operations against Hong Kong, Burma and the Malay Straits – Singapore itself may be in danger. In addition to all this, the loss of these important ships weakens us at sea, not only in the Pacific but also in the Atlantic. It looks to me as if very strenuous times are ahead of us

[4] The loss of this battleship and battlecruiser, recently sent by Churchill to Singapore to act as a deterrent but lacking adequate air cover, was a humiliating blow to British naval prestige and removed the chance of preventing Japanese landings in Malaya. The ships were sunk by bombs and torpedoes dropped from aircraft by conventional means, not by suicide attacks as surmised here.

... I feel very gloomy – but my colleagues in the HofC I am glad to say preserve their usual equanimity and have devoted a good part of their proceedings today debating whether or not they should be 'reserved'.[5]

Thursday 11 December   It was cheering to hear today that over 2,000 men were saved from *Prince of Wales* and *Repulse* – one always feels the personnel is what matters most. Winston made a statement in the House this morning and does not appear to have said much – I did not hear him as I had to attend a conference at Central Office – of our delegates at the T.U.C. conference[6] – I was elected chairman. We were given luncheon with the T.U.C. people (Eugene Ramsden appearing as our host – but no doubt the Central Office paid the bill, and I can't see why E.R. need have been there at all!) – our conference lasted from 2.15 to 5.10 p.m. – I was in the chair and the proceedings were most amicable. Sir W. Citrine[7] put their case very well – needless to say, making everything seem very simple – the other T.U.C. people were equally plausible – of course they are more Tory than the Tories – but, nevertheless, they are asking for too much. Their game is to put themselves in a position where they will be to all intents and purposes as powerful as Parliament. This would be bad enough even if they were not part and parcel of one of the political parties. We all asked questions – and many of the answers to them were very unsatisfactory I thought. Maxwell Fyfe[8] M.P., who seems rather a nice fellow, is going to draw up a report for us to present to the Executive.

Monday 15 December   ... I had an appointment with Topping

---

[5] Workers whose skills were essential for the war effort were classed as 'reserved occupations' and exempted from conscription into military service.

[6] The meeting of delegations nominated by the National Union and the T.U.C. to discuss the latter's request for the amendment of the 1927 Trade Disputes Act.

[7] Walter McLennan Citrine (1887–1981), Sec., Electrical Trades Union 1914–20, Ass. Gen. Sec. 1920–23; Ass. Sec., T.U.C. 1924–25, Gen. Sec. 1926–46; member of Nat. Production Advisory Council 1942–46, 1949–57; Chairman, Central Electricity Authority 1947–57; kt. 1935, cr. Baron Citrine 1946.

[8] David Patrick Maxwell Fyfe (1900–1967), Con. M.P. Liverpool W. Derby 1935–54; Solicitor-Gen. 1942–45; Attorney-Gen. 1945; Home Sec. 1951–54; Lord Chanc. 1954–62; Recorder of Oldham 1936–42; Dep. Chairman, Con. Post-War Problems Central Ctte. 1941–43, Chairman 1943–45; Dep. Chief Prosecutor at Nuremberg War Crimes Trials 1945–46; Chairman, Ctte. on Party Organization 1948–49; kt. 1942, cr. Viscount Kilmuir 1954, Earl of Kilmuir 1962.

at 11 a.m. He was anxious to hear about our T.U.C. discussion – later in the day he rang me up to say that Maxwell Fyfe had sent him his report, which he seemed to doubt whether I should like.

Tuesday 16 December   ... I went to the HofC where I made the acquaintance of the man who is to issue tickets for sleepers to M.P.s – I was lucky enough to get one for tonight and another for tomorrow night – in the future the situation won't be so pleasant – one's chances of getting 1st class sleepers looks poor – I listened in despair to what Llewellin[9] had to tell us north country M.P.s at a little conference we had with him this morning. I also attended with a deputation upon John Anderson by the request of Erskine Hill – we got an assurance from him that nationalization by stealth should not be indulged in – that the Party should not always be finding itself faced by the *fait accompli*.[10]

Monday 22 December   Winston's arrival in Washington is announced today – how he travelled is not stated, but he is stated to have dropped from the air in the U.S.A. capital – and no doubt is going to enjoy himself right royally. I fancy that he is likely to be a huge success with the Americans: after all, he is half a Yankee by birth[11] and has many American traits. Let us hope that he will do a good job of work.

Friday 26 December   We all listened to Winston's speech to the American Congress tonight – it came over wonderfully well and certainly was one of his best efforts – 'grim and gay'. He had a magnificent reception and was clearly enjoying himself. His success in the U.S.A. I should imagine is assured. General Pownall[12] has

---

[9] John Jestyn Llewellin (1893–1957), Con. M.P. Uxbridge 1929–45; P.P.S. to W. Ormsby-Gore 1931–35; Ass. Whip 1935–37; Civil Ld., Admiralty 1937–39; P.S. Supply 1939–40, Aircraft Production 1940–41, War Transport 1941–42; Pres. Bd. of Trade 4–21 Feb. 1942; Min. of Aircraft Production Feb.-Nov. 1942; Min. Res. in Washington for Supply 1942–43; Min. of Food 1943–45; Gov.-Gen., Rhodesia & Nyasaland 1953–57; cr. Baron Llewellin 1945.

[10] translation: accomplished fact, i.e. something now impossible to reverse.

[11] Churchill's mother, Jennie Jerome, was a wealthy American heiress.

[12] Henry Royds Pownall (1887–1961), army career; Dir. of Military Operations, War Office 1938–39; Chief of Staff, B.E.F. 1939–40; Inspector-Gen., Home Guard 1940; C. in C., N. Ireland 1940–41; Vice-C.I.G.S. 1941; C. in C. Far East 1941–42, Ceylon 1942–43, Persia & Iraq 1943; Chief of Staff to S.A.C. South-East Asia 1943–44; kt. 1940.

succeeded Brook-Popham[13] at Singapore – he is said to be a good man – let us hope that he has more in him than his brother[14] in the HofC who, by universal consent, is one of the biggest – if not the biggest – ass in the House.

Saturday 27 December   ... Winston, quite rightly, is going to Ottawa to make a speech in the Canadian Parliament. He certainly is having the time of his life and one only hopes that he won't crack up – for, rightly or wrongly only time will show, the whole people not only here but throughout the Empire have decided that he is the organizer of victory. We are lucky to have such a man – for in war a 'leader' is absolutely essential – I suppose that L.G. fulfilled this function of leadership in the last war, but nothing like to the same extent as Winston does in this war. In those days there were other men who might have stepped in to fill L.G.'s place at any time – today one cannot see anyone at all capable of replacing Winston – whether one believes [in] him or not he is our only leader for the time being.

Wednesday 7 January 1942   ... Onslow who is coming on to my constitutional sub-committee I am sorry to say – and takes it all too seriously as might be expected – suggested that we should have Hailsham on it which I promptly refused. Saw Topping later in the afternoon: apparently all the other members of our delegation[15] agree with me rather than Maxwell Fyfe, so there is no need for a meeting which is a mercy.

Thursday 8 January   ... I went to the HofC where Attlee made a statement about the war (Mr. Shinwell, Eddie Winterton & Co. had insisted upon our all being dragged up to London for one day to hear it). I did not hear Attlee, got to the House too late, and what little of the debate I did hear was beneath contempt – all the

[13] Henry Robert Moore Brooke-Popham (1878–1953), Commandant, R.A.F. Staff College 1921–26; A.O.C. Fighting Area, Air Defence 1926–28; A.O.C. Iraq 1928–30; Commandant, Imperial Defence College 1931–33; C. in C. Air Defence of Britain 1933–35, Middle East 1935–36; Gov. & C. in C. Kenya 1937–39; C. in C. Far East 1940–41; kt. 1927.

[14] Assheton Pownall (1877–1953), Con. M.P. Lewisham E. 1918–45; P.P.S. to Sir L. Worthington-Evans 1923, to Sir A. Steel-Maitland 1924–29; Chairman, Public Accounts Ctte. 1943–45; kt. 1926.

[15] Which negotiated with the T.U.C. on the Trades Disputes Act; see above.

usual gang spoke and there was something rather ridiculous in Percy Harris and his ilk criticizing the Government on ill-preparedness and bad strategy: I never can understand how all these peacemongers and League of Nations Union cranks can dare to open their mouths about the war.

Saturday 10 January   I have been reading today *Hitler Speaks*, by Hermann Rauschning[16] – I have only glanced at it before. It is extraordinarily interesting, I think, and worth study, because it shows what an astonishing being Hitler must be – it seems almost unbelievable that a man of his type and upbringing should be filled with such amazing ideas – still more unbelievable that he should have been able to bring so many of them into fruition. It shows how little man had [*sic*] advanced in his ethical outlook after all these years of Christian teaching – that there should be any nation in existence in Europe today that holds for the sort of world that Hitler contemplates is astounding – but how many Germans, I wonder, have any real grasp of what the Nazi policy really means? Very few I should imagine – world conquest, yes – but surely not the reintroduction of slavery, etc., etc. How odd it is to remember that I have met this madman Hitler – odder still that I was not in the least impressed by him and failed to recognize a superman.

Sunday 11 January   The Japanese are still pressing forward in Malaya and it looks as if they were going to take the town of Kuala Lumpur – we are recalling Mr. Duff Cooper! It will be interesting to hear what that eminent man has to say for himself when he gets home again – of course his appointment was quite absurd – nothing more than an expensive joke – for even granted that a Minister's presence was required out in these parts, the last one to have been selected for the job was an ill-tempered, tactless, lazy little failure like Duff.

Wednesday 14 January   I went to the Central Office at 10.30 a.m.,

[16] Hermann Rauschning (1887–1982), President of the Senate, Danzig Free City 1933–34; an early member of the Nazi Party and colleague of Hitler, he became disillusioned and fled to Switzerland in 1935, living in the U.S.A. after 1948. He was the author of two influential books which exposed the ruthlessness and dangers of Nazism: *The Revolution of Nihilism* and *Hitler Speaks* (English translations of both published in 1939).

where a committee presided over by Eugene Ramsden, composed of some of us and some agents, considered Topping's after the war scheme for instituting a board to administer a central fund (provided by the better-off constituencies!) for supplying agents to the less well-to-do constituencies. It is all rather hopeless I feel, but we spent 2 hours or more discussing the plan this morning. Lunched at the Constitutional Club again as a guest to listen to a speech by Harold Balfour – not a very interesting entertainment – then to the Caxton Hall for the Executive meeting. I presented our report of our interview with the T.U.C. people and our recommendations (the committee – our delegates, I mean – had all preferred my views to those of Maxwell Fyfe). The Executive adopted the recommendations *nem. con.*[17] – Lord Salisbury congratulated us profusely!

Tuesday 20 January   Winston made his reappearance at Westminster today, but he does not seem to have got as big a reception as might have been expected, judging at any rate by what was said on the wireless – people are too much worried about the Far Eastern situation to be all over him I fancy. His proposal to broadcast his speech in the House on the war situation is, I think, a mistake and I should doubt very much whether the House will fall in with his wishes. It would be a bad precedent for obvious reasons – if the practice were started it would be impossible to say the P.M. might broadcast his speech and that a similar privilege should not be conceded to the Leader of the Opposition, etc.

Thursday 22 January   At the House this morning I had a talk with Erskine Hill, chairman of the '1922 Committee'. He is reputed to be a coming man but I find him a bit heavy in hand and I doubt somehow whether he is really the man to get a move on among the Tories – however, he professes to be trying to do so and I have agreed to work in with him. There is no doubt today a feeling of great unrest in the Party, and in the House generally, against the Government. The muddle and failure in the Far East is of course the main reason for this and, in a lesser degree, the slowness of our operations in Libya where we have clearly failed so far to smash

[17] translation: with no one opposing; the abbreviation of the Latin phrase *nemine contradicente*, commonly used in this form in the minutes of meetings, etc.

up Rommel.[18] The truth of the matter is that we are still sadly lacking in war material and people, not unreasonably, are beginning to wonder why this should be so after $2\frac{1}{2}$ years' war. Winston is too cock sure of himself and thinks that he can go on carrying everything on his own back, and I don't think that the HofC will stand this indefinitely.

Saturday 24 January   The news today is not exhilarating: our retreat in Malaya continues: we are also withdrawing in Burma: Rommel appears to be attacking again and driving us back. ... the Australians are screaming for help as the Japanese are now in New Guinea and the Solomon Islands. We must be hopelessly outnumbered on land and the enemy has the sea-power and air-power ... It will be interesting to hear what kind of a defence Winston will put up on Tuesday.

Tuesday 27 January   Winston made a very effective speech today – he demanded a vote of confidence and will of course get it. His line was that although faults had admittedly been made here, there and everywhere – and very little had gone according to plan – considering our original unpreparedness, the fall of France, etc., etc., we might have fared a deal worse. His defence of the Far Eastern mess was not very convincing: it only amounted to what Attlee said the other day – with our available military potential we could not be strong everywhere and that we had to run the risk of Japan coming into the war. I suppose, if the truth were told, they had banked on the U.S.A. carrying the baby for us – and had not anticipated Pearl Harbour – but obviously he was right when he said that we were not in a position to take on Germany, Italy and Japan single-handed. He professed – for the first time, so he said – to see a gleam of light on the horizon – why he did not explain but some people appeared to be cheered by the information.

Wednesday 28 January   The Speaker was tiresome this morning

[18] Erwin Rommel (1891–1944), German army career; G.O.C. 7th Panzer Div. 1940–41; Comm. of Afrika Korps (German forces in N. Africa) 1941–43, where his tactical brilliance earned the nickname of the 'Desert Fox'; Comm. Army Group B, Italy 1943 and France 1944; seriously wounded by air attack 17 July 1944, implicated in the anti-Hitler bomb plot of 20 July 1944 and commited suicide, as the alternative to arrest and trial, on 14 October.

and would not call me – or rather would not say whether he would or would not. He really is getting quite intolerable and his one idea is to call the same people in every debate – a good many of us who speak seldom are beginning to get very restive – but of course we can do nothing but grouse as the Speaker is a law unto himself and has one in the hollow of his hand. The debate today, what I heard of it, was not on a very high level – the same sort of criticisms made as are always made by the same people who usually make them in the same sort of way. Attlee spoke – rather better than usual so I was told – but I did not hear him ...

Thursday 29 January   The Speaker was unpleasant again this morning. One would not mind so much if one was not well aware that the creature tells other people when he proposes to call them – Shinwell, for instance, and young Randolph Churchill[19] were going about telling their friends the time at which they were going to speak. It really is all wrong, this differentiation in treatment between Members. ... Winston wound up the debate this afternoon – another first class effort – and he has given way *re* production – inasmuch as he proposes to put it all under one man – but, needless to say, the man is to be Beaverbrook and some of us feel that he is not the man for the job. I personally cannot believe from all that I have heard about this creature's performances since he was brought into the direction of the war that he really is any good. All that I have heard said in his favour is that he is of real use in *any* department for about a fortnight, to clear out the inefficient and futile and to cut out red tape – then the sooner he is away, the better – for he has no knowledge of administration or experience in industry. He and Winston are boon companions – and there it is, so long as Winston continues, so long will the Beaver – but a few more votes of confidence such as today's, unless he can show some successes and a greater efficiency, will be the end of Winston.

Saturday 31 January   Cosmo Gordon *Cantuar*[20] announced his intention of retiring at an early date a few days ago. I found in the HofC last week that Conservative Members were much exercised

---

[19] Randolph Frederick Edward Spencer Churchill (1911–1968), Con. M.P. Preston 1940–45; only son of Winston Churchill.

[20] The Latin title for the Archbishop of Canterbury.

in their minds as to the succession – a very strong feeling, which I confess I share, against Willie *Ebor*.[21] Of course the man is among the other Bishops a triton among minnows – but it always seems to me that he lacks judgement and a sense of proportion in political matters – and his open adherence to the Socialist, or Christian Socialist, programme is all wrong for an Archbishop. If he would only keep out of active political controversy and politics, home and foreign, generally – and devote himself to the reform and edification of the Church, I personally would make him Archbishop of Canterbury tomorrow – but as he makes a point of being a politician, I would leave him where he is. I had a word with Brendan Bracken (who is Winston's bishop-maker!) the other day. He told me that it was a very difficult business – W. *Ebor* is the outstanding man among the bishops and none of the others appears to wish to stand in his way.

Sunday 1 February ... the Japanese are reported to be massing their forces in Johore for a big attack on Singapore – I suppose that their idea is to storm the fortress and as their forces must be largely in excess of ours one must, I think, be prepared for the worst. To me it is difficult to believe that we can relieve Singapore for several months at any rate. Rommel is said to be moving east from Benghazi – and nothing is said to show that we are in any position to check his progress. If we cannot be strong everywhere, one would have thought that by this period in the war we might be strong somewhere – and as we have chosen to fight in Libya, surely we might by now have been ever so much stronger than we seem to be? There must be something radically wrong with our war direction, and one can only suppose either that the P.M. is running the show against the advice of his experts or that he is relying on his experts who are not good enough for their job.

Tuesday 3 February I got a letter today from Onslow enclosing a memorandum on HofL reform which I suppose I must read. I

---

[21] The Latin title for the Archbishop of York; refers to William Temple (1881–1944), Fellow, Queen's College, Oxford 1904–10; Headmaster, Repton School 1910–14; Rector of St. James's, Piccadilly 1914–18; Canon of Westminster 1919–21; Bishop of Manchester 1921–29; Arcbishop of York 1929–42, of Canterbury 1942–44; Pres., Workers' Educational Assoc. 1908–24; inaugurated British Council of Churches 1942.

fear that he is going to be a nuisance on our sub-committee – still, on the whole, it is more amusing to have stalks[22] than logs on committees, at any rate they keep things going. I wish I felt keener and fitter – for the time being the life has gone out of me and I feel as if I did not care a damn about anything.

Wednesday 4 February   Changes in the Govt. announced tonight – the Beaver is Minister of Production, Andrew Duncan back at the Ministry of Supply, Llewellin goes to the Board of Trade, Harold Macmillan leaves Supply for the Colonies and is made a P[rivy] C[ouncillor] and there are other minor changes, shiftings of under secretaries – Noel Baker[23] appears to be the only new man in the show. He is quite a pleasant fellow with good manners, and full of energy and I should imagine ability. He knows almost everything – and having been the leading exponent of disarmament, etc., has now developed into a critic of strategy and an expert upon war. He will now be muzzled as Under Secretary for War Transport. ... Probably because I feel so seedy I feel extremely depressed about the war. Unlike Winston I can see no silver lining to the clouds which at present surround us – indeed I am beginning to wonder whether we can win the war under the present regime – it seems to be incapable of getting a move on and to be unable to get production really going – everywhere we appear to be short of all the essential machinery of modern warfare. Whether this is because we are not producing these things in sufficient quantities (which one imagines to be the case) or whether there is not sufficient shipping available to carry them where they are required, one does not know.

Thursday 5 February   ... in Libya Rommel still appears to be doing much as he likes and now is reported to be about sixty miles

---

[22] Presumably means 'storks', a reference to the fable in which the inactive 'King Log' is replaced by the active 'King Stork'.

[23] Philip John Baker (1889–1982), assumed surname Noel-Baker 1923; Lab. M.P. Coventry 1929–31, Derby 1936–50, Derby S. 1950–70; P.P.S. to A. Henderson 1929–31; P.S. War Transport 1942–45; M.S. For. Office 1945–46; Sec. for Air 1946–47; Commonwealth Sec. 1947–50; Min. of Fuel & Power 1950–51; Chairman, P.L.P. For. Affairs Group 1964–70; member, P.L.P. Parl. Ctte. 1936–40, 1951–59; member, N.E.C. 1937–48, Chairman 1946–47; cr. Baron Noel-Baker 1977; a conscientious object in the First World War, lifelong advocate of internationalism and disarmament, awarded Nobel Peace Prize 1959.

from Tobruk – the next thing, I suppose, will be for us to be told
that we have lost that place – one begins to feel that R. is too good
for us – that his 'stuff' is better than ours and that we never have
enough men and equipment in the right place at the right time –
however, it is no doubt a very difficult business and it does not do
to sit in judgement upon those in authority. The real clash at
Singapore has not yet begun – but Wavell has told the garrison to
stick to it till help arrives. I don't envy them the job – and, as I
look at the map, I simply cannot see how they can hold out for
long, always supposing that the Japanese are in great force and
don't mind getting killed.

Sunday 8 February   Clearly the defence of Singapore is not
going to last much longer ... One feels terribly depressed – more
depressed, I think, than after Dunkirk – to be beaten and humiliated
in this way by Asiatics is almost more than a Victorian Englishman
can bear!

Tuesday 10 February   Everywhere we are on the defensive and
everywhere we do not seem to have the means of defence. Surely
there is no excuse for these things – our air weakness everywhere
is what annoys me most: I feel sure that it is largely due to the
wretched dual control[24] which one always feared would be our
undoing – but it must also be due to our production being
terribly behindhand – surely if it were anything like as large as
Beaverbrook & co. have led us to believe we should have been able
to get sufficient air support of the right type to the Far East during
the last year. Everyone one meets is gloomy and anxious and there
is no doubt that the P.M. is losing ground. He is an obstinate devil
and full of *hubris*[25] – no one apparently can persuade him to see
reason and he is developing the Baldwin tendency of looking upon
anyone who dares to criticize him or to take a contrary view to
him as a traitor not only to him personally but to the country. He
is bound to come a cropper unless he can see reason. His departure
would be a great loss in many ways – but I am coming to the
conclusion that it would be better to have a B+ man who listened

[24] The division of responsibilty between the Royal Air Force and the Navy's Fleet
Air Arm; the question of the control of air forces was a matter of much debate
during Headlam's time at the Admiralty in the 1920s.
[25] translation: arrogant pride.

to good advisers than a superman who persists in trying to run the entire show and knows better about everything than his experts.

Wednesday 11 February   Gossip in the Smoking Room at the HofC has it that Winston is becoming more and more determined to continue running the show in his own way and people are getting more and more uneasy. It is a bad business because Winston is by far the best man for the job if he would only see reason. No one wants him to go – but almost everybody feels that he cannot possibly run the show single-handed – and what we all feel in the HofC will before very long be the feeling of the man in the street. This continuous run of ill success with worse still to come must have its effect on the public.

Friday 13 February   The first news which greeted me this morning in Newcastle was that the German ships at Brest, which have been so constantly bombed since last March (*Scharnhorst, Gnieisenau* and *Prinz Eugen*), have escaped through the Channel and are now back in the Heligoland Bight – apparently they got out of Brest in the dark and were not observed in the Channel until 11 a.m. – then they were attacked by our bombers and fighters – and, later, by destroyers and other small craft – but they were protected by any amount of aircraft and destroyers and it is scarcely surprising that they got away. In this business we lost *40* aircraft – the enemy 16 – we lost no seacraft and claim to have hit one or two of the enemy's craft – but clearly the damage cannot have been great. It is rather a startling affair and one wonders how it happened: it is creating a good deal of concern to the man in the street who is startled that German ships should be able to run through the Channel with impunity.

Sunday 15 February   Tonight at 9 p.m. we listened to Winston announce the fall of Singapore. He spoke for about 35 minutes and, as usual, spoke well. He appealed for us all to keep up our hearts and to stick loyally together – such an appeal was uncalled for and may be misinterpreted as an appeal to stick to him – but, on the whole, he said the right things in the right way and one felt terribly sorry for the man. He did not allude to the escape of the German ships: no doubt we shall have a statement about that episode in the House on Tuesday. Winston has a bad press today –

the *Sunday Times* speaks very straight to him and I think fairly. The man takes too much upon himself – too great a burden and it is quite absurd that he should go on doing so. His War Cabinet as at present constituted is a farce – no one except himself in it counts at all. ... It is absurd that so much of his time should have to be devoted to the HofC. Well, we shall see what the great man decides: he is his own worst enemy and his little coterie of admirers don't help him.

Monday 16 February   Travelled to London with Charlie Grey and Eddie Winterton – the latter had been speaking for the Ministry of Information ... We dined together here on arrival – and he talked away very vigorously about the situation. His views *re* Winston are much the same as mine. The problem is how to induce the man, whom everyone wants to remain P.M., to realize that he must reduce his burden and reorganize his present team on different lines. Everyone realizes his great qualities – but clearly things are going too badly everywhere for us to rest content with the conduct of the war and war production as they are today. Eddie W. seems convinced that Winston simply will not budge an inch or give way to the feeling in the House. I hope that this opinion is wrong – but, presumably, we shall know tomorrow as the P.M. is to make a statement of some kind.

Tuesday 17 February   Winston made a little statement about the German ships – rather suggesting that it was just as well they had left Brest! – but he succeeded in appeasing his critics by telling them that he had appointed a High Court judge, an admiral and an air marshal to inquire into the business. He declined to have a debate today or this week about the general war position, but said that we could have one next week – but even he appears to realize that it is not possible to ask for another vote of confidence. My own view is that his best plan is to resign and be given the job of forming a new Ministry; I gave that opinion for what it is worth to James Stuart – such a course would give Winston a little time to reconsider the situation – would enable him to get rid of a few of his present team – and to reshape his War Cabinet on lines which would satisfy the critics – he could go on being P.M. and need no longer call himself Minister of Defence or appoint anyone else to the job which really is not in the least a necessary one. It will be interesting to see what happens as I honestly don't think the present situation can continue much longer – everyone has the same story to tell, and reports a feeling of disquiet and uneasiness among his constituents.

Wednesday 18 February   There is no doubt that it is indescribably dull living in London nowadays as I do. The House is usually up about 5 p.m. and from then onwards I find nothing to do except to sit in the [Travellers] Club which [is] no longer comfortable and usually very cold. It is filled with people I don't know coming mainly from Windham's Club I imagine.[26] Hardly any of the servants are left and we are waited upon at meals by a collection of alien young women who don't know one or appreciate one's idiosyncrasies. I suppose if one were younger one would venture out at nights and seek amusement – but I never cared about restaurant life, or dancing at night clubs or going to cinemas and now that I am aged I like such things less. I should like to dine with friends now and then, but I never know where they are to be found – so many people have shut up their houses and left London. The hotels are crammed and unless one engages rooms long in advance, there is no chance of getting them. In some ways we appear to be living in a beleaguered city – Winston presumably intends to make his last stand in Whitehall where the wire entanglements and machine gun posts strike the eye. There is one of these latter in Parliament Square camouflaged to look like a newspaper stall and guarded by a Guardsman armed to the teeth – it is very ridiculous. The only good thing about all this war business, so far as the appearance of London is concerned, is the removal of so many ugly iron railings: I hope that they will never be replaced.

Thursday 19 February   Tonight we heard the new War Cabinet – i.e., the changes which Winston has made in it to meet criticisms. Attlee becomes Deputy P.M. and Secretary of State for the Dominions; Stafford Cripps[27] becomes Lord Privy Seal and is to lead the

---

[26] Due to bomb damage at the latter Club.

[27] (Richard) Stafford Cripps (1889–1952), Lab. M.P. Bristol E. 1931–50, Bristol S.E. 1950 (expelled from the Lab. Party 1939, readmitted 1945); Solicitor-Gen. 1930–31; Amb. to Russia 1940–42; Lord Privy Seal & Leader of the House 1942; Min. of Aircraft Production 1942–45; Pres. Bd. of Trade 1945–47; Min. of Economic Affairs 1947; Chanc. of the Exchequer 1947–50; kt. 1930.

HofC; John Anderson, Bevin and Eden remain members of the W[ar] C[abinet]; Kingsley Wood leaves it but continues to be C[hancellor] of E[xchequer] (more's the pity) and thank God the Beaver goes, as does Arthur Greenwood, and Oliver Lyttelton is brought in to exercise a general supervision over production. Winston still continues to call himself Minister of Defence. To me it all amounts to very little – *plus ça change, plus c'est la même chose*[28] – but I expect the majority of people will be pleased, imagining that changes must make for increased efficiency.

Friday 20 February   All the papers seem to be impressed by the Cabinet changes – but clearly the entry of Cripps into the Government excites most interest. He is regarded as the coming man, who may prove something extra special – it is rather ridiculous really for so far the man has done nothing to warrant such a belief – a very clever lawyer with advanced Socialist ideas, his only claim to fame so far is that he quarrelled with the Labour Party because they were not red enough for his taste. Then he went as Ambassador to Russia where Stalin & Co. would have none of him and whence he came, if report is true, on leave a disillusioned man – then when he was on holiday in England Hitler invaded Russia and Stalin became our 'ally' – now the B[ritish] P[ublic] attribute Russia's entry into the war as a result of Cripps's efforts and he is alluded to in the press as our most successful diplomat. He may turn out a success and a leader – for he is honest, absolutely sincere (so they say) in his beliefs, very able and a good speaker. I think that he should lead the HofC well – but whether he is to become leader of the Conservatives or of the Labour lot I really cannot venture to prophesy.

Sunday 22 February   The Sunday papers are all very busy pressing for Cabinet changes – clearly they must come. It is absurd to try and run a one man show in a war of this magnitude – even if Winston were a heaven-born strategist and statesman (which I personally don't believe he is) the responsibility and actual work entailed would be far too great for a single individual. In his present War Cabinet there is no one capable of standing up to him and no one who carries much weight in the country – one would like to

[28] translation: the more things change, the more they remain the same.

see Attlee, Bevin and Greenwood go – also the Beaver and Kingsley Wood – and I would pick their successors elsewhere than from the HofC.

Monday 23 February　　Congratulated the Archbishop of York, who was on the train, on being promoted to Canterbury. He was very affable – I gather that one or two other prelates and divines were approached before him, but that they all stood back for him – presumably he is the mental superior of them all and 'the Church' wanted him. Perhaps now that he has reached the top of the tree he will be wiser politically, less left wing – such is the hope – but I doubt it. The Bishop of Winchester goes to York – I suggested that he should go to Canterbury and so save us from Willie Temple, but I gather that he would not.

Tuesday 24 February　　Attended a committee (*re* supply of agents etc.) at 10.30 a.m. at the Central Office – a plan of Topping's to raise money out of 'richer constituencies' to help finance agents in 'poorer ditto' – the old, old, hopeless story. Went from Palace Chambers to Caxton Hall where I spoke at the annual meeting of the South-Eastern Area (Kent, Surrey, Sussex), Lord Ebbisham in the chair – about 70 people (mainly women) present, speech quite a success – I missed Winston's speech in the House, but he did not say much except about the changes in the Govt. It is good that the Beaver is gone – but Bevin remains – Oliver Lyttelton's duties seem undefined. People appear to be sorry for David Margesson who has been thrown out – but I cannot help remembering the way he spoke to me when Oliver Stanley was made Minister of Labour and Hore-Belisha was put in as Minister of Transport over my head – if I recollect rightly I wished then that David might some day realize a similar fate.

Wednesday 25 February　　Spent a lot of time in the House jumping up and trying to get called but the damned Speaker would not call me – so I gave up the unequal struggle ... got back to the House about 4 p.m. in time to hear Stafford Cripps wind up for the Government – needless to say, he did the job very well.

Thursday 26 February　　A good deal of gossip going on in the Smoking Room – but I have heard little that is interesting. No one very happy about anything which, in the circumstances, is not surprising. The changes in the Government don't seem to have impressed people with the idea that there will be much gingering up – so long as Bevin is left in charge of Labour nothing will be done to make people work. What horrifies me most about this HofC is the way in which the Labour and Liberal people go on day in and day out talking 'class' shop – always insinuating that all our troubles are due to the 'old school tie' and social inequalities. It is really too ridiculous, but there is no end to it – it is trotted out on all and every occasion.

Friday 27 February   No one at all honoured me with a visit in Jesmond Road this afternoon,[29] but some of our women supporters were having a monthly meeting of some kind ... Our show is really a most depressing affair – but I can see no way of getting it going: it certainly is not up to me to worry my head about it. If I do stand again, I suppose people will vote for me – and that there will be people ready to work for me. Nevertheless, it is a bit disheartening that in a constituency like North Newcastle scarcely anyone belongs to the Conservative Association or subscribes a penny piece to it.

Saturday 28 February   Beatrice and I attended a meeting in the City Hall today to inaugurate the Warships Week – the Lord Mayor presided and Alexander, the First Lord of the Admiralty, was the principal speaker. He has been specializing in these speeches and been criticised in the HofC for doing so on the grounds that he ought not to be so much away from Whitehall in these grim days – but personally I should imagine that he is better employed in making fighting speeches in the country to boost the Navy than in pretending to conduct the sea war at the Admiralty. He is a good platform speaker and made an excellent speech today. As usual the trade unionist, Bowman, moved the vote of thanks and was far too long-winded – a tiresome, swollen-headed fellow I think. It has been a wet and miserable day and Newcastle was crammed with people to see the show – a march past Alexander by the forces – they say unkindly that the man will go anywhere,

---

[29] Weekly constituency 'surgery', at the North Newcastle Conservative Association's offices.

if he can be allowed to take the salute. He told us privately that a sea fight was in progress in the Java Sea and that we were not doing too well.

Monday 2 March   A great relief not to be going to London today: I am taking a week off for no other reason than a feeling of complete repulsion for the HofC. I hope that this feeling is only temporary, but for the time being I can scarcely bear the place or the people in it – all of them seem so ineffective and most of what they say so futile. The debates seem to me one worse than the other, and there is little or no variety in them for the Speaker rings the changes on the same people over and over again – one is sick to death of the views of men like Archie Southby,[30] Stokes,[31] Aneurin Bevan, Mander, Percy Harris, McGovern, etc., etc.

Thursday 5 March   Fresh changes in the Government are now announced – they none of them make me feel that they will help us win the war any more quickly – some nonentities go and others come – *viz.* one Henderson[32] (son of Arthur Henderson, I think – a Labour M.P.) replaces Ned Grigg at the War Office (possibly one reason for this change is that you could not well have 2 Sir Griggs[33] as Sec. of State and Under-Sec. in the same department!); Austin Hudson[34] is replaced by one Pilkington[35] as Civil Lord of

---

[30] Archibald Richard James Southby (1886–1969), Con. M.P. Epsom 1928–47; Whip 1935–37; cr. Bart. 1937.

[31] Richard Rapier Stokes (1897–1957), Lab. M.P. Ipswich 1938–57; Min. of Works 1950–51; Lord Privy Seal & Min. of Materials 1951; member, P.L.P. Parl. Ctee. 1951–52, 1955–56.

[32] Arthur Henderson (1893–1968), Lab. M.P. Cardiff S. 1923–24, 1929–31, Kingswinford 1935–50, Rowley Regis & Tipton 1950–66; P.P.S. to Sir W. Jowitt 1929–31; jt. U.S. War Office 1942–43, F.S. 1943–45; U.S. India & Burma 1945–47; M.S. Commonwealth 1947; Sec. for Air 1947–51; cr. Baron Rowley 1966; son of Arthur Henderson (1863–1935), Lab. Leader 1931–32.

[33] On 22 Feb. 1942 Sir Percy Grigg, the senior civil servant at the War Office, was appointed to be Secretary of State for War; this placed him above Sir Edward Grigg, who had served as Under-Secretary of State for War since 1940.

[34] Austin Uvedale Morgan Hudson (1897–1956), Con. M.P. Islington E. 1922–23, Hackney N. 1924–45, Lewisham N. 1950–56; Ass. Whip 1931, Whip 1931–35; P.S. Transport 1935–39; Civil Ld., Admiralty 1939–42; P.S. Fuel & Power 1942–45; Chairman, Metropolitan Area 1932–34; cr. Bart. 1942.

[35] Richard Antony Pilkington (1908–1976), Con. M.P. Widnes 1935–45, Poole 1951–64; P.P.S. to O. Stanley 1938–39; Civil Ld., Admiralty 1942–45; kt. 1961.

the Admiralty; Grimston,[36] a dull little whip, becomes Assistant
P[ost]-M[aster]-G[eneral] *vice* one Chapman[37] who replaces Wedderburn[38] at the Scottish Office; Emrys Evans supersedes Shakespeare at the Dominions Office – Sir W. Jowitt[39] becomes Paymaster-
General *vice* Hankey and is to take charge of the reconstruction
job vacated by Arthur Greenwood. Maxwell Fyfe is the new
Solicitor-General and Henry Strauss gets a job – these last two are
supposed to be the flower of the young Conservatives -neither has
impressed me very much. I fear that Ned Grigg will be a bit cast
down – but he has not been a great success as a Minister by all
accounts – for a man of undoubted ability he carries rather light
guns. The appointment of Emrys Evans surprises me for he has, in
my opinion, no abilities of any kind except for wire-pulling – but
he is very thick with Eden and Bobbety Cranborne which no doubt
has helped him. Charles Peat, of Darlington, becomes Under-
Secretary to the Ministry of Supply – another strange appointment.

Tuesday 10 March   In the House today Eden confirmed the
reports regarding Japanese brutalities to our people in Hong Kong.
. . . a lot of bitter comment in the Smoking Room today about the
Singapore disaster. It seems to have been a terribly bad show if
only half of what one is told is true – bad leadership and no guts
anywhere – the Australians appear to have behaved abominably,
giving up the unequal battle and boarding ships in the harbour – I
suppose that all this will be kept secret to spare their feelings – at
any rate such I am told is the reason why the Government is

---

[36] Robert Villiers Grimston (1897–1979), Con. M.P. Westbury 1931–64; P.P.S. to
D. Hacking 1933–36, to H. Ramsbotham 1936–37; Whip 1937–42; Ass. Postmaster-
Gen. 1942–45; P.S. Supply 1945; Dep. Chairman of Ways & Means 1962–64; cr.
Bart. 1952, Baron Grimston of Westbury 1964.
[37] Allan Chapman (1897–1966), Con. M.P. Rutherglen 1935–45; P.P.S. to W.
Elliot 1938, to Sir J. Anderson 1938–41; Ass. Postmaster-Gen. 1941–42; jt. U.S.
Scotland 1942–45.
[38] Henry James Scrymgeour-Wedderburn (1902–1983), Con. M.P. Renfrew W.
1931–45; U.S. Scotland 1936–39, jt. U.S. 1941–42; Min. without Portfolio 1958–61;
M.S. For. Office 1961–64; Con. Dep. Leader in Lords 1962–64; suc. 13th Viscount
Dudhope 1952, 11th Earl of Dundee 1953; cr. Baron Glassary 1954.
[39] William Allen Jowitt (1885–1957), M.P. Hartlepools 1922–24, Preston 1929–31,
Ashton-under-Lyme 1939–45 (Lib. until June 1929, Lab. 1929–31, Nat. Labour
1931–36, rejoined Lab. Party 1936); Attorney-Gen. 1929–32; Solicitor-Gen. 1940–
42; Paymaster-Gen. Mar.-Dec. 1942; Min. without Portfolio 1942–44; Min. of Nat.
Insurance 1944–45; Lord Chanc. 1945–51; Leader of Opposition in Lords 1952–55;
kt. 1929, cr. Baron Jowitt 1945, Viscount 1947, Earl 1951.

unwilling to have and enquiry – possibly Winston fears one too!

Wednesday 11 March Winston announced in the House today that Stafford Cripps was to go to India to find out whether the Cabinet's proposals for a new Indian constitution would be acceptable to all parties – I suppose that this decision to send Cripps is a wise one – he, at any rate, cannot be looked upon as an 'Imperialist' and it may be that the Congress people will be more ready to accept something presented to them by him than by anyone else – all the same I shall be surprised if any terms offered will be acceptable to all the various interests concerned. I don't believe either that the Congress people are particularly keen (whatever they may say to the contrary) to be saddled with real responsibilities at a time of crisis like this – nor, if they were willing to accept the task of Government, do I believe that the Army in India would accept their rule.

Thursday 12 March Winston announced today that Oliver Lyttelton is to become Minister of Production, though he did not go into much detail as to what the functions of the new Minister are to be – however whatever they may be I feel sure that Oliver will be able to cope with them. He is certainly having a good war though he may regret being recalled from the Middle East.

Tuesday 17 March At the House coal was discussed. Dalton – now President of the Board of Trade – and Grenfell did their best to justify coal rationing – and there was the usual slobber over the miners by their many representatives in the House. I intervened to suggest that if you must ration coal (and incidentally rationing is only needed as a result of the hopeless blundering of Grenfell ever since he came into office and, indeed, the bungling since the war began) it should be rationed according to the number of people in a house and not by the house – I gathered from Dalton that reason would be recognized by the local coal supervisors. We are to adjourn on the 26th until the 13th of April which is rather a longer Easter recess than usual – personally I feel that the less the House sits the better.

Wednesday 18 March   The Australians have got McArthur[40] to command all their forces – and apparently are going entirely American. I wonder what the future of the British Empire is going to be? Is it passing away whatever the issue of the war may be? Are Canada and Australia going to join up with the U.S.A., and what is going to happen to India? It looks to me as if G.B. might really sink into being a mere island in the North Sea, or become one of the members of a sort of pan-American group, if the Americans will take us on. But they may prefer to cut adrift altogether from Europe and leave us out of the picture – and if we were to join some European federation, we should only be a very insignificant portion of it – and if we stayed out of it, we should be at its mercy. The future certainly does not look very alluring for the British – and yet to a mid-Victorian like me it seems inconceivable that we should pass entirely out of the picture and become of no account.

Thursday 19 March   In the afternoon I went to the All Party Committee to hear an address from Sir James Grigg[41] the new Sec. of State for War. He is said to be a wonder and the rudest and most able man in the Civil Service – but his real claim to his present exalted post is that he was Winston's Private Secretary when he was at the Treasury. His performance today was a complete fiasco: he was fool enough not to consume most of his time with his speech: he said he preferred to speak as shortly as possible and then to answer questions. The result was that everybody had a shot at him and he was bombarded with questions many of which he could not answer. He has made a bad start which may or may not be good for him – [it] depends on whether or not he possesses common sense in addition to the power of being rude! I also

[40] Douglas MacArthur (1880–1964), American army career; Chief of Staff 1930–35; C. in C. Phillipines 1935–42; S.A.C. South West Pacific 1942–45; C. in C. Occupation Forces in Japan 1945–51, U.N. Forces in Korea 1950–51.
[41] (Percy) James Grigg (1890–1964), joined Treas. 1913, Private Sec. to Chanc. of the Exchequer 1921–30; Chairman, Bd. of Customs & Excise 1930–31, Bd. of Inland Revenue 1931–33; Finance Member, Govt. of India 1934–39; Perm. U.S. War Office 1939–42; Sec. for War 1942–45; Nat. Con. M.P. Cardiff E. 1942–45; kt. 1932.

listened to Harriman[42] the American. He made a good, little speech
and answered his questions very well. He told us to buck up, we
had done marvels and were fools not to tell the world about all we
had done. He explained the American point of view and told
us not to worry our heads about the nonsense talked by his
countrymen.

Friday 20 March   Stafford Cripps with his olive branch to 'India'
and the 'Indian people' has reached Cairo where he is to stay for
some days to consult the British military and civil authorities –
what about God only knows. I am not one of those who have
much use for Cripps who has never done anything (so far as I
know) to prove himself a good negotiator or administrator. To me
he seems to be nothing more than an idealist with very extreme left
wing views who can get on with nobody and has never done
anything to justify his present job. Presumably he is sent to India
to please the Indian politicians – will he please them any more than
he pleased the Bolshies?

Monday 30 March   I went into Newcastle today to preside over
the Area Executive Committee – there was a scant attendance,
Appleby and Wilkin conspicuous for their absence and not an
apology from either of them. If our so-called Conservative leaders
take no interest in politics nowadays what can one expect of the
rank and file? I have no doubt that old Appleby is shy of meeting
me after his ridiculous attitude towards the North Newcastle
Association – at first he refused to give it anything out of his fund –
then he agreed to do so if we (Sykes, Lawson and I) gave him a
written 'indemnity', his line being that he is only entitled to assist
the 3 other divisions – it really is a very fatiguing business and the
sooner we forget all about Appleby and his fund and proceed to
some kind of federation for the City, the better it will be. It really
is monstrous that one out-of-date old wire-puller should be able to

[42] (William) Averell Harriman (1891–1986), American businessman; head of Lend-
Lease administration in London 1941–43, U.S. head of mission to Moscow to
arrange supplies for Russia 1941; U.S. Amb. in Moscow 1943–46, in London 1946;
Sec. of Commerce 1946–48; U.S. rep. in Europe for Marshall Aid programme 1948–
50; Director, Mutual Security Agency 1951–55; Gov. of New York State 1954–58;
Ass. Sec. of State for Far East 1961–63, Under. Sec. 1963–65; Amb.-at-large 1965–
69.

hold such a prominent position in politics because he is in sole control of a fund subscribed by a few rich men many years ago – it is monstrous, too, that the Central Office should recognize his so-called Newcastle City Association which has no members and only exists on paper. Sooner or later I shall have to ask him all about it.

Saturday 4 April   Perhaps I am feeling too gloomy, but this long continuance of bad news is affecting my morale more than I would admit in public. We seem to lack something in this war which we had in the last war – what exactly it is I don't know – there is courage and endurance today as there was then – but today there seems a lack of direction, a lack of foresight, and a lack of organizing ability. Presumably the real source of the trouble is not any of these things, but a lack of all the necessary impedimenta of modern warfare and a strange difficulty in producing them. We started practically from scratch – then lost most of what we had got in the Dunkirk episode – and so far have not made up our deficiencies – and the Americans have not helped us at all sufficiently.

Monday 6 April   The news today is that the Japanese have begun to bomb India – a port just north of Madras – meanwhile the Indian politicians are still being tiresome – and Stafford Cripps has delayed making his 'announcement' until Wednesday – this may mean much or little; President Roosevelt's special envoy in India has been seeing the Indian leaders and the American press is busy telling them what to do. One wonders how much real difference their acceptance or refusal of the Government's proposals will make? Not much I imagine: no one expects the 'Indian people' to rise like one man and become a fighting race just because they are promised Home Rule – the fighting races in India will fight whatever happens, the others won't whatever happens.[43] Certainly the Indian politicians won't play a very prominent part in warlike operations. My own personal opinion is that the whole business is excellent shop-window dressing for us – we are showing our readiness to

[43] A reference to the Muslim and Sikh regions of northern India, from which most of the ranks of the Indian Army were recruited; conventional British opinion regarded the Hindu population as being intrinsically less martial.

oblige – if our offer is refused, it cannot be helped; if it is accepted, the 'democracies' will say how splendid – and that is about all there is to it.

Saturday 11 April   The Cripps mission has failed – Sir S. spoke on the wireless this evening and delivered a message to 'India' – it was I thought rather poor stuff – but then I object to his talking all the time to the 'Indian peoples' as if they were enslaved and assuring them that we are quite in earnest about giving them their 'freedom' – Home Rule, yes, when they can agree about it themselves – but free they are today as free as any of us – and it is quite ridiculous for any intelligent or sane man to talk as if the Indians were kept in slavery. I expect that all the cranks will be bothering the Government about India – nothing seems to teach them sense, and whatever happens to go wrong is always the fault of the British. If the British Empire falls, its fall will be largely due to the Liberal tradition – the attitude of mind which was more concerned with making money than anything else and invariably pandering to the selfishness of the individual, which despised all military preparedness and fondly imagined that one could live at peace with the rest of the world because we were satisfied and rich – we are having our lesson now ...

Tuesday 14 April   I did not waste time listening to Kingsley Wood opening his Budget: apparently he read his speech from beginning to end and took 2 hours and 17 minutes doing so – everyone tells me that he was intolerably dull ... met Walter Dalkeith[44] in the Lobby this morning and had a long talk with him. He is much annoyed because he is accused of being a Fascist – for no other reason than because like a good many other people he thought that this war might have been avoided had we been a little less foolish with Germany in the years after the last war – I confess that I belong to this 'suspect' body of persons. Whether we were right or wrong no one will ever know – but because we held this view, it does not mean that we were believers in Fascism. This

---

[44] Walter John Montagu-Douglas-Scott (1894–1973), Con. M.P. Roxburgh & Selkirk 1923–35; Ld. Steward of the Household 1937–40; Lord Clerk Register 1956–73; Ld. Lt. Roxburghshire 1932–73; styled Lord Whitchester 1894–1914, styled Earl of Dalkeith 1914–35, suc. 8th Duke of Buccleuch 1935, K.T. 1949.

afternoon[45] I presided over a meeting of our Central Office sub-
committee on Constitutional Reform in the Moses Room, HofL –
Onslow not present as he has had to cancel all his engagements
and rest owing to heart trouble – Agnes turned up, having recovered
from her jaundice – Douglas Jerrold, Clark[46] (the Cambridge don),
Kenneth Pickthorn, and Matt Ridley.[47] We talked away for a
couple of hours, and it was left to the Headlams to make something
out of all the blather.

Thursday 16 April   The news from Burma is depressing – we keep
on withdrawing and the oil fields seem to be lost, though we are
said to have destroyed the workings. No one is particularly cheerful
at the HofC – but there is less criticism of the Government: the
feeling now is, I think, that we must grin and bear things for some
considerable time longer – until the Americans get going!

Thursday 23 April   Winston's speech in the Secret Session this
morning was grim in the extreme – I knew that our naval losses
had been severe, but not how severe. Apparently Italian death or
glory boys got into Alexandria harbour and succeeded in blowing
holes in the bottom of *Queen Elisabeth*[48] and a cruiser, putting
them out of action for months – this on the top of all the other
calamities has severely crippled our overworked navy – indeed,
almost to breaking point. If the French fleet were to join the Italians
we should be hard put to it in the Mediterranean. In Burma our
main difficulty is to keep the few troops we have there supplied –
and it will take us a long time to bring our air force in the Far
East up to strength – clearly Burma must go. He wound up in a
more cheerful strain assuring us that President R. was more certain
of victory than ever, and that production in the U.S.A. was
proceeding by leaps and bounds – but of course this is the stock
ending of all his speeches. Today's effort was, I thought, a very

---

[45] A correction in the diary entry for the next day notes that the meeting in fact
took place on 15 April.

[46] George Sidney Roberts Kitson Clark (1900–1975), historian; Fellow of Trinity
College, Cambridge Univ. 1922–75; Reader in Constitutional History, Cambridge
Univ. 1954–67.

[47] Matthew White Ridley (1902–1964), Regional Controller for the North, Min.
of Production 1942–49; Chairman, Northumberland County Council 1940–46, 1949–
52; suc. 3rd Viscount Ridley 1916; owner of over 10,000 acres in Northumberland.

[48] One of the most powerful battleships in the fleet.

fine one – and none of his critics made any reply to it – not even complaining at his refusal to hold an inquiry on Singapore – they prefer to speak in public so that they can advertize themselves.

Friday 24 April   Spent the morning at the Northern Counties Club ... all the experts extremely angry and worried about the coal-rationing scheme which they assure me would be quite unnecessary if only the miners were to work an extra half-hour during the summer months – but of course this is exactly what a man like Dalton would never dream of asking them to do. The miners nowadays are a law unto themselves and treat the rest of the community like dirt – and all because we are living in a sentimental age and because the miners have so many M.P.s in the HofC. They don't even obey their own leaders – and they do just as little work as they choose.

Sunday 26 April   [Oliver Lyttelton's broadcast] speech was rather interesting for it looked like, or rather sounded like, a political feeler. He was expressing his after-the-war ideas. They were not particularly original – but they seemed to be designed with the object of expressing his political views – which appear to me to be such that he can fit himself into any political party without much difficulty! He may do well, I fancy. He has a great opportunity on the Conservative side for really, except for Eden, there is no sort of competition so far as I can see – and Oliver, so far as politics are concerned, has a clean slate.

Tuesday 28 April   Lunched at the Cafe Royal – and lunched excellently. The entertainment was given by Sir George Broad-bridge, M.P. for the City of London, in honour of Tommie Dugdale – about 30 people present representing the City of London and selected M.P.s. I sat between Edward Campbell[49] M.P. and a City brother of Douglas Clifton Brown, opposite to Ned Grigg. Tommie made a very good, little speech – I fancy that he will be a success in his job: he is very popular, has great tact and charm of manner, and has guts which Hacking had not. He has, however, a very difficult job ahead of him as the Party is in a moribund

---

[49] Edward Taswell Campbell (1879–1945), Con. M.P. Camberwell N.W. 1924–29, Bromley 1930–45; P.P.S. to Kingsley Wood 1931–43; kt. 1933, cr. Bart. 1939.

condition and seems to have entirely lost confidence in itself – and of course Winston is an utterly futile leader.

Thursday 30 April   Dalton came to the '1922 Committee' this afternoon and explained his rationing scheme. He was inundated with questions and parried them with ability – when I asked him why he did not ask the miners to work an extra half-hour during the summer months which experts tell me would solve his problem, he replied that he was assured that such a plan would be ineffective.

Sunday 3 May   On the wireless tonight I heard that little Patrick Munro,[50] M.P., had died suddenly at the HofC as a result presumably of overstrain training with the HofC H[ome] G[uard] – I was only having tea with him in the Smoking Room at the HofC last Thursday – such a pleasant fellow – and absolutely straight I should imagine. He was a famous international Rugger player in his time and until recently a Government whip – I suppose that he was too old to run about like a boy playing at soldiers. ... Tonight Stafford Cripps spoke on the wireless – a full-blooded Socialist oration about the new world, and the Archbishop of Canterbury seems to have made a similar pronouncement in a sermon at Manchester – really these well-intentioned people will cause a revolution if they are not more careful – why should men be so utterly different after the war and are they really so very bad nowadays? We might have been living in hell all these years from the way the wise men, or considered wise men, are talking today. It is all very disquieting and one gets more and more nervous about the future. A planned world seems to me impossible without some form of political despotism – and is it this despotism which we are now fighting against – a democratic despotism is not an alluring prospect.

Tuesday 5 May   We have sent an expeditionary force to Madagascar and it appears to be strong enough to take possession of the island, although the French are opposing it. This is a good move so far as one can judge, as with Laval in power it was

[50] Patrick Munro (1883–1942), Con. M.P. Llandaff & Barry 1931–42; joined Sudan Political Service 1907, Gov. of Khartoum Province 1925–29; P.P.S. to E. Wallace 1935–37; Whip 1937–42.

probably fairly certain that the island might have been handed over to the Japanese as was Indo-China. ... went to the HofC, where there was nothing much doing – everyone delighted about the Madagascar move.

Wednesday 6 May   I attended the '1922 Committee' this afternoon: a very full attendance: unanimous against the fuel rationing scheme: I spoke against it and also took strong exception to Cripps's B.B.C. Socialist speech the other night, as did several others.

Thursday 7 May   It is odd how all and sundry appear to be obsessed with the idea that the Russians are going to beat the Germans and then 'steam roll' into Berlin. I only hope that the idea may turn out to be correct, but I confess I shall be greatly surprised if it does – my only hope is that the Russians may be able to hang on, killing Germans and using up their war material, until such time as we and the Americans can put a huge army onto the Continent – but when that will be God only knows. Our difficulty is to find the necessary shipping – and that difficulty increases every day – for I gather that the shipping losses are very heavy.

Friday 8 May   I visited Tydeman this morning: he had no news of any kind and is going very slow with his scheme of federation – I wonder whether he has been got at by Sir Alfred or Wilkin? One would imagine not, but he is such a tricky, disloyal little beast that one is never certain what he may be up to – it is quite on the cards, too, that he has consulted Central Office and that Topping is playing a hand in the game – however, there is no great hurry about the thing and I can let [the] matter be for a time. Lunched at the Conservative Club and then attended a meeting of the Women's Advisory Committee (Northern Area), Rebe [Bradford] in the chair – Donald Scott gave an excellent little address on after the war. He is a man, I think, who should do well in politics – I should be certain about his chances if only he were not quite so serious and dull! He has all the requisite ability and is an admirable speaker – but he lacks charm and personality.

Saturday 9 May   A line from H.V. Armstrong informing me that I have not been elected Chairman of the [National Union] Executive –

which is disappointing as I had hoped to beat Sir Eugene – however, no doubt he had the support of all the Central Office clique and they certainly will have registered their votes which others may not have troubled to do. It was, perhaps, silly of me to let my name go forward – still it gave people the chance of getting rid of Eugene if they so wished – and one can only suppose that they prefer him to me from the result of the ballot.

Sunday 10 May　　Winston broadcast tonight – a review of the progress of the war during the last two years – it was good of its kind, but he was not so full of vim as usual I fancied though his outlook was optimistic enough. He had nothing to tell us that we did not already know and was, as usual, sarcastic at the expense of Mussolini who, if he were wiser, he ought to be treating more kindly. ... The Government has won the Putney bye-election – a very small poll – after Winston's personal intervention in the contest by means of his letter attacking ... the Independent candidate, the result was pretty certain. Nevertheless, it is satisfactory – though I don't fancy that the Government's stock is very high at the moment – nor is it likely to rise until we succeed in scoring a win somewhere or other.

Tuesday 12 May　　From the dentist's chair I went to the HofC – not a very enlivening day there – Scottish estimates of one kind or another. James Stuart informed me that he had withdrawn the 'whip' from Cunningham-Reid,[51] M.P., did not I think he was right in view of the man's Rugby speech? Not having read the speech I could not offer an opinion but Cunningham-Reid is better outside the Party than in it – though he really does not count either way – a rotten bad type if there ever was one – apparently he, Mr. W. Brown[52] (the Civil Service extremist who won at Rugby as an independent) and one Granville,[53] a Liberal M.P. who has quarrelled

[51] Alec Stratford Cunningham-Reid (1895–1977), Con. M.P. Warrington 1922–23, 1924–29, St. Marylebone 1932–45 (whip withdrawn May 1942, sat as Ind. Con. 1942–45; P.P.S. to Sir J. Baird 1922–24, to W. Ashley 1924–29.

[52] William John Brown (1894–1960), Sec., Civil Service Clerical Association 1919–42; Lab. M.P. Wolverhampton W. 1929–31 (resigned whip & sat as Ind. Lab. Mar.-Oct. 1931), Ind. M.P. Rugby 1942–50.

[53] Edgar Louis Granville (1899–1998), M.P. Suffolk Eye 1929–1951 (Lib. to 1931, Lib. Nat. 1931–42, resigned whip & sat as Ind. from Feb. 1942 to Apr. 1945 when rejoined Lib. Party, joined Lab. Party 1951); P.P.S. to Sir H. Samuel Aug.-Oct. 1931, to Sir J. Simon 1931–36; cr. Baron Granville of Eye 1967.

with his friends, are forming a new party[54] – no doubt the Speaker will recognize them and call them on more frequent occasions than the rest of us!

Wednesday 13 May I looked in at the Executive meeting today and saw Eugene re-elected as Chairman – several people came up to me and said how sorry they were that I had failed in the contest. I suppose Topping was against me – and he is an admirable puller of strings behind the scenes – but I confess that I am surprised that Ramsden beat me because I have never heard anyone say a good word for him as Chairman. I suppose that I was the wrong man to stand against him – my action in North Newcastle shocked a good many of the orthodox Central Office gang and I have never been popular with them – I ought to have got Proby or someone of that type to stand – and then probably I should have effected my purpose and got rid of Eugene! I confess that I have not forgotten his reception of me in the Smoking Room of the HofC after the Newcastle election – and no wonder. From the Executive I went to the 1922 Committee – Erskine Hill & Co. are very much pleased with themselves at having got the Govt. to withdraw the Beveridge[55] [coal] rationing scheme and imagine that they have done the Party a good turn – I doubt whether this is the case, but I am glad that the coupon plan is 'off' – I fear, however, that the Govt. will now try and produce some plan of Govt. control of the pits to placate the miners – and such a policy is bound to lead to trouble. I am getting rather nervous about Cripps, and wonder whether it was a wise thing to make him Leader of the House – I fancy he is the kind of man who is quite likely to resign if he does not get his own way, and his resignation would cause a bad effect in the country even though he has yet to prove that he is of any use in the Cabinet.

[54] The withdrawal of the whip was announced in *The Times* on 15 May 1942, and reason given was Cunningham-Reid's announcement of the formation of the 'People's Movement', whose object was 'to attain total efficiency in this total war'.
[55] William Henry Beveridge (1879–1963), civil service career, Dir. of Labour Exchanges 1909–16; Ass. Gen. Sec., Min. of Munitions 1915–16; 2nd. Sec, Perm. Sec., Min. of Food 1916–19; Dir., London School of Economics 1919–37; Master, Univ. College, Oxford 1937–45; Chairman, Inter-Departmental Ctte. on Social Insurance & Allied Services, 1941–42; Lib. M.P. Berwick 1944–45; kt. 1919, cr. Baron Beveridge 1946.

Saturday 16 May   I have decided not to go to London next week for the war debate – one will hear no more from the Govt. than what one already knows and one has heard the critics too often to want to hear them again!

Sunday 17 May   Winston made rather a bombastic speech at Leeds yesterday: 'If Hitler plays rough,' he said, 'we can play rough too.' Let us hope we can – but let us hope equally that we shall not do anything foolish or jump off before we are really ready – I am always nervous where Winston is concerned.

Tuesday 19 May   In Burma things appear to be going slower, but Alexander[56] says that he has got most of his troops away which is a relief. He has fought a wonderful rearguard battle and deserves a lot of praise – he is a grand fighting soldier.

Wednesday 20 May   The war debate (1st day) in the HofC yesterday appears to have been much the same as usual – the usual speakers + Oliver Stanley and Ned Grigg. I don't think that I have missed much – though perhaps had I been present and sat tight all day I might have been called as apparently the House sat fairly late.

Sunday 24 May   ... the Russians admit that they are no longer on the Kerch peninsula and the fact that they are digging in on the Kharkov sector seems to indicate that the Germans have brought their offensive to a standstill. The papers still go on emphasizing the German losses and suggesting that the Russians are doing splendidly – perhaps they are – but it seems to me a pity to be so optimistic as it leads people here to imagine that victory is a deal nearer than it can possibly be – all this emphasis, too, on the bad living conditions in Germany and Italy is unfortunate for one is fairly certain that however bad conditions in those countries may be the peoples are unlikely to give in so long as the Nazi domination lasts and that will last until the German armies really break down.

---

[56] Harold Rupert Leofric George Alexander (1891–1969), army career; C. in C. Southern Command 1940–42, Burma 1942, Middle East 1942–43, 18th Army Group N. Africa 1943, Allied Armies in Italy 1943–44; S.A.C., Med. 1944–45; Gov.-Gen., Canada 1946–52; Min. of Defence 1952–54; kt. 1942, cr. Viscount Alexander of Tunis 1946, Earl 1952.

I give the war another full year at least – probably longer if we are really going to win it – and the war against Japan may take fully as long. Much must depend on the U.S.A., not only upon her war production but also upon her naval, air and military forces. From all one hears of her soldiers and sailors it is going to take a considerable time before they are ready to meet the German in the field.

Tuesday 26 May I had a letter today from Topping who, in answer to my inquiry, tells me that Eugene Ramsden got 38 votes to my 22 – which was a bigger majority than I had expected – I wonder how it was secured – I mean I wonder if any lobbying was done? I never lifted a finger in my own interests. Topping also told me, again in answer to my inquiry, that this is Ramsden's fifth year of Chairmanship: it really is typical of the Executive Council or Committee or whatever it is called that it can put up with such a chairman for so long. I always feel in despair when I attend meetings of the Executive because to me it always appears to be so utterly out of touch with the realities of politics. It is just a clique of old-fashioned, orthodox Conservatives almost all of whom are still living in the atmosphere of the Primrose League.[57]

[57] A semi-official Conservative organisation popular in the late-Victorian and Edwardian era, founded in memory of Disraeli and taking its name from his favourite flower; it had a deferential social atmosphere, and a large female membership.

9

'AS BAD AS EVER'

May to October 1942

Thursday 28 May 1942   The Labour Party has been airing its views at its conference in London during the last two days – it stands for the usual things and its speakers bawl out the usual platitudes. In the old days one did not bother much about what was said at Labour conferences, but nowadays one realises that all this claptrap has a bigger and bigger following of people – unthinking people, I think. The left wing intelligentsia always strike me as the most unthinking of men: their theories are all based on the old worn out, futile, untrue assumption of equality – all men may be equal in the eyes of God, but He never made all men equal to the tasks which they are set. To institute a new order of society on the basis of equality is doomed to failure – because it implies bringing men down to the level of the least fit among them to cope with the problems of life. In such a society progress in the true sense of the word would, I am certain, be impossible – unless, indeed, it were possible to change all the human instincts. Is it likely that a man would give of his best if he were to gain no reward for his efforts? Would not the natural instinct of each one of us be to sit back and do as little as possible, if he knew that he would be kept by the State?

Friday 29 May   I went to a Boys Club near Byker Bridge and afterwards went on the Byker and Heaton Conservative Working Men's Club. Everyone there was very civil to me and I drank a lot of beer – I also spoke for about five minutes which I gathered was as much as they wanted. Several men came and talked to me, asking questions – clearly the Russian complex has taken possession of some of them – it is odd how quickly propaganda has an effect upon the crowd – one might think that Russia was of more importance to us than our own country.

Saturday 30 May   The Government has made an 'appeal' to the miners (many thousands of them now on strike) to go back to work while the matter of the increased wages they are demanding is being considered. It really is disgraceful that men should behave as they are doing in the crisis of the war – and what to me seems almost worse is that the press appears to condone their action – it is incredible.

Sunday 31 May   We made a tremendous bombing raid (1,000 bombers) over Cologne and the Ruhr last night. It is stated to have been a huge success: about 4 per cent only of the machines not returning, which I gather is what one has to expect – 4 to 5 per cent is all right: 10 per cent is high: 14 to 15 per cent is more than can be suffered.

Tuesday 2 June   ... I went to the HofC. Winston appeared and read a report from Auchinleck on the Libyan battle immediately after questions. It was optimistic in tone and so far it seems we have done well – but the General was wisely guarded in what he said – Winston was clearly in high glee, but mercifully he did not let himself go too much. ... We are to have the Government's white paper on coal tomorrow evening. It is to be taken in whole or cast away – and I gather is likely to please no one and I should imagine will not increase production – the miners appear to be entirely out of hand. They are a curious lot – and really the only thing is to put public opinion against them, but the press unfortunately always takes their side for sentimental reasons.

Wednesday 3 June   The War Damage Bill began its committee stage today and I suppose I must try and say a few words tomorrow when the mortgage business comes up – but Kingsley Wood has told me that he means to be sticky on the subject and so it will be pure waste of time to say anything. People are more cheerful as a result I suppose of the P.M.'s statement yesterday – but personally I wish that he had not made it. I can see no use in discussing a battle until it is over – more especially one in the Libyan desert and against Rommel who has sprung so many unpleasant surprises upon us in the past. Looking at the map, however, it does seem that, if we have sufficient tanks, etc., and tolerable luck, we might check him pretty effectively this time.

Wednesday 10 June　　I was lucky today – Dennis Herbert came up to me in the Smoking Room and told me that I was to be called comparatively early in the Coal debate – and so I was. I spoke for about a quarter of an hour (the Speaker had made an appeal for short speeches) and did not do so badly though I failed to say much of what I had intended to say. However, I was listened to – and Tom Magnay and a few others whom I saw later on, including D. Clifton Brown, congratulated me – I think sincerely. ... I find that people are getting a little uncomfortable about the show in Libya – Rommel is undoubtedly very strong and is pushing his drive for all he is worth, and what worries people here is that we don't seem to be strong enough for the job of holding him, let alone attacking him. Everyone is much pleased that the Free French are fighting so well at Bir Hacheim – but again one wonders why it does not seem possible for us to go to their assistance in strength – obviously they won't be able to hold the place much longer unless they are reinforced.

Thursday 11 June　　The Government carried its coal proposals by 329 votes to 8 – I did not listen to much of today's debate, but I heard some of Dalton's performance and Cripps winding up. Their tone – indeed, the tone generally – was all that the miners could ask for – admonitions to the wretched mineowners and never a word of expostulation to the miners. I have no brief for either party in the industry – but it seems to me all wrong to go on for ever placating the miners and never reminding them of the duty they owe their country to produce more and more coal. ... At the end of today's proceedings Anthony Eden announced the making of a treaty with Russia. It has been an open secret that Molotov has been over here (and apparently he has been to the U.S.A. too) and now we have the result of his visit. To my mind the Treaty (which is to last for 20 years) does not amount to much – but no doubt it will cause delight to the great majority of people in this country who for the time being are intensely pro-Russian. All reference to the future state of the Baltic states is omitted – so perhaps we are not going to be tiresome to Stalin about them! The rest of the Treaty is pretty obvious stuff and means just as much as the Russians find it convenient to themselves for it to mean.

Friday 12 June   The U.S.A. authorities now state that the Japanese lost in the battle of the Coral Sea 1 aircraft carrier, 3 heavy cruisers ... all of which are said to have been sunk. ... The Americans are also optimistic enough to think that the Japanese lost 4 aircraft carriers in the Midway Island battle. These aircraft carrier losses are very satisfactory if only they are really true.[1]

Saturday 13 June   The Russian Treaty is getting a lot of kudos both in the press here and also with the Allied nations generally. To me it seems to have been a good move – though I don't for a moment suppose it that it would prevent Stalin making peace with Hitler at any moment should he deem it in the interests of the U.S.S.R. Treaties in these days really mean very little – they really are 'scraps of paper' – however, it does not do to suggest any of this sort of thing in public. The public in this country is firmly convinced not only of the *bona fides* of the Bolshies but also that they are fighting Hitler for *us*. It is a really astonishing belief, but perhaps not altogether surprising in view of the tremendous Russian propaganda which is being carried on today.

Thursday 18 June   The shipping situation one hears is really becoming very serious and the strain on the navy is terrific – the Americans don't seem to be able to cope with the U-boats. Winston, so a little bird told me today, is away to the U.S.A. again to talk with Roosevelt – what more they can have to say to each other God only knows – perhaps Winston's idea in going is to strengthen his position here – if Tobruk falls, and it looks as if it would, he is going to get a big jolt – not only in Parl. but also in the country. He would be well advised to cease to be Minister of Defence – it would really make no difference to his position if he remained P.M. – and might satisfy critics.

Friday 19 June   ... arriving at Coldstream a few minutes before

---

[1] The sinking of four Japanese aircraft carriers in the Battle of Midway was a turning point in the Pacific theatre.

seven where the Dunglass people met us. ... a neat square Georgian or early Victorian house – dower house of the Home family – with a fine view of the river, Alec Dunglass[2] can now walk about a bit (after nearly a year on his back) and they hope that he is now on the road to recovery and will be all right in another six or seven months. He looks twice the man he did and has put on 2 stone in weight. He is an extraordinarily good fellow and his patience and courage throughout all this trying time have been wonderful.

Sunday 21 June   Tobruk has fallen after a very short blitz, the Germans apparently overrunning our defences and our garrison (about 2 divisions) surrendering – it is an odd affair and makes one somewhat anxious both as to the capacity of our leaders and also of the fighting qualities of our men ... It looks as if we had been out-generaled, out-gunned, out-manoeuvred – it is all very depressing and one is extremely nervous as to what more in the way of disaster is ahead of us. We must be much weakened on land – at sea we know how weak we have been and still are [and] in the Middle East and in the air we don't appear to possess any kind of superiority.

Monday 22 June   Maureen Stanley's death is announced in the press today – I feared from what Malcolm Bullock[3] told me the other day that there was little hope of her recovery – but one had hoped against hope. I was very fond of her and she was always so nice and friendly to Beatrice and me – she had great charm and an astonishing *joie de vivre*.[4] Poor Oliver: he will be more than ever a lonely soul without her – and I am terribly sorry, too, for Charley Londonderry who was so fond and proud of her.[5]

Tuesday 23 June   In the House Attlee, after questions, read out a report from Auchinleck regarding the fighting up to the 20th of June – it did not tell us much more than we already knew. The

[2] Alec Douglas-Home, styled Lord Dunglass 1918–51 (q.v.).
[3] (Harold) Malcolm Bullock (1890–1966), Con. M.P. Waterloo 1923–50, Crosby 1950–53; Chairman, Political Educ. Ctte, N.W. Area 1935–45; Chairman, N.W. Area 1936–37; cr. Bart. 1954; married 1919 Oliver Stanley's sister, Victoria, who died in a riding accident in Nov. 1927.
[4] translation: joy of living, i.e. vitality.
[5] Maureen Stanley was the daughter of the 7th Marquess of Londonderry.

papers today are full of reports from correspondents who tell us that the troops fought well, but were overwhelmed by superior armaments – the criticism of our leaders has begun and there can be little doubt that Rommel has outclassed them. There is a feeling of grave disquietude in the HofC – and of course all kinds of rumours and gossip are floating about – undoubtedly the opposition to Winstonian control is gathering force. Beaverbrook is said to be behind a lot of this – influencing, so they say, Winston's critics who sit on both sides of the House. We are to have a debate next week and it looks as if it might be acrimonious – but as the Speaker is certain to call only the usual people it won't be easy in all probability to know how far opinion generally has turned against the P.M. Oliver Lyttelton (just back from the U.S.A.) told me that he thought it quite likely that things went too fast for us to evacuate Tobruk – but I don't think that he knows any more about things than the rest of us.

Wednesday 24 June   In the HofC there was a colonial debate and I am told that Harold Macmillan did well – I had a glass of beer with him and Dorothy whom I met as I came out of lunch – they refreshed themselves at one of the bars where the food (sandwiches, sausages, etc.) looked rather good I thought – one finds oneself always studying food nowadays – not that there is any real lack of it, but because one tries to find variety and the most one can get for one's money. ... Roger Keyes,[6] whom I talked with in the Lobby today, congratulating him on his son's posthumous V.C.,[7] was very bitter at the way in which Sir A. Cunningham[8] had been sacked by Winston – he, after all, did splendidly in his East African campaign.

Tuesday 30 June   Rommel seems to be doing very much as he

[6] Roger John Brownlow Keyes (1872–1945), naval career; Commodore, Submarine Service 1910–15; Chief of Staff., Med. 1915–16, Grand Fleet 1916–17; Dir. of Plans 1917; commanded Dover Patrol 1918–19, Battle Cruiser Squadron 1919–21; Dep. Chief of Naval Staff 1921–25; C. in C. Med. 1925–28, Portsmouth 1929–31; Dir. Combined Operations 1940–41; Con. M.P. Portsmouth N. 1934–43; cr. Bart. 1919, Baron Keyes 1943.

[7] Victoria Cross, the highest award for bravery in battle.

[8] Andrew Browne Cunningham (1883–1963), naval career; Dep. Chief of Naval Staff 1938–39; C. in C. Med. 1939–42, 1942–43; Head of Admiralty Delegation in Washington 1942; 1st Sea Lord 1943–46; cr. Bart. 1942, Baron Cunningham of Kirkhope 1945, Viscount Cunningham of Hyndhope 1946.

likes in Egypt and is now reported to have passed El Daba and to be only 90 miles from Alexandria – presumably we intend to fight him somewhere. Winston informed the House this morning (I was not present) that Auchinleck had taken over the command from Ritchie[9] and was running the show himself. Let us hope that he is up to the job – I don't know him – nor does anyone I have met. He was a successful brigade commander on the N.W. Frontier[10] and knows nil I should think about tanks or desert fighting or air cooperation or, indeed, anything of what he should know to meet a specialist like Rommel. One can't help feeling a bit gloomy about his chances – and everyone I meet appears to be equally gloomy. ... There was a meeting of the 1922 Committee this afternoon which I attended – I spoke very strongly against the vote of censure motion and got a lot of support – indeed, if I had challenged a division I believe I should have got a majority to ask Wardlaw Milne[11] to withdraw. James[12] told me that W.M. had offered to postpone his motion if Winston would like him to do so, but Winston said that in the circumstances as it was on the paper he would prefer to have it taken as arranged – James told me this later. ... James looked and seemed seedy (he has had some tummy trouble), but says that he is finding Winston less difficult to deal with than he imagined would be the case.

Wednesday 1 July   The Censure debate began today: it has been a poor show so far. It began at 12 noon – I sat through most of it, until 8.30 p.m. – kept bobbing up and down but was not called ... John Wardlaw Milne made quite a good speech – and carried on successfully even after his proposal to make the Duke of Gloucester[13] C.-in-C. had interrupted it for several minutes – the

[9] Neil Methuen Ritchie (1897–1983), army career; G.O.C. 51st Div. 1940–41; Dep. Chief of Staff, Middle East 1941; G.O.C. 8th Army, 1941–42, 52nd Div. 1942–43, 12th Corps 1944–45; C. in C. Scotland 1945–47, Far East Land Forces 1947–49; Commander, British Army Staff in Washington 1950–51; kt. 1945.
[10] The north-west frontier of India; much of the British Army was stationed here in peacetime, mainly involved in small-scale policing operations.
[11] John Sydney Wardlaw-Milne (1879–1967), Con. M.P. Kidderminster 1922–45; Chairman, Select Ctte. on Nat. Expenditure 1939–45; Chairman, Con. Party India Ctte. 1930–35, & Foreign Affairs Ctte. 1939–45; kt. 1932.
[12] James Stuart, Conservative Chief Whip.
[13] Henry William Frederick Albert (1900–1974), styled Prince Henry 1900–28, cr. Duke of Gloucester 1928; Chief Liaison Officer, B.E.F. 1939–40, Home Forces 1940–41; third son of King George V.

whole House bursting into ribald laughter at this quite unexpected solution of the problem of a better central control of our war effort! Oliver Lyttelton who replied for the Government was not a success. He showed that he has still much to learn as to managing the House and he spoke very indifferently – and of course it was not an easy job to explain why after nearly 3 years of war we are still lacking the war armament we require. Oliver will have to improve a lot as a debater if he hopes to do any good in Parliament – so far things have been too easy for him. No one else made a decent speech all day and the Speaker, as usual, called most of the usual people – the rest of them, I suppose, will be called tomorrow. ... The news today is worse than ever – Sevastopol has fallen and Rommel's progress does not appear to have been checked – though we are told that a big battle is raging and that our troops have been reinforced, presumably from Syria where no doubt we shall soon hear of the Germans – a mess if ever there was one.

Thursday 2 July   Winston spoke for an hour and a half this afternoon in a very full House – and I thought did very well. He is a giant among pygmies when it comes to a debate of this kind, and I think that everybody realizes it – but of course he had a pretty simple job today because the censure motion was so stupidly framed. To vote for it was out of the question because if it had been carried it meant the fall of the Government in the middle of a great battle – had it been framed so as to condemn the work of the Ministry of Supply and demand a thorough overhaul of its machinery I certainly could not have voted against it. The Govt. won by 475 to 25 and there were, I believe, about 20 abstentions including that ass Eddie Winterton who is always willing to wound but is afraid to strike. The news today is still extremely alarming. The enemy claim to be past El Alamein – we say that we are still holding out in that area. Clearly the situation is critical in the extreme and it seems pretty certain that our troops must be entirely disorganized or surely we could break up Rommel's long line of communications – presumably we can have little or no armour left ... It is a disconcerting business and there is an all-pervading gloom ... I remember March 1918 and refuse to believe that God has deserted us.

Friday 3 July   There are moments nowadays when one is inclined to become downhearted and to feel that the issue of this great struggle is in doubt. It is taking us such a hell of a long time to get going and we still seem to be so hopelessly inferior in material to the Germans – one cannot help feeling that there is something radically wrong in our war production – a lack of decision and initiative, too much committee work, too little drive. When my eye rests on the great stupid face of Sir John Anderson on the Treasury bench, I feel that the Civil Service mind is too much in charge of things in this war and that until some new man turns up to take control of everything we shall do no good. I had hoped that Oliver Lyttelton might be such a man, but I am beginning to be somewhat doubtful of him. Beaverbrook is a crook and a charlatan by all accounts and everyone is agreed that we are well rid of him – surely there must be someone who could do the job? Are we really so destitute of talent in these days? One hears so much about this being a young man's war: no one over 50 need apply – surely, it is a mistake, except in the actual fighting – it seems to me that the young men have not shown up so far: time to look round to grown up people – and they should not be civil servants.

Saturday 4 July   I had to go to Newcastle again today to attend a conference of northern Conservative and Unionist Clubmen summoned to meet Lord Clanwilliam,[14] the Chairman of the Association of C. and U. Clubs. I lunched with Clanwilliam and his party (which of course included Sir Albert [Appleby] and Sir Alfred [Leith]!) at the Station Hotel and then we all went off to the Byker and Heaton Club where the meeting was held. There was a good attendance – some of the men having come from West Cumberland. Clanwilliam gave them an excellent address – I also spoke and seemed to be appreciated. I suggested to the President of the Club that I should pay them a monthly visit and give an address on current affairs. He seemed pleased at my suggestion, but I should doubt whether the offer will be accepted. Beer drinking and not political thinking is the object of Conservative Clubmen – and I for one don't blame them.

Sunday 5 July   Much annoyed to see in the papers today that

[14] Arthur Vesey Meade (1873–1953), styled Lord Gilford 1873–1907, suc. 5th Earl of Clanwilliam 1907.

Winston has thought fit to send a special telegram to the Air Marshal in Libya thanking the R.A.F. for the splendid assistance they are giving the Army! It really is quite absurd to treat the R.A.F. as if it were an ally of ours, not part and parcel of our fighting forces – as long as this silliness continues there will never be complete and full liaison between the Services. Besides why should the P.M. congratulate the R.A.F. and not the land troops who, after all, are bearing the brunt of the fighting?

Monday 6 July   The Germans claim to have crossed the Don – and there is no doubt that they are making a tremendous, and what looks like a successful, effort on the Kursk-Colchank sector. One does not quite know what the Russians will do if their communications are cut between Moscow and the South. ... In London I find that even the War Cabinet knows nothing about Stalin's plans. Everything is wrapped in mystery and practically all we are told is what we read in *Soviet War News* which is just propaganda issued from the Russian embassy in London.

Wednesday 8 July   Dorman Smith, Governor of Burma, who has just got home, addressed the All Party Committee at the HofC this afternoon. His address was excellent and most interesting. He utterly refuted the gossip that the Burmese had welcomed the Japanese – there was of course a 5th column, but it was not a large one – and the enemy was helped by Dacoits,[15] playing their own game – but he assured us that the mass of the people are not ill-disposed towards us and would welcome us back. I don't know the man (he was not in the House with me), but he struck me as sound and sensible. He is said to have done his job in Burma quite admirably – cool, confident and resolute. He spoke very highly of Alexander.

Thursday 9 July   The war at sea is not going well for us and the shipping losses are far too heavy by all accounts – presumably we shall be told a lot of unpleasant things next week. The shipping debate is to be held in secret – quite properly in my opinion. But today in the House (I was absent) Shinwell and co. demanded that the debate should be in open session. This would be a dangerous

---

[15] Organized criminal gangs.

policy calculated to aid the enemy – nevertheless I think that the public should be made to appreciate the full meaning of the shipping position by some kind of Government statement.

Saturday 11 July It is odd how Wilkin loves entertaining – but perhaps it is just as well that he does – I suppose at the back of his mind is a desire sooner or later to become Area Chairman. He wants to become head of the caucus, to pull strings and be the boss. My only complaint against him is that he really possesses no guts and is essentially a wirepuller, not a leader. After luncheon we adjourned to the Conservative Club where Topping explained his scheme for the creation of a special fund to be administered by a board for the supply of agents – as the money for this fund is to be supplied voluntarily by the richer constituencies I don't suppose that the scheme is likely to mature – more especially as there is a strong body of opposition to it among the agents. We had about fifteen chairmen of associations present: the majority of them were in favour of giving the scheme a trial.

Monday 13 July Not much fresh in the war news – certainly it is the day of the Germans, by which I mean that for the time being they have the initiative and are doing much as they like. The only hope that I can see is that they will not succeed in keeping to their time table and will therefore not be in a position to sit still and laugh at us when the winter comes again. If by that time, however, they have overwhelmed the Russians and are in possession of the Ukraine and the Caucasus, they might well say to us – 'now what about it? Here we are with everything we need to carry on the war indefinitely – are you prepared to face it or shall we have an end of it – we want so and so – we are prepared to let you keep the British Empire – is it worth while continuing the fight just for the sake of a few mouldy little countries like Czechoslovakia and Yugoslavia, etc., which are more trouble than they are worth, and Soviet Russia?' Of course our answer would have to be 'to Hell with you' – but I wonder how long we should be prepared to go on fighting? It would be a long drawn out business – unless of course the Germans are a deal harder hit than I imagine.

Tuesday 14 July The House discussed production today. O.L[yttelton] did better than last time – but he is not as yet a good speaker and does not understand the HofC. In time perhaps he will do all right, but I rather doubt it. He is, I think, a bit too self-satisfied with himself. He is quick at the up-take and clever – but he has not much personality and is too much the successful business man for the HofC. I lunched at the Turf Club with Oliver Stanley. He told me that Maureen died from infection due to the operation. He also told me that he never expected that she would conquer the disease, implying that he knew she would never give herself a chance – but what a confession to make for a husband! He intends to come back to the HofC, and says that he would like to have a comeback. I begged him to set out to *lead* the Party – but I know in my own mind that he is incapable of the effort – a pity for he is the only decent and able man available in my opinion, but unfortunately he lacks the necessary drive and personality. He simply cannot push himself forward. Maureen did all she could for him and even with her drive he never took the place he should have done in the party. In the afternoon listened to Halifax on the U.S.A. He was quite happy about their war effort and spoke well – but, somehow or other, he is not to me an impressive persona – heavy and dull – and I doubt whether he is the right man to represent us in Washington.

Wednesday 15 July   All the wild men in the HofC keep calling for a 'second front' – but they don't tell us where it is to be or how we are going to supply our invading forces. And of course all this pother about a second front is doing harm both here and in Russia. Ignorant people here follow the extremists and in Russia the belief must be gaining ground that we don't really mean to help them. It is all very disturbing and one feels that something should be done to check this tiresome propaganda.

Thursday 16 July   I did not hear the earlier part of the debate today on the shipping situation as 40 minutes were wasted in a discussion as to whether or not the debate was to be in secret. The usual bores were at work – *viz.*, Eddie Winterton, Hore-Belisha, Aneurin Bevan, Shinwell, etc. – a division was challenged, but Shinwell could not even get tellers. Obviously the debate had to be in secret mainly because as Winston pointed out at the beginning of the secret session most of the shipping losses are American and it would not do to criticize our allies – our own losses have not been more severe than usual. After Winston had spoken I had to leave for my Liverpool Globe board meeting so I did not hear Alexander who opened for the Govt. I gather that he was not very good – Salter, who wound up for the Govt., did well. He told us that the shipping situation was bad, worse, in his opinion, than it was in 1917. The Govt. apparently are not going to issue any statement in the press which I think is a mistake as I hold that our public should be made to realize – if it is possible to make them realize anything unless they are actually bombed – the terrible gravity of our situation. The Russians are getting it in the neck and it remains to be seen how long they will be able to stand it; if they make a separate peace, which they may be forced to make, we shall have the whole of the German power against us – and with Russia in the bag Hitler can go on indefinitely I should imagine.

Friday 17 July   I went to see the miserable little Tydeman. He has not yet drawn up the memorandum re. the Newcastle amalgamation. He is either hopelessly incompetent or is not playing the game by me – I rather suspect the latter but I am giving him a bit more rope. I dislike and distrust the man and wish to goodness I could get someone else – but Topping will see to it that I don't. Tydeman suits him all right and always plays his game.

Friday 24 July   I lunched at the Northern Counties Club, sat next to Hugh Northumberland[16] who was very civil ... he did tell me something which was of interest – *viz.*, that Walter Buccleuch[17] had shown him a letter from Neville Chamberlain, written only two or three days before the Germans invaded Poland, in which Neville (in his own writing) had added to the typewritten letter that he thought that now the crisis was over and that all would go well or words to that effect. It all goes to prove, I think, how lamentable our Intelligence service must have been before the war, or how completely those in authority neglected it and trusted to their own

---

[16] Hugh Algernon Percy (1914–1988), Lord in Waiting May–July 1945; Lord Steward of the Household 1973–88; member of Northumberland County Council 1944–55, Alderman 1955–67; Ld. Lt. Northumberland 1956–84; Pres., North of England Shipowners' Assoc. 1952–78; styled Lord Hugh Percy 1914–40, suc. 10th Duke of Northumberland 1940, K.G. 1959.

[17] Walter, 8th Duke of Buccleuch (q.v.)

judgement which was based upon an entire misunderstanding of Hitler and what he was up to. Poor Neville was clearly too ignorant and parochially minded to cope with foreign politics – why he should have imagined that he could play a decent game with Hitler and Musso, God only knows – and yet he had met both scoundrels, who must have hoodwinked him completely.

Tuesday 28 July   We had our Constitutional sub-committee meeting this afternoon – there were present, in addition to Agnes and myself, Pickthorn, Douglas Jerrold, Kitson Clark, Phillimore,[18] and Arthur Bryant[19] – such a party as ever was! It really looks as if it would be quite impossible to get a sensible report out of such a team. They are all entirely lacking in any practical experience of political life and only D.J. has any first hand knowledge of administrative procedure. K.C. is just an ordinary history don; Godfrey Phillimore is, I should imagine, a sort of Fascist idealist, Arthur Bryant is just a faddist *sans*[20] any real knowledge and with a head in the clouds; Pickthorn is intelligent enough, but lazy and futile. Agnes and I had drawn up quite a sensible memorandum – but it failed to please our colleagues – but none of them could suggest any practical alternatives to our proposals. They don't seem to understand, for example, that if you have free election by the people, you must submit to their choosing their representatives and that those representatives may not be the 'best type' of people to serve in Parliament. They all profess to accept our particular form of parliamentary democracy – but, obviously, don't in the least appreciate its implications or the method of its working. We talked and talked for over two hours today but got nowhere.

Thursday 30 July   ... to the HofC. There is a great deal of caballing going on – Beaverbrook is supposed to be at the bottom of it all – his idea being (so they say) to break up this Government and the Conservative and Labour parties, and to fix up some new

---

[18] Godfrey Walter Phillimore (1879–1947), suc. 2nd Baron Phillimore 1929.

[19] Arthur Bryant (1899–1985), author of popular historical works; Lecturer in History, Oxford Univ. Delegacy for Extra-Mural Studies 1925–36; columnist, *Illustrated London News* 1936–85; lecturer at Bonar Law Memorial College, Ashridge 1930–39; Chairman, Ashridge Council 1949–49; Chairman, Society of Authors 1949–53; kt. 1954.

[20] translation: without.

National Govt. in which the Beaver would be the power behind the throne with Winston as P.M., and presumably Wardlaw Milne as Chancellor of the Exchequer. If all this gossip has any foundation in fact, it is rather a terrible prospect – I don't believe for a moment, however, that such a plot has a chance of success – the malcontents in our Party have no following and the bulk of the Labour Party is too sound to follow men like Shinwell and A. Bevan. I wish that we had someone who could lead us. I fear that Oliver Stanley is not capable of taking a lead – temperamentally he is unsuited for the part: he has no vim – no thought of any kind – and he won't let one help him, a pity because one could help him if he would give one a chance.

Sunday 2 August   The German advance in the Caucasus area continues and one does not see what is to stop it – clearly the Russians are being driven back without much difficulty ... here the cry for a 'second front' gets more and more noisy: it may prove very troublesome to the Government before long, more especially if the Russians actually collapse – all our left-wingers will then shriek that it is our fault.

Monday 3 August   We attacked Dusseldorf pretty effectively it seems, and most of the town is reported as destroyed. The papers are beginning to gloat on these air raids somewhat too much, I think. They are necessary and excusable in view of what the Germans have done over here – but bombing promiscuously from the air is a beastly form of warfare and the less said about it the better. Civilians must suffer and private property and non-military buildings must inevitably be destroyed – but I don't believe that this sort of thing will end the war.

Tuesday 4 August   The House duller than ever. I find myself out of touch with everybody and bored to death – if only Oliver Stanley were a man and would try and pull things together what fun we might have. There never was such an opportunity for a man of grit as there is today – everyone on our side is looking for a leader – someone who will be ready to take control when Winston passes from the scene either during or after the war. Oliver has the ball at his feet – but he is such a helpless fellow – so completely lacking in initiative and drive.

Saturday 8 August   The miserable Gandhi[21] addressed the All-India Congress Committee in Bombay yesterday and told his audience that he did not want the Japanese in India because that would mean the end of China and perhaps also of Russia. He asked his friends not to harbour hatred of the British and emphasized the importance of non-violence in the struggle against us. How long are we going to tolerate this absurd old man and his friends? Surely the time has come to put them all under lock and key and to show India and the world in general that we mean to govern India so long as the war lasts whatever changes we may decide upon when it is over. It is of course the only policy at the moment and it is a policy which would be accepted in India. One is dead sick of all the nonsense which is being talked in this country about India and it is high time that the Government took a firm line – we have been too weak and feeble for words.

Sunday 9 August   They have at last shut up Gandhi and about 100 other of the Congress leaders which in a time of crisis like this seems to me to be the right and proper thing to do with such creatures. It will be interesting to see whether there is any repercussion in India – from all one knows of the people there will be no trouble – our mistake has been not to govern – so long as we remain in India we must be firm and not stand this incessant political agitation by what after all is a fraction of the population. I expect myself that there will be more outcry from the left wing people than there will be in India – but if I were Mr. Amery[22] that sort of agitation would not upset me. The news from Russia is as bad as ever and I don't envy Winston when he goes to Moscow: he is likely to find Joe Stalin in a very disagreeable mood.

Monday 10 August   The Indian rioting appears to be decreasing and the Government claims to have got it well in hand – now it is only to be hoped that firmness will be maintained and that we shall show all and sundry, here, in India, and elsewhere, that at long last we intend to govern and that until the war is over at any rate we

[21] Mohandas Karamchand Gandhi (1869–1948), Indian nationalist, leading figure in Congress movement from 1915; attended Round Table Conference 1931; imprisoned 1922, 1930, 1933, 1942–45; called 'Mahatma' (great soul) by Hindu folowers; assassinated by Hindu fanatic after supporting partition, 30 Jan. 1948.
[22] The Secretary of State for India.

really cannot go on arguing and pleading with people like Gandhi and Nehru.[23] When Hitler and Musso and the Mikado[24] are just a bad dream, it will be time enough to decide what form of government is to be established in India.

Wednesday 12 August ... the Germans seem to be doing much as they like in the Caucasus – but the Russians are defending Stalingrad for all they are worth. If they can manage to hold the place, all may yet be well.

Thursday 13 August In India it looks as if the Government had got things well in hand: at any rate it does not look as if there was going to be anything like a general strike – Bombay streets are reported to be 'normal'. I am glad that Roger Lumley[25] is there and not frightened Freddy Sykes![26] Roger is not the sort of man to give in to violence and is a man of courage and determination I should say.

Monday 17 August Our press appears to me to get worse and worse. There is literally no really first class newspaper or journalist nowadays, even *The Times* has become completely colourless and just flows with the tide. It was feeble one thought *auspice* Geoffrey Dawson, but under Barrington Ward[27] it has become feebler still – its 'pinkness' is almost pathetic and it appears to be incapable of giving a real lead to the public. It supports all the silly things like family allowances, etc., and never appears to consider it its duty to point out that what we lack is faith in ourselves and a determination to lead harder and more useful lives.

[23] Pandit Jawaharlal Nehru (1889–1964), Indian nationalist; Pres. of Congress from 1929; P.M. & For. Min. of India 1947–64.
[24] The Emperor of Japan: Hirohito (1901–1989), 124th Emperor 1926–1989.
[25] (Lawrence) Roger Lumley (1896–1969), Con. M.P. Hull E. 1922–29, York 1931–37; P.P.S. to Austen Chamberlain 1924–26, to W. Elliot 1931–32, to J. Gilmour 1932–35, to A. Eden 1935–37; Gov. of Bombay 1937–43; U.S. India 1945; Lord Chamberlain 1952–63; suc. 11th Earl of Scarbrough 1945, K.G. 1948.
[26] Frederick Hugh Sykes (1877–1954), Con. M.P. Sheffield Hallam 1922–28, Nottingham Central 1940–45; army career, commanded Royal Flying Corps 1912–14; Chief of Air Staff 1918–19; Chief of British Section, Paris Peace Conference 1919; Controller-Gen. of Civil Aviation 1919–22; Chairman, Govt. Broadcasting Bd. 1923–27; Gov. of Bombay 1928–33; Chairman, Miners' Welfare Commission 1934–36; Chairman of Council, Royal Empire Soc. 1938–41; kt. 1919.
[27] Robert McGowan Barrington-Ward (1891–1948), ass. editor, *Observer* 1919–27, *The Times* 1927–41; editor of *The Times* 1941–48.

Tuesday 18 August   Alexander has been appointed to take Auchinleck's place as G.O.C. Middle East; Montgomery[28] has been given command of the Eighth Army and Lumsden[29] succeeds Gott[30] as commander of 10th Corps – I should imagine that these are all good appointments. Alexander is the only one of these I know personally, and he certainly is a good man who has proved himself in this war – Montgomery has a big reputation. It is now announced that Winston has been in Egypt and Moscow – but he does not appear to have got home again – pray God he has not gone to see Gandhi!

Saturday 22 August   The Dieppe raid is now described as a 'reconnaissance in force' and appears to have been a big scale show – reading between the lines I doubt very much whether it can rightly be described as a success – however, presumably it has been of some use to the G[eneral] S[taff]. I do not myself believe that a full scale invasion between Dunkirk and Dieppe is a feasible military proposition unless we can obtain complete mastery of the air and of the sea. Whether this can or cannot be done remains to be seen - I confess that I have very grave doubt as to whether such a mastery can be obtained even temporarily – that it could be maintained appears to me still more doubtful. Personally I feel that to be successful an invasion of the Continent should be made elsewhere – but against this of course is that the air and sea supremacy would be even more difficult to secure.

Wednesday 26 August   Winston is back in London and apparently in the best of form. There is no doubt that these trips strengthen his position at home immensely and I should think help things along abroad. The rumour that Wavell is coming home to serve in

---

[28] Bernard Law Montgomery (1887–1976), army career; G.O.C. 8th Div. 1938–39, 3rd Div. 1939–40, 5th Corps 1940, 12th Corps 1941; C. in C. South-East Command 1942; G.O.C. 8th Army 1942–44; C. in C. British Group of Armies & Allied Armies, N. France 1944, 21st Army Group 1944–45; British Commander, Allied Expeditionary Forces in Europe 1944–46; C.I.G.S. 1946–48; Chairman, Western European Cs. in C. Ctte. 1948–51; Dep. S.A.C. Europe 1951–58; kt. 1942, cr. Viscount Montgomery of Alamein 1946, K.G. 1946.

[29] Herbert Lumsden (1897–1945), army career; G.O.C. 10th Corps (8th Army) 1942–43; special rep. with Gen. MacArthur, S.A.C. South West Pacific 1943–45.

[30] William Henry Ewart Gott (1897–1942), army career; G.O.C. 7th Armoured Div. in N. Africa offensive 1941, 10th Corps (8th Army)1942; selected to command 8th Army but shot down and killed whilst returning to Cairo on 7 Aug. 1942.

the War Cabinet is denied – also the report that Auchinleck was to go back to the Indian command.

Wednesday 9 September   Winston's speech yesterday in the House does not seem to have told us much more than we knew already – apparently the debate which was expected did not materialize and the House was nearly counted out after the P.M. had finished. A strange place the HofC – one can never tell what is going to happen there – possibly in this lies one of its main attractions.

Saturday 12 September   One feels that in Victorian days there were a great many more big men in politics than there are today – our people are so colourless and half-baked, lacking in scholarship and education. On both sides in Victorian days there were men who might easily have taken on the Premiership – nowadays when one looks round for someone to succeed Winston there is literally nobody of any stature. Perhaps one is inclined to underrate one's own contemporaries – and of course familiarity breeds contempt – but I try to be fair to men like Eden, Oliver Stanley, Kingsley Wood, Greenwood, Attlee, Morrison & Co., and I find them lacking in every way.

Monday 14 September   The attack on Stalingrad grows more and more intense – clearly the Germans mean to have the place at all costs...

Thursday 17 September   Another planning report has just been published – the Uthwatt report – it deals with agrarian problems, and I gather does not recommend the nationalization of land. One simply cannot keep pace with all this planning – and I for one don't propose to attempt to do so – most of the proposals are likely to be consigned to oblivion I should imagine.

Thursday 24 September   I went to see Bobbety Cranborne at the Colonial Office this morning to talk about the HofL.[31] He looks deplorably sick and emaciated and, if he were not a Cecil, one would suppose that he was about to expire – however, he appeared to be quite fit and alive. I was rather pleased to find that his ideas

[31] Cranborne had been Conservative leader in the Lords since 22 Feb. 1942.

about a reformed HofL rather tally with mine, so that one can proceed with a knowledge that what one proposes may get a little support from among the peers.

Monday 28 September   One wonders what is going to happen after the war, what new follies men will commit – whether after the fighting there will be revolution and what kind of 'New Order' will be established. If we are to have a proletarian heaven on earth, it will lead to chaos and more wars – and yet this looks the sort of thing towards which we are heading. I fail to understand why all and sundry should be ready to accept in wartime all the silly gospel of the Socialists which they wisely turned down in time of peace. Today the most old-fashioned Tories and Liberals keep assuring one that practically everything they have hitherto stood for is no longer either right or feasible. It is all amazing to me, for though I realize that many changes must come and that the old-fashioned individualism is no longer possible, I cannot believe in 'the State' and unlimited public control, either national or local.

Thursday 1 October   I attended the Party [Central] Council this morning at Caxton Hall – there was a large attendance. I proposed a motion for the holding of a Party Conference (the first since 1937) in London next March – it was carried with only two dissentients. Then R.A. Butler read us an essay (a very nicely written one) on the work of the party committees, and then one Faber,[32] chairman of the Education committee, defended his plan for youth. He was very long-winded and I could not wait to the end of his speech as I had to go to my Liverpool, London & Globe board meeting. I returned to the House after the board meeting and heard one or two speeches in the coal debate – they were not very illuminating. They tell me that Robin Castlereagh made a good speech this morning and that G[wilym] L[loyd] George[33] did not do too badly. I asked the Speaker to put my name down for Tuesday when the debate is to be continued.

[32] Geoffrey Cust Faber (1889–1961), author and publisher; Chairman, Faber & Gwyer Ltd. 1923–27, Faber & Faber Ltd. 1927–61; Chairman, Publishers Assoc. 1939–41, Nat. Book League 1945–47; kt. 1954.

[33] Gwilym Lloyd George (1894–1967), Lib. M.P. Pembroke 1922–24, 1929–50, Nat. Lib. & Con. M.P. Newcastle N. 1951–57; P.S. Trade 1931, 1939–41; P.S. Food 1940–42; Min. of Fuel & Power 1942–45; Min. of Food 1951–54; Home Sec. 1954–57; cr. Viscount Tenby 1957.

Saturday 3 October   The defence of Stalingrad continues and the Russians say that they are holding the German advance in the Caucasus. They are putting up a marvellous show and deserve success if any people ever did. We seem to have made a little push in Egypt 'to improve our line' (how well one remembers the expression and what it usually entailed).

Tuesday 6 October   I spoke in the coal debate this afternoon – not well – Clifton Brown called me – spoke also in the '22 Committee later in the day, against prolonging or altering the present hours of sittings, at any rate during the winter months. Oliver Stanley proposed longer hours and later ones – why I don't know. He had support from Eddie Winterton, etc. – but, on the whole, people were against it I fancy though we had no vote today. The whips are against it and I think rightly. Had a talk with Onslow regarding HofL reform: his views are much the same as mine. Pickthorn informed me that the intelligentsia of my committee are not going to accept my memorandum and are preparing one of their own – it looks, therefore, as if we were in for a tiresome time and as if my committee at any rate would come to grief – for my intelligentsia are entirely ignorant of practical politics and know little about the working of Parliament.

Wednesday 7 October   A dull day at the House – a long wrangle resulting from a report against some company by the Public Accounts Committee. The company is run by the new M.P. for Grantham whose name I forget, but who is not a particularly attractive chap.[34] Walter Elliot, chairman of the Public Accounts Committee, did badly I am told in the debate, the other chap did well and was defended by the Minister of Aircraft Production, whose department, when *auspice* the Beaver, was in the business - one's natural inclination is to feel that there is never smoke without fire, but I did not listen to the debate. Oliver Lyttelton spoke very well at the '22 Committee this afternoon – a speech which went down well and made one quite hopeful about his future. He has a

[34] William Denis Kendall (1903–1995), Ind. M.P. Grantham 1942–50, Lib. cand. Grantham 1951; Dir. of Manufacturing, Citroen Motor Company, Paris 1929–38; Managing-Director, British Manufacture & Research Co., Grantham 1938–45; Pres., American M.A.R.C. 1955–61, Dynapower Systems, California 1961–73, Kendall Medical International, California 1973–82.

wonderful opportunity if he only knows how to use it. A lot of gossip about the war, to the effect that Winston has been prevailed upon to have a go at a 'second front', on a small scale which cannot possibly be successful – pray God it is not true.

Thursday 8 October   The House discussed India today on a bill brought in by Amery, rendered necessary owing to the present situation. He made rather a good speech moving the second reading but I could not hear it all ... everything was delayed by one thing or another, the most interesting being some remarks by Herbert Williams drawing attention to the Speaker's methods of selecting speakers in the House – I thought he did a difficult job very well – and clearly the House, our people at any rate, were in sympathy with what he said. The Speaker did well too, better than I liked: but clearly he will have to go – why he should stay on is a mystery to me – he is obviously bored to tears with the business and has had his day. Oliver Stanley, they say, made an admirable speech in the Indian debate but I did not hear it – of course he made a good speech – but how much further will he ever go over and above making good speeches? and what good do good speeches do a man unless he can form a party round him and show himself a leader?

Thursday 13 October   Spent most of today at the HofC – but took little or no part in the proceedings – by this I mean that I was very little 'in the Chamber'. I am finding it more and more difficult to listen to people making speeches – I was never a good hand at the job and nowadays I find it almost impossible to listen to the turgid eloquence of the Socialists who form the bulk of the orators. They most of them speak with fatal fluency – very few of them appear to be able to condense their eloquence – they repeat themselves *ad nauseam* and can never manage to close down after they have made their points. Aneurin Bevan who is, I suppose, about the ablest of them, in addition to a vast conceit, is clever and can make a good debating speech, but he has the usual failing and is always far too long. Shinwell to my mind is by far the cleverest man on the Labour side (out of the Government I mean). He can be very nasty and is a clever critic – but his unpopularity with all and sundry, his own people as well as ours, is not going to make it easy for him to get on. I am told that he refused an under-secretaryship when Winston formed his government – which was foolish conceit – for had he taken a humble place, by now he would probably have been in the Cabinet.

Thursday 15 October   I had a talk this morning with Rab Butler *re* my sub-committee's revolt. He rather surprised me by saying that he had found their memorandum interesting – my reply was interesting as an abstract work having no relation to actual facts or realities. We discussed new people to come on the committee – Oliver Stanley, Plymouth,[35] Bridgeman,[36] Castlereagh, Taylor[37] were my suggestions – he agreed.

Saturday 17 October   Matt [Ridley] ... does not look well and has evidently been through rather a serious time – a sort of blood poisoning I gather – however he is now out and about again and very busy with his production job. He is the local despot for Oliver Lyttelton and should, I imagine, do the job well – for he is not only very able but also very popular in the area. We discussed post-war conditions up here. He is fussed about the position as all the new factories and war work are in other parts of the country (ours being held to be a vulnerable area before the war) – the result will be that we shall start at a disadvantage when peace comes. He is going to try and induce those in authority to build more factories in the north.

Thursday 29 October   The news from Egypt continues good and everybody is greatly cheered by it – the papers so far are not writing it up too much – which is a good thing – for it may only be a tactical success – though of course it may develop into something bigger ... I am hopeful that something bigger is on the *tapis*[38] – *viz.* a landing somewhere on the coast of northern Africa to attack Tripoli from the west. Then, indeed, things might begin to move

---

[35] Ivor Miles Windsor-Clive (1889–1943), Con. M.P. Ludlow 1922–23; Chief Whip in the Lords 1925–29; U.S. Dominions 1929; P.S. Transport 1931–32; U.S. Colonies 1932–36; U.S. For. Office 1936–39; Ld. Lt. Glamorgan 1923–43; styled Viscount Windsor 1908–23, suc. 2nd Earl of Plymouth 1923.

[36] Robert Clive Bridgeman (1896–1982), army career 1914–37; Dep. Dir., Home Guard 1941; Dir.-Gen., Home Guard & Territorial Army 1941–44; Dep. Adjutant-Gen. 1944–45; Alderman, Shropshire County Council 1951–74; suc. 2nd Viscount Bridgeman 1935.

[37] Charles Stuart Taylor (1910–1989), Con. M.P. Eastbourne 1935–74; kt. 1954.

[38] translation: cards.

in conjunction with Alexander's advance from Egypt – would the French forces in northern Africa fight us I wonder? and what would the French fleet do? It is all very exciting and one feels somehow or other that the war is coming to a crisis – meanwhile Stalingrad is still holding out.

10

THE TIDE BEGINS TO TURN
November 1942 to May 1943

Tuesday 3 November 1942 ... this war is becoming more and more tremendous and one can see no end to it – one doubts, indeed, whether one will live to see the end of it – I should like to and yet I dread all that is to come after it – I foresee so much disappointment and discontent as the result of all the nonsense that is being given tongue to nowadays. Why should human nature be changed for the better as a result of war? Why should we expect a better world because everyone will be poorer and yet expect to live more easily and do less work? To me the future looks very bleak and I fancy that there will be a rude awakening to realities particularly in this country where, despite all that is now said to the contrary, the bulk of the population was well off and prosperous before the war.

Thursday 5 November The battle in Egypt has taken a big turn in our favour – we have broken through Rommel's line, destroyed a lot of his tanks, taken a goodly number of prisoners – and he with what is left of his force is said to be in retreat. It is a cheering performance – I had not dared to hope that we should make such good headway in such a comparatively short space of time. ... Now it looks – if only we can keep up our pressure on Rommel – that at any rate he will be driven out of Egypt, and possibly – who knows – a good deal further. We at last seem to have not only air superiority, but also better equipment and plenty of it.

Monday 9 November The news of the landing of a big Anglo-American force in northern Africa has come at last. It seems to have been kept as a real secret this time and to have been managed very effectively – Casablanca, Oran and Algiers appear to be in our hands. Our troops have had to do a bit of fighting, but nothing excessive – and the local population seems to be welcoming them. The American C-in-C is in charge of the expedition, and it looks as if our First Army were with him. Well – now things should begin to hum – we must get hold of Bizerta as quickly as possible, before the Germans can get a large force there – and then we should be able to hold north Africa and use it as a jumping off base for yet bigger things.

Tuesday 10 November   I went to the HofC early this morning as I thought it possible that Winston would make his war survey, but it is to be reserved until tomorrow. Everyone one met was highly elated at the war news – but no one I came across was unduly optimistic or imagined that we were more than 'at the end of the beginning' (to quote Winston's happy expression in his Mansion House speech today). The session was brought to an end today and tomorrow the King opens the new one.

Wednesday 11 November   Spent my 2 minutes' silence standing with Boulton[1] (one of the whips) in George Street on my way to the House. The King opened the new session, but I did not attempt to go and hear his speech – no room for M.P.s in the present HofL. Winston spoke for well over an hour: an admirable speech, not too hopeful or boastful (though many of us are a bit dubious about ringing the church bells next Sunday).[2]

Thursday 12 November   The debate on the address began this morning. Had a talk with Oliver Stanley in the Smoking Room – he has decided to try and get our people to revive the party in the House – and to advocate the ending of the '1922' Committee and to turn it into a regular party meeting.[3] This seems to me an

---

[1] William Whytehead Boulton (1873–1949), Con. M.P. Sheffield Central 1931–45; whip 1940–44; cr. Bart. 1944.

[2] Church bells had been silent since the summer of 1940, when it was decided that they would be used as the alarm signal in the event of an invasion; it was now proposed to ring them in celebration and thanksgiving for the victory at El Alamein.

[3] The 1922 Committee originated as an independent initiative and was not formally a part of the Conservative Party organization; membership was confined to backbench M.P.s, and thus it was not a forum for the whole parliamentary party.

excellent plan and I am all for it – but, needless to say, he does not intend himself to become the Party Secretary – too busy, etc., etc. – nor will he join my constitutional sub-committee. He never will come out into the open or take any kind of lead. He is going to raise the party question next Wednesday at the meeting of the '22 Committee – unfortunately I cannot be there...

Sunday 15 November   The bells rang out today all over England ... But for God's mercy I don't imagine the bells would have been ringing today, for without divine help one feels that we would not have survived after Dunkirk. What a crisis we lived through in the summer of 1940 and how few of our people seemed to realize it – or do now for the matter of that! We are a strange race – such a mixture of stupidity, sound common sense, kindness of heart and self complacency there never was in this world and never will be again.

Saturday 21 November   The German position in Europe is so immensely strong and one does not see how we can ever be strong enough to force our way through into Germany – on paper it looks almost an impossible task – and yet one knows that it can and must be done – the Allies have got to beat the Germans to a frazzle in their own country. But I wonder whether the Americans fully realize this? I should doubt it – and yet it is up to them to supply the manpower. What always makes me feel happier about things is when I begin to think of what Hitler and Co. must be thinking. They must realize well enough by now that the game is up, so far at any rate as a German victory of a full-blooded type is concerned. The best they can hope for – bar accidents – is a draw, and that can only come about if the Allied nations get too fed up to go on fighting. This I hope and believe is unlikely, but one can never be sure of anything in this world. Even the people of this country might become tired of the war if they saw no end to it and if their food supply got really bad – and one never knows how long the Russians and Americans may be willing to carry on.

Sunday 22 November   Some changes in the War Cabinet are announced tonight. Stafford Cripps for some reason or other leaves it to become Minister of Aircraft Production (Llewellin, the present

Minister, is going to the U.S.A.); Morrison[4] enters the W.C.; Oliver Stanley becomes Secretary of State for the Colonies *vice* Bobbety Cranborne (whose health I imagine is none too good). O.S.'s appointment is rather disconcerting: perhaps his motion in the '22 Committee has induced the Government to absorb him – but he has always told me that he could not serve under Winston. Well, it is never easy to refuse a job in the Cabinet I suppose and O.S. is very ambitious. Anthony Eden is to lead the HofC *vice* Cripps. I wonder what all this means?

Tuesday 24 November   In the Smoking Room at the HofC today I found a lot of people much exercised in their minds about our employing Darlan[5] – of course it is a pity to have to use the services of such a man – but one feels that Dakar would never have come in with us without him – not without a fight I mean – nor probably would the French administrative officers in Algiers [have] cooperated with us against Vichy had not Darlan been on our side. In any case people who are not in the know cannot judge a matter of this kind: it must be left to the Government and they in their turn must be guided by the men on the spot. I only wish that the French fleet would hearken unto Darlan and come out of Toulon before it is too late.[6]

Wednesday 25 November   Mrs. Tate and her friends had a day out in the HofC today – equal compensation for injuries received when fire-watching by women and men. On the face of it there would appear to be nothing against such a suggestion – but the War Cabinet having gone into the matter say that such a change would upset the whole business of compensation allowances and are not prepared to make the change without first having made the

---

[4] Herbert Morrison (q.v.), Home Secretary from 3 Oct. 1940 to 23 May 1945.

[5] Jean Louis Xavier François Darlan (1881–1942), executive head of French Navy 1933–39, C. in C. 1939–40; Min. of Marine in Vichy Govt. 1940–42, Chief Min. Feb. 1941-Apr. 1942; was in Algiers when Allied troops landed on 8 Nov. 1942, disassociated himself from Vichy when German forces entered the 'unoccupied zone' in the following days, ordered French forces in N. Africa not to fire on Allied forces and offered to collaborate. Darlan was regarded more favourably by the Americans, leading to inter-allied frictions; he was assassinated in Algiers on 24 Dec. 1942.

[6] French warships at the main naval base of Toulon scuttled themselves on 27 Nov. 1942 in order to avoid capture by the German forces occupying the Vichy zone.

House appreciate what the results would be – so they proposed the appointment of a Select Committee to go into the whole thing. As they did this I felt obliged to support the Government – Mrs Tate & Co. seized the opportunity to divide the House – mainly for advertisement no doubt – and she and her friends will get much kudos for doing so – she made a first class speech into the bargain. I find her a nasty, hard, conceited, little creature – but she undoubtedly has great ability and the courage of her convictions.

Wednesday 2 December   The Beveridge report[7] was available this afternoon – it seems to me to make big promises on an insufficient basis – a vast increase of expenditure on social services based on the supposition that our trade and industry will be as great after the war as it was before the war and that unemployment figures will not exceed a million odd. I am, and always have been, in favour of the consolidation of all the insurance schemes – and of course I should like to see higher benefits – but it seems to me sheer folly to promise higher benefits unless you are sure you can guarantee them – and this seems to me [is] what Beveridge is doing. ... Anthony Eden wound up for the Government this afternoon on the Labour amendment to the address. He devoted himself mainly to foreign affairs and said the usual things not particularly well. But of course I have a low opinion of his mental capacity and do not regard him as a great Foreign Secretary. I don't think that he is improving as a speaker – and I cannot think that he is [a] suitable man to lead the Party – not unless he comes along a lot.

Thursday 3 December   I lunched and 'boarded'[8] in Lombard Street today – the insurance pundits were rather upset by the Beveridge plan. They say that it must cost a deal more than he has estimated for and is going to be much more difficult to work than Beveridge seems to think. Our group of companies luckily are not much involved in industrial insurance and so will not be greatly affected by the scheme if it comes in[to] force. In the House we had the I.L.P. amendment to the Address – it was defeated by over 300

---

[7] The *Report on Social Insurance and Allied Services*, written mainly by the chairman of the Interdepartmental Ctte., Sir William Beveridge (q.v.); it attracted great popular attention, and is regarded as the founding charter of the 'Welfare State'.

[8] A board meeting of the Liverpool, London & Globe insurance company.

votes to 5. To me it seems all wrong that the Speaker should always accept this I.L.P. amendment – it is the same thing over and over again and it is absurd that the time of the House should be wasted so often by such a ridiculously small group of members.

Saturday 5 December   A raw, beastly day – felt that I ought to go to a meeting of the Tyne District Council of the League of Nations Union – to see what they are up to – they always invite me to their meetings. Found a dreary little group of people at 66 Jesmond Road and heard an address by one K. Zilliacus[9] who for 20 years was an official of the Information Section of the L[eague] of N[ations] Secretariat at Geneva. He spoke of the world future, not too badly, but of course most of what he had to propose was in my opinion impracticable. He seemed to hover between a revival of the old League and some species of federation – it was all rather vague and visionary – but the man put his arguments well, even if they were based on fallacies – and of course he pleased the band of silly old and young Liberals who formed the audience. It is odd how people of a certain type cling to old beliefs and really imagine that the world can be put right by agreements on paper and leagues etc. According to Zilliacus Germany, Italy and Japan are not to be permitted to join in his new world order until they have set up egalitarian governments. I asked him one or two questions – but tired of the business, and went off to catch my train earlier than was necessary. The more I see of the L. of N. Union and the half-baked intelligentsia which constitutes its membership, the more depressed I become. Their wishy washy internationalism and little England outlook fills me with rage that such people should still exist. They seem to visualize a new world in which we as a nation should step out of the picture for good and all and hand over our heritage to all the cranks and faddists who preach an international gospel – meaning nothing but leading to chaos – and this after 2 great wars.

Sunday 6 December   The news today is that we have clearly had a setback in Tunisia and that the Russian offensive is slowing

[9] Konni Zilliacus (1894–1967), Lab. M.P. Gateshead 1945–50 (Ind. Lab. 1949–50), Manchester Gorton 1955–67; worked in Information Section, League of Nations Secretariat 1919–39; expelled from the Lab. Party May 1949, readmitted Feb. 1952; a member of the 'Labour Independent Group' 1949–50.

down – undoubtedly the Germans are fine fighters – but they are on the defensive now, however much they pretend they are not, and it is only a matter of time for them to collapse as they did in 1918 – but it will take a longer time in this war than it did in the last to smash them and there is always a danger of the Allies tiring. Italy really looks like collapsing already – but one doubts whether the Germans will let them break away from the Axis and so long as Mussolini remains in power he will keep his people going I should imagine. Colville has been appointed Governor of Bombay to succeed Roger Lumley – a good sensible man I should imagine, without much imagination – safe rather than showy – presumably what is wanted today in India. The rumours as to Linlithgow's[10] successor continue – I see that Greene's[11] name is now mentioned. I like him personally but should doubt his being a forcible enough character for the times. He is one of the Edward Halifax type and has a host of admirers – the usual All Souls success. Of course he is a brilliant lawyer and is, I gather, a great success as Master of the Rolls – he might be better than some of the others who are tipped.

Tuesday 8 December   ... a long heart to heart ... with Charley this afternoon in Londonderry House where he was lying in bed recovering from his operation. He is a weak, rather vain, man – but when you get to know him has a heart of gold. Today he could talk of nothing but his difficulties (wholly imaginary) about making recommendations to the Bench to the L[ord] C[hancellor]. If only he would keep a tighter hold of the Labour people, there would be no trouble at all. He told me today that he was recommending Lawther[12] as a J.P. – a wholly unnecessary thing to do – it will be severely criticized by law-abiding citizens.[13] I advised him strongly to reconsider the matter – and I think persuaded him: I hope so at

[10] (Victor) Alexander John Hope (1887–1952), Civil Ld., Admiralty 1922–24; Con. Party Dep. Chairman 1924–26; Chairman, India Joint Select Ctte. 1933–34; Viceroy of India 1936–43; styled Earl of Hopetoun 1887–1908, suc. 2nd Marquess of Linlithgow 1908, K.G. 1943.

[11] Wilfrid Arthur Greene (1883–1952); Lord Justice of Appeal 1935–37; Master of the Rolls 1937–49; Lord of Appeal in Ordinary 1949–50; kt. 1935, cr. Baron Greene 1941.

[12] William Lawther (1889–1976), Lab. cand. S. Shields 1922–24, M.P. Barnard Castle 1929–31; Pres., M.F.G.B. 1939–54; Pres., T.U.C. 1949; kt. 1949.

[13] Lawther had been jailed for two months for intimidation and interference with food distribution during the General Strike of 1926.

any rate. I honestly don't think that one should go out of one's way to put a man with Lawther's record on the Bench just because he happens to be President of the Miners' Federation.

Wednesday 9 December   This afternoon I listened to Leo Amery deliver an address to the '22 Committee on constitutional reform – most of his suggestions we have already considered in our sub-committee. ... No one with whom I have spoken approves of our taking over Darlan – but presumably the Americans would not have accepted him unless it seemed the best thing to do. These wretched French are all at sixes and sevens and it may well have been that unless we had taken on Darlan, some of them might have turned nasty.

Thursday 10 December   Winston made an excellent speech this morning in secret session on the Darlan business. He made it quite clear that we had nothing to do with regard to the recognition of the man – were not even consulted – nor apparently was the American Govt. The whole thing was settled by the American G.H.Q. on the spot – and the reason for taking on Darlan was that he was the only man all the other Frenchmen would agree to obey. We had intended that Giraud[14] should be the big noise and we brought him out of France by submarine for that purpose – but apparently some of the French generals and officials in North Africa wouldn't agree to his overlordship. To get hold of Dakar, Oran, Algiers, etc., and to have no trouble with the French administration were the reasons which influenced the Americans and one must hope that their decision was a right one – at any rate as the men on the spot they were best qualified to make it. I did not hear any of the rest of the debate as I had to lunch ... and then had to preside over my constitutional subcommittee in [the] Moses Room. We had quite a good attendance which included Bridgeman, our newest recruit. Hankey came to tell us his views regarding a standing committee on the F[oreign] O[ffice] and war departments. He was quite interesting and I am glad to say did not look favourably on the suggestion – he plumped as I have done on

[14] Henri Honoré Giraud (1879–1949), French army career; G.O.C. 9th Army 1940; imprisoned 1940–42, escaped 1942; High Comm., French N. & W. Africa 1942; Co-President, French Ctte. for Nat. Liberation, May-Oct. 1943; C. in C. Free French Army 1943–44.

utilizing the C[ommittee of] I[mperial] D[efence] as an educational centre for opposition M.P.s.

Friday 18 December   The papers today say that Rommel's forces are cut in two – that advanced troops of the Eighth Army have managed to get between his retreating columns ... The Russians claim further progress near Stalingrad, south-west of the town; they are also said to be advancing on their central front – altogether the news is cheering today – even the French ships at Dakar and Alexandria are promised to us by – Darlan! I have no confidence, I fear, in Darlan, or, for the matter of that, in any of these Frenchmen. They are at sixes and sevens among themselves and none of them – not even De Gaulle & Co. – really [is] well-disposed towards us. It is to be hoped that they will play the game by the Americans – but even that is doubtful I should imagine. They are disgruntled and ashamed of themselves – and envious of us and the Americans and the Russians.

Sunday 20 December   The Jews are in a state of panic as they assert that the order has gone out for their total extermination in Europe, and really the stories of German atrocities are almost past belief. It is strange that any civilized human beings – even in war time – should behave as they do – it proves their innate stupidity more than anything else – for the whole teaching of history is that brutality in the long run never pays.

Monday 21 December   ... things in general seem to be going all right – but what a long time we have to go before these bloody Germans are beaten – to say nothing of the Japanese: I sometimes wonder whether we and the Americans will have the patience and guts to fight the thing to a finish? It is heresy at the moment to suggest that we may grow tired of the eternal struggle and the immense effort that it must entail. Here, and still less in the U.S.A., do people realize all that we shall have to endure before it is over. So far, except for the bombing raids, our people have scarcely suffered at all during the war – indeed, a large section of them are probably better off than they ever have been. But soon we shall begin to suffer as regards rations I expect – and probably from renewed bombing – nor will things at the front move in our favour nearly as quickly as so many people imagine will be the case. The

Nazi leaders have no intention of giving in and will continue fighting to the last gasp – and so will the Japanese – it is war to the death. They are counting on tiring us out – and it does not seem to me that this is impressed upon our people half enough; on the contrary, the papers are always emphasizing our successes and leading the public thereby to believe that an early end of the war is to be anticipated – it is a very dangerous delusion to foster.

Tuesday 22 December   The death of Apsley,[15] M.P., in an air crash in the Middle East is announced today. He is a loss to the HofC – the type of Member who can least be spared. I knew him slightly (I doubt whether many people knew him well – he did not much frequent the Smoking Room and was not gregarious) but I liked him. His death makes the seventh vacancy to be filled in the House of Commons: I see that some of the other vacancies are going to have contested elections – which, on the whole, seems to me to be [a] good thing. The only pity is that most of the so-called 'Independent' candidates are such useless freaks.

Friday 25 December   Darlan has been murdered in Algiers – by someone whose 'nationality is unknown' according to the wireless report, which seems rather a silly business – presumably the murderer is a 'Free Frenchman'[16] ... On the whole I should say that this was the best way of disposing of Darlan – his record of treachery and deceit is a bad one and obviously the De Gaulle people could not be expected to have any dealings with him – so he is better out of the way...

Wednesday 30 December   The Russian advance continues – it really is beginning to look rather impressive on the map and if half of what they (the Russians) report is true ... things are beginning to look rather awkward for the enemy.

Friday 1 January 1943   Some new Government appointments were announced yesterday. Harold Macmillan comes off best – he is to go to North Africa as our ministerial representative. He should

---

[15] Allen Algernon Bathurst (1895–1942), Con. M.P. Southampton 1922–29, Bristol Central 1931–42; P.P.S. to J.T.C. Moore-Brabazon 1925–28, to T. Inskip 1936–39; styled Lord Apsley 1895–1942, heir of 7th Earl Bathurst but predeceased him.

[16] The assassin was in fact a fanatical French royalist.

do well if he has the guts to stand up to the Americans and is clever with the French. Harry Crookshank is to succeed W.S. Morrison at the G.P.O. – the latter is to be the new minister in charge of post war house planning or whatever the ministry is to be called.[17] *Oi evteλλoi*[18] certainly don't seem to have much use for Crookshank: I never can make out why – because he always appears to be efficient and to know his job. Ralph Assheton[19] succeeds him as Financial Secretary: he strikes me as an able fellow and he has good manners – but not one of them has much personality or is anything more than 'clever' – where is our leader of the future?

Wednesday 13 January ... to the Caxton Hall for the meeting of the Conservative Executive, Eugene Ramsden in his usual form – Lady Hillingdon asked me if I would stand again for the chairmanship of the Committee – I said I thought that they had better get some more generally popular figure.

Sunday 17 January The news today from Russia is very cheering even if one feels inclined to discount even half of the Russian claims. They say that they have made a big break-through south of Voronezh ... and that they have the German Stalingrad forces in their pocket. It is a tremendous performance, and they show no signs of stopping ... In north Africa the Eighth Army is attacking Rommel, and the report tonight is that he is again on the run ...

Thursday 21 January ... the debate in secret session on manpower – its second day – Bevin, they tell me, has done well in it and on the whole gave a satisfactory account of the situation. ... presided over my sub-committee ... we discussed the Civil Service and came to interesting decisions. Archie James[20] was present as representing the 'Central Committee' – apparently he is now Rab

---

[17] Ministry of Town and Country Planning.

[18] translation: those in command.

[19] Ralph Assheton (1901–1984), Con. M.P. Rushcliffe 1934–45, City of London 1945–50, Blackburn W. 1950–55; P.P.S. to W. Ormsby-Gore 1936–38; P.S. Labour 1939–42, Supply 1942–43; F.S.T. 1943–44; Con. Party Chairman 1944–46; Chairman, Public Accounts Ctte. 1948–50; cr. Bart. 1945, Baron Clitheroe 1955; also suc. his father as 2nd Bart. Sep. 1955.

[20] Archibald William Henry James (1893–1980), Con. M.P. Wellingborough 1931–45; P.P.S. to R.A. Butler 1936–38, 1943–45; Hon. 1st Sec. in Embassy at Madrid 1940–41; kt. 1945.

Butler's P.P.S. – I suppose that there is something to him, but he always strikes me as rather a tiresome little fellow who rates himself too highly. ... Clifton Brown has been made Chairman of Committees *vice* Dennis Herbert – no sign of the Speaker resigning I regret to say.

Tuesday 26 January   We had a secret session at 5 p.m., when Attlee informed us that Winston and Roosevelt had met at Casablanca and that Giraud and De Gaulle[21] had shaken hands, that a tremendous war council had been held between the chiefs of the British and American staffs, etc. It all sounded very nice and exciting, but I am told that Fleet Street knew all about everything early this morning – naturally Shinwell, Bevan & Co. were annoyed – but what did it really matter? Someone asked where the P.M. now was, but this information was not vouchsafed to us. He is certainly not back in England and the general impression is that he has gone off to Russia – sooner or later one feels that he will disappear into the blue never to return.

Tuesday 2 February   The Russians have finished off the Germans at Stalingrad – truly a colossal triumph – a smashing defeat for the Germans – one wonders how even Hitler's popularity can survive such a disaster – still more how the German army can survive it – and yet there are no visible signs that either Hitler's prestige or his army's morale is cracking. We have a long way yet to go before this war is won – my own belief is that it will last a deal longer than the last one: I only hope that I may be wrong. I spent most of the day at the HofC. The place, I think, gets duller and duller – a certain number of people spend their time in the usual game of caballing, but this game cannot be played with any semblance of reality these days because there is no possible chance of upsetting the Government and no kind of an alternative leader to Winston – nor, as a matter of fact, are there very obvious alternatives to the existing Ministers. Some of them may not be of a very high calibre

---

[21] Charles André Joseph Marie De Gaulle (1890–1970), career in French army from 1909; commanded a division in May 1940, escaped to Britain after fall of France; established the 'Free French', became leader of French Ctte. of Nat. Liberation in Algiers, June 1943; entered Paris Aug. 1944; his regime recognized as French govt. by the Allies Oct. 1944; Pres. of provisional govt. 1945–46; head of 'govt. of national safety' 1958–59; 1st Pres. of 5th Republic 1959–69.

but there are, so far as I can see, no people in the House nowadays who would cut better figures in office than they do.

Wednesday 3 February   I lunched at the House with Douglas Clifton Brown and Austin Hopkinson. The last named is more pig-headed and conceited than ever, but one cannot help liking the man despite his egotism and self-sufficiency. Late in the afternoon we had quite an amusing episode, and succeeded in making the Government withdraw, or promise to withdraw, a most all-embracing and dictatorial order of the Minister of War Transport. Had there been a division we should have beaten the Govt. Noel-Baker, the Parliamentary Secretary, had a difficult job and did not do particularly well – the Labour people were as usual very silly and asserted that we were only objecting to the order in order 'to humiliate' a Labour minister. They really are the silliest lot of children without the slightest sense of humour, always on the lookout for anything that can be construed as an attack upon their own friends – they still suffer from an inferiority complex.

Thursday 4 February   Had a talk with Onslow about our sub-committee, whose work he takes very seriously – I wish I did! I am sick to death of our intelligentsia, especially of Douglas Jerrold whose conceit and certainty about everything annoy me. The more I see of these literary pundits who write about history, etc., the more I realize how hopeless it is for people, however intelligent they may be, to appreciate political and parliamentary matters without practical experience. For instance not one of these men on our sub-committee – Phillimore, Jerrold, Bryant or Kitson Clark – has an idea of the practical working of the HofC or even a glimmer of knowledge about constituency work. Their theories are superb, but they fail to appreciate the realities – nor do they understand in the least how the machine works. Their one idea is that Parliament has lost public confidence and that this confidence can only be revived by doing away with professional politicians and replacing them by bright young business men, Ministers must also be assisted by councils (consultative) representing industries, etc., and the Civil Service must be taught business methods etc., etc. It is all so very silly.

Friday 5 February   I suppose – if the war ends within a year or

so – there will be an election and I will stand again, but that will
be the last election for me presumably – and whether or not my
Fridays in Newcastle will help me to win the seat next time is
somewhat doubtful. The seat is on the face of things quite a safe
one – I suppose that by lunching every week in the Conservative
Club I am getting better known to my constituents which is all to
the good.

Saturday 6 February   Winston has been in Tripoli, reviewing the
Eighth Army and no doubt enjoying himself vastly. He must have
an amazing physical toughness to do so much air travelling, but I
can't help thinking that he must be taking a terrible lot out of
himself.

Thursday 11 February[22]   Winston made a fine speech today – in
his best style – the man's vitality and self-confidence are superb.
... I have spent the usual 'busy' day – mainly at the HofC. There
was not much gossip – but Winston's speech has given general
satisfaction. I am glad that he gave so much attention to the 'U'
boat difficulties because obviously everything hangs upon our being
able to cope with this danger at sea – unless we can overcome it
the invasion of the continent is going to be a difficult business and
the lengthening of the war is a certainty. On the whole he was
optimistic but not, I am glad to say, too optimistic – and in all he
said he was careful not to enter too hopefully into the realms of
prophecy or boasting. I had a word with Douglas Hacking. The
large anti-Govt. vote he got against the second reading of the
Catering Bill has pleased him – and he thinks that the Govt. will
be more amenable than they were at first as a result of it. I confess
I rather doubt this – Bevin is an obstinate brute and Winston, they
say, believes in him. In addition to this, so many of our party –
more especially the younger members – are more 'left' than the
Labour Party – terribly afraid of being thought unprogressive –
and nowadays to be progressive you must be all out for totalitarian

---

[22] The diary entry of 10 Feb. was written by mistake on the first three-quarters
of the page intended for 11 Feb.; Headlam drew a line across the page and then
wrote the first part of the entry of 11 Feb. below this, continuing the rest of the
entry on the page intended for 10 Feb. and amending the printed title on both
pages.

methods of administration however much you may condemn such methods in Germany or in Italy.

Tuesday 16 February   The first day of the Beveridge debate has not been very entertaining. The Govt. put up John Anderson to state their case and he read out a brief which detained the House for an hour and a half and bored and irritated everybody – no doubt it will read all right, but it was a weary thing to listen to. The Labour people were, or professed to be, very angry that the Govt. did not accept Beveridge's recommendations *en bloc* – others of us thought that they were accepting too many of them. Clearly the whole scheme is dependent upon finance, and I am glad to say that Anderson rubbed this in all the time.

Wednesday 17 February   I fired off a little speech on the Beveridge report this afternoon – not the least what I had intended to say, or rather a much curtailed edition of what I had intended saying – however, it went quite well and pleased the saner Conservatives – Eddie Winterton did not approve of it and took the opportunity of being grossly rude to me on the front opposition bench, for the second time since I have been back in the House. He really is an insufferable creature as I felt obliged to tell him this afternoon. The kindest thing I feel is to regard him as scarcely *compos mentis*[23] and this I gather is the general feeling with regard to him. I listened this evening[24] to William *Cantuar* appealing to us to feed Europe

---

[23] translation: in possession of one's faculties, i.e. sane.

[24] The location of this address is unclear: Temple does not seem to have spoken publicly on these issues at this point, either in a radio broadcast, in the House of Lords, or in a meeting reported in the press. However, exactly two weeks previously, on Wednesday 27 Jan. 1943, he had addressed a private meeting of M.P.s and peers on this topic. That meeting decided to send a deputation to the cabinet and to adjourn for a week to await their report. This may either have been that reconvened session postponed by a further week, or another private meeting. It is unlikely that Headlam is referring here to the 27 Jan. meeting. The earlier part of the entry refers to Headlam's speech on the Beveridge report which was delivered on 17 Feb., and this section flows directly on from this and would seem to have been written at the same time. There are no missing days in the diary during this period, and no reason why Headlam would misplace an event by two weeks. Furthermore, it would seem that he was not at the 27 Jan. meeting as the diary entry for that day mentions an appointment at 5.00 p.m., after which Headlam had 'a lonely dinner' at his Club 'and am off to bed 9 p.m.'

and save the Jews.[25] He did not tell us how we were to do these two things and I feel very strongly that a man in his position should not go talking so 'bigly' without a little more balance. I fancy that he is beginning to bore people by being so constantly in the limelight. He is far too much a politician to make a really great Archbishop of Canterbury.

Thursday 18 February   I always feel relieved after I have made a speech in the HofC – mainly because I feel that I need not make another one for some time. My little effort yesterday seems to have been better than I suppose, as several people have congratulated me upon it and it does not read too badly. I suppose I shall be attacked by the Beveridge maniacs but I anticipate the approval of sane people. I lunched ... then I went back to the House to vote for the Government. Practically the whole Labour Party voted in the other lobby – it was of course just a party move for after Herbert Morrison's winding up speech (which was quite excellent) there was no earthly reason for dividing against the Govt. In my opinion all this fuss about the Beveridge report will fade out: it ought never to have been had the Government acted more wisely and not allowed it to be published until after they had studied it and made up their minds about it, and most certainly Beveridge ought to have been forbidden to puff it on the B.B.C. etc.

Saturday 20 February   There has been a bulletin about Winston today which has rather fussed one – he is said to be suffering from 'severe catarrh' which may mean trouble I should imagine. I little thought in the past that I should feel anxious regarding Winston – but his departure from this world today would I feel be a real calamity. There is virtually no one of any calibre to succeed him – he is as nearly indispensable at this moment as any man could be. The Russians still report progress, but there are reports of an early thaw which may upset things – the German resistance, too, is clearly getting more stiff.

[25] The two issues were not directly connected; there was evidence that the blockade was leading to starvation conditions in parts of occupied Europe, in particular in Greece and the Low Countries, whilst on 16 Dec. 1942 Eden had made a statement in the Commons which for the first time affirmed that the Nazi regime was murdering the Jewish population.

Sunday 21 February   Beatrice and I went into Newcastle after luncheon by car and attended the 'Red Army' demonstration in the City Hall – Oliver Lyttelton represented the War Cabinet. He made a good speech but he certainly has not yet achieved the knack of 'putting it over'. The other speakers were Charles Trevelyan[26] (who fairly let himself go politically: among other things he asserted that every second man in the Russian Army had received a secondary education) [and] Arthur Lambert. The audience was mainly composed of sailors, merchant seamen, soldiers, airmen and representatives of trades and industries, A.R.P., Fire Service, etc. with of course a large attendance of extremists in the galleries for whom the whole business was a political demonstration. On the platform were all the swells – generals, admirals, air marshals, M.P.s, the nobility and gentry. The show was well done ... The news regarding Winston is better: Oliver assured me that he was not really bad – but personally I never like catarrh and patches on the lung for men with thick necks and double chins. The news from Russia is satisfactory, but from Tunis not so good...

Thursday 25 February   I listened to Grigg introduce the Army Estimates – he read out rather a good statement and he has now learned a bit and can make himself heard. I met him later in the day in the Smoking Room having tea with James Stuart and Tommie Dugdale – I find him rather an unpleasing little man but presumably he is able. He was quite civil. He told us that Alexander had cabled to say that the trouble was that the Americans were not yet a capable fighting force – which I think that we all of us had already realized. The Speaker is said to be very ill – indeed, Dennis Herbert ... spoke as if he were on the point of death.

Friday 26 February   I presided over the Area Executive this afternoon: quite a good attendance, even one of the Cumberland people turning up. I dined at the Conservative Club and later in the evening received a deputation from a body which calls itself the 'Voters Policy Association' – quite decent people who appear to represent middle class opinion and are opposed to the growth

[26] Charles Philips Trevelyan (1870–1958), Lib. M.P. Elland 1899–1918, Lab. M.P. Newcastle Central 1922–31; P.S. Educ. 1908–14; Pres. Bd. of Educ. 1924, 1929–31; Ld. Lt. Northumberland 1930–49; suc. 3rd Bart. 1928.

of bureaucracy, etc., etc. – about eight of them, men and women, came to see me tonight and talked more or less intelligently with me for over an hour – whether or not I satisfied them I am sure I don't know, but I am glad to find that such a body does exist in Newcastle and that it seems 'alive'.

Monday 1 March   I cannot remember so early a spring as this ... all the fruit trees, lilacs, etc., are green in the bud ... The early thaw in Russia is unfortunate ... The German Army is undoubtedly an amazingly efficient machine and its discipline [is] beyond all praise. The suggestion now is that Hitler has more or less faded out and that the German generals have taken full control of the direction of operations in the field: no longer is the show to be directed by the *Führer*'s 'intuition'. One wonders how much truth there is in all these rumours about Hitler – some suggest that the man is dead – my own belief is that he is very much alive, though it may be that he is not so near the front as he would have us believe.

Tuesday 2 March   The House got through its work very early today and I might, I think, have spared myself from this week's visit to London. ... No one seems greatly worried by Hitler's changes in his naval command – to me they seem to be rather interesting – it looks, in my opinion, as if the German fleet were going to be utilized much more actively in the coming months – commerce raiding possibly and in an effort to interfere with our operations on the Continent. Certainly Hitler & Co. won't allow it to remain in port: it will die in battle this time – and will give us a lot of trouble before it is sunk. The Speaker apparently is dying – his heart is very weak and from what Ralph Verney[27] told me tonight he cannot last long. I suppose one must regard him as a successful Speaker – but it is unfortunate that he did not retire some years ago – latterly he has clearly been bored with his work and always adopted the line of least resistance. Personally he has always been friendly towards me, but I have never known him well. I hope that his successor will be Douglas Clifton Brown – he has

---

[27] Ralph Verney (1879–1959), Military Sec. to the Viceroy of India 1916–21; Sec. to the Speaker 1921–55; Examiner of Private Bills, House of Commons 1927–44; kt. 1928, cr. Bart. 1946.

done well as Chairman of Ways and Means and everybody likes him. It will be interesting to see whether, if he becomes Speaker, he will remain equally accessible & friendly.

Wednesday 3 March   The Speaker died today whilst the House was sitting – the first time I believe that a Speaker has died while the House was *actually* in session. Verney (the Speaker's secretary) came into the House and told Clifton Brown who was in the chair – C.B. slipped out of the chair without a word and the Clerk assistant got up and told us that it was with extreme sorrow that he had to inform us that Mr. Speaker died this afternoon – a few words from Anthony Eden, the Leader of the House, and from the leaders of the other groups – then the Clerk by direction of the House put the question and we adjourned till Tuesday next. Without a Speaker we are incapable of doing anything, being a body without a head. Attended the 1922 Committee later in the afternoon – the succession to the Speakership was discussed – except for Ned Grigg and a few others, almost everybody was in favour of having Douglas Clifton Brown as Speaker. I spoke strongly in his favour – no one wanted Milner[28] to become Chairman of Ways and Means, but I don't see how he can be passed over – the mistake was ever letting him be made Deputy Chairman.

Thursday 4 March   ... I attended the 1922 Committee – a large attendance to discuss the succession to the Chair, etc. Almost everybody was clearly anxious for Douglas [Clifton] Brown to be Speaker, but some people did not like the idea of Milner becoming Chairman of Ways and Means – and of course he is not the right type of man for the job – however, the impression is that the Labour Party will make a fuss if he is not promoted and so I suppose promoted he will be. The only other man mentioned for the Speakership was G[wilym] Lloyd George – but no one seemed keen to have him.

Tuesday 9 March   Douglas Clifton Brown was duly elected Speaker today. He made an excellent little speech and seemed to

[28] James Milner (1889–1967), Lab. M.P. Leeds S.E. 1929–51; P.P.S. to C. Addison 1930–31; Chairman of Standing Cttes. 1935–43; Dep. Chairman of Ways & Means Jan.-Mar. 1943, Chairman & Dep. Speaker Mar. 1943-May 1945, Sep. 1945-Oct. 1951; cr. Baron Milner of Leeds 1951.

enjoy the performance. I sat in the Smoking Room with him previous to the meeting of the House and watched him drink his last drink in that room – I am afraid that he will miss the social side of the HofC a deal more than he imagines. Old Dennis Herbert who was also there was taking all the credit for having discovered Douglas and I believe that he is justified in all he said. He told me that when he suggested to Douglas that he should become deputy chairman of Committees Douglas doubted his ability to take on the job – but eventually did so saying that he was sure of one thing – that the House of Commons could not frighten him. This I am sure is the secret of his success – at any rate it is the first essential to success in the chair. Lunched in the House with Archie Southby who is nowadays a very busy ass – a good fellow all the same. ... Dined at the Travellers. Ralph Verney told me that Algie Fitzroy had quite decided to leave the chair even after war was certain and only agreed to stay on at the personal request of Neville Chamberlain, then P.M. If he had retired then, no one could possibly have said a word against him – today Cunningham-Reid in a very ill-advised intervention said what a good many people have been thinking.

Wednesday 10 March   James [Stuart] much relieved to have got over the Speaker and Chairman of Ways and Means crisis – Milner had to have the latter job apparently or there would have been a Socialist revolt – Charles Williams[29] delighted to be deputy chairman: he got the job after Wedderburn had refused it.

Thursday 11 March   No particular news or gossip today – everyone rather gloomy about our Russian allies who are clearly getting a knock. They are asserting that 12 fresh divisions have been brought against them from the Western Front – and no doubt our left wingers will be attacking the Govt. for not having embarked upon 'a second front' – it looks to me as if we have done all we can do in north Africa for the time being ... meanwhile our General Montgomery is talking too big to please me – I hate boasting in time of war: it really serves no useful purpose and often makes you look rather silly.

[29] Charles Williams (1886–1955), Con. M.P. Tavistock 1918–22, Torquay 1924–55; P.P.S. to Sir A. Griffith-Boscawen 1921–22; Dep. Chairman of Ways & Means 1943–45, Chairman & Dep. Speaker 1945.

Sunday 14 March I am afraid that the Russian offensive has now about run its course and all that one wants to know is whether or not our allies will be able to hold on to what they have captured. The Germans seem to have pulled themselves together but whether they are in a position to renew the offensive is quite another matter. Goebbels has thought fit to deny the rumours about Hitler but not very convincingly: personally I hope that the man is still in supreme command of the German Armies, but I don't suppose that he is.

Monday 15 March I have practically cleared up all my correspondence which is a mercy – on the whole I am, I think, more lucky than most M.P.s as regards letters. Someone told me at the HofC the other day that his average post was fifty letters a day which may or may not be true – but I have noticed that many people seem to have a larger pile of letters handed to them at the HofC post office than I do.

Tuesday 16 March Winston was back in the House today and apparently was given a great reception which I missed. Anthony Eden has gone off to the U.S.A. to discuss things: somehow or other I have no great confidence in the man: he always strikes me as mediocre and futile – but I fear that he may become leader of the Conservative Party when Winston goes. His stock is not very high in the present HofC – but there appears to be no one else to compete with him and he has a strong backing in the press and I think also in the country. It is a pity that neither Oliver Stanley nor Oliver Lyttelton cuts more ice – both of them are abler men than Anthony – but no one seems to feel well disposed towards either of them as a leader. People are a bit depressed about the Russian reverses and nervous as to their results.

Wednesday 17 March Rab Butler attended the Conservative Committee (no longer the 1922 Committee)[30] and talked about education. He spoke well but did not disclose much about his

---

[30] When the decision was taken on 10 Mar. 1943 to widen the membership to all M.P.s in receipt of the Conservative whip, and so include serving Ministers, the name was changed to 'the Conservative and Unionist Members' Committee'. However, the shorthand term '1922' remained in common use, and by 1951 the 1922 Committee had reverted to both its former composition of backbenchers only and its former name.

proposed bill – people, however, seemed quite pleased with what he said: he has a certain following in the House, but I have never heard anyone talk of him as a prospective leader. Nevertheless, in my opinion, there is more in him than there is in Anthony Eden – but unfortunately he has little or no glamour and perhaps, too, is a little too careful about making a false step. If you want to get to the top (and I believe Rab is ambitious) one has to take risks some time or other.

Thursday 18 March   I meant to speak today in the debate on the Govt.'s proposals for the reform of the 'Foreign Service', but there were a lot of would-be speakers ... I don't think that the changes in the 'Foreign Service' amount to much though they sound much more 'democratic' – I fancy that the same type of man will go on running the show in the various embassies and ministries – politically at any rate – obviously a wider entry for the service is desirable, and ... a development of the commercial side of diplomacy is essential. The ignorance of, and contempt for, this side of the business displayed by the professional diplomatists has always amazed me when I have visited them abroad.

Friday 19 March   I have spent most of today reading – I began by reading Charley Londonderry's book *Wings of Destiny*, which he has sent me. It is not very exciting and mainly a defence of his conduct as Air Minister – however, it is not nearly as bad as I expected from what Robin Castlereagh had told me about it. Personally I should not have written it had I been in his place, but as he chose to write it he might have done it infinitely worse. What he naturally does not appreciate is that he is not, and has never been, a big enough man to be a Cabinet Minister – but, considering his limitations, he did well enough and in the main, I imagine, he took good advice and in very difficult times did all in his power to promote the efficiency of the Air Service – but like almost every air-minded man could not understand the Army and Navy point of view.

Sunday 21 March   Winston spoke on the wireless tonight for about fifty minutes – almost entirely about the 'brave new world'. It was a very carefully prepared oration and, while he was careful to tell us all that nothing could really be done until the war was over, he assured us that he was all for keeping us from the cradle to the grave – so I suppose that he will satisfy all the progressives. It was a pity, I think, that he did not emphasize more the duties of the citizen – but one refrains [from] judgement of his effort until one has seen it in print. It is certain to be greeted by a round of applause and undoubtedly was a fine performance of its kind. Though one does not really like him or trust him one cannot help admiring his amazing vitality and power of leadership – and if one knew him better, perhaps one might like him more – at any rate he is a man and a patriot. The Eighth Army has begun its attack on Rommel and Winston told us that so far Montgomery was satisfied with the progress being made.

Tuesday 23 March   I have just been listening to the B.B.C. record[ing] of the Requiem Mass for Cardinal Hinsley[31] ... Hinsley is a real national loss – a big man – a patriot and a great churchman. It is amazing how quickly he made himself felt here – one read his speeches and pronouncements with such admiration and respect because one seemed to feel his absolute sincerity and complete disinterestedness – there was nothing of the politician about the man – one could regard him as a leader and a real exponent of Christian tradition and principle.

Saturday 27 March   The Axis are said to have 250,000 men in north Africa – this theatre is clearly becoming 'a second front' for Hitler, but, needless to say, the Russians don't admit it. I see that that little swine Maisky[32] is still suggesting that we are not doing all we can to help his people – not in so many words of course but by suggestion – I distrust this man greatly: from all I hear of him he is a real danger in this country politically.

Wednesday 30 March   In the House ... the Catering Bill was in Committee. I intervened once, but only to ask a question. Bevin was very stiff and not accepting any of the many amendments and

---

[31] Arthur Hinsley (1865–1943), Roman Catholic clergyman; ordained 1893; Rector, English Coll. at Rome 1917–30; Archbishop of Sardis 1930–34, of Westminster 1935–43; cr. Cardinal 1937.

[32] Ivan Mikhailovich Maisky (1884–1975), Soviet Amb. in Helsinki 1929–32, in London 1932–43; Dep. For. Min. 1943–46.

our people who were proposing them did not strike me as very effective.

Thursday 1 April   This morning much to the surprise of us all Douglas Hacking, who has been leading the opposition to the Catering Bill, announced his intention to retire from the contest – his strange reason for so doing was that as it was evident that Bevin did not intend to give way about anything, it was sheer waste of time to go on proposing amendments! This strange new doctrine of parliamentary practice was very properly severely criticized (even by M.P.s on our side who were in favour of the Bill) and they continued to move amendments with the result that the time of the Committee was fully occupied and another day has had to be given to the Bill.

Saturday 3 April   Dick Proby[33] has been preferred to me by the Executive in London: he will do the job very well – just the sort of chap for it – much more the required type than I am. I am sorry I stood – but no harm has been done – in other words Lady Davidson[34] has not slipped in as a result of a divided vote!

Monday 5 April   Lord Woolton[35] keeps preparing us for more stringent rationing in the coming months, suggesting that we cannot run a second front on the Continent without utilizing a vast amount of shipping for military purposes which have hitherto been employed in carrying food. One is quite ready to believe this – but, nevertheless, I cannot help wondering whether there is not a real shortage of shipping nowadays due to U Boat depredations.

[33] Richard George Proby (1886–1979), landowner and farmer; Chairman, Eastern Area, 1938–48; Chairman, N.U. Exec. Ctte. 1943–46; Chairman, N.U. 1946, Pres. 1958; Chairman, Country Landowners' Assoc. 1943–46, Pres. 1947–51; High Sheriff, Huntingdon & Cambridgeshire 1953; cr. Bart. 1952.

[34] Frances Joan Dickinson (1894–1985), married 1919 John Colin Campbell Davidson (1889–1970), Con. Party Chairman 1926–30; styled Viscountess Davidson after husband raised to peerage 1937, & suc. him as Con. M.P. Hemel Hempstead 1937–59; member of N.U. Exec. 1955–85, Pres. N.U. 1964–65; founder of the Young Britons, and the first woman to be elected to the Exec. of the 1922 Ctte.; cr. Dame 1952, Baroness Northchurch 1963.

[35] Frederick James Marquis (1883–1964), business careeer; Min. of Food 1940–43; Min. of Reconstruction 1943–45; Lord Pres. May-July 1945, 1951–52; Chanc. Duchy of Lancaster 1952–55; Min. of Materials 1953–54; Con. Party Chairman 1946–55; kt. 1935, cr. Baron Woolton 1939, Viscount 1953, Earl 1956.

Tuesday 6 April   In the House this morning Winston announced that the Eighth Army was through the Wadi Akarit and in hot pursuit of Rommel – it looks as if he were making for Sousse. We are in touch with the American II Corps, but I personally don't expect that we shall collar R. He knows his job too much for that, and in these days of land mining a delaying action can be pretty effective – still we have done amazingly well and everybody is highly elated. No gossip of any interest – Eden is back and is said to have had a great success in the U.S.A. He still has little backing in the House, and yet it seems generally agreed that in the event of Winston's demise he would lead the Party and become P.M. The reason for this is that there is no one else – all the other possible runners have failed in one way or another – Oliver Stanley, W.S. Morrison, Walter Elliot, etc! The man who had the chance of a lifetime had he known how to use it is Oliver Lyttelton – but so far he has nor done well in the HofC and shows no sign of improvement.

Thursday 8 April   I asked a question in the House this morning – worth recording as I don't suppose that I have asked 20 questions throughout my parliamentary career. My policy is to go to ministers personally if I want anything done – it does not advertize oneself, but one has far more chance of getting what one wants than by asking a question on the floor of the House. ... I dined tonight as usual at the Great Northern Hotel[36] and gossiped with 3 M.P.s – Jennings, Harvie-Watt[37] and Sir Douglas Thomson.[38] Watt told me that Winston had had quite a severe attack, but was supposed to be all right again now. The unhappy Watt has to write a daily report of Parliament for the P.M. – it seems that Winston is very susceptible to HofC opinion and anxious to miss nothing.

Friday 9 April   Saw Tydeman in the morning – he is a wearisome

---

[36] This had become Headlam's practice in wartime on a Thursday evening before catching the train north, due to the problems of obtaining cabs in the black-out.

[37] George Steven Harvie-Watt (1903–1989), Con. M.P. Keighley 1931–35, Richmond (Surrey) 1937–59; P.P.S. to E. Wallace 1937–38; Ass. Whip 1938–40; P.P.S. to W. Churchill 1941–45; Chief Exec., Consolidated Gold Fields 1954–69; Dep. Ld. Lt., Greater London 1966–78; cr. Bart. 1945.

[38] (James) Douglas Wishart Thomson (1905–1972), Con. M.P. Aberdeen S. 1935–46; P.P.S. to W. Mabane June–Oct. 1939, to various Min. of Shipping Oct. 1939–May 1941, to J. Llewellin 1941–42; suc. 2nd Bart. 1935.

little man, but I am getting used to him now – I don't trust him very far, but I think that he is now definitely on my side, even if this is only because there is for the time being no other side to be on! The worst of him is that he is convinced that he knows the north country and really does not. We discussed the Hartlepools vacancy, due to poor old Gritten's death. There is, I should imagine, bound to be a fight there against 'Common Wealth'[39] – after its victory at Eddisbury (due to a split Liberal vote) it is almost certain to have a go at the Hartlepools, and we shall need a good candidate.

Sunday 11 April   The Queen made a really admirable broadcast tonight addressed to the women of the Empire. It could not have been better either in matter or in delivery. We are very lucky to have such a pair in charge of things as the present King and Queen – they are quite admirable and wherever they go they are successful. Their recent visit in this area went off splendidly so I am told – but what a life the poor people live! One wonders how in the world they can carry on so splendidly – more especially as with them it is a life sentence!

Monday 12 April   I decided not to go to London today to hear Kingsley Wood 'open his Budget' – a Budget speech nowadays is a tedious performance as a rule even when it is made by a good speaker – but to listen to Kingsley read out a long memorandum in his squeaky voice for 2 hours is really not worth one's while – after all, one can read it for oneself if one feels so inclined.

Tuesday 13 April   People seem quite satisfied with the Budget – Kingsley is said to have done his reading very nicely and his stock has gone up considerably – he is now described as a great success as C. of E. – perhaps, after all, it may be he who will dish Mr. Eden – one can never tell what may happen in political life: it certainly is never safe to prophesy.

[39] A recently formed left-wing pressure group, able to contest by-elections as it was not bound by the wartime truce agreed between the main parties. Common Wealth had a broad radical agenda of nationalization and welfare reform, and was able to mobilise popular aspirations for post-war reconstruction and to benefit from the unpopularity of the Conservative Party. Between 1943 and the end of the war Common Wealth won a series of by-election victories in Conservative or National Liberal defended seats, in several cases with candidates who were members of the Labour Party.

Wednesday 14 April   I attended a meeting of the National Union Executive this afternoon – Dick Proby, the new chairman *vice* Eugene Ramsden, in the chair – they preferred him to me which is not surprising as he is a deal younger than I am and much more the Central Office type – more amenable and all things to all men than I am. He is a very capable fellow, and, if he goes into the House, should do well. I walked to Caxton Hall (where Executive now meets) with George Jeffreys[40] – I asked him if he knew Montgomery – he replied that he had known him as a staff officer in France in the last war and had had him as a b[attalio]n commander under him in India. He said that the man was efficient but unattractive and that his Bn. in India was a thoroughly 'cowed' body of men – well trained in tactics, but bad at shooting and not good in the field – Monty drove them a deal too hard. Went to pay a call on Douglas Clifton Brown, Mr. Speaker. I was told that he would be glad to see me – apparently he is not yet used to his Olympic seclusion and dignity – we chatted away for about half an hour and I think that he was pleased that I came.

Thursday 15 April 1943   There is little war news, and we are not to have a war statement before the Easter recess – I suppose that our forces in Tunisia are 'regrouping' for the next stage in the campaign, and the Germans are said to be regrouping in Russia for another big push. They certainly are formidable enemies and one feels that they have a tremendous amount of fight still in them. I cannot understand why the press is so optimistic – I cannot see how the war can be brought to a victorious conclusion for many a long day to come.

Sunday 18 April   I have been skimming through some books on the last war today and am struck with the similarity of things then with what they are today – muddle and confusion everywhere: quarrelling and intriguing and ignorance in high places not only in this country but also in Germany. Indeed, on the whole, it seems to me that in this war things are better than they were then. I suppose we have to thank Winston for this – he is the undisputed

[40] George Darell Jeffreys (1878–1960), army career; G.O.C. London District 1920–24, Wessex Div. 1926–30; C. in C. Southern Command, India 1932–36; Aide-de-Camp Gen. to the King 1936–38; Con. M.P. Petersfield 1941–51; kt. 1924, cr. Baron Jeffreys 1952.

leader in this war – whether for good or ill – he has no rival. ...
In the last war Labour was pampered and wages were increased
just as in this war – but strikes were more prevalent between 1914
and 1918 than they have been since 1939 and I should imagine that
the spirit of the people is better in this war than in the last. We
don't promise quite so much today as we did before – but we all
approve the Beveridge report!

Friday 30 April   I saw Tydeman in the morning – he says
that young Kellett did not seem keen to become candidate for
Hartlepool – and that the other man Greenwell[41] entirely charmed
the Selection Committee. I am sorry about Kellett as he would, I
think, have done well in the HofC. ... In Burma it is reported that
the Japanese have been 'checked' – but clearly we are too weak in
this theatre and can only hope to hold the enemy for some time to
come – I think that one dislikes being hustled by the Japanese more
than anything else. It seems so terribly humiliating to have 'to take
it' from this horrible yellow race and it is going to take a long time
for us to regain our lost prestige in the Far East – nothing but a
smashing victory will do.

Saturday 1 May   ... it is so maddening to be thought useless
when we are both full of life and could help so much in many ways
up here ... and I feel being out of everything even worse, I think,
in London when I look at the Front Bench and see all the people
sitting there so smugly and I know that had I only been given a
fair deal by Baldwin, Margesson & Co. I ought to be a leading
member of the Government today – well what good does it do to
feel bitter? Things might have gone a deal worse for us – and I
quite realize that other people may be doing just as well as I should
have done.

Sunday 2 May   I must frankly confess that I am getting very
tired and disgruntled – it is, I suppose, largely my own fault for I
might get busy in the HofC and take things seriously if I only had
the required energy. But I have no kind of urge to do so – I am

---

[41] Thomas George Greenwell (1894–1967), Con. M.P. The Hartlepools 1943–45;
Chairman, Northern Counties Area 1946–48; High Sheriff, Co. Durham 1951–52;
Chairman, N.E. Coast Ship Repairers Assoc. 1937–40.

too old and out of favour with those in the seats of the mighty to
expect to be given a job or a mission of any kind and I don't want
to butt in and criticize Ministers who, so far as I can see, are doing
their best to win the war some of them may not be all one could
desire, but the majority of them are as good men as there are to
be found in the House at the present time.

Friday 7 May   I visited Tydeman: he is very important nowadays
as he is running the by-election at West Hartlepool. He is pleased
with the man Greenwell who has been chosen as our candidate.
There is to be a Common Wealth candidate – some woman – no
Independent has turned up at present, but no doubt someone will.
I should imagine that if it is a mix up Greenwell is pretty certain
to get in provided that he turns out to be a good candidate.
Tydeman, who has had plenty of experience, assures me that the
man is all right – I have conflicting reports – I have never met him.
We had the annual meeting of our Association tonight – we were
lent the Central Division room and our attendance was about 30!

Saturday 8 May   Grand news today – we have captured both
Bizerta and Tunis – a tremendous achievement ... Our campaign
seems to have been amazingly well organized and run by Alexander – a really fine show and I only hope that he is given the
credit for it.

Tuesday 11 May   The news tonight is exhilarating – there are
now reported to be over 100,000 prisoners in Tunisia and apparently
we have cut through the German defences on the front of the Cape
Bon peninsula – some German units are still holding out vigorously,
but apparently others are surrendering readily – a crack in the
German morale is a really welcome sign and once the rot has begun
it may spread. But it does not do to be too optimistic – these Nazis
are not going to give way yet awhile and I fear that it will be a
long time before we beat them – and we shan't do it without a
holocaust of casualties – so far casualties don't appear to be heavy
compared with those of the last war which is a great relief.

Wednesday 12 May   Winston is in America today, with his
military and other experts – no doubt at the top of his form
planning a new victory somewhere or other. He certainly is a big

man nowadays and I hope that he will see the thing through and go down in history as the man who weathered the storm. In Tunisia the enemy is [in] a state of complete collapse ... but it would be foolish to suppose that because these troops in Tunisia have collapsed, that it means that a rot has set in [in] the army as a whole – still it does show that when hard put to it, the Germans are not prepared to fight to a finish. In north Africa they seem to have lots of food and munitions, but clearly they were thoroughly disorganized and dismayed by the hammering they were getting and instead of fighting in the last ditch they were glad to surrender. What an amazing success it has been – our leadership and staff work must have been superb – and clearly our men fought magnificently and never gave the enemy any respite. Our losses are said to have been comparatively light which is also good news. There is little news from the Russian front but what there is [is] good – but clearly the Germans are bound to make a big push on that front.

Thursday 13 May　　I went to the House this morning – the few people I saw in high spirits. The extent of the victory has surprised and excited everybody – few people expected anything of the kind – the general anticipation was that it would take some little time to clear the Germans out of the Cape Bon peninsula positions ... the catch of prisoners continues to mount.

11

THE ALLIES ADVANCE
May to December 1943

Friday 14 May 1943   The great news of the north African victory
is becoming clearer and clearer – though whether the effect on
German morale is as great as the papers would have us imagine
remains to be seen … so long as they are assured that the German
defences are so strong in Europe that we cannot surmount them,
they will carry on despite the air bombing, etc., etc. – at least such
is my conviction. We simply have got to go through with it – or
make up our minds to that effect – we have got to beat the German
army in Germany – and it is going to be a terrific job.

Thursday 20 May   I attended the Party Conference this morning
at the Central Hall, Westminster. It was well attended and everyone
I met seemed pleased that it was being held – I can truthfully say
that had it not been for my pressure it would not have been
held – needless to say, no one recognizes that now! Anthony
Eden deputized for Winston: I was not at all impressed by his
performance, but the *mot d'ordre*[1] was to express admiration for it
and to explain away the orator's obvious inability to get across
what he was saying by reminding us all that Anthony was suffering
from a bad throat – perhaps he was – but I cannot rate him high
as a leader. … This afternoon I attended the Party Finance
Committee at 24 Old Queen Street – and heard the Party boss of
Birmingham explain how they raised money for the Party in that
city – it sounded as easy as shelling peas – and so it would be in

[1] translation: required word.

Newcastle if we federated the place and made Wilkin our party boss.

Saturday 22 May   The interesting news today is an announcement from Moscow that the Comintern[2] has been abolished or closed down. This is a big decision by Stalin if it is to be taken seriously – it means presumably the end of Communist propaganda for world revolution emanating from Moscow. If it is really a change of policy, it should do much to facilitate friendly intercourse between Russia and us and the U.S.A. It should also cramp the style of the Communist Party here and in America.

Wednesday 26 May   I lunched today at the House with James Stuart and Charles Waterhouse – the former, as usual, very friendly – I think that he is genuinely fond of me, but knows that he can do nothing for me and feels a little uncomfortable about it – no reason why he should – I realize well enough that at my age and not being one of Winston's lot I must resign myself to being on the shelf. The only way off it would be to keep asserting myself in the House and 'waiting'. I am too tired and lazy to do either – and so in obscurity I shall remain. James had no news – he said the 'Boss's' success in the U.S.A. was going to his head, which I can well believe.

Saturday 29 May   I see that the T.U.C. are now threatening to accept the affiliation of the union of the Post Office workers – a direct challenge to the Trades Disputes Act – if the Govt. gives way to a challenge of this description during the political truce, it will be disgraceful – but I should not be in the least surprised if it did. We have, I think, reached a stage in our constitutional development when parliamentary government is really for the first time threatened from outside – and it seems to me that the Party should make a real stand – but I am afraid that it may submit to Winston if he deems it expedient to give way to the T.U.C. – and he is *capable de tout*.[3]

Monday 31 May   ... went to Hartlepool this evening where I

---

[2] The short title of the Third International, established by Soviet Communism in March 1919 as the organizing body to promote Marxist world revolution.

[3] translation: capable of anything.

addressed 2 meetings – 'eve of the poll' at the by-election. ... Peat, M.P., was the Government spokesman – the candidate (Colonel Greenwell) did not impress me very favourably – rather a common looking little creature: his wife the better man of the two I should say. They seem confident of winning and as there are three 'independent' candidates, the Conservative ought of course to get in. The meetings were not too badly attended, but there was no kind of excitement at them – or in the town – clearly by-elections are not popular events in time of war and quite right too.

Thursday 3 June   Alexander, First Lord of the Admiralty, has made a very reassuring statement regarding the U Boat war – this is really cheering – because if we are really getting the upper hand in this business, one can begin to feel that victory is certain. ... So far in this war one has been left more or less in ignorance as to how things were going – at any rate since they ceased to publish the monthly returns of sinkings – and so one has been very nervous as to what was happening – one has been told of course from time to time that we were just holding our own but that the sinkings were very serious – now Alexander definitely says that we appear to be gaining the upper hand.

Tuesday 8 June   Winston was at his best this morning – he spoke for just under the hour and never put a foot wrong – and yet he told us nothing we did not already know. He wisely did not indulge in boasting, nor was he unduly optimistic ... He looks ever so much better for his change of air and scene.[4]

Wednesday 9 June   I attended the House practically the whole of today, but I can't say that I heard anything worth hearing. I intervened for a few minutes on the Committee stage of one of Ernest Brown's bills – he is a Minister who appears to be losing ground in the House.[5] People are getting tired of him for some reason – but I don't see much difference in him myself – he seems to know what he is about, even if the policy he is pursuing may look foolish. He is said to be failing to get on with the doctors:

[4] Churchill had recently visited the U.S.A. and the North African theatre.
[5] In Nov. 1943 Ernest Brown (q.v.) was moved from the Min. of Health to the lesser post of Chanc. of the Duchy of Lancaster.

they very naturally are not at all keen to be turned into a State Medical Service to please the planners – Eustace Percy told me the other day that in his opinion it would take years to bring the medical profession into line with the Beveridge scheme, and he is fairly closely in touch with all the doctoring clique in Newcastle.

Thursday 10 June　　... there was nothing on but the adjournment debate – in which Walter Womersley Min. of Pensions was, I believe, attacked. He seems to have gone downhill a lot recently and is losing any command of the House. His is a rotten job in any case – one can never satisfy anyone about a pension case – and the doctors, as I know from experience,[6] rule the show – the whole business is really left to them and I am quite sure that it should not be so. ... Matt Ridley had tea with me in the Smoking Room. He is now anxious to get the northern M.P.s to press the Govt. for more preparation for post war needs in the north. I said that I would gladly do anything I could in the matter and advised him to get in touch with Jack Lawson as well as myself so that, if possible, we might all work together irrespective of party.

Tuesday 15 June　　The Labour Party conference is sitting – Arthur Greenwood has defeated Herbert Morrison for the post of Treasurer which both were after. Morrison is not a popular character among the T.U.C. people or indeed among the Labour M.P.s – he is too clever for them. Bevin seems to be lying low – but should anything happen to Attlee I would back Greenwood before either Morrison or Bevin as political leader of the party. As regards the amendment of the Trade Disputes Act the conference, so far as I can make out, is supporting the T.U.C., but is advised by its Executive to let the matter rest for the time being – I fancy this means that nothing will be done as regards the postal workers.

Sunday 20 June　　Archie Wavell has been appointed Viceroy of India – he should do the job all right, but it does seem an odd thing to remove your best general from the Army in the middle of a major war – it also seems odd that there was no civilian available for, or ready to take on, the job. Well, I personally am glad that neither Sam Hoare, nor John Anderson, nor Archie Sinclair is to

[6] Headlam served as junior minister at the Ministry of Pensions 1931–32.

go to India – I have not a high opinion of any of these gents – not
at any rate for India.

Tuesday 22 June   Lunched at the House with James Stuart,
Shakes[7] Morrison and R. Grimston who is now second string at
the Post Office. James had little or no gossip, nor had Morrison –
the latter is a very charming person, but I always look upon him
as lacking in political push and drive – Baldwin always predicted
that he would be the next but one P.M. after him. In this he has
already been proved wrong – and I don't find anyone today backing
Morrison as a future P.M. – however, it [is] never safe to prophesy
regarding persons in political life – reputations are so constantly
changing, and such small things seem to change them

Monday 5 July   The aeroplane conveying General Sikorski,[8] the
Polish P.M. and C.-in-C., from Gibraltar to England crashed into
the sea just after it started and everyone in it except the pilot has
been killed ... including Victor Cazalet – poor little man – he was
so very full of life and such a friendly soul – I am terribly sorry
for his mother (whom I don't know) and Thelma[9] M.P. who simply
adored him. He was not an eminent member of the House, but he
was a busy one – and I don't suppose that anyone ever had a
grouse of any kind against him. He was so entirely simple, and
even his pleasure in knowing the right people was harmless because
it was so undisguised. He had great charm of manner and was I
am told wonderfully kind to all and sundry.

Tuesday 6 July   For a wonder I have spent practically all day at
the HofC. I went there at 11 a.m. and stayed till the House rose
soon after 6 p.m. There was nothing particular to take me there,
still less to keep me there, but I had no other appointment today.
There was a debate on the Third Reading of the Finance Bill which
I did not find interesting and another on the 'remaining stages' of
the Foreign Services Bill: I 'intervened' for a few minutes – more
to get my name into *Hansard* for a change than for any other
reason – next session I really must speak more or what was said of

[7] The nickname of William Shepherd Morrison (q.v.).
[8] Wladyslaw Sikorski (1881–1943), Polish soldier and statesman; P.M. 1922–23;
P.M. & C. in C. of Polish Govt.-in-exile in London 1939–43.
[9] Thelma Cazalet-Keir (q.v.), Victor Cazalet's sister.

old Grattan-Doyle will be said of me: 'he never makes a speech!'

Thursday 8 July   In the House this morning the Speaker administered a snub to Eddie Winterton who, as usual, was tiresome – claiming his 'considerable experience' to prove that Rob Hudson was out of order in reading out a statement of policy after questions without asking the leave of the House. It was a small matter but I liked the way Clifton Brown handled it and still more I liked to see Eddie W. made to look an ass.

Saturday 10 July   News this morning that an Allied force – British, American, Canadian – has invaded Sicily – the landing was effected against considerable opposition under air and sea cover and is said to be proceeding according to plan ... it is going to be a stiff fight I should imagine if there are really as many Axis troops on the island as are reported to be there by the press. The battle in Russia continues and according to Russian reports the Germans are being held – if they continue to be held, well and good – but I never attach too great importance to the Russian reports of German losses – certainly the war is quickening up and one feels all strung up and nervous – one remembers what an offensive meant against prepared defences in the last war!

Tuesday 13 July   There was a debate on the Colonies today opened by Oliver Stanley in rather a dull speech – I had intended to say a few words but did not do so ... my style of speaking is not that practised in the House nowadays – I simply cannot write out a long oration and then get up and calmly read it out which is the practice now adopted by most M.P.s.

Wednesday 14 July   I went back to the House after luncheon and fired off a little speech in the shipping debate. It was rather a success and I was cheered when I sat down and congratulated by several people – it did one good!

Thursday 15 July   In Sicily things are said to be going well – but it looks as if opposition were hardening and it is too early to be *too* confident. However, so far as I can gather, those in the know are pleased with our progress. ... I don't find in the House of Commons anyone who possesses any sense in the ultra-optimistic mood which is a bit too prevalent in other quarters.

Sunday 25 July Stalin has published an 'order of the day' announcing that the German offensive has been smashed – and I must say that it looks as if he were speaking the truth – what next I wonder? Hitler cannot keep his armies in Russia doing nothing or their morale will quickly evaporate – but what new offensive can he stage on the Eastern Front? Prisoners in Sicily now total over 10,000 and the Italian soldiers are surrendering *en masse*: the Germans are still said to be fighting desperately in the north-east corner of the island – one wonders how many of them will succeed in getting away.

Monday 26 July Mussolini is a thing of the past – his resignation is announced in the press today ... The King of Italy[10] and Marshal Badoglio[11] are now in charge so presumably Fascism goes with Musso. They tell us that Italy will fight on, but I should imagine that the end of the war for the Italians is in sight – somehow or other I cannot see the Germans fighting to keep us out of Italy with the Italian Army as it is today. My own view still is that Hitler means to evacuate Italy and I should say that Musso's fall is a result of this decision. The Italians will go on with the war until the Germans are gone and then will surrender – and we shall have the unenviable task of having to feed them and look after them ...

Tuesday 27 July Winston made an admirable speech in the HofC this morning – not too gloating or 'splashy'. The only expression I regretted was when he said that we should allow Italy 'to stew in her own juice' for a time – an excellent policy but stated somewhat crudely – however 'it suited the mood of the House'. Everyone I meet is filled with exhilaration and one might imagine that the war was already won – which of course is very far from the case. I gather that Musso's fall came as a surprise to those in authority. I

---

[10] Victor Emmanuel III (1869–1947), King of Italy 1900–46; assumed titles of Emporer of Ethiopia 1935 & King of Albania 1939 after Italian occupations; abdicated May 1946, died in exile in Egypt.

[11] Pietro Badoglio (1871–1956), Italian soldier and statesman; Chief of Staff, 1925–28,1940–41; Gov. of Tripolitania & Cyrenaica 1928–34; C. in C. Italian forces in Abyssinia 1935–36; P.M. 1943–44.

listened this afternoon to Wavell make an oration on the war in the Far East at the All Party Committee, Amery in the chair – I was not much impressed by it and the man told us nothing which we did not already know. He attributed our feeble display in Malaya and the fall of Singapore to our own 'carelessness, complacency and contempt of the Japanese' – no doubt true enough. He also said that our Intelligence was very bad in the Far East. He anticipates a long, stiff fight before we have done with the Japanese. He told us that there was a certain feeling of disgruntlement among British troops in India who had many of them been there too long: this will have to be attended to.

Wednesday 28 July   This evening at the Beefsteak where we had rather a pleasant little party of five, Harold Nicolson told us that he had recently had breakfast with Stanley Baldwin whom he found supremely happy! apparently without any kind of uncomfortable feeling regarding his responsibility for our present discontents. He had had a letter from David Kirkwood[12] assuring him that the national unity today was largely due to his (S.B.'s) conciliatory attitude towards the working-class population. He (S.B.) had also lunched with Winston and had a 2 hours' heart to heart with him – they were now the best of friends. This delighted S.B. who told Nicolson that there was a 'golden streak in everyone and that war seemed to bring out the best in everyone.'

Friday 30 July   Our bombing of Hamburg has been (and continues to be) terrific. By all accounts this unhappy town has literally been wiped out – and now they are talking in Germany of evacuating Berlin which they imagine will be our next target. One wonders how long the German people will stand up to such colossal air attacks – there have been no previous bombing raids on anything like the present scale. Hitherto I have always been inclined to think that bombing could not break a people – now I am beginning to wonder whether this view was a right one. If town after town can be pulverized out of existence, the cumulative effect on the morale of the people must be stupendous – and from what one hears the bombing of their homes and families is having an effect on the

---

[12] David Kirkwood (1872–1955), Lab. M.P. Dumbarton Burghs 1922–1950, Dunbartonshire E. 1950–51 (sat as I.L.P. M.P. 1931–33); cr. Baron Kirkwood 1951.

morale of the German armies in the field – this may lead to big results.

Tuesday 3 August   In the House there was a debate on women and their work, woes and worries and all the women M.P.s had their say – to me it is quite ridiculous to have sex representation in Parliament – after all women M.P.s represent men as well as women. ... a debate on foreign policy raised by A. Bevan on the Consolidated Fund Bill. The fellow made a mischievous speech – and was followed by others of the same kidney – the idea apparently of these left wing extremists is that we should only deal with left wing politicians in Italy and in the other occupied countries. It is an idea which, if acted upon, would lead to trouble – it is not our job to tell other countries what form of government they are to adopt.

Wednesday 4 August   Lunched at the HofC with James Stuart, Donald Somervell and Ralph Assheton. They also spoke very highly of Kingsley Wood – he is, they say, such a keen, loyal and intelligent little man who can always be depended upon and is always bright and cheerful. He certainly is doing ever so much better in the House than I expected he would.

Thursday 5 August   The House rose for the Recess today ... Everybody is very cheerful – unduly so I think – the general view is that we shall soon be called back to London to discuss peace terms with Italy. Personally I rather doubt it – I fear that the Germans are too strong in Italy to permit an Italian surrender – besides which, short of a revolution, I cannot see Badoglio and co. accepting an unconditional surrender. I always thought that the Casablanca declaration was a mistake at any rate so far as Italy was concerned.

Wednesday 18 August   I went to Newcastle today ... I attended a memorial service at the Cathedral for David Adams. He died a few days ago – very suddenly – he seemed well and hearty when I saw him at the HofC the day Parliament adjourned. There was a large attendance of the City Council headed by the Lord Mayor who made a speech making out what a fine fellow David Adams was – perhaps he really was – who knows? but one has heard a lot of gossip about him, as one has heard of most of the Newcastle business men. In the HofC he was known as 'the undertaker' because he looked like one and had such a lugubrious manner.

Friday 20 August   I saw Tydeman and sent off the 'Federation' letters to the four Newcastle chairmen:[13] it remains to be seen how they will receive it – it will depend mainly on Wilkin I suppose - and he, so Tydeman tells me, is once again in a nursing home, poor man. ... the papers suggest that an invasion of the Continent may come at any moment – one only hopes that we shall not make a big move until we are really ready – the Russian propaganda for invasion continues with unabated vigour – apparently no account is taken in Moscow of our Sicilian victory or of our incessant bombing of Germany or of the material help we are giving.

Saturday 21 August   The Post Office union has withdrawn its application to join the T.U.C.: a fresh effort is now to be started by the T.U.C. and the Labour Party to find a settlement of the question of the relations of the Civil Service unions to the T.U.C.: what this means I really can't think – but I only hope that the Government is not going to give way a jot – it really is nothing but a try on – let them wait until they have a majority in the HofC and then repeal the Trade Disputes Act and make the T.U.C. supreme in the land, something above Parliament and the Courts – but don't let us help them in any way to this end.

Tuesday 24 August   The Quebec Conference[14] has come to an end and we are assured that everything has been arranged very nicely – the invasion plans are settled and the plan of campaign against Japan decided upon. The Russians claim to be following up their Kharkov success and I only hope they are – for everything depends on keeping up their push. We bombed Berlin last night and claim to have wrought great havoc: we lost 58 bombers in the process – a very heavy toll and one wonders whether smashing up Berlin was worth it.

Wednesday 25 August   ... it is interesting to note the statement

---

[13] A proposal for an overall Conservative organization for the city of Newcastle.
[14] A summit conference attended by Churchill, Roosevelt and their staffs.

that at Quebec the main subject under discussion was the war against Japan ... without inner knowledge one scarcely dares to believe that the beginning of the end of the German war is at hand. Perhaps Himmler's appointment to supreme control of the Home Front means this – but can any man keep a people in a war merely by terror? I doubt it – terror will keep people going for a time but if it has lost faith in its leaders even terror will fail – and then there must come a collapse. But even if the Nazi Party has to go, the Army might carry on for a long time – until, indeed, it is knocked out – after all what has Germany to gain by giving in? So long as we demand 'unconditional surrender' we must be prepared to go on fighting to the bitter end – at least so I think.

Saturday 28 August   Francis Fremantle's[15] death is recorded in the press today – yet another M.P. gone. He was a nice creature – but oh! so dull – no one more earnest and sincere in all he said: no one more boring to listen to. I have known him for years and can remember him when I was a schoolboy at Canterbury and went to tea in his father's house – a friend of my father's and then a Canon of Canterbury, afterwards Dean of Ripon.

Sunday 29 August   I have been re-reading today Arnold Wilson's[16] *Walks and Talks* abroad: they are exceedingly interesting and worth re-reading first to recall the events of the years before the war and what our reaction to them was, and second to see how wrong a very able man was in foreseeing what was going to happen – and yet Wilson is undoubtedly right to point out what was good and efficient in Fascism and Nazism and how much we had to learn from them – of course today anyone who would venture to say anything in favour of either regime, or who dared to suggest that both Hitler and Musso were both heavily backed by the people in Germany and Italy, would be dubbed a traitor and a fool, and yet, perhaps without knowing it, many of our left wing extremists are

---

[15] Francis Edward Fremantle (1872–1943), Con. M.P. St. Albans 1919–43; County Medical Officer of Health, Herts. 1902–16; kt. 1932.

[16] Arnold Talbot Wilson (1884–1940), Con. M.P. Hitchin 1933–40; career in Indian Army; Chairman, Industrial Health Research Bd. 1929–33; identified as sympathetic towards the German & Italian Fascist regimes in the 1930s; joined R.A.F. as an Air Gunner Nov. 1939, missing in action & presumed killed 31 May 1940.

practically preaching the same kind of social politics and economic changes which were set going by Hitler and Musso in their respective countries.

Tuesday 31 August   Winston spoke tonight on the wireless, but someone had to read his stuff as owing to 'atmospheric' conditions he did not 'come across' satisfactorily. There was nothing new in what he said and I don't think he was at his best – however, this may have been due to the speech being delivered by a B.B.C. announcer.

Friday 3 September   This morning I attended the official service at the Cathedral on the fourth anniversary of the declaration of war – a big congregation with all the City [of Newcastle] dignitaries. ... This morning we invaded the toe of Italy, landing forces near Reggio – one wonders whether this is the right place to land – but no doubt Monty & Co. know what they are doing. There is very little news so far, but we are warned that it is not going to be an easy job as the German troops who evacuated Sicily are reported to be waiting for us. At last, at any rate, we are on the mainland of Europe and let us hope that the Russians and their admirers in this country may consider this landing to be the beginning of a 'second front'.

Monday 6 September   Stalin has sanctioned a religious revival in Russia and the Holy Synod is to be set going again. This is an interesting piece of news – for it must mean that there is a popular move towards religion in Russia – a result no doubt of the war – very soon it looks as if the Soviet Republic will return to the normal – just when we are toying with the idea that we ought to try and copy the Bolshevik system – by 'we' of course I mean our intelligentsia for I don't believe for a moment that the bulk of the people in this country would be foolish enough to wish to adopt the teaching of Karl Marx. The 'class war' is waged by a few extremists and the mistake is to be fearful of them – our danger is that we are apt to allow ourselves to be led to do foolish things and adopt a wrong policy because we are influenced by a comparatively small but noisy minority and are ready to take their word for it that they represent the vast majority of the working class. Our 'young Conservatives' are so much afraid of being considered non-progressive that they adopt Socialist ideas without due consideration and surrender the fort without fighting when it is easy to defend and the enemy are much weaker than they suppose. Changes of all kind must come – but it foolish to accept them just because you feel that they will be forced upon you.

Tuesday 7 September   Winston spoke at Harvard yesterday where he was given an honorary degree – a fine speech in which he emphasized the world importance of the British Commonwealth of Nations and the U.S.A. sticking together after the war. He also advocated the maintenance of an American-British staffs committee, and drew special attention to the vast importance of the English language which might some day lead to a common citizenship – the speech seems to have been well-received in the U.S.A. Of course an Anglo-American alliance or understanding – a practical union of the English-speaking races – is the only real way of bringing permanent peace to the world. Had there been such an under-standing after the last war we should not have had to face this war – but, nevertheless, I shall be agreeably surprised if we and the Americans remain good bed fellows once the war is over. There is too much foreign blood in the U.S.A. I fear to permit of permanent good relations between the 2 countries – however, we have both had our lesson and common sense may prevail.

Wednesday 8 September   Great news today – Italy has surrendered unconditionally and the Russians announce that they have cleared the whole of the Donetz Basin and are still advancing on their other fronts. ... presumably Hitler will hold on as long as he can in northern Italy – but his difficulties are going to be increased considerably – not only will he be fighting in a hostile country but he will also now have the difficult job of holding down the Balkans on his own – hitherto much of the police work has been done by the Italians. We have broken the Axis – and though, I suppose, we shall now have to feed and supply Italy with coal, etc. We have secured our hold of the Mediterranean and Adriatic and so are infinitely stronger for an attack on Germany by air – and also by land. Let us hope that the beginning of the end is in sight.

Monday 13 September   Musso has been liberated by German parachutists from confinement in some hotel at the top of some mountain somewhere in Italy – it sounds like a film story – and no doubt will be one before we have heard the end of it. It certainly is an odd affair and one wonders how it happened and why we did not insist on the man's being handed over to us – however, I do not set the same importance on Musso's release as the Germans appear to – I don't fancy that it is possible for him to regain his prestige and certainly not with German aid. Hitler may set up some sort of puppet government under him, but it won't cut much ice I should imagine with the Italian people. The fact that the Germans have succeeded in releasing the man may impress the Balkans, but one hopes not for long.

Saturday 18 September   I visited Wilkin yesterday in his nursing home. He looks terribly ill and has had to have blood infusions to keep him going – and yet he tells me that they propose to carry out a very severe operation on him to remove two ulcers in his stomach next Tuesday. To me it seems sheer madness – but I suppose the doctors ought to know what they are about. We had a heart to heart ... we are entirely agreed as to federation, and he has had a row about J.P.s with Appleby and is all out to do down the old gent. I wonder whether he will survive an operation: I doubt it and I fear that he also doubts it – poor man – he has overtaxed his strength and energy.

Tuesday 21 September   Winston spoke for the best part of 2 hours (with a luncheon interval) and, needless to say, had a big reception – the House was packed and he looked in the pink – truly an amazing man for his age. He gave an excellent account of things, but I am glad to say made it quite clear that we have a long way to go before we can talk of winning the war. On the whole, however, he was cheerful and sensible, and left little for his critics to get hold of except of course in his attitude about what they are pleased to call 'political war'. He made it quite clear that it was not his intention to hand over Italy to the extreme left wing people and that he treated with the Badoglio government because it was the *de facto* government of the country which had surrendered to the Allies – all quite sensible – but not pleasing to asses like Aneurin Bevan & co. I did not listen to much of the debate which followed Winston's speech but I am told that it was not inspiring. I dined here tonight with the Devonshire family which lives in the [Mayfair]

Hotel – Eddie[17] tells me that he finds it a great economy which no doubt it must be to a chap who in normal times lives at Chatsworth...

Wednesday 22 September   I made a little speech in the war debate this afternoon – not of my best – but James Stuart was kind enough to say that it was helpful to the Government and one or two other people assured me that it was excellent, which of course it was not. Anthony Eden wound up for the Government and spoke with more vim and force than usual. He is coming on – developing as Charles Ponsonby[18] says – and it looks as if he had the leadership of the Party in his pocket when Winston goes. He has been a lucky man – but he has known how to utlilize his chances which his rivals have not – perhaps he may turn out to be a bigger man than I have ever imagined him to be – I still think that it was he who brought Musso into the war against us.

Thursday 23 September   There has been a debate on manpower today ... I gather that Bevin got away with it about the calling up of the older women – however, he has assured us that he will go canny with them and I don't suppose that many will be really 'directed' to jobs.

Saturday 25 September[19]   I dined tonight at the Station Hotel – a dinner given by the City to Stafford Cripps who is visiting aircraft production centres in this part of the world. ... Cripps made an excellent, little speech – the sort of stuff for the occasion and quite

[17] Edward William Spencer Cavendish (1895–1950), Con. M.P. Derbyshire W. 1923–38; U.S. Dominions 1936–40; U.S. India 1940–43; U.S. Colonies 1943–45; Ld. Lt. Derbyshire 1938–50; styled Marquess of Hartington 1908–38, suc. 10th Duke of Devonshire 1938, K.G. 1941.

[18] Charles Edward Ponsonby (1879–1976), Con. M.P. Sevenoaks 1935–50; P.P.S. to A. Eden 1940–45; Chairman of Council, Royal Empire Soc. 1954–57; Pres., Royal African Soc. 1962–71; cr. Bart. 1956.

[19] Headlam's activities for this day were described by mistake on the page intended for 24 Sep., with the entry for 25 Sep. noting 'I see that I have written most of today's happenings in my remarks of yesterday, which is carelessness.' As it was not a case of entries being simply transposed, Headlam did not follow his normal practice of amending the printed page headings by hand. The first part of this extract, as far as 'perfectly blue nose', appears on the page allotted to 24 Sep.; the remainder, commenting upon the ministerial appointments, is on the page intended for 25 Sep.

exemplary as regards politics. He is a strange, aloof creature and one wonders what his views are now – is he still a Communist?[20] My own opinion is that he is just Cripps – a freak and not a person who will ever be a controlling force in political life – he is too aloof and impersonal. I thought tonight what a bad advertisement he is – and looks – for non-drinking, nut-eating etc. – he has a perfectly blue nose. ... The new appointments are out. John Anderson has succeeded Kingsley Wood at the Exchequer[21] – he is a dreary dog but everyone assures me that he is efficient and he is not likely to try and be clever. What infuriates me is that Beaverbrook has been brought back to the Government. He is Lord Privy Seal *vice* Cranborne who returns to the Colonial Office. It really is too much that so utterly rotten a man as the Beaver should be reimposed upon us – Winston is quite incorrigible and just does as he likes. Presumably he likes the Beaver and, for all one knows, may be beholden to him, but this is no reason for employing him as a Minister of the Crown against the wishes of all decent men in the HofC. It is not as if the Beaver were any good – all those who have had anything to do with him assure me that he is a wrong 'un and that he has no idea of administration or anything but second-rate journalism. His record is bad, his manners are bad, his appearance is bad – and, in addition, he is no chicken.[22] In these days his age alone should debar him from public service. Dick Law has been made 'Minister of State' but appears to be going to remain at the F[oreign] O[ffice] as second string to Anthony.

Wednesday 29 September   The strike mania continues – the one at Barrow is a serious stoppage I should imagine and the men appear to be quite out of hand – in Scotland a lot of miners are out and I see in today's papers that there has been a lightning strike in one of our Durham pits. It is difficult to account for this 'unrest' – the men won't listen to their own leaders and no one seems to grasp the situation. My own view is that people are getting a bit stale and seize any excuse to stop work for a bit – they have

[20] Cripps was expelled from the Labour Party in Jan. 1939 for advocating a 'Popular Front' with anti-appeasers and Communists against Fascism, but he was never a member of the Communist Party; Headlam's reference is rather to the ideas of state control with which Cripps was identified as a leading figure in the Labour radical left during the 1930s.

[21] Kingsley Wood, Chanc. of the Exchequer, died suddenly on 21 Sep. 1943.

[22] Beaverbrook was 64 years old in 1943.

got it into their heads that the war is nearly won and there has been no hostile bombing to disturb their equanimity. It is an unfortunate business and, as we are not in the habit of enforcing obedience by drastic means and as managers no longer have the right to sack bad hats owing to the essential work order, there would appear to be no way of dealing with the men except propaganda and appealing to their reason – as they won't listen to reason and are not convinced by propaganda, the situation is pretty grim. I shall be curious to hear what Bevin has to say when we meet again.

Thursday 30 September ... things appear to be going all right in Italy although clearly we are to have a hard tussle there. Our Fifth Army is almost in Naples – the Germans presumably are retiring to some other defensive position further north. If reports are true they have entirely smashed up Naples and, if they continue this process, there will be precious little left standing in Italy by the time they have been expelled. What Vandals they are – I hope and trust that one of the peace conditions will be that the swine are made to build up what they have destroyed in other countries before they are allowed to start repairing things in their own beastly country. It would be a punishment fitting the crime: they have forced hundreds of thousands of foreigners to work for them during the war; let them be forced to work for the rest of us when the war is over.

Saturday 2 October I went into Newcastle after an early lunch and presided over the Area meeting. I said a few words about Wilkin, but not so well as I had hoped. Matt Ridley made a dull speech about the industrial situation after the war and seized the opportunity, somewhat tactlessly, to assure a political audience that he took no interest in party politics! He is very stupid about politics. I got Londonderry to move a vote of thanks. It was a dull meeting and not so many attended as last time – clearly the interest in politics among Conservatives grows less and less – and there seems to be no way of arousing it. Charley came back here for the weekend and is in one of his most friendly moods. He is a kindly, simple creature and I feel very sorry for him. He is worried to death about Robin who apparently has resumed his excessive drinking and is most unpleasant to his people. It is interesting to hear both sides of a story – I am prepared, on the whole, to accept Charley's version.

Sunday 3 October   Have spent a quiet day – mainly listening to Charley Londonderry's views on men and things. He is very naive and simple-minded and tells one the most common-place things as if they were something new and wonderful – but one cannot help appreciating his obvious sincerity and anxiety to play his role well and to help people. I wish I could help him with Robin – but it looks to me as if the situation were fairly hopeless. It is not as if Robin were a boy – he is forty and this breach with his father and mother has been going on for a long time – it is the old story of an inferiority complex – Robin it seems has always had one – and the effect upon him has been to make him assert his individuality in the wrong way.

Thursday 7 October   Lunched in Lombard Street after wasting 2 hours at the Party Central Council meeting at the Caxton Hall – I returned to the meeting after luncheon and moved a resolution (which we had passed last year at the Area meeting to please Central Office) advocating the formation of 'Looking Ahead Circles' ... the resolution was accepted – it certainly did nobody any harm even if does nobody any good. Hacking accused me of being nasty and untruthful about Central Office in my speech – whether he was serious or chaffing I really don't know or care – I merely described what they said and did at the beginning of the war regarding Party activities – my remarks appeared to amuse everybody in the room except Douglas Hacking.[23]

Tuesday 12 October   It makes one's heart ache to think of all the agony and sorrow caused by these foul Germans for the second time in one's lifetime – and perhaps it makes one still more sad and depressed that neither in 1914 nor in 1939 need we have had war if we as a nation had realized our danger and faced the situation – shall we be equally foolish again I wonder? For the time being the mass of the population would be ready, I think, to submit to military service, etc. – but I doubt whether as a race we shall ever face up to our responsibilities for long – we forget far too

---

[23] Hacking (q.v.) had been Chairman of the Party at the start of the war.

easily – once the danger is past, once the enemy's brutalities are not green in our memories, we are liable to sit back, to sentimentalize, to take the line of least resistance.

Wednesday 13 October   The coal debate seems to have been much the same as usual yesterday – [Gwilym] L.G.'s speech as reported in the *D[aily] T[elegraph]* was a pretty feeble effort – it seems quite impossible for any Minister to speak the truth fearlessly about the coal situation – and the same thing applies to the miners' M.P.s in the HofC.

Thursday 14 October   In the HofC yesterday Winston 'intervened' and told the Socialists that nationalization of the pits was not practical politics during the war – of course as a matter of fact the pits are 'nationalized' at the present time and Lawther & Co. know this well enough and what nationalization means – however, the play acting goes on – on and on – and there seems no one in authority who can tell the miners the truth and make the fool public realize the situation. The longer I live the more clearly I see that more than half of our industrial troubles today are due to causes which no longer exist, but which are kept going in order to furnish propaganda for political changes which are no longer needed and a social revolution which has already taken place. It is a strange world.

Tuesday 26 October   Went to the HofC ... nothing to interest me there nor did I hear any gossip – indeed, I saw no one whom I wanted to speak to – I really must try and get to know more people and to mix better. It is no use being in the House unless one does – but nowadays I am so little there – my business affairs keep me so busy that I am not much in the House – so long as it meets at 11 a.m. it really is not easy for people who have other things to do to be regular attenders.

Wednesday 27 October   I looked in at the HofC this morning and listened to Winston make a speech about the rebuilding of the

HofC[24] – a Select Committee of the House is to examine plans etc. – but I gather that the Government intends to rebuild the place much as it was before and if the present site is to be utilized I don't see how any great alterations can be made – Winston was effective this morning and the House was all in favour of his ideas. He is certainly the leader – no one else counts for the time being and he is enjoying every moment of his leadership – rumour has it that it is his intention to stick on for as long as he can and in that case it would surprise me if he retained his popularity long after the war.

Monday 1 November   Mr Quintin Hogg[25] has denied that he proposes to cross the floor of the House – this must be a great relief to every true blue Tory! – at the same time Hogg is certainly an able man and when he grows up a bit more and becomes less Oxford Unionish should do very well – a pity that he will have to go to the HofL[26] – unless of course my committee's reforms are accepted!

Thursday 4 November   ... we had a constitutional sub-committee meeting in the Moses Room – quite a successful one – we are really beginning to make progress and are generally agreed, but of course each one of us has a better method of expressing what we want than has the other. Agnes ... was very talkative but no wonder – she has studied the subject and written most of the stuff and does not want her work improved – unlike me she has little experience of parliamentary committees and their ways. The essential thing is to let every member have his say and, when he is tired, to go on as if nothing had happened – you then alter your wording as little as possible, and when it is referred to him again he has forgotten

---

[24] The Commons chamber was destroyed by an incendiary bomb on the night of 10–11 May 1941. After a short interval at Church House, the Commons met in the Chamber of the House of Lords until the rebuilt Commons chamber was opened in Oct. 1950.

[25] Quintin McGarel Hogg (1907-), Con. M.P. Oxford 1938–50, St. Marylebone 1963–70; a founder of the Tory Reform Ctte. 1943–45; jt. U.S. Air 1945; 1st Lord of Admiralty 1956–57; Min. of Educ. 1957; Con. Party Chairman 1957–59; Lord Pres. 1957–59, 1960–64; Lord Privy Seal 1959–60; Min. for Science 1960–64; Leader of House of Lords 1960–63; Educ. Sec. Apr.-Oct. 1964; Lord Chanc. 1970–74, 1979–87; suc. 2nd Viscount Hailsham 1950, disclaimed peerage 1963, cr. Baron Hailsham of St. Marylebone 1970.

[26] Hogg was the son and heir of the 1st Viscount Hailsham.

what he actually said and is quite happy as a rule with the thing
as he finds it.

Monday 8 November   I attended a meeting today in the Town
Hall – presided over by the Lord Mayor – got up by the Tynemouth
and Wallsend councils and trade union people connected with
shipping. The employers of labour had not been invited to attend:
various Tyneside M.P.s present – *viz.*, Magnay, Lawson, self,
West Russell,[27] Nunn – the demand was for the reopening of the
Northumberland dock and assurances from the Government as to
post-war ship building etc. West Russell made an oration and a lot
of town councillors and Labour people aired their views – we M.P.s
said that we would arrange for a deputation to see Ministers if
they so desired.

Tuesday 9 November   The House rose unexpectedly today – at
12.30 after we had voted God knows how many millions for the
war in about ten minutes – no one was ready with any motion on
the adjournment and so we all went home. I returned later in the
afternoon to see a coloured motion film made by Billy Brass,[28]
M.P., of the recent tour of M.P.s in Canada – one got rather tired
of seeing the M.P.s being photographed, but otherwise it was an
admirable show and I should like to have it up here – the work
people on the Tyne would, I think, be interested to see Canadian
workmen building ships and tanks. ... The Italian advance is a
slow one and I shall be much surprised if we succeed in taking
Rome before Christmas – the terrain is very difficult, the supplies
problem must not be easy, the enemy is in considerable force in
prepared positions.

Wednesday 10 November   I lunched with the Speaker and Mrs.
Clifton Brown today. They now have a very nice flat to live in and
seem comfortable and happy – the other guests were Austin
Hopkinson M.P. and Andy MacLaren[29] M.P. ... MacLaren is now

---

[27] Alexander West Russell (1879–1961), Con. M.P. Tynemouth 1922–45; kt. 1937.
[28] William Brass (1886–1945), Con. M.P. Clitheroe 1922–45; P.P.S. to N. Chamberlain 1922–24, 1924–27, to L. Amery 1927–28, to J. Moore-Brabazon 1940–42; kt. 1929, cr. Baron Chattisham 1945.
[29] Andrew MacLaren (1883–1975), Lab. M.P. Burslem 1922–23, 1924–31, 1935–45 (Ind. Lab. from Mar. 1943).

an independent Labour M.P. – he is a clever fellow who has strong views of his own and says rather caustic and amusing things about people, especially about his former Socialist colleagues – in the House the other day when Hore-Belisha was making a speech and alluded to someone as his Honble. friend,[30] MacLaren, I am told, shouted out 'You have not got an Honble. friend in this House.' Today he and Hoppy were very scathing about all and sundry ... I spoke to the Speaker about Ramsay[31] M.P. and told him that I thought it was high time he should be released – the Speaker told me that he too was beginning to get uncomfortable about the unfortunate man and had him in mind, but that the decision of the Committee of Priv[elege]s had rather complicated matters – he promised to do what he could.

Thursday 11 November   ... went to the Conservative Executive Committee meeting at the Caxton Hall – a lot of talk about the unfairness of the B.B.C. towards Conservatives. Tommie Dugdale had interviewed the Governor of the B.B.C. and protested – and protested. He was told that the trouble was that so few Conservative M.P.s could 'come across' on the wireless – was there ever such rot – they might ask me who can come across – if it was not for the trouble of preparing something to say I would ask Tommie Dugdale to put forward my name.

Friday 12 November   Changes in the Cabinet announced today, the most important of which is Lord Woolton's appointment to be Minister of Reconstruction. He is clearly a very able man who should know his job and as he is to be in the War Cabinet he should be in a position to get what he wants done. Llewellin, now our Minister in the U.S.A., is to succeed Woolton at the Ministry

---

[30] 'My Honourable Friend' is the form used in debate when referring to another M.P. who is of the same party.

[31] Archibald Henry Maule Ramsay (1894–1955), Con. M.P. Peebles & Midlothian S. 1931–45. Ramsay was strongly anti-Semitic and prominent in upper-class circles sympathetic to Nazi Germany. Documents found when Tyler Kent, a diplomat at the U.S. embassy in London, was arrested for espionage on 20 May 1940 linked him to Ramsay and other members of the Right Club. This led to an extension of the terms of Defence Regulation 18B by the Privy Council and on 23 May, together with Sir Oswald Mosley and leading figures of the British Union of Fascists, Ramsay was arrested and interned. He was detained in Brixton Prison until 26 Sep. 1944, but was never charged with any offence.

of Food – he is always being shifted from one job to another and is said to be a good man – though I have never noticed any great sign of ability in him. Willink,[32] K.C., who is an able man, is to succeed Ernest Brown as Minister of Health – Ernest B. becomes Chancellor of the Duchy of Lancaster *vice* Duff Cooper who they say is to be ambassador to De Gaulle – a hard job I should say.

Sunday 14 November   [Herbert] Morrison as usual has made a speech this weekend – he says that employers must have new ideas and our Will Lawther also has much the same thing to say. Morrison also tells the Labour Party to stop fooling and stick together or they will come to grief – which is good advice that will not be taken. The trouble of the Labour people is that loyalty to their leaders is quite unknown among them – when a man gets to the top there is always another fellow who is determined to pull him down. From a Conservative point of view the longer this peculiar trait in the Labour make-up continues, the better.

Saturday 20 November   Mosley[33] and his wife[34] have been released and their release appears to be exciting the left wingers who don't appreciate the impotence of the wretched man to do any harm and fail to understand that 18B is not a punitive instrument.[35]

Tuesday 23 November   Mosley's release was discussed today – Morrison made out quite a good case – but all the outside Bolshies of one kind and another, including the genteel Citrine, are up in

[32] Henry Urmston Willink (1894–1973), Con. M.P. Croydon N. 1940–48; Special Comm. for Rehousing for London Region 1940–43; Min. of Health 1943–45; Master of Magdalene College, Cambridge 1948–66; High Bailiff of Westminster 1942–67; Dean of Court of Arches & Vicar-Gen. of Province of Canterbury 1955–70; cr. Bart. 1957.
[33] Oswald Ernald Mosley (1896–1980), M.P. Harrow 1918–24 (Con. to 1920, Ind. 1920–24, Lab. from 1924), Smethwick 1926–31 (Lab. to 1931, then New Party); Chanc. Duchy of Lancaster 1929–30; Leader of New Party 1931–32, of British Union of Fascists 1932–40, of Union Movement 1948–66; interned 1940–43; suc. 6th Bart. 1928.
[34] Diana Mitford (1910–), daughter of 2nd Baron Redesdale; married 1929 Bryan Walter Guinness, later 2nd Baron Moyne (divorced 1934), married 1936 Sir Oswald Mosley; closely involved with him in British Union of Fascists during 1930s, visited Hitler, regarded as pro-German and interned with her husband.
[35] Defence Regulation 18B, under which Mosley and other British Fascists had been imprisoned since 1940, permitted internment without trial on grounds of national security; the Con. M.P. Ramsay was also held under this wartime regulation.

arms – however, the Government is not going to allow itself to be bullied.

Wednesday 24 November   My amendment to the Address has been selected by the Speaker, so I shall have to make a speech – and shall try and make a good one – I am certainly *au fait*[36] with the subject. ... Winston is again on the jaunt – gone to Teheran for a conference with Stalin and Roosevelt so we were told in secret today. The miserable little Attlee read out a prepared statement about the loss of Leros designed to make us all believe that our strategy is all right.

Thursday 25 November   ... we had a meeting of the constitutional committee. I am heartily sick of the committee and wish to God we could make our report and have done with it – but the position is still the same – I have been foolish enough to leave the thing to Agnes: and she has failed me ... I ought to have written it myself – my only excuse for not having done this is that I thought that she would do it better and that latterly I have been so tired and out of sorts that I have not had enough energy to concentrate properly on anything. ... I see no sign of ever ending our labours. My committee contains too many cranks: I was a fool to take on Phillimore and Douglas Jerrold – however, it is no use fussing – one always knows that even the worst dream must come to an end.

Headlam's lassitude heralded a breakdown in his health. He recorded 'feeling none too well, nursing my cold which is in the head but not very tiresome' on 26 November, and the next day travelled as planned to Bushton Manor in Wiltshire for the weekend. Here he was taken more seriously ill, and the entry for 27 November breaks off in mid-sentence after only three lines. He then spent nearly four weeks in the nursing home of Beatrice's physician, Dr. Todd, in Bristol, and the diary remains blank until 23 December. On Christmas Eve the Headlams travelled back to Holywell; Cuthbert was relieved to be home but noted in the diary 'I have been very ill and there it is – I am lucky I suppose to be alive and kicking – even kicking feebly.' The diary resumes from this point, but Headlam remained convalescent; on

---

[36] translation: familiar.

30 December he recorded that 'it looks as if I should take a long time to get going again.'

Friday 31 December And so ends 1943 – it has been a great year for the Allies and I only hope that 1944 will be as successful. I cannot understand, however, why there is such a fixed determination that the war is nearing its end in Europe – even some people who ought to be in the know are amazingly optimistic. I can see no sign of an immediate breakdown in German morale – the Germans must be fighting hard in Russia and they are certainly fighting well in Italy. They have had heaps of time to prepare for our continental invasion and we shall have to fight all out – of that I am fairly certain. ... Thank God I am better and glad to be still alive – perhaps I may still be of some use to some people – not so completely on the shelf as I imagine – but for the next few months I shall have to lie very low.

12

THE SECOND FRONT

January to September 1944

Headlam spent the first six weeks of 1944 recuperating at Holywell; he kept the diary regularly, but his knowledge of events was restricted to that provided by the press and radio. Towards the end of January he began to return to his normal routine and attended some meetings in Newcastle. However, his first visit to London in mid-February brought on further illness and he was confined to bed for the following three weeks. After this Headlam's strength recovered sufficiently for him to engage in local affairs, but he did not make another visit to the House of Commons until 21 April and only resumed a regular pattern of attendance at the end of May.

Tuesday 4 January 1944   The Russians report that they are now only 8 miles from the old Russian–Polish border: Montgomery is home again and evidently going to enjoy a lot of publicity – his farewell speech to the Eighth Army fully reported in all the papers.

Friday 7 January   The papers and wireless busy today boosting a new kind of aeroplane – it is 'jet-propelled' and is said to be a success and likely to revolutionize flying.

Sunday 9 January   The Common Wealth candidate has got in at the Skipton by-election, beating the Conservative by 221 votes: a big surprise I imagine to the party wirepullers. The Sunday press suggest that the farmers voted against the Government candidate as a mark of their disapproval of Rob Hudson who they say has broken his pledge to them regarding food prices.

Tuesday 11 January   In the wider sphere of the war the news is much the same as that of yesterday – a continued advance by the Russians who are now said to be at Sarny, a place about 30 miles into Poland – a slight advance in Italy – but the best news in my view is a statement by Winston and Roosevelt to the effect that the battle of the Atlantic is still going well: [the] total of merchant tonnage sunk in December was again low despite an extension of [the] U-boat operation area – fewer U-boats were destroyed during the month mainly owing to increased caution on their part: in 1943 the U-boats only sank 40 per cent of the merchant tonnage they sank in the previous year – on the other hand United Nations' tonnage constructed for 1943 nearly doubled the tonnage constructed in 1942. All this is good reading, but we must never forget that the battle in the Atlantic can never be won until the war itself is won

Wednesday 19 January   Winston has returned and must have recovered a deal quicker than I have – at any rate he arrived in London yesterday morning; presided over 2 Cabinet Councils; answered questions in the House and lunched with the King. He must have enjoyed every moment of his day – cheered by all and sundry and well in the limelight. The Russians are now making a new push in the Leningrad area which seems to be going well … the enemy's position in the eastern theatre would appear to be deteriorating more and more…

Thursday 20 January   [Tydeman] brought me a list of the candidates for the Area – apparently several constituencies are without candidates – 2 have been killed in the war. He asked whether it was true that Agnes was withdrawing[1] … I said not to my knowledge…

Monday 24 January   The news today is that a Common Wealth candidate has come out against me in North Newcastle. His name is H.A.C. Ridsdale and he is chairman of the Common Wealth people in the division. He is an employee of N.E.S.Co.[2] and is said

---

[1] As prospective Conservative candidate for Barnard Castle.
[2] North-Eastern Electric Supply Company, of which Headlam was a non-executive director.

to belong to the 'intellectuals'. It is tiresome but what one expected: one knows that in Newcastle there is a lot of soft stuff especially among the University people, and naturally such stuff responds to the Common Wealth appeal. I am told that a lot of young people, too, are fascinated by the doctrines of Acland[3] – I shall have to study it.

Tuesday 25 January   I met Mr. C. Wilton, the man who has succeeded Wilkin as chairman of the Central[4] division, at the Conservative Club. We had a long heart to heart and lunched together – I liked the man and was impressed by his keenness and evident desire to pull his weight. Denville,[5] apparently, has tried hard to put him against me and the federation scheme – Denville, he told me in confidence, was jealous of me! This I was already well aware of: he is a tiresome little man. After lunch I went and rested in the Northern Counties Club for a couple of hours – until Beatrice called for me and we went to Saville Row[6] ... Sykes has resigned and Temple was elected Chairman in his place. He is not the ideal man – but he seems keen to have the job and assures us that he will try and pull things round. One asks for nothing else – the present state of the Association is deplorable – even the women's branch can only boast of 120 members!

Wednesday 2 February   Winston has apparently upset people in Brighton by his letter to the Conservative candidate, but I should hardly imagine that there is any danger of losing the seat: it would be a slap in the face for him if the Conservative did not get in. He is far too self-satisfied and pleased with himself (perhaps not unnaturally) and of course does lack judgement. By-elections are becoming more interesting.

Saturday 5 February   The Government have held Brighton but only by 1,959 votes: the poll was a low one. The faithful Berry

---

[3] Richard Thomas Dyke Acland (1906–1990), M.P. Barnstaple 1935–45 (Lib. until Sep. 1942, then Common Wealth), Lab. M.P. Gravesend 1947–55; suc. 15th Bart. 1939; founder of the Common Wealth movement.

[4] Headlam wrote 'north' by mistake; Wilkin (q.v.) had been Chairman of Newcastle Central Division Conservative Association.

[5] Denville (q.v.) was Con. M.P. for Newcastle Central 1931–45.

[6] The office of the Newcastle North association, for a meeting of the executive committee.

press is trying to make out that it was only Winston's letters (which his candidate did not even send out as a pamphlet) which saved the seat. I hope to hear all the gossip about it from Tommie Dugdale when I get back to London.

Tuesday 15 February I went to the House this morning and people were very kind to me – Anthony Eden and James Stuart especially – both of them seemed really pleased to see me back again (for how long I wonder?) and regretted that I was not fit enough to be a member of the Speaker's Conference. The Speaker, too, whom I went to see, was equally nice.

Wednesday 16 February I am no worse today – but no better and I have been very careful of myself – but it has been a foul day – cold and foggy. Went to the House this morning ... everyone I meet has been ill, 'M & B'[7] seems to have saved several M.P.s from dying of pneumonia – Ned Grigg with whom I lunched has had jaundice very badly, etc. – altogether I appear to have escaped more lightly than many others! I have heard little or no gossip – the general impression is that the Italian show has gone wrong,[8] but no one seems to know quite why – Winston is to speak next week. I have not seen him about, but they tell me that he is quite recovered – which I find it difficult to believe. I called on Tommie Dugdale this evening. He was as usual charming. He tells me that the scheming and underground work by Beaverbrook, Bracken, Belisha etc. is almost more than he can stand and is bound to lead to trouble before long. I can well believe it – it is quite deplorable that such crooks should be in control of everything.

Wednesday 23 February In bed all day – Winston seems to have made a good speech yesterday, telling people that we are a long way off winning the war – it was high time that he did this as, despite the slowness of the Italian advance, there is still a deal to much optimism about. Winston assured the House that everything was being done to reconcile the Russians and Poles – but he

[7] A medicine which Headlam had also been prescribed – 'a marvellous drug': Headlam diary, 24 Feb. 1944.

[8] The Allied advance had been held for a long period at Monte Cassino, whilst the landing farther north at Anzio had not secured a large beachhead and was now under severe pressure from German counter-attacks.

plumped all out for the Communist 'Marshal' Tito[9] in Yugoslavia which will cause a lot of trouble I should imagine with the Yugoslav Government over here – clearly we are letting the Russians lead us by the nose so far as eastern Europe is concerned.

Sunday 27 February   ... all the Seaham Colliery miners are out on strike ... one really does despair of the miners – they have covered themselves with shame during this war – and the odd thing is that the mad British public still regards them as a combination of all the virtues. Today the papers tell us that coke is to be rationed.

Tuesday 7 March   I am beginning to feel a bit stronger and more like one's own self – but it is no use trying to believe that I can resume my ordinary life – I get so easily tired and have less energy than ever to concentrate on work of any kind.

Thursday 16 March   The Government have declared their housing policy in the Commons. Their proposals appear to me sensible and practical – not attempting anything more than can be done immediately after the war – needless to say all and sundry in the House profess to be outraged or disappointed, as the case may be, at the meagreness of what is proposed. Such criticism is inevitable and it is a thousand pities that all these controversial matters have to be discussed at a time like this. If only Winston had adhered firmly to the policy of not introducing such measures as must arouse party strife until the war crisis is past, how much better it would have been – but, presumably, the pressure of the press and the noisy people has been too strong.

Friday 17 March   We have given Stuttgart a terrific bombing – all this destruction of German industries and communications must be helping the Russians, but I doubt very much whether they recognize our help. This is understandable, but extremely unfor-

[9] Josip Broz (1892–1980), known as 'Tito' from 1922; Yugoslav Communist organizer, imprisoned 1928–34; Gen. Sec., Yugoslav Communist Party 1937–80; leader of 'Partisan' (Communist) resistance from June 1941, named 'Marshal of Yugoslavia' at the Jajce Congress of the Anti-Fascist Nat. Liberation Ctte., Nov. 1943; head of the provisional & federal govt. 1943–45; P.M. 1945–53; Pres. 1953–74, Pres. for life 1974–80.

tunate for the future – the Russians will say that they beat the Germans single-handed and all our help to them in materials, etc., and in our bombing campaign will be lost sight of. Until our armies are operating on the continent no Russian will consider that we are pulling our weight in the war – and who knows where the Russians may have got to by the time the 'Second Front' gets going?

Sunday 19 March   The Russians announce that the Germans are in flight over the Dniester and that a big catastrophe is in store for the enemy. The Russian advance is certainly a great military achievement and seems to have completely upset the German defence – instead of flagging it seems to gather momentum as it goes forward. Strategically and tactically it is a marvellous performance and the organization behind the front must be of the first order. The wags, so they say, are telling how Winston was rung up on the telephone the other night by Stalin – 'Who's there?' asked Winston – 'It's Joe speaking' was the reply – 'Where are you speaking from?' – 'Calais – do you want me to come any further?' What happens, I wonder, if the Russians get to Berlin before we start the 'Second Front'? – as things are going now, such a thing might happen.

Saturday 25 March   Simon[10] seems to be stupider and stupider about his rules and regulations – no one over 60 to be made a J.P., the appointment of schoolmasters to the Bench advocated, etc. It strikes one as rather absurd that a man over 70 can be L[ord] C[hancellor] or a Judge of the High Court and that a sound man of 60 should be debarred from being made a J.P. It quite rules out a Conservative working man being on the bench – for no one pays him for his day's work and he really cannot afford to give the time until he gives up work. The Labour J.P.s, up here at any rate, all get paid for their public services by the Unions or the Party. It is a sorry business.

Sunday 26 March   Winston spoke on the wireless tonight for fifty minutes – it struck us all that he spoke less vigorously and I don't think that it was the sort of speech that the public was expecting –

[10] Lord Simon, the Lord Chancellor.

not enough about coming events in the war and too much about all the planning business for after the war – a defence of the Government's reconstruction policy about which the average man is getting a bit tired I fancy despite all that is said by the planners.

Tuesday 28 March   The Govt. has been beaten by 1 vote on an amendment to a clause in the Education Bill moved by Mrs. Thelma Cazalet – the amendment laid down that in the teaching profession women sh[oul]d receive the same salaries as men. This amendment emanated from the Tory Reform Group and is typical of its attitude of mind. Obviously if such a rule were made for women teachers, it would have to be made to apply to women in the Civil Service, and could not stop there. In equity there is no reason why women should not be paid equal wages to those paid to men for equal service – but such a change would greatly change existing conditions and must be carefully considered in all its aspects before it is hastily adopted for one profession. I doubt very much whether the change would really work out in the interests of women as a whole, but I have an open mind on the subject. Had I been in the House, I should have voted against Thelma and her friends who included the Labour Party as well as the Tory reformers.

Wednesday 29 March   A telegram from James Stuart[11] this evening asking me to come and vote for the Government tomorrow – replied in the negative. The Government is sure to have an overwhelming majority – its mistake is to have given way to the clamour for controversial legislation in war-time. There must be a division of opinion upon such legislation and this means party politics – once you have party politics in active play anything may happen. The loss of a division, however, by one vote on a clause in a Bill in a House of 233 in my opinion does not call for a vote of confidence. Why not have put the matter right in the HofL?

Friday 31 March   I went into Newcastle this morning in order to preside over the Area Executive Committee in the afternoon ... really the Conservative apathy prevailing in this Area is lamentable

[11] Con. & Govt. Chief Whip; Churchill chose to regard the defeat on the 'equal pay' amendment as an attack on the govt., and its reversal was to be moved on 30 March and treated as a Vote of Confidence.

... The Government won their confidence division in the HofC yesterday by 425 to 23 and so the sensitive Winston is once again in a good humour – but these silly affairs should not be in wartime.

Saturday 1 April We have made a big bombing attack on Nuremberg and lost 94 bombers on the job – apparently a desperate resistance was put up by the *Luftwaffe* all across Germany, but the bombers report that they got through and gave Hitler's city[12] a real dosing – one marvels at the courage and pertinacity of our bombing crews: God only knows how they stand it.

Wednesday 5 April Bevin has 'spoken out' against the strike and is threatening all and sundry with terrible things unless they go back to work – he asserts (with truth I should say) that there are subversive influences behind all this industrial unrest in S. Wales, on the Clyde and on Tyneside, and generally among the miners – then why to goodness has he allowed it to go on so long undenounced even, certainly not punished. He locks up scores and scores of perfectly harmless people and leaves out of jug[13] these agitators who are really injuring national interests.

Saturday 15 April I attended the Lord Mayor's luncheon in honour of James Grigg who opened the City 'Salute the Soldier' week – sat between Irene Ward and Allendale[14] – the former more than usually skittish and above herself, the only woman present. Much to my surprise I was asked to move a vote of thanks to the L.M. for his hospitality – the first time I have ever been invited to open my mouth at a civic entertainment. I presided over the Area Council conference in the afternoon. It was addressed by the Vice Chairman of the Party central organization (Harold Mitchell,[15] M.P.) in a rather long, dull speech – I moved a resolution about

[12] Nuremberg was the location of the Nazi Party rallies from 1933 to 1938, and the site of Hitler's planned monumental buildings.

[13] A colloquial term for prison.

[14] Wentworth Henry Canning Beaumont (1890–1956), Lib. peer; Lord in Waiting 1931–32, 1937–52, 1954–56; Pres., Northern Lib. Fed. 1925–49; Chairman, West Riding Unemployment Centres 1936–41; suc. 2nd Viscount Allendale 1923.

[15] Harold Paton Mitchell (1900–1983), Con. M.P. Brentford & Chiswick 1931–45; P.P.S. to J. Colville 1931–35, to R. Assheton 1939–42; British Liaison Officer with Polish Forces 1940–41; Con. Party Vice-Chairman 1942–45; Lecturer in Hispanic American Studies, Stanford University, California 1959–65; cr. Bart. 1945.

the location of industry which Donald Scott seconded. The attendance was not too bad. I brought Mitchell back here for dinner and
he left by the night train for London – not a bad fellow – rich,
amiable and well-meaning – quite suitable for his job.

Friday 21 April   I spent the morning at the HofC and lunched
there ... I find that there is little gossip here – all and sundry are
fairly cheerful, but there is, I think, considerable anxiety about
coming events. People don't say much about it, but it is obvious
that the invasion is in everyone's mind – and no wonder – the more
one hears about the German preparations for our coming, the more
one realizes what kind of a campaign we are in for – and I
personally am fearful that our and the American forces may not
be as fully a disciplined and organized and well-led an army as will
be required for such a struggle as is before them.

Tuesday 25 April   The Budget today – I listened to most of John
Anderson's speech – a sensible, well-written essay which he read
much better than he usually reads his speeches. It was well-received
and as there were no new taxes, everyone was pleased. The fact is
that we have over-budgeted so persistently since the war began that
the Treasury can afford to be lenient – nevertheless, Sir John's
stock has risen and people are beginning to regard him as a great
financier and as a possible successor to Winston – but this means
nothing because in the HofC Smoking Room a new leader is
decided upon almost every other day.

Friday 28 April   I spent most of today at the HofC listening to
the debate on Bevin's proposed regulation dealing with the penalties
to be inflicted on people who encourage other people to strike. I
should have liked to say a word or two in this debate, but the
whips did not wish us to intervene and so I refrained from trying
to get in. Aneurin Bevan made a deplorable speech which helped
Bevin a lot when it came for him to reply. He did very well and
Bevan's prayer was heavily defeated. I lunched at the House with
James Stuart, Donald Somervell and Charles Waterhouse who were
all very pleasant. James retains all his old charm and sense of
humour and, I should say, is doing his job as Chief Whip admirably,
though I should doubt whether he has much control over Winston –
but then who has?

Thursday 18 May　　The news today is that Cassino[16] has been captured – 'evacuated' by the enemy – and that the whole of the 'Gustav' defence positions are in our hands – good progress has been made and it sounds very satisfactory – what one wonders is why we ever made a frontal attack on Cassino?

Friday 19 May　　The newspapers are still gloating over the capture of Cassino and all it implies ... Winston has made a good speech in London at a luncheon given to Mr. Curtin,[17] the Australian P.M., in praise of a limited monarchy. He pointed out what I am always saying – how odd it is that we who do so well under our form of monarchy are always advocating a republican form of government in other countries. I suppose our foolish left wingers think that such counsel is a sign of the democratic spirit which they would have people believe inspires them.

Sunday 21 May　　I feel so utterly useless nowadays with nothing to do and one thing and another – this is all wrong, because I am lucky to be alive and improving in health. I have a lot for which to be thankful, and it useless to be out of spirits because I have no job of war work and am doing nothing *pro bono publico*.[18] What should one's own concerns matter – all that does matter is winning the war – and for the first time I feel that the war may come to an end – the war in Europe I mean – this year. The Italian campaign is showing that the Germans are weakening – if our people can drive them from prepared positions in the mountains I feel that they can be driven out of any defences – perhaps 'Monty' may yet be proved to be right and that even the invasion of Europe may turn out to be 'a simple affair'.

Wednesday 24 May　　Milner promised to call me this morning in the Foreign Office debate, but when the time came I funked it – very silly of me, but I simply could not face the ordeal – I was tired after listening to Winston for an hour and a half – needless

---

[16] German forces holding the monastery on Monte Cassino had delayed the Allied advance in Italy for some time, resisting heavy bombing and frontal assaults.

[17] John Curtin (1885–1945), Australian trade union and Labour leader, Lab. M.P. (at Canberra) Fremantle 1928–31, 1934–45; Lab. Leader 1935–45; P.M. Australia 1941–45.

[18] translation: for the public good.

to say the moment after I had said I did not want to speak I regretted it. Winston I did not think as good as usual. He has got into the habit of speaking in a conversational tone and this does not carry in the HofL.[19] The substance of his stuff was good so far as I could hear it, though he really had nothing we did not know to tell us. We are to have an international Council and a police force, but as this (at any rate to begin with) will be run by us, Russia and the U.S.A. (if the other two play which I doubt) it won't mean all the folly of the League of Nations over again. My own view is that any kind of international organization to maintain peace is doomed to failure – neither this country nor any other independent nation is likely to fight a preventive war, unless its own interests are threatened – besides when the next war comes along there will be two parties in Europe just as there have always been in the past. This view is rather a gloomy one, but it is, I believe, in accordance with human nature.

Thursday 25 May　　The debate on foreign affairs went on today but I did not listen to much of it – however, I heard Anthony Eden wind up and thought that he made a good speech – but he is not a really first class speaker and I doubt whether he ever will be. He lacks fire and distinction and never impresses one as a formidable personality or, indeed, as a real master of his subject – but I am very critical and I may underrate his efforts – he appeared to satisfy most people today though he really said very little more than Winston said and left some of us wondering what our foreign policy is.

Saturday 27 May　　The Government's White Paper explaining its proposals to provide 'full employment' is published in the press today. I have not examined the proposals carefully but ... I doubt whether any scheme which man can devise can guarantee employment for so many workers as exist in our small country – everything really depends on our ability to regain and develop our foreign trade, political sanity and a peace established and maintained by our military power.

---

[19] Due to the bomb damage suffered by their own chamber, the Commons were meeting in the House of Lords during this period.

Tuesday 30 May　　The invasion of Dutch New Guinea has apparently come as a complete surprise to the Japanese and is proceeding satisfactorily. One is apt to overlook the war in the Pacific, but it certainly seems to be being carried out very effectively, considering its enormous difficulties. One wonders why the Japanese fleet is doing so little – presumably it is being husbanded for the bigger struggle yet to come.

Thursday 1 June　　... the important announcement today is that the Germans announce their retreat on a wide front in Italy which must mean that we really have broken the line of defence to which they have been clinging so long. I feel that if we can drive them out of a defensive system of this kind in a country such as Italy, we can drive them out of any system of defences anywhere in Europe – it is a very cheering sensation. [De] Valera is winning the general election in Ireland – but who cares? I suppose that we shall not even trouble about 'Eire' after the war – and yet what a menace the beastly, little country has been to us all through this war – first, as a 'U' boat shelter, and always as a haven for German spying. What other nation in the world would have tolerated such a situation? ... Perhaps the best policy might be to cut Eire out of the Empire and treat it in the future as a foreign country.

Sunday 4 June　　The news from Italy today is good ... It looks as if we had reached the last stage of the drive to Rome. The 'pre-invasion blitz', as the newspapers call it, continues with increasing vigour and we are said to be doing a vast amount of damage on German communications and supply bases in western Germany and France. We are also, I am glad to say, going for German oil supplies – oil is the most necessary war supply and surely the enemy must be running short of it? Where will the invasion come I wonder? Not the Calais region I think – it is too obvious and too strongly guarded I should imagine. The Antwerp approach looks tempting, but, somehow or other, I fancy a landing in France – either in the Cherbourg area or in Brittany. We must have a good port and Cherbourg would fit the bill – and Brest, as a U-boat base, must be tempting. Whatever has been settled upon, the secret is being well kept which is the great thing – the enemy must be surprised if we are to effect a successful landing.

Tuesday 6 June   The invasion of France has begun. We have succeeded in effecting landings between Havre and Cherbourg and, so far, things are reported to be going well – but Winston in the House today, where he made a statement, warned us not to be too optimistic and that very heavy fighting was ahead. It looks to me as if we must have succeeded in effecting a tactical surprise, otherwise how could we have pierced the 'wall'[20] so quickly.

Wednesday 7 June   The news today from France is still satisfactory, but the Germans have brought up their reserves and the fighting seems to be pretty severe – everything, I should imagine, depends on our ability to keep pushing in our troops, guns and tanks and piling up supplies. I spoke in the House today (Committee of Supply, Location of Industry) – Dalton made a speech on the portion of the Gov.'s White Paper dealing with the subject. What he said was fairly satisfactory I thought, so far as the north east coast was concerned – but he took over an hour to get out what he had to say – and some Labour Front Bencher who followed him spoke for 45 minutes! Milner called me next and I spoke for a quarter of an hour – not too badly considering all things – anyway I have not neglected the interests of my constituents which is the great thing! and it is a relief to have got off a speech at last. It is over six months since I spoke in the HofC.

Tuesday 13 June   I have spent a dull day at the House, but voted against the Government – a rare thing for me to do – but Rob Hudson was impossible. He proposes that his office should have the right of deciding whether or not a farmer should be allowed to produce milk for sale, and that a man's only appeal should be to a tribunal of 3 on which one of the members should be an officer of the Ministry. We got him to say that he would feel bound to accept the decision of this tribunal if it were unanimous – but this of course did not go far enough, seeing that one of its members would be one of his officials. I felt fully justified in recording my vote against Rob – and I was amused to find 2 Common Wealth M.P.s voting in the same lobby – of course their party is dead against private enterprise but they both happen to represent agricultural constituencies! It would seem that these carefully selected, public-

---

[20] German propaganda had made much of the defences of the 'Atlantic Wall'.

spirited, state-minded creatures are very much like the average, much despised M.P.s when it comes to a division. The campaigns in Normandy and Italy are progressing satisfactorily, but it will be some time, I fear, before the progress in France is as rapid as it now is in Italy. It is still a long road to Berlin and yet I am beginning to be hopeful that the war in Europe may be over much more quickly than I have hitherto thought possible.

Wednesday 14 June   De Gaulle is in France and apparently receiving a big reception – surely we ought to recognize him and his Govt? Harold Nicolson, who is, or professes to be, well informed, told me today that the only trouble is Roosevelt who dislikes and distrusts De Gaulle who he says has continually lied to him. We are too much influenced by American ideas and opinions – what is important for us is not to let the Free French turn to the Russians. It is all important for us to maintain good relations with France after the war, if it is at all possible. The French dislike us enough now: we don't want them to dislike us more.

Thursday 15 June   ... to the Central Office where the Sub-committee met to hear what old Lord Salisbury had to say about HofL reform: shortly – he is resigned to the Parliament Act, to qualifications for hereditary peers, to a limited number of life peers – so really the only difference between his ideas and ours are the nature of the qualifications for hereditary peers and the number of life peers – he is afraid of 'swamping', we are not.

Friday 16 June   I half intended to speak in the Ramsay debate (18B)[21] today and I think that I might have been called – but after hearing Morrison I felt that perhaps in Ramsay's own interest it was better to keep him detained than to let him out. Irving Albery[22] and Archie Southby each put his case well, but they were silly to have a division – there were too few people present. I abstained from voting as, although I hate 18B, I fancy that it must still be necessary from what Herbert Morrison said, and that it is less cruelly administered than it used to be. We had a noisy night last

---

[21] The M.P. detained under Defence Regulation 18B (q.v.).
[22] Irving James Albery (1879–1967), Con. M.P. Gravesend 1924–45; kt. 1936.

night – several alerts and a deal of gunning. The Germans have used one of their new secret weapons – a 'pilotless plane'[23] and I fancy that it is going to give us some trouble...

Sunday 18 June   Tommie Lascelles ... gave us some interesting war gossip (he has been to the front with the King). Our landing was a complete surprise to the enemy – it seems that as a result of our false reports he was expecting a landing in the Calais area and possible landings in Holland and Norway. We have some kind of device (a contraption of some kind attached to the tail of an aeroplane which vastly multiplies the noise of the machine and gives the impression of there being a host of machines): single machines so equipped were flown over in the Calais area: this resulted in all the *Luftwaffe* available being sent there – and when they came back saying they could find no enemy machines, they were sent back again as the German instruments still were hearing the noise of many planes. The landing really was cheaply made – the only people who suffered badly were the Yanks, one of whose div[ision]s came up against a German division which was practising a defence scheme. Tommie said that the 'synthetic' harbours (invented by Louis Mountbatten[24]) are proving a huge success.

Monday 19 June   ... alerts have been going all day and I saw 2 of these beastly [V-1] robots in the air this morning. They go at a terrific pace and it is difficult to see how aeroplanes can account for many of them and what science is to do about them it is difficult to see. The only real remedy that I can see is to drive the Germans far enough east to prevent their sending over the Robots.

Tuesday 20 June   The House met today in the 'Annexe'[25] – much

[23] The V-1 rocket, also known as the 'flying bomb'.
[24] (Albert Victor Nicholas) Louis Francis Mountbatten (1900–1979), naval career; Chief of Combined Operations 1942–43; S.A.C. South East Asia 1943–46; last Viceroy of India Mar.-Aug. 1947, and first Gov.-Gen. 1947–48; 4th Sea Lord 1950–52; C. in C. Med. 1952–54; 1st Sea Lord 1955–59; Chief of Defence Staff 1959–65; assassinated by I.R.A. bomb; cr. Viscount Mountbatten of Burma 1946, Earl 1947, K.G. 1946.
[25] Church House (q.v.); near to the Palace of Westmister, this more modern and stronger building had been used during periods of heavy bombing in Nov.-Dec. 1940 and Apr.-June 1941. Since then the Commons had used the chamber of the House of Lords (their own House being destroyed by a bomb on 10–11 May 1941), but the V-1 attacks caused a temporary return to Church House from 20 June to 3 Aug. 1944.

to everyone's annoyance – it is such a beastly, uncomfortable, inconvenient place. Winston, it seems, insisted upon our going there as he believes that the German robots have the Houses of Parliament taped and that we shall all be safer in a better constructed modern building – it all seems to me rather silly, but there it is ... The news today is good, and our grip on the Cherbourg peninsula is said to be tightening. The French *Maquis*[26] movement appears to be working effectively behind the German lines and to be gathering strength – if this is really the case, it should materially assist us. Winston has made a speech in which he seems to suggest that the war against Germany may come to an end by the late summer – even if he thinks so, I feel that it is a mistake to say so.

Monday 26 June Fighting is now going on in the streets of Cherbourg and it looks as if the place was ours. It is rather a pity that it should have fallen entirely to the Americans: it will only make their countrymen more certain than ever that they are winning the war. I am told that our efforts are scarcely noted in the American press. I fancy that the Americans after this war are likely to be more swollen-headed and tiresome than after the last war: they may well be more troublesome to us than the Russians.

Tuesday 27 June There was little doing in the Annexe and the attendance was not large – the 'p[ilotless] p[lane]' raids and the disinclination to go to the Annexe will keep a lot of people away I expect. The raids go on day and night and I fancy that the damage done already is pretty considerable. The morale of the people, too, is a bit shaken – crowds of people are said to be leaving London and the tubes are again crowded at night time.[27] A sign of the exodus, which rather amused me today, was evident at Simpsons [restaurant] – usually the place is simply packed with 'business' people – Jews especially – today the place was almost empty and the manager told us that all the Jews had vanished into the country.

Wednesday 28 June I dined at the 'Rag' with Martel,[28] the

[26] The term for the French Resistance.

[27] The Underground railway stations were used as air raid shelters at night.

[28] Giffard Le Quesne Martel (1889–1958), army career; C. in C. Mesopotamia 1936–38; Dep. Dir. of Mechanization, War Office 1938–39; G.O.C. 50th (Northumberland) Div. 1939, Royal Armoured Corps 1940; Head of British Military Mission at Moscow 1943; Colonel Commandant, Royal Engineers 1944; Con. cand. Barnard Castle 1945; kt. 1943.

General, and Robin Turton[29] M.P. The former who commanded the 50th Division for a time is anxious to find a north country seat, vainly imagining that he will get a lot of votes from his ex-service men. I suggested Berwick as the most likely chance – but both Turton and I agreed that if he won the seat he would have to live in the division. He promptly replied that his wife would not live in the north. I then suggested the Durham City division and I am to make inquiries regarding it.

Monday 3 July   The news today is good from Normandy so far as it goes – we have held some pretty severe German counter-attacks and are consolidating our tactical positions round Caen. The Russian advance continues and it really does look as if the Germans were being given a tremendous shaking – at the rate they are going the Russians look like getting to East Prussia before we get to Caen – one wonders what has happened to the Germans in the East.

Wednesday 5 July   The 'p[ilotless] plane' war continues and one is beginning to hear stories of the death and disaster they are causing – probably most of these stories are exaggerated, but certainly people are getting the wind up – this new 'air blitz' is the subject of all the scraps of conversation one overhears in the street and tubes etc., and M.P.s discuss little else. I gather that the exodus from London is considerable and the shelters are full – it is not surprising and up to a point Hitler should be pleased – but it does not seem to occur to anyone that we shall have to make a patched up peace or give up the struggle a day earlier because of this new weapon – it is regarded as a nasty new form of nuisance which is upsetting to the nerves and a cause of additional suffering.

Thursday 6 July   Winston spoke this morning in the Annexe – a statement regarding 'p[ilotless] planes' which has cleared the air. He did not attempt to minimize the damage and inconvenience they are causing, and he prepared us to expect worse things of the kind to come – but he assured us that everything was being done

[29] Robert ('Robin') Hugh Turton (1903–94), Con. M.P. Thirsk & Malton 1929–74; P.S. Nat. Insurance 1951–53, & Pensions 1953–54; U.S. For. Office 1954–55; Min. of Health 1955–57; Father of the House 1965–74; Chairman, Commonwealth Industries Assoc. 1963–74; kt. 1971, cr. Baron Tranmire 1974.

to cope with the new weapons and told us that a good many 'p[ilotless] planes' were already being destroyed in one way or another. On the whole I think that this statement will do good: there has been so much gossip and exaggeration about the casualties, etc. ... to the Central Office where we had a meeting of the Sub-committee – Jerrold, Taylor, Lady Davidson were the other members present. We discussed Lord Salisbury's views about HofL reform and decided that we would try and meet his opposition to our life peers' proposal by limiting their number to 250 – this should reduce the danger of 'swamping' which he considers so dangerous. Next meeting we are to begin consideration of the draft report – I should be thankful when we have done with it.

Tuesday 11 July　Morrison moved the second reading of his planning bill – no one likes it, but if such a bill has to be, this one seems to me comparatively harmless. The Labour people and the local authorities are said to disapprove of it, the former because it does not nationalize the land, the latter because they were not consulted about it – which seems rather stupid on the part of the Government. The Labour Party is said to be going to vote against the 2nd reading although their leaders are supporting it. Really the attitude of the Labour people whose own people are in the Cabinet and who profess to support the Government is intolerable. They just do as they choose and are playing the party game all the time. Lunched at the House with Lady Apsley[30] – she is a charming woman and I admire her pluck tremendously – but she is rather too earnest a parliamentarian for me, a trifle boring after a bit, and, as I had dear Eddie Cadogan on my other side, I was not really in luck.

Wednesday 12 July　The 2nd reading of Morrison's bill was carried by 214 votes to 14, or something like that. The Labour Party decided not to vote against the bill but to abstain – a mean decision. The Labour people in the Government voted for the bill. What a strange method of supporting the Government this is – the Labour leaders go into the lobby with the rest of us – Greenwood and the rank and file sit on the fence.

[30] Violet Emily Mildred Meeking (1895–1966), married 1924 Allen Algernon Bathurst, styled Lord Apsley; Con. M.P. Bristol Central 1943–45 (seat previously held by her deceased husband); Dir., Western Airways 1936–55.

Friday 14 July   The French state that the S.S.[31] troops in France
are perpetrating the most ferocious massacres on the civil population, exterminating whole villages – there is probably a good deal
of exaggeration in these reports – and yet these S.S. people are
capables de tout[32] as we already know. We go on assuring all and
sundry that those responsible for these crimes will be punished, but
how in the world they are to be discovered and proved guilty one
does not know – of course Hitler, Himmler, Goering, Goebbels &
Co. are the responsible parties – but when it comes to the point
shall we even hang them?

Saturday 15 July   The Russians have stormed Pinsk – the
Germans, as usual, report that they have abandoned the town. The
capture of Pinsk is a big step forward I should say to the capture
of Brest-Litovsk and Warsaw – really the Russians are steam-
rolling this summer and one can see no real reason why – if they
can keep going at this pace – they should not be in Berlin by the
autumn. It all must depend, of course, upon the German will to
resistance, and the strength of Hitler's reserves – one is beginning
to wonder if he has any worth considering. The drain upon the
German armies for the last 4 years must have been stupendous and
the greater part of the able-bodied man-power must surely be
mainly used up by now? War material, too, must be running short –
above all, oil. I should not care to be in Hitler's shoes today –
what will be the end of the man, I wonder? I don't believe that he
will commit suicide, but I should imagine that he stands a good
chance of being bumped off before long by his own people.

Thursday 20 July   ... to the Central Office where we had a
meeting of our Sub-committee ... I had a talk with Tommie
Dugdale after we had finished. He does not look well, but assured
me that he was better. He tells me that my little talk with Anthony
Eden the other day regarding Conservative policy and reorganization has impressed that great man – which is satisfactory so far
as it goes – but of course Winston is the snag. He thinks that some
kind of compromise can be made with the Labour Party so that

---

[31] The elite force of the Nazi Party; its military wing, the *Waffen S.S.*, grew to
include several fully-equipped divisions and fought alongside the regular army
forces, but was responsible for atrocities against civilians and captured prisoners.

[32] translation: capable of anything.

his National Government may continue, and so he is disinclined to give his own party a lead. I think that he is living in a fool's paradise and that as soon as the war in Europe is ended the Labour people, whatever their leaders may wish, will go their own way.

Wednesday 26 July The House was as dull as usual – living in the Annexe appears to be bad for morale – people cannot face its deadliness and lack of all amenities.

Monday 31 July The German losses every day on all their fronts must be terrific – one wonders how it is possible for them to carry on. ... In Germany all kinds of exciting things are said to be going on[33] – but it looks to me as if the Nazis had got the situation well in hand for the time being at any rate. Here the line is as usual rather absurd – everyone seems pleased that the Generals should try and murder Hitler, but they are accused of doing so only to save the *Junkers*[34] and the military caste. The argument is that they only want peace now in order to set to work to prepare for another war. This may or may not be true, but that does not prevent their wanting to end this war because they see that their army is beaten and to save further bloodshed – Germany is certain to make another war sooner or later if she is given an opportunity whatever the Generals may do now.

Tuesday 1 August The news today continues good – clearly we are on the move in France all along the line. The Americans are approaching Rennes and we are beginning to make progress from the Caen line – it looks as if we were doing a fine job of work and treating the enemy as he treated us in 1940 – but he is not beaten yet! The Turks have decided to break off diplomatic relations with Germany ... I expect that it is fear of the Russians and not any particular affection for us which has induced the Turkish government to take this step – the fear of what Russia may do must be all pervading now in the Baltic States, the Balkans and Turkey. It looks as if the Baltic would be a Russian lake after this war for

---

[33] The purges after the unsuccessful attempt to assassinate Hitler by Colonel von Stauffenberg on 20 July, and the failure of the following army coup in Berlin.

[34] Originally the term for the agrarian gentry of Prussia, this was extended in common British usage to embrace the whole of the traditional German upper classes.

some time to come and presumably they will also obtain access to the Mediterranean – a nice look out for us in the years to come.

Thursday 3 August   Winston's speech yesterday has not told us much more than we knew already, but it was couched in an optimistic tone. He clearly expects a fairly early end of the war unless something goes wrong. He was wise enough, however, not to rule out our having a worse time at home before the end comes. The 'p[ilotless] plane' trouble is not yet overcome – and Winston seems to anticipate the coming of the 10 ton torpedo bomb.

Monday 7 August   The war news continues good – full of big possibilities. The Americans are stated to have 'sealed off' the Brest peninsula ... our people are doing the hard job of holding the greater part of the German forces while the Americans are doing the more spectacular part of the business – but it is a fine show and the team work and organization appear to be all that could be desired. If all goes well, I can visualize a really big coup coming – we may quite possibly get right round all the German forces on the south side of the Seine if only they are fools enough to hang on where they are long enough – and as Hitler now must be running the show and not the great General Staff this is quite likely to happen. I am beginning to think that we may be in Paris a deal sooner than I ever thought possible when this campaign in Normandy began.

Tuesday 8 August   The Liberals guided by that stupid fellow Lord Perth have put out proposals for Germany after the war. They pin their faith on the control of arms and education. The former proposal is all right, the latter seems to me absurd – how can we possibly hope to make the Germans good little boys and make them love us? It is a typical Liberal idea and no doubt will delude a lot of warm-hearted people.

Saturday 12 August   Winston has gone to Italy – and as we are bombing southern France heavily it may be that a new invasion plan is maturing in that area and that Winston has gone to see the show. What strength the man must have to do these trips and what fun he gets out of it all – well, he deserves all the fun he can get now – he must have passed through some hectic moments since he became P.M. .... Mannerheim,[35] who is now President of Finland, is said to be negotiating peace terms with Russia – I fear that that damned Stalin will drive a hard bargain. His attitude, too, towards the Polish Govt. in London is becoming very unpleasant and I am afraid that our Government may play the dirty on the decent Poles here, which would be a terrible mistake, covering their policy under the sacred word of 'democracy' as interpreted by Stalin. To allow the Russians to set up a Bolshevik form of government in Poland and set up what frontier they like would be a pitiable thing to do, ruinous to our prestige in Europe.

Sunday 20 August There is now no doubt that the Germans in France are being well beaten and for how long they can remain in the country unless they can be heavily reinforced – which would seem to be out of the question with the Russians pounding against their eastern front – it is difficult to forecast – but not for long I should say. ... It seems to me that Hitler will be lucky if he gets many of his troops out of France to defend the Fatherland. I am sure that Paris will be in the bag before many days are past, and I hope before long that we shall get the Pas de Calais.[36]

Monday 21 August A body of M.P.s, Conservatives headed by Wardlaw-Milne, have produced a scheme for Germany after the war. It sounds all right on paper as all such schemes do, but I doubt whether it could be worked.

Wednesday 23 August Tonight on the wireless we heard that Paris is liberated – apparently the deed was done by patriot forces aided by the citizens within the city – this is as it should have been – a great thing for French *amour propre*.[37] We continue our pursuit of the enemy on the lower Seine – in southern France American forces are said to have reached Grenoble, and they are closing round Marseilles. It all sounds very good. In the eastern

[35] Carl Gustaf Emil Mannerheim (1867–1951), Finnish soldier and statesman; acting Head of State 1919–20; resumed command of Finnish Army 1939, entered war against Russia in alliance with Germany June 1941; Pres. 1944–46; secured armistice with Russia Sep. 1944, joined Allies and entered war against Germany Mar. 1945.

[36] The area of the launching sites of the short-range V-1 'flying bomb' rocket.

[37] translation: pride, self-belief.

theatre the Russians have renewed their offensive in the Jussy area and claim to be making rapid progress. King Michael[38] of Rumania is reported to have dismissed Antonescu[39] and to have broken with Germany. Well – things are moving fast – one ought to feel tremendously elated and yet my feelings are more of thankfulness for a great danger past rather than of triumph. We thoroughly deserved to be beaten and had not God loved us we should have been beaten – our stupidity and laziness and lack of patriotism between 1918 and 1939 were almost unbelievable – the nation was sound enough at bottom, but we allowed ourselves to be led astray by cranks and faddists, by extreme left wingers, some of whom were honest enough but some most undesirable. Pacifism and materialism took possession of us and I don't think that it was altogether surprising that foreigners thought that we were thoroughly decadent. We gave the appearance of a people who were not prepared to fight and who looked to other peoples for assistance in time of trouble. We have had a near squeak – will it teach us to be wiser in future? – I wonder.

Saturday 26 August   The Rumanians have actually declared war on Germany, and Bucharest has now been bombed by the *Luftwaffe* – a strange thing for a place to be bombed by both sides in the same war. The Russians now control Rumania and Bessarabia as far south as the Danube, and must be collaring a lot of Germans. They will soon have Galatz and the Ploesti oil fields – how Hitler is going to manage for oil beats me – even if he can have a *levée en masse*[40] of the German people, he cannot do much in modern warfare without oil – his bolt is about shot I fancy ... I feel that once we can settle down to fighting the Japanese, the war in the Far East should not take very long even if the Russians stand out of it. We – the Allies – will have a tremendous strength at sea and in the air and once the Japanese Navy is destroyed, Japan's forces

[38] Michael II (1921-), King of Rumania (under regency) 1927–30, replaced by his father Carol II, returned to the throne 1940–47, abdicated 1947.

[39] Ion Antonescu (1882–1946), Romanian officer, linked to Fascist movement; Chief of Gen. Staff 1937; imprisoned for plotting against govt. 1938–40; Min. of War 1940; P.M. 1940–44, effectively dictator, proclaimed himself *Conducator*; arrested in coup staged by King Michael 23 Aug. 1944; executed for war crimes May 1946.

[40] translation: mass mobilisation; the term originates from the armies raised in the early 1790s to defend revolutionary France from invading forces.

in China etc. would be cut off from the mainland.

Tuesday 29 August It will be interesting to see what the attitude will be in France towards us after the war. I only hope that it will be less unfriendly than after the last war – but I doubt if it will. The French and the English have never really got on well together – they will remember how we 'deserted' them in 1940 and how we bombed their towns, and we shall remember the way in which they crumpled up and threw in the sponge.

Friday 1 September I spent most of the day in Newcastle and, on the whole, satisfactorily. I saw Tydeman in the morning and he advised me to have a straight talk with Temple – and I had one at the Northern Counties Club where he lunched with me. He professed complete loyalty to me, but admitted that Lawson and Mrs. Fenwick[41] disliked me! I said that I was quite aware of this and that I knew what they were up to – I pointed out to him the entire absence of any kind of organization, the inadequacy of membership, the futility of Mrs. F., etc., etc. He agreed with all I said, and was most amenable – but, somehow or other, I don't much trust him. However, what he said about himself appeared to be quite frank. He said that of course sooner or later he intended to go into the HofC and naturally he was thinking of N. Newcastle as a likely seat – but that it would suit him best if I stood at the next election, thus giving him time to build up his practice at the bar. He said that he was going to give me all the help he could – but I must give him time, etc., to get the money – I said that time was the essence of the contract, etc. – on the whole the interview went all right.

Sunday 3 September In the eastern theatre the Germans claim to have checked the Russian attack in the Warsaw area and the unhappy Polish troops in the city are having a bad time of it. This Warsaw business is deplorable and one hates Stalin & Co. more than ever. I wrote a letter to Anthony Eden on the subject a few days ago, but I don't suppose that I shall get a satisfactory reply

[41] (Mary) Beatrice Fenwick, member of Newcastle City Council, Sandyford Ward 1945–53; she was married to Christopher Fenwick, K.C., and was not related to the owners of Fenwick's department stores, which originated in Newcastle.

from him. He is not the man to stand up to Stalin I fear.

Tuesday 5 September   We pushed on yesterday into Belgium and beyond the Meuse and the Moselle – but our advance is meeting with more opposition and our supply difficulties are increasing which is not surprising in view of the fact that we still only have the beachheads and Cherbourg for disembarking supplies. To me it is simply amazing that we have been able to go forward as far and as fast as we have. ... An account of the manner in which we have dealt with the flying bomb has been published: it is a great record of achievement – nevertheless, this business should give us seriously to think – in the future this form of attack might well mean national disaster for us, and the lesson that the 'p[ilotless] plane' has taught us [is] that never again must we allow any European Power to be in a position to wage war against us – it will mean incessant vigilance on our part and preparedness for war – even of a preventive nature.

Tuesday 12 September   The Quebec Conference has opened, but Marshal Stalin is conspicuous by his absence – Winston and F.D.R[oosevelt] must be enjoying the popular ovation which they are getting. What these two men will find to do when the war is over, goodness only knows. Winston, I think, would be well advised to retire from public life and to sit down and write his reminiscences.

Thursday 14 September   At the meeting of the [National Union] Central Executive this afternoon there was the usual sort of discussion – Tommie Dugdale told me that he did not expect a general election until the spring – some people (notably Herbert Williams) expect it in February. If we have one then, I should say that defeat for us was a certainty – I gather, however, that the Labour Party are frightened of a 'khaki election',[42] but clearly they intend it to be a party one when it comes.

[42] An election fought under wartime or immediate post-war conditions in which the Conservatives would benefit from popular feelings of patriotism and military success; the term was originally applied to the 1900 general election, held during the Boer War, and refers to the colour of the army uniform at that time.

Tuesday 19 September   Young Hartington[43] has been killed in France – I fear that it will be a sad blow for his parents ... To judge by a notice in *The Times* today written by Charles Waterhouse, he must have been a very promising young man – one does not realize until one reads obituary notices how many people one knew were 'remarkable', 'spread infectious gaiety', 'radiated happiness', etc., etc. It only shows how unobservant one is and how little one realizes the effect which some people have upon their fellows. I often regret my lack of the bump of veneration and my critical outlook upon people.

Thursday 21 September   Our tanks are reported to be five miles north of Nijmegen today – the air-borne people are fighting a desperate action at Arnhem – but are said to be holding their own. I shall feel a deal happier when I hear that they are relieved – the Germans claim to have taken 2,000 prisoners, including a General. The Russians are again, according to our press, 'smashing up and encircling' the enemy in the Baltic States – they have captured 'nearly 2,000 places' – one would not have thought there were so many places to capture in Esthonia – however it is the fashion nowadays to wax almost lyrical about what the Russians do, both in the press and on the wireless, and one must just bear with it. The main thing, however, is that our ally is a long time getting into East Prussia.

---

[43] William John Robert Cavendish (1917–1944); styled Marquess of Hartington after suc. of father as 10th Duke of Devonshire 1938; married 1944 Kathleen Kennedy, sister of John Kennedy, Pres. of U.S.A. 1960–63.

13

THE REVIVAL OF PARTY POLITICS
September 1944 to March 1945

Friday 22 September 1944   The Govt.'s demobilization plans have been published and seem to be devised as fairly as possible, but there are certain to be plenty of hard cases which will cause the likes of me a lot of trouble later on! Men, who are retained in the forces after the war in Europe, are to be given higher pay which is right and proper – it is estimated that this increase will cost £100 million a year – a lot of money and where it is to come from goodness only knows, and yet I gather that some of [the] press consider that it is a niggardly business. All sense of proportion about the spending of money is gone nowadays – millions mean nothing – 'nothing is too good for our bairns', as the Labour people used to say in the Durham C[ounty] C[ouncil]. The idea that we can afford anything and everything after peace is restored is based on the assertion that, if we can spend so much in the war, we can spend just as much in peace. No one seems to realize that because we have to spend so much in war, we must have less to spend when it is over.

Wednesday 27 September   Tonight I took part in a sort of 'Brains Trust'[1] affair got up by the Workers' Education Association, described as 'politicians in the witness box'. I represented the Conservative Party, Charlton Curry the Liberals, and there were also representatives of Labour, I[ndependent] L[abour] P[arty] and Commonwealth. The last named party was represented by my opponent Ridsdale – a nasty-looking little man with all the Gol-

---

[1] A popular radio programme, in which questions were put to an expert panel.

lancz[2] tit-bits at his fingers' ends ... Curry seized the opportunity to expound 'Liberalism', but, in the main, he said what I said in 3 times as many words. The other four[3] spouted 'Gollancz' and flattered 'the common people' whom they constantly reminded us they all represented. Their supporters of course were present in force, but behaved very well – the room (the Connaught Hall) was packed, and I am told could easily have been filled twice over. Certainly politics – party politics – are very much alive among 'the common people' – and what the result of it all is going to be God only knows.

Friday 29 September   Young Peter Thorneycroft[4] made a first class little speech this morning – full of vim and confidence and exceedingly well expressed and delivered. He has, so it seems, all the things that matter for parliamentary success. Yesterday Quintin Hogg, they tell me (I did not hear him), did well – made a 'remarkable speech' so Anthony Eden said today – it certainly reads well. These 2 'Young Tories' and Alec Dunglass seem to me to be the rising hopes of the moment – and two them are destined for the HofL before so very long,[5] unless that assembly is reformed as my sub-committee recommends. Eden did not say much in his reply – but led us to understand how very sticky 'Uncle Joe' [Stalin] is to deal with – and this I can quite believe – but he is likely to become more and more tiresome, so it seems to me, if we give way whenever he becomes nasty. Apparently nothing we do or say seems to overcome the Russian suspicion and dislike of us. What the future has in store for us God only knows – everyone in the debate kept on harping on the necessity for the 3 great Allied Powers – G.B., U.S.A. and Russia – to stick together after the war – but how can they when we alone are willing to play the game? The Russians don't trust us and the Americans dislike us –

[2] Gollancz was well known as the publisher of the successful 'Left Book Club' series and other left-wing pamphlets and books.

[3] There was also a Communist representative.

[4] George Edward Peter Thorneycroft (1909–1994), Con. M.P. Stafford 1938–45, Monmouth 1945–66; P.S. War Transport May-July 1945; Pres. Bd. of Trade 1951–57; Chanc. of the Exchequer 1957–58; Min. of Aviation 1960–62; Min. of Defence 1962–64 (Sec. of State, Apr.-Oct. 1964); Chairman, British Overseas Trade Bd. 1972–75; Con. Party Chairman 1975–81; cr. Baron Thorneycroft 1967.

[5] Hogg and Dunglass were the heirs of peerages (Viscount Hailsham and the Earl of Home) which they were likely to inherit in the course of the next few years.

once the common enemy is destroyed, the troubles will begin.

Tuesday 3 October   At the HofC most of the morning ... the parties – Conservatives and Labour – are rapidly drifting apart, I fear. The reason for this, I think, is that the rank and file of the Labour Party firmly believe that they can sweep the country in a general election, and it may be that they are right – some of them are a bit nervous about what would happen if they got a big majority – whether or not they would be capable of running the show – but I fancy that this section is a small one! There are others who think that if they got a reasonable majority they might form another National Government to carry us over the treaty-making business and get Conservative co-operation in post-war reconstruction. This section, I fancy, includes the wiser heads of the Party who realize the unfitness of Labour to govern. What we are thinking I really cannot make out – some of our more active M.P.s seem to think that we should win if there was an election – on what grounds they think so it is hard to determine – each man seems to judge the position from his own position: he is sure he can hold his seat, and can see no reason why other people should not. None of us has an inkling of what the P.M. has in mind – what his intentions are and when he is going to disclose them. Never was a party so leaderless as is the Conservative Party today. It is, I think, drifting to its doom – at any rate to a temporary eclipse – and perhaps it is the best thing that could happen to it if it is to revive.

Thursday 5 October   I am sorry for the poor Dutch – being 'liberated' is not all beer and skittles: it means being smashed to pieces by both sides. It is sad to think of that trim, neat, prosperous little country, so much of it saved from the sea by the efforts of its inhabitants, being flooded and ruined – and now the Germans are said to be setting fire to places like Amsterdam and Rotterdam – if it is true, it is too damnable. The brutes are beat to the world – and they know it – and yet they do these things – one feels that there is no punishment too harsh for them. They should be made the Helots[6] of Europe for 100 years.

[6] The slaves who worked as servants of the Spartans in ancient Greece.

Saturday 7 October I wonder what good there is in trying to interest women in politics? There are and always have been a small minority of women, mainly spinsters, who have busied themselves with social and humanitarian matters – but the great mass of women have left politics to men and it is better so for the nation – for women are not fitted for politics – and their cry for equality with men is only raised by the disgruntled ones – not, as a rule, by the mothers and wives. The more women come out in politics the worse it will be for the future of our race.

Sunday 8 October ... I have thought a bit over one thing and another, more especially of politics and all the fools who deal with them – now why should these futile Labour politicians decide to return to the party business when they are getting most of what they want – certainly most of what their leaders know to be good for them – from the Coalition? The truth of the matter is that the Labour leaders in the present government prefer to remain in a coalition for some time to come – they realize that this would be the wise thing to do – best for the country – but their followers won't let them. The rank and file of the Labour Party is convinced that there is gong to be a swing over to the left at a general election: they expect to get a real thumping majority – at the worst they hope to be the largest party in the House – they could form a new coalition if the worst came to the worst. Morrison, Bevin & Co. are fearful of their political future – but none of them dare stand out on his own and stand up to his followers.

Monday 9 October I am afraid that the Germans are pulling themselves together effectively and I doubt very much whether we shall be able to get much forwarder yet awhile. The Russians of course may be able to move faster than we can – but as the German defensive perimeter decreases the better he is able to defend it. ... Anthony Eden has given what I suppose is meant to be a lead to Conservatives in a speech at Bristol – it does not give me much inspiration, but I hope I am the exception not the rule among his followers.

Wednesday 11 October I have been reading today a little book by Quintin Hogg, the leader of the 'Young Tory' movement in the

HofC.[7] It is called *One Year's Work* and reprints his speeches in the HofC with some additional matter. I always admire people who admire themselves – self assurance is a tremendous asset to a young man especially in politics, even if it makes people angry with you – at any rate it keeps you in the public eye. Q.H. is a fine speaker and will be better when he has had more practice – the House is certainly beginning to listen to him. I can find little or nothing to find fault with or unorthodox in the views expressed in this book – whenever 'Young Tories' try to be 'progressive' they quote Dizzy[8] and produce a watered down Socialist programme, very much like the Conservative Party programme only expounded vigorously – sometimes almost ferociously, as something entirely new. In the House today Q.H. (who clearly takes great trouble in preparing a speech) makes his appeal or his criticism with force and eloquently; Hinchingbrooke[9] speaks moderately well, but is utterly lifeless and carries no weight; Hugh Molson[10] is tremendously earnest and knows everything – but bores people to tears; Thorneycroft has a pleasant and fluent style of speaking and I like listening to him - but, on the whole, I don't think that the country has gained much by any of these young men taking off their uniforms and devoting their attention to politics and their own political futures.

Thursday 12 October   Winston and Anthony are busy talking in Moscow with 'Uncle Joe' – no doubt their main job is to try and bustle on the Russians to invade East Prussia – the next business I suppose is to try and get the decent Poles to give way to the indecent Poles who are being run by Uncle Joe. It really should begin to open people's eyes a bit about the brave new world to watch the way in which Russia is treating Poland – never was there a more bare-faced or grosser policy of aggression and interference

---

[7] The 'Tory Reform Committee', of which Hogg was a founder and leading member.

[8] Benjamin Disraeli, leader of the Conservative Party 1868–81 and author of romantic Tory novels.

[9] Alexander Victor Edward Paulet Montagu (1906–1995), private Sec. to S. Baldwin 1932–34; Treasuer, Junior Imperial League 1934–35; Con. M.P. Dorset S. 1941–62; Chairman, Tory Reform Ctte. 1943–44; Pres., Anti-Common Market League 1962-; styled Viscount Hinchingbrooke 1916–62, suc. 10th Earl of Sandwich 1962, renounced peerage 1964.

[10] (Arthur) Hugh Elsdale Molson (1903–1991), Con. M.P. Doncaster 1931–35, High Peak 1939–61; P.S. Works 1951–53; P.S. Transport & Civil Aviation 1953–57; Min. of Works 1957–59; cr. Baron Molson 1961.

by one country against another – not only do the Russians propose to take a big slice of Polish territory but they tell the Polish Govt. what it is to do with regard to the internal government of Poland. Needless to say our Govt., the press here and the Socialists are lying low about the whole horrid business.

Thursday 19 October It looks as if we are going to have a rumpus over the Govt. Planning Bill. It is, in my opinion, too big a measure – it should have been limited to the blitzed area and designed to raise as little controversy as possible – instead of which it is made to apply to what they are pleased to call the 'blighted' areas as well – and the row is about property condemned by local authorities for town improvement, etc. I have not heard much of the debates, but clearly they were getting acrimonious on party lines.

Monday 23 October Lunched at the Station Hotel in Newcastle – the luncheon got up by a newly organized body representing the light engineering firms in the area – rather an imposing affair – about 100 present including 8 or 9 M.P.s, B[oard] of T[rade] officials, Matt Ridley, etc. ... The feeling of the gathering was that there ought to be vigorous self-help in the area, sensible planning, and that the Government should give a helping hand in every possible way by enabl[ing] people to get a move on – exactly the last thing which it seems inclined to do. We seem to be drifting badly already and it makes one feel gloomy as to the future.

Tuesday 24 October Have spent the day at the House, where the proceedings were dull. Talked with various friends as to tomorrow's business – compensation under Morrison's new Bill. The Govt.'s 'concessions' are most unsatisfactory – but I feel that it would be a mistake for the Party to divide against them unless we are prepared to vote our full strength and make the Govt. resign or to withdraw the Bill. We cannot afford to turn the Govt. out and most of us don't want to – so the only thing to do, it seems to me, is not to divide. However I gather that Herbert Williams and co. are determined to do so – and there it is – all that [will] result from the business will be ill-feeling and recrimination within the Party. The whole business has been quite unnecessary, I think, and is the obvious result of introducing controversial legislation before the war is ended.

Wednesday 25 October   The opposition to the Housing Bill rather fizzled out today and the Govt. got a large majority – I did not vote – and was too lazy to explain my reason for not doing so in the C[ommittee of the] W[hole] H[ouse]: I told James Stuart in private and he entirely understood my point of view – a good many other people, I gather, shared it.

Thursday 26 October   William Temple, Archbishop of Canterbury, died today. He is a great loss to the Church, I should imagine, which does not possess too many men of mark in these days – I personally disapproved of his political 'business', because it seemed to me calculated to lead people astray. He seemed to believe that Socialists must be Christians which is not the case as most of us realize – however he was no doubt a good and a sincere man, learned and eloquent. ... to the HofC, where I listened to the closing stages of the Planning Bill. Bouquets all round – what a queer place the HofC is – here is a Bill which all Conservatives dislike and disapprove of – an unsatisfactory compromise has been arrived at, both illogical and unjust, and yet we all agree to say how clever, tactful and conciliatory the Minister has been. Well, compromise is the basis of our political system and it works well – after all, that is what really matters.

Monday 30 October   Dined ... with Jasper Ridley[11] – he much exercised in his mind as to who should be the next Provost of Eton – I could not suggest anybody – after dinner Tommie Lascelles was equally exercised in his mind as to who should be Archbishop of Canterbury – both he and Jasper Ridley plumped for the Bishop of London who they both considered a statesmanlike chap ... Then Tommie asked us who were to be made K[nights of the] G[arter] – apparently there are 2 vacancies already in the Order and 2 or 3 more likely in the near future – apparently it is difficult to find suitable people – the idea nowadays is that the K.G. should be

[11] Jasper Nicholas Ridley (1887–1951), Con. cand. Morpeth Jan. 1910, Newcastle Dec. 1910; Chairman, Coutts & Co., Nat. Provincial Bank; Fellow of Eton College; kt. 1946; second son of 1st Viscount Ridley.

given to persons of merit not merely to big noises[12] – an excellent
idea. Bobbety Cranborne was the only man any of us could think
of except Wavell, after he has finished being Viceroy. Tommie told
us that Alex[ander] has been made a F[ield] M[arshal] but that it
has been kept dark for political or rather diplomatic reasons –
when the appointment is announced, it is likely to be ante-dated
to make him senior to Monty.

Tuesday 31 October   Winston spoke today – we are not to have
a spring election – I did not hear him, but he is said to have been
in good form. His Moscow expedition appears to have done him
good: truly an amazing man with a constitution and physique of
an ox. He thrives on war and the conducting of it – perhaps he
will just fade away when it is all over. Probably that would be the
best thing that could happen for him – to vanish in a blaze of
glory, and not to linger on the stage when he has done his job. ...
I spent a good deal of time in the Smoking Room at the HofC
today, but heard little or no gossip. The appointment of Ralph
Assheton to succeed Tommie Dugdale has rather surprised people –
not because they don't think him suitable for the job, but because
it seems surprising that a man who has the job of Financial
Secretary to the Treasury should give it up to become Chairman
of the Party – I suppose he has been told that he won't be forgotten
later on – still it is a risk to leave the ladder when one is half way
up. Personally I am very sorry that Tommie D. has gone – I liked
him and knew him well – this new man I scarcely know – but they
tell me that he is very able and should do well.

Wednesday 1 November   I spoke in the shipping debate today –
a poor little effort if there ever was one – Greenwell spoke well and
so did Shinwell – the latter is becoming more and more Conservative
in his views – his speech today might have been made by any of
us. No one speaks well of the man, but I doubt whether he is such
a swine as he is always described. He is out to make his way in the
world like other people and he may be unscrupulous and pushing –
but he is a damned sight cleverer than most of the other Labour
people – I suppose the real trouble is that he knows it and does
not suffer the other fools gladly. If Labour gets in at the next

---

[12] The honour was normally given to the holder of a great aristocratic title.

election, it is not easy to see how he can be left out of the Cabinet. Winston's speech on Tuesday has rather cleared the air – a great relief to hear that he does not intend to have an election in the spring. I am told that he contemplates another 2 years of war before Japan is brought to her knees and does not expect German resistance to end until the summer. Of course the right thing to do would be for this Govt. and Parliament to go on until both wars are over – it is an opportunity to get our 'social' legislation carried out in a reasonable manner...

Thursday 2 November   I did not listen to Sir W. Jowitt introduce his security plan, nor did I hear much of the debate. He and everybody else was, I gather, tumbling over himself to tell us how the people of this country are to be made 'free from want', etc., etc. We are all mad, I think, but there it is – if a man like John Anderson, in his role as Chancellor of the Exchequer, assures us that this grandiose scheme can be financed – well, then it can be – we cannot but take his word for it – but he at any rate does say that he is supposing that all of us will be ready to work hard, etc., etc. My own view is that this is the real crux of the situation – my impression is that the general idea is that we should all work less and enjoy a better standard of living – if this impression is correct, what of the future?

Saturday 4 November   We have had the quarterly meeting of the Area Council today – not too badly attended. Nunn, M.P., was our speaker and made a good speech – he is a curiously disillusioned man whom I never know whether to like or dislike. Fergus Graham moved a vote of thanks and Greenwell seconded it – the former was as usual – like a revivalist preacher – the latter all right. Greenwell is on the crest of a wave after his successful speech in the House the other day and much in the public eye up here – I am wondering whether he would be the right man to succeed me as Area Chairman? Old Appleby was most forthcoming and gave us all tea after the meeting.

Sunday 5 November   The death of Jack Dill in the U.S.A. was announced on the wireless tonight – I had no idea that he was ill. I am terribly sorry that he has gone. He was a great friend of mine and I looked upon him as one of the ablest and most efficient men

I have ever come across. He was without doubt the best staff officer
of our time. He has, I am told, been an outstanding success in the
U.S.A. and will be a difficult man to replace.

Tuesday 7 November   Everyone much shocked about Walter
Moyne's[13] murder – it appears to have been perpetrated by Jews –
members of the Terrorist gang at present so busy in Palestine.
What they expect to get from it God alone knows – I should
imagine that outrages of this kind are calculated to do a lot of
harm to the Zionist movement. Lunched with James Stuart and
Lloyd George, the younger, at the House ... The general opinion
is that he is about the most ineffective of all the coal ministers there
have ever been – but doubtless his job is a very difficult one – a
section of the miners is quite out of hand – even their own leaders
admit it – and all they (the leaders) can do is to go on saying that
production would be better if the pits were nationalized. It is too
ridiculous – but the public can be made to believe anything if it is
repeated often enough – and today of course nationalization is all
the rage because the Russians have fought so bravely! I told James
that I should be absent next week and he evinced no surprise – it
seems to me that for a man who takes no interest in politics –
indeed, has no knowledge of them – he makes an admirable Chief
Whip – but I cannot imagine how he manages to keep Winston
sweet – I fancy that his real troubles lie ahead of him when the
Coalition comes apart.

Wednesday 8 November   Geoffrey Dawson's death is announced
today ... I have known him since 1895 and he has, I know, been
a good friend to me. He was a very able man – quick brain and
wise, perhaps a bit too wise – on the whole, he was a good editor
of *The Times* – he was absolutely honest and stood for what he
believed – but his inclination was 'Round Table-ish',[14] and I think
that this outlook of mind sometimes made him disinclined to take

[13] Walter Edward Guinness (1880–1944), Con. M.P. Bury St. Edmunds 1907–31;
U.S. War Office 1922–23; F.S.T. 1923–24, 1924–25; Min. of Agric. 1925–29; P.S.
Agric. 1940–41; Colonial Sec. 1941–42; Dep. Min. Res. Middle East 1942–44, Min.
Res. 1944; cr. Baron Moyne 1932; assassinated in Cairo by the Stern Gang 1944.
[14] The *Round Table* was the journal of the imperial federation movement; it was
non-party and came to be identified with compromise and conciliation in imperial
affairs, and later with support for 'appeasement'.

a really strong line where a strong line was needed. ... Attended the Party Executive Committee this afternoon. Ralph Assheton, the new Chairman [of the Party], made his first appearance – he told us that we must be ready for an election in May – a bad month for Conservatives to choose for an election.

Thursday 9 November   Winston this morning made an announcement about V II,[15] asserting that it had done but little damage so far – so far we have said nothing about it, but the Germans a few days ago asserted that much damage was being caused by it, and stated various places in and around London where it had fallen – some of the places they mentioned were accurate enough, some were not. I suppose that the Government considered that the time had come to say something. Personally I don't like V II a bit – it is rather uncanny to feel that at any moment it may drop unannounced from the sky and extinguish you – however, I suppose that one would know nothing about it and that there are worse ways of ending one's life. One hears V II plumping down two or three times a day and I gather that it makes a beastly mess where it falls – but, so far, it has not done anything like the damage done by V I. The trouble about it is that there is no answer to it, except to destroy its starting off places – and this can only be done by beating the Germans.

Wednesday 22 November   Changes in the Government are announced today. Portal[16] retires (a lucky escape for him I should say) from the Ministry of Works and Duncan Sandys, Winston's son-in-law, is to reign in his place. I don't know the man, but he does not strike me as anything to write home about and I have [not] heard anyone say a good word for him. Ned Grigg is to succeed Moyne as our Minister Resident in the Middle East. I am glad that he has been given the job – he is very hard-working and earnest and of course capable. Harold Balfour is to be our Minister Resident in West Africa. He, too, deserves promotion and is, I

---

[15] The successor to the V1 'flying bomb', the V2 was a chemical-fuelled rocket which had a longer range and could reach London from sites in northern Germany; it travelled faster than the speed of sound and thus gave no warning of its approach.

[16] Wyndham Raymond Portal (1885–1949), businessman; P.S. Supply 1940–42; Min. of Works & Buildings 1942–44; presided over 14th Olympics 1948; suc. 3rd Bart. 1931, cr. Baron Potal 1935, Viscount 1945.

should say, capable. Brabner,[17] a nice young man, succeeds Balfour as Under-Secretary at the Air Ministry, and John Wilmot[18] (who won a pacifist by-election and frightened Baldwin![19]) is to take Sandys's place at the Ministry of Supply.

Sunday 26 November   The Sunday papers tell one that six Allied armies are 'driving forward' towards the Rhine and are 'grappling with the massed German army in what may be the last great battle of the West' – it sounds so grand but what a false picture it gives of what is actually going on! One wonders whether this sort of stuff really takes in the man in the street? I doubt it – people must by this time realize that the fighting is going to be a long and laborious affair – at one time, when we were racing through France, it looked as if we really had got the enemy on the run and that the war was only an affair of weeks. The way in which the Germans have pulled themselves together is a wonderful performance and I think that we are all agreed on that – now we are up against the enemy's carefully constructed system of defences and there can be no more smashing forward. So long as his manpower lasts it is clear that the enemy intends to fight out the battle – how long it will last remains to be seen – in the end our superiority in men and material must prevail – always supposing we are in deadly earnest. We are – but we are now only a small part of the Allied forces. The Russians are in earnest – it depends, therefore, on the Americans – I don't see how they can give way now, but one never can tell.

Tuesday 28 Novemeber   Parliament was prorogued today and I suppose that its last session will begin tomorrow. My own view is still the same – I don't think that there should be a general election until the war is really over and the boys come home. Why should the choice of a new Government be left to the people who have

[17] Rupert Arnold Brabner (1911–1945), Con. M.P. Hythe 1939–45; joined Fleet Air Arm 1939, served at sea; Technical Ass. to 5th Sea Lord 1943–44; Ass. Whip July-Nov. 1944; U.S. Air 1944–45; his aircraft was lost near the Azores 27 Mar. 1945.

[18] John Charles Wilmot (1895–1964), Lab. M.P. Fulham E. 1933–35, Kennington 1939–45, Deptford 1945–50; P.P.S. to H. Dalton 1940–44; jt. P.S. Supply 1944–45; Min. of Supply 1945–47, & Aircraft Production 1945–46; Alderman, London County Council 1937–45; cr. Baron Wilmot of Selmeston 1950.

[19] The East Fulham by-election, Oct. 1933; Baldwin later cited its result as having influenced him to be cautious about public willingness to accept rearmament.

stayed at home? – many of whom have done precious little to help the war effort. Thousands of soldiers while still serving will not vote – I am sure of that.

Friday 1 December   I attended a meeting at the City Hall this morning presided over by the Lord Mayor at which Willink, M.P., Minister of Health spoke quite well about housing, but he really told us nothing. Housing in my opinion is the matter about which the man in the street is more concerned than anything else – he is far more concerned to find a house than he is about insurance. I don't think the Government is sufficiently alive to this fact. After the meeting Willink opened a housing exhibition. He was then entertained to luncheon at the Mansion House, but I was not asked to meet him – certainly M.P.s don't count for much in Newcastle.

Tuesday 5 December   There was little gossip in the Smoking Room today – people are resigned to the war going on for some time and election talk is not so much heard – nevertheless, it is now clear that an election will come very soon after the war with Germany is over and it is not a pleasant prospect. I cannot make up my mind whether I want to stand again – an election fight is a strenuous affair and I don't look forward to it.

Wednesday 6 December   I have spent most of today at the HofC writing letters – I did not go into the House much, but there was not anything of much interest. People are naturally upset by the position in Greece where the so-called patriots are busy attacking the Govt. There are three possible policies for us to adopt – (1) to leave Greece and let them have their little civil war and starve, (2) to take over the government of the country ourselves, (3) to support the Greek Govt. in restoring order. Winston and co. have plumped for no. (3) which is probably the best course to adopt – needless to say our left wing creatures are furious and assert that we are doing our best to scupper democracy – why it should always be considered by our Socialists and Communists here that any attempt to preserve law and order is undemocratic is one of those things which is beyond my understanding.

Thursday 7 December   A debate in the House today on Housing. I heard little or none of it – but I gather that Duncan Sandys did

well, speaking for the first time as Minister of Works and Buildings.
... The news from Greece today is as bad as ever – our people
have had to support the Greek Govt. with arms and the Communists
are apparently fighting hard – using our weapons against us and
Germans are said to be with them. It is a bad business and I am
sorry not to be able to be in the House tomorrow when there is to
be a debate on Greece – I should have liked to speak in it. The
attitude of some of the Labour Party is really deplorable and makes
one despair of the future – one feels that nothing but trouble is
ahead of us in Europe.

Saturday 9 December Winston made a fighting speech in the
HofC yesterday and the Reds were well beaten. I wish that I could
have been there – I should have liked to say a word about the true
meaning of democracy: whatever it may or may not mean, it
certainly must not be another word for anarchy.

Monday 11 December The German assertion ... that even if the
collapse comes and the main areas of the *Reich* surrender, a guerrilla
war will be continued *ad infinitum* does not impress me greatly –
once their armies in the field are done in and their country is
occupied, I don't see the Germans carrying on a war of partisans -
though no doubt a few 'fanatical Nazis' may prove troublesome
for a time. Once the Hitler spell is broken, I fancy that the Germans
will prove very subservient until they feel fit to have another war
if we are silly enough to give them the chance. What worries me
far more than the Germans are the Russians – God only knows
what their line is going to be after the war – they are worrying
enough during the war from all accounts and are likely to be even
more truculent when it is over.

Tuesday 12 December Spent most of the day at the HofC –
debates on Burma and Rural Housing. I listened to a good deal of
the Burma talk – young de Chair,[20] Godfrey Nicholson[21] and other
'progressive' young Conservatives appear to have taken that rather

[20] Somerset Struben de Chair (1911–1995), Con. M.P. Norfolk S.W. 1935–45,
Paddington S. 1950–51; P.P.S. to O. Lyttelton 1942–44; author and historian.
[21] Godfrey Nicholson (1901–1991), Con. M.P. Morpeth 1931–35, Farnham 1937–
66; P.P.S. to R. Assheton 1943–44; Chairman, Estimates Ctte. 1961–64; cr. Bart.
1958.

unforthcoming country to their hearts and written a report about its future Government – today they enlarged upon the subject and spoke very well, I thought. I wish I had the energy to be 'busy' like all these little people and fill more columns in *Hansard* than I do. It looks important and pleases one's constituents, if nothing comes of all one says. But I never have been keen to make myself heard in the HofC, and now that I am old and on the shelf there is little or no inducement to make me do so. Donald Scott, they tell me, spoke well on rural housing, but I did not know that he was going to speak and so missed him. I lunched at the House – heard a certain amount of gossip, but nothing worth recording. People are clearly depressed by the military situation – the toughness of the German resistance appears to have come as an unpleasant surprise – one hears much less about an early election.

Wednesday 13 December   I listened to Winston speak today. I did not think that he was at his best – but I am glad to say that he is looking fitter and stronger than he has been looking recently. How much depends on this man nowadays – if he were removed to a better world, what would happen I wonder? I don't see the precious Government carrying on without him and I fancy a general election would be inevitable – but even worse than this, would be our position *vis à vis* our allies – without Winston's prestige and personality, where should we be with Roosevelt and Stalin? They are tiresome enough as things are – but how could Anthony Eden, or Attlee, stand up to them? No – I have never been a Winstonian, but I do realize that today if a man can ever be indispensable, Winston is that man.

Thursday 14 December   I lunched today at the Dorchester with Ralph Assheton – it was a luncheon for 'Area Chairmen' and I felt I ought to attend it ... At the luncheon were 7 or 8 Area Chairmen, Miss Maxse,[22] Harold Mitchell M.P. and Topping – we had quite an interesting talk and I was pleased with Ralph Assheton who seems keen and anxious to help us all in every way. He strikes one as having more energy and ideas than Tommie Dugdale – but he

---

[22] (Sarah) Marjorie Algeria Maxse (1891–1975), Dep. Principal Agent (Women's Organisation) 1921–30; Chief Organisation Officer 1930–39; Vice-Chairman, W.V.S. 1940–44; Con. Party Vice-Chairman 1944–51; cr. Dame 1952.

has a big and thankless task ahead of him which I don't envy him. He has, somehow or other, to get the party organization going again – and it is as near dead as any organization can be. Without agents and women organizers and with a vast majority of antique and moribund chairmen of associations all over the country and with precious little money, I simply cannot see how Assheton or anyone else can be expected to do much – however, perhaps I am so gloomy because I am faced with such a hopeless state of things in this part of the world – perhaps elsewhere our prospects are less depressing.

Friday 15 December   I spent most of today at the HofC and listened to most of the debate about Poland. I did not hear all Winston's speech but what I heard was rather a sorry performance – he tried to explain away our surrender to Russia and he was not convincing. He and Anthony have failed utterly to make any impression on Stalin – and that is the long and the short of it – instead of a combined determination by us and the U.S.A. to show that neither of us can approve of the Russian policy we have given way and are now trying to make out that Russia is right to deprive the Poles of a huge slice of their territory and to dictate to them the kind of government they are to have. It is a bad business which will do us untold harm in Europe. The Polish case was well put by Victor Raikes,[23] Pickthorn and others – Eden spoke well, and made a better case than Winston. He told me afterwards that it was hopeless to try and reconcile the Poles and the Russians – that his great fear was that unless we had agreed to the partition the Russians would set up an independent government in Poland – my fear is that they will do so, confident now that we shall not interfere.

Saturday 16 December   I paid a call on Miss Maxse at Central Office this morning – she was very pleasant and friendly and sympathetic when I told her some of our troubles. I think that she means to be helpful and I am glad that she is back again 'at headquarters', because she is sensible and efficient. ... The leader in today's *Times* about Poland sickens me – a vain attempt to show

---

[23] (Henry) Victor Alpin MacKinnon Raikes (1901–1986), Con. M.P. Essex S.E. 1931–45, Liverpool Wavertree 1945–50, Liverpool Garston 1950–57 (whip withdrawn May 1957, resigned seat Nov. 1957); Chairman, Monday Club 1975–78; kt. 1953.

that our pledge to the Poles only referred to German aggression! I agree that we cannot prevent Russia from doing as she likes with Poland, and the Baltic States and the Balkans – but we should not try an excuse ourselves on any other score than our inability to prevent the Russians from their acts of aggression – we should not attempt to condone them – what we are doing now is to make ourselves a partner in a new partition of Poland. The consequence of this policy will be to reduce our prestige in Europe and to lay the foundation for future trouble. We are really fighting this war to preserve the balance of power in Europe which is essential for our own preservation – all that we have succeeded in doing is to knock out German hegemony and set up a Russian hegemony – which in the longer run may be much more dangerous to us both in Europe and Asia.

Sunday 17 December   This German counter-offensive against the American 3rd Army looks as if it were on a big scale – a seventy mile front – but there is little information available at present.[24] But even if a big break-through has been effected (and this is probably what has happened) I cannot believe that there can be sufficient weight behind it for the enemy to get very far.

Thursday 21 December   The newspapers tell us today that the German push is being held ... the American flanks are holding firm ... The weather is wet and foggy on the Western Front which, I suppose, helps the Germans because it reduces our air superiority – however, I cannot see how this push can go very far, unless things go wrong. We must by now have sufficient forces on the scene of action to check the invaders – then we ought to be able to cut their retreat ... The Russians are 'thrusting' into Czechoslovakia where the Germans are said to be in full retreat – one always wonders how much truth there is in these Russian reports – all that is certain is that Budapest is still in German hands – however, all the time Germans are being killed and their manpower reduced – this is the thing that matters most.

Saturday 23 December   The news today is that the German

---

[24] This was the start of the 'Battle of the Bulge', the last major German offensive in the west, intended by Hitler to repeat the success of 1940 and drive a wedge between the Allied forces and reach the Channel ports.

offensive seems to have been 'switched' southwards towards Bastogne, which looks from the map as if it was a road centre of some importance. ... The German push has now penetrated between 40 and 50 miles – but I don't think that it should go much further, unless Rundstedt[25] has better supply lines than I imagine he has. The Germans report that British troops have been sent to support the Americans – but, though this is likely enough, there is no official information from our side to confirm the report. There is a new army call-up of 250,000 men – the need for men on the Western Front is growing – the drain of this kind of war in this kind of weather, as one knows, is terrific. ... The trouble in Greece continues – if every 'liberated' country is going to start a civil war – and it seems not unlikely – it looks as if our troubles would never end – and yet we have our Socialists here doing all they can to encourage the malcontents in Greece to fight against their own Government.

Sunday 24 December   The 'doodle bomb' appears to have fallen at Tudhoc, not a mile I should say, as the crow flies, from this house [Holywell] – perhaps, indeed, less – 2 people are reported to have been killed. Let us hope that we are not going to have more of these beastly things in this peaceful area – and yet their coming might make the miners realize more that there is a war on. They are said to be doing worse than ever – and we are being warned to consume less electricity and gas because of the coal shortage. It is a bad business, and yet the public (by reason of our absurd press articles) still seems more inclined to blame the owners for their inefficiency than the miners for their absenteeism. We all have to be 'progressive' and 'democratic' and 'sloppy' nowadays. The employers are always to blame ... all this rubbish gushes from the press, from *The Times* downwards, and is prated from every platform by half-baked, half-educated young people who pose as the intelligentsia. It is a sorry state of things and I fear that we shall have to pay for all this foolishness before we are much older.

---

[25] Gerd von Rundstedt (1875–1953), German army career; C. in C. Army Group South, Polish campaign 1939, Army Group A, invasion of France & Low Countries 1940, Army Group South, invasion of Russia 1941 (relieved of command after retreating from Rostov contrary to Hitler's order, Nov. 1941); C. in C. Western theatre 1942–45.

Sunday 31 December   And so 1944 comes to an end – it has been a great year, even though it has not brought an end to the war as some people fondly hoped it would. We have still a big job ahead of us both in Europe and in Asia – neither of our enemies looks like giving in at present – but their doom is certain always supposing that the Allies are prepared to stick to the business and don't fall out among themselves. If only one could really trust the Russians, one would feel a deal happier – but one cannot. Clearly they are playing their own game and that game seems to me to be directly opposed to all that we are fighting for. They are working for a Russian hegemony over northern and eastern Europe which would be most dangerous for us – and yet none of our left wingers appears to appreciate the situation – Russia, they assure us, is a great democratic country – Russia can do no wrong – have we not a treaty of alliance with Russia for the next twenty years? ... Poland, the Baltic States, Sweden and Norway, and the Balkans are or soon will be in the Bear's grip and we can do nothing to prevent it. Nor can we trust France or the U.S.A. ... after nearly six years of war we have not any real friends in the world and the seeds of future discord are already sown in Europe and Asia.

Monday 1 January 1945   The New Year's Honours are not very interesting or exciting – Mark Hodgson,[26] a very fine type of trade union leader, secretary to the Boiler Makers, gets a knighthood: Tommie Dugdale becomes a baronet: Portal gets a step up in the peerage: Chapman[27] for some reason or other is given a C.B.E. (he is a great collector of ribands): Ellen Wilkinson and Florence Horsbrugh become Privy Councillors: etc., etc. I am all in favour of 'honours and awards', but am often left wondering on what principle (if any) they are given – I expect that a good many other people are equally perplexed – but it does not much matter anyway – no doubt deserving people do now and then get recognized. I

[26] Mark Hodgson (1880–1967), member of Exec., United Soc. of Boilermakers, and Iron & Steel Shipbuilders 1913–36, Gen. Sec 1936–48; Pres., Confederation of Shipbuilding & Engineering Unions 1943–45, 1947–48; Chairman, Northern Regional Bd. for Industry 1949–65; kt. 1945.

[27] Robert Chapman (1880–1963), Con. M.P. Houghton-le-Spring 1931–35; Chairman, Northern Counties Area 1954–58; member of S. Shields council 1921–52, Mayor 1931–32; Army Welfare Officer, Co. Durham 1939–52; High Sheriff, Co. Durham 1940–41; Chairman, North Eastern Trading Estates Ltd. 1940–48; kt. 1950, cr. Bart. 1958.

cannot imagine why L.G. has decided to become an Earl – let alone to call himself Earl Lloyd George! Probably the new Mrs L.G.[28] wanted to be a Countess – but it seems rather hard on Gwilym[29] – that it is to say, if he has political aspirations. Now, unfortunately, Eddie Winterton does really become 'father of the HofC'[30] and he is likely to be more in evidence than ever – a father who is always retailing his experiences and giving you advice is a trying individual.

Wednesday 3 January ... we are making an effort to cut the German communications – the battle is said to be a fierce one, and the country most difficult. However, the crisis of this German offensive would now seem to have ended – the enemy's westward advance effectively stopped – and I don't mind betting that this has been done by Monty and his merry men – sooner or later, we shall be told all about it I suppose, but at present the censorship seems to be strict – a good thing too. The press men are allowed a lot more licence in this war than in the last and the enemy must learn a lot from them.

Saturday 6 January ... we had a comfortable journey to Carlisle + Tydeman – Fergus Graham met us, as charming and as good mannered as ever ... later I addressed about 50 members of the [North Cumberland Conservative] Association in a Cinema Hall designed to hold 500 people. ... I fancy that the Association is all to pieces and that the seat will need a deal of work and a really good candidate if it is to be won back.

Friday 12 January ... addressed a meeting of the N[ewcastle]-upon-T[yne] Branch of the 'National Federation of Business and Professional Women's Clubs of G.B. and Ireland'. There were about 30 or 40 earnest women present and I spoke for 35 minutes and then answered questions – clearly most of the questioners were

[28] After his first wife died in 1941, Lloyd George had married his former secretary and mistress of many years, Frances Stevenson, on 23 Oct. 1943.

[29] In fact Gwilym Lloyd George (q.v.) was the younger son; he did not inherit the Earldom when his father died on 26 Mar. 1945, and remained in the Commons.

[30] The honorary title of the M.P. who has sat for the longest continuous period; this does not need to be for the same seat, but it cannot be counted across an interval out of the House. For this reason Lloyd George (an M.P. since 1890) was succeeded by Winterton (who had sat since 1904) rather than Churchill (who was first elected in 1900, but was out of the Commons in 1922–24).

left wingers and one heard all the usual tripe about female rights and wrongs, social security, etc., etc. Whether or not the meeting was a success I have no idea – they professed to be pleased with one, but very few of them, I fancy, agreed with what I said – which amounted to ladies don't be in too much of a hurry, don't get carried away by sentiment, do please remember that men must be considered a little, etc., etc.

Monday 15 January   I had a long, rather pathetic letter from Charley Londonderry a few days ago about Robin – was there a Durham seat which he could contest, if he decides to give up his Ulster one? I doubt whether Robin would want one nowadays, and I doubt very much whether any Association (except a very derelict one) would want him. He and his father have been too long absentees from the county.

Wednesday 17 January   After luncheon representatives of the Industrial Insurance Companies came to see me at Saville Row. Personally I can see no reason why their business should be taken from these people, but the Government thinks otherwise and is determined to take over everything to give us 'social security'. What a catch phrase this 'Social Security' is becoming, almost as tiresome and misleading as 'collective security', and yet we all have to swallow it as the government was foolish enough to allow Beveridge to coin it and get it across – Beveridge who knows as much about real men and women as I know about statistics!

Thursday 18 January   ... nor did I hear anything worth recording at the HofC. It is a lifeless place nowadays – the only people who appear to find it amusing are Aneurin Bevan and his nasty little coterie, and the young Tories who are busy being busy. It amuses me to see them moving about mysteriously in the Library, consulting among themselves and preparing amendments and concocting speeches! It is good to be young. I wish that I had got into the House when I was young and keen and half fledged – then perhaps I should have joined a group, and advertized myself, and learned the business and got on. I was too old, too disillusioned, too critical when I got into the House to make a success of it. I simply could not take myself seriously – to take oneself seriously is really most important for success in the HofC – if you don't take yourself seriously, no one else will – and you must not mind if people laugh at you when you are doing it – this is inevitable – but if you go on taking yourself seriously and are not an absolute dud, sooner or later you won't be laughed at – on the contrary, you will begin to count – then the ball is at your feet!

Friday 19 January   I spoke shortly in the War debate today – Milner kindly called me no. 2 so I had no waiting – it was not too bad an effort and several people were kind enough to congratulate me and I think that they meant what they said – but I was not deemed worthy of a mention in the B.B.C. report tonight – it only mentioned at any length, Percy Harris(!) Hore-Belisha (who made an excellent speech), Acland (who, they tell me, talked outrageous nonsense for nearly an hour), Aneurin Bevan who appears to have been more intolerable and insolent than usual, and Anthony who wound up the debate with considerable vigour and success. Acland challenged a division and got seven malcontents to vote with him. The government had 340 supporters – and yet from the B.B.C. report the world may well imagine that we are a House divided amongst ourselves! It is all wrong that such reports should be allowed in war time – but no one seems able to control the B.B.C. – and it certainly cannot control itself.

Saturday 20 January   Douglas Clifton Brown[31] was in the Club this morning. He was indignant with the B.B.C. report of yesterday's debate – more still with Bevan's performance. He told me that this comparatively young and fit man did not even serve as a fire-watcher at Westminster – it really is a scandal that such a fellow should be tolerated.

Monday 22 January   I don't myself see how the Germans at the present stage of the war can keep going much longer against an invasion on two fronts – always provided that they are given no respite. If the Russians can drive them out of Silesia and deprive them of its coal and industrial potential, and if we can bomb their western industrial areas continuously and contain a large part of their armed forces, it is difficult to see how they can go on producing arms and munitions of war. Manpower, too, must be strained to

---

[31] The Speaker of the House of Commons.

the uttermost. I suppose that but for this 'unconditional surrender' business the Nazis could not keep things going and one regrets sometimes that Winston and Roosevelt ever stated so categorically this matter – it has enabled Hitler and Goebbels to assert that it means a deal more than it really does mean and one can understand their countrymen's reaction to what they tell them – still, even so, human flesh & blood must give way.

Tuesday 23 January   Finance for industry was discussed in the House today – it all sounded splendid, but no one appeared to take much interest in what John Anderson had to say. I suppose the man knows what he is about, but surely there never was a Chancellor of the Exchequer so ready to distribute money in such vast quantities for every scheme that comes along – where he gets it all from passes my understanding – but then I never was a financier and I have an uneasy feeling that Anderson is not one either. Surely the time has come to think about a reduction of taxation, not more spending.

Wednesday 24 January   There was a debate today about compulsory service for A.T.S. overseas – I did not listen to much of it because it seemed to me much ado about nothing – clearly if the services of the women are needed abroad and enough don't volunteer, there must be conscription. There is no reason to suppose that the women will not be looked after properly or in more danger than they are at home. Grigg for a change was conciliatory when winding up the debate, and the storm, if storm it was, fizzled out. ... The Russians announce the capture of Bromberg which is sixty-five miles north-east of Poznan on the railway to Danzig which latter town presumably must now be cut off. The Russians have also reached the Oder in the neighbourhood of Breslau – I suppose the betting now is odds on their getting to Berlin before we cross the Rhine at Cologne – but I fancy that they will have a lot more fighting and probably some setbacks before they get to Berlin – still for the time being at any rate they are swinging along merrily and one wonders where and when the enemy will stage a really big counter-attack. The important thing in the Russian advance is the over-running of Silesia where the Germans get so much of their coal and where the war industries have been largely concentrated as a result of our bombing of the Ruhr area so persistently.

Thursday 25 January   At luncheon today at the HofC those two great pundits, Eddie Winterton and Malcolm Robertson, were airing their views about Germany. If Hitler and Ribbentrop had only listened to E.W. when he visited them, there would have been no war – E.W. spoke very strongly to them – he and Malcolm are convinced that once the Germans crash a long and very difficult guerrilla war will begin and that fanatical Nazis will go about murdering all and sundry – especially Allied officers in control of civil affairs – everything will be done to make the administration of the country impossible – incidentally Malcolm stated that he was positive that Hitler was dead.

Tuesday 30 January   Went with Turton and some other M.P.s to interview James Grigg (Sec. of State for War) about the 50th Division – apparently it has been reduced to a cadre – said to be worn out and no longer of any fighting value. It seems all rot – but apparently (according to Grigg) such is Monty's opinion. There is nothing to be done except to try and keep all this from the people of Northumberland and Durham – we impressed this view on Grigg who seemed to appreciate our point of view.

Wednesday 31 January   Returning to the House I presided over the 'Northern Group' at 4 p.m. – Denville, Irene Ward, Storey and Donald Scott turned up.[32] I told them about the arrangements for the T[rade] U[nion] meeting on the 3rd of March and about the building people's wishes as expressed to me and Magnay last Saturday. Denville thought that all we need do *re* the future of the North East coast was 'for a few of us to have a heart to heart with Hugh Dalton'. He apparently has been going behind our backs to Dalton who 'deplores' a public meeting – I said that this particular meeting was a T.U. affair – no concern of ours – except as onlookers – that I was going to it and that the rest of the Tyneside Members could come or not as they pleased.

Thursday 1 February   There is still no news of poor Bernays[33]

---

[32] Headlam listed Scott twice, the wording in the original being 'Denville, Scott, Irene Ward, Storey and Donald Scott'; this is probably a simple error, but there may have been a further unidentifiable M.P. present in addition to the named four.

[33] Robert Hamilton Bernays (1902–1945), Lib. M.P. Bristol N. 1931–45 (stayed on govt. benches in 1933, joined Lib. Nat. Party 1936); P.S. Health 1937–39; P.S. Transport 1939–40; Dep. Regional Comm. for Civil Defence, S. England 1940–42; the aircraft he was travelling in was lost on 23 Jan. 1945.

M.P and one Campbell[34] M.P. (whom I did not know). It is now thought that their machine flying from Rome to Greece must have fallen into the sea – a sad business. Bernays was a strangely retiring shy little man – but extremely earnest and hard working – a Liberal, but an intelligent one.

Friday 2 February   ... there is no push as yet on the Western Front – how one wishes that the Americans were not in charge on this theatre – one feels that they are all amateurs and that they don't know how to get a move on. The idea here seems to be that they are neglecting this theatre of operations and are concentrating their main effort in the Pacific which, I should imagine, was quite likely. The House spent its time today on the second reading of a bill to make the carrying of a back lamp compulsory on cyclists after the war – an example of the detachment of Parliament in wartime.

Tuesday 6 February   The 'Big Three' are said to be conferring somewhere in the Black Sea[35] and to be agreed upon this, that and the other – let us hope they are – but I fear that brother Stalin must be getting all he wants. The Russian position is very strong for the time being and one wonders what Russian policy is out for? I have met one or two people today who say that they agreed with Hitler's latest speech and are just as frightened by the Bolshies as he is. We have certainly got to make up our minds for a very different Europe with Soviet Russia as top dog to what it was in the past. Clearly Russian influence is going to be preponderant in the Baltic and in the Balkans, and probably in Germany for some time to come – whether this will lead to a new kind of peaceful stability or to another war only time will tell. For some years to come I should think that all the world and his wife will be too much exhausted for anything but peace – the crux of the situation I should say lies in the attitude of the Russian Army and its leaders after the war. The Russian Army is now, I believe, the principal

[34] John Dermot Campbell (1898–1945), Con. M.P. Antrim 1943–45; member of N. Ireland parliament for Carrick 1943–45; Dep. Flax Controller, N. Ireland 1940–45.
[35] The last major inter-allied conference of the war, attended by Churchill, Roosevelt and Stalin, was held at Yalta on the Crimean peninsula on 4–11 Feb. 1945.

factor to be taken into consideration – it has learnt its strength and if its leaders are aggressive there may be trouble – Stalin, like every dictator, may have difficulty in pursuing a policy of peace, even if he wants to, and it won't be easy for him to liquidate victorious generals so easily as he liquidated his military opponents before Hitler invaded Russia.

Thursday 8 February   I attended the Conservative Executive where we had Willink M.P., Minister of Health, to talk about houses. His speech was considered effective, but it struck me as rather a helpless exhibition of impotence. How can there be a really effective policy of house building when one Ministry deals with the house planning, another with the labour required for the building and another with the materials?

Monday 12 February   ... to Whitley Bay where we attended the Ladies Luncheon Club which was started by the Conservative Association in the Wansbeck division in 1936 and has had a monthly luncheon ever since – rather a fine record especially as the period includes five years of war. Today there were nearly 80 ladies present (a larger gathering than usual, so I was assured ...).

Tuesday 13 February   In the House we had the second reading of the Govt.'s Requisitioned Lands Bill which is so unpopular – John Anderson made a conciliatory speech and I got him to say that the Govt. had no intention of not repairing the damage done by outcrop coaling operations.

Wednesday 14 February   The whole world, according to *The Times*, (always excepting Germany and Japan) is elated by the agreement reached in the Crimea – only the Polish Government in London (and not unnaturally!) among the Allies has revolted – it has (perhaps rather too hurriedly) said that it will not recognize a fifth partition of Poland. One cannot blame them – they know what the Russians are: we don't – or if we do, keep our knowledge to ourselves. We are quite helpless: we cannot break with the Russians and have to accept whatever they want – I suppose that Winston and Anthony feel that in the circumstances it is best to do this with a good grace and maintain that the Russians have a real claim to the Curzon Line[36] and are justified in settling what kind of a government should be set up in Poland.

Friday 16 February   I lunched at the House, but heard no gossip: very few people there and those present (except for the Tory Reform youths who were busy looking up facts and figures in the Library for some future debate presumably) not of the more interesting. ... Tokyo has had a big bombing, something on a large scale which is said to have done a deal of destruction – Dresden also is being smashed to pieces – it is an abominable business – but it cannot be helped in these enlightened days and no one now seems to have any compunction in killing crowds of civilians, so long as they are Germans or Japanese. It is not surprising in view of all that has been done by these two nations – it is none the less hateful to me – and one's only consolation is the hope (a faint one) that it will sicken people of war.

Monday 19 February   The North Newcastle Association *soirée*[37] tonight at the Station Hotel was a huge success for Mr. William Temple – there were nearly 200 people present and everybody seemed keen and awake. It was a pleasant surprise for us.

Tuesday 20 February   Winston is home again and there are the usual pictures of the great man shaking hands with his colleagues. The foreign affairs debate is to come off next week and it will be interesting to hear how he gets away with this new partition of Poland. It is reported that he is going to ask for a vote of confidence – the usual trick to force us to vote against our convictions in order to impress the world by our national unity.

Saturday 24 February   I had a talk with Tydeman ... apparently the situation in North Cumberland is more tiresome than ever – there is now a party for Fergus Graham – and a party, including ... the chairman of the Association, against him. ... Lunched at the Mansion House to meet Lord Woolton he addressed a meeting afterwards in the Durant Hall. He spoke for an hour on the

---

[36] The settlement of the Russo-Polish border proposed in July 1920, named after the British Foreign Secretary at that time, Lord Curzon; it excluded from Poland territory mainly inhabited by Ukranian, Lithuanian and Russian population.

[37] An evening social function.

National Insurance business and told us nothing new about it. He did not impress me either as a speaker or as a man – very pleased with himself and rather pompous.

Tuesday 27 February   Winston spoke for 2 hours today (with a luncheon interval) – it was a fine performance – but his line about Poland annoyed several people, self included. He tried to ride off criticism by assuring us that the Crimean agreement was in the best interests of the Polish nation and that they ought to welcome losing their eastern territory, etc., in view of what they were to get from Germany. His assurance that the new Polish Government would be fully representative of Polish political views was not very convincing and one is left with the feeling that he and Roosevelt have given way to Stalin. It is a bad business I think, and it is obvious that Russia is determined to put Poland in the bag just as she has put Finland and the Baltic republics and Yugoslavia, Bulgaria and Rumania. Winston is so much obsessed by the beating of Germany that he seems to be oblivious of the new danger he is creating for us in eastern Europe by assisting the aggrandisement of Russia and the promotion of Communism as far west as Vienna.

Wednesday 28 February   A good deal of talk today at Westminster on the subject of Poland – nobody seems pleased with what Winston said, but I heard no one suggest what else he could have said in the circumstances – if he and Roosevelt could not persuade Stalin to be a gentleman and they were not prepared to quarrel with him, there was no alternative but to try and make the decent Poles acquiesce in the new partition and to appreciate how nice it will be for them to have a semi-Russian government in Poland. Some of our more pronounced Conservatives are going to move an amendment against the Government. I don't think that I can vote for it – for, if it were carried, it would mean a condemnation of the Yalta agreement and one could not agree to that. But it is a rotten business – one gets more and more fussed about Russian policy – God knows what will be the end of it. All one feels is that we are face to face with a new menace to world peace – because the present Russian Govt. is pursuing the national policy of Russia since the days of Peter the Great – a purely national policy of aggrandisement which bodes no good to us. Indeed the danger is greater than it has ever been before for Russia is immensely more powerful now than she has ever been before and in the west she has no longer to consider Germany.

Thursday 1 March   The Government carried its vote of confidence by 413 votes to 0 this evening – only the two I.L.P. were against the resolution and they of course had to act as Tellers. I voted for the Government. The debate was not on as high a level as yesterday but I heard little of it – Anthony replied for the Government – not a particularly effective speech in my opinion – but it served its purpose – Winston there in high spirits. He has accepted Henry Strauss's resignation – which is not surprising. He has also lost the services of Harcourt-Johnson,[38] Minister of Overseas Trade. He voted in the division yesterday – but then had a stroke and died soon afterwards. He was a financial pillar of the Samuel – Sinclair – Bonham-Carter[39] section of the Liberal Party – and so was given office. He did not shine in the HofC. I remember him as the man who gave £200 to that miserable Liberal carpet-bagger[40] in the '35 election whose intervention was largely the cause of my losing the seat – and now the Liberals are going to play the same game against me in Newcastle. They are a sorry lot and entirely unnecessary nowadays – for all they can do is to help the Socialists win Conservative seats.

Friday 2 March   There was a debate on the Government's proposals to assist industry financially after the war – and the C[hancellor] of [the] E[xchequer] seized the opportunity of telling us all that there was no chance of any reduction in high direct taxation yet awhile. It is of course the one thing really needed to help a national revival – but if we will go on paying out more and more millions on Social Security, etc., etc., how can there be any reduction

[38] Harcourt Johnstone (1895–1945), Lib. M.P. Willesden E. 1923–24, S. Shields 1931–35, Middlesborough W. 1940–45; Whip 1931–32; Sec. for Overseas Trade 1940–45.

[39] (Helen) Violet Asquith (1887–1969), daughter of H.H. Asquith, Lib. P.M. 1908–16, styled Lady Violet after father cr. Earl of Oxford & Asquith 1925; married 1915 Maurice Bonham-Carter; Pres., Women's Lib. Fed. 1923–25, 1939–45; Pres., Lib. Party Organisation 1945–47; Lib. cand. Wells 1945, Colne Valley 1951; a leading figure on the Asquithian wing of the Liberal Party, prominent in the 1950s; cr. Dame 1953, Baroness Asquith of Yarnbury 1964.

[40] A nineteenth-century term for a candidate who has had no previous connection with a constituency before appearing to contest it in an election.

in taxation? We are rapidly descending the slope to national chaos and catastrophe – and no one seems to care a damn or even to realize what is going on.

Saturday 3 March   ... went to the Trade Union meeting at the City Hall – Bowman (A.E.U.)[41] in the chair – Denville, Ellen Wilkinson, Aske,[42] Nunn, Lawson, Magnay, the M.P. for Consett[43] (I forget his name) and myself. The floor of the hall was pretty full, but it was nothing like as big a meeting as was anticipated – shop stewards representing 80,000 workers on the Tyne. The Trade Union leaders did the speaking (poor stuff) then there were questions (the usual ones!) – then the M.P.s said a few words. I left before the end – it was a dull affair – no Communist disturbance of any kind.

Wednesday 7 March   I lunched at the House – but heard no gossip – people are cheerful, but the over-optimism of last autumn is conspicuous by its absence. The Speaker, who has been visiting the Western Front, told me that out there there was an evident feeling of optimism among those in authority – they don't apparently regard the Rhine any longer as a serious obstacle.

Tuesday 13 March   I spent most of today in the HofC, hoping to speak on the Army Estimates – but at 8.30 p.m. I felt too tired and angry to stay any longer. The Speaker and Milner had promised to call me but the chair seemed to be mainly in possession of Charles Williams, who kept putting me off – tiresome little Jack in office, if ever there was one. It is, nevertheless, annoying in the extreme that the chair has not more sense and justice in calling people – people like myself, who rarely speak, have some standing and are ancient should not be kept jumping up again and again as I was today. ... Grigg (Sec. of State for War) read out rather a well written essay about the recent doings of the Army. He was more successful (during his hour and a quarter at the Box) in his effort to disguise the fact that he was reading every word of his

[41] John ('Jack') Bowman, District Sec., Amalgamated Engineering Union; see entry for 14 Sep. 1941.
[42] Robert William Aske (1872–1954), Lib. M.P. Newcastle E. 1923–24, 1929–45 (Lib. Nat. from 1931); kt. 1911, cr. Bart. 1922.
[43] James Edward Glanville (1891–1958), coalminer, member of Exec. of Durham Miners' Assoc.; Lab. M.P. Consett 1943–55.

speech than was Henderson (his Under-Secretary) who read out a long statement about demobilization later on in the debate (forty minutes or thereabouts). This habit of reading speeches is growing into a positive nuisance as it lengthens speeches terribly. Grigg was jubilant in having read his stuff more clearly than Henderson did his. He is rather an entertaining little man and I should like to know him better – he certainly has courage and knows his own mind.

14

LABOUR LANDSLIDE

March to October 1945, May to July 1946

Wednesday 14 March 1945   Spent most of the day at the HofC –
nothing of much interest – lunched with James Stuart and one or
two others. It surprises me to find how many of our younger leaders
appear to be convinced that we shall win the election – a reduced
majority very likely – but defeat no. They base their confidence
very largely on Winston's popularity and also on the futility of the
opposition – I much doubt whether Winston will retain his popularity very many months after the war, and futile though the
opposition may be, it does, I think, represent the futility of the
electorate – so many people fail to appreciate how much they would
dislike Socialism – it sounds all right and only *experentia docet*.[1]
But of course I don't pretend to know the feeling of the public
outside the Northern Area where the Labour Party is so strong.

Thursday 15 March   Beatrice and I attended the Conference[2]
again this morning and listened to Winston's oration. He was in
good form and had a fine reception. So far as I could gather his
intention is to carry on for a bit with a reformed Government after
the Socialists and Archie Sinclair[3] leave him, and, if he is returned
after a General Election, proposes to form a new Govt. – not
entirely Conservative but of the best men available. I suppose his
idea is to keep on Anderson, Grigg, Oliver Lyttelton, Duncan,
Woolton, etc., who are no doubt not all of them Conservatives
avowedly. Whether this arrangement will please the Conservative

[1] translation: experience teaches.
[2] The Conservative Party conference held in London on 14–15 Mar. 1945.
[3] The leader of the independent Liberal Party.

Party remains to be seen: it will at any rate enable Winston to call his new Cabinet a national one.

Friday 16 March   I spent most of today at the HofC – not because there was anything to take me there but because there was nowhere else very obvious to go to. I believe that the Bill to continue the life of the Ministry of Fuel and Power was being discussed, but I did not go into the chamber so little was I interested in the business. It seems to me to be a futile Ministry, but so are most ministries – so why worry about any of them? ... Someone in the Smoking room today, I forget who it was, told me a story which he assured me Anthony Eden had told him – apparently the party of M.P.s, headed by Walter Elliot, which has recently been in Russia, was given half an hour's interview with Stalin. Walter E. with his usual loquacity had used up half the time gushing about the Russians and their achievements – then Joe could stand it no longer and told the interpreter to ask whether this man was sincere in all he said – would it not be better for the M.P.s to ask him questions? But why send such an ass and wind bag as Walter to head a deputation anywhere – who is responsible for this sort of thing I wonder?

Monday 19 March   Winston has at last told the T.U.C. people that he does not intend to amend the Trade Disputes Act in this Parliament – so that is all right. The repeal or the amendment of the Act is be one of the planks of the Labour programme – not an exciting one.

Tuesday 20 March   There is a deal too much writing at the present time and it seems to me that the written word is of no avail to check the follies of our age. No one reads the things that matter – education so far has, I think, been singularly ineffective – so far as politics and civil government are concerned the present generation seems to me either totally ignorant or singularly ill-informed – otherwise how could so many young people be toying after vain things – things that have been advocated, tried out, in the past and always ended in failure? It is odd, too, how unconcerned with the teachings of history the modern intelligentsia seems to be [and] determined on reviving the follies of the past – how it shuts its eyes to all the progress [that] has been made socially and politically through the ages and will risk the damages of revolution in order to achieve their aims – from all of which it may be gathered that I have been reading a little left wing literature today.

Friday 23 March　　The rumour of the Nazi last stand in the Bavarian alps is being spread a good deal – 50 divisions are said [to be] being kept for this job by Hitler – and the stand is going to last for 2 or 3 years, etc. It all sounds rather absurd but then the Nazis are absurd – and the whole of this war has been absurd – and the whole of the immediate future looks as if it were going to be absurd.

Monday 26 March　　This crossing of the Rhine has been a splendid performance – the incessant bombing goes on and must be wrecking German concentrations. Winston is reported to have crossed the Rhine – how the man must be enjoying himself and what amazing vitality he has – I only hope that he will live to see the thing through – but if he does, how wise he would be to retire from public life – but he will never do that I imagine of his own free will – he loves the lime light and probably would quickly expire without it.

Tuesday 27 March　　Young Lambton[4] (Durham's son) came to have lunch with me. He is anxious to contest a seat in the county at the next election. He is only 23 – but seems keen and intelligent. I liked him, but what he knows about politics, etc., and whether he has any facility of speech remain to be seen – however, we need candidates badly and he is the right type if he really means business.

Monday 9 April　　The enemy is done to the world and he must know it well enough – one wonders why he continues the fight – even from the Nazi point of view it would appear to be a fatal mistake, because it is the youth of the country which is now being killed off – surely it cannot be a wise policy? If Germany is to revive and have another go for 'world supremacy' why kill off the present generation and the rising one? I don't see how the Germans

---

[4] Antony ('Tony') Claud Frederick Lambton (1922–), Con. M.P. Berwick 1951–73; P.P.S. to S. Lloyd 1955–57; U.S. Defence (Air Force) 1970–73; styled Viscount Lambton after death of elder brother in 1941, suc. 6th Earl of Durham 1970 but disclaimed peerage, continuing to use the courtesy title of Lord Lambton.

will be fit to have another war for a hundred years – Napoleon's wars put France out of effective action very effectively and it looks as if Hitler may be doing the same thing for Germany.

Tuesday 10 April   There was nothing exciting at the House – a certain amount of talk about the Bevin-Bracken speeches,[5] and a general feeling that the Government cannot last much longer. Winston was in one of his cheerful moods and no doubt the Cabinet mean to hang together a bit longer.

Wednesday 11 April   I have spent most of today in the House and more time than usual in the Chamber – Requisitioning of Land Bill (or whatever the thing is called) in Committee. I intervened on one amendment speaking for it, but I did not divide against the Government – I never see much point in these small anti-Government divisions – they seem to me to serve no useful purpose and are liable to mislead public opinion – to make it appear that the Party is not fully supporting the Government in war-time. If the subject in dispute were a serious one, and party feeling were more or less united, it would be another matter – then the right thing to do, in my opinion, would be to bring pressure on the Government to reconsider its proposals before the subject came up in the House – it would have to do so if the pressure were strong enough. I lunched and dined in the House, but heard little or no gossip. It surprises me how many of our people appear to be in favour of a June general election – surely the hay season is not the moment for us to go to the country?

Thursday 12 April   ... I went to the Central Office [National Union] Executive meeting which was as dull an affair as usual. The coming general election is the only subject which influences people's attention at the moment – from what Ralph Assheton told me it is beginning to look like a summer general election – a great mistake, I think. However I am perhaps not in a position to judge as I am not in the know – some say that an early election will catch the Left Wingers on the hop – that they are not so nearly ready for it

---

[5] Bevin attacked the Conservative Party's pre-war record and probable election tactics at the Yorkshire Labour conference on 7 Apr.; on 9 Apr. Bracken, speaking at a luncheon at Holborn C.A., replied and criticised Bevin in partisan terms.

as they would have us believe. The idea, too, is that Winston may be a greater asset for us in June than he may be in October – my own view is that Winston is not going to be so great an asset at any time as some people believe – once the war is over, his war record will be forgotten and his past misdeeds will be remembered. He never was a popular politician with the people.

Friday 13 April   Roosevelt's death is announced in the papers today – a very sudden affair, and a sad calamity I should say. ... The HofC adjourned this morning as a mark of respect to Roosevelt – the first time I believe it has done so for a foreign chief of state – everybody sorry for Winston who was clearly much upset and no wonder! Lunched at the House with Austin Hopkinson, Manningham-Buller,[6] Perkins[7] and Petherick[8] – much gossip about Beaverbrook, Critchley[9] etc. as might be expected – according to Hoppy, the Beaver is the real ruler of England.

Tuesday 17 April   The war news continues good and Germany is rapidly being cut in two parts – one does not see how in either part a prolonged resistance can be possible. The tales of atrocities in concentration camps which are coming in as they are reached by the Allies are really too revolting for words. It is almost inconceivable that such cruelty could be possible and one realizes with shame how little man has improved since Christ died – how bestial he can be. What on earth can be done to punish the perpetrators of these iniquities I don't know – where are they to be found? how are they to be caught? The danger is that the troops may be so righteously incensed at what they see that they may take the law into their own hands and begin slaying Germans indiscriminately.

Saturday 21 April   ... we had the Area meeting which was well

---

[6] Reginald Edward Manningham-Buller (1905–1980), Con. M.P. Daventry 1943–50, Northamptonshire S. 1950–62; P.S. Works May-July 1945; Solicitor-Gen. 1951–54; Attorney-Gen. 1954–62; Lord. Chanc. 1962–64; Ld. of Appeal in Ordinary 1969–80; kt. 1951, suc. 4th Bart. 1956, cr. Baron Dilhorne 1962, Viscount 1964.

[7] (Walter) Robert Dempster Perkins (1903–1988), Con. M.P. Stroud 1931–45, Stroud & Thornbury 1950–55; P.S. Civil Aviation May-July 1945; kt. 1954.

[8] Maurice Petherick (1894–1985), Con. M.P. Penryn & Falmouth 1931–45; F.S. War Office May-July 1945.

[9] Alfred Cecil Critchley (1890–1963), Con. M.P. Twickenham 1934–35; contested Islington E. as a Beaverbrook-sponsored 'Empire Crusade' cand. Feb. 1931; Dir.-Gen. of B.O.A.C. 1943–46; Chairman, Skyways Ltd. 1946–54.

attended by all the 'old and true'. Ralph [Assheton] made a good sound speech, but the success of the afternoon was young Lambton who made a splendid little speech which pleased people. He should do well in time if he has the health for the game. Thorp,[10] the Berwick candidate, did quite well too – but whether he can beat Beveridge remains to be seen.

Sunday 22 April   Ralph Assheton ... departed this morning – called for by Peat M.P. who was as dull and unforthcoming as usual. Tydeman is dubious as to his chance of keeping Darlington at the next election – no doubt the Peat-Vickery row has not done any good to the Conservative party in Darlington – however it is Peat's affair not ours. He has always run his own show and kept aloof from the Area organization.

Tuesday 24 April   Anderson's budget speech today was dull, long and uninteresting – however, he clearly expects that there will have to be a second budget this year if all goes well.

Wednesday 25 April   In the Smoking Room listened to Wickham,[11] one of the M.P.s who has been to Germany to see the atrocities. His account the same as what has been published in the papers – too horrible for words – it only shows how foul human beings can be when they are given a chance – and their chance comes when the dregs of the population come to the top as they invariably do in revolutions be they Bolshie, or Nazi, or Fascist. Berlin is now surrounded so Stalin announces ... The Speaker lit up 'Big Ben' last night: a great event.

Friday 27 April   The news is excellent – the official link up of the Russians and Americans is reported at Targau just north east of Leipzic – I don't see how the Germans can carry on much longer – indeed, I feel that the end is very near. I lunched today at the House with James Stuart, Harry Crookshank and G. Lloyd George. They were cheerful – but the result of the Chelmsford by-election

    [10] Robert Allen Fenwick Thorp (1900–1966), Con. M.P.Berwick 1945–51; Whip 1947–48.
    [11] Edward Thomas Ruscombe Wickham (1890–1957), Con. M.P. Taunton 1935–45; served in Indian Political Dept. 1919–35; P.P.S. to F. Horsbrugh 1939, to L. Hore-Belisha 1939–40, to Sir V. Warrender 1940, to D. Margesson 1941–42.

where Common Wealth has won with a 6,000 majority rather made them sit up. It has not surprised me – because I feel that the country is going left – there is so much foolishness on all sides – I suppose that it is only a temporary phase – but It Is going to cause us all a lot of trouble in the near future. I cannot understand why our Conservative pundits are so blind to the situation. Their faith in the magic of Winston's name is to me rather pathetic – but let us hope that there may be more justification for their faith than I can see cause for.

Tuesday 1 May   Everyone was expecting a statement today from Winston about peace – the idea being that Himmler was going to give up – but Winston had nothing fresh to tell us and it looks as if there were a hitch somewhere – though what it can be no one seems to know – possibly it may be that Himmler is not in a position to speak for Germany – what has become of Hitler seems to me the crux of the situation. ... Had a talk with Oliver Lyttelton this afternoon – he is just back from the U.S.A. He says that the new President[12] strikes him as a sensible little business man. He has no imagination but takes a point quickly – of course he has not the power or the position of Roosevelt and Congress will have far more control than it had – all this I had already appreciated – whether or not it is good for us remains to be seen. Oliver says that Halifax now has an immense position in the U.S.A. – greater than even Lothian had he thinks – due entirely to his acknowledged moral superiority to all and sundry. It is a great triumph for him – 'the great Christian nobleman' as G. Dawson used to call him.

Wednesday 2 May   It has been a great day – this morning the death of Hitler and Goebbels announced in the newspapers ... Berlin is practically in Russian hands and the 'Southern Bastion' is almost gone, as Winston told us in the House at 7.30 p.m. this evening. He announced that the Germans in Italy and in most of Austria had surrendered to Alexander – a force of approximately 1,000,000 men. It is a wonderful triumph and everyone in the House who heard the news were delighted that it had come to

---

[12] Harry S. Truman (1884–1972), Democratic Senator, Missouri 1935–44; Vice-Pres. of U.S.A. Jan.-Apr. 1945, Pres. 1945–53 (suc. Pres. on death of Roosevelt Apr. 1945, re-elected 1948). The single letter 'S' which was Truman's second name was chosen as a compromise reference to the forenames of both his grandfathers.

Alex. He is more popular there than the great Monty. One can hardly realize that the war in Europe is practically finished – that the end of this long horror has come – one has a great feeling of relief and thankfulness – but, somehow or other, one is not wholly happy as one should be – one is so nervous about the future – whether our people will behave sanely – whether we shall be able to maintain our solidarity and common sense. And one is nervous, too, about the general state of things in Europe. What of the Russians? What will be the next moves of Stalin & Co. – what claims will they make – what backing have they got politically? I personally have no faith in them and dread their political aims in Europe and Asia.

Friday 4 May   ... it 'does not do' to count upon a collapse in Japan and if they decide to go on fighting, the war must be a long one – and the difficulty we shall have here is that once the European war is over, people will get slack about the war in the Far East – all the old party troubles will begin and we shall lose that unity of purpose and decision which will be required to guide our policy in Europe and to organize the new world. It is a thousand pities that it should be deemed necessary to have a hurried General Election, no sane man really wants one – certainly not the Labour Party leaders – it is the result of incessant extremist propaganda which has been steadily pursued during the war years and bodes no good to this country. Well, it is no use fussing – if we have to have an election, we must do our best to win it – if we fail and Labour comes into power, we must endeavour to prevent their tail wagging the dog – but it won't be an easy job.

At this point Headlam fell ill, and the diary is blank from 6 to 11 May. On 12 May he was able to travel from London to Todd's nursing home in Bristol where he convalesced, returning to London on 23 May.

Sunday 13 May   ... I am glad that Winston in his broadcast tonight at long last spoke pretty strongly about the Russian policy in Poland – not by any means too strongly. He did not drop a hint that I could gather as to when the election is to be.

Wednesday 16 May   A letter from R.A. Butler politely turning down our report – he thinks that Jerrold better print it; clearly it is likely to be controversial, especially about HofL and so should not emanate from official quarters. All this is rather what I expected – and now it is up to us to decide what to do Jerrold will probably not print it on his own – Agnes, methinks, will have to find someone [else] to look after her offspring. I doubt whether the Committee will care to father it on their own – I mean admit to having shared in its production which R.A.B. now tells us is the right thing to do – he and his coterie have let us down pretty badly – odd how little I seem to mind!

Monday 21 May   The Labour Party have not accepted Winston's proposal to keep the Coalition going until the war against Japan is over – they would be willing to carry on until October – but the 'Tories' won't have this, and so presumably the election will be early in July. Personally I am extremely nervous about it, but I may be unduly perturbed. We shall see – in North Newcastle I have not an idea of what our fate may be – but clearly the sooner one gets there the better as nothing is being done so far as I know to get the organization going again. ... This Russian cloud all over the horizon has completely ruined any happiness one might have had as a result of the German war – Hitler must be chuckling in his grave I should imagine as the new dictatorship over Europe develops.

Tuesday 22 May   I certainly feel a deal better and less fearful of an election battle – there seems no doubt now that we are in for the beastly thing. The Labour Conference is out for a fight – and a beastly one it is going to be. The more one thinks about it the less necessary an election seems to be – we are only having one because the left wingers think that they will win and feel that, even if they don't, their position can only be strengthened in any new Coalition. Winston is about the only asset we have in this election because I doubt whether argument or common sense can help us much with a new electorate which has been brought up on left wing nonsense without any kind of contradiction for five years.

Tuesday 29 May   I went into Newcastle this morning and went to Temple's chambers to see him as he said he had something of importance to tell me. It seems that the Executive Committee –

some of its members at any rate – are unwilling to adopt me as candidate. Temple was discreet but I gather that Lawson and Mrs. Fenwick are the ring leaders in the business. They assert that I shall lose the seat if I stand – I am so unpopular in Newcastle, etc. It may well be that I shall loose the seat, if things go wrong – but, if I do, the fault will not be mine – they, the Executive, have done nothing for the last five years – there is no organization and I have not been allowed to try and get it going again, though I have begged them to let me do something for the last twelve months. I suppose that these beastly people have been waiting to have a go at me – but they have left it too long – a new candidate now would find things very difficult.

Saturday 2 June   I was asked to receive a deputation from the Executive Committee this afternoon in Saville Row. Temple on their behalf handed me a resolution which they had drafted saying that they were not prepared to recommend me to the Association for adoption! I asked for the reasons and was told that they considered I could not win the seat as I was too old, not physically fit and unpopular. I replied that I would think the matter over and consult my friends and give them my answer on Monday – but I could tell them at once that I should leave the matter to the Association.[13]

Sunday 3 June   Saw Leith and Appleby yesterday – both rather surprised at the action of the Committee. The former rather aggressive to me personally – apparently he considers that I have been rude to him since I have been chairman of the Area: not consulting him about political matters – I reminded him that during the last six years there have been no such matters to discuss with anyone! He telephoned to me tonight that if I will give an assurance not to stand again after this election, it might be all right! I have drawn Matt Ridley into the business and Bloxam[14] is busy in Newcastle roping in new members to be at the Adoption meeting.

Monday 4 June   I saw Temple at the Station Hotel and gave him

---

[13] i.e., to a general meeting of the Association.

[14] Miss Rosalie Bloxam had been helping Headlam in the constituency since the autumn of 1944, acting as an unofficial organiser and secretary.

my written reply to the Executive Committee's resolution – then we went to see Alec Leith. He was friendly, but not expansive – of course he does not like me and showed it tonight when he rang me up to tell me that Temple had told him that if I gave an undertaking not to stand again after this time he thought that his Committee might change their attitude. I said that this did not seem likely as their objection was to my standing at this election – whereupon Alec grew abusive and washed his hands of the whole business! What a man! We (B. and I) lunched with the old Applebys who were both very kind and sympathetic – Dudley Appleby is also standing by me. It is a beastly business and is taking a lot out of us ... Winston opened the battle on the air tonight. He went all out – rather overdid the business I thought, so far as sensible people are concerned – but then there are few sensible people and the rank and file of the party may welcome a fighting speech from the leader.[15]

Tuesday 5 June　　It has been a trying day, and I am tired – though not unduly. I saw the Applebys – *père et fils* – this morning and they were both most friendly and helpful – both advised me not to compromise with the enemy as advised by Alec Leith. Alec was furious with me – but of course he always has a grievance of some kind against me – and it cannot be helped. Tydeman also counselled me to let the business go to the Association and have nothing more to do with the Committee. I saw Temple later in the day and told him so – so now there is nothing more to be done until Friday – for which the Gods be praised. Temple again assured me that he had no wish to stand at this election – which is true no doubt – but he wd. be 'persuaded' to stand if I were turned down! Saw Matt Ridley at the Club and told him my tale: he promised to come to the meeting on Friday if at all possible. Attlee's broadcast tonight was in a minor key – a clever bit of work I thought designed to try and make people believe that the Socialist policy was very moderate – all the old stuff of course but put across quite well.

Friday 8 June　　The Adoption meeting has passed off quite successfully – a large assembly and, so far as I could make out, only

---

[15] This was the broadcast in which Churchill asserted that a Socialist government would need to use 'some form of Gestapo' to enforce its measures.

5 objectors – Mr. Fred Allen (a Grattan-Doyle supporter in the by-election) and 4 women whom he brought with him. Temple proposed me (he took the chair very well) and Councillor Chapman[16] seconded me – Matt Ridley supported me (his appearance was a great asset as I had anticipated it would be: he eclipsed Lawson who sat in the background) – old Appleby, Alec Leith, Dudley Appleby and one or two others spoke. I gave a short address. It all went like a marriage bell – if only the election ends as well as it began tonight, all will be well.

Saturday 9 June   ... I spoke tonight at Spennymoor for Douglas Nicholson[17] – quite a good meeting – over 300 present so they told me – I spoke for about 40 minutes and was in good form – no trouble with my voice – a good many questions afterwards most of which were addressed to me. The Vicar of the parish ... was rather tiresome – he is a Christian Socialist and I scored off him to the great pleasure of our people in the hall – apparently he bores them with his politics and Socialist study circles. ... Douglas N. is working very hard – and spending a lot of money – but I don't think he has a chance of winning.

During the hectic period of the election campaign Headlam often did not have time at the end of the day to write the diary, and the pages for 12–19 and 25–29 June are blank.

Wednesday 20 June   I spoke for Martel tonight in the Witham Hall at Barnard Castle – quite a full attendance and my speech went down well – saw a good many old friends and they seemed pleased to see me.[18] Martel spoke after I had finished for 50 minutes – a military lecture on his experiences while our military representative in Moscow. It was quite interesting (if one had not heard it all before) but hardly the stuff for an election speech. He seems quite happy for some reason or other about his chances –

[16] Norman Hackworth Chapman (1884–1972), Managing Dir., N.H. Chapman & Co., furnishers, from 1919; member of Newcastle City Council, St. Nicholas', Walker & Jesmond Wards 1936–49, Alderman 1949–61, Chairman, Finance Ctte. 1940–45, Sheriff 1949–50, Lord Mayor 1950–51; one of the city's largest ratepayers.

[17] (Frank) Douglas Nicholson (1905–1984), Con. cand. Spennymoor 1945; Chairman, Durham Police Authority 1955–64; High Sheriff, Co. Durham 1948–49; Jt. Managing Dir., Vaux Breweries 1937–52, Chairman 1953–76.

[18] Headlam had been the M.P. for Barnard Castle in 1924–29 and 1931–35.

he certainly has a very weak opponent and no Liberal opponent, and it is the turn for a Conservative. Philip Pease[19] was in the chair and wound up the meeting, bidding all and sundry to vote for Martel and so help 'to return Mr. Baldwin with a good majority'. This brought the proceedings to a close in a merry mood!

Thursday 21 June   I spoke tonight [in Newcastle] – the meeting was not a large one – but it was said to be larger than the other people have had. Meetings are clearly not going to be well-patronized – holidays, wireless and fine weather account for this – but also, I think, the people have made up their minds one way or the other – which way I don't know – I still am convinced that this hurried election is a mistake. Elections cannot be won without organization – and our organization has been in cold storage for too long while the Left Wing people have been busy all the time ... If we had waited until October for the election, the Labour people would have been no stronger than they are today and we should have been able to get our organization going again.

Friday 22 June   Saw Denville, Nunn and O'Sullivan[20] at the County Club. They are terribly worried about the food worry. They all seem to think that it is going to defeat them – agreed as they wished me to join with them to add my name to an S.O.S. to Winston, asking him to get out at Newcastle on his way back from Scotland. The man is touring the country but proposes to omit the north east coast in his tour – a great shame – but I doubt whether our S.O.S. will do any good – and I regard it as undignified – however, there it is – if one is one of four members one must play with the team. My meeting tonight was a success I think – Temple, who turned up today from the Assizes and is very affable, took the chair for me – about 100 present – not too bad for such a fine night – but the general apathy and lack of interest in the election is rather odd and, I think, rather ominous – but it may be that the majority of the people have made up their minds about their voting, and of course the wireless has done a lot to spoil local meetings unless you have big noises on the platform – if one can hear all the

[19] A member of the Pease family, major figures in southern Co. Durham; originally a Quaker and Liberal industrial dynasty based in Darlington, they became increasingly identified with Conservatism between the 1880s and 1930s.
[20] R. O'Sullivan, Lib. Nat. cand. Newcastle E. 1945.

leaders on the air, why should one worry to go and listen to lesser people?

Sunday 24 June   ... we really are badly neglected by our leaders in this part of the world – we have not even been able to get a Cabinet Minister to speak in Newcastle – either they are frightened to come here or the Central Office has written off the industrial north and is not prepared to waste ministers upon us. The shortage of speakers is appalling in this election.

Saturday 30 June   Winston made his last broadcast tonight – it was, I think, the best he has done – I wish he had begun on a less provocative note – however, all the broadcasting is over now, thank God – what its results may have been one cannot say, but I am sure that propaganda of this kind is not good – far better keep politics off the air. My view is that it lowers the prestige of the leaders and confuses the electors – this spate of speeches on the wireless ruins the political meetings everywhere – however, I suppose the practice once adopted of an air campaign has come to stay.

Sunday 1 July   Winston has now stated quite clearly that he would not serve in a Labour Govt. – so let us hope that this statement will silence the Lib-Lab cry that it makes no difference what party is returned to power Winston will still be P.M. Beveridge has been crying out this nonsense very vigorously – I am glad to think that there is a good chance of this particular gent loosing his seat. The Nicholsons came in for drinks – Douglas is still quite confident that Spennymoor can be won. Young Macmillan[21] dined here. He is not so confident of beating Shinwell – but he has done very well I am told.

Monday 2 July   Back to Newcastle – saw several deputations today – people bothering about their questionnaires – I have answered all of these futile things when they have been sent to me by Newcastle bodies – otherwise, I have torn them up. Winston is

---

[21] Maurice Victor Macmillan (1921–1984), Con. M.P. Halifax 1955–64, Farnham 1966–83, Surrey S.W. 1983–84; Economic Sec., Treasury 1963–64; Chief Sec. Treasury 1970–72; Employment Sec. 1972–73; Paymaster-Gen. 1973–74; eldest son of Harold Macmillan, styled Viscount Macmillan of Ovenden after cr. of father as Earl of Stockton 1984; unsuccessfully contested Seaham 1945.

still worrying away at Laski[22] – presumably this must be considered 'good tactics'. Laski's intervention only confirms what most of us knew before – *viz.* that a political Labour chief can never be the master in his own house. He has to meet his political followers in the HofC every week and be badgered by them – he has to listen to the pundits of the T.U.C. and apparently also to the Chairman of his party caucus – I don't see how there is ever to be a strong and independent Labour Cabinet – and this of course is the tragedy of the Labour Party as an alternative Government. I doubt, however, whether the man in the street realizes all this – and I doubt whether the Laski business will change a single Labour vote – I am not bothering about it very much. Wavell in India is still busy interviewing all the political leaders – Gandhi would appear to be amenable, but the other fellows are giving a lot of trouble – one doubts whether it is humanly possible to get the Moslems and the Congress leaders to pull together – well, India is not a matter which appears to be interesting the electors here!

Tuesday 3 July   Another day of electioneering ... Beatrice and I visited 2 R[oman] C[atholic] convents ... I gather we have what is called 'the Catholic vote' – I always doubt very much whether it means much nowadays. The same applies to the Jewish vote ... It will be interesting to see whether the animosity against Temple will survive the election – if we lose the fight, I fancy that disappointment and anger will sweep him out and all the old gang as well – if we win, he will probably survive – but I doubt whether he ever will secure the seat. There is no news of much interest in the papers – a lot of election gossip of course – but no one, not even the most enterprising journalist, is daring to prophesy the result – no one anywhere seems to be able to grasp which way the country is going. I think the result depends on the women.

Wednesday 4 July   I made my last speech tonight – not a bad meeting – but I am still quite incapable of sensing the political atmosphere – I am inclined to think that it is going to be a close thing either way. If it were not for the Liberal intervention – this

---

[22] Harold Joseph Laski (1893–1950), Prof. of Political Science, L.S.E. 1926–50; member of Fabian Society Exec. 1922–36; member of Lab. Party N.E.C. 1936–49, Chairman 1945–46.

complicates matters considerably – my own view is that the Labour vote in this division has greatly increased and it may well be that we cannot afford to lose Liberal support. I don't fancy that the Liberals are strong enough to win the seat, but they may well ruin our chance of success. ... Winston's London tour seems to have drawn huge crowds and he has been treated rather rudely in some places, but I suppose that his tour has done good. The Labour press is more bitter than ever: its only cry is class warfare – one wonders how far this will be successful? My own hope and belief is that it won't have much effect – it has failed before and will fail again unless I am far wrong – and if I am far wrong, it is a bad look out for the country.

Thursday 5 July   Well, it is all over bar the deferred shouting.[23] Beatrice and I drove round the polling stations and committee rooms all the morning – polling, they told us, was going on steadily and they expected a heavy poll – this is said to be a good thing for me – for it may mean that the Tories are turning out! Labour always does. We have not had enough cars all day and those that we have had don't appear to have been used to the best advantage. Report tells me that Scanlan[24] has been much rattled and tiresome. He certainly has not sat in his Central Office, but been wandering about all day. Temple has also been doing the same thing and has had Scanlan with him telling people to go to the poll by 'loud speaker' – what a job for an agent! If we loose this election it will be largely due to Temple – he has done nothing to revive the organization during the last year and has been in collusion with Mrs. Fenwick all the time – she has not even troubled to come back from London to vote! We have had a lot of good helpers tumbling about all day!

Saturday 7 July   Our troops are in Berlin and the Union Jack has been hoisted in Germany's capital. It will be difficult this time for the Germans to say that they were not defeated – still I expect that Germany will rise again and I go further and consider that it would be bad for Europe if she did not – I do not contemplate the

---

[23] In order for the votes cast by men serving in the forces overseas to be included, the count and declarations took place three weeks after polling day.

[24] T.M. Scanlan (b. 1893), army officer 1914–36, 1939–45, retired as Colonel; Con. Agent Newcastle N. 1945–51; the son of a Newcastle city councillor.

introduction of a Russian civilization in the west – at this moment it looks as if that was in store for us – Stalin has merely to take possession of France and Peter the Great's Testament will have been carried into effect – there are, I fear, hectic days ahead of us unless we can put aside domestic brawls and trivialities and face the future realistically.

Monday 9 July   The policy of appeasement with the Russians seems to be on the increase and is bound to make them more grasping and obnoxious. The war with Japan shows no sign of coming to an end – though I hear that the egregious Dr. Dalton in a speech out of doors to a crowd in Darlington assured his hearers that in strict confidence he could tell them that it would only last another six months! Was there ever such a man! The Japanese are said to be expecting us to invade Malaya and are busy evacuating civilians – they are done to the world of course but evidently are going to fight on to the last gasp – and then what are we going to do with them? Kill as many as possible of them – but this won't amount to much as they breed like rabbits.

Wednesday 11 July   I spoke this evening at Morpeth for Morley Longden[25] – his eve of the poll meeting – they postponed this election because the miners at Ashington were on holiday last week. It seems to me quite ridiculous to make such exception and it all comes from having a General Election at this time of year. Goodness only knows how many of my supporters were away from the poll – but they don't count – it is only working men who have big unions behind them whose holidays have to be taken into consideration. The meeting this evening was very hot and crowded – a Conservative gathering for the most part … I thought that the show would never end. It began with 'God save the King' and ended with 'God save the King' – I don't recollect ever before such a fervent exhibition of loyalty. Godfrey Nicholson told us that he could not even make out whether he was going to get in at Fareham and assured us that Oliver Lyttelton might lose Aldershot. It certainly is a very odd business and people seem to be just as uncertain of what is happening in the South as we are in the North. Harold Macmillan

---

[25] Gilbert James Morley Longden (1902–1997), Con. cand. Morpeth 1945, M.P. Hertfordshire S.W. 1950–74; kt. 1972.

who was here yesterday thinks that he has lost Stockton.

Thursday 12 July ... spent the morning in Newcastle where I saw Tydeman and Scanlan. The former was as futile and senile as usual. He thinks that I shall keep my seat, but is very uncertain about the other three seats – as, indeed, we all are. Scanlan is only uncertain about my majority! He now puts it at 7,000 – it used to be 10,000 according to his estimate. He was very affable, but I am not sure that he is to be depended upon: I fancy that he thinks Temple is the man to back. This does not much matter to me but it may lead to more trouble in the Association.

Friday 13 July Winston is still at his French villa – ruminating, I suppose, on what is going to be his fate. It looks rather rocky at the moment – people are now talking of a 'bare majority' or even of a Labour win. It is all very odd and the only thing to do is 'to wait and see' – there may yet be a surprise for the Labour Party as there was in 1931 – when up here, at any rate, they expected to win every Tory seat and were only left with two of their own – I still think that the result depends on the women.

Friday 20 July I gather that the general opinion is that Labour has got a majority – such is my own feeling at any rate – and perhaps if they are to have a majority at all it is best that it should be a working one – nothing could be worse than a repetition of 1923 or 1929. Until the Socialists have really been in power, the electors will not be satisfied – then alone we shall find out whether or not Socialist ideas can be put in practice without a general slump in our national prosperity.

Thursday 26 July We got to Newcastle about 11 o'clock this morning and our result was declared at 12.30 – the figures were self 17,381; Shackleton[26] 10,228; McKeag[27] 5,812; Ridsdale[28] 904. It was a great relief – and a famous victory in this truly catastrophic election – never was such a crushing disaster – the 3 other Newcastle

[26] Lab. cand. Newcastle N. 1945.
[27] William McKeag (1897–1972), Lib. cand. Durham 1924, 1929, M.P. Durham 1931–35, cand. Newcastle N. 1945, Newcastle E. 1950; Dep.-Ass. Adjutant-Gen. 1939–45; Lord Mayor of Newcastle 1951–52, 1953–54.
[28] The Common Wealth candidate.

seats have gone and except for a victory at Berwick where Beveridge was turned out, we have only one other seat in the whole Northern Area – Penrith & Cockermouth.[29] It is the same story all over the country. Labour has a clear majority of 150 or thereabouts over 'the rest' – Winston has resigned and little Mr. Attlee reigns in his stead – it is a sorry business and one feels ashamed of one's countrymen. But there it is – this is democracy – the people wanted a change and, no longer being afraid, voted Labour. The Left Wing propaganda has had its effect and it would seem that the vast majority of the new generation has gone Socialist for the time being. What a HofC it is going to be – filled with young, half baked, young men – mainly from the R.A.F. so far as I can make out – including Aidan Crawley who has turned out one of the Berry family.

Friday 27 July   The more one thinks over this ghastly election, the more wretched one feels. In the U.S.A. people are aghast that the English people should have so wholeheartedly chucked Winston – the Left Wingers throughout Europe are reported to be sitting up and taking notice – no longer is this country looked upon as stable and the consequences will be more political troubles all over the world. The prospect seem to me to be bleak in the extreme – if Attlee and co. had their own way, no doubt they would go slow and not precipitate things – but with a crowd of eager young men pledged to every extreme their job won't be an easy one – especially with Laski and co. bingeing up the extremists. I suppose that the idea of this [*sic*] people will be to force the pace – but I hardly think that the wiser among them will decide to pass an Enabling Bill such as Cripps and Laski have suggested. The fat would then be in the fire with a vengeance and one wonders what would happen: our line, I think, should be to lie low for a time and watch developments in the HofC while setting to work to reorganize the Party in the constituencies. I only hope that there will be a clean sweep at the Central Office and that there is someone who can get it going on lines more satisfactory than the present regime. Ralph Assheton has lost his seat and it may be that he will now devote himself for a time to this reorganization work. He is supposed to be one of our abler younger men and the job of

---

[29] Headlam did not count Hexham, the Speaker's seat, in the Conservative total.

reorganization is by far the more important matter at the moment – we must recapture youth.

Monday 30 July   I hate leaving home as I always do – but there it is – it is good for me to have the HofC to go to – though I know that it won't be a pleasant place for me in these bad days. I shall hate triumphant Labour permeating the place and I am not young enough or strong enough to enjoy being in opposition – still I hope that now and again I shall be able to make a useful speech – who can tell? ... I saw Tydeman and Scanlan. They had no news for me. I wonder how long we are to be left with the former – somehow or other I don't think that he is the man to reorganize the north of England. We shall have to get busy on the job and with some practical plan in our minds. The trouble is that I can see no one capable of taking on the job which I must relinquish – I cannot go on being chairman of the Area indefinitely – indeed, I don't think that it would be within the rules for me to do so even if I wanted to.

Wednesday 1 August   I attended the sitting of the House for the election of [the] Speaker – Douglas Clifton-Brown was duly elected – proposed by Neil Maclean[30] (in an excellent little speech) seconded by Hugh O'Neill[31] in a less successful effort – Douglas himself made an admirable little speech. Morrison and Winston both spoke as well as some Liberal whom I did not know by sight and the inevitable Gallacher.[32] The House was a strange sight – full to the brim with the new boys – the flight lieutenants and other callow youths who are to rule us all for the next five years at least – my heart rather sank within me when I saw their eager, excited young faces and the smug, grinning faces of Morrison and his colleagues on the Front Bench. Some ass on our side thought fit to start

[30] Neil Maclean (1875–1953), Lab. M.P. Glasgow Govan 1918–50; Whip 1919–21, 1922–23; member of N.E.C. 1920–22; member of P.L.P. Exec. 1931–36; Chairman, P.L.P. 1945–46.
[31] (Robert William) Hugh O'Neill (1883–1982), Ulster Unionist M.P. Mid-Antrim 1915–22, Co. Antrim 1922–50, Antrim N. 1950–52; Speaker of N. Ireland Parl. 1921–29; Chairman, 1922 Ctte. 1935–39; U.S. India & Burma 1939–40; Father of the House 1951–52; Ld. Lt. Co. Antrim 1949–59; cr. Bart. 1929, Baron Rathcavan 1953.
[32] William Gallacher (1881–1965), Communist M.P. Fife W. 1935–50; Pres., Communist Party of Great Britain 1956–63.

singing 'For He's a Jolly Good Fellow' when Winston came in – and the enemy responded with 'The Red Flag'.

Thursday 2 August   I spent most of today at the HofC and took the oath late in the afternoon. ... Dalton is the new Chancellor of the Exchequer – Bevin at the Foreign Office is rather an alarming experiment – one wonders what his line is going to be – the appeasement policy with Russia presumably – where will this policy lead? We now have Asia half across Europe – and it does not look as if anyone in this country minds. ... Saw some old friends – 'the orphans of the storm' like myself – no one seems to have expected such a debacle – Herbert Williams, they tell me, who was well beaten at South Croydon, after the election was finished expected to be in with a 10,000 majority – so apparently did many others who were badly beaten – assuredly the Labour people played a very clever game – they knew they had the game in their hand and kept so quiet that few of our people realised the danger they were in.

Friday 3 August   I lunched at the HofC – 2 strange young men (Labour youths of the Aidan [Crawley] type) came and sat themselves down at our table much to our consternation – all of us old stagers are rather pothered – for if the Labour people sit among us it makes it awkward as we cannot talk freely among ourselves. One wonders how the new boys can be made to understand this sort of thing – who is their mentor in these matters? – the good William Whiteley[33] is scarcely qualified to train them in this sort of thing. The whole place (as it was yesterday) was crowded today with the new Labour people pottering about with their female relatives and blocking up all the doors and passages – I hope that this sort of thing won't continue long for it is displeasing to see so many unpleasing males and females – it is an outward and visible reminder of this untoward election.

Saturday 4 August   Tonight Ralph Assheton rang me up and wondered whether I should like to go to the HofL? I rather expected this – they naturally want to get seats for some of the ex-Ministers.

[33] William Whiteley (1881–1955), Lab. M.P. Blaydon 1922–31, 1935–55; Whip 1927–31, 1935–42, Chief Whip 1942–55; D.M.A. Miners' Agent 1912–22.

In some ways I should like to be a peer – to return from the HofC to the HofL would be rather a record and achievement[34] – it would keep me at Westminster for the remainder of my days – but I cannot afford to give up my HofC salary and railway ticket – nor can I very well throw up Newcastle North just after being reelected and in the peculiar circumstances existing.

Sunday 5 August   Saw Ralph Assheton this morning – rather a depressed little man which is not surprising. He was very pleasant and could not have put things more nicely – I told him that I should like to go to the HofL – but did not think that I could do so now – in a year or so perhaps. He pointed out that unless I took this opportunity, it might never occur again. I said I quite realised this – I suggested that they should make me a P[rivy] C[ouncillor] and then in a year's time N. Newcastle might be available – I told the same thing to James Stuart whom I saw this afternoon. Rang up Beatrice who quite approves.

Monday 6 August   The news tonight is that some new and fearful form of bomb – something to do with the 'splitting of the atom' (God help us) – has been dropped in Japan – the havoc so fearful that no one can tell how much damage has been done. It is a ghastly discovery on which our scientists and the Americans have been at work for some years: the Germans were also busy on the same thing and we apparently won the race by a short head – and so, according to Winston, won the war instead of losing it. It seems that this wretched bomb is so devastating in its effect that it wipes out a whole town at one blow – if this is really the case, it means either the end of war or the end of civilization. Apparently its discovery – the discovery of the bomb – has cost 500 million pounds – it is all beyond my comprehension and makes one hate 'Science' more than ever. ... I also had a word with Edward Halifax – I asked him whether he was going back to the U.S.A. He said his return depended upon the wishes of his master Ernie Bevin. I asked him if he knew him and his reply was that he did and that he liked him – to which I replied that there was no accounting for tastes.

---

[34] Headlam had worked as a Clerk in the House of Lords from 1897 to 1924.

Tuesday 7 August   The general subject of discussion is the new bomb, and the general opinion is that it will speedily end the war with Japan – it and the entry of the Russians into the war will give the Warlords an excellent pretext for making peace without losing face one would imagine. Pray God that it may – but what luck it all is for the new Government – why on earth Winston decided on such a rush election when he must have known that the bomb was coming so soon, God only knows. I suppose that he was just too cocksure that he would win and so did not trouble to think where he would be if he lost.

Wednesday 8 August   Someone told me yesterday (I forget who it was) that Winston describes Attlee as 'a sheep in sheep's cloth- ing' – which I think is too clever a description of our new P.M. to be forgotten. The same man also told me the following repartee made by young Randolph Churchill to Noel Coward which is also worth remembering. The latter apparently hates the former – he sent him 3 tickets for the first night of his new play and hoped that Randolph had 2 friends to send the tickets to – Randolph replied that he was sorry that he could not go on the first night, but would like Noel Coward to send him three tickets for the third night if he thought that the play would still be running – rather good, I think.

Saturday 11 August   A letter from Winston this morning telling me that he was proposing to recommend me for a P[rivy] C[oun- cillor]ship. I have accepted his offer – a little unhappy about doing so, but yet much pleased to have got this distinction which I have always wanted and which in my opinion is the nicest thing an M.P. can get.

Tuesday 14 August   My P[rivy] C[ouncillor]ship is announced in the papers this morning – so that's that. I am very pleased about it – it is the only honour worth having in my opinion and I have always felt disgruntled for not having had it before. David Margesson always assured me that Ramsay Macdonald would not give it to me – but I always felt that it was David who did not press it as he should have done – however, here it comes in the end. I think that my getting it will please Conservatives in the

north. Peerages go to Willie Davison,[35] and the Tory members for
the City of London and Bournemouth – so three of the defeated
ministers will find new homes.[36] The more I think of it, the more
sure I am I was right not to take a peerage – my doing so would
have created a bad impression in the constituency and given Temple
and co. their chance.

Wednesday 15 August   The opening [of Parliament] show was
somewhat spoilt by the weather but it was like old times even
though there was no gold coach – everyone was congratulating me
and we felt elated! The HofC crowded with the new boys and all
the passages and lobbies crowded by their women folk – and such
womenfolk! The Speaker was duly elected. He made an admirable
speech. I can't say I envy him his task with over 300 new faces to
get to know by sight – indeed, I cannot think how anyone can do
such a thing. The new Labour M.P.s are a strange looking lot –
one regrets the departure of the sound old Trade Unionists and the
advent of this rabble of youthful, ignorant young men. Today is
'V.J. day' as the Japanese surrender was announced at midnight –
huge holiday crowds and rejoicing.

Monday 20 August   I am feeling aggrieved tonight as everything
went wrong for me in the foreign affairs debate today. Anthony
Eden asked me to speak after Bevin who opened the debate. James
Stuart would arrange it with the Speaker – but when Bevin sat
down and I got up, the Speaker called one of our new boys – then
of course he took a new boy from the other side – indeed 2 – then
he said he would call me. Anthony was to have spoken at 5
o'clock – but Winston (who no doubt wanted to go away) made
him speak at 4 o'clock – after this I was fed up and tired and gave
up the unequal contest – a pity as it was an opportunity to say a
few wise words and to get off with a speech. Bevin's survey of
foreign affairs was a good one whoever wrote it and it is a mercy
that the Govt. proposes to continue the Coalition's policy – from
the silence which greeted his speech on his own benches, it is pretty

---

[35] William Henry Davison (1872–1953), Con. M.P. Kensington S. 1918–45; Mayor
of Kensington 1913–19; Chairman, Metropolitan Area 1928–30; cr. Baron Brough-
shane 1945.
[36] i.e., three by-elections would result in safe Con. seats, giving an opportunity
for some of the Con. leaders who had been defeated to return to the House.

clear that the Labour intelligentsia was considerably disappointed by what he said. My impression is that the Govt has more to fear from its supporters than we have.

Tuesday 21 August   Spent all day at the HofC – Oliver Lyttelton made rather a good speech I thought on the industrial situation – Dalton replied but I did not hear him. He does not appear to have impressed our people. Gossip says that the bright young Labour people are not at all pleased with Bevin's foreign policy speech – which is not surprising for it was far too sane and realistic a policy for the likes of them. This afternoon Winston addressed us in Committee Room 14 – he made a sensible speech telling us how much wiser and better informed we were than the other side and adjuring us to keep ourselves *au courant*[37] with everything and never give the enemy any respite. A lot of committees are to be set up – far too many I think – clearly there is going to be a lot of hard work for us in this Parliament and I (at the moment) am not looking forward to it. James Stuart suggested that I should serve on the committee the Govt is setting up on procedure, but as it is to sit all through the vacation I felt I better not take on the job.

Thursday 23 August   I attended the Executive meeting of the National Union at Caxton Hall – not a large attendance – but the usual outlook on life – nothing can change the attitude of the old fashioned Tories – they forget nothing and learn nothing. There were several ex-M.P.s present including H.G. Williams – he and the rest of them all told me the same story – the result of the poll came to them as a complete surprise. The new housing estates and factories and young people were too much for them. There was no inquest today but there is to be one in October. Proby was in the chair and I thought him rather futile. He is not a man of any initiative or leadership, though he does well enough as a chairman in normal circumstances. Somehow or other we must get a more pushing man to take charge – but I cannot think of anyone suitable at the moment.

Friday 24 August   I was sworn a member of the Privy Council at Buckingham Palace this morning – rather an interesting little affair –

[37] translation: up to date.

there was quite a party of us to be sworn in ... We were rehearsed at the Privy Council office by the Clerk of the Council, who took it all very seriously which was right and proper. Then 'we proceeded' to the Palace: I was given a lift by Mr. Silkin[38] M.P. the new Minister of Town and Country Planning – he is rather an able little man who looks like a Jew (but says he is not one). ... We went into the presence in single file and each in turn shook hands with the King who informed me that it was a long time since he had seen me; I replied in the affirmative and then passed on. We knelt and swore an oath (or rather the Clerk read it to us) and then each in turn knelt before H[is] M[ajesty] and kissed his hand – then we took a longer oath standing, shook hands with the old P[rivy] C[ouncillor]s -had a little chat with each other and the King and then we drifted away.

Sunday 26 August   Keynes[39] and Halifax are off to the USA to see whether they cannot do something about this Lease and Lend business[40] – 2 Etonians to the rescue of the Labour Party! Shinwell in a speech at Cardiff tells the miners to work and the people to tighten their belts for the hardest winter they have yet had to encounter! The outlook is pretty bleak, I fear, and it looks as if we should have to trust to potatoes and brussels sprouts for our winter fare.

Monday 27 August   Billy Brass's death is announced in the press this morning – a sad business – I heard in London that he was laid up in a nursing home and had been very ill, but was thought to be getting better. He had an operation for appendicitis and they bungled it in some way. He was a very good fellow and had just

[38] Lewis Silkin (1889–1972), Lab. M.P. Peckham 1936–50; member of London County Council 1925–45, Chairman of Housing & Public Health Ctte. 1934–40, of Town Planning Ctte. 1940–45; Min. of Town & Country Planning 1945–50; Dep. Lab. Leader in the Lords 1955–64; cr. Baron Silkin 1950.

[39] John Maynard Keynes (1883–1946); civil servant, India Office 1906–08, Treasury 1915–19; Principal Treasury rep. at Paris Peace Conference 1919; Lecturer in Economics, Cambridge 1908–15; Fellow of King's College, Cambridge; member of Ctte. on Finance & Industry 1929–31; Economic Adviser to the govt. 1940–46, chief rep. at Bretton Woods conference 1944; a member of the 'Bloomsbury group' of intellectuals; influential economic theorist, author of *General Theory of Employment, Interest and Money* (1936); cr. Baron Keynes 1942.

[40] On 17 Aug. 1945 President Truman had abruptly terminated the Lend-Lease Act of Mar. 1941, which Britain had depended upon to purchase essential materials.

been given a peerage after over twenty years in the HofC – full of life and go – one will miss him greatly ...

Friday 7 September   The Americans are beginning to publish details of Japanese cruelties to prisoners which are just as revolting as those perpetrated by the Germans. How one is to punish these beastly creatures, I cannot imagine – something spectacular, I imagine, should be done, but short of hanging the Emperor and all his war lords I cannot think of anything calculated to impress the Japanese nation. The only sensible thing to do really would be to drop atomic bombs wholesale over the country and thus to destroy the Japanese race as fully as possible – one cannot see what good service they render to humanity.

Thursday 13 September   In the afternoon I called at the Central Office where I had a talk with Jim Thomas[41] M.P. (he is Vice Chairman in succession to Harold Mitchell I suppose). He is a pleasant individual and always very civil. He says that Topping is leaving early in October and that then presumably the Area Agents would be decided upon – I put in a word for Ledingham in the Northern Area and left it at that. Thomas had not much gossip about reorganization or anything else, except the bye elections – of course they cannot find seats for all the defeated ministers!

Monday 1 October   I went into Newcastle by train this morning to attend a luncheon given by the Light Engineering Association people – their object being to get to know all the new M.P.s for the northern area – a lot of them were there – Thorp of Berwick and I being the only Conservatives – the Labour gents were very busy displaying an interest in the views of the employers. They always amuse me: they are such very new brooms and are so eager to display their keenness to do all they can for the area. None of them strikes me as anything out of the common and some of them are very common stuff – and useless except to record their votes for the Government.

[41] James Purdon Lewes Thomas (1903–1960), Con. M.P. Hereford 1931–56; P.P.S. to J.H. Thomas 1932–36, to A. Eden 1937–38, 1939–40; Ass. Whip 1940, Whip 1940–43; F.S. Admiralty 1943–45; 1st Lord of Admiralty 1951–56; Con. Party Vice-Chairman 1945–51; cr. Viscount Cilcennin 1956.

Wednesday 3 October   The conference of Foreign Ministers has come to an end – disagreement about anything and everything that matters – M[onsieur] Molotov and Ernest Bevin almost at each other's throats if the newspapers are to be believed. Contrary to what Stafford Cripps assured us during the general election, the Russians seem even less disposed to be accommodating with the Labour Government than they were with Winston and Eden – perhaps old Bevin stands up to them better than the others did – but the result is not satisfactory and one wonders how we shall ever be able to draw up a final settlement of the European situation and get things going again if the Russians continue their present tactics and refuse to play ball with us? Their present attitude is quite impossible and must end in trouble I should imagine. How long will it be, I wonder, before the Socialist rank and file will realize what the Russian foreign policy really is and how dangerous it is for us.

Saturday 6 October   The Area meeting went of all right and, despite Greenwell and D. Nicholson, I got the Committee of Inquiry I wanted. Irene Ward made rather a silly speech, but otherwise people were sensible. The attendance was not more than the average. Fergus and Mary Graham ... gave us tonight a lot of amusing gossip about the Northern Cumberland, Mid Cumberland and Carlisle elections – apparently Spears and Dower[42] were hopeless.

From 15 October onwards the remainder of the 1945 volume is blank, and Headlam did not keep a diary at all in 1946. However, in the Headlam papers there are four letters written in mid-1946 which include the following comments on political affairs:

Cuthbert to Beatrice Headlam, 7 May 1946   This morning I went to a function at Church House to see Winston made a Freeman of the City of Westminster. It was a good show and Winston made a good speech – all the swells were there. Today the excitement here is the Government's announcement that they have decided to remove the British troops from Egypt forthwith: the news was greeted with boisterous cheers by the Comrades: Winston moved

---

[42] Alan Vincent Gandar Dower (1898–1980), Con. M.P. Stockport 1931–35, Penrith & Cockermouth 1935–50.

the adjournment of the House and there is to be a debate at 7 p.m. It is an attempt, I imagine, to please the Egyptians and placate the Arab League – a fruitless business – just giving away our position and only likely to induce the other people to ask for more. One really is beginning to despair about the future of this country.

Cuthbert to Beatrice Headlam, 18 June 1946   Everyone here [House of Commons] seems much the same – the same 'much ado about nothing', and 'the comrades' as pleased with themselves as ever – although some Conservative M.P.s are optimistic enough to assert that they have discerned a certain amount of discontent with the Government beginning to show itself in their constituencies.

Cuthbert to Beatrice Headlam, 24 July 1946   It looks now as if the House would rise next Friday week (2nd August) ... There is no news here: everyone seems bored and tired – and certainly it is time to close down shop for a time. Some people profess to see 'the turn of the tide' in the by-election results: I cannot confess that I am unduly elated: I can see no real sign of a change of heart among the people.

Cuthbert to Beatrice Headlam, 30 July 1946   I have just been listening to Winston addressing the Conservative M.P.s – telling them how well they have done during the Session, etc. Chaps got up when he had finished (not yrs. truly!) and told him that he had given them 'food for thought', which reminded me of what the old Tory ladies say of my speeches. He really said nothing at all which everybody in the room did not know already.

15

OPPOSITION AND CRISIS

January to July 1947

When Headlam resumed keeping a diary at the start of 1947, the Labour government was facing a serious crisis due to the combination of an unusually severe winter and a shortage of coal, resulting from low productivity in the recently-nationalised mines.

Wednesday 1 January 1947　　I gave up keeping a diary in the autumn of '45 and I don't quite know why I am starting one again this year. I doubt very much whether I shall succeed in keeping it going – or whether, indeed, there is any real point in doing so. However, I find my old diaries rather interesting reading – interesting to me that is to say – and so one might as well try and continue the series for one's few remaining years – they can only make the funeral pyre of my life's records a wee bit bigger. ... I have neither the energy nor the inclination to publish my life's history, or to advertize my views about men and things – after all, what have I done worthy of note? and of what value are my opinions?

Friday 3 January　　Things do look too gloomy for words both in this country and all the world over. The Terrorists in Palestine are at it again – and one wonders what the Government can do to repress them? Surely they will come to some kind of decision on policy before long? As things are now, no one has the least idea of what our policy in Palestine is ... One sign of the times is that synagogues in London are being set on fire – in any other country there would be a pogrom of Jews if Jewish terrorists were allowed to behave to people as they are behaving to our troops and police and officials in Palestine today.

Wednesday 8 January	The Government have produced yet a new major bill – one for a 'land plan in Britain' – by which landowners are to be deprived of the right to build on their own land except in accordance with proper planning requirements – owners who lose development value under the measure will not be entitled to compensation but £300 million of Mr. Dalton's paper will be available to meet cases of hardship.[1] There is to be the usual Board and ministerial control and functions for local authorities. It is all too complicated and tedious for me to attempt to understand. The strike of lorry drivers continues ... meanwhile food supplies in London are being held up...

Thursday 16 January	I think that the middle classes are beginning to sit up and take notice, but it is late in the day – locking the stable door after the horse has escaped. In addition to which the middle class ladies and gents are too lazy to do any work and too genteel to mix with the lower classes. I think that they are doomed to go under here as elsewhere against organized Labour – and then it remains to be seen whether organized Labour will be able to keep the Communists in check.

Thursday 23 January	Harry Crookshank turned up from London 2 hours late: all the trains make a point of being 2 or $2\frac{1}{2}$ hours late nowadays ... H.C. says that everyone is becoming more and more nervous and that some kind of financial crash would appear to be inevitable. He spoke in Durham Town Hall tonight and spoke very well. The hall was full but it only holds about 350 to 400 people.

Saturday 25 January	A long and dreary day in Newcastle – I attended two of Greenwell's[2] new committees – one committee took all the morning – the other all the afternoon – the agenda was the same for both committees. Greenwell did a lot of talking, wasting our time and his breath, but he took it all very seriously and

---

[1] Dalton was Chancellor of the Exchequer 1945–47.
[2] Thomas Greenwell (q.v.) had succeeded Headlam as Northern Counties Area Chairman in May 1946.

perhaps it is not a bad thing to have all this palaver: it makes people think that they are really functioning. However the attendance at these committees was not large and there were only the usual people present, those who always attend such meetings: no new faces.

Tuesday 28 January   I went down to the House after luncheon and came back here for dinner as we did not divide against the Government's Agriculture Bill. It seems that H. Crookshank spoke very well yesterday leading for us. His stock is high nowadays, and rightly so, I think. He is a first class HofC man – is quick at the up-take – always knows his subject and puts his stuff across good naturedly and effectively. He is now our leading agriculturalist *vice* Rob Hudson who apparently rubbed up our Agricultural Committee so violently that they refused to go on working if he remained chairman. He has also had the same effect on the Nat[ional] Farmers' Union – so he has been made chairman of the Fuel and Power Committee (of which I am an unobtrusive member) where he will probably be equally unpopular before long – meanwhile he will lead the opposition to the Electricity Bill. It is a pity that Rob has such bad manners, such a complete self assurance, for he is a capable man and has courage and ought to be of the greatest use to the Party were not his arrogance so intolerable. I have never had a row with him, but this is probably due to the fact that I have never had much to do with him.

Wednesday 29 January   Attended a Jerusalem Board meeting. Shearer[3] was very friendly and full of gossip – City gossip – about the debacle that is in store for us at some unspecified date! He asserts that Attlee and the more intelligent of his ministers are fully aware of the mess we are in and would gladly form a new Coalition with John Anderson as P.M. – if only Winston would keep out of it. I should doubt whether this were true – but I cannot see our people agreeing to throw over Winston in order to follow J.A. nor do I think that it would be possible for us to join in a Coalition with the present Labour Party in such a vast majority in the HofC – nor do I see the present Labour Party with such a large extremist

[3] Eric James Shearer (1892–1980), service in Indian Army 1911–29; Jt. Managing Dir., Fortnum & Mason 1933–38, United Kingdom Commercial Corporation 1942–45, Caltex Trading & Transport 1950–60; a businessman and Lloyd's Underwriter.

section being willing to join a Coalition under the leadership of Anderson or any other 'moderate' man of his type. Got back to the House about 4 p.m. – Silkin spoke, or rather read a brief, for 2 hours and 10 minutes moving 2d [reading] of his Town and Country Planning Bill – a very thin House – no one understands the Bill or cares 2d. [two pennies] about it.

Thursday 30 January   We voted against the 2nd reading of the Town & Country Planning Bill tonight – a reasoned amendment. No one that I have met on either side of the House professes to understand the Bill. Dalton, I am told, made a particularly offensive speech today – but I did not hear it and shall not read it. He is obviously always out to play to the most extreme men on his side of the House and his game is fairly transparent – Morrison is sick: Bevin not popular: who then?

Monday 3 February   Shinwell spoke at length on the 2d of his Electricity Bill, but I fell asleep while he was speaking – however, he said very little worth hearing so I am assured. Rob Hudson moved the rejection of the Bill in quite a good speech.

Tuesday 4 February   What a strange, odd creature Oliver [Stanley] is – he hardly ever approaches me nowadays – clearly Maureen was the one who liked me. Oliver is good in opposition – and yet he has not the least appeal and though no Conservative Cabinet would be complete without him, I doubt whether he will leave any mark when he is called to his fathers.

Wednesday 5 February   In the House there were no divisions and I hardly went into the Chamber: I ought to take more interest in things, I suppose – but I simply cannot. I grow lazier and lazier and more disgruntled than ever – which I think is due to old age, and despondency about the country's future. I cannot see a ray of sunlight anywhere – and not a sign of these dreadfully inefficient people losing ground in the country or even falling out among themselves. I went off to the Beefsteak about 7 p.m. where I dined –

John Maude[4] K.C., M.P., and Colonel Lancaster,[5] M.P., 2 rising hopes of our party were there ... I like John Maude – he is very intelligent, I think, has charming manners and is a good speaker: certain to be a Law Officer in [the] course of time. Lancaster I hardly know. He is rather above himself I should say – but able.

Thursday 6 February   There was a debate on conditions in our zone in Germany: they don't seem to do much credit to us and, if about a half of what one hears about the people who are running the control is true, we appear to have been very remiss in our choice of them and still more remiss in not getting rid of a lot of them. Dick Law led the opposition and made a very dull speech I thought. I like what I know of him and presumably he is intelligent, but he is not a great parliamentary performer and I don't suppose he would have ever been given a job if he had not been the son of his father[6] and a friend, I believe, of Bobbety Cranborne – however, these are both excellent reasons for giving a man a chance and I am not complaining.

Friday 7 February   I left Euston at 12.10 for my ... meeting at Lancaster. The meeting was a good one: they were expecting to get an audience of a thousand and there were there, I was told, nearly 700 people – which, considering the bitter cold night and that most of the roads were ice bound, was a good show. I was the 'star turn' of the evening (replacing Rob Hudson) but Ian Fraser[7] who is M.P. for the adjoining constituency was put up first (half an hour) then a little local man asking for money (a quarter of an hour) then a collection – so I did not rise until 8.30 or thereabouts. I don't fancy that Rob Hudson had he been in my place as intended would have stood for this!

[4] John Cyril Maude (1901–1986), Con. M.P. Exeter 1945–51; Recorder of Devizes 1939–44, of Plymouth 1944–54; Additional Judge, City of London Court 1954–65, Central Criminal Court 1965–68.
[5] Claude Granville Lancaster (1899–1977), Con. M.P. Fylde 1938–50, Fylde S. 1950–70.
[6] Andrew Bonar Law, Conservative Party leader 1911–21 and 1922–23, Prime Minister 1922–23.
[7] (William Jocelyn) Ian Fraser (1897–1974), Con. M.P. St. Pancras N. 1924–29, 1931–37, Lonsdale 1940–50, Morecambe & Lonsdale 1950–58; Pres., British Legion 1947–58; kt. 1934, cr. Baron Fraser of Lonsdale 1958; blinded at the Battle of the Somme 1916.

Sunday 9 February The fuel situation is very grave – Shinwell's casual announcement of a big electricity cut in his speech in the House on Friday last has caused consternation and indignation. It will throw thousands of people out of work and cause the maximum of inconvenience and discomfort to everybody. One realises the Government's difficulties due to the inadequate coal stocks but one feels that a little more foresight would have made things easier and avoided this present mess – certainly the country should have been warned. Industrialists then might have been able to prepare what was always inevitable, if we were to have a hard winter. I am curious to hear what Attlee and Shinwell have to say for themselves tomorrow – no doubt their followers will accept their excuses whatever they may be – but the public at large may not be so easily satisfied – of course Shinwell ought to be sacked. He is clearly a bad administrator and unfitted for his job – but to sack him would be an admission of failure by the Government and that is not to be expected. I don't expect any sudden political crisis.

Monday 10 February Shinwell's defence in the House today was poor stuff and Dalton I am told – for I never listen to the man if I can help it – was little better – nor was Attlee's opening statement at all effective. Everything was put down to the weather and the bad management of the coal owners in the past – the awful inheritance which Shinwell came into. Rob Hudson and Winston spoke for our front bench. I was not much impressed by either of their speeches. It seemed to me that they might have hit harder – however, their indictment was pretty severe and the Government had a bad day, though there was little criticism from their own side. There was little or no gossip in the Smoking room – things are really too serious for gossip. If this weather continues the situation may really become disastrous – coal cannot be moved and the railway lines are congested – sea transport largely suspended.

Tuesday 11 February The cold continues: and gas and electricity decrease – it is a sorry business and I am afraid that things are likely to get worse before they are better. The unemployment increases and the charming slogan 'work for all' is beginning to seem slightly ridiculous – but 'the comrades' in the HofC still seem quite cheerful and pleased with themselves and blame the coal owners for the present shortage of coal. The whole situation would be ridiculous if the position of the nation were not so much in peril – our whole livelihood depends on production and production with the present coal shortage is impossible. They are now talking of importing coal from the U.S.A. and paying for it out of the American loan! All the world from reports in the press appears to think that we really are down and out this time – are we?, I wonder. I sat next to William Scott,[8] M.P., at dinner tonight. He was M[ilitary] S[ecretary] both to Jack Gort and Alex[ander] in the war (God only knows why!). He told me that he was urged by the soldiers as an M.P. to tell Chamberlain early in 1940 of the dangerous weakness on the Western Front. He did so and Spears M.P. was sent out to report on the French Army – that Spears returned to England and stated that the French had got the finest army they had had since Napoleon's *Grande Armée* – Scott says that it was on the strength of this report that the French 4th Division and one of our divisions were sent to Norway and the Western Front still further weakened.

Wednesday 12 February   … at the Constitutional Club political luncheon given to R.A. Butler who subsequently made a political oration to the Club. … Herbert Williams who was in the chair at the luncheon called upon Boyd-Carpenter[9] and me to say 'a few words' – he as representing the younger brand of Conservatives, I the 'old Brigade'. R.A.B. assured me that I made 'a very good speech' – which was very cheering! He is quite certain that he is one of our leading lights and has been successful, so far, in making other people think the same of him. He is ambitious and means to be the leader sooner or later. He may be – everything is possible in politics – but he never strikes me as having much personality or go – he is a don and an intellectual – not, I fancy, the type of man who could inspire a crowd – and so long as 'safety first' is his guiding principle it is difficult to see him leading a party effectively.

[8] William Walter Montagu-Douglas-Scott (1896–1958), Con. M.P. Roxburgh & Selkirk 1935–50; styled Lord William Scott after suc. of father as 7th Duke of Buccleuch 1914.

[9] John Archibald Boyd-Carpenter (1908–1998), Con. M.P. Kingston-upon-Thames 1945–72; F.S. Treasury 1951–54; Min. of Transport & Civil Aviation 1954–55; Min. of Pensions & Nat. Insurance 1955–62; Chief Sec. Treasury & Paymaster-Gen. 1962–64; Chairman, Public Accounts Ctte. 1964–70; Chairman, Civil Aviation Authority 1972–77; cr. Baron Boyd-Carpenter 1972.

Thursday 13 February   In the HofC Attlee informed us that the crisis was not quite so acute: the public, as usual, is playing up to the restrictions: a good deal of coal is being saved and the coal ships are now beginning to come up the Thames. The situation, however, is still 'serious' – indeed, it is! Cripps moved 2d of a new Bill this afternoon, designed so far as we could gather to put the whole of industry more or less under the State – we voted against it. In the '22 Committee' there was a discussion on a woolly production produced by Peter Thorneycroft designed to bring Lib[eral]s and Conservatives together and produce a common policy. It is a hopeless business and nearly everybody who spoke in the Committee, including Winston who damned it with faint praise, was against it – but P.T. is going to publish it.

Friday 14 February   According to the papers the coal situation in London is slightly better – the coal ships are arriving – but of course it will take ages to replenish the stocks and meanwhile industry is coming to a standstill. It is assuredly a sorry business – and it is, whatever they may [say] to the contrary, largely the Government's fault. They have been warned and warned again during the last eighteen months how little coal there was at the power stations and gas works. In the debate in the HofL yesterday there was a loud demand for Shinwell to be sacked – and of course he ought to go – he is wholly incompetent as an administrator.

Wednesday 19 February   ... the Electricity Bill ... surely there never was a more futile thing than to bring in a Bill of this kind at the moment – all that is required for the electricity industry is a readjustment of areas – otherwise the industry is flourishing, efficient and progressive – no possible advantage to the public can be derived by nationalizing it – on the contrary, the price of electricity supply is more likely to go up than to go down under State ownership. Galloway[10] lunched with me at the Conservative Club (food filthier than ever and another guinea to be put onto the subscription). We discussed North Newcastle. He is very angry with Scanlan who apparently is the only agent up here whom he

---

[10] Jack Galloway (b.1910), Con. Agent, S.E. Leeds 1931–34, The Wrekin 1934–36, Cannock, 1936–39; war service, Royal Tank Regiment 1939–46; C.O. Agent, Northern Counties Area 1946–1956, West Midlands Area 1956–1975.

cannot get on with. He agrees with me that we must do all we can to get rid of the Town Councillor control of the organization and prevent Temple getting the seat.

Thursday 20 February   Then to the HofC where the P.M. announced the latest Government policy for India. We are to leave to country in June of next year – apparently whether or not the contending factions in India have come to a settlement or not – Wavell is sacked and made an Earl – and Mountbatten is to go out as Viceroy in March. It seems to me to be a tremendous gamble and a needless policy of despair – unless there is a settlement by the appointed day what will our position be? Shall we really withdraw our troops and leave India to anarchy and chaos? Such a policy would in my opinion be wholly wrong and a great betrayal of the whole Indian population. I think that Attlee's statement today came as a shock to the whole of the House and he did not seem very comfortable about it himself.

Monday 24 February   A long and dull day at the House where we had the 2d of a Scottish Town and Country Planning Bill – I did not listen to the debate, no more did most other people. I had a good deal of letter-writing to do and dined at the House. There is a lot of gossip again which is only natural in the circumstances – it does not amount to much however – according to our pundits the Government is at sixes and sevens and much worried. This may be the case, but its position is solid enough here, and in the country there are no signs that its mistakes and mismanagement have made us any more popular with the electorate – amongst ourselves there is the usual wondering as to when Winston will go and who will succeed him. I am told that Anthony's stock here is not so good – but no one else seems to be much in favour and even those who don't think much of Anthony as a leader have to admit that he is the only one of our 'leaders' who appears to have any following in the country. Young Thorneycroft and his friends have published their pamphlet but it does not appear to have cut much ice. I saw Thorneycroft today. He is coming North next Sunday for the meeting in Newcastle on Monday – cannot possibly spare more time, etc. – his head is swelling almost visibly!

Tuesday 25 February   Bevin made, in my opinion, a good speech today on Palestine – incidentally he said that if it had not been for Truman's sudden announcement of his intention to aid 100,000 Jews to enter Palestine he thought he that he might have reached a settlement – this information will cause a flutter in Washington I expect – but American politicians deserve a show up. I agree with Bevin's statement that Jews and Arabs would live quite happily together if it were not for the extremists on both sides and outside interference. The reference of the matter to U.N.O. appears to have been the only course to adopt in the circumstances, but Oliver Stanley's criticism that the reference might well have been made earlier is sound. Winston mercifully – owing to his brother's death – was absent so we were spared a speech from him which might well have caused trouble in view of his Zionist attitude.

Wednesday 26 February   The HofL debate on the Government's Indian plan ended today without a division rather to everyone's surprise – apparently Edward Halifax made a speech to the effect that he could think of no other plan which offered any better result than that of the Government – and this statement decided the peers not to vote against the Government.[11] It is odd what an influence Halifax has – for he never seems to have any definite views about anything. In this case, however, he may be right – all those entrusted with the Indian business have made such a mess of things that it may be too late for us to do anything but scuttle – and so perhaps it is not a bad thing to state the date for the scuttle – but God help the 'Indians' when we go.

Friday 28 February   The decision of the Government announced today to give special food concessions to miners, more consumer goods in mining villages, more pre-fabricated houses, etc., to me seems all wrong. The miners, in my opinion, have blackmailed the country in 2 wars – continuously, indeed, since the General Strike – why should the miners be dealt with differently to workers in the other heavy industries – and who are the miners? – perhaps special privileges should be given to the actual hewers of coal – but why to the other workers in pits, many of whom never go underground? One simply cannot understand why so much should be done for the miners – or as we now call them 'the shock troops of industry'!

---

[11] Halifax (then titled Lord Irwin) had been Viceroy of India 1925–31.

Sunday 2 March   The mess and confusion everywhere – at home and abroad – continue and things seem to be getting worse not better. The Government clearly cannot cope with the situation and we appear to be heading for economic disaster – but the mass of the population is entirely unaware of the situation and still imagines that 'less work and higher wages' is the order of the day – now the Government is making frantic efforts to disillusion the public, adjuring people to work, etc. – but how can the public be expected to take what they are now told seriously after they have been brought up to believe quite the contrary!

Monday 3 March   Beatrice drove me into Newcastle this evening for the Thorneycroft meeting at the City Hall – I found the young man having 'a press conference' at the Conservative Club – he was playing the part of an important statesman very effectively! He and I were entertained to dinner at the Club by the Political Committee. The meeting has been a success – there were about 1,600 or 1,700 people present and Peter Thorneycroft made a good speech which he put across very effectively. He certainly has an attractive personality.

Tuesday 4 March   ... in London ... I find everyone very gloomy – even the Socialists are getting a bit rattled – which is not very surprising for they are in the hell of a mess – of course they can blame the weather – but though the weather may be abnormal it is not the real cause of their troubles. They have simply not looked ahead and now have to face all the difficulties, financial and economic, that every intelligent man knew must inevitably arise after the war. They have concentrated their energies on nationalization – a policy which cannot possibly help at the moment whatever its future possibilities may be. They now have to tell the people the truth and entreat them to work harder and produce more – and this after leading them to suppose that a Socialist regime would mean less work and higher wages. It is a sorry business – and if ever there was a time for political unity it is now – but this Attlee and Co. cannot admit – and while they scream for help from us all and the 'Dunkirk spirit', they persist in forcing through Parliament their silly policy of nationalization which so many of us believe is wholly wrong and against the national interest. It is a hopeless business.

Wednesday 5 March   The 2 days' Indian debate began today – a long, and from his point of view, a very good speech from Cripps – answered very effectively by John Anderson. Cripps maintained that the risk of 'fixing a date' was well worth taking. Anderson asserted that the Government's policy was a wild gamble. The whole thing to me seems almost incredible – that we should calmly state our intention to walk out of India in June 1948 – whatever the situation in that country may be – is a terrible confession of failure – and may also mean handing over the vast bulk of the Indian population to rapine and murder – our duty is to continue to govern India until such time as the people of India can be assured of peaceful Home Rule.

Thursday 6 March   I meant to speak in the Indian debate this afternoon, but Winston and others spoke at length ... Winston made a good speech today, less violent than one might have expected – Alexander who replied to him was very poor.

Friday 7 March   Went to the HofC this morning and stayed there until 4.30 p.m. No divisions – food supplementary estimates – we seem to have spent a lot more money last year for a great deal less food, but I did not hear Dr. Edith Summerskill's[12] explanation for this. She is an unattractive female but manages to get through her work in the House pretty well. Her charming Minister (Strachey[13]) is still in the U.S.A. searching for food – buying turkeys it is reported in the press for the restaurants, not for the housewives – which, if true, will not make him any more popular with the housewives – I am always getting postcards now from ladies, demanding that Strachey and Shinwell should be sacked for incompetence. There is a body called the League of Housewives (or some such name) which runs all this, but whether it is or is not a political force I have no idea – it is certainly an active body.

[12] Edith Summerskill (1901–1980), medical practicioner; Lab. M.P. Fulham W. 1938–55, Warrington 1955–61; P.S. Food 1945–50; Min. of Nat. Insurance 1950–51; member of P.L.P. Ctte. 1951–57, 1958–59; member of N.E.C. 1944–58, Chairman 1954–55; cr. Baroness Summerskill 1961.

[13] (Evelyn) John St. Loe Strachey (1901–1963), Lab. M.P. Birmingham Aston 1929–31 (joined New Party Feb.-June 1931, sat as Ind. June-Oct. 1931), Lab. M.P. Dundee 1945–50, Dundee W. 1950–63; U.S. Air 1945–46; Min. of Food 1946–50; Sec. for War 1950–51.

Sunday 9 March   I have been trying to put together some notes for a speech in next week's debate – have not succeeded in thinking of anything original to say: odd how difficult I find it 'to prepare' a speech – but this is not the result of old age – I never could sit down and write a speech as most of my friends appear to be able to – I always have to trust to the inspiration of the moment and outside the HofC this inspiration has not really ever failed me – inside the HofC I dare not trust to inspiration and this is the reason, I suppose, why I find it so difficult to speak there.

Monday 10 March   The Economic Debate began today – Cripps led off for the Govt. and spoke for about 2 hours. His speech was of course lucid and fluent and from his point of view well argued – but really all it amounted to was a fuller exposition of what is in the White Paper. Oliver Lyttelton who spoke first for us was better than usual, I thought, and made a lot of good points – but he is not a good speaker and somehow or other does not have much effect in the House. The 'dirty doctor' [Dalton] spoke later in the debate for the Govt. but I did not hear him – apparently he had not much to tell, and did not seem to have as much 'joy in his heart' as usual. ... The comrades were not in such good heart today. They had been addressed by Attlee this morning: according to the press this evening some of them had a good fling at him, but they will all vote against our vote of censure that is certain – I can see no sign of a real break up among them yet. They can all unite in the class warfare business and lay the whole burden of their maladministration and failure upon the shoulders of the Tories whose past misdeeds are the cause of all our troubles today – and the worst of it is that this sort of tripe still goes down with the public.

Tuesday 11 March   Isaacs,[14] the Minister of Labour, opened for the Government today. He rattled off lists of figures, etc., for 40 minutes, which did not carry things much further – even for those

---

[14] George Alfred Isaacs (1883–1979), Lab. M.P. Gravesend 1923–24, Southwark N. 1929–31, 1939–50, Southwark 1950–59; P.P.S. to J.H. Thomas 1924, 1929–31, to A.V. Alexander 1942–45; Min. of Labour & Nat. Service 1945–51; Min. of Pensions Jan.-Oct. 1951; Mayor of Southwark 1919–21; Gen. Sec., Nat. Soc. of Operative Printers 1909–49; Pres., World Trade Union Conference 1945.

who like myself tried to follow what he was saying – Clem Davies[15] for the Nat. Libs[16] followed him, but as usual there was an exodus from the Chamber when this bore got up. I was among the number who did not listen to him – but I am told that for once he attacked the Govt. Lady Grant,[17] the new member for South Aberdeen, made a first class maiden speech – well delivered, an excellent manner, and good sound stuff – she was a real success – and added to her fine style of speaking, she had the advantage as McGovern put it of the additional attribute of being 'kindly to the eye'. I spoke -but only for twelve minutes, not too badly – but too short to be effective – a pity, but it is no use worrying. Dined at the House late and for once rather enjoyed the meal, at the Opposition table with James Stuart, Oliver Lyttelton, and Hinchingbrooke – quite a pleasant little party – friendly – O.L. less above himself than usual and not endeavouring to be amusing.

Wednesday 12 March   Winston excelled himself today in moving the vote of censure – an admirable fighting speech which seemed to me quite unanswerable. Alexander was put up later in the evening to answer him and apparently bungled the business badly – just party abuse which did not strengthen the Government's case though his attack on Winston pleased the comrades they tell me. He was so long a rubber stamp to Winston that I suppose it pleased him to stand up to him – more especially as W. was not in the Chamber – even a worm will turn. Alexander I think is rather ashamed of being a Socialist – he is said to have social aspirations – I have always thought him a flat catcher. Thorneycroft made a good speech. In the division we got 198 for our amendment; the Govt. 374. In the second division we rose to 204 (the Liberals

---

[15] (Edward) Clement Davies (1884–1962), Lib. M.P. Montgomeryshire 1929–62 (Lib. Nat. 1931–39, Ind. Lib. 1939–42, Lib. from Aug. 1942); Chairman of the 'All Party Action Group' in May 1940; Lib. Leader 1945–56.

[16] Davies was at this time Leader of the Liberal Party; Headlam's reference to 'Nat. Libs.' is a mistake, probably resulting from the fact that Davies had sat as a Liberal National from 1931 to 1939 (he resigned the Nat. whip in Dec. 1939 and rejoined the Liberal Party in Aug. 1942, becoming Leader on 2 Aug. 1945).

[17] Priscilla Jean Fortescue Thomson (1915–1978), married first 1934 Sir Arthur Lindsay Grant of Monymusk, 11th Bart. (killed in action, 1944), second 1948 2nd Baron Tweedsmuir; Con. M.P. Aberdeen S. 1946–66; U.S. Scotland 1962–64, M.S. 1970–72; M.S. For. Office 1972–74; delegate to U.N. General Assembly 1960–61, Chairman of U.N. Ctte. for Refugees 1961–62; cr. Baroness Tweedsmuir of Belhevie 1970.

voting with us) and the Govt. got 371. Ours was a good showing, but of course we are in a hopeless minority and voting against the Government does little to help the country – we are in the devil of a mess and one can see no way out of it. Several people including Harold Macmillan and Shakes[18] Morrison are suggesting that to avoid responsibility for the crash they see ahead Attlee and Co. may go to the country in the autumn – I have thought this not unlikely for some time past.

Thursday 13 March   ... to the House where Army estimates were being discussed – most of the talking was done by Labour left wingers who had a lot to say about reducing the army, still further 'democratizing' it, etc., etc. The usual tripe ... Eddie Winterton led for us assisted by Grimston – a curious pair to represent military views – James Stuart casually suggested that I might speak, but the suggestion came too late.

Wednesday 19 March   I went into Newcastle by train this afternoon and attended the Lord Mayor's dinner at the Mansion House given in honour of the Soviet delegation which is visiting Newcastle – the usual one horse affair – poor food and deplorable wine – 40 people crowded into a space inadequate for 20 comfortably ... The Lord Mayor, who is an even more stupid and third-rate man than is usual even with Newcastle Lord Mayors, made a speech – and then Charles Trevelyan (wearing a red shirt, collar and tie) held forth – a fiery political utterance assuring the Russians that the British working classes would never tolerate a war with Russia. It was a silly performance – and quite out of place at a party of this description – but no one smiled except myself.

Friday 21 March   I spent the morning and afternoon at the HofC where we discussed the Dog Racing Bill, limiting Grey hound racing to one day in the week, and passed it through all its stages. It is one of the Government's major efforts to meet the economic crisis – the suppression of 'mid-week' sport, they contend, will be to reduce absenteeism. My own view is that it will not do much to

---

[18] W. S. Morrison (q.v.) was known as 'Shakes': shortened from Shakespeare, the nickname derived from both his initials and his love of Shakespeare's works.

prevent absenteeism and is rather hard upon workers (e.g. people who work in shops, etc.) whose weekly holiday is in the middle of the week – however, against this it may be urged that such people are not producers as a rule, mainly distributors – how far this is true I don't pretend to say. I moved a manuscript amendment in C[ommittee of the] W[hole] H[ouse] to gratify certain people in Newcastle who were keen about it – but Chuter Ede[19] was not prepared to accept it and I did not press it, not minding in the least whether the Bill was amended or not. Our leader was Osbert Peake[20] and [he] was all for letting the Govt. have its Bill in the day – I should have preferred to hold it up – but again it was not a matter worth worrying about: it was a Bill said to be necessary in the national interest and therefore perhaps it would have been wrong for us to delay it in any way, utterly futile though we believed it to be.

Monday 24 March   A debate on Imperial Preference – Walter Elliot spoke well, I thought – he seems to be more effective and less verbose and confused than he used to be – more vigorous too. Cripps assured us that no decisions on the matters involved by our Agreement on the American loan regarding Empire trade would be made at this approaching Economic Conference at Geneva without the House being given an opportunity to debate them. He also asserted that the Government here was acting in concert with the Governments in the Dominions – with these assurances we must be content, I suppose – I wish to goodness that we were not so closely bound to the U.S.A. economically – but I suppose that the war made such a position inevitable – what the outcome of it all will be time will alone show – but unless we can pull ourselves together and get going again on our own volition, the British Empire is well and truly ended.

[19] James Chuter Ede (1882–1965), Lab. M.P. Mitcham Mar.-Dec. 1923, S. Shields 1929–31, 1935–64; P.S. Educ. 1940–45; Home Sec. 1945–51, & Leader of the House Mar.-Oct. 1951; Chairman, Surrey County Council 1933–37; Chairman, London & Home Counties Electricity Authority 1934–40; Pres., County Councils Assoc. 1953–61; cr. Baron Chuter-Ede 1964.

[20] Osbert Peake (1897–1966), Con. M.P. Leeds N. 1929–55, Leeds N.E. 1955–56; U.S. Home Office 1939–44; F.S.T. 1944–45; Min. of Nat. Insurance 1951–53; Min. of Pensions & Nat. Insurance 1953–55; Chairman, Public Accounts Ctte. 1945–48; cr. Viscount Ingleby 1956.

Tuesday 25 March   There was a debate today on rural housing to which I am afraid I did not listen – after questions Byers[21] (the Liberal whip) on behalf of W.J. Brown (M.P. for Rugby – Independent) raised a rather interesting matter of Privilege. Brown was Secretary of the Civil Service Clerical Association which he founded and organised – his Association agreed to his going into Parliament as an Independent – now because he has voted against the Government on occasions they have told him that they won't continue him as Secretary of the Association. Such is Brown's version of the case and the Speaker said that there were grounds for the matter being referred to the Committee of Privileges. I don't care about Brown – who is a clever, bumptious little man – but my sympathies are with him. The tyranny of these unions nowadays is very alarming – they are primarily political organizations and claim a complete dominion over their members – to deprive a man of his livelihood because he exercises his own judgement in political matters unconnected with his union or his job is a monstrous infringement of liberty – and to threaten an M.P. in the way in which Brown is being threatened must surely be an infringement of parliamentary privilege.

Thursday 27 March   ... how one hates this 'planned economy' which gives such unlimited power to officials to worry the ordinary man and woman – how long will the people of this country stand for it, I wonder? The worst of it is that the new generation has never known anything different and takes it as natural to stand in queues and to be 'regulated' for all and everything and therefore does not resent the modern procedure as those of us of the older generation do.

Friday 28 March   ... to South Shields this evening and I addressed the annual general meeting of the Conservative Association which was restarted last October – I was told that there was to be an attendance of 150 or 200 – there were actually 38 people present in a big, cold hall – a gloomy show ...

Monday 31 March   The second reading of the National Service

---

[21] Charles Frank Byers (1915–1984), Lib. M.P. Dorset N. 1945–50; Chief Whip 1946–50; Chairman, Lib. Assoc. 1946–63; Chairman, Lib. Party 1950–52, 1965–67; Lib. Leader in the Lords 1967–84; cr. Baron Byers 1964.

Bill in the House today. There is said to be a Labour revolt against it – the anti-conscription cry – I don't suppose that when the division comes tomorrow night the 'revolt' will be very noticeable. Winston spoke in support of the Bill, and was in excellent form – poking fun, as he well might, at Attlee and Alexander who are now fathering conscription which they opposed so vigorously in 1939. He also chaffed the Liberals who are voting against the Bill and again was highly successful. I dined at the House, but retired early as I found the debate boring. It is hard to listen to a series of impassioned utterances by people like Rhys Davies,[22] Zilliacus, Campbell Stephen, etc.;[23] whether what they say is sincere or not, it is wholly unrelated to realities and in many ways clearly calculated to mislead the public.

Tuesday 1 April   We had the division on the National Service Bill tonight – we supported the Government – 386 to 85 – the number of malcontents was greater than I expected, as, in addition to those who actually voted against the Government, a good many others were absent or abstained from voting.[24] This came as a shock to the leaders who were hoping that, after the exhortations of Attlee at a party meeting this morning, only a small number would go into the Lobby against the Bill. Our people are very jubilant and are already hoping for a real split among the Socialists. I don't myself expect this to happen yet awhile – much more likely that the Cabinet gives way to its opponents.

Wednesday 2 April   There was a debate on the fuel situation today ... a much subdued Shinwell opened the debate for the Government and he was very gloomy – even admitting that we must expect a reduced output of coal as a result of the 5 day working week which the miners have forced the Government to accept. Private consumption of all forms of fuel must be kept as low as possible, etc., etc. It is all monstrous of course and the subjection of the nation to the miners is all wrong and I believe quite unnecessary. Anthony Eden and Rob Hudson both spoke

---

[22] Rhys John Davies (1877–1954), Lab. M.P. Westhoughton 1921–51; U.S. Home Office 1924; Pres., Manchester & Salford Lab. Party 1917–20, Trades Council 1920–22; member of P.L.P. Exec. 1923–24; member of N.E.C. 1921–27.

[23] i.e., Lab. M.P.s on the far left or of Pacifist opinions.

[24] As well as the Liberals, the No vote included 72 Lab. and 1 Con. M.P.s.

well from our front bench and there was little worth hearing from the other side. It does not seem to strike any of the Comrades what a disastrous situation lies ahead of us if we are ever to regain our industrial position without an adequate supply of coal – it will never be obtained if the matter is left to the discretion and good behaviour of the mining population unless there is a complete change of attitude on their part as a result of nationalization and this has yet to be proved. ... I am tired and in a wholly despondent mood and heartily sick of the House of Commons.

Monday 7 April   ... I can't help feeling that we are going downhill morally and socially as a result of the general trend of ideas – there is certainly less sense of responsibility – less honesty, less willingness to work – a greater materialism, and less spiritual sense than there used to be – I suppose all old men have thought as I am thinking of the degeneracy of the new age into which they have survived – and so I may well be wrong in my pessimistic view of things – pray God I am. Old Lord Salisbury has died – one of the old school – a very courteous, charming man – not a clever man, but a wise one whose opinion was worth having. To me on the occasions when I came into contact with him – mainly about HofL reform – he was always most kind and helpful and no one could have expressed his views more modestly and with greater charm. His successor is of a similar type – probably cleverer, but equally sound and sane in his outlook.

Tuesday 15 April   ... into Newcastle this evening – I drank sherry with Dudley Appleby and his wife. I told him that I had no intention of making any public declaration of my intention to stand again – and I thought that it was up to him and other active members of the Association to clear out Temple and his clique and to get a decent new Executive to run the Association. He agreed with all I said, but I doubt whether he is the man to get a move on – I fancy that his wife is anxious for him to go into the HofC, but that he is only half-hearted.

Thursday 17 April   ... a general feeling of spring in the air – cheering as far as it goes – but the economic gloom continues – no one I met at the House this afternoon was anticipating anything but more trouble – greater shortages of food – and financial disaster. David Eccles[25] told me that he had talked with Dalton last night and that that great man fully admitted the disastrous state of things – but that his view was that, if the people were told all the further austerities that were coming, they would lose heart and would cease to work at all and that then Communism would come to its own. If this is really the 'dirty doctor's' view of 'the people', what a fraud the man must be and what a dismal fate is awaiting him. The terror the Socialists have of the Communists is amusing – but all the same there is reason for the fear. If things do go really wrong, it may well be that the Russian Fifth Column may get their chance – and yet somehow or other I don't see this country going Communist, though it is likely enough that there will be trouble and disorder unless a firm hand is maintained – and what Government nowadays is capable of being firm about anything?

Friday 18 April   I spent from 12 noon to 4.30 p.m. at the HofC, and voted 3 times against the Government – but with no effective results I regret to say – we only had about 70 of our people present and, as usual, the Comrades' 'quorum' was in full force – I notice, however, that the Comrades are less full of bounce than they were and some of them, I am told, are seriously perturbed about the way things are going. Attlee's Cabinet changes announced today it is said have disappointed some of the younger men who expected jobs. But the changes are merely a reshuffle – Arthur Greenwood (who was noticeably tight[26] in the House yesterday – more noticeably than usual) becomes Minister without Portfolio, and a scarcely known individual called Lord Inman[27] succeeds him as Privy Seal. 'Pethwick'[28] in a letter in *The Times* has said goodbye to 'Clem'

---

[25] David McAdam Eccles (1904-), Con. M.P. Chippenham 1943–62; Min. of Works 1951–54; Min. of Educ. 1954–57, 1959–62; Pres. Bd. of Trade 1957–59; Paymaster-Gen. & Min. for the Arts 1970–73; Chairman, British Library Bd. 1973–78; kt. 1953, cr. Baron Eccles 1962, Viscount 1964.

[26] Under the influence of alcohol, but not completely inebriated.

[27] Philip Albert Inman (1892–1979), businessman, dir. of publishing, hotel and industrial companies; Lord Privy Seal Apr.-Oct. 1947; Chairman, Hotels Exec., British Transport 1948–51; a Church Comm. 1946–57; cr. Baron Inman 1946.

[28] Frederick William Lawrence (1871–1961), assumed additional surname Pethick on marriage 1901; Lab. M.P. Leicester W. 1923–31, Edinburgh E. 1935–45; F.S.T. 1929–31; India & Burma Sec. 1945–47; cr. Baron Pethick-Lawrence 1945.

and Lord Listowel[29] succeeds him as Secretary of State for India –
I don't suppose that it matters much who is Secretary of State
nowadays – but who has ever heard of Listowel, except that he
calls himself a Socialist and is in the HofL. Frank Pakenham[30]
takes Hynd's[31] place as Chancellor of the Duchy in charge of
Germany under Bevin, and little Mr. Paling[32] hands him [*sic*] the
Ministry of Pensions and becomes P[ost]-M[aster]-G[eneral] in
succession to Listowel – presumably the Government is strengthened by these changes, but some of its younger supporters are sure
it is not!

Saturday 19 April   Winston made an oration today to the Primrose League which is being revived – God only knows why. He
made a frontal attack on the Government but seems to have said
nothing new and certainly nothing constructive – by which I mean
that he did not attempt to declare a policy for the Party – quite
right, too, in my opinion – and yet everyone is asking what we
should do if we were in power – and it is not easy to answer the
question for how the present mess is to be cleared up it is hard to
say – it seems to me that the one and only way out of our troubles
is a financial clear up – real economies at home and some kind of
settlement of our foreign indebtedness – surely neither of these two
things should be beyond the wit of man?

Tuesday 22 April   In the House we discussed the Budget resolutions. The resolution regarding tobacco occupied most of the
time – Dalton, as a result no doubt of party pressure, made it

[29] William Francis Hare (1906–1997), Lab. Whip in Lords 1941–44; P.S. Burma
1944–45; Postmaster-Gen. 1945–47, & Min. of Information Feb.-Mar. 1946; India
Sec. Apr.-Aug. 1947, & Burma 1947–48; M.S. Colonies 1948–50; P.S. Agric. 1950–
51; Gov.-Gen., Ghana 1957–60; Chairman of Cttes., House of Lords 1965–76; styled
Viscount Ennismore 1924–31, suc. 5th Earl of Listowel 1931.
[30] Francis Aungier Pakenham (1905-), Lord-in-Waiting 1945–46; U.S. War Office
1946–47; Chanc. Duchy of Lancaster 1947–48; Min. Civil Aviation 1948–51; 1st
Lord of Admiralty 1951; Lord Privy Seal 1964–65, 1966–68; Colonial Sec. 1965–66;
Lab. Party Leader in the Lords, 1964–68; cr. Baron Pakenham 1945, suc. 7th Earl
of Longford 1961.
[31] John Burns Hynd (1902–1971), Lab. M.P. Sheffield Attercliffe 1944–70; Chanc.
Duchy of Lancaster 1945–47; Min. of Pensions Apr.-Oct. 1947.
[32] Wilfred Paling (1883–1971), Lab. M.P. Doncaster 1922–31, Wentworth 1933–
50, Dearne Valley 1950–59; P.P.S. to M. Bondfield 1924; Whip 1929–35, Dep. Chief
Whip 1935–41; P.S. Pensions 1941–45; Min. of Pensions 1945–47; Postmaster-Gen.
1947–50.

pretty plain that he was going to allow some kind of rebate for old age pensioners – personally I don't see why this should be limited to old age pensioners as there are lots of other people nearly or equally as poor who ought also to be included in any rebate. ... We voted against the tobacco proposals on the grounds that if tobacco was to be reduced the only fair and certain way of bringing down dollar expenditure (the object in view) was to limit the amount of American tobacco imported.

Thursday 24 April   At the House there were no excitements and I wrote a lot of letters. The Library has no heating of any kind and is most uncomfortable. The Comrades entirely spoil it – littering their correspondence on all the writing tables, sleeping and snoring in all the armchairs when they are not clustered together chattering away like school children at a bun feast. They certainly are intolerable and are rapidly destroying all the amenities of Parliamentary life – A. Bevan's noisy laughter in the Smoking Room infuriates me!

Friday 25 April   Went to Jarrow about 6 p.m. and spoke at two meetings. They were both very poorly attended: none of the enemy present so far as I could make out. Our candidate – Scott[33] – is a pleasant spoken man and said to be very 'well-liked' in Jarrow – but I don't suppose that he has much chance of winning – however one really knows nothing about his chances – nor does Handy who is running the election. He thinks that the result will depend upon how the women vote rather an uncertain quantity – all the workers seem full of confidence and the canvassing is said to be going well. ... no one offered me a bite or drink in Jarrow – but then there is no one to do so in that God forsaken hole – surely one of the most depressing places in England.

Monday 5 May   ... we had the 3rd reading debate of the Transport Bill. I did not listen to much of it – Mr. Barnes[34] was terribly dull – David Maxwell Fyfe was good, but I find him rather a tiring man to listen to. He is the blue-eyed boy of our Party and is

---

[33] William Scott, Con. cand. Jarrow 1947.
[34] Alfred John Barnes (1887–1974), Lab. M.P. East Ham S. 1922–31, 1935–55; P.P.S. to W. Graham 1924; Whip 1925–30; Min. of Transport 1945–51; Chairman, Co-Operative Party 1924–45.

unquestionably very able – I like him personally and hope that he will be as successful as people expect him to be and he intends. A new member – Poole,[35] M.P. for Oswestry – wound up for us in an admirable speech – he is a pleasant fellow and clearly one of the best of our new members.

Tuesday 6 May ... at the HofC until nearly midnight – we had the first day of the Committee stage of the Nat[ional] Service Bill. I listened to most of the discussion, some of which was rather entertaining – only two amendments were considered – the age for conscription – the Socialists (recalcitrant) wanted it to be 21. We voted with the Government for 18. The I.L.P. members (now reduced to 2 as McGovern has joined the Labour Party) wanted to have Scotland out of the Bill, Clem Davies wanted Wales out of the Bill and Hugh Ross[36] wanted North[ern] Ireland in the Bill – the Bill was not amended, we voted with the Government. I hope to say a few words tomorrow against reducing the period of service from 18 months to 12, but I expect Winston and Alexander will use up all the time. Kesselring[37] has been sentenced to be shot – I suppose that it is a just sentence but somehow or other it rather revolts me. It is time, I think, to end all these trials of war criminals – but perhaps I am too tender-hearted? And yet I feel that enough has been done to show Germans how naughty they have been – more especially as the crimes they committed are no worse than those committed by the Russians – however, I suppose one cannot put forward this argument in public.

[35] Oliver Brian Sanderson Poole (1911–1993), Con. M.P. Oswestry 1945–50; jt. Con. Party Treasurer 1952–55; Con. Party Chairman 1955–57, Dep. Chairman 1957–59, jt. Chairman Apr.-Oct. 1963, Vice-Chairman 1963–64; Gov., Old Vic Theatre 1945–63; cr. Baron Poole 1958.

[36] This is a reference to Ronald Deane Ross (1888–1968), Ulster Unionist M.P. Londonderry 1929–51; P.P.S. to Sir B. Eyres-Monsell 1931–35; Chairman, Ulster Unionist Parl. Party 1939–41; Recorder of Sunderland 1936–51; N. Ireland Govt. Agent in London 1951–57; suc. 2nd Bart. 1935; Headlam's use of the forename Hugh was a mistake possibly resulting from the fact that the other leading Ulster Unionist M.P. of the period was Sir Hugh O'Neill (q.v.)

[37] Albrecht Kesselring (1885–1960), German army career 1904–35, then transferred to the air force; Chief of Staff, *Luftwaffe* 1936–38; C. in C. Air Fleet I (Berlin) 1938–39, Air Fleet II 1940–41; C. in C. South, commanding all German forces in the Mediterranean theatre 1941–45 and the Italian front 1943–45; C. in C. North-West Europe, March–May 1945; sentenced to death by a British military court in Venice, May 1947, for Ardeantine Cave massacre of Italian civilians in March 1944, sentence commuted to life imprisonment, released on health grounds 1952.

Monday 12 May I saw Galloway in the afternoon – he is just beginning to recover from the Jarrow election. He told me that our candidate was a complete wash out – lost his nerve completely and could hardly be induced to go on a platform in the later stages of the campaign. On the whole, therefore, the result was as good – perhaps a little better – than he had expected. Galloway told me also that there is a lot of trouble about finding candidates for most of the divisions in the Area – things altogether don't seem to be going well and Greenwell seems to have no power of leadership.

Tuesday 13 May After luncheon ... to the HofC where I remained until 12.30 – Town and Country Planning Bill report stage. We had a few divisions – but it was a slow and dull business. The principal result of sending Bills to Standing Committees is that no one who has not been a member of the Committee knows anything about it, or takes the slightest interest in it, when it is reported back to the House. This means that important Bills are really only dealt with by about fifty members after their second reading – of course this is not right or proper but it is inevitable in the circumstances – and is, I think, an unfortunate change in parliamentary practice – it comes of course from there being too many important Bills in a Session.

Wednesday 14 May Another day of Town and Country Planning – guillotine[38] at 9.30 p.m. I went home after the division, but I gather that Anthony Eden made a protest of some kind after the Speaker had read out all the hundreds of amendments that had not been discussed. Suppression of discussion is inevitable if a Government insists on so heavy a programme as this Government is insisting upon. Of course it is all wrong in theory – but I doubt whether inveighing against it has much propaganda value. The public really takes little interest in the procedure of the HofC and does not in the least understand what is going on – it does not appreciate that our parliamentary system of government is being replaced by something akin to the methods of dictatorship.

Friday 16 May I spent the morning at the HofC where the debate on Foreign Affairs dragged on – I did not listen to much of it.

[38] The procedure by which a debate is closed at a previously fixed time.

Harold Macmillan wound up for us in one of his clever, well-prepared speeches which are always worth listening to, even though his manner of delivering them always irritates me. He is so profoundly certain that he is doing the job so well and that H.M. is the man to back.

Saturday 17 May   Mountbatten is flying here from India to consult with the Cabinet – I gather that the mess in India is getting worse than ever. Anthony Eden told me yesterday that the Princes are now sitting up and taking notice – are anxious to stay on in the Empire and have no intention of playing second fiddle to Congress – the present troubles centre round the Moslem demand for the division of the Army – this of course would make for trouble and lead to a complete break-up – but surely we can do no good by leaving India even before June next year which is said to be the Cabinet's present idea? It would be a monstrous thing to do and disastrous for the future.

Monday 19 May   Went down to the House after luncheon. The menu for the day was the 2nd reading of the Finance Bill against which we divided – but I did not listen to the debate so I cannot say why we did so – it is rather an unusual proceeding and I must study *Hansard* for our reasons – the considered wisdom of our 'Shadow Cabinet' ... Had a long talk in the Smoking Room tonight with Harold Macmillan – he, like me, regards the Indian situation as the most alarming matter of the moment. He has been in India recently and the conditions then were pretty bad – now they are infinitely worse – absolute chaos will result if we go – and what is to become of our own people and their business interests under Indian rule? Harold says that a very large part of Macmillan & Co.'s book sales mainly educational are in India. Wavell said that he could not guarantee preservation of law and order without having six more divisions at his disposal – these the Government would not or could not give him.

Tuesday 20 May   We finished off another Bill tonight – the Town and Country Planning Bill – guillotined at 9.30 p.m. I don't profess to have read one word of this most important measure, but can only hope that it may not be as devastating in its effects as some people say that it will be. I have an instinctive distrust of planners and always feel that 'planning' merely makes confusion worse confounded – but then I am out of date and prefer things to grow up in their own way, only correcting them when they have proved to be wrong and are no longer suited to the times – and by things I mean institutions and customs and methods of life as well as the land system and the building of houses and designing of towns.

Thursday 22 May I made a short speech in the HofC this afternoon on the 3rd reading of the National Service Bill – spoke for eighteen minutes and ought to have gone on a bit longer – it might have been better and it might have been worse – and at any rate it is a relief to have got it off the chest. The debate was not an interesting one – no one wants conscription, but everyone, except the pacifists and pro-Russian left wingers, appreciate that we cannot do without it for the time being at any rate, and many of us feel as I do that conscription is the only fair way of having an army in these days and that national service is good for the health of the community. There was a poor attendance at the HofC today – a lot of people have evidently taken an extra day's holiday – and one cannot blame them. The House is tired out and sick to death of the endless business in Standing Committees on Bills which no one really cares a pin about and which will not help us out of our present discontents – even the comrades are beginning to wonder about things in general and how all the Government's legislation is going to help them at the next General Election, unless they can show some tangible results – more houses, more food, more goods in the shop windows.

Saturday 24 May I went to Tynemouth last night to attend the annual dinner of the Conservative Working Men's Club. It was quite a good show – everyone friendly and cheerful – and I think pleased to see me again – I used to visit the club in the old days. I had to respond to the toast of 'The Empire' – I seized the opportunity to speak about the present situation in India, but, needless to say, there is no report of my speech in the *Newcastle Journal* today – it really is the least useful paper we could possibly have in this area – it is run on the cheap and no attempt is made to make it a real local newspaper. How I wish that we could start a really good rival to it – but of course no one would put up the money – perhaps the Labour Party may do the job for us – they are talking about setting up local newspapers.

Monday 26 May   A report of yet another virulent speech from Shinwell at Margate. It seems odd that Attlee and Morrison cannot shut up this horrid little man – but perhaps they are using him as Asquith and the respectable Liberals of those days used L.G. Shinwell may [be] being used to keep alive class hatred and tickle the fancy of the extreme Left – I doubt, however, whether abuse of Winston goes down very well even among the Reds: it certainly does not please the better type of Labour man in this part of the world, and even at Margate, if the newspapers are to be believed, Shinwell was shouted down when he alluded to Winston as a 'garrulous old man'. Personalities never pay in politics in the long run – not in this country at any rate. I make a point – and always have done – of never alluding to my political opponent in an election, except of course to contradict any untrue statement he may have made against me or Beatrice which was common enough when Will Lawther was my opponent in the old Barnard Castle days.

Tuesday 27 May   The Labour Party Conference at Margate has endorsed the National Service Act by a big majority – how the times have changed! but it is all to the good. The comrades were at loggerheads about foreign policy – Zilliacus extremely angry about a pamphlet just published by Transport House called 'Cards on the Table', explaining Bevin's foreign policy *vis á vis* Russia. I have not seen it – but if it annoyed Zilliacus it must contain some sound views.

Wednesday 28 May   Attlee yesterday at the Margate Conference defended the Civil Servants and warned his followers not to strain them too much or the whole Civil Service machine might break down – some of us think that the machine has already broken down. The growth of the Civil Service has certainly not increased its efficiency – and its long and glorious tradition of service no longer survives.

Friday 30 May   ... to the Housewives' [League] meeting in the City Hall – about 700 to 800 people present, mainly women. We listened to a speech by Miss Dorothy Crisp[39] who it appears is the leading light in the League. She spoke very fluently for an hour and ten minutes, but we were not much wiser at the end of the speech of what the policy of the League is and what they intend doing in order to get rid of Strachey and Shinwell. It seems from what Miss Crisp says that women are much wiser than men – that all 'politicians' are fools or knaves – etc., etc. – I am disappointed with Miss Crisp of whose oratory I had heard so much.

Sunday 1 June ... we are to have a statement about India the day the House meets – it looks as if some kind of agreement has been arrived at about partition – the only possible solution of the present impasse – indeed, it has probably been the only possible solution since all the pother began, but Cripps and Co. would never admit it, being infatuated believers in the Congress Party. But it is difficult to see how partition can be brought about or made to work ... It is certainly an interesting situation, but one rather doubts the capacity of the Government to deal with it – it is not the kind of denouement they had in mind.

Tuesday 3 June ... to the HofC ... no gossip – but Attlee's statement about India which I had heard earlier in the day was well received on both sides of the House. It was much as had been expected – partition – 2 dominions until such time as 'the Indians' can bring about a union among themselves. The situation is saved, I hope, at any rate for the time being.

Friday 6 June I went to the HofC this morning for a short time and listened to Stafford Cripps move the second reading of the Companies Bill. He certainly has the gift of clear exposition – a pity he is such a crank.

Monday 9 June The situation as regards Russia remains the outstanding trouble of the day – it is full of menace and one simply cannot see what more can be done to bring about a better relationship between the Russians and ourselves and the Americans.

[39] Dorothy Crisp (b. c.1910), married 1945 John Neil Becker; Ind. cand. Acton 1943, St. George's 1945; Chairman, British Housewives' League 1947–48; she used her maiden name throughout her involvement with the League, although she was expecting her second child in 1948.

It seems to me quite useless to go on trying to be friends with a Government which never attempts to play ball with us – and yet what is the alternative? Is Europe to be cut in two? Is the eastern part of it to remain a Russian preserve? Can we allow Germany to be split in two? Are we prepared to fight a preventive war against Russia? If not, what is left open to us to do?

Tuesday 10 June   The Finance Bill in Committee today – the 'dirty doctor' [Dalton] in his usual form. I simply cannot bear to listen to the man – so glib – so pleased with himself – so spiteful – so terribly anxious to score cheap debating points – so essentially a party man on the make. Somehow or other, however, I doubt whether he will ever lead his party. He is clever enough to do so, but, despite all his efforts to please the Toms, Dicks and Harrys, I don't think from what I hear he is at all popular with his back-benchers – some of whom see well enough that the man is on the make. With us he is more disliked than any other man on the Front Bench – this is natural enough for he is regarded as a renegade, as indeed he is.[40] For the moment, however, the only thing that counts is his financial ability – can he save us from a financial crash? Is his Budget a wise one? I cannot believe it is because he is making no real attempt to lighten the burden of taxation and [is] not reducing expenditure. I don't see how we can pull through and bring about a sound reconstruction of trade and industry so long as we maintain our present high expenditure – but neither party seriously faces the situation – neither party will bring itself to cutting down the Social Services – and it is the Social Services bill which in our present economic destitution we cannot afford at its present level.

Thursday 12 June   I lunched and 'boarded' in Lombard Street. We had Lord Woolton to lunch with us – he is a director of 'The Royal'. He is a pleasant man – a bit deaf but otherwise with all his faculties. He told us that during the war he was constantly getting letters telling him how badly he ran the Food Ministry, etc., etc. – 'Now', he remarked, 'I find that I was the blue-eyed boy! My successors have made a reputation for me.' This is probably very

---

[40] Socially rather than politically: Dalton had an upper class background and education, but had not been involved in politics other than in the Labour Party.

true. He also told us how difficult it is to get money for the Party. This I can well believe – even if firms which have everything to lose under Socialism were to subscribe to Party funds, the auditors would not pass their subscriptions – whereas Trade Unions and Co-operative Societies are allowed to have political funds which go to support Socialist and Co-operative candidates – it really is rather farcical. In the old days of course the Conservative Party was largely financed by a few very rich men – and the rank and file paid little or nothing to the Party – now there are no longer rich men and still the rank and file pay little or nothing. I don't see what more can be done to raise money than is being done, and if Woolton cannot get money out of his business friends, I don't see who can.

Saturday 14 June   I lunched with [Tony Lambton] and Galloway at the Station Hotel – the former broke to me the news that the new report of the Boundary Commission for the distribution of seats recommends only 3 seats for Newcastle and the doing away of the North division. This has come as a considerable shock to me as it means the end of my parliamentary career – one would have naturally expected that if one division had to go, it would be the Central division which is by far the smallest, but of course the North division is a Conservative seat and so it is to go – now it will not be easy for a Conservative to win a seat in Newcastle – one of the objects of the Commission was, as I understood it, to try and get all divisions to about 50,000 voters – by this arrangement this Newcastle Division will have about 70,000 electors! Barnard Castle is also to disappear as a separate constituency and is to be merged in B[isho]p Auckland – Tony Lambton now thinks of standing for B.A. – let us hope that if he does, he will unseat the 'dirty doctor'.

Wednesday 25 June   I went to the memorial service at St. Margaret's this morning to the late Erskine-Hill – a sound, sensible man who died recently at a comparatively early age. He was chairman of the '22 Committee in the last Parliament and did well. He was, I am told, ambitious politically but I don't think that he would have achieved much success – sound rather than showy, and not in the political or party swim! He lost his seat at the last election very much to his surprise. I liked what I knew of him.

Thursday 26 June   There was a debate today on the Board of Trade vote initiated by the Lib-Nats – the subject they were worried about was the lack of consumer goods in the shops, but the debate was allowed for some reason or other to roam over the whole of Cripps's policy. He was not very happy and assured us that things would get better he hoped in the course of time, meanwhile we could all lump it and leave it to him. Oliver Lyttelton made a strong attack on him which all the young Tories thought wonderful. It was a good speech and I propose to do it the honour of reading it in *Hansard* – an honour which I seldom give to speeches I have listened to in the HofC. ... Had a talk with Arnold Gridley[41] today *re* the Electricity Bill. He is very gloomy about the Bill in particular and the Government's attitude about industry in general – clearly nationalization is going to put an end to individual effort and without it it is difficult to see how this country can maintain its individual position in the world – all these public boards and committees of management will never have the same enterprise as private boards of men working for their own interests and ready to take their risks.

Wednesday 2 July   I went to the HofC afterwards where there was a debate on the Post Office – our side was lead by Mr. Grimston who is a dull dog – I did not listen to the debate but I gather that our side attacked and that all the comrades were concerned about was that less hours of work and higher wages should be given to postal employees – an expensive postal service and rotten telephone service were matters of minor importance. Had a long talk in the Smoking Room with Hinchingbrooke – he is, I think, a pleasant fellow and an able one – like so many people he is concerned about the leadership of the Party, and like me is not very happy about the present and prospective leaders – not one of them stands out above the others, and not one of them shows any real initiative or drive. Hinch's young Tory group[42] apparently has ceased to exist and I gather that he is tired of Peter Thorneycroft and Molson.

Thursday 3 July   ... went to the HofC – where there was a debate

---

[41] Arnold Babb Gridley (1878–1965), Con. M.P. Stockport 1935–50, Stockport S. 1950–55; Chairman, 1922 Ctte. 1945–51; Controller, Electric Power Supply 1916–18; kt. 1920, cr. Baron Gridley 1955.

[42] The Tory Reform Ctte., of which he was the first Chairman in 1943–44.

on productivity in industry – it was not wildly exciting. David Maxwell Fyfe opened for us – I suppose that he is a very able man, but he is a terribly dull speaker I think. John Maclay[43] made an excellent speech on the shipping industry – he is a Lib-Nat and an able fellow. Isaacs wound up for the Govt. – he is a sound little man I should say, but is an out and out trade unionist and really believes, I think, that our economic prosperity is assured if only the trade unions were allowed to run industry. Like so many of the Labour leaders he fails to realize that the days of trade unionism are over if we are to have prosperity unless their leaders can control the shop stewards the majority of whom today are Communists – so long as these people run the show there can be no real peace in industry.

Tuesday 8 July   Halifax told us that he had to see Roosevelt once in order to tell him all about Eden who was then about to visit the U.S.A. He says that R was not interested in Eden, but showed him a copy of a telegram which he (R) had sent to Neville Chamberlain immediately after Munich – all that the message contained were the two words 'Good man'. Halifax was anxious to get hold of this message to give to Neville's biographer – but no trace of it could be found at the F[oreign] O[ffice] or in the Chamberlain archives – that it was sent was confirmed to H. by Sumner Welles[44] – an odd affair.

Wednesday 9 July   The Finance Bill report stage today . . .to me it seems that this habit of Dalton of first taking off the purchase tax and then putting it on again, and then altering the tax on some things and not on others, is wholly wrong and intolerable for manufacturers.

Thursday 10 July   The second reading of the India Bill today –

---

[43] John Scott Maclay (1905–), Lib. Nat. M.P. Montrose Burghs 1940–50, Renfrewshire W. 1950–64; Head of British Merchant Shipping Mission to U.S.A. 1944; P.S. Production May-July 1945; Min. of Transport & Civil Aviation 1951–52; M.S. Colonies 1956–57; Scottish Sec. 1957–62; Pres. of Assembly, Western European Union 1955–56; Pres., Nat. Lib. Council 1957–67; Chairman, Jt. Exchequer Bd. for N. Ireland 1965–72; cr. Viscount Muirshiel 1964, K.T. 1973; a shipowner; his father, the 1st Baron Maclay, was Min. of Shipping 1916–21.

[44] Sumner Welles (1892–1961), U.S. diplomat; Ass. Sec. of State 1933–37, Under. Sec. 1937–43; a close friend of Roosevelt.

Attlee moved it, and Harold Macmillan spoke first on our side. The former's speech was good I thought – he made as good a defence as was possible for the measure. Harold was good too – but he is growing more and more pompous as a speaker – I am sure that he imagines himself a new Pitt!

Sunday 13 July   Mrs. Moore[45] spent her whole time here abusing Miss Fletcher,[46] the Central Office woman agent in Newcastle – the latter is a bad tempered, ill mannered, masterful woman and is not popular up here – however, these worries don't affect me nowadays – now that I am no longer Area Chairman – a pity all the same that my successor, Greenwell, is such a dud.

Tuesday 15 July   The question of privilege raised by W. Brown, M.P., was considered today on the report of the Committee for Privilege. There was a poor debate – Pickthorn and H. Strauss who moved the rejection of the report made long and confused speeches, and no one else had anything to say worth hearing – needless to say the House supported the Committee's report which was drawn up on party lines. I had meant to say a few words against the political bias of the Committee and the conduct of the Attorney-General who acted on the Committee as if he were the advocate of the Trade Union point of view – but I got no opportunity. The 3rd Reading of the India Independence Bill was passed – a series of higher plane speeches. They made one rather tired – and I think that all sensible men were left wondering what would happen to India and whether in passing the Bill we were doing the best for the great masses of the Indian peoples.

Thursday 17 July   There was a debate on coal today in which I had intended speaking – but Clem Davies raised as a matter of 'urgent national importance' the cut in newspaper print – and the Speaker allowed it – so the coal debate ended at 7 p.m. and I had no opportunity of speaking – Shinwell and Rob Hudson, who led for us, spoke so lengthily. The former made a poor show and Rob

---

[45] A leading supporter of Headlam in the Newcastle North C.A.

[46] Florence Fletcher (d.1961), Con. Woman Organiser, Rugby 1934–39; wartime service in A.T.S., rising to rank of Chief Commander; Con. Agent, King's Norton CA, 1945–46; Dep. C.O. Agent, Northern Counties Area, 1946–47; Secretary, Women's Nat. Advisory Ctte. of N.U., 1947–60.

had no difficulty in demolishing him – clearly the coal situation is deteriorating.

Thursday 24 July   The House apparently sat until 9.30 or thereabouts this morning – David [Maxwell] Fyfe told me fairly late yesterday (and he was in charge of the show on our side) that the business would go on until about 3 a.m. and that there would only be about 7 divisions. It only shows how little anyone can prophesy what will happen in the HofC – there were 20 divisions and D.F. was six hours wrong in his forecast. Had I known that it would be such a long drawn out affair I might have stayed and so improved my division list which is none too good – one can get home at 9 a.m. – at 3 a.m. it is an impossibility unless one hires a car and, if one decides to do so, one never knows what time to order it. ... I listened to a good deal of the talk on the Lords amendments to the Electricity Bill – the Government disagree with some of them - all the more important ones which was only to be expected – now I suppose the Lords will give way. Cranborne is determined I gather not to make any use of the Parliament Act. He wishes to run no risk of a row with the Socialists – what use there is in a Second Chamber like the HofL nowadays I cannot see except to improve the grammar of our legislation.

Saturday 26 July   Our present hopeless economic position is largely due to the miners who have played their own selfish game ever since the days of the late A.J. Cook[47] – ca'canny and continual disputes about hours and wages, with a set policy of not allowing large coal stocks to be maintained: now we are all suffering because of an insufficiency of coal, and the Government's only policy is to try and placate the miners in every way possible at the expense of the rest of the community – it really is quite ridiculous and must lead to disaster. Meanwhile the absurd Nat. Coal Board is losing money hand over fist so I am told, and it is fairly certain that the price of coal will have to be raised – perhaps as no coal is obtainable by the ordinary consumer this won't hurt us as much as might be supposed – but of course our industries will suffer and recovery of trade will be gravely impeded.

[47] Arthur James Cook (1883–1931), Sec., M.F.G.B. 1924–31; a leading figure in the General Strike of 1926 and of the miners' strike of 1926–27.

16

RESHAPING THE PARTY

July to December 1947

Sunday 27 July   The Sunday papers are full of the approaching crisis and the *Sunday Times* and *Observer* are beginning to drop hints about a National Government. My own view is that there ought to be a national coalition of some kind which would drop Socialism like a hot potato and get back to common sense. But such a coalition in the present Parliament would be madness – with such a large Socialist majority it could not be a success and would hamstring us.

Thursday 31 July   Spent the remainder of the day at the HofC. James Stuart is back again after his 'illness' – looking very fit and well – I don't imagine that there has been much the matter with him. Apparently Winston turned up unexpectedly at the 22 Committee this afternoon – I did not attend the meeting ... but I am told that he was in excellent form – telling us that country must come before party in the national emergency, etc., etc. The boys all seemed pleased and that is the great thing. They are all busy wondering what is going to happen. I gather that Attlee gave satisfaction to his rank and file at yesterday's party meeting – they are all thoroughly frightened, but anxious at all costs to keep in. They realize, I think, that they are now exceedingly vulnerable and that an early election might be disastrous for their party.

Friday 1 August   [at Binderton House, Chichester] This is a charming house but too close to the main road – still one has a pleasing view towards the Downs – Goodwood in sight. No one here except Anthony [Eden] and his son – a very tall youth of 16 at Eton. There are some charming pictures, some quite good furniture and the internal decoration of the house is pleasing – a fine staircase of the Charles II period and a finely moulded ceiling. A gave me a good welcome and I am well lodged for the weekend. We have discussed men and things this evening. A was communicative and friendly. He has great charm and one realises that he has ability – but one wonders whether he has the patience and forbearance which are required in a party leader, and whether he is a good judge of men.

Saturday 2 August　　It has been hot and sultry all day ... Anthony and his boy played some lawn tennis and gathered early apples. A has been very friendly and forthcoming telling me all about his difficulties both domestic and political – his wife and Winston seem both to be worrying him. The former appears to have gone potty about some American who has now left her and gone back to his own wife – the latter is always being tiresome about one thing and another, and shows no sign of retiring from the active leadership of the party. A appears to be resigned to his wife's behaviour and is waiting for her to return to him – she is at present in Bermuda. He is restive about Winston – talks about giving up politics etc. My advice to him was to stick to the job – to abide in patience – not to retire when the ball was at his feet. We discussed most of the other 'possibles' – he says that O[liver] S[tanley] is all right – plays the game – he is not so happy about H[arold] M[acmillan] and R.A.B[utler]. He thinks that O[liver] L[yttelton] is getting more the hang of things.

Monday 4 August　　A long and weary day discussing Lords amendments after a debate (the same debate as usual) on Germany. I can see little use in fussing about Lords amendments which the Lords don't intend to stick to – but presumably we cannot let the Government refuse them without a protest. Today the protests went on until midnight (when I left the House) and looked like going on all night – this seems to me overdoing things.

Wednesday 6 August　　Today we have had the first day of the 'Crisis' debate. Attlee's speech was long, dreary and futile – the Government's proposals are just the cuts and little devices forecast by the Press, and they demand a new Bill to give them powers to do whatever they like. They are a set of frightened men – quite incapable of leading for they know not what to do – indeed, if they did know what to do, they would not dare to do it unless they got the permission of the T.U.C. I should have liked to say a few words – indeed, I have prepared a speech – but the Speaker told me he had 120 names on his list and I resigned from the competition.

Thursday 7 August   We had the second day of the 'economic crisis' debate today. ... The Government has come out of the show badly – Attlee was hopeless enough yesterday, but Dalton and Cripps were little better today – neither of them really addressed himself to the present situation – the former tried to defend his cheap money policy, the latter explained the changes which had resulted from England no longer being the workshop of the world. They both gave the cumulating causes of our troubles, but neither of them told us how the Government intended to cope with them – except of course by assuring us that it was intended to carry on with nationalization. This information cheered their left-wing followers. Anthony Eden wound up for us – and did the job well I thought – he is developing more vim and this goes down with the Party. Gossip says that the Comrades are more than ever at sixes and sevens after this debate – Attlee has certainly lost ground, but who has gained ground it is difficult to say – I myself don't think that the Government will split – yet awhile at any rate – but they are no longer a happy family. I lunched and boarded as usual in Lombard Street, where I learned that the City is not impressed by the Government's plans to 'meet the Crisis'.

Friday 8 August   Today the House sat until 4 p.m. Winston in a very effective speech moved the rejection of the Government's Bill to obtain further powers to meet the national emergency. David [Maxwell] Fyfe wound up for us; Chuter Ede for the Government – the latter's speech was pretty feeble. There is no doubt that the Government is in a sorry mess and has not an idea what to do – no kind of a lead has been given to the country and the Socialists are divided among themselves. The extremists want to push on with Socialist legislation at all costs: the less extreme Labour people are terribly frightened and uncertain what course to take – Attlee and his cabinet don't know whether to allow themselves to be pushed from behind or to assert a real leadership. To my mind they are lost – this would be excellent if it were not for the plight in which we are in. The only hope today is national unity, but unless there is a cessation of party politics this is impossible – we cannot get together unless there is a pause in Socialist legislation. The right thing today would be an appeal to the country.

Thursday 14 August   We finished up the Session with a division on the length of the adjournment. Anthony Eden spoke well and effectively – but the Government stuck to their guns and we adjourned to the 20th of October. In ordinary circumstances this would have been a sound policy – but, in view of the real crisis we are faced with, it would have looked better for the House to take a shorter holiday – however, it really is not a matter of much moment either way as we can always be summoned if an emergency should arise. I lunched at the House – Arnold Gridley told me in strict confidence that Shinwell had pressed him to become chairman of any one of the area electricity boards which he might choose to have and that he had refused the offer as he had felt so strongly against the whole scheme. He did right, I think – but after all Shinwell has said in the House against appointing opponents of the Bill to jobs in the new administration which it sets up it is typical of the little beast that he should try his best to get Gridley to help him – Gridley who was his most effective opponent in the House.

Sunday 17 August   ... clearly things are moving very fast and the Cabinet is being very busy – one wonders how they are going to get us out of the mess and what new privations and unpleasantness we are to suffer – certainly there is nothing very cheering in life nowadays and one feels that we might be a deal better off if only we had decided 2 years ago to cut our clothes according to our cloth – we ought to have begun trying to live within our means then instead of spreading our expenditure in the way we have done. We are spending ever so much more than we can afford, for example, on our Social Services – and yet since the war we have increased this expenditure considerably. I suppose, had we had a Conservative or National Government, the Beveridge business would have been carried out – and perhaps the school age would have been raised – we are almost as stupid as the Socialists and as frightened – but presumably we should not have gone in for all these silly nationalization schemes – and the Americans would, I imagine, have played ball better with us than they [are] doing with Attlee & Co.

Thursday 21 August   ... the crisis is said to be coming more and more acute and Mr. Herbert Morrison is busy warning us all of the increasing hardships which are coming to us. The usual cry 'Exports first – targets must be secured'. How I am beginning to hate this wretched word 'target' – the Government is always fixing a target but it never seems to be reached – a target is like an 'objective' in my war – it is seldom reached, and if it is, it only means another objective further on, and trouble all the way. We have suspended 'convertibility of sterling' temporarily at any rate – what exactly this means and how it will help us I don't quite know – but it means that we shall be able to save a little of what is left of the American loan I gather, and that we shall be less able to buy in the hard currency countries – so a reduction in meat and fat rations at an early date is certain.

Friday 22 August   The Government is still trying to make up its mind what to do – this Cabinet, I imagine, must be hopelessly divided – the left wing led by Bevan is said to be determined to go on with the nationalization policy, getting to work with iron and steel as soon as the new Session begins – Herbert Morrison, on the other hand, is said to be anxious to call a halt on nationalization and concentrate on solving the economic crisis. Obviously such would be the wiser course in the circumstances – what is required now is national unity and we cannot be expected to work whole-heartedly with the Government so long as it pursues an industrial policy which we believe to be wholly wrong – but I gather that the left wingers in the HofC are gaining strength and may be strong enough to upset the apple cart – and yet I don't see Bevan resigning yet awhile to lead the left wing backbenchers against Attlee.

Thursday 28 August   The Govt. have announced their immediate plans to meet 'the crisis' – cuts in food and doing away with the basic petrol allowance, and money for foreign travel. ... The positive proposals for expanding home production and for a redeployment of industrial resources to increase the volume of exports are being worked out in consultation with employers and the inevitable trade unions – we are supposed to be informed about these matters in the second week of September. To me it all appears very hopeless, just tinkering with the business – what is needed now is drastic economy in expenditure, a cutting down of public expenditure, even if it means reductions in the social services and the giving up temporarily of many desirable projects. It is ridiculous going on living as if we were a solvent nation when we are not.

Tuesday 2 September　　I was lucky enough to find in one of the Sunday papers an article by Bob Boothby which enlightened me considerably. He has been right about this American loan from the beginning – what a pity it is he made such a mess of things for he is a very able man, and one of the best speakers in the HofC. I have never spoken to him since he returned after his debacle[1] – but I feel that I ought to make it up with him – everybody else has and who am I to uphold an attitude of moral rectitude which nowadays is completely *demodé*?[2] My grouse against Bob is not so much what he did, but his returning to the HofC and carrying on as if nothing had happened – no man who has been condemned for improper conduct by the House should in my opinion ever return to it.

Wednesday 3 September　　The Yorkshire coal strike instead of ending at the bidding of Lawther & co. is spreading – today there are said to be 30,000 idol in 23 pits and 180,000 tons of coal are estimated as having been lost as a result of the strike. It really is a bad business: how we are ever to get going again with this spirit of unrest in the mining industry I cannot image. The miners are no more prepared to do their job under the N[ational] C[oal] B[oard] than they were under private ownership and no more ready to obey their leaders – I suppose Communist agitation is behind the whole thing – but no one cares to say this openly. In India matters are no better – riots everywhere, and the Indian politicians are helpless, so it seems, to quell them.

Thursday 11 September　　The Government has held the Liverpool seat with a reduced majority – the Liberal candidate forfeited his deposit, getting only a little over 900 votes: the 2 other candidates

---

[1] For details, see note to entry for 21 Jan. 1941.
[2] translation: out of fashion.

hardly scored at all. The result is disappointing but is what I expected – the seat is a working class one and the working classes still do not realize the mess they are in. They have good wages and as much work as they care to do – and they have been taught to believe that if the Tories were to come back their wages would be reduced and they would be faced with unemployment – until they really are forced by circumstances to face the situation they will continue to support the Socialists. I can see no sign of light on the horizon.

Friday 12 September   The Cripps plan for our national recovery is much what one expected – a real concentration of industry to promote the export trade ('targets' *ad lib*), less of everything for home consumption, reduced rations, possible reduction of capital expenditure, possible direction of labour. The 'capitalist' press professes to welcome this plan – to me it seems rather ridiculous because I firmly believe that most of the 'targets' are unobtainable and because I don't believe that people generally will respond to the call to work as they have never worked before – nor do I believe that, even if we can make all the goods required, we shall be able to sell them abroad at the prices we shall have to demand to meet the heavy charges of their production ...

Friday 19 September   Reid[3] gave the inaugural address at the Conservative School which is to run for a week in Durham Castle. His address was a good one and the students appeared to be interested and certainly asked more sensible questions than is customary at these gatherings. Conservative youth appears to be very anxious to be given some cut and dried policy – what the reason for this is [is] amply apparent – Conservatives have as a rule not the slightest conception of what Conservatism stands for and never know what to say when they are faced with Socialist conundrums – it is all rather silly and depressing.

Sunday 21 September   Spent most of the remainder of the day discussing politics and politicians with James Reid – his views

[3] James Scott Cumberland Reid (1890–1975), Con. M.P. Stirling & Falkirk 1931–35, Glasgow Hillhead 1937–48; Solicitor-Gen. Scotland 1936–41; Ld. Advocate 1941–45; Dean, Faculty of Advocates 1945–48; Ld. of Appeal in Ordinary 1948–75; Chairman, Malayan Constitutional Comm. 1956–57; cr. Baron Reid 1948.

about the latter are much the same as mine. He has no great
admiration for any of our Tory leaders – he ranks Oliver Stanley
(as I do) as possessing the best brain of the lot, but does not regard
him as a leader – nor does he regard R.A.B. and Harold Macmillan
as possible leaders. He himself has political ambition and I should
like to see him Sec of State for Scotland when we come back. He
is not very hopeful about the future and somewhat a defeatist
about our capacity to remain a Great Power – all for giving up the
Middle East which rather horrified me.

Saturday 27 September   There is no news – apparently our decision to leave Palestine is 'final' and we are, it seems, prepared to
see a Jew–Arab war as complacently as we are viewing today the
communal upheaval in India. We are an odd people nowadays and
perhaps the time has come when we should sink into obscurity –
we have neither the vision nor guts required for holding a commanding place in the world. We can today take interest in nothing
but material things at home – our social welfare, our wages, etc. –
but I fear that we are entirely forgetting that all these things depend
primarily on our position in the world – upon our trade and
commerce and industrial efficiency. Sooner or later I hope that
confidence in ourselves will revive, but this won't be so long as
false political and economic doctrine prevails among the masses
and is held, too, by a considerable section of the educated classes.
How, except by hunger and unemployment, common sense is to
prevail, I cannot see – for there is no sign as yet of a Conservative
revival, and the people are far from the disillusionment with
Socialism without which there can be no recovery.

Tuesday 30 September   The news today is that Stafford Cripps has
been appointed to be Minister of Economic Affairs – Greenwood is
put on the shelf where he ought to have been put some time
ago, and J.H. Wilson,[4] Cripps's former Under Secretary, is made
President of the B[oard] of T[rade]. I know him by sight – he is, I

[4] (James) Harold Wilson (1916–1995), Lab. M.P. Ormskirk 1945–50, Huyton
1950–83; Dir. of Economics & Statistics, Min. of Fuel & Power 1941–44; P.S. Works
1945–47; Sec. Overseas Trade Mar.-Oct. 1947; Pres. Bd. of Trade 1947–51; P.M.
1964–70, 1974–76; Lab. Party Leader 1963–76; member of N.E.C. 1952–76, Chairman 1961–62; Chairman, Public Accounts Ctte. 1959–63; K.G. 1976, cr. Baron
Wilson of Rievaulx 1983.

believe, an ex-Oxford don who started life in a council school and is only 31 years old – he will presumably do what Cripps tells him. Cripps, I suppose, will be more the King of the Castle than ever, and greater and greater austerity will be the order of the day.

Saturday 4 October   The Party Conference appears to be going well – it has adopted the 'Industrial Charter' almost unanimously, only poor old Waldron Smithers[5] seems to have spoken against it. He considers it to be milk and water Socialism which perhaps it is – but, so far as I have studied it – and that is not a great deal – it seems to lay down as an 'industrial policy' the practices that exist today between employers and employees in the best managed firms – there does not seem to me much harm in this. Smithers has sent me a long memorandum attacking the Charter but the attack is not formidable.

Tuesday 7 October   Churchill wound up the Party Conference at Brighton – he seems to think that we shall have a general election in the near future – I doubt it very much unless there is a material change in the situation whether for better or worse. I feel that these people mean to stay in for their full time if they can possibly do so in the hope that conditions will improve – if they were to go now, it is possible that they would be returned but with a greatly reduced majority – they could not, therefore, claim that the people were so solidly behind them as they can now with their huge majority in the HofC and they would find it more difficult to carry out their full programme of Socialization. However, there is every reason for us to work up our organization for all we are worth in case of an early election. Whether Woolton will get the million pounds he has asked for remains to be seen – I doubt it – but perhaps he will be satisfied with half a million.

Wednesday 8 October   The changes in the Government are announced – Shinwell has been moved from Fuel and Power to the War Office, but leaves the Cabinet – to make such a creature Secretary of State for War is an insult to the Army. Wilmot,

---

[5] Waldron Smithers (1880–1954), Con. M.P. Chislehurst 1924–45, Orpington 1945–54; kt. 1934.

Westwood[6] and Bellenger[7] are sacked and none of them will be missed ... most of the new Under Secretaries belong to the Intelligentsia which won't please the trade union section of the party.

Thursday 9 October   The changes in the Government have aroused little comment – why should they? Captain Blackburn,[8] M.P., whom I spoke to last night at the Café Royal professed to take no interest in the reshuffle, but said that he thought that the move was rather to the right than the left. He was careful to tell me that he had been staying the night *chez* Vansittart – 'dear old Van, a great friend of mine' – I said 'oh', and then we parted. ... The general impression is that Cripps's stock has gone up, and that both Bevin and Morrison have lost ground – I wonder – I cannot see Cripps as Attlee's successor or as a future P.M.

Sunday 12 October   Tom Inskip's death is announced. He has been ill for a long time – a good, sensible man who at one time was supposed to be in the running for the leadership of the Party for no very apparent reason that I could see. He was what one calls a 'sound man' and made an admirable A[ttorney-]G[eneral] in the House of Commons – lawyers did not rate him very high, but he managed to become both Lord Chancellor and L[ord] C[hief] J[ustice] – I doubt whether any other lawyer has achieved so much. At one time I was pretty friendly with him, but latterly have seen nothing of him.

Tuesday 21 October   The Government are apparently going to amend the Parliament Act, reducing the period of delaying legis-lation to one year instead of two. Their object is clear enough and is what we should have always anticipated – now the question is

[6] Joseph Westwood (1884–1948), Lab. M.P. Peebles & Midlothian S. 1922–31, Stirling & Falkirk 1935–48; P.P.S. to W. Adamson 1929–31; U.S. Scotland Mar.-Aug. 1931, 1940–45; Scottish Sec. 1945–47; Political Organiser, Scottish Miners' Fed. 1918–29; killed in a car accident 17 July 1948.

[7] Frederick John Bellenger (1894–1968), Lab. M.P. Bassetlaw 1935–68; F.S. War Office 1945–46; Sec. for War 1946–47; a Con. member of Fulham Borough Council 1922–28.

[8] Albert Raymond Blackburn (1915-), Lab. M.P. Birmingham King's Norton 1945–50, Birmingham Northfield 1950–51 (resigned whip Aug. 1950, sat as Ind.); Common Wealth cand. Watford 1943.

whether the HofL will refuse to pass the Bill – if it does, then will the Government give way or will it go to the country on a peers v. people stunt? I imagine that this is their plan – well – if it is their plan, I doubt whether it would be successful. Arthur Henderson[9] and co. firmly believed that the dear food cry would triumph in the election of '31 and got the shock of their lives – we must not be frightened this time, if the occasion arises. But I am fearful of our party leaders – they have no guts. My own view is that the Labour people have made a false move this time by attacking the Lords without any cause for the attack and that we are in a good position.

Friday 24 October   There is no doubt that the Conservative women, like the Young Conservatives, are improving a lot – really trying to understand things and far more politically-minded than they used to be in this area – if only they will get down to work, they ought to make a great effect upon public opinion.

Monday 27 October   I got to the HofC about 2 p.m. and had luncheon with Tom Moore,[10] M.P.. He, like most of the other people I have spoken to today, assured me that there was a 'tremendous change' in the country – that the Government had lost a lot of ground – that we should win an election today. I wonder how true all this is? – if all the wobblers would vote Conservative, it might be so – but would they vote at all? Well, perhaps the municipal elections will give us some genuine indication of the feeling of the country. Germany was discussed on the Address Debate today – I did not listen to much of it, but my feeling is that our control policy has been all wrong and that we have failed miserably. I went with Kenneth Pickthorn and Harry Strauss for dinner at the Beefsteak. They are at the extreme right of our party and take themselves very seriously – it was rather amusing to hear what they thought of Rab [Butler], Harold [Macmillan], Oliver Stanley, etc.

[9] Arthur Henderson (1863–1935), Lab. M.P. Barnard Castle 1903–18, Widnes 1919–22, Newcastle E. 1923, Burnley 1924–31, Clay Cross 1933–35; Lab. Party Treasurer 1904–12, Chairman 1908–10, 1914–17, Sec., N.E.C. 1912–35; Pres. Bd. of Educ. 1915–16; Member of War Cabinet 1916–17; Home Sec. 1924; For. Sec. 1929–31; Lab. Leader 1931–32.
[10] Thomas Cecil Russell Moore (1888–1971), Con. M.P. Ayr Burghs 1925–50, Ayr 1950–64; Food Controller in Russia 1918–19; kt. 1937, cr. Bart. 1956.

Tuesday 28 October   Winston made a long and 'fighting' speech in the House today, moving the opposition amendment to the Address. His vitality and physical endurance are amazing – he spoke for nearly an hour and a half – and never faltered in any way. Except in his economic ideas I thought what he said was good stuff, and I think most of our side were pleased with the speech – always excepting R.A.B., Harold Macmillan & Co. I find that this pinkish portion of our party are more prominent but less popular with the rank and file than they used to be. People instinctively dislike their economic planning and plotting and yet can see no alternative to some policy of the kind in present conditions. In this I fancy they are right – the great thing, however, is not to emphasize the necessity for controls so much – if and when we come back into power, it will be time enough to decide how much Govt. intervention in the conduct of industry is required – that there will have to be some general direction is certain. Winston's speech today was naturally seized upon by Herbert Morrison to envisage a return to *laissez faire*, though as a matter of fact it was not – his speech was clever debating but not a really good performance, though it appeared to please his party. He seems to have entirely recovered from his illness.

Wednesday 29 October   Got to the HofC about 4 p.m. and listened to Harold Macmillan indicting the Government – a lengthy and able speech – and no one was more pleased with it than was Harold. Oliver Lyttelton spoke from our front bench to wind up for us (but I did not hear him) and Attlee wound up for the Govt. – I am told that his speech was mainly an attack on Winston which pleased his party. Afterwards Boyd Carpenter moved a prayer against basic petrol abolition – the Government only got a majority of twenty-seven and had all our people stayed after the division on the amendment to the address I think that we might have beaten the Government on basic petrol – so many of their people were absent or abstained from voting. It seems to me that our whips might have foreseen this opportunity and kept our people – but they are not very clever in matters of this kind.

Thursday 30 October   The House spent the whole of today's sitting on discussing its 'privilege' and how to punish the two members who had offended it.[11] Allighan,[12] M.P., was expelled and Walkden,[13] M.P., was reprimanded by the Speaker as was also the editor of the newspaper which had offended. I am glad to say that no one seemed inclined to press the point that disclosing matters discussed in party meetings should be treated as a breach of privilege. ... I did not hear Quintin Hogg's speech unfortunately – apparently it was far the best of the day. The whole business, however, was rather sordid and unpleasant. It did no credit to the Mother of Parliaments and that the 'people' should have sent such men to Parliament as Allighan and Walkden, neither of whom I know personally. Another Labour M.P., one Weitzman,[14] has been sentenced to twelve months' imprisonment for misdemeanour today[15] – so the Party is a bit unhappy for the time being – if this kind of thing were to continue, even their supporters might begin to wonder whether the right type of man was being selected to reform and remodel English public life!

[11] Allighan had published an article in *World's Press News* on 3 Apr. 1947, alleging that M.P.s were disclosing information from confidential party meetings to the press in return for payment. Walkden was identified as having done so, but Allighan's offence was regarded as the more serious as he had made a sweeping allegation against the conduct of M.P.s in general.

[12] Garry Allighan (1900-), Lab. M.P. Gravesend 1945–47; Radio Editor, *Evening Standard* 1931–39; News Editor, *Daily Mirror* 1941–44; Industrial Editor, *Daily Mail* 1944–46; member of London County Council 1937–42; Principal, Premier School of Journalism, Johannesburg 1963–73.

[13] Evelyn Walkden (1893–1970), M.P. Doncaster 1941–50 (Lab. to Nov. 1947, resigned whip and sat as Ind.); Organiser, Nat. Union of Distributive & Allied Workers 1928–41; P.P.S. to Sir W. Jowitt Mar.–May 1945, to Sir B. Smith 1945–46.

[14] David Weitzman (1898–1987), Lab. M.P. Stoke Newington 1945–50, Stoke Newington & Hackney N. 1950–79.

[15] A practising barrister since 1922, Weitzman had financed a business managed by his younger brothers called the Newington Supply Co. The firm ran into difficulties after the war and, as principal creditor, Weitzman brought in an official reciever. This led to the discovery that in 1939–40 the company had deliberately breached the wartime controls on the production of toileteries. On 29 Oct. 1947 Weitzman and four others were found guilty of conspiracy to contavene defence regulations; he was sentenced by Mr. Justice Denning to twelve months imprisonment and a £500 fine, a verdict reported in a letter from Denning to the Speaker read out in the House on 30 Oct. However on 1 Dec. Weitzman was granted bail pending the hearing of an appeal, and on 16 Mar. 1948 his conviction was quashed by the Lord Chief Justice, who criticised Denning for allowing the case against the M.P. to proceed when the evidence indicated that he had not been involved in the actual management of the business. Weitzman therefore remained an M.P., and became a King's Counsel in 1951.

Saturday 1 November   The municipal elections are on today and it will be interesting to see what happens. My own view is that we shall see a considerable change in areas which have been Conservative – I doubt whether there will be any change in our part of the world ... The interesting thing in these elections will be to see what happens now that so many of them will be fought on strictly party lines – perhaps the Conservatives may go to the poll more readily to vote [in] a straight political fight than has been their practice hitherto in the 'non-political' days.

Monday 3 November   All our people were much elated at the House today as a result of the municipal election returns. The anti-Socialist vote has undoubtedly increased tremendously – my own view is that the heartening thing about these results is that clearly so many more Conservatives have gone to the polls than is usually the case.

Tuesday 4 November   Today the House was occupied by the consideration of the Third Report from the Select Committee on procedure. The Government thought fit to amend the proposals of the committee on several matters on which the committee had been unanimous – a strange and I should imagine an almost unprecedented proceeding – however, their own supporters backed them. The only object Herbert Morrison has in view is to expedite business which of course means as a general rule the cutting down of the powers of the House as opposed to the wishes of the Executive – gradually but surely the authority of the House over its own proceedings is being whittled away and the rule of the Executive [is] being made stronger – it is of course the result of Socialist totalitarianism or whatever you choose to call it – the determination to put party before Parliament.

Wednesday 5 November   In the HofC Winston moved the rejection of the 2nd reading of the Burma Bill – rightly I think – but his language was as usual too violent for my taste.

Thursday 6 November   Yesterday James Stuart asked me if I would care to be a member of a special committee to consider the Parliament Bill – our policy regarding it and the preparation of amendments – I said that I should like to be on the committee –

but this evening the whole business was brought up after the usual meeting of the '22 Committee' for all and sundry. Winston spoke and Bobbety (Salisbury) – the latter I thought more effective than the former. It was decided to move a reasoned amendment against the 2d of the Bill rather than a direct negative. Personally I strongly favoured the reasoned amt. idea – but Harry Strauss and some of the other would-be constitutional experts preferred the other course as stronger – the Lords are going to put up a reasoned amendment against the 2d when it goes to them – no one at today's meeting suggested openly that the Lords should pass the Bill, but I gather that there are those who advocate this policy. I am against it, because I think that such pusillanimity would serve no useful purpose.

Friday 7 November   Woolton told me yesterday that he is getting lots of small money, but that big money was not forthcoming so far – this is quite understandable for who has got the big money nowadays – the Labour Party can utilize Trade Union money and the Co-op[erative]s apparently can use the money of their subscribers – but we cannot avail ourselves of the money of public companies and all the big subscribers have ceased to subscribe. Of course it is infinitely better that there should be thousands of small subscribers £1.1/- to £10.10/- but it takes a lot of these to make a million £.

Monday 10 November   The Speaker was kind to me today – calling me no. 4 in the Parliament Bill 2nd Reading Debate. I spoke for twenty minutes – my notes as usual handicapped my delivery, but the speech should read all right – people, I think, realized that my effort was a serious one – certainly they listened to me attentively. The debate was singularly dull and ill-attended – clearly the Comrades would much have preferred a bill to do away with the HofL entirely – they are most of them Single Chamber men. Morrison's opening speech was a poor one – half would-be facetious and entirely unconvincing. David [Maxwell] Fyfe who opened for us (Winston having a cold not being present) was as always painstaking and sound – but I always find him dull to listen to. Q. Hogg was vigorous, but his effort as a whole was not up to his usual standard – too much repetition, too much back chat with the Comrades.

Tuesday 11 November　　Winston turned up today and made a wonderfully effective speech on the Parliament Bill – full of wit and humour – it was an election speech and went down with the Party. Anthony Eden also spoke well in winding up for us – indeed, his speech seemed to me more fitting for the occasion than Winston's because it dealt, and dealt very effectively, with the Bill under discussion. The P.M. who replied for the Government made some rather obvious points, but looked smaller and spoke more feebly than ever – he is, I should think, a thoroughly tired and harassed man. How he manages to carry on with such a team as he has beats me – it is a scratch crew if there ever was one. Harold Macmillan for once in a way conversed at length with me today. He considers that this Govt. is practically down and out and that it is only a matter of months to a general election – I doubt this myself unless the financial situation is so desperate that they cannot carry on. Harold evidently foresees another Coalition after a fairly close drawn election – this of course is a possibility.

Wednesday 12 November　　Dalton introduced his supplementary budget this afternoon. He has raised 200 million additional taxation in various ways – but has not increased income tax or surtax or increased the price of tobacco ... The 'dirty doctor' was as irritating as ever – but he certainly has done nothing to increase his reputation as a financier by this latest effort – nor did he attempt to tell the House what is our real financial position today. It was a disappointing and misleading performance and one felt that it was quite unnecessary to introduce an emergency budget at all if this was the result – it does not enlighten the nation as to the true state of things financially and does little or nothing, so far as I can see, to check inflation. I fancy that the dirty doctor is played out, and I am sure that the enormous increase in purchase tax is wholly bad for the development of our trade and industry if a long view is taken. There was a considerable amount of talk today which is unusual on Budget day – but all the Comrades appeared anxious to air their views – I did not listen to the debate which I am told was pretty feeble.

Thursday 13 November　　The sensation today has been a grave 'indiscretion' on the part of the Chancellor of the Exchequer – in answer to a private notice question put by Victor Raikes he admitted that he had revealed his budget proposals to a lobby correspondent on his way into the House! A strange thing to do and so far as one can see for no purpose whatsoever. Dalton admitted his error and apologised to the House – he looked pretty miserable poor man and I could not help feeling sorry for him. Clearly, however, the matter cannot be left where it is and our people and the Liberals are tabling a motion tonight asking for an enquiry. I cannot see myself what other course Dalton has but to resign – it remains to be seen whether he will. Salisbury came to the 22 Committee again this evening and spoke sensibly about the Parliament Bill issue – the Lords will have a reasoned amendment against passing the Bill and leave it at that – holding up the Bill for 2 years from its second reading in this House. This really is the only course they can pursue.

Friday 14 November   The 'dirty doctor' has resigned and Cripps has been made C[hancellor] of E[xchequer]. He also remains Minister of Economic Affairs. I expect that we shall now be whipped with scorpions! but presumably this process is what is required if we are to be saved – an unpleasing prospect nevertheless. No one seems particularly sorry for Dalton – indeed, his fall has bucked up our people no end. It has rather overcome the Comrades – a real shock for them. It is a very odd happening – how any man in Dalton's position can have been such a fool as to betray his own budget is incomprehensible. Most people think that it was due to his ridiculous wish to be popular – but this seems rather a futile idea in the circumstances, if they are what is supposed – why give away all your budget proposals to a little Lobby correspondent? Some day perhaps we shall hear the whole truth of the business, but I hope that our people won't press for a parliamentary inquiry now as they had intended last night.

Monday 17 November   Went to the House ... and got there about 3 p.m. – too late for luncheon, but I had 2 nasty sausage rolls and a cup of tea in the tea room to keep me going. People are still talking about *l'affaire* Dalton – there is to be an inquiry into his performance, but I don't suppose that anything new will result from it. Some of our fellows are now recalling the leakage of last

year which Gurney Braithwaite[16] drew attention to. He tried to
trace its origin from the City end and a report was submitted to
Dalton who said there was not sufficient evidence to go on, if I
recollect rightly – now people are not unnaturally wondering
whether the leakage last year originated from the same source as
has the leakage this year – it may have done, but of course no one
can raise the matter again. The general debate on the budget was
concluded today – I did not listen to much of it. I fancy that Cripps
will be a far more efficient and more difficult a C. of E. for our
people to deal with than was Dalton, and I am certain that he will
prove a better C. of E. for the Government because he is an abler
and more honest man than his predecessor – being popular with
the Comrades will not be his main preoccupation.

Tuesday 18 November   Aneurin Bevan introduced – or rather
moved the second reading – of his Local Government Bill this
afternoon – I listened to most of his long speech which was an able
one. His fluency is amazing and he is an undoubtedly a fine
parliamentarian – odious creature though he is – I wonder what
this man's political future is? He is clearly the ablest of the left
wing section of the Socialists and is therefore a possible leader of
the party – supposing the party swings to the left, which it may
well do, he may be Attlee's successor, and might be acceptable to
the T.U.C. people – on the other hand, I don't see Bevin giving
way to him without a struggle – and then there is Cripps. Somehow
or other I fancy that he cannot be in agreement with Bevan and if
he is successful as C. of E. in this economic crisis and can pull the
Government out of the mess it is in, he will be in an immensely
powerful position and likely to command the support of the more
moderate and sensible Comrades.

Wednesday 19 November   Tonight as I was leaving the HofC
people were already taking up their positions for tomorrow's show[17]
... There is a good deal of disgruntlement about tickets for the
Abbey – only a few tickets given to the HofC, and these are allotted

---

[16] Joseph Gurney Braithwaite (1895–1958), Con. M.P. Sheffield Hillsborough
1931–35, Holderness 1939–50, Bristol N.W. 1950–55; P.S. Transport & Civil Aviation
1951–53; cr. Bart. 1954; regular speaker in Hyde Park for the '1912 Club' 1927–31.

[17] The marriage of Princess Elizabeth, later Queen Elizabeth II, to Philip Moun-
batten.

according to the strength of parties, so we are getting very few and they are balloted for – I gather that a good many ex-Cabinet Ministers have not been invited to the Abbey – and very few Privy Councillors as such. Personally I don't mind, but Beatrice is disappointed, poor dear ... Dalton disgruntled us all by turning up here this evening – joking and laughing with the Comrades who were patting him on the back as if he were a hero – we certainly do live in strange times, and old codes of manners and behaviour are flopping every day.

Monday 24 November   There was a Bill (2d) in the Chamber to do away with the Poor Law, and the Comrades were indulging in much sob stuff – however, there was a poor attendance for such an epoch-making measure – which – so far as I can see – merely changes the method of public assistance for the old and destitute and gives it another name. I dined at the Beefsteak ... Tommie [Lascelles] told me that Philip Mountbatten[18] is a 'nice boy', but not much educated – should do all right he thinks for his job.

Tuesday 25 November   The Second Reading of the Finance Bill today – it was moved by Glenvil Hall,[19] the Financial Secretary, in what, I am told, was a poor speech – I can well believe this for he is a rather feeble little man, though personally I like him. He is one of the few Comrades I know. Harry Crookshank opened for us – a good, sound speech, but not anything out of the way. Ralph Assheton wound up for us – he is a poor performer. Cripps wound up for the Government and I thought his performance extremely able – how one envies anyone who can put up a good case for any conceivable subject – and this is exactly what Cripps can do.

Thursday 27 November   Lord Woolton came to the '22 Committee this afternoon and discussed the Gravesend election result. He said that he had not expected to win the seat – our candidate not good enough – he considered the result was satisfactory on the whole – it showed that although there was no great swing over as yet there

---

[18] Philip Mountbatten (1921-), son of Prince Andrew of Greece; married 1947 Princess Elizabeth (1926-), Queen Elizabeth II 1952-; cr. Duke of Edinburgh 1947.

[19] William George Glenvil Hall (1887–1962), Lab. M.P. Portsmouth Central 1929–31, Colne Valley 1939–62; F.S.T. 1945–50; Chairman, P.L.P. 1950–51; member, P.L.P. Ctte. 1951–55.

was, nevertheless, a change for the better. In this I think he is right – but when he went on to say that if there were a G[eneral] E[lection] in a month's time we should have a small majority, and if that one were to come in March or April we should have a working majority, I though him somewhat optimistic. I was pleased to hear that he had already got £600,000 of the million he is asking for and expected to get the rest before the end of the year. He strikes me as a keen and confident man, but I doubt whether he understands much about politics. ... In the House we had the second reading of the Criminal Justice Bill. The decision 'to hang or not to hang' is to be left to the free vote of the House. but the Home Secretary said that the opinion of the Govt. was that this is not the moment to change the law – in this I agree with him.

Friday 28 November   The visitors to the House are a real nuisance to M.P.s, especially nowadays when they come in such numbers – even from constituencies like mine. There are queues of them waiting all day – I should say that the HofC is now the most popular place of entertainment in the country – odd because never since I knew the place have the debates been of poorer quality – I suppose the Comrades and their friends are new to the business and 'visiting the House' is an experience which interests them.

Saturday 29 November   The Socialists have retained the Edinburgh seat with a slightly reduced majority: we have won the Howdenshire seat with a bigger majority than at the general election – 14,000 as against 10,000. These three by-elections show, I think, fairly clearly that there is no real swing over at present. The average voter still feels that he has nothing to gain by turning out the Government – so far as the 'working man' is concerned, this is quite understandable – he has better wages (in money) than he has ever had before, he has employment and as much to eat as anybody else – if the 'Tories' came back, he fears that there will be unemployment and harder times – so naturally he votes Socialist – until hard facts show him that Socialism means national disaster, he will continue to vote 'Labour'. The only satisfactory thing about these elections is that the Liberal candidates in H. and E. forfeited their deposits – at any rate there is no Liberal revival.

Thursday 4 December   ... spent the afternoon at the House. I noticed that our people are less certain now for some reason or other that the Comrades are down and out – one hears less of the coming disaster which we have been hearing about for the last few months. I suppose our not winning Gravesend has somewhat dispirited our young men – they are beginning to realize that it takes time to disillusion the masses, especially when they are feeling themselves better off than they ever remember being before. The bulk of the people have no idea that we are bankrupt and cannot afford to maintain our present standard of living – and if a gent like Sir John Anderson suggests that paying subsidies to provide us with food at a reasonable price is all wrong, he is considered to be an enemy of the people. I am sure – as I always have been since the general election – that the Comrades will need a deal of getting rid of – and that they won't risk another general election until the last moment possible. Time I fancy is on their side – besides we really have nothing to offer the people – the 'Industrial Charter' is feeble stuff compared with the Socialist utopia to which they are looking forward, and the mass of the workers still believe that Toryism means exploitation for them and a return to the 'bad old days'.

Sunday 7 December   Winston has made another fighting speech – this time to 6,000 Conservatives at Manchester. In my opinion he always overstates his case – but our rank and file like this – from him at any rate – and so I suppose it is all right.

Wednesday 10 December   We had the 3rd reading of the Parliament Bill today. I did not speak again – there really was nothing more to be said and the debate was a fairly poor one. Herbert Morrison's winding up speech for the Government was beneath contempt – semi-facetious and wholly futile. The Bill is entirely unnecessary, just like the Bill repealing the Trades Disputes Act of 1927 – inasmuch as both the Parliament Act of 1911 and the Trades Disputes Act have worked well and are measures the practical usefulness of which is abundantly clear to any sensible man who can look ahead whatever his politics may be – unless of course he happens to be a Communist – and yet neither of these amending bills has caused any stir in the country. The present electorate seems incapable of appreciating measures of this kind – not realizing in the least how easy it will be for some future left wing Government to destroy our constitutional machinery and end our present form of parliamentary democracy within the duration of a single Parliament – nor can trade unionists of the old-fashioned type see how the Trade Disputes Act of 1927 enabled them to hold their end up against extremists within their own ranks.

Thursday 11 December   The Palestine debate opened today – Creech Jones[20] read out a long statement of Government policy. We are to give up the Mandate in May and to have cleared out of the country by the 1st of August. ... Oliver Stanley opened for us. He is all for clearing out as quickly as possible – he tried his best to make out that but for the Govt.'s two years' of procrastination we might have contrived to carry on – but what he said was not very convincing. The only way for us to remain in charge is to enforce law and order – and neither we nor the Socialists are prepared to do that – another sorry affair, the results of which it is not easy to forecast. In my opinion the villains of the piece are the Americans who have abused us all along in order to please the Jews in New York.

Friday 12 December   The second day of the Palestine debate ... Anthony [Eden] wound up for us and did so effectively – Bevin finished for the Government, speaking better than usual I thought ... I lunched at the House sitting between Oliver Stanley and Anthony – the former has been in the limelight this week – 4 speeches – all of them good – on a variety of subjects. He is more forthcoming with me recently – less sticky and more like old times – an odd creature whom one simply cannot get in touch with – otherwise quite charming.

Monday 15 December   Stanley Baldwin's death is announced. He died in his sleep – I should imagine what is called a merciful relief – for he was tired and old and unhappy. In the past I never knew whether I liked him or disliked him – and I am still quite uncertain in my mind about him. When I first knew him he seemed to me a simple, honest little man – and he was in those days before the

[20] Arthur Creech Jones (1891–1964), Lab. M.P. Shipley 1935–50, Wakefield 1954–64; P.P.S. to E. Bevin 1940–44; U.S. Colonies 1945–46; Colonial Sec. 1946–50; Nat. Sec., Transport & General Workers' Union 1919–29; Organising Sec., Workers' Travel Assoc. 1930–40.

[Lloyd George] Coalition came to an end. From then onwards I think that his character changed – he posed as still being the plain man – the man in the street – but he became something quite different. He was a very astute politician and a clever parliamentarian and at times an orator who could sway the HofC. He was not a really big man – and could never see ahead – 'peace in our time' at almost any price was his aim at home – and of foreigners and their affairs he knew nothing and cared less.

17

THE COLD WAR

January to July 1948

Saturday 3 January 1948   The news today is that (1) Winston is better (he has been laid up with a cold at Marrakesh for some days and as Lord Moran[1] and Mrs. Winston[2] are going there I should imagine that he must have been worse than was made out) and (2) there is one less in the Cabinet – Lord Listowel whose job as Secretary of State for Burma has come to an end is now made Minister of State for the Colonies without a seat in the Cabinet. I am told that he is a half-wit – but I don't even know him by sight and expect that a great many other people are in a similar position – Socialist peers are fairly inconspicuous persons. Several hotels have been searched for black market food – one dislikes black marketing and no doubt it is all wrong (as human nature generally is) but one dislikes still more the continual spying and police methods which now go on – shall we ever get back to 'normality' I wonder?

Wednesday 7 January   I had a word with Tony Lambton ... He certainly is doing his share of work nowadays and ought to make a fine leader for the Conservatives of Durham county in a few years' time. He is coming on by leaps and bounds – but I fear that he won't beat the dirty Doctor and will still be minus a seat in the next Parliament – sooner or later I suppose he will have to emulate Anthony Eden's example and find one outside his own county.

[1] Charles McMoran Wilson (1882–1977), medical career; Dean, St. Mary's Hospital Medical School 1920–45; Pres., Royal College of Physicians 1941–50; kt. 1938, cr. Baron Moran 1943; Churchill's personal doctor from 1939.
[2] Clementine Ogilvy Hozier (1885–1977), married 1908 Winston Churchill; Chairman, Red Cross Aid to Russia Fund 1939–46; cr. Baron Spencer-Churchill 1965.

Monday 12 January   The civil war continues in Greece and is clearly being kept going by Tito and co. no doubt on the orders of Moscow ... unless something is done before long to make the Bolshies understand that we do not intend to let them turn Turkey and Greece into Soviet republics they will continue to play 'cold war'[3] until such time as it seems good to them to make real war. It is a serious state of things – and all the time their 'Fifth Column' in this country is playing up their game for all it is worth – I see that the egregious Mr. Zilliacus made a speech in Newcastle yesterday or the day before in the course of which he said that Attlee in his broadcast the other day spoke like a governess correcting naughty children – I expect that this will be the attitude of other Labour M.P.s besides Zilliacus in the foreign affairs debate next week.

Tuesday 20 January   I lunched at the HofC – the same old faces, the same old food. Returning to the place after a recess is much like returning to school after the holidays – one feels fed up and bored, but one soon gets used again to the routine of the place. ... Winston is back – also Anthony – the former assured us all that he was feeling very well and he certainly looked very fit – the latter may not feel as pleased about this as the rest of us said we were – but perhaps this is rather a malicious suggestion for me to make. ... [after dinner] to White's where I saw James Stuart – he is going to the U.S.A. to recover after his illness.

Thursday 22 January   Today has been the first day of the Foreign Affairs debate. Bevin made a terribly long speech which as usual was read – and read very badly. Still it was a sound and well reasoned *résumé*[4] of his foreign policy and there was no mincing about what he said regarding the Russian conduct of affairs. He said nothing calculated to offend the Americans and he made it quite clear that we did not intend to allow the Bolshies to run Europe if we could help it. He stood for an economic and, if possible, a political union of western Europe. Anthony, who followed him, backed him up – Zilliacus did not, and made a clever, mischievous

---

[3] This is the first use of this term in the diary.
[4] translation: summary.

speech for Moscow which was received favourably by a section of the Comrades.

Friday 23 January   Winston made a first class speech today – one of the best I have heard him make I think, because there was nothing *outré*[5] or overdone in it – and it was as usual full of good stuff admirably put across.

Sunday 25 January   ... [Cripps's] brilliant powers of exposition – I know no one who can make things clearer to the average man than he can. How one wishes that he was not such a political crank – then indeed he might be of inestimable value to the country for he has a first class brain.

Monday 26 January   There really was no need to go to the House today as it was a 'Welsh day' which to the ordinary man is as dull as a 'Scottish day' – the only difference being that the Welsh men get more excited and talk quicker and less intelligibly than the Scots. Cripps made his statement about the devaluation of the franc – a very guarded one and he did not enlighten us much further. He clearly is much worried about the position, but professed to believe that there would be no reason for a devaluation of the £. Some people here who consider themselves currency experts seem to think that devaluation of the £ is inevitable.

Tuesday 27 January   A dull day in the House – requisitioning of land Bill in C[ommittee of the] W[hole] H[ouse] – a day out for Mr. Turton and Ralph Assheton – the former is a most hard-working and able man – but a little too serious – however, I always regard him as one of the most efficient younger members of the Party. In the HofL they began the second reading of the Parliament Bill and then adjourned until Monday in order to have discussions with the Government. What the purpose of such discussions is to be I don't know – because unless the Government are prepared to give way on the period of delay I cannot see how a compromise can be arrived at or what use it is discussing a change in the composition of the House. No second chamber can be of any good unless it has a reasonable power of delaying legislation – at least

[5] translation: excessive, bizarre.

so it seems to me. I am afraid that our people don't take the matter very seriously and are afraid of the silly, old cry of Peers v. People[6] – it is a sorry business and makes one despair of the Party.

Thursday 29 January   At the '22 Committee Anthony appeared and spoke rather sensibly about things in general – but somehow or other it seems to me (as an observer) that there is a growing lack of leadership or drive in the party and that the younger people are losing confidence – I can see no sign of any initiative among them – on the other hand, I think that the Government have pulled themselves together at last and are showing more leadership than before Christmas. Getting rid of Dalton has been a Godsend for them – for Cripps is an entirely different type and has the courage of his convictions and is not always trying to placate the various sections of the Comrades as Dalton was – he does not court popularity all the time.

Monday 2 February   I rather like Darling[7] – an ex Lord Provost of Edinburgh and rather a character – also rather a poseur who plays the funny man rather well, but who is really a very able politician – a sound, old-fashioned Tory.

Tuesday 3 February   I heard from Temple and Scanlan today – but neither of them mention anything about the meeting[8] – really they are quite intolerable – and apparently there is to be a big Association party tomorrow to which Beatrice and I have not been invited! It is difficult to know how to proceed with Temple & Co. – clearly he is doing all he can to dig himself in and no one appears to mind – it is an odd constituency if ever there was one. But if you have the chairman and agent working together against the member, backed up by a packed executive, it is difficult to see what

[6] The slogan used effectively by the Liberals in the general elections of Jan. and Dec. 1910.

[7] William Young Darling (1885–1962), Con. M.P. Edinburgh S. 1945–57; Treasurer, Edinburgh City Council 1937–40, Ld. Provost 1941–44; Comm. for Civil Defence, S.E. Scotland 1939–41; Chairman, Scottish Council of Industry 1941–46; kt. 1943.

[8] Of the chairmen of the Newcastle constituencies to discuss the scheme for a city-wide federation; Temple, the only chairman now opposed to the proposal, had failed to attend the previous meeting (which Headlam had chaired): diary, 16 Jan. 1948.

the M.P. can do – except to sit tight – and this is what I propose to do. Sooner or later I hope that there will be a revolt in the Association against the autocracy of Temple.

Sunday 8 February   Cripps made a speech in Edinburgh yesterday – painted everything as black as he could (quite right and proper to do so) and said that unless people buckled to and worked and did not keep asking for higher wages, there would be nothing for it but some form of totalitarian State – what exactly he meant by this I can't say, but it was rather an odd expression to use unless he is prepared to compel people to work which would be a rather difficult thing to do. He also seized the opportunity to attack the doctors for not falling in with Bevan's plans – Grant Waugh[9] told us that he was now pretty confident that the doctors would not give way – I only hope that this may be the case for they are fighting the battle for freedom for all of us.

Thursday 12 February   ... to the HofC, where the 2nd reading debate of the Gas Bill continued. We divided against it – I did not listen to much of the debate, but I heard Herbert Morrison's closing speech which was in his customary flippant and would-be jovial style which pleases his supporters but is hardly worthy of a Leader of the House. Winston turned up at the '22 Committee this afternoon and spoke strongly against our moving an amendment to the Representation of the People Bill marking our disapproval of the universities being disfranchised and the City of London representation being taken away. He had Woolton to support him – their argument was that we should do nothing to give the Government an opportunity of withdrawing the Bill which would give us more seats – and that we could give back the seats to the universities when we return to power. Personally I don't believe that we should do that – but Winston pledged himself to the task. In the circumstances those who wished to move an amendment

[9] William Grant Waugh (1887–1960), medical practitioner, qualified 1910, Fellow of Royal College of Surgeons, Edinburgh 1924; practised in Sunderland from 1910; war service, Colonel, Royal Army Medical Corps; assistant surgeon Sunderland Royal Infirmiary 1924–46, consultant surgeon from 1946; President, Northern Counties Medical Society, 1939; specialised as an orthopaedic surgeon, pioneered treatment of arthritic joints with lactic acid; he had an extensive practice in the north-east and in Harley Street, and was consulted by Cuthbert and Beatrice for many years.

gave way – they could not very well do otherwise, when Winston said that he would stay away from the House if an amendment were on the order paper. I was less impressed than ever by Woolton.

Friday 13 February I spent the morning and early afternoon at the HofC. I wrote a good many letters and talked to a few people, mainly about Winston's performance yesterday – which most people think was well done. I am never much of a believer in 'tactics', but I don't fancy that we should have done ourselves much good by moving the rejection of the Bill.

Monday 16 February ... the 2nd reading debate on the redistribution bill ... Winston spoke first for us and personally I did not think much of his effort – but it stirred up the Socialists and this no doubt was what its author intended to do. Chuter Ede who opened the debate was very poor and his defence for doing away with the University seats and the City of London representation was feeble in the extreme. The proceedings today were opened by the presence at the bar of the Sheriffs of London who came in full state to present a petition from the City Council against the loss of the London seats – it was an unusual ceremony and well performed. ... There was no gossip at the House except that it looks as if we might lose the North Croydon seat at the coming by-election. The Liberals are putting up Air Vice-Marshal Bennett[10] who is said to be a strong candidate who may get a lot of votes in which case Harold Nicolson (the Socialist![11]) may get in – our candidate is said to be not good enough.

Tuesday 17 February ... went with a delegation of M.P.s to the Ministry of Health where we interviewed A. Bevan about some grievances our local authorities had against the Local Govt. Bill.

---

[10] Donald Clifford Tyndall Bennett (1910–1986), career in Royal Australian Air Force and R.A.F.; Commander of Pathfinder Force, Bomber Command 1942–45; Lib. M.P. Middlesbrough W. May–July 1945, Lib. cand. Croydon N. 1948, Norwich N. 1950, Ind. cand. Nuneaton 1967; Managing-Dir., British South American Airways Corporation 1946–48; Chairman of Exec. Ctte., United Nations Assoc. of Great Britain 1946–49; Chairman, Nat. Council of Anti-Common Market Organisations 1973–76.

[11] Nicolson (q.v.), a National Labour M.P. from 1935 until his defeat as a Nat. candidate in 1945, joined the Labour Party in 1947 and was chosen as Lab. candidate for the Croydon N. by-election.

Mr. Wilkes[12] was the only other M.P. from Newcastle – apparently Newcastle had no grievance at all and Mr. Wilkes and I looked rather silly. I was struck more than ever by the quickness and ability of Bevan who completely knocked out all his opponents – a pity it is that he is not a better type of man and on the 'Right' side.

Wednesday 18 February   The Local Government Bill was the bill of fare today – re-committal stage – the agricultural and other local government experts on our side were busy. The doctors' vote[13] has resulted in an overwhelming division not to accept the proposals of the present Act – nevertheless the Government are determined to bring the Act into force just the same – presumably some compromise will be arrived at. The obvious course would be to drop Bevan if he remains intransigent, but I gather that Attlee and co. are frightened of doing that as Bevan might become a terrible nuisance to them if he left the Cabinet and took the lead among the left wingers. My fear is that there will be a break-away among the doctors when the issue has really to be faced – meanwhile Colonel Perón[14] has decided to take over the Falkland Islands and Chile some other islands over which the British flag flies, and the Argentine Fleet is being sent to the Falklands! Ye Gods! what are we coming to?

Thursday 19 February   ... spent the remainder of the day at the House – at dinner tonight William Scott made a violent attack on Winston whom it seems he has no use for. In his opinion so long as Winston remains leader there is no hope of a Tory revival – I rather share this opinion, but I lay low tonight – so did Walter Elliot who was next to me. It never does to express one's opinions too strongly, especially when there is nothing to be done. The Tory Party cannot give Winston his *congé*,[15] especially at a time when

---

[12] Lyall Wilkes (1914–1991), Lab. M.P. Newcastle Central 1945–51; Ass. Recorder of Sheffield & Newcastle 1960–62; Dep. Chairman, Co. Durham Quarter Sessions 1961–64; Judge of the County Courts 1964–82.

[13] The British Medical Association's ballot of its members on Bevan's National Health Service proposals, and in particular the question of state control.

[14] Juan Domingo Perón (1895–1974), Argentine army career; one of the Group of United Officers who seized power in June 1943; Min. of Labour & Social Security 1943–46; Pres. 1946–55, 1973–74; in exile 1955–73.

[15] translation: notice of dismissal.

he is the only really 'big noise' it possesses. The only way of getting rid of Winston is for him to retire of his own accord and this he will never do. The mistake was ever to make him leader and at the time when Neville died it was almost impossible not to do so – he had to be invited to become leader and he with the experience of what happened to L.G. in his mind naturally jumped at the chance of leading a party.

Tuesday 24 February   The 3rd reading of the Local Government Bill today – we voted against it – rather foolish of us I think as on the whole the Bill is not too bad, even though it does help the ratepayer at the expense of the taxpayer and is a direct incentive to progressive local authorities to spend more and more money! – with a Socialist Govt. in power a measure of this kind was inevitable and this one might have been worse – but once it is law we are not likely to repeal it, so why vote against it? The Communists are wining in Czecho[slovakia] ... The Soviet dictators are certainly playing their game extraordinarily successfully – and no wonder – we are entirely powerless – and the Americans are not going to take a strong line – they are no more anxious for war than we are. The Russians know this well enough and just carry on as they like – short of atomic bombs they won't stop – everybody knows this well enough, but no one is prepared to use atomic bombs – the Russians may not be so squeamish when they get hold of them.

Wednesday 25 February   In the House this afternoon we had the second reading of the River Boards Bill from the Lords. Tommie Dugdale led off for us and made a good speech – he read all of it, but did his reading very well. He is a popular little man and will no doubt be rewarded with a job if and when we get in again. He is the recognized type of Conservative members who proceed as of course to jobs of one kind or another – an excellent type – sound, practical, agreeable men who often make good administrators and colonial governors.

Monday 1 March   ... a debate on the Government's White Paper on Defence – a terribly feeble document and a very feeble speech by Alexander in defence of it – it is absurd that such a man should be our Minister of Defence. Attlee who wound up for the Government was equally feeble. We are spending 700 millions on our defence forces and have no navy, air force or army – it is a terrible state of things. Anthony Eden made a good speech for us and so did Head[16] who closed the debate on our side.

Wednesday 3 March   There was a debate today on the subject of questions in Parliament. There is a growing habit of Ministers to refuse to answer questions dealing with the administration of the various boards and corporations which run the nationalized industries – up to a point this is reasonable, though it illustrates the snares which nationalization causes and the dangers that it may lead to, but the complaint we make is that the [clerks'] Table is declining more and more to accept questions as 'out of order' because Ministers will refuse to answer them – our contention is that questions ought not to be quashed in this way, but that Ministers should be left to say whether or not they will answer them in the House. The debate was interesting – Harry Crookshank put our case admirably and he was reinforced by John Anderson in his ponderous, official way. Herbert Morrison who would up for the Government was flippant and futile – his parliamentary style seems to me to get worse and worse every time he speaks. He is always trying to score cheap points and plays up to his Party all the time.

Friday 5 March   I went to the House this morning: the report and 3rd reading of the National Assistance Bill – a measure which I have not even looked at I am afraid. It apparently finds favour with all parties in the House and I suppose, therefore, that it is one of the 'humanitarian' measures which are so fashionable nowadays – designed to improve the lot of the people, but calculated to make them less and less responsible for their own welfare and self-preservation – no people which is a 'kept people' can for long remain a great nation – such I believe to be the teaching of history – when national self-confidence declines it is generally due to spoon-feeding.

Tuesday 9 March   ... the debate on the Army estimates – I ought

---

[16] Antony Henry Head (1906–1981), Con. M.P. Carshalton 1945–60; Sec. for War 1951–56; Defence Sec. 1956–57; High Comm. Nigeria 1960–63, Malaysia 1963–66; Chairman, Royal Nat. Institute for the Blind 1968–75; cr. Viscount Head 1960.

to have spoken, but did not feel up to the effort. Shinwell, I thought, made a pitiable speech. Edward Winterton 'led' for us – he was, I thought, better than usual. I wish that I possessed his supreme confidence in himself and complete indifference to what people think of him in the HofC – it enables him to play a part in the House to which neither his abilities nor his manners entitles him. I did not listen to much of the debate. My own view is that the Army can never be satisfactorily remodelled on the lines proposed by the Government – a Territorial Army cannot be a success when it [is] half volunteer, half conscripted – nor will the conscripted men be really well trained and disciplined with only 12 months' training.

Wednesday 10 March　　Today in the House we had a debate on the 2d of the Palestine Bill – a measure which is apparently necessary to give a legal covering to our surrender of the Mandate and handing over the country to U[nited] N[ations] O[rganization]. Creech Jones, the Colonial Secretary, read (very badly) a long dreary speech explaining the Bill – and Rab Butler (as Oliver Stanley is still absent) led for us. He agreed that the surrender of the Mandate is our only possible course of action in the circumstances. Everybody appeared to be of the same opinion – and except for some left wing people mainly of the Zionist persuasion, there was no serious objection to the Bill. We surrender the Mandate on the 15th of May and hope to get out our troops and belongings by the beginning of August – after 15th May we are no longer responsible for law and order, and only God knows what the mess will be like – one can only hope that all our military measures have been carefully taken.

Thursday 11 March　　This afternoon in the House I attended an All Party Committee formed to support a speedy formation of a Council for Western Europe to produce a scheme of social, economic and defence union – apparently this organization is already being considered on the Continent and is approved by Winston in the background: it is not as yet looked on with favour by the Govt. and Socialists have been urged not to join the All Party Committee. However a good many of them have done so and our game obviously is to keep in touch with the business – we discussed this afternoon a resolution in support of the scheme which is to be put on the order paper. The resolution had already been drafted by a sub-committee and was passed after about 2 hours' discussion usefully amended I think. It will be interesting to see what results it brings forth – needless to say, a good many 'pushers' are behind it and I doubt whether I shall have much part or lot in the business, but I have put my signature to the resolution.

Friday 12 March   The North Croydon election result is very cheering – our man in by nearly 11,000 votes over Harold Nicolson, the 'Socialist' candidate, and the Liberal (the man Bennett, Air Vice Marshal, 'the Pathfinder') forfeits his deposit. The poll was considerably higher than at the general election. It is a highly important election result because it does really show a return to sanity – Harry Willink[17] only held the seat by 800 votes in 1945 – of course N. Croydon is a Tory seat in ordinary circumstances – nevertheless, the enemy when this election began fully intended winning it and has spared no effort in the fight – our candidate they tell me did wonderfully well and he claims to have won on Rab Butler's 'Social Charter'[18] – which is satisfactory if his assertion is true, but I doubt it very much. I went to the House this morning and did a little 'sitting on the [Front] Bench' to please the Whips – I was the only P[rivy] C[ouncillor] present bar Oliver Lyttelton and he, having fired off a speech on the 2d of the Government's Bill for subsidizing cotton firms which group themselves, left the Chamber. The Bill it seems is welcome to everybody so scarcely anybody attended to give it a welcome.

Saturday 13 March   Apparently our 'resolution' *re.* 'European Federation' has already been put on the order paper with 71 signatures attached. It has attracted a certain amount of attention in today's press, mainly favourable – no doubt the 'long term' policy will be criticized in some quarters as a betrayal of national sovereignty, etc., and a break-up of Empire Union etc. Personally I feel that the policy is so unlikely of ever being agreed to by all concerned that it is scarcely worth fussing about one way or the other – but that if it could be brought into fruition, it would be highly desirable and would not in any way weaken the strength of

[17] Henry Willink (q.v.).
[18] i.e., the *Industrial Charter*.

the Commonwealth. Anthony Eden has been operated on for appendicitis and is reported to be going on very well. I wonder which of his colleagues will act as deputy leader in his place – a bit of a scramble I should imagine!

Monday 15 March   Beatrice dropped me at the HofC and I have been there all day – Service Estimates: not exciting – but the new system of taking the report stage of all 3 services on one day is absurd and gives no real opportunity of thorough or even semi-thorough consideration of the various Votes. Oliver Stanley after his operation and Rob Hudson after his South African trip have returned to the fold – both looking 'in the pink' and busy making themselves amiable to the rank and file. They are both assets to the Party in their respective ways – but I don't see either of them as 'the Leader'. There has been a strike here today of the boiler stokers, maintenance men and lift men, and as a result we have had no heating or hot water or lifts running – mercifully it has not been a cold day though considerably colder than yesterday. I am told that the men have a good case having been claiming higher wages for a considerable time and that the Treasury has been haggling with them unduly – but of course it is the usual wage increase demand which is going on all round despite the Government's exhortations. Attlee made a statement in the House telling us that the Government was going to keep Communists out of certain posts in the Civil Service – how they can succeed in doing this I fail to see, so long as Communists are allowed to be civil servants.

Friday 19 March   I went to the House this morning where the last stage of the Palestine Bill was under discussion – a lot of talk and progress was slow – mainly attacks on the Government by their Jewish supporters. On the whole I found myself agreeing with Silverman[19] & Co. – for it seems to me a rotten business for us to clear out of Palestine in the way we are doing. This Government is gravely to blame for the mess we find ourselves in – for, having promised Palestine to the Jews before the general election, they have gone back on their promise and wasted two and a half years

---

[19] Samuel Sydney Silverman (1895–1968), Lab. M.P. Nelson & Colne 1935–1968 (whip withdrawn 1954–55, 1961–63); member of N.E.C. 1956–57.

muddling about quite unable to make up their own minds what to do – now they have decided to clear out of the country lock, stock and barrel – on a specified date whether or not there is any form of government to take our place. It is in my opinion a pitiable display of incompetence, cowardice and callous indifference to the consequences wholly unworthy of our nation. The pitiable performance of Creech Jones, the Colonial Secretary, was lamentable.

Thursday 25 March   We have not won the Brigg by-election – the Socialist is in by about 4,000 votes – this is a reduction of majority, but not one, in my opinion, worth making a fuss about – our people are voting better, but Labour's followers are still faithful to 'the Movement'. How we are to break the industrial vote I cannot imagine – despite all the pundits of the Rab [Butler], Harold Macmillan type, I don't believe that the 'Industrial Charter' will do the trick – we cannot offer the people (so-called working classes) any form of policy which will be a greater bribe than the Socialists are giving to them – nothing but clear proof that Socialism must cause a national collapse will convince the ignorant voter that its gospel is fallacious – only hunger and unemployment will get rid of our present rulers – it is a depressing view of the situation, but I am sure it is a correct one.

Friday 2 April   The Russians are continuing to tighten the control on traffic between Berlin and the West – our reply it appears is to suspend all rail services between [Berlin and] the British and American zones and to start air services instead. It is a sorry mess and our position is a truly humiliating one – how in the world this situation can continue without real trouble I can't see – surely the time has come for a show-up of some kind? – an ultimatum in other words.

Saturday 3 April   The news in today's papers from Berlin shows no sign of improvement and one does not know [what] to think about it. It is hard to believe that the Russians intend to go to war – and yet how can one make out what they are up to otherwise?

The Marshall Plan[20] is through, but what real good it is going to do us I don't know – it cannot get us out of our mess unless we really put our backs into the production drive and give a chance to keen men to make money – so long as we submit to the dictation of the trade unions and kow-tow to 'organized labour' we simply cannot carry on.

Monday 5 April　There is said to be an 'easier atmosphere' in Berlin but what this amounts to it is hard to say ... I don't see how matters can go on like this without leading to serious trouble before long – a series of 'incidents' must end in disaster one day or the other ... and so, without either side wanting war, we may find ourselves at war – some people, indeed, assert that Stalin & Co. mean war and are only deterred from starting war because they are frightened of the atom bomb. There may be some truth in this, but my opinion is that they (S. and Co.) are just seeing how much they can get without war and will back down if we stand up to them. The Foreign Aid Bill was signed by President Truman yesterday – so the Marshall Plan will come into operation and the economic situation will be eased for Messrs. Attlee & Co.

Wednesday 7 April　*The Times* describes Cripps's Budget as a 'brave one' – perhaps it is – but I cannot quite make out why. It certainly faces 'hard facts' more squarely than was the habit of the 'dirty Doctor' in his Budgets – but the continual raising of taxation from the rich continues and the beginning of a Capital Levy seems to me quite unjustifiable. Cripps describes it as a once-for-all exaction – but one knows what this means – and the 'dirty Doctor' and the Comrades generally are already asking for more. ... it will mean selling out investments for almost all concerned as few people can pay the additional levy out of income. Certainly it is a bad epoch to live in for those who have inherited, or earned and saved, enough to keep them in their old age.

Friday 9 April　I went to the HofC this morning ... The general feeling among our people is that the capital levy part of the Budget

---

[20] Proposed by Gen. George C. Marshall, U.S. Sec. of State 1947–49, the European Recovery Programme provided American financial aid to stimulate economic revival and co-operation; Russia and its satellite states rejected participation in the scheme.

is monstrously unjust and City people tell me that it will have a staggering effect upon investments – the markets are already reacting badly and Government securities are dropping – but I don't pretend to understand what this means – my experience is that big drops are usually very temporary affairs – and that City prophecies are usually wrong.

Monday 12 April   The debate on the Budget continued today. I listened to an oration by Oliver Lyttelton and part of a reply to it by Wilson, the President of the B[oard] of T[rade] – but I cannot say that I was greatly impressed by either of them – both were dull – and the debate was unimpressive. ... The Russians are now barring our route to Vienna and the murdering of Arabs by Jews and Jews by Arabs continues. Creech Jones in the House was more helpless and hopeless than ever about what is going on – a hot, and slightly incoherent man who always cuts a poor figure 'at the Box'.[21] A 'private letter' from Jim Thomas[22] to me today asking whether I intended to retire at the end of this Parliament, as my seat might suit Walter Elliot – this gives one to think!

Wednesday 14 April   The HofC (free vote) decided tonight to put the death penalty for murder into cold storage for 5 years which presumably will mean the abolition of capital punishment in English law. The Home Secretary and the Cabinet advised the House that in their opinion this was not the moment to make the experiment – the police and the judges are said to be against the change – but the Comrades as a body were not convinced. Human life is sacred, hanging is no deterrent to murder, other countries have abolished it without any increase of murder – why should not we? All very plausible – all very noble-minded – but what does all the fuss amount to? Chuter Ede gave us figures to show that about 11 or 12 people are hanged every year – that a majority of murder cases are reprieved – that the chance of a miscarriage of justice is very slight (much had been made in the debate of an innocent man being sent to the Gallows) – that not only was there the High Court trial, but there was also the Court of Criminal Appeal and

---

[21] The Despatch Boxes sit on the table between the two front benches and have become the customary place for Ministers or Opposition front-bench spokesmen to stand when delivering a speech, as they provide a convenient resting place for notes.
[22] The Vice-Chairman of the Party responsible for candidates.

the HofL, and finally the Home Secretary's decision. We are asked therefore to do away with capital punishment against the advice of responsible authority at a time when criminal violence is on the increase ... The speeches today were good, bad and indifferent – and each speaker in turn congratulated the one who spoke before him on his high morality and sincerity. There was a deal of sob stuff which depressed me as it always does.

Thursday 15 April ... I fear that my age is against me – if the G[eneral] E[lection] does not come until 1950, I shall be rising 75 or thereabouts and everyone will consider me too old for the job – there may well be unpleasantness about in N. Newcastle when one remembers all the little people who are after the seat and who want to get rid of me. Well, we will see what Beatrice has to say about it, and Galloway – if only I were better off and would not miss the money so badly and my free trips to London, I don't really think that I want to stay on in the HofC – I only wish that I had taken the chance of going to the HofL when it was offered me, but at the time it was not possible. ... The division last night is the subject of discussion today – apparently 40 Ministers of one kind and another did not vote or absented themselves – 14 Conservatives voted with the majority, but only 140 odd were present. If I were Chuter Ede, I think that I should be inclined to resign – but I don't fancy that this will be his decision – nevertheless it is a funny Government which offers advice to the House and then does not support whole-heartedly its point of view, even if it allows a free vote for the rank and file of its followers.

Friday 16 April Galloway came here [Holywell] to luncheon and we discussed the North Newcastle business. He is, I think, all for me but he fears (as I fear) that if I want to stand again in 2 years' time a cry will be engineered against me on the score of age – not openly by Temple, but either engineered by him or his competitors for the seat. I should hate this – and so perhaps the best course is to make up my mind to retire and do all I can to get the seat for Walter Elliot if he wants it – I don't want it to go to a rotten Town Councillor type of candidate. Young Tony Lambton came here this afternoon on his way to a meeting at B[isho]p Auckland. He was friendly and communicative – he clearly knew all about the intriguing in N. Newcastle against me and was most indignant and sympathetic.

Saturday 17 April   Rosalie Bloxam lunched here ... She told us that the wards from the West [division] which are to join the North are dead against Temple, and she thinks when there are so many locals in the field eager for the seat an outstanding outsider would be generally acceptable – she even mentioned Walter Elliot's name. Her view appears to be the same as ours. The question now is how to deal with the situation for Temple will fight hard I expect and may get the North to support him, if he is given time – I fancy that I had better leave the matter to Thomas and Galloway.

Sunday 18 April   We went over to Wynyard this afternoon and 'took tea' with the Castlereagh[23] family. Robin looks fit and well – he has entirely given up drinking and seems far more alive – she[24] has grown to look a deal older, thin and haggard. ... Robin says that his father is done for – that the doctors tell him that the poor man will never be able to speak again or think consecutively – though physically he may last for some time to come. It is a terribly sad business and I can imagine no worse end for any man – Robin consoles himself by believing that his father is really happier as he is than he was before his breakdown, because he worried and repined so dreadfully – there may be something in this though it is not easy to understand.

Monday 19 April   The matter of the telegram[25] sent by some of the left wing Comrades was again raised today – and the pushing, little right wing Comrade, Captain Blackburn, proposed that this affair should be referred to a Select Committee of the House. Personally it seems to me that this is a matter of party discipline and no concern of the House – if a number of Members decide to support the Socialists in Italy who ally themselves with the Communists and send them a telegram to that effect, and then quarrel among themselves as to who did or did not sign the

[23] The eldest son and heir of the Marquess of Londonderry was known by the courtesy title of Viscount Castlereagh.
[24] Romaine Combe (1906–1951), married 1931 Viscount Castlereagh, suc. 8th Marquess of Londonderry 1949.
[25] The 'Nenni telegram'; see entry for 23 Apr., below.

telegram, it is their business not ours. Anthony [Eden], who was back in the House for the first time since his operation, reserved our view on the matter which is being 'handled' by Herbert Morrison – he clearly is getting tired of his left-wingers.

Wednesday 21 April   I dined with James Willoughby de Eresby[26] at the Turf Club ... I am very fond of James who is one of the simplest, unspoilt men in the House. He is also a good critic of the rest of us – more critical than one would have expected. He has little use for a good many of our rising men, but I was surprised to find that he was no admirer of James Stuart – he does not think much of him as Chief Whip – and in this of course I agree with him, though I infinitely prefer him as such to Bobbie Monsell and David Margesson – James says that he is so rude to people and loses his temper so badly – this is a side of J.S. which I have never seen.

Thursday 22 April   I had a talk with Anthony Eden this afternoon and told him about North Newcastle. He saw no reason why I should be in any hurry to make a decision. He seemed pleased that I was going to The Hague and agreed with me that a defence scheme should be the first step in any scheme for Western European Union. He does not appear to be so nervous about the Russian menace as I am – but this may be because he has had more experience of the Soviet leaders than I have. He cannot believe that they want war – about this I am by no means certain.

Friday 23 April   The row in the Labour Party about the Nenni telegram[27] continues and trouble is also being raised about the M.P.s who are going to The Hague to the conference against the wishes of the Government. The idea that a federation of Europe must be founded on Socialism is really too absurd to be taken

---

[26] Gilbert James Heathcote-Drummond-Willoughby (1907–1983), Con. M.P. Rutland & Stamford 1933–50; Ld. Great Chamberlain 1950–52; Ld. Lt., Lincolnshire 1950–75; styled Lord Willoughby de Eresby 1907–51, summoned to the Lords as Baron Willoughby de Eresby Jan. 1951, suc. 3rd Earl of Ancaster Sep. 1951.

[27] Twenty-two left-wing Lab. M.P.s had signed a telegram of support sent to Pietro Nenni, the leader of the pro-Communist group of Socialists contesting the Italian election. The N.E.C. demanded an apology and promise of future conformity, which most of the M.P.s involved gave; the N.E.C. meeting on 23 Apr. 1948 also expelled from the party the left-wing M.P. John Platts-Mills (q.v.).

seriously – if really such is the intention of the Government, the scheme is doomed to failure *ab initio*.[28] Their only reason for boycotting this conference at The Hague is because Winston will be the leading figure there – it is too mean and petty a bit of work to be credible – and yet it is typical of the attitude of mind of our present rulers.

Monday 26 April   Today has been perfect for the Royal Silver Wedding show ... Certainly the King and Queen have done their job admirably and the Monarchy stands as firmly as ever it did – indeed, perhaps it is firmer today as a consequence of Socialist rule – for it does offer a little glamour and show in a very drab and dreary state of things. In the Chamber today we went on with the Committee stage of the Representation of the People Bill. I looked in now and then for a few minutes at a time, but found the proceedings exceedingly boring – one M.P. after another getting up and asking for something for his own constituency – something which would improve the chances of his party to retain it by extending or reducing its boundaries – I am glad that I had not to bother about North Newcastle. We are urging that eight new constituencies should be made in the Home Counties – I don't suppose we have much chance of getting them – but the matter is to be referred to the Boundaries Commission.

Tuesday 27 April   I am 72 years old today and presumably my race is nearly run ... no doubt in theory the mass of the people in this country are better off than they used to be, and it may be that they are more healthy – but to me it seems they have lost much of their moral strength and mental balance, and I very much fear that they will find themselves up against it before long. This country is too overcrowded and too spoilt to put up with a lower standard of living – and its people are too lazy to work hard. The competition all over the world is going to be severer than it has ever been before ...

Wednesday 28 April   I had luncheon with Walter Elliot at the House today and discussed N. Newcastle frankly with him. He clearly would like to have the seat but is not 'interested' in it if I

[28] translation: from the start.

want to stay on. We left the matter open for the time being, at any rate until after the Redistribution Bill becomes law. The more I think over it all the less attractive is the idea of fighting another election, especially with a prospect of a battle with Temple & Co. probably in store for me, in which this time I might not be so successful as I was in 1945. If it were not for the money and a free ticket to London, I don't think that I should hesitate for two minutes – would that we were not so desperately hard up! – a Scottish day in the Chamber – so I, like a good many other people, left early.

Thursday 29 April   The Comrades are all very busy chattering excitedly in the Smoking Room about their private quarrels – the Central Executive of the [Labour] Party has decided to expel the man Platts-Mills,[29] and the others who signed the Nenni telegram are given a week in which to write and apologize or they too will be turned out into the wilderness. I don't suppose that we have heard the last of all of this – but I doubt whether the Labour Party is 'disintegrating' as some optimistic Tory M.P.s are prophesying.

Friday 30 April   At 5 o'clock we had our federation [of the Newcastle seats] meeting. Temple was present – as odious as ever – and he won the battle easily – all the others ratted – the only thing we got out of the proceedings was that the 4 divisional chairmen and candidates should hold a monthly meeting and work together. I am afraid that this won't mean much, but it is a step in the right direction – nothing sensible or effective can be done in Newcastle so long as Temple & Co. continue to run the show – but they will all do so unless we can bring about a central authority.

Headlam was unwell during May and the diary is blank from 2 May to 19 June, when he returned to London after spending two weeks in the Channel Islands as the guest of the Dame of Sark.[30]

---

[29] John Faithful Fortescue Platts-Mills (1906-), Lab. M.P. Finsbury 1945–50 (Ind. Lab. 1948–50); expelled from Lab. Party Apr. 1948, member of Lab. Ind. Group 1949–50.

[30] The reason for this visit was the marriage of the Dame's daughter, Jehanne, to Headlam's former secretary and agent, Harry Bell (Henry Parkin Bell, q.v.), who had lived with the Headlams at Holywell since 1925. He served in a staff post in the Home Guard at York 1942–45 and was then employed as secretary to Lord Ridley's Northern Industrial Group; he was currently jointly managing the pig-farming venture at Holywell with Beatrice.

Monday 21 June　　Lunched at the Travellers and then went to the HofC – the policemen and the attendants were glad to see me back again and most sympathetic about the cause of my absence – few if any of my colleagues seem to have noticed my absence – indeed, I think that Anthony Eden was the only one of them who asked me if I was all right again. Well, one cannot expect people to notice one's absence if one never makes oneself conspicuous, and when all is said and done I have few friends in the HofC nowadays. The time has come for me to say goodbye to the place and to sink into obscurity – I should not hesitate for a moment to flit if only it was not for my impecuniosity – but even so I think that I ought not to stand again. ... The Report stage of the Finance Bill was the day's business and I recorded a few votes against the Government. They tell me that things have been very dull recently and that I have not missed much.

Tuesday 22 June　　In the House we went on with the report stage of the Finance Bill – our side was run by Oliver Stanley, Harry Crookshank and Osbert Peake. Everyone is much concerned about the position in Berlin which is very delicate. The Russians seem determined to make us clear out – and, if they mean to do so, it is difficult to see how we can stay there – apparently, in addition to being able to cut our communications, they control the gas and electricity supply of the city, its water supply and sewage system. It is a pretty mess – how we can ever [have] agreed to allowing the Russians to come west of Berlin I cannot imagine. Harold Macmillan told me that he was ready to take a bet that we should be at war by December or should have a million unemployed – he is inclined to talk in this way – but certainly things are in a bad way – and this dock strike in London is a serious matter, which the Government is not attempting to tackle properly.

Wednesday 23 June　　The strike continues – the P.M. made rather a feeble little statement about the situation assuring us that steps were being taken to ensure food supplies etc. – Isaacs, the Minister of Labour, is still in the U.S.A. The union leaders are being howled down by the strikers and only a few men have gone back to work. The complete failure of the accredited leaders to control their men, which is becoming more and more obvious in each successive strike, is a very alarming sign of the times – this strike is being run by the

Communists whose power is increasing all the time. The wretched Government realize this well enough, but have not the courage to act with vigour. We had the 3rd reading of the Representation of the People Bill today – I heard Chuter Ede make a wearisome little speech, but just as Winston got up Miss Wilson of Newcastle turned up and I did not hear him – they say that he was very amusing ... I could not get her into the House which I am afraid was a great disappointment for her – really the difficulty of getting anyone into the Chamber nowadays is almost intolerable. The queue for admittance gets longer and longer – people were still waiting – crowds of them – when I left the House at 10 p.m.

Tuesday 29 June   I had a word with Walter Elliot today – he says that he would 'definitely' like to succeed me in North Newcastle – I again emphasized the difficulty of arranging the business – and also said that I was still undecided whether or not to stand again – but the more I think of it, the less inclined I am ...

Wednesday 30 June   There was a debate on Germany in the Chamber this afternoon – I listened to Bevin who spoke well I thought – he certainly was pretty definite about the Berlin business. We and the Americans and the French intend to remain in Berlin – for the time being we are feeding the population by air – but how we can continue doing this for long, and how we can send coal by air, remain to be seen.

Thursday 1 July   ... I attended the '22' Committee and another special party committee presided over by Anthony Eden to consider our attitude towards the E[uropean] R[ecovery] P[rogramme] debate next week. Oliver Stanley began by setting out the pros and cons - he did this very ably – it is the sort of thing in which he excels – his advice was to accept the Marshall Plan agreement, but to attack the Govt. for its extravagance and bad use of the original American loan – this policy was generally accepted – I think rightly. To oppose the agreement would be misinterpreted by the Americans and the electorate here – and the acceptance of the agreement does give us a fresh chance of recovery, if only it does not have the effect of making our people less inclined than ever to do any work.

Saturday 3 July   There is nothing new in the papers, but I feel that we are living on the edge of a volcano and that any day there may be some new incident which may lead to a situation of the utmost gravity – we are living under the sword of Damocles.

Sunday 4 July   ... the Berlin business remains as it was – no sign of any Russian change of attitude ... that the Russians mean war sooner or later is quite probable – but that they will start it so soon is another matter – the answer would be, I suppose, that they are mobilized to all intents and purposes and nobody else is – that they could get to the English Channel in a very short time – and so control the continent of Europe – but everyone seems convinced that they have not got the atom bomb, and surely they won't risk war until they have it? Well – it is never safe to prophesy in matters which are controlled by dictators – where prestige is at stake they may have no alternative but foreign war and to them it matters very little how many Russian citizens may be destroyed – Stalin & Co. may well be in difficulties behind the 'Iron Curtain'.[31]

Monday 5 July   Galloway turned up for dinner tonight. He is as ebullient as ever – full of energy and vim – but I am glad to say quite conscious that the North is not in the least inclined to turn away from 'Labour'. We discussed North Newcastle and he is as much at sea as to the best way of tackling the problem of succession as I am ...

Tuesday 6 July   Today was the second day of the Marshall Plan debate. Yesterday's debate they tell me was very dull – Cripps's speech a mere lecture and recapitulation of facts which everybody knew. Today's debate was not very different – Oliver Stanley and Oliver Lyttelton spoke for us. The former's speech I heard – it was clever and witty – O.L.'s effort I did not hear – but it does not seem to have been anything to gush about – he is not, and never will be, a successful performer in the HofC, but I suppose he will be a Cabinet Minister again if we come back to power. It is odd that these 2 men (O.S. and O.L.) who used to profess such friendship for me, neither of them ever evinces the slightest wish to speak to me, or the slightest interest in me – both of them are entirely self-

[31] The first use of this term in the diary.

centred and each of them is terrified that I may ask something of them.

Wednesday 7 July   Much ado in the House today on 2d of [the] British Nationality Bill from our side – apparently it turns us into 'British citizens' – or rather into 'citizens of the U.K.' – and the expression 'British subject' as applying to all the subjects of the Crown ceases to count for much. I confess that I dislike the word 'citizen' – but one has to get used to it nowadays, and if the Dominions wish to have their 'citizens', by all means let them have them. However I must admit that I did not listen to David Maxwell Fyfe setting forth all his grand objections to the Bill – I find him, as I think I have said before in these pages, somewhat ponderous to listen to, but must admit that he invariably knows his subject and presents sound arguments – he is a more formidable opponent, I should imagine, in a legal debate than James Reid who, it seems to me, is not gaining ground.

Friday 9 July   In the morning at the House I had a talk with Tommie Dugdale about men and things (I don't know whether he is pleased that Patrick Buchan-Hepburn[32] has been made our Chief Whip – and I did not allude to the matter, though I consider it a bad appointment and feel that T.D. would have been a much better choice – but perhaps he did not want the job[33]). T.D. says that Winston is now more full of vim than ever – more especially since the defeat of Smuts[34] – and he keeps pointing out that 'this Great Statesman' although he is 78 is continuing to lead his party and remains in the political fight. I asked what Anthony's feelings were – and we both grinned. Waiting to step into a dead man's

[32] Patrick George Thomas Buchan-Hepburn (1901–1974), Con. M.P. Liverpool E. Toxteth 1931–50, Beckenham 1950–57; P.P.S. to O. Stanley 1931–39; Ass. Whip 1939, Whip 1939–40, 1944–48, Chief Whip 1948–55; Min. of Works 1955–57; Gov.-Gen. of West Indies 1958–62; cr. Baron Hailes 1957.

[33] Dugdale had been Dep. Chief Whip 1941–42 before moving aside to serve as Party Chairman 1942–44; it might be considered that he had a greater claim to the succession than Buchan-Hepburn, and should have been considered for the post.

[34] Jan Christian Smuts (1870–1950), Gen. commanding Boer forces in Cape Colony 1901–02; Min. of Defence, Union of S. Africa 1910–19, P.M. 1919–24, 1939–48; Min. of Justice & Dep. P.M. 1933–39; S. African delegate to Imperial conference 1917, member of Imperial War Cabinet 1917–19; one of the few contemporaries of Churchill still to be on the world stage .

shoes is always a tiring business, but when the 'dead' man persists in remaining alive it is worse than ever.

Tuesday 13 July ... to the HofC – a lawyer's day – much argumentation on the Govt.'s British Nationality Bill amendment ... our people appear to be much upset about the matter, not caring much about the term 'citizen of the U.K. and the colonies' – nor do I, but it does not seem to me to matter much nowadays what we are called, provided that we stick together. If Canadian, Australian, etc., 'citizens' continue to look upon themselves as 'British subjects' as well, and Canada, Australia, etc., continue to owe allegiance to the British sovereign and fight for the same flag, the two-tier citizenship does not matter a damn.

Wednesday 14 July In the House today there was a debate on housing. I did not sit in the Chamber very persistently, but I made a point of listening to Bevan who wound up the debate – as usual he made a lot of clever debating points and, if all he said was true, he is building a lot of houses. Our line was to give the man a quiet hearing and not reply to his sallies – on the whole the best policy to adopt though the impression left on my mind was that he had the best of the deal as a consequence.

Thursday 22 July ... the Whips had asked us all to be back at 9.30 to vote in favour of accepting the Lords' amendments to the Criminal Justice Bill (i.e., the omission of the compromise clause on hanging). The division did not actually come until 12.15 or thereabouts ... The Govt. stood up to their critics and accepted the Lords' amendment – but when I say the Govt., I mean Herbert Morrison and Chuter Ede – the greater number of the Govt. did not vote at all – and a great number of the Labour Party – however the anti-hangers only mustered 34 when the division came – 130 odd of their supporters voted with Chuter Ede and 80 of us.

Monday 26 July I had a word with Walter Elliot the other day and told him that I had nearly made up my mind not to stand again, but that I would tell him definitely my decision in September – meanwhile he must let me know if he had any other seat in mind. I told him again all the difficulties about N. Newcastle which he fully appreciated – I don't want to retire, but I feel that it is no use going on in the HofC as I am going on now, and I have not the energy to do more – this is the truth.[35]

Tuesday 27 July Very warm again today ... and I shall be glad to get away from London – having decided to speak in the foreign [affairs] debate tomorrow, it is only to find that the debate has been cancelled. Anthony Eden, with whom I had a talk, tells me that it is largely on our initiative that the debate has been put off. He says that this was because he and Winston were afraid that the Comrades would take the opportunity of saying unpleasant things about the Americans and condemn a defensive policy as a basis of Western Security. Perhaps they are right – the Comrades are undoubtedly a most dangerous crew – a fifth column if there ever was one.

Headlam was suffering from some minor health problems, and when Parliament rose for the summer recess on 30 July he returned home to Holywell. The diary continues with intermittent breaks until 19 August, after which there are no further entries for the rest of the year.

---

[35] By the end of 1948 the problems of Newcastle North and Headlam's continuing uncertainty had led to Elliot's prospective candidacy fading away, and in 1950 he contested and regained his former seat of Glasgow Kelvingrove. Headlam's decision to stand again seems to have evolved gradually but definitely by mid-1949: see diary entries for 31 Mar. & 21 June 1949, below.

18

WAITING FOR THE TORY REVIVAL

January to June 1949

Saturday 1 January 1949   I have started another diary – though I doubt very much whether I shall have the energy to go on with it for any length of time – one's life nowadays is no longer of much interest and one no longer has much *joie de vivre*[1] – all that one has lived for appears to be passing away and the 'brave new world' is singularly unattractive to those of us lived fifty years ago. One's only hope is that this new generation will 'grow up' in course of time, and realize that the things we stood for in the past were the things which matter in life – the things for which it is worth living...

Sunday 2 January   [Councillor] Frame[2] came over at my request to discuss the constituency business. He professes to be very indignant about it – and asserts that Temple is in with the Roman Catholics who are determined to get back the seat[3] – apparently Temple's wife is an R.C. and so too is Scanlan – there may be something in this – at any rate it is worth looking into. Frame swears that if Temple stands he himself will stand as an independent Conservative. He begs me not to resign and assures me that if Temple stands, there really is a chance of his losing the seat. He is

[1] translation: joy in life.
[2] Alexander Frame, member of Newcastle City Council, Arthur's Hill & Walker Wards 1942–52, Alderman 1952–58 (resigned from the Progressive Party group 1954, and sat as Ind).
[3] The Member from 1918 to 1940, Nicholas Grattan-Doyle, was a Roman Catholic and the religious issue was an element in arousing opposition to his son succeeding him in 1940.

going to get busy – I said that I had no wish to stand again, but that I did [not] want to see Temple succeed me.

Saturday 8 January   Mr. Marshall's[4] resignation of his State Secretaryship is announced. He will be a great loss to Truman I should imagine – his successor is Mr. Dean Acheson,[5] the present Under-Secretary. He is said to be an able man and well-disposed towards this country – nowadays an appointment of this kind in the U.S.A. is almost a matter of as much importance in this country as it is on the other side of the Atlantic – we are so terribly dependent on America and I don't suppose that this dependency is likely to decrease. We are told that the Cease fire order has been given in the Negev[6] – whether this order by U[nited] N[ations] O[ganization] will be obeyed by the Jews remains to be seen – my impression is that the blood has gone to their heads and that they will go on penetrating into Egypt. What a mess we have made of the whole business! – it makes me ashamed to be an Englishman in these bad days – if our policy of scuttle and surrender had led to peace, it would not be so humiliating – but it has not had this result – and we are of no account and no good purpose served. I have never thought much of Bevin as a Foreign Minister – now I imagine my view of him is shared by most people on both sides of the House.

Sunday 9 January   The Jews in the Negev area have shot down 5 of our aeroplanes which apparently were taking photographs on the frontier of Egypt[7] – it is an outrageous proceeding on the part

[4] George Catlett Marshall (1880–1959), American army career; Chief of Staff U.S. Army 1939–45; Sec. of State 1947–49; Sec. of Defence 1950–51; awarded Nobel Peace Prize 1953.

[5] Dean Gooderham Acheson (1893–1971), U.S. citizen; legal career; Under Sec. Treasury 1933; Ass. U.S. Sec. of State 1941–45, Under-Secretary 1945–47, Sec. of State 1949–53.

[6] When the British mandate in Palestine ended on 14 May 1948 the establishment of the Jewish state of Isreal was proclaimed. This was immediately followed by an invasion from the neighbouring Arab states which was defeated by Israeli forces, and the war concluded with a series of cease-fires in early 1949.

[7] During their drive south to secure the Negev region, victorious Israeli units crossed the Palestinian border and on 3 Jan. 1949 were confirmed to be on Egyptian soil. The purpose of the reconaissance flight was to determine if the promised withdrawal had taken place; this was linked to the British aim of invoking the disputed Anglo-Egyptian Treaty of 1936.

of the Jews but I feel that it was very foolish to send out our machines in this particular area – it was courting trouble – we are powerless in Palestine as things are and in this matter we shall have U.N.O. and the Americans against us – surely our Mr. Bevin must be out of his mind? It is useless to try and assert yourself unless you can support your case with armed force – and this is exactly what we cannot do nowadays, specially in Palestine.

Monday 10 January   We have sent a protest to Telaviv about the shooting down of our five aeroplanes – the Jews complain of our 'unilateral intervention' in the Palestine conflict and pay no attention to our protest – of course our Mr. Bevin has so far refused to recognize the Israeli Government – a very unrealistic line of policy in my opinion, but he is a stupid, obstinate man whose diplomacy has failed miserably.

Thursday 13 January   This morning I attended a meeting called by the Lord Mayor for M.P.s and officials to explain the housing difficulties – apparently there is still a lot of slum clearance to be done and the rate of building new houses is far too slow – a deputation is to be sent to the Ministry of Health to ask for a bigger allocation, etc., etc.

Tuesday 18 January   ... at the House ... my colleagues appear to be back in force, but they are by no means so confident and pleased with themselves as they were before Christmas.

Wednesday 19 January   The Palestine debate is to be next week, by which time no doubt we shall have recognized Israel and Mr. Bevin's critics on his own side of the House will be silenced – but what a mess he has made of things and how terribly he has lost us prestige. He is not the type of man to be Foreign Secretary – too stubborn and self-opinionated, too ignorant of foreigners and too conceited for the job – all that one can say is that bad as he is, Dalton would be infinitely worse. It may sound snobbish but one does need a gent and an informed man at the F[oreign] O[ffice].

Thursday 20 January   [Guy Dawnay][8] had no use for his niece by marriage, Mrs. Archer Clive,[9] and could not imagine how an old hand like J[ames] S[tuart] should have got entangled by her.[10] Tommie Dugdale told me this afternoon that the case was settled early in December and that there was no publicity – R[achel] S[tuart][11] had behaved splendidly and J.S. thought that all was well – and then the little cad Beaverbrook who does not like J.S. thought fit to publish portraits of him and Mrs. A.C. in yesterday's *Daily Express* – bad luck on James – but in these days affairs of this kind are soon forgotten.

Saturday 22 January   ... the less I feel inclined to carry on with North Newcastle – I have had two unpleasant battles there with my own side, why at my time of like should I have another? And yet I hate knuckling down to Temple and his friends and I also feel that to allow him a walkover would be the worst thing for the constituency. My trouble really is that my supporters are so feeble. They are not people of any importance personally nor have they any following – and of course the fact that Temple and Scanlan are working so closely together makes the business so difficult for the attackers. It is a sorry end-up to my political activities. The death of J.H. Thomas is announced at the age of 74. I never cared for him. He was able and self-confident, but a man one could not trust – Nancy Astor, who at one time was a great believer in him, was disillusioned with him at the time of the General Strike, feebly bewailing that he was only behaving so badly because he was drinking too heavily. He liked the good things of this life and I don't blame him – he liked being in with the nobs and used to

---

[8] Guy Payan Dawnay (1878–1952), army career 1899–1911, war service 1914–18; Chairman, Dawnay, Day & Co., Gordon Hotels Ltd., Liverpool, London & Globe Insurance Co., Central Insurance Co., Army & Navy Stores Ltd., President, Anglo-Norwegian Holdings; Vice-Chairman, *Financial Times* Ltd.; Headlam's closest friend since the First World War, original founder with him of the *Army Quarterly*.

[9] Penelope Isobel Portman (b.1913), daughter of 7th Viscount Portman, married 1934 Archer Francis Lawrence Clive (b.1903), divorced 1949; she married on 1 Mar. 1949 David Arthur Bowlby (b.1907). Archer Clive was the eldest son of (George) Sidney Clive (1874–1959), kt. 1933, married 1901 Madeline Buxton (d.1957), daughter of Francis Buxton (1847–1911), Lib. M.P. Andover 1880–86; Guy Dawnay married 1906 her sister, Cecil Buxton.

[10] James Stuart was cited as co-respondent in the Archer Clive divorce, although this was given very little publicity at the time; see also 1 Feb. 1949.

[11] Rachel Cavendish (1902–1977), styled Lady Rachel Cavendish after suc. of father as 9th Duke of Devonshire 1908; married 1923 James Stuart (q.v.).

address all and sundry by their Christian names even if he did not know them.

Sunday 23 January   Chiang Kai-Shek[12] has retired and gone to visit the tombs of his ancestors – a pity perhaps that he did not adopt this line many months ago for clearly he is a useless and probably corrupt creature. He was invented by us and the Americans during the war as China's great national leader – all the time, however, he was probably playing his own game and filling his own pocket – now the Communists would appear to be in almost complete control of China. What this means no man can tell, but on paper it looks pretty bad for the western world – and yet I don't fancy that Communism is likely to be the same sort of nuisance in China as it is elsewhere – China is too vast and old-established to adopt *in toto* the doctrines of Marx or the over-lordship of Soviet Russia – it will go its own way and for a time at any rate I should doubt very much whether the Communist victory would make much change in the everyday life of the Chinese or in their attitude in trading with foreigners.

Tuesday 25 January   In the House today we had the report stage and 3rd Reading of the Wireless Telegraphy Bill – a measure in which I have taken no interest and which we don't appear to have opposed to any extent – so presumably it is innocuous. There is a feeling of fatigue and boredom about the House which is not confined to any particular party or group. I think that this Parliament has about run its course – by which I mean that the energy and drive have gone out of people – more especially the Government side – they are out of breath – have over-strained themselves – don't quite know what to do for the remainder of the Parliament – whether to go on nationalizing or to try and consolidate what they have already nationalized – what course is calculated to gain votes: I am wondering whether we may not have a general election in the autumn? I hope not personally.

[12] Chiang Kai-Shek (1887–1975), Chinese army career; emerged as leader of the Kuomintang (Nationalist Party) 1926–28; Pres. and effective dictator 1928–49; C. in C. of Nationalist forces in war with Japan 1937–45, attended Cairo conference 1943; defeated by Communists in civil war 1947–49, resigned as Pres. on fall of Peking Jan. 1949; withdrew to Taiwan, where he was Pres. 1950–75.

Wednesday 26 January   The Palestine debate today was not a very exciting affair – but the Government only had a majority of ninety on the division we forced on the adjournment – about sixty of their supporters sat in the House during the division and about forty others did not turn up for the debate. Bevin spoke, or rather read his statement, for nearly an hour and a half – Winston made a fierce and rather overdone attack on Bevin for another hour or so – then Clem Davies ranted for forty-five minutes, a fierce Zionist oration – then some Labour backbencher (an ex engine driver) from Nottingham spoke quite unintelligibly for over half an hour – then the Speaker called me and I spoke for ten minutes on the one point that we should recognize the Israeli Government as soon as possible. It was not a bad little effort and I was congratulated afterwards by several people for having put my case so shortly and yet so effectively – I was pleased. ... There is little or no gossip – at the 1922 Committee this evening Q. Hogg suggested that we ought to advocate the expulsion from the House of Mr. Belcher[13] in the forthcoming [Lynskey] Tribunal[14] debate. I am against this – and so, I think, were the majority of those present. The man ought to go – but if we were to press for his going, we should be accused of kicking a man when he is down.

Tuesday 27 January   Today in the House a debate began on the 2nd reading of the American Aid and European Payments (Financial Provisions) Bill – Cripps spoke at considerable length and very effectively – he reads his stuff but he does so well and one feels that is a complete master of his subject. I listened to most that he had to say but I confess (in the privacy of this book) that I could not understand a lot of it. It seems, however, to me that we are going to pay rather heavily for American aid and that much of the European recovery will depend upon our financial help. However, no doubt I am all wrong – I hope so at any rate. R.A. Butler (who apparently is a financial expert as well as an expert on

---

[13] John William Belcher (1905–1964), Lab. M.P. Sowerby 1945–49; P.S. Trade 1946–48; resigned his seat in Feb. 1949 after findings of Lynskey Tribunal; employed by British Railways 1949–63.
[14] The Tribunal, presided over by Mr. Justice Lynskey, was established by the govt. on 27 Oct. 1948 to investigate rumours that Ministers had accepted gifts from businessmen in exchange for favourable treatment on licences and contracts. The report, published on 25 Jan. 1949, uncovered only relatively minor indiscretions on the part of Belcher and the trade unionist George Gibson.

everything else) opened for us – I am afraid that I did not stay and listen to him. The Tribunal's report came out yesterday – as was expected only Gibson[15] and Belcher have been dropped on of the Government and civil servants concerned.

Friday 28 January   The debate on the second reading of the American Aid and European Payments (Financial Provisions) was continued and finished – very few people in the House. David Eccles led off for us and Harold Macmillan wound up – both spoke well. The former is clever but to me not an agreeable type – too obviously self-satisfied and sure of himself, determined to push to the top – which I think that he may well do. Harold is the same as ever – he, too, is making ground I think.

Monday 31 January   I find it always exceedingly difficult to work in the Library of the HofC – people are always on the move and the habit of the Comrades is to gossip and joke among themselves, so that one is continuously disturbed and annoyed. There is one non-speaking room but it is of no use to me as a workshop as smoking is *verboten*.[16] There really ought to be a silent smoking room. The business today was dull in the extreme (3d [reading] of the special Roads Bill) and the divisions which we were asked to stay for never materialized.

Tuesday 1 February   Another uninteresting day in the House. There is singularly little gossip nowadays – indeed, I have [heard] nothing of any interest for a long time. Young Thorneycroft I see in the newspapers is to be divorced by his wife – an undefended case. He is about as usual – no one nowadays has any awkwardness about such matters. I have no particular regard or admiration for this bright young man of the Conservative Party whose abilities seem to me to be overrated – he has not been in the limelight so much lately and I fancy has lost ground – but he is a good platform speaker and is, I believe, in much request in the country. I had a talk with James Stuart this afternoon – he is very sorry for himself

---

[15] George Gibson (1885–1953), trade unionist; Gen. Sec., Confederation of Health Service Employees 1946–48; member of T.U.C. Gen. Council 1928–48, Chairman 1940–41; Chairman, N.W. Regional Bd. for Industry 1945–48, N.W. Area Power Bd. 1948–49; N.W. Industrial Estates Ltd. 1946–48.

[16] translation: forbidden.

and disturbed about his affair, or rather of its outcome.[17] He says that he may have to give up his seat – seemingly Scotland is more old-fashioned about divorce than is this country. Rachel is sticking to James which is a relief to him I imagine.

Wednesday 2 February   It has been a dull day in the House. I attended a meeting to discuss the best way of fighting the 'anti-sport' [Bill][18] which is to be introduced by Seymour Cocks[19] – it excludes fox-hunting from the prescribed list of prohibited sports – this is supposed to be a clever move because lots of people, it is said, who don't mind cruelty to foxes condemned cruelty to stags.

Tuesday 3 February   We had the Lynskey Tribunal debate in the House today. Belcher made his apologia – on the whole I thought with dignity and courage – a horrible ordeal for any man. But I don't think if I were ever in such a position I should attempt to make a speech on such an occasion – I should do as Jim Thomas did, apologize and go away as quickly as I could. Attlee and Churchill both did well – but why the latter should have gone out of his way to express his sympathy for Gibson and boost up the T[rade] U[nion] leaders generally I cannot imagine – by all accounts Gibson is not an attractive personality and his habits and mode of life are not so different to those of others of his kind. I did not listen to most of the other performers in the debate, but I listened with pleasure to the A[ttorney-]G[eneral][20] administering rebuke to the awful little Silverman who tried to make out that the Tribunal had not acted in accordance with the rules of law. The A.G. is

[17] Stuart had been cited as co-respondent in a divorce case: see 20 Jan. 1949.

[18] Time for Private Members' Bills was allowed in this session of Parliament, for the first time since the outbreak of war in 1939.

[19] Frederick Seymour Cocks (1882–1953), Lab. M.P. Broxtowe 1929–53; Chairman, Foreign Affairs Group, P.L.P. 1945–47.

[20] Hartley William Shawcross (1902–), Lab. M.P. St. Helens 1945–58; Attorney-Gen. 1945–51; Pres. Bd. of Trade Apr.-Oct. 1951; Chairman, Enemy Aliens Tribunal 1939–40; Dep. Regional Comm. for Civil Defence, S.E. England 1940–41, Regional Comm. N.W. England 1942–45; Chairman, Catering Wages Commission 1943–45; Recorder of Salford 1942–45, of Kingston-on-Thames 1947–61; Chief British Prosecutor, Nuremberg War Crimes Trials 1945–46; Chairman, Bar Council 1952–57; British Member, Court of Arbitration, The Hague 1950–67; Chairman, Medical Research Council 1961–65, Panel on Take-overs & Mergers 1969–80; cr. Baron Shawcross 1959.

undoubtedly a very able man, and it is a thousand pities that he decided to be a Socialist.

Tuesday 8 February   I wrote letters all the morning and most of the afternoon at the HofC – a heavier post than usual. A lot of my constituents appear to be interested in the 'anti-sport' Bill – more against it, I am glad to say, than for it. The opponents are usually women. The Northumberland Farmers Union is violently opposed to it. I don't myself think that the Bill will get through the HofC as I hear that the Government are frightened about it – an interference by the urban population in the affairs of the countryside. ... I dined at the HofC – the usual unwholesome unappetizing food – why it cannot be better I cannot imagine.

Wednesday 9 February   This has been the dullest week in Parliament which I ever remember – nothing [to] do – and a poor attendance – no gossip in the Smoking Room – no sign of a Tory fighting spirit. I am beginning to be more and more afraid that there will be a snap election in the autumn and that the enemy will be returned to power.

Thursday 10 February   I do not remember so dull a week in the HofC in my parliamentary experience – all the interest of this Parliament is over and, bar the Iron and Steel Bill now in Committee upstairs, there is no excitement that one can foresee ahead of us. My own private opinion is that a general election may come in the autumn – though this is not the general opinion. My reason for this opinion is that the Government may well decide to go while the going is good and may think that it is wiser to go to the country earlier than late – they are, I think, in as good a position now as they are likely to be next year.

Friday 11 February   News came this morning that poor Charley Londonderry died yesterday – a merciful release, I suppose[21] – but none the less one deeply regrets his death. I was very fond of him and looked upon him as a real friend – a man who one could have gone to in difficulties and who one knew would do all he could to

---

[21] Londonderry had been an invalid and unable to speak since suffering a serious stroke: see entry for 18 April 1948.

help one. He was extraordinarily conscientious – modest and unassuming – and is a real loss to the community – he was often misunderstood and never rightly appreciated.

Saturday 12 February   I attended a dinner at the Station Hotel organized by the 'British Anti-Partition of Ireland' League in honour of de Valera – Professor Savory[22] M.P. was with me. It was a big 'do' – all the Romans there in force – mainly women of Irish nationality I fancy who listened to Dev as if he were God and cheered everything he said. He is rather a striking looking man but no orator – he put his case across well nevertheless – not very convincingly perhaps to anyone like myself who knew the case against him, but well enough for his audience. He was terribly long-winded and I thought that he would never stop – we did not get back home until nearly midnight.

Wednesday 16 February   This afternoon I attended one of these European Union[23] meetings in a Committee Room of the HofC – all the old hands were present – Gilbert Murray, Lord Layton,[24] etc. – in addition to our HofC experts – Bob Boothby, Mackay,[25] etc. – and a lot of odds and ends representing the various societies interested in Europe in one way or another. The object today was to elect our representatives to the Council and there was a deal of talk from the pundits. Lord Layton was elected our Chairman – I cannot say that I took much interest in the proceedings, but I realize the necessity for some kind of union among the western nations if any halt is to be made on Russian and Communist

[22] Douglas Lloyd Savory (1878–1969), Ulster Unionist M.P. Queen's Univ. Belfast 1940–50, Antrim S. 1950–55; Chairman, Ulster Unionist Parl. Party 1953–55; Prof. of French, Queen's Univ. 1909–40; kt. 1952.

[23] This meeting founded the United Kingdom Council of the European Movement; Layton was elected Chairman, and Duncan Sandys (q.v.) was elected Chairman of the Exec. Ctte.

[24] Walter Thomas Layton (1884–1966), Lib. cand. Burnley 1922, Cardiff S. 1923, London Univ. 1929; Dep. Lib. Leader in Lords 1952–55; Dir. of Economic & Financial Section, League of Nations; Dir.-Gen. of Programmes, Min. of Supply 1940–42; Chief Adviser, Min. of Production 1942–43; Head of Joint War Production Staff 1942–43; editor, *The Economist* 1922–38; Chairman, *News Chronicle* Ltd. 1930–50, *Star* Newspaper Ltd. 1936–50; Vice-Pres., Consultative Assembly of Council of Europe 1949–57; kt. 1930, cr. Baron Layton of Danehill 1947.

[25] Ronald William Gordon Mackay (1902–1960), Lab. M.P. Hull N.W. 1945–50, Reading 1950–51; delegate to Council of Europe, 1949–50; Ind. Lab. cand. Llandaff & Barry 1942, member of Common Wealth, rejoined Lab. Party Jan. 1945.

progress westward – of course the main thing is to achieve a system of defence and this does appear to be being taken seriously nowadays as usual, however, the active co-operation of the U.S.A. is essential and how far this can be depended upon remains to be seen.

Thursday 17 February   In the House today an attack was made by Walter Elliot on Mr. Bevan's monstrous Supplementary Estimates for the national health business. Winston fulminated against them the other day and threatened a vote of censure – but I gather that we are not going to move such a vote after all. It seems to me that Bevan, who is to wind up the debate, will make considerable party capital out of this – it is silly to speak big and act small.

Friday 18 February   The Socialists have kept the Batley seat with a reduced majority. We don't make much headway in the country which is disappointing, but not surprising – until a slump comes I don't see how the man in the street is to be made to understand the ghastly financial position that we are in – he gets all he wants – has as much work as he feels inclined to do – and no longer worries about controls.

Wednesday 23 February   The undercurrent of discontent in the party about Winston's leadership is growing – of the course the truth is that he is not, and never has been, a party man. He has always been too much interested in himself to run a party – and now of course he is too old and too busy about his book,[26] etc., to trouble about 'leadership' and all it entails.

Friday 25 February   The debate on the 'anti-sport' Bill sponsored by Seymour Cocks was a good one – no doubt the press will describe it as 'the HofC at its best'. (This means that we are all supposed to have voted and spoken according to our consciences and not at the bidding of the Party whips). Today the only Tory who voted for the Bill was young Edward Carson[27] – he explained his position very clearly and moderately, and has greatly improved

[26] Much of Churchill's time during this period was taken up with preparing his multi-volume history and memoir, *The Second World War*.

[27] Edward Carson (1920–1987), Con. M.P. Thanet 1945–53; son of Sir Edward Carson, later Lord Carson (judicial life peerage).

his parliamentary position. Seymour Cocks spoke with his usual ability and presumably meant all he said – but if it is so cruel to hunt a hare, a deer or an otter, why is it less cruel to hunt a fox? Tom Williams[28] as Minister of Agriculture advised the House to vote against the Bill – apparently 20 years ago he himself introduced an anti-sport Bill – but when twitted with this he admitted quite frankly that he had learnt wisdom with years. Eddie Winterton made an amusing, vigorous speech which pleased the House – I had meant to speak but as there were so many would-be speakers, I did not bother the Speaker. The second reading was defeated by 214 to 102 – a satisfactory result, but presumably the humanitarians will continue the fight.

Tuesday 1 March   I have spent most of the day at the HofC – a debate on Civil Aviation – we voted against Lord Pakenham's estimate – I did not listen to much of the debate which does not seem to have been of much interest except for a speech from Harvey[29] M.P. for Macclesfield – rather a nice fellow – an ex-airman who knows what he is talking about. There is no news – our people are all much depressed about the Hammersmith [South] election result – they cannot get over it.[30] I think that their mistake is to make too much fuss about any by-election (but I think that I must have said this many times before in this diary of mine). The enemy is certainly going strong at the moment and we have got to face the fact – we must go on working as hard as possible and not be fussed.

Wednesday 2 March   At the House this afternoon I attended two committees – one to consider our course of action when the anti-fox hunting Bill comes along next Friday week – the other to

[28] Thomas Williams (1888–1967), Lab. M.P. Don Valley 1922–59; P.P.S. to N. Buxton 1924, to M. Bondfield 1929–31; P.S. Agric. 1940–45; Min. of Agric 1945–51; member of P.L.P. Ctte. 1931–40; cr. Baron Williams of Barnburgh 1961.

[29] Arthur Vere Harvey (1906–1994), Con. M.P. Macclesfield 1945–71; Chairman, 1922 Ctte. 1966–70; adviser to Southern Chinese Air Forces 1932–35; service in R.A.F., Air Commodore 1944; Chairman, Ciba-Geigy (UK) Ltd. 1957–74; kt. 1957, cr. Baron Harvey of Prestbury 1971.

[30] The Conservatives had confidently expected to win this seat from Labour; it had been Conservative in the inter-war period and was a more residential and middle-class area than had been the case in other recent by-elections.

consider a resolution by one Commander Pursey[31] M.P. attacking the political action of Ian Fraser M.P. as President of the British Legion. Eventually the motion was withdrawn – Fraser made a very dignified speech and he had a large majority in his favour – I said a few words.

Thursday 3 March ... the Defence Ministry debate today ... was a poor debate and Alexander was too feeble for words. Oliver Stanley for us made a good speech. He is gaining ground. Winston attended the 22 Committee this afternoon – he listened patiently to a good deal of criticism and then told us how optimistic he was about the result of the coming G[eneral] E[lection] – luckily he did not give us the 'V' sign! for people were rather critical and disgruntled and not at all impressed by his optimism – why should they be? For the time being at any rate clearly the Socialist star is in the ascendant and our star is entirely obscured.

Monday 7 March It has been a very dull and dreary day at the HofC – at least for me as I take no interest in the Landlord and Tenant (Rent Control) Bill which was in Committee – our Walter Elliot and Commander Galbraith[32] were in charge of it, and we had 2 or 3 divisions. Our people are in a somewhat gloomy and discontented mood, and there is an undercurrent of anti-Winstonism – though one and all would deny it. It is not really surprising for Winston is a poor leader of a party – principally because he is so entirely egotistical. A man cannot hope to be a successful leader (however great and grand an individual he may be) unless he concentrates entirely upon the job. He must be in the House all the time – he must be friendly with all and sundry and show an interest in other people's speeches, not only upon his own. Winston is relying solely on his war record – he is seldom in the House – and when he comes into the Smoking Room he does not mix with his party, only with his own little clique of admirers and hangers-on – he is not a good judge of men. He is not really a

[31] Harry Pursey (1891–1980), Lab. M.P. Hull E. 1945–70; entered Royal Navy 1907, retired with rank of Commander 1936.
[32] Thomas Dunlop Galbraith (1891–1985), Con. M.P. Glasgow Pollok 1940–55; jt. U.S. Scotland May-July 1945, 1951–55, M.S. 1955–58; Chairman, N. of Scotland Hydro-Electric Bd. 1959–67; cr. Baron Strathclyde 1955.

party man – all he wants is to get back to power – people are beginning to realize this.

Thursday 10 March   I meant to speak in the Army debate this afternoon ... Shinwell's statement [was] most unsatisfactory – he gave us no real information, but it was tolerably clear that we have not a single formation ready for war in this country, that recruiting is bad both for the Regular Army and the T[erritorial] A[rmy], and that we should be well nigh helpless if war began tomorrow. Anthony Head who opened the debate for us made an excellent speech – he is, I think, about the best of our young men. ... We have not won the election in St. Pancras – a reduction in the Socialist majority is all we have to write home about – certainly the enemy is holding his ground well and there is no real sign (*pace*[33] Lord Woolton) of a Tory revival – it is very disappointing, but there it is. My own view is that the worst thing that could happen would be for us to be returned to power with a small majority.

Friday 11 March   The second reading of the new spelling Bill[34] was only defeated by 3 votes today – 87 to 84. The reason for the small majority was that as the anti-fox hunting Bill had been withdrawn most of our people were conspicuous by their absence. I did not listen to much of the debate – the facetiousness of Mr. Follick,[35] who moved the second reading, bored me and letters from Bernard Shaw[36] in support of the measure did not interest me. I suppose that the silly business will be repeated next year if this Parliament is still in existence.

Tuesday 15 March   Public meetings are no longer of much use: people simply don't attend them, least of all the enemy. Broadcasting has knocked out platform speeches except during the actual election fights – a pity in many ways. After the meeting was over

---

[33] translation: despite, notwithstanding.

[34] A Private Member's Bill to introduce a phonetic system of spelling.

[35] Mont Follick (1887–1958), Lab. M.P. Loughborough 1945–55; founder, Regent School of Languages; Prof., English Univ. of Madrid; advocate of spelling reform and of decimal currency.

[36] George Bernard Shaw (1856–1950), playwright and author; founding member of Fabian Soc. 1884; awarded Nobel Prize for Literature 1925; left the residue of his estate to promote an alphabet of at least forty letters.

we went to the Jesmond [Conservative] Men's Club – very few men there – apparently few people can afford to drink beer at its present price which is not surprising. The removal of coupons for clothes, etc., has, Scanlan tells me, not led to [a] rush of buyers in Newcastle – only the miners' wives have money and they are ready to buy as many blankets as they can get – other people have no money ...

Wednesday 16 March   In the House this afternoon we had the second reading [of the Housing Bill]. I did not listen to the debate: I never can bear listening to Bevan – apparently there was a row about him on Friday when he let himself go in his most abusive way, maintaining that Peter Thorneycroft had introduced his Bill (I forget what its title is) for easing the pains of childbirth for political motives – he is [a] low creature if ever there was one. I find that people are still wondering why Vyshinsky[37] has taken Molotov's job as Foreign Secretary – and what change it may mean in Soviet foreign policy. I don't pretend that I know anything about the business – who can in this country? – but of one thing I am fairly certain – no change of personnel at the Kremlin means that the Soviet has become, or intends to become, any more well disposed towards us – a change of personnel may mean a change of method but not a change of policy.

Thursday 17 March   The Socialists have held Sowerby with a reduced majority – we do not seem to be making much progress in the country – our M.P.s are not very happy! – one hears a good deal of grumbling.

Friday 18 March   *The Times* correspondence about Conservative policy continues – what good it does I fail to see – a long letter today from Amery deploring the decline of British agriculture, all leading up to Empire co-operation, etc., etc. It is a good letter and I agree with what he says in the main. It is only by working together that we can prosper unless we are to remain dependent upon the U.S.A. The trouble is that when one tries to work together each unit of the Commonwealth can never look beyond its own imme-

[37] Andrei Yanuarievich Vyshinsky (1883–1954), State Prosecutor in the major trials of Stalin's purge 1936–38; transferred to foreign service 1940, assisted Molotov 1940–45; Soviet delegate to United Nations 1945–49, 1953–54; For. Minister 1949–53.

diate needs – and as each unit becomes more self-supporting and more conscious of its own individuality the desire for co-operation becomes less apparent.

Saturday 19 March   Bevin announced in the HofC yesterday that the Eight Power Agreement on the North Atlantic Pact (published yesterday) was one of the greatest steps towards peace and security taken since the end of the First World War.[38] I should say that probably he is right – nevertheless, I should be happier about the preservation of peace, if the powers which have signed it were prepared for war – this clearly not one of them is – whether or not the Russians are remains to be seen – probably they are not – in which case presumably the 'Cold War' will continue, and when all is said and done that serves Russian policy well enough for the time being. Communism is spreading all the time – however, this Pact is a step in the right direction and one welcomes it – only Messrs. Warbey[39] and Piratin[40] appear to have spoken against it in the House – one is a 'fellow-traveller', the other a Communist – neither of them is of much account.

Tuesday 22 March   As a result of the row between Fascists and Communists the other night Ede has put a ban on political processions in London for three months. He really had no alternative – in the House apparently Silverman and Piratin got little change out of him – Ede, I think, is an excellent Home Secretary and a very reasonable man. If Attlee retires I think that the Socialists would do well to put Ede in his place – but this would not please the Left Wingers or Herbert Morrison.

Wednesday 23 March   It is announced in the press today that there is to be a Commonwealth Conference in April. Mr. Nehru, we are told, is going to raise the matter of the 'status' of India –

---

[38] The North Atlantic Treaty, which established N.A.T.O., was signed in Washington on 4 Apr. 1949 by nine European countries, Canada and the U.S.A.

[39] William Noble Warbey (1903–1980), Lab. M.P. Luton 1945–50, Broxtowe 1953–55, Ashfield 1955–66; editor, *Look & Listen* 1952–55; Exec. Dir., Organisation for World Political and Social Studies, 1965–80; Sec., World Studies Trust 1966–80.

[40] Philip Piratin (1907–1995), Communist M.P. Mile End 1945–50; London Organiser, Communist Party, from 1939; Circulation Manager, *Daily Worker* 1954–56; member of Stepney Borough Council 1937–49.

presumably he will tell us that he intends to declare India a republic, and presumably he will demand that we should treat her as we are treating Eire. What a farce it all is! and how will it all end? The British Empire was a strange enough affair – but at any rate all sections of it acknowledged the same ruler and owed allegiance to him – now this bond is broken and what is to take its place? I can see nothing that can do so – certainly not with India – nor do I believe that India can hold together, or protect herself. What is to happen if there is war with Russia? Chaos – then Communism would appear to be the future for the 'vast sub-continent' – a horrible prospect. Thousands of controls, it is announced, are to be ended – the Government is clearly making ready for the General Election and I still should not be surprised if it comes this year. 'Final shape' is said to have been given to the Socialists' policy and when this has been confirmed at their annual conference, there is really nothing left for them to do before appealing for a new period of power – and what are we doing? Precious little in my opinion – and we are not gaining ground in the country.

Tuesday 29 March   I 'intervened' in the debate on the Committee stage of the Army and Air Force Bill. It was unexpectedly rather a good little debate, and a good many people spoke – Eddie Winterton and Harold Macmillan spoke from our front bench and the latter made a very good little speech ... The gloom of our side is very noticeable – unduly so – but on the whole, I prefer it to the over confidence of a few months ago – that always struck me as rather ridiculous and somewhat dangerous. My own view is that the Socialists are now on the top of their form – things have gone unexpectedly well for them – and that before long they will begin to lose way – much of course depends on the Budget, but I cannot see that it is likely to bring much satisfaction to the Comrades because Cripps is not likely to ease taxation – indeed, I don't see how he can – or to do anything to reduce the cost of living – lower prices are what the Comrades are demanding.

Wednesday 30 March   A dull afternoon and evening in the House – Oliver Stanley came and sat with me at dinner. He was very friendly for him (what an odd, aloof creature he is) – I noted how the young men as they came into dinner gravitated to our table – had I been alone this would, needless to say, not have been the case!

Thursday 31 March   In the House today we had the first day of a debate on the second reading of the Bill to provide 'National Parks' – I listened to the greater part of the man Silkin's speech and, as I fell asleep, I still am not quite sure what 'National Parks' are to be – Harold Macmillan with whom I had a talk in the Smoking Room (or rather whom I heard talking, for, as usual, one had little chance of saying anything oneself) asserted that they are intended to stop grouse shooting – perhaps this may be so if we are to have paths and right of way here, there and everywhere – however, I fancy that the B[ritish] P[ublic] *en masse*[41] is not likely to take to walking over the hills – charabancs, main roads and pubs are what the majority of holiday-makers like. ... I had a word with Jim Thomas about Newcastle (North) and suggested that he should have a nice young man ready should I succeed in defeating Temple and then fall by the way – I am not particularly enamoured of J. Thomas but presumably he is all right.

Tuesday 5 April   The general mania for being shown round the Palace of Westminster is much on the increase – shoals of visitors from morning to night – a positive nuisance for M.P.s. The food debate this afternoon and evening was full of incident and ended in a row – due largely to Strachey's insolent style of oratory and Milner's complete inability to enforce order – ultimately we had a division and the Govt. majority was only a little over sixty – this was surprising as there were no abstentions or cross-voting by those M.P.s present – we had a 3 line whip out: the Socialists had not for some reason. I heard today unofficially that Jack Lawson is really going to be appointed Lord Lieutenant of Durham[42] – I suppose that his appointment will be looked upon as a new triumph for democracy but I am old-fashioned and don't like it a bit.

[41] translation: in the mass.
[42] The position of Lord Lieutenant had mainly formal and ceremonial functions, but it had considerable historic and social prestige and had previously been confined to the higher levels of the landed aristocracy. It was therefore symbolic that Lawson, a former coal miner, should succeed the recently deceased 7th Marquess of Londonderry.

Wednesday 6 April   I gave the Budget a miss today – I have always found it extremely tiring to sit through a Budget speech, and as I grow older I find it more and more wearisome. Today Sir Stafford appears to have excelled himself in a $2\frac{1}{2}$ hour speech – he undoubtedly is a brilliant creature with a real gift for putting a case forward with logical clarity and force. ... I don't myself see how any other Budget was possible in the circumstances – but no doubt it will be difficult for the Comrades and the T.U.C. people to make their people grasp the simple fact that you cannot eat your cake and have it too.

Thursday 7 April   ... the first day of the debate on the Budget resolutions – Harry Crookshank opened for us. He gave a general approval to Cripps's proposals – the general opinion is that the latter has done what in the circumstances was inevitable. He met his party this morning and the official version of the meeting is that he satisfied the recalcitrant Comrades – nevertheless, in the debate today Hewitson[43] (of Weardale), who represents the second biggest union in the country, assured us that the Unions would not tolerate a reduction in the standard of living or be able to check demands for higher wages any longer. I wonder whether the Govt. will stick to their guns if the T.U.C. becomes really truculent? ... I have had a notice informing me that I have [been] 'appointed' to be a member of Standing Committee 'B' – this won't do – to be on a Standing Committee at my time of life would be intolerable – and, needless to say, I don't intend to accept my 'appointment'!

Saturday 9 April   Beatrice ... had luncheon with Miss de Jonghe[44] yesterday and heard a deal of gossip about conditions of things in the Area – they are not at all satisfactory – no leaders – no decent candidates – etc., etc. – it is all rather disheartening, but much as

---

[43] Mark Hewitson (1897–1973), Lab. M.P. Hull Central 1945–55, Hull W. 1955–64; member of N.E.C. 1939–40, 1947–53; Nat. Industrial Officer, Gen. & Municipal Workers' Union, until 1964; Pres., Public & Civil Service International 1937–40; Pres., Gen. Factory Workers' International 1945–50; member of Durham County Council 1930–40.

[44] Jeanne De Jonghe (1910–91), Con. Woman Organiser, 1938; Con. Agent, Birkenhead 1945, Stalybridge 1946, Heywood & Radcliffe 1946–47; Dep. C.O. Agent, Home Counties North Area 1947, Northern Counties Area, 1947–55, North West Area 1955–58, East Midlands Area 1958–71.

I expected when I retired from the Chairmanship.[45] There was no one to succeed me except Donald Scott, and he, so it appears, does not count for much – every little Tom Noddy is playing his own game, and everybody is squabbling and scheming on his own account – unfortunately, too, Galloway has no one to control him and is far too big for his boots. I wish that I could take charge again, but of course this is out of the question, and the same thing applies to Beatrice – even if I am appointed President of the Area in succession to Charley [Londonderry], it won't be possible for me to take any practical lead.

Sunday 10 April   The Labour people on the C[ounty] C[ouncil] in London have announced their intention of maintaining their majority in the Council by appointing an outside chairman and juggling with the Aldermen – presumably they can do this if they so choose – I don't profess to understand how it can be done – but it is of course more or less what the Durham people always do as far as the Aldermen are concerned. What our riposte will be I don't know – so far the County Council elections have gone pretty well, though in Durham we only succeeded in winning 3 seats and losing 3 which we already possessed – so all Mr. Cherry's and the Conservative Party's united efforts have done nothing at all to reduce the 'Socialist domination' over the county.

Tuesday 12 April   [a week before there had been] nearly a row owing to the offensiveness of Strachey and the inadequacy of Milner ... Quintin Hogg has raised the matter by insisting on putting up a motion accusing Milner of a lack of impartiality – a silly business – but the young man is far too big for his boots, and there it is. This place (HofC) is pretty dead – Herbert Morrison and Co. are now thinking more of what the programme is to be for the next election than of providing more legislation for this Parliament, and the Comrades are more anxious to be in their constituencies than here – meanwhile my position still remains somewhat obscure, and I feel that whether I am to stand again or not to stand again must be settled soon – if we are to stand again, we must begin to do a bit of work.

---

[45] Headlam stood down as Chairman of the Northern Counties Area in May 1946; his successors were Thomas Greenwell (q.v.), May 1946-May 1948, and Lady Graham (q.v.), May 1948-May 1951.

Monday 18 April Eire declared herself a republic today[46] – a bad, sorry business in itself, but to make the wretched King send a message of congratulation to the Irish President seems to me to be the limit – now the agitation to get hold of Northern Ireland will be intensified.

Friday 22 April The Chinese Communists have shelled a British sloop (*Amethyst*) and a destroyer (*Consort*) on the Yangtse – killed over 20 seamen and done a lot of damage to the ships – a bad business and one wonders why this has happened and what we shall do. I should imagine that Russian influence may be behind this affair though of course there is not likely to be any proof – we shall, I suppose, take it lying down ... all we do, or can do, nowadays is to protest and refer the matter to U[nited] N[ations] O[rganization] or some outside arbitration body – and, even if such a body awards us 'compensation', there is no means of obtaining it – or even an apology – from the offending party. What a world we live in – and what a very minor position we hold in it compared with what we held in the world when I was young. The odd thing nowadays is that the public does not seem to care what happens, or how we are treated, and this apathy to me is the worst sign of the times – we seem to have lost entirely our national pride and self assurance.

Monday 25 April Beatrice drove me into Newcastle this morning where I attended the opening by Mr. Blenkinsop[47] M.P. (Parly. Secretary to the Ministry of Health) of a new factory for Scott & Turner at Coxlodge on the outskirts of Gosforth. This firm manufactures a powder called 'Andrews Liver Salt' which it seems is drunk in vast quantities all over the globe especially by black and brown people – in this new factory they can make 3 million tins a month. Blenkinsop who is a smug little man made a smug little speech and everyone seemed pleased – quite a lot of people were there and there was plenty to drink which I take it was the reason why most people came.

Tuesday 26 April Attlee's statement about China was not very

[46] Easter Monday, in commemoration of the 1916 Easter Rising.
[47] Arthur Blenkinsop (1911–1979), Lab. M.P. Newcastle E. 1945–59, S. Shields 1964–79; Whip 1945–46; P.S. Pensions 1946–49, Health 1949–51.

illuminating and not satisfactory. Clearly neither the Government
or those in authority on the spot anticipated what happened – and
clearly they were unprepared – no air support of any kind. Winston
emphasized all this (especially the lack of air support and I could
not help remembering the ill-fated *Prince of Wales*!).[48] The day was
devoted to a discussion on War Pensions – the Govt. refused a
Select Committee or Royal Commission inquiry.

Thursday 28 April   Attlee announced the new formula for the
retention of India and other republics within the Commonwealth –
Winston accepted the new arrangement for the Party in the House
and then came upstairs to the [19]22 Committee to tell us why he
had done so! – a sorry, foolish business, but presumably it is as
well to have India in the Commonwealth.

Saturday 30 April   It looks as if the Russians were anxious to
end the Berlin blockade – why one wonders – is it that they are
now concentrating their attention on what is going on in China, or
is it because the effects of the blockade are worse for them in their
part of Germany than they are for us in our part? It is difficult to
judge with the little information one gets in the press, and no one
I meet in London seems to be any better informed than I am.

Sunday 1 May   I had rather a gloomy letter from Robin Londonderry yesterday – Charley, he says, has left his Irish property
and most of his money to Circe[49] and Mary Bury[50] (the money
presumably only for life) – and he (Robin) will be terribly hard
up – what especially annoys him (and no wonder) is that Lord
Nathan[51] has been appointed Chief Trustee and Executor – why
on earth Charley should have appointed such a creature I cannot

---

[48] The battleship *Prince of Wales* and battlecruiser *Repulse* were sent by Churchill
to defend Singapore, but lacking air cover were easily sunk by Japanese aircraft in
December 1941; this was one of the most embarassing débâcles of the war.

[49] His widow, the Marchioness of Londonderry (q.v.).

[50] Mairi Elizabeth Vane-Tempest-Stewart (1921-), youngest daughter of 7th Mar-
quess of Londonderry, styled Lady Mairi; married 1940 Derek William Charles
Keppel (1911–1968), heir of 9th Earl of Albemarle but pre-deceased him, styled
Viscout Bury (divorced 1958).

[51] Harry Louis Nathan (1889–1964), M.P. Bethnal Green N.E. 1929–35 (Lib. until
Feb. 1933, resigned whip and sat as Ind., joined Lab. Party June 1934), Lab. M.P.
Wandsworth Central 1937–40; U.S. War Office 1945–46; Min. of Civil Avaition
1946–48; cr. Baron Nathan 1940; qualified as a solicitor 1913.

imagine. Of course Robin has only himself to blame – for he was a rotten son – and yet it seems to me strange that Charley should have handed over his Irish estate lock, stock and barrel to a daughter thus severing the connexion of his family with Ireland – I thought so when he told me of his intention – but did not remark upon it, for it was no affair of mine.

Tuesday 3 May   It has been the usual dull, ordinary day – we had the report stage of the Iron and Steel Bill – I cannot say that I listened to much of the debate but what I did hear was not interesting or in the least exciting – more in the nature of a sham fight which indeed it is – neither side can get up any steam under the guillotine – and, in this case, neither side can take the Bill too seriously because even if it does become law (under the Parliament Act) during this Parliament's life its effective life must depend upon the result of the next General Election. I notice that our people are beginning to be a bit less gloomy than they have been of late – presumably the results of the County Council elections have cheered them a bit – they always grasp at any straws. My own view of course is that the C.C. elections and L[ocal] G[overnment] elections in general are not much of a guide for parliamentary elections – indeed, there is no real guide because the electorate nowadays is more of an uncertain quantity than ever and one cannot tell until a few weeks before a G[eneral] E[lection] what the feeling of the country may be.

Wednesday 4 May   Today in the House we discussed water supplies, and there were several divisions. Bevan, the Minister responsible, did not take any part in the proceedings (leaving the job to Blenkinsop, his Parly. Secretary). This was fairly insolent first because the Bill (a confirmation order) was being worked under new procedure used for the first time, and secondly because the man was actually in the precincts of the House and had no excuse for his absence from the Chamber – of course attention was given to his non-attendance, but it had not the effect of bringing him into the Chamber. He is an arrogant brute if there ever was one, but a clever parliamentarian – one wonders whether he will become P.M.

Thursday 5 May   The news today is that the Russians have agreed to raising the Berlin blockade – so the air lift is to be raised. It looks as if Bevin has scored, but I cannot believe (unless Stalin & co. are having real difficulties at home) that this implies a more friendly spirit in Moscow. It looks to me like a typical example of Russian policy – finding that the air lift was too strong to be beaten Stalin has decided to give way – *reculer pour mieux sauter*[52] – the pressure in the west to be relaxed, the pressure in the Far East to be intensified – I cannot feel unduly elated by the removal of the blockade, but no doubt it will be hailed as a famous victory by Bevin & co., or at any rate by their supporters.

Monday 9 May   In the House we had the 3rd reading debate on the Iron and Steel Bill – Oliver Lyttelton 'led' for us and made what seemed to me to be about the best speech I have ever heard him make in the HofC. He has improved considerably since his first arrival in the House, but I doubt whether he will ever be really able to impress himself upon his audience. There is something lacking in his mode of speaking – and his manner is more that of a chairman addressing a board meeting than of a statesman 'putting it across' in the HofC – which perhaps is not surprising in view of his upbringing. They tell me that his ambition is to be made C[hancellor] of [the] E[xchequer], but I fancy that Oliver Stanley is the more likely man to get the job if and when we come back.

Tuesday 10 May   I went this morning with my two Newcastle colleagues (Wilkes and Popplewell[53]) to interview Dr. Edith Summerskill at the Ministry of Food – the subject for discussion was the amount of Danish butter, bacon, etc., allocated for unloading at Newcastle. My colleagues did a deal of talking, especially Popplewell who takes his duties very seriously, and the Dr. was extremely affable and reasonable – she always strikes me as a very able woman who knows her job and I am told that her officials think well of her. Tonight I had intended going to the Literary Society dinner to which I have not been for some time – however the whips were so confident that we were to have a lot of divisions on the report stage of the Licensing Bill that I did not like to go

---

[52] translation: stepping backwards in order to better jump forward.
[53] Ernest Popplewell (1899–1977), Lab. M.P. Newcastle W. 1945–66; whip 1946–55, Dep. Chief Whip 1955–59; cr. Baron Popplewell 1966.

out – as things turned out I could have gone to the dinner as there was no division until past 9 o'clock. The whips nowadays never seem to know much about what is going to happen but today they don't seem to have been to blame as Chuter Ede was more amenable than was expected.

Wednesday 11 May   The Govt.'s Ireland Bill had its second reading today – I intended to speak, but the Speaker was not very anxious for me to do so – and as, when it came to the point, I was only (as usual) half-hearted about speaking, I did not press the point. I must try and get in on the 3rd reading. I voted for the 2nd reading with the rest of the party – I hate allowing these beastly Irish to have the rights of British citizens – or indeed to allow them to have an independent republic – but clearly we can't (under the Statute of Westminster) prevent them having a republic, and if we treated them as aliens it would be a troublesome business not only for them but also for us. Attlee made a good speech I thought when moving the second reading and Anthony Eden spoke well for us – I did not listen to much of the subsequent debate. For the division a hundred or more Labour people were absentees – not because they were opposed to the Irish point of view, but because they did not like the guarantee to Ulster and because a lot of them were busy at the local election meetings throughout the country.

Thursday 12 May   Today in the HofC we had a motion on the North Atlantic Pact – Bevin read out a more than usually dull memorandum from the Foreign Office. He really is the dreariest man to listen to – he reads so badly. He was not particularly optimistic about the future and clearly does not believe that the Russians intend to cease from troubling us. Winston spoke after Bevin and I am told that he was less optimistic than the Foreign Office. His speech does not seem to have been quite up to his usual standard – except for Zilliacus and a few other pro-Bolshies the Pact was generally welcomed – it certainly would seem to be a step forward to a real collective security – though not a very big step. In the '[19]22' Committee Winston (in a very felicitous little speech) presented a writing table and chair to James Stuart – a mark of esteem from the Party ... James made an admirable little speech of thanks.

Monday 16 May   In the House we had today the Committee stage of the Ireland Bill. The attitude of the bulk of the Comrades on the Irish partition business is odd – they favour the anti-partitionists presumably because they dislike the 'Toryism' of the Northern Ireland Govt. – in their view it is 'reactionary' – in other words, its representatives in Belfast and London wish to remain within the U.K. and naturally they support the Unionist party in this country. The Comrades try to make out that this is not the view of the Ulster working class population and assert that the inhabitants of Fermanagh and Tyrone are dying to join Southern Ireland and are being tyrannized over by the Unionists in Belfast. I listened to most of the talk today and was, as usual, amazed at the foolishness and futility of the Socialists – why should they take the side of the Irish Roman Catholics? After all, the religious difference is the cause – or the main cause – of all this Irish imbroglio.

Tuesday 17 May   I attended a meeting this afternoon of the 'U.K. Council of European Movement' – I am afraid that like all these efforts at European union οξ εν τελλοι[54] are trying to go too fast and attempt to run before they can walk. Today's discussion was not impressive and the proposals for setting up a Judicial Body struck me as unworkable and far too detailed at this early stage – far better to leave over matters of this kind for the time being – what is the use of overloading the ship before you know what its requirements may be – or, indeed, whether you can get it to sail at all. The usual collection of cranks and enthusiasts were conspicuous at the meeting – I cannot say that they impress me very favourably. Duncan Sandys was present – I don't know him, but I have never met anyone who appears to be a friend of his: not a congenial personality by all accounts – and only occupying his present job in the 'Movement' because he is Winston's son-in-law and had nothing particular to do – neither reason being particularly adequate for his appointment – so much depends on the personality of a man in his position.

Wednesday 18 May   We had the second reading of the Finance Bill this afternoon – W.G. Hall moved the second reading and read

[54] translation: those in command.

out a dull speech not too cleverly – he is a feeble, little man – Cripps sat beside him and was as usual sneering and patronizing throughout the debate, I did not stay [for] his winding up speech – nor did I listen to R.A. Butler's speech, who led for us – presumably because Oliver Stanley was away in Liverpool being inducted as Chancellor of the University in place of his father.

Thursday 19 May   A debate on coal and electricity in the Chamber this afternoon – our chief spokesmen were Rob Hudson and Brendan Bracken – I don't care for either of these two statesmen, nor have I much respect for what they say. They certainly had not anything new to say today. I did not hear Gaitskell's[55] speech, but they tell me that it was full of statistics, etc., explaining why motor petrol has to be so strictly rationed – the usual reason: lack of dollars coupled with the need for collecting them.

Monday 23 May   ... [from Liss] Beatrice and I travelled back to London this morning – a very nasty luncheon in the train – it seems to me that each section of our 'British Railways' vies with the others in providing the nastiest food to travellers. There really is no need why meals should be so nasty – they have always been bad on English railways but it has been left to the new organization to make them even nastier. Beatrice dropped me at the HofC. There was a debate this afternoon against the new telephone rentals and charges proposed by Cripps in his Budget – I said a few words against them and no one on either side of the House said a word in favour of them. It looks as if the great man might have to withdraw the increased charges which are iniquitous and really raise only a comparatively small sum.

Tuesday 24 May   It has been a Health Ministry day in the Chamber – this means a lot of chatter from Walter Elliot. I like him very much as a man, but I dislike listening to him speak – his Scottish (Glasgow) accent is jarring – he speaks far too fast – overflowing with verbosity – and I don't think that he is particularly effective. He is not a match for Bevan as a debater – at least such

[55] Hugh Todd Naylor Gaitskell (1906–1963), Lab. M.P. Leeds S. 1945–63; P.S. Fuel & Power 1946–47; Min. of Fuel & Power 1947–50; M.S. Economic Affairs Feb.-Oct. 1950; Chanc. of the Exchequer 1950–51; Lab. Party Treasurer 1954–55; Lab. Leader 1955–63; Vice-Chairman, N.E.C. 1962–63.

is my opinion. He is usually assisted by Tom Galbraith – a pleasant little man, very keen and hard working, determined to get on – but he, too, has a bad voice and is inclined to be somewhat aggressive – this would not matter if his aggression were effective, but it seldom is.

Saturday 28 May   Beatrice and I went to Newcastle today for the Area meeting – it was held in the Station Hotel and I suppose that there were about 250 to 300 people present – a lot of new faces to me, but some of the old bores were there to greet me. Mary Graham was in the chair – I was duly declared President[56] in succession to Charley Londonderry ... Irene Ward made a nice little speech and then I replied. Scanlan was not present, though I had written to him a few days ago saying that I hoped to see him at the Area meeting – Temple was at the extreme back of the room and went off before the meeting ended making no effort to speak to me – really the situation is becoming intolerable. ... I suppose that it is a good move to have become Area [President][57] – my election at any rate shows that the Area Council do not regard me as too old [or] futile to go on leading the Party in the north – what the would-be leader thought about things is another matter!

Wednesday 8 June   The Labour Party conference does not seem to be very exciting. There has been little or no opposition (*coram publico*[58] at any rate) to the party bosses – and Cripps again reminded his followers that they could not eat their cake and have it too. Griffiths,[59] M.P., the chairman, declared definitely that there would not be an election in the autumn – this need not necessarily mean there won't be one, but it looks as if an election were not contemplated sooner than next year – to me I don't think that it

[56] This honorary position with few duties was held by a senior figure in the region: either an 'elder statesman' who was no longer in the front line but was still active, or a prominent aristocrat from an old and prestigious family.
[57] By mistake, Headlam wrote 'Area Chairman' – this was a separate position which he had held from 1936 to 1946.
[58] translation: before the public.
[59] James Griffiths (1890–1975), Lab. M.P. Llanelli 1936–70; Min. of Nat. Insurance 1945–50; Colonial Sec. 1950–51; Welsh Sec. 1964–66; Dep. Lab. Leader 1956–59; member of N.E.C. 1939–40, 1941–59; member of P.L.P. Ctte. 1951–59; Pres., S. Wales Miners' Fed. 1934–46.

matters much one way or another – but of course we ought to begin working at once.

Sunday 19 June　There is little of interest in the Sunday papers in which the absurd Brendan Bracken gets far more space for his speech than does Anthony Eden. It is the same old story – anyone who has influence with the press (as B.B. has) is bound to be better reported than people who have no such direct influence.

Monday 20 June　This afternoon Jock McEwen and his wife and youngest son aged six (the eldest son is twenty-one and the family consists of seven, six sons and a daughter) came over to see us.[60] They were very pleasant ... Jock has grown rather fat but he appears to be well and fit. He is not trying to return to the HofC – I gather that he spends his time writing poetry – he also presides over the Conservative Party in Scotland. He was in the chair at Anthony [Eden]'s meeting on Saturday and says that A. made a fine speech. He told me that A. was getting more and more disgruntled – waiting interminably for Winston to retire was galling him. Jock's fancy for Conservative leader is Oliver Lyttelton – I said that I did not think that the party in the HofC would stand for him – nor do I – O.L. tries hard to be hail fellow well met with all and sundry, but I don't think that he has any following among our back benchers – however, I may be wrong and influenced in my judgement by my own feelings about O.L. – I find him a *faux bon homme*.[61]

Tuesday 21 June　I saw Scanlan in Newcastle. They have fixed the annual general meeting for the 30th of June without consulting me – I fancy that this is going to be another packed gathering – mainly to re-elect Temple as Chairman. It is a bad business – most of my supporters I gather are away on holiday. I suppose that this

---

[60] Headlam was staying at the home of a family friend, Gladys Hotham, at Milne Garden, Coldstream, recovering from a mild illness. Beatrice and he had begun a trip to Scotland on 8 June but on reaching Milne Garden, their first stop, his temperature, cough and tiredness forced a change of plan. Headlam spent a few days in a nursing home in Edinburgh and then rested at Coldstream from 16 to 21 June, when he returned to Holywell.

[61] translation: false friend. In the difficult period after Headlam lost his seat in 1935, Lyttelton had raised his hopes that he might help him to find directorships in the City, but nothing had come of it.

is a sign that Temple still means to challenge my renomination. It is depressing, but I don't see how if he does stand against me, I can defeat him – it looks like a sorry end to my active political career, but there it is.

19

DEVALUATION AND DESELECTION
June 1949 to February 1950

Sunday 26 June   The papers today are full of the financial difficulties – the drain on our gold reserves and the proposed convertibility[1] of sterling – I don't profess to understand the intricacies of finance, but clearly our main trouble is that we cannot sell our goods cheap enough.

Monday 27 June   Today in the House we began the Committee stage of the Finance Bill – it will go on again tomorrow. Cripps is not giving way on a single point. He assumes rather an irritating, superior attitude in the House which is rubbing our people the wrong way. There is general gloom about our financial position and the Socialists are fussed about the industrial unrest in the docks and on the railway – I suppose they will solve the railway problem by giving the extra pay.

Thursday 30 June   Our [constituency] annual meeting was in the Old Assembly Rooms. The hall was almost full – mainly by the usual collection of Jesmond women. Temple of course was re-elected chairman and the other officials were re-elected – what a farce it all is and of what avail are our friends?

---

[1] The lifting of controls to allow Sterling to be freely exchangeable with U.S. dollars. Due to the relative strengths of the British and U.S. economies, when this had been previously introduced in July 1947 it had caused severe economic and financial pressures, and had been suspended after only five weeks.

Sunday 3 July   To luncheon[2] came the Honble. D. Berry[3] and his wife – the former is the new manager of the Kemsley press up here – a common, little man if ever there was one, though perhaps less common than his predecessor. His wife I rather liked. They came in grand Rolls-Bentley which Berry described as 'a nice little bus'. ... Berry expressed himself as pleased with the [Royal] Commission's report on the press: he also said that he had not read it.

Friday 8 July   [Belinda Lambton[4]] is an oddity, but I think that she is sound enough not to make a mess of things – she has not had much chance in her bringing up and her parents were, I should imagine, a pretty hopeless couple. I cannot make out whether Tony cares much about her – nor do I know him well enough to judge whether he will stick to her – clearly she irritates and bores him at times, and he himself is an irritable and impatient man who does not suffer fools gladly. What his moral basis may be I don't know – everything really depends upon that – but it is fairly clear that he needed a different type of wife – more especially if he is to have a political career.

Monday 11 July   I lunched at the HofC and spent the rest of the day there. It has been very hot (the hottest day of the year according to the press) and everyone here is feeling the heat, I think, for everyone is rather flat – and no wonder, for the economic situation is pretty hopeless and the dock strike and railway trouble are, to say the least of them, full of danger. Attlee moved the Emergency Powers measure. He is not an impressive man in a crisis.

Tuesday 12 July   The 3rd reading of the Finance Bill this afternoon – not a very exciting discussion – then amendments (Lords) on various bills. I stayed until midnight (I can't think why) and

---

[2] Headlam was spending the weekend at Biddick Hall, Lambton Park, the home of Lord (Tony) Lambton.

[3] Denis Gomer Berry (1911–1983), second son of 1st Viscount Kemsley; appointed Managing Dir. of *Newcastle Journal* in 1948; dir. of Kemsley Newspapers; married, as second wife, 1947 Pamela Wellesley (b.1912), elder daughter of Lord Richard Wellesley. Berry was heir-presumptive to his elder brother, the 2nd Viscount Kemsley, but pre-deceased him.

[4] Belinda Bridget Blew-Jones, daughter of Major Douglas Holden Blew-Jones, of Westward Ho!; married 1942 Antony Lambton (q.v.).

voted in a few divisions. This afternoon I listened to the pundits of the Party discussing our line of policy in the economic debate next Thursday and Monday – Oliver Lyttelton in the chair. He was not very impressive and there seemed considerable divergence of opinion as to what our line should be. Everyone appears more or less nervous about saying anything which may be used by the enemy to say that we intend to cut down the social services – but the enemy will make this assertion whatever we may say. The dock strike is spreading.

Wednesday 13 July In the House Attlee moved the Emergency Regulations and we had 2 divisions as the Pritt[5] faction[6] and the 2 Communists insisted on having them. The Government had a 3 line whip. The debate was not at all an outstanding one – it is entertaining, however, that this Government should have to move for the regulations and I don't think that it will increase their popularity among their own supporters – meanwhile the dock strike continues – indeed, more men have come out on strike. I suppose that the strike won't last for long, but it has already cost the country a lot and no doubt checked our 'export drive' whatever that may be worth at the present time.

Thursday 14 July The first day of the economic situation debate has not been very exciting – Cripps began the business with his usual dull explanation of our financial difficulties – nearly an hour and a half of it – then came Oliver Lyttelton – his speech will no doubt read better than he made it appear – he is not a speaker who 'gets it across' well. To me the best speech of the day came from Bob Boothby who can get his stuff across very plausibly – whether it is sound finance or not may be another matter.

[5] Denis Nowell Pritt (1887–1972), M.P. Hammersmith N. 1935–50 (Lab. 1935–40, Ind. Lab. 1940–50); member of P.L.P. Ctte. 1936–37; member of N.E.C. 1937–40; expelled from the Lab. Party in Mar. 1940 after defending the Russian invasion of Finland; sat as Ind. Lab., defeating official Lab. candidate in 1945; Chairman, Labour Independent Group 1949–50; awarded Stalin Peace Prize 1954.

[6] The 'Labour Independent Group' was formed in June 1949 by a handful of left-wing M.P.s who had been expelled from the Labour Party: Pritt became Chairman and the other founding members were J. Platts-Mills (expelled Apr. 1948), L.J. Solley and K. Zilliacus (both expelled May 1949); they were shortly afterwards joined by H.L. Hutchinson (expelled July 1949). All five members were defeated by official Labour candidates in the 1950 general election, after which the Group disbanded.

Friday 15 July   I ruminated about the 'economic situation' at the Club and began constructing a speech which I hope to deliver next Monday. To me the situation seems to be desperate, and frankly I cannot see a way out except by the most drastic economies and a lower standard of living for the country. We are living far above our means and 'full employment' is a fraud – for so many workers who are supposed to be fully employed are in reality only partially employed – costs are too high, production is not good enough and strikes are too prevalent – Cripps & Co. are concealing the truth from the nation and the 'common man' has no idea of the peril he is in. Things are far worse than they were in 1931 and nobody seems to realize the situation – by nobody I mean the Socialist party in Parliament and the working class community. What the end of it all is to be God alone knows.

Monday 18 July   I wanted to speak on the economic situation debate today, and spent the morning here preparing a speech, but the Speaker was annoying and clearly expressed a wish that I should stand down – of course I did so, but I am feeling aggrieved – I speak so seldom and when I do speak am so 'un-long winded' that he has no right to be tiresome with me – more especially as I am a P[rivy] C[ouncillor]. However it is not worth worrying about – clearly I am a past number – every day I realize it more. The debate today was not very exciting – the usual speakers were called and made their usual speeches – on the whole it seemed to me that we did not make the most of the opportunity. Cripps's illness does not appear to be anything much – merely a rest cure I should say. One would imagine that he might take his rest in this country just as well as in Switzerland – and if he were anybody else, I imagine that is what the Medical Committee would tell him.

Tuesday 19 July   Today we had the report and third reading of the National Parks and Access to the Countryside Bill *auspice* Mr. Silkin. It seems to me to be a wholly unnecessary and futile measure meaning more expenditure for no particular purpose – because there is today access to the countryside inasmuch as 'ramblers' and 'poachers' and other unauthorized persons just go wherever they like, and only very rarely (if ever) are they prosecuted for so doing.

Thursday 21 July   There was a debate on foreign affairs this afternoon, opened by Macmillan for us: one of his usual 'well prepared' and dramatically delivered orations – sound criticism on the whole. I did not listen to Bevin's reply which I am told was pretty dreary – but he did say that our 'unconditional surrender' policy was responsible for a good many of our difficulties in Germany. Winston then informed the House that F.D.R[oosevelt] was solely responsible for this policy.

Friday 22 July   I went to the HofC in the morning where Chuter Ede announced that he had ordered the deportation of 3 aliens who have just arrived in this country – their job being to foment the dock trouble. David [Maxwell] Fyfe said the stuff for us approving the Home Secretary's action. We were also told that the dockers had signified their intention of resuming work next Monday, so it looks as if this strike had petered out – and now no doubt the Communists will set to work to organize a strike in some other essential industry.

Monday 25 July   We had the Lords' amendments to the Iron and Steel Bill today and an all night sitting – a deal of talk carried on by our people (most of whom had been on the Standing Committee) and a lot of divisions. I thought that our people were decidedly effective and showed more fight than they generally do.

Tuesday 26 July   I slept without turning round from 2.30 a.m. to 8 a.m. when I got up and returned to the House which was still sitting – it went on sitting until 12.30 p.m. – an absurd business (an all night sitting), but now and then it appears to amuse M.P.s and the public to have one. This morning Members were patting themselves on the back for having lasted through the show and scored so many divisions – most of them were useless (more or less) for the rest of the day – however, it did not matter much as there was nothing much on – a debate on fuel and power which I did not attend.

Thursday 28 July   ... I went to the House, where people are busy clearing up and clearing out. It has not been an interesting session so far as I am concerned – I have said very little and that little not very effectively – I am I suppose 'gently fading away' – however, I

still hope that I may say something worth remembering before I
finally depart.

Sunday 31 July   I called on Temple this afternoon and was
ushered into a room where I found him and Mrs. Fenwick and
Sherrif Chapman! My first impulse was to go away – but I decided
to stay and we had about an hour's talk. Temple explained that
after his experience with Lord Woolton he was running no risks or
words to that effect – I replied that I considered this remark
extremely rude to me – then we had a conversation *re* the Woolton
business, etc. It was not very satisfactory – clearly these people are
going to do their utmost against me and the fight is on. It is all
very unpleasant and disagreeable – but I feel that I must make an
effort to beat them not only for myself, but in the interests of the
Party and more especially my supporters in N. N[ewcastle]. But I
shall not go to the length of standing against Temple if he is
adopted by the Association – I told the trio quite definitely that I
was anxious to stand again.

Monday 8 August   I attended a meeting of northern candidates
called to consider Mr. Butler's declaration of policy – *The Right
Road for Britain* is, if I remember correctly, the title of this rather
tepid little production. Miss de Jonghe was in charge (Galloway
on holiday), about a dozen candidates [present] ... They were not
a *distingué*[7] looking lot – but they all seemed to be keen and to
have their ideas – we talked for nearly two hours ...

Friday 12 August   ... the Consultative Assembly of the Council
of Europe which held its first session yesterday at Strasbourg.
Winston was present and apparently was busy upholding the
position of the Assembly as opposed to the Council of Ministers –
he and Herbert Morrison performing as if in the HofC. Personally
this sort of things I find displeasing – Winston is a childish,
mischievous creature and nothing will change him – but he is a
marvel for his age.

Friday 26 August   ... to the Byker Conservative Working Men's
Club ... about 70 men present and I talked with a good many of

---

[7] translation: distinguished, impressive.

them – Grey, the Chairman of the Club, told me that they are down by £1,400 on last year's drink taking – he says that people are feeling the pinch more and more. What effect this will have when it comes to voting remains to be seen – tonight most of those with whom I spoke assured me that the working man was beginning to 'think' – I can scarcely believe this.

Saturday 3 September   At Strasbourg our Socialists and Tories appear to be at loggerheads – Mr. Crawley *v.* Mr. Eccles (rather an unequal contest I should imagine); Mr. Macmillan *v.* Dr. Dalton – I wonder whether the European Assembly is really cutting any ice? I fear me not. The Lord Davidson who it seems is Chairman of the Governors at Ashridge[8] is having a row with Mr. Bryant and Gen. Sir B. Paget[9] – the latter is Principal of the College. What the row is about, and what the College does or professes to do, I really don't know – but I prefer Paget to Davidson any day – he is a very sound, sensible fellow, though not a very amusing one.

Tuesday 6 September   The correspondence between J.C.C. D[avidson], Arthur Bryant and Paget continues – I take no interest in it, though presumably it is a matter which should interest a patriot – but I don't believe that these high-brow efforts to interest people in world citizenship serve a really useful purpose simply because the people who attend these 'schools' and 'colleges' are not, as a rule, the people who really matter – if the right ideals of citizenship were planted in the minds of children and young people in their school days, it would be another matter ...

Monday 12 September   In Germany – Western Germany – they

[8] Ashridge House, Hertfordshire, had been acquired by the Conservative Party in 1930 as a residential centre for its educational organization, and named the Bonar Law Memorial College. Davidson, Party Chairman 1926–30, had raised the money for the project and was strongly committed to it; Arthur Bryant had been actively involved as a lecturer at the College from its opening. The College was inactive during the war and the property was requisitioned by the government; in the post-war austerity, and with a Party education centre now operating at Swinton in Yorkshire, the future role and usefulness of Ashridge was far from clear.

[9] Bernard Charles Tolver Paget (1887–1961), army career; Commandant, Staff College 1938–39; G.O.C. 18th Div. 1939–40; Chief of Staff, Home Forces 1940; C. in C. South Eastern Command 1941, Home Forces 1941–43, 21st Army Group 1943, Middle East Force 1944–46; Principal, Bonar Law Memorial College 1946–49; Gov., Royal Hospital, Chelsea 1949–57; kt. 1942.

have elected a President and are about to elect a Chancellor. There is a familiar ring about all this and one only hopes that history is not going to repeat itself. Two things are fairly clear – one, that Germany is recovering faster than we are, and two, that we have not succeeded in making the Germans friendly towards us – a thing which was all essential for the peace of the world.

Sunday 18 September   Tonight Cripps announced the devaluation of the £ (on the wireless). I did not listen to his speech: I shall read it tomorrow and find out the reasons which have induced him to go back on all that he has been telling us against devaluation. What good it is going to do I myself cannot see – or how this policy is really going to get us straight unless the Americans lower their tariffs – and, even if they do, we shall still have foreign competition against us in the U.S.A. markets, for the whole sterling area I should imagine will now devalue – harder work, greater productivity, lower taxation, reduced cost of production are the only means of increased trade.

Monday 19 September   Cripps's speech is not very cheering reading – the £ is devalued from 4.03 to 2.80 dollars – this takes effect immediately – food subsidies (as already decided) are not to be increased – the $4\frac{1}{2}$d. loaf will go up to 6d. and flour correspondingly in about a fortnight – etc., etc. The man assures us that nothing will be done to reduce the Social Services or our defensive organization. How hopeless it all is! – a truly desperate state of things and I for one cannot see any way out of the mess so long as we don't face the facts – we are living above our means, are not working hard enough and have too many mouths to feed. We cannot afford our present standard of living and unless we cut it by common consent we shall have to do so sooner or later or face financial disaster and vast unemployment. I am curious to see what the reaction of Winston and his Shadow Cabinet is going to be to Cripps's statement – will they face the facts and tell people the truth, risking unpopularity? I doubt it – but it seems to me the only wise policy, even if it may mean losing the election – but I don't believe it would – England votes Conservative when frightened.

Wednesday 21 September   The T.U.C. not unnaturally are somewhat upset about devaluation and all it means. They had a meeting yesterday and after a discussion lasting for over 3 hours failed to endorse the Government's decision to devalue the £. Will Lawther & Co. are in a quandary and know it – but presumably, with a general election so near, they are bound to toe the line – and, if we have a division next week, I don't fancy that many of the Government's followers will be in our lobby.

Friday 23 September   It is reported that the Russians have reached the 'Atom bomb' stage – whether this brings us any nearer to another war remains to be seen ... The House is to meet next Tuesday and to sit for three days – I shall not go to London until Tuesday night and so shall miss the explanation of Cripps: I don't envy him his job, but no doubt he will make an excellent speech – though it is not likely to please a great number of his supporters.

Sunday 25 September   ... all the [press] pundits seem to expect an election in November – this has always been my view, for I cannot see what the Socialists have to gain by deferring the election to the spring. Things may well be worse by then – they can scarcely be any better. The truth of the matter is that both parties are not particularly anxious to be returned to power next time – neither expects a large majority – and the mess to be cleared up is going to be formidable. What the leaders would like is a Coalition – but of course they cannot admit it – because in their opinion a coalition will alone be capable of dealing with the extremists of the Left and Communism which is the danger of the moment. I hate the idea of another coalition, but I don't see how it is to be avoided unless and until there is a regrouping of political parties – moderates versus extremists.

Monday 26 September   The Government are going to treat the devaluation policy as a vote of confidence – they have no alternative – so far, however, they do not seem to have got the T.U.C. to acquiesce in the business, though no doubt they will. I only hope that our leaders will not say anything very silly or calculated to upset our more moderate supporters.

Tuesday 27 September   Cripps's speech yesterday was rather a feeble one, and his explanation of his *volte face*[10] over devaluation is scarcely likely to increase his reputation or to enhance the prestige of the Govt. – indeed he has admitted that devaluation is not part of an economic policy, but yet another 'expedient' rendered necessary by the very difficult financial situation into which we have drifted. Oliver Stanley's reply reads well – but no doubt I shall hear more about it tomorrow – I rather wish that I had gone to London yesterday.

Wednesday 28 September   In the afternoon ... I missed Winston's speech – they tell me that he was 'at his best' – *viz.*, a strong attack on Cripps – Wilson whom I heard was very feeble I thought – and so were most of the other speeches I heard!

Thursday 29 September   The debate ended today – not a very remarkable one – Winston and Bevan made the 2 speeches of note. The former, as I have already said, was in good form and the latter this afternoon made a clever debating speech which caught on with his supporters – the stuff they needed to stimulate them which they certainly did not get from Cripps or Wilson or Attlee. Eddie Winterton (who is very amiable to me nowadays!) told me that Bevan's speech was up to the level of L[loyd] G[eorge]'s speeches in his earlier days – it was intended as high praise, but I never can admire speeches which are based on party prejudice and misstatement of facts. I spoke for 10 minutes this evening, and cannot say that my speech electrified the House – but at any rate it was listened to as my little efforts always are. ... The general opinion in the Smoking Room is that we shall have an autumn election. Bevan's speech certainly looks like this – it was so essentially an electioneering effort just as Winston's was. This HofC is as dead as the dodo – and a good thing too – but I can see no confidence on either side as to what the result of a Gen. Election may be – certainly I cannot venture on prophecy.

Saturday 1 October   The Tito-Stalin imbroglio is becoming more strenuous and it looks as if it would end in a fracas – and what then I wonder? It seems rather futile for us to rush to the help of Tito – if, indeed, we could do anything to help him – and yet we

[10] translation: about turn.

clearly cannot afford to allow the Bolshies to occupy Yugoslavia which presumably would be the result of the suppression of Tito. I suppose this is really a matter more for the U.S.A. than ourselves – but we have always got to remember that if war comes, we and not the Americans will be the first sufferers.

Wednesday 5 October   Cripps made a rather feeble speech last night at the Lord Mayor's dinner to the bankers – it looks to me as if he were a sick and disillusioned man. There was nothing new in what he said and no sign of a constructive Govt. policy – only a hint of still higher taxation to preserve us from inflation, and a confession that devaluation must result in an increased cost of living and a rise in prices other than the rise in the price of bread.

Wednesday 12 October   This afternoon I went to the Party Conference held in a huge ice rink near Earl's Court – too vast a place for such a gathering – no doubt the hall will be packed for Winston's speech on Friday, but today it was only about half full.

Thursday 13 October   The P.M. has announced that there is not to be a G[eneral] E[lection] before Christmas – this news is a surprise for me as I quite expected an election in the near future. What advantage the Socialists expect to gain by putting off an election I cannot imagine – it may be that Morrison & Co. are not ready for the contest, or maybe they are against an immediate election because Bevan & Co. are anxious for one – my impression is that the Socialist leaders are at sixes and sevens, and find it difficult to carry on together.

Monday 24 October   I went into Newcastle this evening and met the [constituency] Executive Council; Temple was the 'impartial' Chairman. It was a very unpleasant meeting and several of those present, notably one Councillor Henderson,[11] were extremely rude to me. I made a very straight speech, which my supporters approved of, but it had no effect upon my opponents whose minds were clearly made up. There were more women than men present, and of course all my enemies – Lawson, Chapman, Mrs. Fenwick, etc.

[11] Robert Mills Henderson, member of Newcastle City Council, Westgate Ward 1947–63.

They lay low while I was in the room – after I had 'retired', a good deal of nastiness was aired apparently, and my renomination was turned down by 28 votes to 9. They never invited me back to tell me the result – I happened to meet Temple going away from the meeting and he told me the news. My supporters ... were all highly excited and enraged ... I have a lot of friends but I doubt whether they will be strong enough to beat the other side assisted by Scanlan.

Tuesday 25 October   The more I think about last night's performance the more angry I am. The rudeness with which I was treated is what annoyed me most – it was so uncalled for, and one knows that it was all worked up behind the scenes by Temple, Scanlan & Co. At the same time I feel that mine is a pretty hopeless fight – I am up against a highly organized conspiracy and have to help me only a few inexperienced people who are anxious to help me but who have no organization and no leader – I myself am too tired and too old to carry on without experts to help me, and the time (even if I had them) is too short to work up a really strong body of supporters. ... I have at any rate the sympathy of all decent people in the division.

Wednesday 26 October   Today has been an unpleasant one – it seems that the news of the Executive Committee's decision has 'leaked out', and the press has got hold of it. I have been rung up continuously by north country papers – and I am told, though I have not seen them myself, that there are already paragraphs in the papers on the subject – 'sacked M.P.', etc., etc. It is very tiresome and no doubt this is all part of the 'plot' – whether it will help me or the reverse remains to be seen. Galloway, who dined with me at the House tonight, was not much use – the more I see of him nowadays the less I have confidence in him. I listened to Cripps for an hour and a half this afternoon – a terribly dull speech – a lecture on economics rather than a parliamentary oration – Anthony who spoke after him was good I thought – I did not listen to any of the others ... I hear that a Liberal candidate for N. Newcastle has been adopted.

Thursday 27 October   The debate today was not very exciting – Winston made a good speech – Anderson, whom I did not hear, was I am told a bit clumsy and not altogether helpful to our side – I cannot understand why we go on employing him. I voted in the division on our amendment, but had to leave before the division on the Profits tax in order to catch my train.

Tuesday 1 November   ... I went to the Central Office where I had another talk with Uncle Fred[12] – he was sympathetic rather than helpful. Of course (and I never expected he would) he won't put anything into the press, but he may let the Association know that he is not prepared to suggest candidates to them as he understands that Temple has already been selected by the Executive.

Wednesday 2 November   I had a letter from Temple today inform- ing me that 'in the interests of the Association' he was calling this [general] meeting. I replied that I saw no reason for the meeting, but that until I saw the agenda I did not know what it was all about – if, however, it was intended to get the meeting to agree with the Executive's decision about me the meeting was out of order (or words to that effect) – we shall hear what he says in reply – then I can make up my mind whether or not to boycott the meeting. I feel very depressed about the whole business and feel inclined to retire from the contest! I had a telephone call from Beatrice saying that she is told that feeling is running strong for me.

Wednesday 9 November   This Parliament is dead: there is no doubt about it. It strikes me – as a result of conversations, which I engage in or overhear in the Smoking Room – that neither side is very sure what the verdict of a General Election will be. Shinwell, Bevan and Co. may prophesy a victory for Socialism but I doubt whether this is the true opinion of their Party – as for our people, one says one thing, one another – but it largely depends upon the constituency which they represent. Those who hold industrial constituencies are naturally less sure of their fate than those who represent safer seats – but, generally speaking, very few people feel it safe to prophesy one way or the other.

Sunday 13 November   Naturally this Newcastle business is both-

---

[12] The popular nickname of Lord Woolton, the Chairman of the Party.

ering both of us a lot – personally I have no great wish to fight yet another election, but I feel more and more strongly that I cannot – if I can help it – let Temple and Co. run away with the seat. It means the triumph of the wrong people and a perpetuation of the 'clique' government in Newcastle. I have always opposed this kind of domination of the Association by a group of people lusting for power, and I don't propose to cease fighting them. Their calling this extraordinary General Meeting with so little notice and on a Saturday afternoon shows that they imagine that they have a majority of the Association behind them – they certainly have a solid block of supporters, but if my friends will turn up at the meeting, they may get a surprise.

Monday 14 November   Beatrice and I went into Newcastle today and saw various of our friends – a lot of discussion about tactics, etc., at the coming meeting. I confess that all this 'discussing' tires me a lot – but of course one has to go through with it. My own private view is that the result of the meeting will depend largely on the way in which I can present my case against the Executive – it is a very strong one, and I feel that if I can put it across well enough it might well secure me a majority – if of course the voting is to be by ballot which we intend to be the case. They tell me that the correspondence in the press is having its effect in Newcastle and that Temple and his friends are steadily losing ground. This is all to the good, but of course he has a steady body of supporters (mainly women) in the Association who are certain to attend the meeting in full force and may well win the day for the man. However, if we lose on Saturday we are going to demand another special meeting with our own agenda – and even if that fails I could still have a public meeting on my own.

Tuesday 15 November   Lord Runciman[13] has died – 'a merciful release' I should imagine as he has been so helpless for so many years. I did not know him at all intimately, but he was always friendly and pleasant both in the HofC and when we met outside. He was a very able man and more broad-minded than most Liberals. At one moment after the formation of the National Govt. in 1931 it looked as if he might become a big noise – possibly

---

[13] Walter, 1st Viscount Runciman (q.v.)

leader of the Liberals – but he did not pull it off. Asquith used to say, I believe, that he preferred 'the old Pirate' (Runciman's father[14]) to 'the Alabaster Statesman' – and I don't fancy that R. (who has just died) was ever a popular character – clever, etc., but lacking the human touch.

Saturday 19 November We won a famous victory today – and though both of us are very tired tonight, we are content and relieved in mind. .... The meeting in the Old Assembly Rooms was packed, but it was said that all who wanted to be at the meeting had got into the hall – so the question of the meeting being null and void did not arise. Matt[15] by Temple's request was in the chair and conducted the proceedings admirably. Temple moved the resolution in a very inferior speech (at least I thought so) and Beatrice Fenwick seconded it formally, reserving her right to speak (she never opened her lips again!) – a lot of people, for and against, had their say – then I spoke for about half an hour, and Temple spoke in reply. Then came the ballot – 301 for the resolution; 481 against – a fine result – to me unexpected – and to Temple and his friends also, I imagine, judging by their faces. Beatrice superb.

Thursday 24 November I lunched today with Winston[16] – or rather with Mrs. Churchill as Winston was in bed with a cold. However, after luncheon, we went upstairs and had coffee with him. There did not appear to be much the matter with him. He was in good spirits, and talked mainly about the coming election. I gathered rather thankfully that he did not intend to perambulate the country again and realized that he must be more careful about his broadcasts. Neither he nor Mrs. Churchill seem at all confident about the result of the election which is perhaps not a bad thing. The party was not a very amusing one – Charles Williams, Frank

[14] Walter Runciman (1847–1937), Lib. M.P. Hartlepools 1914–18; leading shipowner in the north-east, founder of the Moor Line 1889, acquired Anchor Line 1935; Pres., Shipping Fed. 1932–37; cr. Bart. 1906, Baron Runciman 1933.

[15] Lord Ridley, President of the Association and a prestigious figure in the northeast. He had been a personal friend of Headlam's since the 1920s, and was firmly on his side; Cuthbert and Beatrice lunched with him before the meeting.

[16] After criticism of his absences from the Commons and remoteness as leader in 1946–47, Churchill began to host a series of lunches to which eventually all Conservative M.P.s were invited; six was the usual number attending, and this must have been one of the last in the series.

Sanders[on],[17] Wakefield,[18] Tommie Moore, one Spence[19] and myself – I suppose the sweepings – however, the luncheon was excellent – good wine, good food, and some excellent brandy.

Friday 25 November   Beatrice seems pretty well, but is worried about what is going on in Newcastle. The enemy shows no sign of giving way and our people are fussing. It is difficult to know what we are to do more than we are doing till the enemy shows his hand – I fancy that the game he is playing is to delay matters – then to call another Executive meeting, to choose a candidate and call another meeting of the Association to adopt him. I myself think that we ought to demand another general meeting at once to get rid of the Executive officers and to demand my nomination, but we might before we do this get Matt to see Temple and urge him to retire. The man will probably not do this but it seems to me worth trying. ... this evening to Newcastle, for David Eccles's meeting – about 1,500 present. B[eatrice] and I were given a good reception. D.E. made an excellent speech. He came back here for the night and was most pleasant – we both liked him. He spoke freely – despaired of all our leaders except Winston – no guts and no go in any of them.

Monday 28 November   It has been an easy day, spent mainly at the HofC – people cannot believe that my episode in Newcastle is still proceeding after my big victory at the general meeting – and of course it is quite absurd – if Temple & Co. had had a majority, they would have counted me down and out – now they are saying that it is absurd when there are 3,000 members of the Association to regard a meeting of 700 as fully representative of the views of

[17] Frank Bernard Sanderson (1880–1965), Con. M.P. Darwen 1922–23, 1924–29, Ealing 1931–45, Ealing E. 1945–50; cr. Bart. 1920.
[18] William Wavell Wakefield (1898–1983), Con. M.P. Swindon 1935–45, St. Marylebone 1945–63; P.P.S. to Marquess of Hartington 1936–38, to R. Hudson 1939–40, to H. Balfour 1940–42; Dir., Air Training Corps 1942–44; kt. 1944, cr. Baron Wakefield of Kendal 1963; Captain of England at Rugby, Pres. Rugby Football Union.
[19] Henry Reginald Spence (1897–1981), Con. M.P. Aberdeenshire Central 1945–50, Aberdeenshire W. 1950–59.

the Association! ... Spaak,[20] the Belgian minister, addressed the
'22 Comtte. today on Western union – good.

Thursday 1 December   In the House there was a debate on the
£20 million railway losses – I thought that David [Maxwell] Fyfe
made a very forcible speech criticizing the whole Govt. transport
scheme. He is a very able man – whether he will be Lord Chancellor
(if and when we come back) or P.M. remains to be seen – I don't
mean P.M. straight away of course.

Friday 2 December   It seems that Temple & Co.'s game now is
to nominate me at the Executive Council and then beat me at the
adoption meeting – they are busy working up the wards against
me. Our plan is to go on making new members and to try and
keep up the enthusiasm of our people – nothing apparently can be
done before Christmas.

Saturday 3 December   A body called 'the Newcastle and District
Trade Council' asked me and the other Newcastle M.P.s to attend
a meeting today – a conference on employment ... The meeting
was in the Connaught Rooms and it was a pretty full one. First
the Secretary of one of the big unions read out a long and gloomy
report about the slackening off of work in the shipyards, and then
the meeting was thrown open for discussion. There was a lot of
plain speaking about the failure of the Socialists to plan successfully
for full employment which I rather enjoyed, even though almost
every speaker was certain that there was no hope of the Tories
doing better – then the man Bowman was unfortunately given a
chance and shouted away for 20 minutes telling us all what
magnificent work the Regional Board of which he is a member is
doing, but I doubt whether it impressed the audience. I made a
non-committal little speech which was well received, and went away
before Wilkes, Popplewell and Blenkinsop had their say.

[20] Paul-Henri Spaak (1899–1972), Belgian P.M. 1938–39, 1947–49; For. Min. of
Belgian govt. in exile 1940–45, For. Min. 1954–57, 1961–66; presided over first Gen.
Assembly of United Nations; Pres., consultative Assembly of Council of Europe
1949–51; Sec.-Gen. of N.A.T.O. 1954–57; chairman of the meeting of European
Coal & Steel Community For. Ministers at Messina 1955 (the 'Spaak Ctte.'), whose
proposals led to the Treaty of Rome in 1957.

Monday 5 December   My meeting in Newcastle last Saturday has created a certain amount of interest – Anthony Eden and several other people have spoken to me about it today – and apparently it has given me a certain amount of kudos – the fact that I was not shouted down has impressed people whereas the Socialist M.P.s are reported to have been given a bad time.

Thursday 8 December   Polling today in Bradford (South) – no one expects a Conservative win – the Socialists anticipate a reduced majority. Their candidate's wife has died and this domestic bereavement will, so the pundits say, mean an increase in the Socialist poll – sympathy for the bereaved husband on the part of the female voters – such is human nature and how universal franchise works. Winston addressed the 22 Committee this evening – not a very exciting oration.

Saturday 10 December   The South Bradford election has gone as expected – a reduction of the Socialist vote, but this is accounted for by Liberal votes and there is still no sign of a revulsion of feeling against Labour – not surprising perhaps because there is full employment in Bradford – but there is 'full employment' almost everywhere – so what? I confess I feel fairly hopeless about the result of the G[eneral] E[lection], though of course voting at a G.E. is not at all the same thing as voting at a by-election. I expect that the result at Bradford will decide Attlee & Co. to have the G.E. as soon as possible. I wonder whether they really wish to come back again? The troubles lying ahead are not calculated to attract anyone – except perhaps Winston!

Wednesday 14 December   The strike in the London power stations seems to be growing – but so far it does not appear to have caused much public inconvenience and for once the Government seem to be standing up to the strikers. What it is all about is not very clear but presumably it is a Communist effort more or less disguised in the usual way – sooner or later we shall have a more serious attempt I expect to hold up the country by a seizure of the power stations.

Tuesday 20 December   Strachey is home again from where the nuts[21] are supposed to be growing. He asserts that everyone employed in their growth is well and happy – the only trouble it seems has been caused by ill-informed political criticism. I wonder whether Strachey has any political future? To me he seems to be utterly without charm or personality, though possessed of brains – nevertheless, a woolly-minded man, of the Dalton type.

Wednesday 21 December   There is strong criticism of the Govt. depts. in the report of the Catering Wages Commission which has just been published. It is the usual story of delay and frustration and of one dept. playing against another. How long, I wonder, are we going on with this bureaucratic folly? Today it seems is the 70th birthday of Stalin – Communists all over the world are celebrating it – odd that such a man should be such a hero to people of so many nationalities. I suppose that no Tzar was ever more autocratic than Stalin is, or represented a more absolute form of government, and yet half the world appears to think that his regime of the 'Police State' is the highest form of democracy. One wonders how long men will submit to such a dictatorship – and yet it is difficult to see how it is possible to bring such a complete despotism to an end when the bombs, the machine guns, the tanks are all on the side of the despot.

Thursday 22 December   The General Affairs Committee of the Council of Europe at Strasbourg is being busy – Harold Macmillan and the 'dirty Dr.' [Dalton] are said to be working in accord – determined not to go too hurriedly – in this, I think, they are right. I do not agree with that cock-sure gent (Mackay, the Socialist M.P.) who will keep pressing federalism for all he is worth. It is far too early to attempt any such policy in Western Europe, and to press it [un]successfully[22] would be fatal at the present time – no one is ready for it.

Wednesday 28 December   The sentence passed on Field-Marshal

---

[21] The Colonial Development Corporation (an initiative of the Colonial Sec., Creech Jones) ran into difficulties with a project to grow ground-nuts in the East African colony of Tanganyika. The venture was advanced £25m. by the Treasury but mismanagement and incompetence led to heavy losses, and the scheme became a subject of popular ridicule.

[22] Headlam wrote 'successfully' but, given the context, must have meant 'unsuccessfully'.

von Manstein[23] (18 years' imprisonment) has filled me with rage –
I feel that not only is the sentence too severe but that it is all wrong
to have Generals tried for obeying orders from their political
superiors. I never liked the Nuremberg trials – but presumably they
were inevitable – but to go on trying soldiers and sailors for all
these years after the war seems to me an outrageous proceeding,
more especially as most of them have been in prison since 1945.

Saturday 31 December   The last day of another year and half the
century gone – and what a half century it has been – two world wars,
political and social upheaval, amazing scientific developments – and
is mankind any the better for it all I wonder – not so far as I can
see, but living as I have through this period of revolutionary
changes I suppose I am unfitted to judge the results – I can only
see the immediate effects, not the ultimate ones – I can only deplore
what has been smashed up and wonder what is going to take its
place – for so far politically and socially all is confusion and
uncertainty. The brave new world has yet to emerge and it is yet
to be seen whether our Christian civilization is gone – whether
Communism is to be the basis of the new civilization – or whether
this world is doomed to destruction by atomic energy or made a
heaven upon earth by its further development. ... it is very painful,
nevertheless, to have lived to see the end of an epoch when England
meant so much to the rest of the world and when one had such
pride in being an Englishman. Perhaps – and pray God it may be
so – this strange new 'British Commonwealth' which is emerging
into existence (on paper at any rate) may fill the place of the 'British
Empire' which my generation knew about and served? I should be
happier if I were at all confident that it would.

Tuesday 3 January 1950   Nothing in the newspapers except guess-
ing about the election – most of the journalists seem to think that

---

[23] Erich von Manstein (1887–1973), German army career; head of Operations
Section, Army General Staff 1935–38; Chief of Staff, Army Group South, Polish
campaign 1939; devised the plan for the invasion of France, 1940; G.O.C. 38th
Infantry Corps 1940, 56th Panzer Corps 1941, 11th Army 1941–42, Army Group
Don 1942–43, Army Group South 1943–44; dismissed by Hitler after advocating
tactical retreats, retired to his estate for the rest of the war; captured by British
forces 1945, convicted by a British military court of failure to protect civilian life
during Russian campaign, Dec. 1949, sentence of 18 years' imprisonment later
commuted to 12 years, released 1953.

it will be on 23rd February – and I think that the general impression is that the Socialists will be back again. It is odd how our people have so little fight in them – how they fail to stand up against these absurd left wingers and allow everything they believe in and which is in their own interest go by default – my firm belief is that the vast majority of people in this country are not in favour of Socialism, but that they have no fight in them – and so the Revolution goes on. What the outcome of it all is going to be God alone knows, but there is plenty of trouble ahead – and it will be largely due to the inertia and futility of the middle classes of this country.

Wednesday 4 January   It seems that we are to recognize the new Communist government in China – what good it is going to do I cannot imagine, but presumably the experts think that it is the only course to adopt – I doubt, however, whether it is likely to save our investments in China: Communists in China are not likely to behave any better than Communists elsewhere – I think, too, that it is a pity that we should recognize the new government sooner than the Americans –and of course for us to recognize a Communist govt. in China and not to recognize a Christian govt. in Spain is too ridiculous for words.

Monday 9 January   The papers still insist that the election is to be on the 23rd of February and Attlee has had an interview with the King – so it looks as if the papers might be right. It is a terrible month to choose – so far at any rate as country districts are concerned – should the weather be really wintry voters will in many districts not be able to get to the polls – but of course the strength of the Socialists is in the industrial centres where weather conditions don't matter so much.

Tuesday 10 January   Well – we have won the 'civil war' in Newcastle (North) conclusively – 704 to 201 – and I don't think, had Temple been a bit cleverer (or well-intentioned), there need have been a division. ... our people turned out splendidly and were most enthusiastic ... Matt Ridley turned up: Lawson and Mrs. Fenwick were conspicuous by their absence! When I noted that neither of them were on the platform I knew that we were safe home. Both Beatrice and I are naturally much relieved though both

of us dread the election. We heard tonight that it has been fixed
for the 23rd of February – so our worries are near at hand.

Saturday 14 January   Winston is home again, and our Party
leaders are in council – one can visualize the gathering and one can
imagine exactly the views expressed by each one of them – are they
really the chaps to lead us to victory? I wonder – but as they are
all we have got, we must put our trust in them I suppose – and
each of us must take his own course in the election, by which I
mean that every candidate will have to go all out and make the
best of any policy produced for him by our rather second rate and
uninspiring pundits. My great fear is that the infernal Liberals are
going to queer our pitch all over the country – perhaps even in
North Newcastle. It is really amazing that there should be this
division in the anti-Socialist ranks and that people who realize the
menace of Socialism should continue to fight each other because in
the past their parents and grandparents fought each other as Tories
v. Whigs, or as Conservatives v. Liberals, and when you look upon
the present leaders of Liberalism – Clem Davies, Violet Bonham-
Carter, etc. – how can you have any confidence in them to run the
country!

Tuesday 17 January   The Labour manifesto is not a very ingenu-
ous [*sic*] document – it is, indeed, more noticeable for what it does
not mention, or just passes a stray remark upon, than for what it
does say – a lot about 'full employment', 'fair shares for all' etc. –
but nothing about foreign affairs, defence, devaluation, reduction
of expenditure, etc. Clearly Herbert [Morrison] & Co. are trusting
to nothing except to frighten the electors about what the wicked
Tories will do if they are given a chance, and a reminder of the
terrible times between the wars.

Saturday 21 January   We listened to Winston's broadcast tonight.
It was a different affair to his opening performance at the last
election – I suppose that Woolton & Co. had begged him to be less
truculent – the result was to my mind very dull – indeed, I fell
asleep before it ended – so did Beatrice.

Wednesday 25 January   The Party programme is a good production – well put together and effectively written – even *The Times*

appears to approve of it, and admits that it is a far better thing than the Socialist manifesto. All the Conservative papers are pleased with it and they tell me that the *Daily Herald* seems a bit nonplussed by it – of course 20 years ago one would have taken it for a Socialist pamphlet – but times have changed.

Saturday 28 January Spent all day in the Connaught Rooms, listening to [Leo] Amery, Marples[24] M.P., Harold Macmillan M.P., and Julian Raikes[25] M.P. Each of them spoke for about half an hour, and then answered questions – all of them spoke very well – and the meeting was well attended by candidates, agents, divisional officers etc. from all over the Area – a good show. I 'wound up' badly – I was given a splendid reception which rather overwhelmed me and for some reason put me out of stride. Harold was somewhat cocksure I thought – I mean as to the result of the G[eneral] E[lection] – the idea being that our manifesto is 'a winner': I wonder – my fear is that the working man won't change his attitude until he is in want – and that is not yet. It is no use counting upon him – our only chance is a change of heart in the wobblers who voted Socialist in 1945, and who may or may not be anti-Socialist this time – and they may vote Liberal!

Friday 3 February Parliament dissolved today – no longer am I M.P. – shall I be M.P. again? One cannot help wondering – although in ordinary circumstances one would feel pretty safe – but really one cannot be altogether confident when one knows so little about the new wards[26] and when Jesmond is said to be full of Liberals – nor can one altogether trust the *bona fides* of all my ex-opponents who are now supposed to be working for 'the official candidate'.

Saturday 4 February There is little news – the speechifying begins today – how boring it all is, and what a lot of over-statement and

[24] (Alfred) Ernest Marples (1907–1978), Con. M.P. Wallasey 1945–74; P.S. Housing & Local Govt. 1951–54; jt. P.S. Pensions & Nat. Insurance 1954–55; Postmaster-Gen. 1957–59; Min. of Transport 1959–64; cr. Baron Marples 1974.
[25] This refers to Victor Raikes (q.v.), who, together with the others mentioned here, assisted Central Office during the election: 'General Election 1950, Review of Speakers Department', CPA CCO/500/24/31.
[26] Added to the constituency as a result of the 1949 boundary revisions.

lying there is going to be. The Socialists have nothing fresh to tell us and so are going to content themselves with a reiteration of their charges against the Tories during the years between the wars. My own fear is that this abuse will be effective – after all, one knows by experience how people's views today are influenced by prejudices aroused by the grievances and sufferings of their grandparents, and how conditions (thought normal 50 years ago) – now condemned by all – are used by politicians to their own advantage. The ignorance and stupidity of the average citizen can be relied upon to accept anything a clever agitator chooses to put up to him. This is why we as a party are handicapped, especially in industrial areas, where we have to contend against the actions of industrialists 40 or 50 years ago – gents who ground down their workers and lived on the poor & needy!

Tuesday 7 February   I opened the campaign tonight, speaking in the West Jesmond School in Forsyth Road. There was quite a good attendance – mainly my supporters and I think that the meeting may be set down as a success. ... The trouble is that there is so much to talk about – though, as a matter of fact, the only thing the average elector is interested in is his or her particular case – how much more can I get out of the State? can I get a house? can I count upon continued employment? can I get a higher salary or wage? will my pension be increased to meet the higher cost of living? will the 'bad times' come again if the Tories get in? etc., etc. No one seems to realize the importance of foreign affairs – or to appreciate the fact that another war would end any chance for our recovery. It is amazing how people cannot look beyond their own noses or try to understand what the Russians are up to.

Wednesday 8 February   In an election the only thing to do is to forget entirely the enemy and to concentrate upon bringing one's own followers to the poll – if one is worrying one's head about the progress of the enemy, one only gets perturbed and one can do nothing to defeat them, except to deny any particular lie they may put out. Tonight we had the adoption meeting in the Connaught Rooms – to my surprise there was quite a large attendance and I had to make a speech. The creature Temple was in the chair, but I don't think that many of the Executive were present. I only hope that the feud is over and that I shall have full support – but I cannot help feeling a bit nervous on this matter. The feeling against me was too carefully worked up to leave any real harmony among those who were against me suddenly to become my adherents – even for the 'Party's sake'!

Thursday 9 February   Anthony Eden's visit today has passed off satisfactorily – I took the chair for his City Hall meeting and then went on with him to Gateshead where he had a very successful meeting. ... Anthony was very pleasant and in good spirits. He says that he had a magnificent meeting in Liverpool and that people in Lancashire were optimistic – Winston, he said, was in fine form. ... I am far from confident myself – we have such an immense leeway to make up if we are to have a decent majority.

Saturday 11 February   A cold day – bitter wind – snow showers – I have spent it touring round the constituency with Bazin[27] and the Tory cinema car – the sort of thing I dislike most doing – however, it was not so bad today as I sat most of the time in Bazin's car, and, except for the waste of time, was not so badly off. It was an absurd performance – the film, etc., I thought extremely poor – but it amused a certain number of children – scarcely anyone else even stopped to look at the performance – a few women out shopping and a few old gents – spoke to some of them, but nobody really evinced any interest in the show or in me.

Monday 13 February   Very little heckling in this election – much the same in this respect to 1945. People are not showing their colours – and probably Socialists have been told to boycott our meetings – usually this is not a good sign – however, it is no use worrying.

Tuesday 14 February   There is certainly no swing our way and it is equally certain, I imagine, that most people have made up their minds how they are going to vote and nothing which I can say, or Winston can say, will change their views. ... Political views are today so cut and dried that the mass of the electors have fixed

---

[27] Michael Bazin, a local businessman who had been one of Headlam's most active supporters during the struggles within the Association; he also volunteered to assist with the election campaign.

opinions and nothing can change them. There are, however, 'wobblers' and upon them depends the result – unfortunate or not as it may be. These people may vote this time 'to give the Liberals a chance' – in that lies our danger. However – so far – the canvassers have failed to find many Liberals and they may be making less headway than I feared?

Thursday 16 February   I spoke in Canning Street School tonight off Elswick Road, and had a well attended meeting – mostly on the other side. However I was given a good hearing – after I had had my say there was a lot of questioning, mainly by rather excited Socialist females – all the old miseries and grievances trotted out. Men hecklers came in after I had finished my speech, and I fancy that they meant to break up the meeting – however, they did not do so. It all ended happily, some crying 'Vote for Popplewell' (Socialist candidate in the neighbouring constituency), others giving 3 cheers for Headlam. . . . In the afternoon we had 3 house meetings which went off quite successfully. Let us hope that they are doing good – people seem to enjoy them and presumably it bucks them up to see us and get to know us. Beatrice was with me all the time, not too tired and full of energy.

Saturday 18 February   There is not much in the newspapers today – both we and the Socialists profess to be winning – we are like boxers trying to binge ourselves up before a fight. Personally I am still unable to express an opinion – the atmosphere is as obscure as it was in 1945 – but of course the swing over our way may be as great as it was against us last time.

Tuesday 21 February   The candidates in the East and West divisions are optimistic of their chances, and even from Wallsend reports are good. I shall be agreeably surprised, however, if any one of these three seats are won. Reports in the press are fairly confident – but it looks as if the finish would be a close one. There is certainly no swing to the right on a big scale, and I don't believe that the Socialist hold in the industrial areas is much less strong than it was in 1945 – in the Northern Area it is certainly as strong (if not stronger) than it was then.

Wednesday 22 February   We have had another full day, winding up the campaign with two more 'house meetings' and two excellently attended public meetings tonight ... My public meetings in this election have been much better attended than in 1945 – our own supporters turning out much more keenly. We have had very little opposition, which may be a good or a bad sign – as a rule a boycott of our meetings has not portended success for us – but I don't feel any sense of foreboding this time. Beatrice is still 'quite sure' we are winning – George White[28] (who is having a bad time of it in the Central division) assures me that, despite everything, he 'senses a sweep in our favour' – let us hope that he may be right – personally I feel no such sensation – nevertheless I think that we shall do ever so much better than in 1945 – but whether we can score heavily enough to turn the Socialists out is another matter – it is a big job to win as many seats from them as to give us a majority especially when there are so many Liberals in the field.

Thursday 23 February   It has been a terribly long day. We went to record our votes soon after 9 a.m. at Brancepeth and then drove into Newcastle. Scanlan's plan was for us to visit each of our 20 Committee rooms and polling stations 3 times during the day – going all out we only succeeded in doing one complete tour. Voting was brisk all day and the general impression we gathered was that things were going our way. Everywhere – except near the Elswick Road, where the children were noisy and aggressive – was entirely peaceful. ... It has been a damp day – drizzling rain – but not cold. After the poll closed we all gathered in our little hotel where we had engaged a private room and had food and drink. We gathered again in the Laing Gallery (where our votes and the Central division votes were counted) shortly after midnight. The count was interminable, lasting until just on 6 a.m.! – a badly organized business, if there ever was one – and not a cheerful affair inasmuch as bad news kept pouring in all the time – news which greatly pleased all the Socialists present – it looks as if they had returned most of the industrial seats. Our success here was never in doubt – we got back to Holywell about 7 a.m. dead to the world but very happy – (Headlam, 25,325; Shackleton [Labour], 16,860; Herbert [Liberal], 4,839. Majority, 8,465. Electorate, 56,205.)

[28] George Campbell White (1900–1974), Con. can. Newcastle Central 1950.

Friday 24 February   The election has left the Government with a majority of ten or thereabouts over us and the Liberals – the latter have about 9 or 10 representatives in the new House – most of their remaining candidates have forfeited their deposits. It is a strange and unsatisfactory state of things and will entail, I suppose, another G[eneral] E[lection] before long – in the meantime, however, there must be a pause in the process of our 'nationalization' – and this must be to the good. Attlee has decided to carry on – he had no alternative – and this leaves him with the initiative – if he can control his wild men, and go canny, and choose the moment for the next G.E., he may well win it – such, at any rate, is my first impression of the present state of things. If, on the other hand, he has to be sticky about the Iron and Steel Act and insist on its coming into force next October, I cannot see how another G.E. can be avoided this year, possibly in the summer – then, too, if the Budget is not a satisfactory one to us there may be trouble.

20

THE LAST PARLIAMENT

March to May 1950, January to February 1951

Thursday 2 March 1950   Went to the House ... and took my seat. The place very full: everyone rushing about and congratulating everyone else – the Comrades more subdued than they were in 1945! The only persons I saw 'in the know' were Harold Macmillan and James Stuart – but neither of them had anything to tell me which I did not already know or surmise. Neither Attlee and Co. nor our people want another election until the autumn at the earliest, and so every attempt will be made to avoid a political crisis – until we see the King's Speech, however, it is not safe to prophesy what may or may not happen – I expect that this will be a very tepid document.

Tuesday 7 March   Winston spoke this afternoon – he moved our amendment to the King's Speech on [the] Iron and Steel Act – we are to divide on it – rather a mistake I think. I did not think much of the speech – rather an uncalled for attack on Clem Davies & Co., and then an ill-considered proposal to appoint a Select Committee to consider P[roportional] R[epresentation], etc. – I must find out whether this suggestion was spontaneous or had really been considered & approved by his 'Shadow Cabinet'.

Thursday 9 March   We had our first division tonight on Winston's amendment (*re* iron and steel) to the Address. The Government won by 14 votes – this was as expected – mercifully for us – for had we won we sh[oul]d, I think, now be in the soup. I thought it running an unnecessary risk to press the am[endmen]t to a division. But the interesting thing today was at the '22' Committee where

Winston attended to discuss his suggestion about 'Electoral Reform'. I disapproved this suggestion when he made it – apparently, as I suspected, the suggestion was entirely off his own bat – and from what I have been told, he had not even consulted his own 'Shadow' Cabinet. This evening he made a somewhat ineffective defence of his ill-considered proposal – Quintin Hogg and others spoke pretty straight against it – and it was clear that the majority of people in the room were also opposed to it. Clearly this upset Winston terribly and for a moment I thought that he was going to threaten to resign the leadership. However, he pulled himself together and the matter was postponed for further consideration. I don't imagine that it will be raised again, but the mischief was made when the proposal was made, and will cause us a lot of trouble I fear – also Winston's prestige in the Party has been lowered – 'W[inston] M[ust] G[o]'[1] is already being whispered. He certainly lacks political judgement as I have always asserted.

Monday 13 March   We had our second division tonight and the Govt. had a majority of 25, the Liberals voting with the Govt. against Walter Elliot's housing amendment. I did not listen to much of the debate, but what I did hear was not very inspiring. Bevan's reply was not effective – not as effective as usual I should say, for the man is always, in my opinion, an effective debater.

Tuesday 14 March   A dull day in the HofC – our attack on the gigantic amount of the Supplementary Estimates. Crookshank opened for us, and I am told made a good speech – Cripps defended and it seemed to me made a pretty good case for the overspending. Bevan, against whose health services the main attack was delivered, made a characteristic reply which greatly pleased the Comrades – nevertheless, our tactic of not interrupting him seems to be rather cramping his style. He is a most virulent fellow – but exceedingly clever and quick at the uptake. The Government had a majority of nineteen.

Wednesday 15 March   Today we had a little relaxation: no 3 line whip. There was a debate on the Transport Supplementary Estimates which I did not listen to. People told me that Peter Thor-

[1] A deliberate echo of the original 'B.M.G.' [Balfour Must Go] slogan of 1911.

neycroft made a good speech – nevertheless, I don't think that this
ambitious young man has regained the position he once had – I
think that he is considered to be too clearly on the make – but one
never can foretell any man's political future – everyone is liable to
ups and downs. Made the acquaintance today of one or two new
Members including Wood,[2] Irwin's[3] younger brother. He seemed
to me an attractive personality – he has lost both legs, but manages
to walk wonderfully well – a marvellous performance.

Thursday 16 March   I meant to speak today in the Defence
debate, but there was such a crowd of would-be speakers that I
stood down. As a matter of fact, Winston (who opened the debate
on our side) said practically everything I had intended saying – his
speech, I thought, was excellent and certainly impressed his hearers.
He did not minimize the danger of our position and military
unpreparedness for any major war, which might come upon us at
any time without warning. He wants a Secret Session so that we
can be supplied with more information to enable us to appreciate
how we really stand. I did not listen to much more of the debate,
which I am told was not on a high level. ... A Socialist M.P. has
died suddenly tonight – one A.S. McKinlay,[4] M.P. for Dunbartonshire West. He only had a majority of 613 – however, he
had a Communist as well as a Conservative against him – the
former got 1,198 votes.

Sunday 19 March   Tim [Nugent[5]] told me that the Royal Family
were delighted with the French President and that his visit was a

[2] Richard Frederick Wood (1920-), Con. M.P. Bridlington 1950–79; P.P.S. to D.
Heathcoat-Amory 1951–55; jt. P.S. Pensions & Nat. Insurance 1955–58; P.S. Labour
1958–59, Power 1959–63; Min. of Pensions & Nat. Insurance 1963–64; Min. for
Overseas Development 1970–74; cr. Baron Holderness 1979; wounded in action
1943; younger son of 1st Earl of Halifax.
[3] Charles Ingram Courtenay Wood (1912–1980), Con. M.P. York 1937–45; Chairman, E. Riding of Yorkshire County Council 1968–74; Ld. Lt. of E. Riding 1968–
74, of Humberside 1974–80; styled Lord Irwin after his father was cr. 1st Earl of
Halifax 1944, suc. 2nd Earl of Halifax 1959.
[4] Adam Storey McKinlay (1887–1950), Lab. M.P. Glasgow Partick 1929–31,
Dunbartonshire 1941–50, Dunbartonshire W. Feb.-Mar. 1950; member of Glasgow
City Council 1932–37, 1938–45.
[5] Terence Edmund Gascoigne Nugent (1895–1973), army career 1914–36; Comptroller, Lord Chamberlain's Dept. 1936–60; extra Equerry to the King 1937–52, to
the Queen 1952–73; Permanent Lord-in-Waiting 1960–73; kt. 1945, cr. Baron Nugent
of West Harling 1960.

huge success – apparently those in authority were fearful that it might be a huge flop.

Monday 20 March   Strachey, the new Secretary of State for War, who obviously knew nothing he was talking about, spoke for about an hour about the reorganization of the Army, but told us nothing about the present situation should war come suddenly – and no one did raise this urgent matter in debate except George Jeffreys – I had intended doing so had I spoken. We certainly are a happy-go-lucky people and deserve what may be coming to us. I lunched and dined in the House but heard no gossip. The early excitement is over and we are settling down to the usual routine existence. As usual on ordinary days very few of our leaders were present and I was called upon to sit 'on the Bench'[6] for nearly two hours alone except for the whip. This is now the only work I do for the Party in Parliament: useful perhaps but hardly flattering to my abilities!

Tuesday 21 March   The Air Estimates were on and I ought, I suppose, to have stayed to hear Aidan[7] make his debut as Parliamentary Secretary to the Air Ministry, but I did not somehow or other take any interest in him – I never have cared about him and I don't think that he has ever cared about me. I find him conceited and lacking in humour and I never can get over his belonging to the Socialist Party – this, I have no doubt, is just an unreasoning prejudice, but there it is.

Friday 24 March   I cannot believe that we can go on in this state of 'cold war' indefinitely and that it is useless to expect that Russian Communism can go on spreading east and west without a terrible denouement – however, I may be a pessimist. If we were as powerful a force in the world as we used to be, we might stave off disaster, but with the Americans in charge, so unversed in world affairs and so self-confident, the position is very different. We may suddenly find ourselves inextricably committed to war – and in the forefront of the battle, unready and unprepared for what is in store for us.

---

[6] To sit on the opposition front bench as the representative of the leadership; as a former Minister, Headlam was entitled to sit there and was sometimes called upon by the whips when no member of the 'shadow cabinet' was available.

[7] Headlam's nephew, Aidan Crawley, had been given junior office after the 1950 election.

It is a terrifying thought – about which very few people in this country is thinking or taking into account.[*sic*]

Monday 27 March   Another M.P. has passed out – a Socialist again with a safe seat – but for the time being the Govt. has only a majority of three over the rest of us. It is difficult to see how this state of affairs can last for long. The attendance required from Govt. supporters will be too exacting and I doubt whether the Comrades will stand up to it.

Tuesday 28 March   There has been a debate on foreign affairs today on the second reading of the Consolidated Fund Bill – Winston excelled himself: I have seldom heard him to better effect. I spoke pretty poorly, but it is a comfort [to] have broken my duck. Bevin, who looks like death, spoke at the end of the debate – I did not hear him, but I gather that he was more dull than ever. The truth of the matter is that the poor man is down and out and ought really not to go on in his job. The situation is desperately precarious and it must demand an all out effort from those in charge of it both here and in the U.S.A. – here we have Bevin, a very sick man; in Washington there is Acheson who is being attacked by politicians and journalists and not allowed to get on with [his] job.[8] One wonders whether the gents in Moscow are equally at sixes and sevens – perhaps they are – but of one thing I am certain, that were they ready for war and sure of winning it, they would not hesitate to go for us – whereas neither we nor the Americans would dream of waging a preventive war even if we were entirely confident we could win it. It seems unfortunate that it should be necessary to wait until the Russians decide that the moment has come for action – and the still great[er] pity of things today is that no war is really necessary for all the world might live in peace – there is no cause for war.

Wednesday 29 March   We have had the satisfaction of beating the Government in a division tonight – it was on a debate on the Committee and remaining stages of the Consolidated Fund Bill –

[8] Acheson was under attack in the U.S. Congress from Republicans over his alleged liberalism and the failure to deter Communist aggression by affirming a clear American commitment to defend South Korea.

the subject of the debate was on Fuel and Power and the division was taken on the motion for the adjournment. I knew some days ago that the whips were plotting a little surprise for the Government, but the secret was well kept and it is clear that the Govt. whips were quite unsuspecting – their followers (who nowadays hang about the Central Hall and lobbies on the lookout for pairs) were equally oblivious of danger. Rather an exaggerated exhibition of excitement followed the announcement of the figures and Winston was given an ovation. Attlee and Co., it is to be hoped, will not resign – there is no earthly reason why they should, but tonight's show cannot be repeated often, if the Government is to remain in office – even if the defeats are on maters of comparative unimportance, they lower the Government's prestige and lower the morale of its followers.

Tuesday 18 April   Cripps's Budget does not sound an exciting one – but it is not an electioneering one. He takes off a little in income tax, but shoves on an extra petrol tax and a tax on commercial motor vehicles – neither of these taxes will be popular – nothing is done to reduce purchase tax and there is not the expected 1d. off beer, but our beer is to be a wee bit stronger. My own view is that this budget will please no one – it certainly holds out no hope of any real reduction of expenditure or of taxation. So long as we have a Welfare State we must submit to heavy taxation is Cripps's point of view and no doubt this is the case – the only question is whether a Welfare State is desirable and, if so, whether any amount of taxation will be able to keep it going, unless the people are prepared to work a deal harder than they do today.

Wednesday 19 April   No one has a good word for the Budget – the only consolation being that it might have been ever so much worse which is true enough – we shall probably vote against the increased tax on the petrol resolution but it is doubtful whether we shall get support from the Liberals – just as well if we don't for I suppose if he is defeated on a Budget resolution Attlee will resign. The Socialists appear to be taking it for granted that if he does resign, he will ask the King to dissolve Parliament and that his request will be granted. I should think that the more correct thing constitutionally for the King to do would be [to] send for Winston – but will he and Tommy Lascelles have the courage to do this?

Monday 1 May   We had a division on some transport matter (I did not trouble to listen to the debate, a field day for Peter Thorneycroft I gather) at 10 p.m. and managed to make a tie with the Govt. – Milner giving his casting vote against us. I fancy that the closeness of the division rather surprised and annoyed Attlee and Whiteley.

Tuesday 2 May   A lot of gossip about last night's debate – we were not intending to beat the Govt., and if we had done so I don't imagine that Attlee would have resigned – but the tie worried them because it was due to some of their people being absent without pairs – if this became a practice, it would soon end the Govt. Personally I don't fancy that the Socialists will stand the strain of continuous attendance for very long – however, I may be wrong. ... Had a little chat about foreign affairs with Anthony Eden today. He had not read my *Times* letter but when I told him about it clearly disapproved of rearmament in Germany – even when I suggested that the Germans would not make their own arms but have to purchase them from us or the Yanks, he said that this would be impossible. He may be right but to me he always seems to think everything impossible when one points out that we must utilize the Germans if we are to keep [the] U.S.S.R. under control.

Tuesday 16 May   ... the Germans seem to be agreeable to the French economic plan,[9] but it looks to me as if French opinion may not be ready to welcome it as willingly as at first seemed likely. Acheson is still here and, so far as I can gather, is scoring a success – of a personal character at any rate. Today we had the we had the second reading of the Finance Bill – it was not a very exciting or entertaining debate. I thought that Anthony and Oliver Lyttelton did well for us – Jay[10] put his case well, I thought, for the Government: I did not stay to hear Stafford [Cripps] wind up.

Apart from three further entries in May and a few lines written on

[9] The Schuman Plan proposed common planning for European iron and steel industries; the resulting agreement was the first step towards the Treaty of Rome in 1957 and the creation of the European Community.

[10] Douglas Patrick Thomas Jay (1907–1996), Lab. M.P. Battersea N. 1946–83; P.P.S. to H. Dalton 1947; Economic Sec., Treasury 1947–50, F.S.T. 1950–51; Pres. Bd. of Trade 1964–67; member of P.L.P. Ctte. 1963–64; cr. Baron Jay 1987.

21 June, the remainder of the 1950 volume is completely blank. Illness was again the cause, as both Cuthbert and Beatrice were seriously unwell in the late spring and early summer of 1950.[11] Headlam told Marjorie Maxse, the Vice-Chairman of the Conservative Party, in early August: 'I have had a bad summer – laid up with bronchial pneumonia from Whitsuntide to the beginning of July.' Whilst he had 'made a wonderful recovery', he still felt low, and the diary was not resumed.[12] However, spurred by Headlam's stationer having automatically supplied him with a new volume, there is a further and final section of the diary in the first two months of 1951. In the meantime, the Korean War began in June 1950, and by late November the United Nations forces had advanced almost as far north as the Chinese border on the Yalu River. However on 29 November a heavy Communist counter-offensive led to a rapid retreat, and the South Korean capital of Seoul fell into enemy hands again on 4 January 1951.

Monday 1 January 1951   Hugh Rees sent me this diary off their own volition, and it is less trouble to keep it than return it – so I shall begin keeping a record of my existence, though whether I shall have the energy or inclination to keep it going throughout the coming year is exceedingly doubtful. ... The news gloomy in the extreme – the Chinese massing in great force for a big offensive in Korea – Tito asserting that the Bulgars and Albanians are massing on his frontier, etc., etc. – and nearer at home a real coal shortage which will hit us all they tell us even worse than in 1947. 'Use less coal' is the advice of the Government to the housewife – not 'dig more coal' to the miners – one feels quite hopeless about the future of this country.

Friday 5 January   Tonight I met the great 'Monty'[13] for the first time, at the O.K.S. dinner at the Park Lane Hotel in Piccadilly. ... 'Monty' is much as one has imagined him to be – self-satisfied and

---

[11] The Deputy Area Agent, Miss de Jonghe (q.v.), reported after a visit to Holywell on 28 June that 'Sir Cuthbert and Lady Headlam have both been very ill indeed, and both appear to be in a very low state of health, particularly Sir Cuthbert.' Memo, 'Newcastle North', Galloway [Area Agent] to Watson [Central Office], 28 June 1950, CPA CCO/1/8/71/1.

[12] Headlam to Maxse, 5 Aug. 1950, CPA CCO/1/8/71/1.

[13] Field-Marshal Montgomery (q.v.), at this time Chairman of the Western European Commander-in-Chiefs' Ctte.

somewhat swollen-headed. Tonight he was of course most affable and genial. He made a speech (for which he insisted on having the waiters turned out of the room as he had some things to tell us which were confidential as he was just back from Berlin), but there was nothing in the speech that one did not know already. He told me in private conversation that none of the Continental countries was really attempting to pull its weight – that the Germans must be brought in or we could not hope to keep the Russians from the English Channel (quite obvious) and that they would not come in except on their own terms – that the French were hopeless and had only one decent General, the man in Indo-China. He did not think that the Russians intended to attack just yet. His contempt for Attlee and Co. was unbounded, and he suggested that he had material enough to send them out of commission for all time. I cannot say I liked the little man, but he struck me as very much alive.

Saturday 6 January   No fresh news from Korea except that the retreat continues – Monty last night confirmed what I had heard in London, that the Americans are not fighting – he said that he got this from the C[hief of the] I[mperial] G[eneral] S[taff], so presumably it is true. It only shows what all sane people know – that you cannot expect success in war with untrained troops.

Sunday 7 January   In Korea our retreat continues and the Chinese appear to be advancing south very rapidly – it is difficult to see how they can be prevented from shoving us out of the country. At home all that is interesting people for the moment is the coal shortage which is hitting everyone very hard. Attlee has issued a personal appeal to the miners to work a bit harder – rather a pitiable effort – and the unhappy 'housewives' are beseeched to use less coal, less electricity, less gas. What a sorry mess 'the planners' have made of things – and yet my own opinion is that if they went to the country tomorrow, they would still get a lot of support, despite their miserable record of failure at home and abroad.

Wednesday 10 January   *The Times* has a heading today 'Groundnuts Plan Modified'. This is something of an understatement, as the Government has decided to abandon the original scheme and is 'writing off' the sum of £36,500,000 which it is estimated will have been advanced to the Overseas Food Corporation by the end of March. It really is a most ignominious business – but of course they (the Govt.) will get away with it and presumably Strachey will not resign as a Minister who has made such a mess of things most certainly ought to – but I suppose if he were to resign the Cabinet which backed him up ought also to resign and that would never do! The 'planners' must go on planning whatever damage they may [do].

Thursday 11 January   Lunch at the Northern Counties [Club] – a lot of people there ... Had a word with Matt Ridley after luncheon and told him of Eustace Percy's idea of re-entering political life as a Conservative[14] – he could scarcely credit the idea - we are to meet some time and discuss N. Newcastle. Then I had a talk with Hughie Northumberland, who has a lot of good sense and a shrewd appreciation of men and things, and went with him to Picton Place[15] – rather to Galloway's surprise. (He had asked Hughie to come and see him about the Area Chairmanship and clearly wanted him to himself!) The usual nonsense going on as to the successor to Mary Graham – it is Northumberland's turn, and as Haswell Peile[16] is going to be High Sheriff, he cannot take on the job as those in authority had intended.[17]

Friday 19 January   I lunched today at the Union Club with Bazin. He told me that he understood that some of the Jesmond clique of women are beginning to raise the question of who is to be the candidate at the next election and that I would not be their choice. He is anxious for me to stand again – but, if I don't want to, he rather surprised me by suggesting Tony Lambton as my successor. ... afterwards I addressed a public meeting in West Jesmond

---

[14] Lord Eustace Percy (q.v.) had been a Conservative cabinet minister in 1924–29 and 1935–36, but had detached himself from party politics during his tenure as Rector of King's College, Newcastle from 1937 to 1952; he became a peer in 1953.
[15] The location of the Conservative Party's Northern Counties Area office.
[16] H. Haswell Peile (1902–1979), war service (prisoner of war in Italy 1942–43) to 1944; Managing Dir., Priestman Collieries, Weardale Lead Co.; Chairman, Peterlee Development Corporation 1957–68, & Newton Aycliffe Development Corporation 1963–68; Chairman, Newcastle & Gateshead Water Co., 1978–79; High Sherrif 1951–52.
[17] Mrs. Stewart Reid became Chairman of the Northern Counties Area, serving from May 1951 to May 1954.

Schools – a poorly attended meeting, about 50 or 60, mainly my faithful supporters ... Mrs. Councillor Chalk[18] moved a vote of thanks – she nowadays is all over me – the reason we think is that she is at daggers drawn with Mrs. Horton who is a firm supporter of Temple. How ridiculous all this bickering is among our female Conservative leaders in this division – but I gather that similar jealousies and self-seeking are to be found in most Conservative associations – the men are bad enough, but the women are impossible.

Friday 26 January   I had an early meal at the Conservative Club – a meal given by the Political Committee to R.A. Butler – he went on to Wallsend when it was over, returning for the City Hall meeting at 8 p.m. It was well attended and he made an excellent speech. He was very friendly to me and most pleasant to all and sundry – one wonders what his future is going to be? I find it difficult to picture him as Leader of the Party – but one never can venture to prophesy about such matters. They tell me that he is very ambitious and confident in himself, and he will certainly not put a foot wrong. He is clever and has ideas, even if one may as a Conservative find it difficult to agree with some of them.

Saturday 27 January   We listened tonight to Bevan's political discourse on the wireless. He kept away from all the burning questions of the day and tried to explain the political philosophy of the Labour Party – it was poor stuff I thought and wholly unconvincing. He seemed extremely nervous and stuttered a good deal – presumably he was sober. Bevin is said to be on the mend – he is being given the new American drug for pneumonia which in this country at present is only for the very rich and V.I.P.s.

Wednesday 31 January   It has been a long, dull day in the HofC[19] – another day devoted to arguments by the lawyers on the Leaseholds Bill. The Government again had a 3 line whip out and our 'leader' decided that we should vote as strongly as possible for appearances' sake. This sort of policy always strikes me as rather

---

[18] Ethel Gertrude Chalk, member of Newcastle City Council, Jesmond Ward 1947–65.

[19] The rebuilt House of Commons chamber had been opened on 26 Oct. 1950.

futile, especially in the case of a measure such as this one – my policy would be to keep the enemy here in full strength as often as possible and not to work our people more than necessary – such a policy would tire out the other people and probably make them less inclined to obey continual 3 line whips – then we might surprise them some day by turning up in full strength quite unexpectedly and beating them.

Thursday 1 February   In the House there was the usual debate on coal – we are to pay another 4/- per ton on coal; 6/6[d.] on coke – it really is a scandal if there ever was one. The Govt. had a majority of 11 – the Liberals abstaining: they are beyond words.

Saturday 3 February   I have been in Newcastle most of the day ... I attended the opening by James Griffiths, M.P., (Colonial Secretary) of what is called 'Colonial Week' ... Griffiths was friendly and civil to me. He is, I think, a decent man – though extreme in his 'political idealism'! He made an excellent speech, I thought, about the Colonies – though he seems to place more confidence in 'native students' than I do – I don't fancy that they will prove an added strength to the Empire! He asked us all to invite them to tea with us – and no doubt this is the wise thing for us to do if we want them to love us. I walked with Eustace Percy to the Mansion House after the opening of the exhibition: he is dull but much less heavy in the hand than he used to be.

Sunday 4 February   Tony [Lambton] got out of bed to see me – he looked ill and was rather gloomy. He is a strange creature – too temperamental, but full of charm. I am beginning to doubt, nevertheless, whether he is physically fit for the House of C[ommons] – but I should like him to succeed me as M.P. for North Newcastle if we can manage it – it is not going to be an easy thing to bring off.

Monday 5 February   We have had another long dose in Committee of the Leasehold Property (Temporary Provisions) Bill and have not yet finished with the beastly thing – a lot of valuable parliamentary time is being wasted on it but presumably the Government can think of nothing better to do. There were 4 or 5 divisions in which I took part, so my score is rising. I have heard nothing of interest today – but I have made the acquaintance of several new M.P.s including Dr. Charles Hill[20] who is rather a pleasant person – he is the 'Radio Doctor'. .... There seems to have been severe fighting in Korea but no one takes much interest in it – we are a strange race.

Wednesday 7 February   Winston moved our Vote of Censure (Iron and Steel) this afternoon – I thought he was a bit too long and abusive, but our people enjoyed his strong language, etc., 'hitting them hard' as it is called. Strauss, Min. of Supply, replied for the Government, and his Parliamentary Secretary, one Freeman,[21] wound up for the enemy – a cock sure young man whom I don't know but dislike intensely. He was good tonight – keeping his head amid considerable noise. The majority against us was 10 – rather larger than I had expected – the comrades much elated. I don't fancy that we shall ever turn them out in a set piece debate. The only hope is a surprise and our whips never seem able to organize one – they don't seem to me to be very subtle people or tactical experts ...

Thursday 8 February   A quiet day in the HofC for me, as I took no part in the food debate except to vote against the Govt. at 10 p.m. The majority against us was 8 – 2 less than in last night's division. Harry Crookshank 'led' for us and made the best speech I have ever heard him make – powerful in attack, well phrased and witty. He certainly scored a parliamentary success and completely showed up the hopelessness of the Govt.'s policy. Poor Webb,[22] the Minister of Food, was ineffective in his reply – the Comrades of

---

[20] Charles Hill (1904–1991), Con. M.P. Luton 1950–63; P.S. Food 1951–55; Postmaster-Gen. 1955–57; Chanc. Duchy of Lancaster 1957–61; Min. of Housing & Local Govt., & Welsh Affairs 1961–62; medical career, known as the 'Radio Doctor' due to his broadcasting activities; Sec., British Medical Assoc. 1944–50; Chairman, Independent Television Authority 1963–67, Bd. of Governors of B.B.C. 1967–72; cr. Baron Hill of Luton 1963.

[21] John Freeman (1915–), Lab. M.P. Watford 1945–55; P.P.S. to J. Lawson 1945–46; F.S. War Office 1946–47, U.S. Apr.-Oct. 1947; P.S. Supply 1947–51 (resigned with A. Bevan and H. Wilson over introduction of prescription charges, Apr. 1951); editor, *New Statesman* 1961–65; High Comm. in India 1965–68; Amb. in Washington 1969–71.

[22] Maurice Webb (1904–1956), Lab. M.P. Bradford Central 1945–55; Min. of Food 1950–51; Lab. Agent, Skipton 1925–29; Propaganda Officer, Lab. Party Headquarters 1929–36; Chairman, P.L.P. 1946–50.

course cheered him but in their heart of hearts I fancy that most of his supporters would have preferred to vote with us. If all one hears is only half true, the Socialists are profoundly disturbed by the food situation and realize what harm the reduction of the meat ration, as a result of Webb's failure to come to terms with Perón, has done them in the country.

Tuesday 13 February   ... the situation in Korea seems to be improving – it looks as if the impetus of the Chinese advance is wearing off. According to American reports the Red losses have been very heavy and if it is true that the enemy has been using his 'shock troops', it may be that he has used them up for the time being and has now only raw recruits to depend on. Unless the Russians intervene themselves I doubt whether the Chinese can keep a big war going very long – nevertheless, American and other troops including our own are being kept busy in Korea – lives are being lost and money expended by U.N.O. while the people in Moscow are sitting back and manufacturing more and more armaments. This cannot go on indefinitely. Bevin is recovering but there is no sign of his returning. Rumour has it that he is sooner or later to be succeeded at the F[oreign] O[ffice] by Oliver Franks,[23] our Ambassador in Washington – I don't fancy that there can be much in this rumour.

Wednesday 14 February   The mania for Votes of Censure continues – I suppose that it is just as well to harass the Govt. by keeping them always on the *qui vive*[24] – but I can see no use in harassing our people all the time – in a set division it is tolerably clear we cannot beat the Govt. – our only chance is to take them by surprise.

Tuesday 27 February   Matt [Ridley] and Robin Houston[25] have announced their resignations – Temple has called a meeting of the

---

[23] Oliver Shewell Franks (1905–1992), Fellow of Queen's College, Oxford 1927–37; Prof. of Moral Philosophy, Glasgow Univ. 1937–45; temporary civil servant, Min. of Supply 1939–45, Perm. Sec. 1945–46; Provost of Queen's College, Oxford 1946–48, of Worcester College, Oxford 1962–76; Amb. in Washington 1948–52; Chairman, Lloyds Bank 1954–62; Chairman, Political Honours Scrutiny Ctte. 1976–87; Falkland Islands Review Ctte. 1982; kt. 1946, cr. Baron Franks 1962.
[24] translation: alert.
[25] The Treasurer of North Newcastle C.A.

[North Newcastle] Executive for next Monday – as he has a majority on this body I presume that it will give him a vote of confidence – then Matt & Co. are going to demand a special meeting of the Association. Odd though it may sound, I have lost all interest in North Newcastle and its affairs.[26] Perhaps this is because I am seedy and not taking much interest in anything for the time being. I hope that this may be the case – for to lose interest in any business which has interested one for so long is bad – a sign that one is running downhill. ... Bevin I observe is returning to London and so I suppose that he is resuming work at the F[oreign] O[ffice] – odd how he hangs on – even his own side would be glad to see him go.[27]

Wednesday 28 February   The grandiose Government egg scheme in Gambia has ended in complete failure apparently – the loss estimated at £825,000. Surely no Government in this country has ever been such a failure as this one, and yet no one seems to mind very much – and by 'no one' I mean the great electorate.

Headlam had been unwell with a cold during much of February, and remained resting at Holywell. Although he was recovering and expecting to return to London in the following week, the diary ends on 2 March 1951. There is no particular explanation of the stoppage other than loss of interest, and he did not keep a diary again. The Headlam papers contain two letters to Beatrice written during his remaining months in the House of Commons; the last of these, written after the announcement of the 1951 general election, is a fitting coda to the diary:

Cuthbert to Beatrice Headlam, 24 April 1951   Opinion here [at

[26] This is the last entry in the diary dealing with North Newcastle Conservative Association. The developments mentioned here heralded the final stage of the conflict: a new and rival Association was formed with Lord Ridley as Chairman, and in July 1951 the National Union disaffiliated the old Assocuation and recognised the new in its place (for a fuller account of these events, see the Introduction, p. 37). Despite his words here, Headlam encouraged the formation of the new Association and assisted it in public and behind the scenes. However, at its inaugural meeting on 2 July he publicly announced that he would not stand again at the next election, and he left the House of Commons when Parliament was dissolved on 5 Oct. 1951.

[27] Bevin resigned as Foreign Secretary on 9 March, and died on 14 April 1951.

the House of Commons] is that – as a result of Bevan's speech yesterday – the Govt. may be able to hang on until August or September – but no one can tell until one sees what amount of support Bevan has in his party.[28]

Cuthbert to Beatrice Headlam, 2 October 1951 ... there was no one at the HofC this morning where I went to clear up a few papers and to return some books I had borrowed. I see in the papers this morning that Winston is to speak in Newcastle on Tuesday 16th of October. It will be interesting to see if I am asked to take the Chair – I ought to of course as President of the Northern Area and ex-M.P., but I shall be agreeably surprised if I am. No more now, my darling – don't fuss about me – my 'depression' is natural enough and will soon pass off – we shall manage all right and will hang on together till death us do part.

Headlam stood down as a Member of Parliament at the general election of 1951. Beatrice and he continued to live at Holywell until 1960, when they moved to Shepton Mallet and then, in 1963, to Bath. Here, at the age of 87, Cuthbert died on 27 February 1964; Beatrice lived for another four years, passing away on 6 April 1968.

---

[28] Bevan resigned from the Cabinet on 23 April, as he could not accept the breach in the principle of a free health service which would result from the introduction of prescription charges in Gaitskell's budget; his resignation statement in the Commons was a parliamentary failure, heard in silence by Labour M.P.s.

INDEX

A biographical note can be found on the page in which each person is first mentioned in the diary text.